An Introduction to Bankruptcy Law

FOURTH EDITION

The West Legal Studies Series

Your options keep growing with West Legal Studies

Each year our list continues to offer you more options for every area of the law to meet your course or on-the-job reference requirements. We now have over 140 titles from which to choose in the following areas:

- Accounting and Financials for the Law Office
- Administrative Law
- Alternative Dispute Resolution
- Bankruptcy
- Business Organizations/Corporations
- Careers and Employment
- Civil Litigation and Procedure
- CLA Exam Preparation
- Computer Applications in the Law Office
- Contract Law
- Court Reporting
- Criminal Law and Procedure
- Document Preparation
- Elder Law
- Employment Law
- Environmental Law
- Ethics
- Evidence Law
- Family Law
- Intellectual Property
- Interviewing and Investigation
- Introduction to Law
- Introduction to Paralegalism
- Law Office Management
- Law Office Procedures
- Legal Nurse Consulting
- Legal Research, Writing, and Analysis
- Legal Terminology
- Paralegal Internships
- Product Liability
- Real Estate Law
- Reference Materials
- Social Security
- Sports Law
- Torts and Personal Injury Law
- Wills, Trusts, and Estate Administration

You will find unparalleled, practical support

Each book is augmented by instructor and student supplements to ensure the best learning experience possible. We also offer custom publishing and other benefits such as West's Student Achievement Award. In addition, our sales representatives are ready to provide you with dependable service.

We want to hear from you

Our best contributions for improving the quality of our books and instructional materials is feedback from the people who use them. If you have a question, concern, or observation about any of our materials, or you have a product proposal or manuscript, we want to hear from you. Please contact your local representative or write us at the following address:

West Legal Studies, 5 Maxwell Drive, Clifton Park, NY 12065-2919

For additional information point your browser at

www.westlegalstudies.com

VILLA JULIE COLLEGE LIBRARY
STEVENSON MD 21153

An Introduction to Bankruptcy Law

FOURTH EDITION

Martin A. Frey
Professor Emeritus
The University of Tulsa
College of Law

Phyllis Hurley Frey
Attorney at Law
Tulsa, Oklahoma

Sidney K. Swinson
Attorney at Law
Tulsa, Oklahoma

THOMSON
DELMAR LEARNING

Australia Canada Mexico Singapore Spain United Kingdom United States

WEST LEGAL STUDIES

INTRODUCTION TO BANKRUPTCY LAW 4E

Martin A. Frey, Phyllis Hurley Frey, Sidney K. Swinson

Career Education Strategic Business Unit:
Vice President:
Dawn Gerrain

Director of Editorial:
Sherry Gomoll

Developmental Editor:
Melissa Riveglia

Editorial Assistant:
Sarah Duncan

Director of Production:
Wendy A. Troeger

Production Manager:
Carolyn Miller

Production Editor:
Betty L. Dickson

Director of Marketing:
Wendy Mapstone

Cover Design:
Dutton and Sherman

Cover Image:
Getty Images

COPYRIGHT © 2005, 1997, 1992, 1990 Thomson Delmar Learning. Thomson and Delmar Learning are trademarks used herein under license.

Printed in the United States
1 2 3 4 5 XXX 08 07 06 05 04

For more information contact Delmar Learning, 5 Maxwell Drive, P.O. Box 8007, Clifton Park, New York 12065.

Or find us on the World Wide Web at http://www.westlegalstudies.com

ALL RIGHTS RESERVED. No part of this work covered by the copyright hereon may be reproduced or used in any form or by any means—graphic, electronic, or mechanical, including photocopying, recording, taping, Web distribution, or information storage and retrieval systems—without written permission of the publisher.

For permission to use material from this text or product, contact us by
Tel (800) 730-2214
Fax (800) 730-2215
http://www.thomsonrights.com

Library of Congress Cataloging-in-Publication Data

Frey, Martin A.
Introduction to bankruptcy law / Martin A. Frey, Phyllis H. Frey, Sidney K. Swinson.—4th ed.
p. cm. — (West Legal Studies series)
Includes index.
ISBN 0-7668-2036-X
1. Bankruptcy—United States. I. Frey, Phyllis Hurley. II. Swinson, Sidney K. III. Title. IV. Series.
KF1524.F74 2004
346.7307'8—dc22
2004045493

NOTICE TO THE READER

Publisher does not warrant or guarantee any of the products described herein or perform any independent analysis in connection with any of the product information contained herein. Publisher does not assume, and expressly disclaims, any obligation to obtain and include information other than that provided to it by the manufacturer.

The reader is notified that this text is an educational tool, not a practice book. Since the law is in constant change, no rule or statement of law in this book should be relied upon for any service to any client. The reader should always refer to standard legal sources for the current rule or law. If legal advice or other expert assistance is required, the services of the appropriate professional should be sought.

The Publisher makes no representation or warranties of any kind, including but not limited to, the warranties of fitness for particular purpose or merchantability, nor are any such representations implied with respect to the material set forth herein, and the publisher takes no responsibility with respect to such material. The publisher shall not be liable for any special, consequential, or exemplary damages resulting, in whole or part, from the readers' use of, or reliance upon, this material.

To my brothers
Norman L. Frey of Highland Park, Illinois
and
the late Arthur J. Frey of Columbia, South Carolina

■

To my sisters and brother
Betty Jean Hurley Riddle of St. Clair Shores, Michigan
Phillip Hurley of Kissimmee, Florida
and
Margarette Ann Hurley Morris Smith of Huddy, Kentucky

■

To my wife and best friend, Caroline

CONTENTS

Table of Exhibits *xx*
Table of Cases *xxii*
Table of Statutes and Rules *xxiii*
Preface *xxxi*

CHAPTER 1

The Evolution of Bankruptcy Law 1

SECTION 1 Brief History of Modern Bankruptcy Law

A. The Appearance of Bankruptcy in Early English Law / 2
B. Treatment of Bankruptcy in the United States Constitution / 2
C. Early American Bankruptcy Statutes / 2
  1. The Bankruptcy Act of 1800 / 2
  2. The Bankruptcy Act of 1841 / 3
  3. The Bankruptcy Act of 1867 / 3
D. The Bankruptcy Act of 1898 / 3
E. The Bankruptcy Reform Act of 1978 / 4
F. Amendments to the Bankruptcy Reform Act of 1978 / 5
G. Future Bankruptcy Reform / 7

SECTION 2 The Dual Nature of Bankruptcy as a Remedy for Both Creditors and Debtors

CHAPTER 2

Bankruptcy Law and Where to Find It 9

SECTION 1 The Bankruptcy Code

A. The Universal Chapters / 13
  1. Chapter 1—General Provisions / 14
  2. Chapter 3—Case Administration / 16
  3. Chapter 5—Creditors, Debtor, and the Estate / 17

B. The Operative Chapters / 17
  1. Chapter 7—Liquidation / 18
  2. Chapter 9—Adjustment of Debts of a Municipality / 18
  3. Chapter 11—Reorganization / 18
  4. Chapter 12—Adjustment of Debts of a Family Farmer with Regular Annual Income / 19
  5. Chapter 13—Adjustment of Debts of an Individual with Regular Income / 19

SECTION 2 The Federal Rules of Bankruptcy Procedure and Official Forms

A. The Federal Rules of Bankruptcy Procedure and Official Forms / 20

B. The Local Rules / 21
  1. District Court Rules / 21
  2. Bankruptcy Court Rules / 22

SECTION 3 Bankruptcy Law Cases

SECTION 4 Secondary Authority

A. Legislative History / 24

B. Digests / 25

C. Loose-leaf Services / 25

D. Treatises / 25

E. Legal Periodicals / 26

F. American Law Reports / 27

G. Legal Encyclopedias / 27

H. Internet Resources / 27

CHAPTER 3

The Cast of Characters and Their Roles in the Bankruptcy Process 29

SECTION 1 The Debtor, the Debtor's Attorney, and the Paralegal

A. The Debtor / 30
B. The Debtor's Attorney / 31
C. The Paralegal / 32

SECTION 2 The Bankruptcy Petition Preparer

SECTION 3 The Creditors and Other Parties in Interest

A. Creditors / 34
  1. Creditors Holding Secured Claims / 34
  2. Creditors Holding Unsecured Priority Claims / 37
  3. Creditors Holding Unsecured Nonpriority Claims / 38
B. Other Parties in Interest / 39
  1. Equity Security Holders / 39
  2. Indenture Trustees / 39
  3. Statutory Lienholders / 39
  4. Lessors / 40
  5. Governmental Regulatory Authorities / 41

SECTION 4 The Administrative Office of the United States Courts

SECTION 5 The Bankruptcy Judge and Staff

A. The Bankruptcy Judge / 42
B. The Judge's Law Clerk, Judicial Assistant, and Courtroom Deputy / 43
C. The Court Reporter / 43

SECTION 6 The Office of the Clerk of the Bankruptcy Court

A. The Bankruptcy Court Clerk / 43
B. The Deputy Clerks / 44

SECTION 7 The United States Trustees, Private Trustees, and Examiners

A. The United States Trustees / 45

B. Private Trustees / 46

1. The Trustee Panel / 46

a. Eligibility to Serve as a Trustee / 46

b. Selection and Qualification / 47

2. Standing Trustees / 48

3. Other Trustees / 48

4. Paralegals / 48

C. Examiners / 49

CHAPTER 4

Information Gathering, Analysis, Counseling, and Drafting 50

SECTION 1 The Debtor-Client

A. Information Gathering / 52

B. Analysis: Nonbankruptcy or Bankruptcy / 65

1. Alternatives to a Bankruptcy Filing / 66

a. Negotiation / 66

b. Consolidation Loan / 69

c. Credit Counseling / 69

d. Assignments for the Benefit of Creditors / 70

2. Bankruptcy Choices / 70

a. Chapter 7—Liquidation / 71

b. Chapter 9—Municipalities / 73

c. Chapter 11—Reorganization / 73

d. Chapter 12—Adjustment of Debts of a Family Farmer with Regular Annual Income / 74

e. Chapter 13—Adjustment of Debts of an Individual with Regular Income / 75

C. Counseling / 76

D. Drafting of Bankruptcy Forms / 76

SECTION 2 The Creditor-Client

A. The Causes of the Creditor's Distress / 77

B. Information Gathering / 77

C. Analysis: If the Debtor Has Filed Bankruptcy / 77

1. If the Debtor Has Filed a Chapter 7 Case / 78

2. If the Debtor Has Filed a Chapter 11 Case / 78

3. If the Debtor Has Filed a Chapter 12 Case / 79

4. If the Debtor Has Filed a Chapter 13 Case / 79

D. Analysis: Alternatives If the Debtor Has Not Filed Bankruptcy / 80
1. Private Alternative / 80
2. State Court Alternatives / 80
a. Prejudgment Garnishment / 81
b. Attachment / 81
c. Receivership / 81
d. UCC § 2–702 / 81
e. Replevin / 82
f. Self-Help Repossession / 82
g. Disposition of Collateral / 82
h. Retention of Collateral / 82
i. Cognovit Judgment / 82
j. Judgment Lien / 82
k. Execution Lien / 83
1. Execution Sale / 83
m. Creditor's Bill / 83
n. Supplementary Proceedings / 83
o. Postjudgment Garnishment / 83
p. Fraudulent Conveyance / 83
q. Consensual Lien / 83
r. Equitable Lien / 83
3. Involuntary Bankruptcy Choices / 84
a. Involuntary Chapter 7—Liquidation / 84
b. Involuntary Chapter 11—Reorganization / 84
E. Counseling / 85
1. Counseling the Creditor-Client / 85
2. Drafting Bankruptcy Forms / 85

SECTION 3 The Debtor-Client in an Involuntary Bankruptcy

A. Information Gathering / 85
B. Analysis / 86
C. Counseling / 86

CHAPTER 5

The Voluntary Chapter 7 Bankruptcy (Liquidation) 88

SECTION 1 The Initiation of a Chapter 7 Case

SECTION 2 The Filing of the Petition

A. The Debtor's Petition (Official Form No. 1) / 103
B. The Filing Fee / 112

C. The Clerk's Notice / 115
D. Corporate Resolution Authorizing Filing of Chapter 7 / 117
E. Disclosure of Attorney's Compensation Statement / 118
F. The List of Creditors / 121
G. Schedules (Official Form No. 6) / 122
   1. Schedule A: Real Property / 122
   2. Schedule B: Personal Property / 125
   3. Schedule C: Property Claimed as Exempt / 135
   4. Schedule D: Creditors Holding Secured Claims / 137
   5. Schedule E: Creditors Holding Unsecured Priority Claims / 142
   6. Schedule F: Creditors Holding Unsecured Nonpriority Claims / 148
   7. Schedule G: Executory Contracts and Unexpired Leases / 152
   8. Schedule H: Codebtors / 154
   9. Schedule I: Current Income of Individual Debtor(s) / 156
   10. Schedule J: Current Expenditures of Individual Debtor(s) / 159
   11. The Schedule of Current Income and Current Expenditures of a Partnership or Corporation / 163
   12. Declaration Concerning Debtor's Schedules / 166
H. Statement of Financial Affairs / 168
I. Statement of Intention If the Debtor Is an Individual with Consumer Debts / 190
J. Debtor's Duty to Supplement the Schedules / 192
K. Debtor's Right to Amend the Petition, Lists, Schedules, and Statements / 193

SECTION 3 The Significance of Filing a Petition

A. The Order for Relief / 194
B. The Estate Is Created / 194
   1. Property of the Estate / 194
   2. Location of Property / 198
   3. Property Acquired after Filing the Petition / 198
   4. Contractual Provisions Limiting Transferability of Property / 200
   5. Possession and Control of Property of the Estate / 200
C. Exemptions / 201
   1. Exemptions under the Bankruptcy Code: State vs. Federal Exemptions / 201
   2. Converting Nonexempt Property to Exempt Property / 206
   3. Waiver of Exemptions and Waiver of Avoidance Powers / 206
D. The Automatic Stay / 207

SECTION 4 The Appointment and Powers of an Interim Trustee

A. Abandon Property of the Estate / 213
   1. Abandonment by the Trustee / 213
   2. A Party in Interest Can Force the Trustee to Abandon / 214
   3. Abandoned by Being Scheduled but Not Administered / 214

B. Assume or Reject Executory Contracts / 214
C. Avoiding Transfers / 215
1. Avoiding Unperfected Security Interests / 215
2. Avoiding Claims That an Actual Creditor Can Avoid under State Law / 220
3. Avoiding Statutory Liens That Arise on the Debtor's Bankruptcy or Insolvency / 222
4. Avoiding Prepetition Transfers of Property of the Estate to Creditors That Are Voidable Preferences / 222
5. Avoiding Prepetition Transfers of Property of the Estate That Are Fraudulent under the Bankruptcy Code / 226
6. Avoiding Postpetition Transfers of Property of the Estate Unless They Are Authorized by the Bankruptcy Code or by the Bankruptcy Court / 228

SECTION 5 Proofs of Claim and Proofs of Interest

A. Creditors' and Indenture Trustees' Proofs of Claim / 230
B. Equity Security Holders' Proofs of Interest / 230

SECTION 6 Motions and Complaints after the Order for Relief

A. Motions / 234
1. Motions by the Debtor / 234
a. Motion to Convert to a Chapter 11, 12, or 13 / 234
b. Motion to Dismiss the Case / 234
c. Motion for a Change of Venue / 234
d. Motion to Enforce the Automatic Stay / 237
e. Motion to Avoid a Judicial Lien / 238
2. Motions by a Party in Interest / 242
a. Motion for Relief from the Automatic Stay / 242
b. Motion to Dismiss the Case / 245
c. Motion for Abstention by the Court / 245
d. Motion for a Change of Venue / 245
e. Motion for Disallowance of a Claim / 245
f. Motion for Examination of Any Entity / 245
3. Motion by the United States Trustee to Dismiss the Case / 247
4. Motion by the Court to Dismiss the Case / 251
B. Complaints / 252
1. Complaints by a Creditor / 252
a. Complaint Objecting to Debtor's Discharge / 252
b. Complaint Objecting to the Dischargeability of a Debt / 255
2. Complaint by the Trustee or the United States Trustee Objecting to Debtor's Discharge / 262
3. Complaint by the Trustee to Avoid Prepetition and Postpetition Transfers / 262
4. Complaint by the Debtor Objecting to the Dischargeability of a Debt / 262

SECTION 7 Order and Notice of Chapter 7 Bankruptcy Filing, Meeting of Creditors, and Fixing of Dates

SECTION 8 Objections by a Party in Interest to Debtor's Claim of Exemptions

SECTION 9 Meeting of Creditors (The Section 341 Meeting) and Meeting of Equity Security Holders

A. The Meeting of Creditors / 270
   1. Examination of the Debtor / 270
   2. Election of a Trustee / 270
B. The Meeting of Equity Security Holders / 271

SECTION 10 Redemption, Discharge and Reaffirmation

A. Redemption / 271
B. Discharge and Reaffirmation / 271
C. Revocation of Discharge / 272

SECTION 11 Distribution of the Property of the Estate

A. Priority Claims / 278
   1. Administrative Expenses / 278
   2. Extension of Credit in an Involuntary Case / 278
   3. Wages, Salaries, or Commissions / 278
   4. Contributions to Employee Benefit Plans / 279
   5. Farmer and Fishermen Claims / 279
   6. Consumer Deposits / 279
   7. Alimony, Maintenance, and Support Claims / 279
   8. Certain Governmental Tax Claims / 279
   9. Insured Depository Institution Claims / 280
B. Nonpriority Claims / 280
   1. Timely Filed Unsubordinated General Unsecured Claims and Tardily Filed Unsecured Claims Where Creditor Did Not Have Notice but Proof of Claim Filed in Time to Make Payment / 280
   2. Other Tardily Filed Unsecured Claims / 280
   3. Penalty-Type Claims / 280
   4. Interest on Priority and Nonpriority Prepetition Claims / 280
   5. Debtor / 280

SECTION 12 Closing the Case

A. Trustee's Final Report and Proposed Distribution / 281
B. Trustee's Final Account after Distribution and Request for Discharge / 281
C. Closing the Case / 281

SECTION 13 After the Case Is Closed

A. Amending the Case without Reopening the Case / 294

B. Reopening a Closed Case / 294

CHAPTER 6

The Chapter 13 Bankruptcy (Adjustment of Debts of an Individual with Regular Income) 298

SECTION 1 The Initiation of a Chapter 13 Case

SECTION 2 The Chapter 13 Plan

A. Contents of a Chapter 13 Plan / 308

1. Mandatory Provisions / 308
2. Permissive Provisions / 309
3. A Sample Chapter 13 Plan / 309

B. The Debtor's Payments under the Plan / 318

C Modification of the Plan before Confirmation / 318

SECTION 3 The Filing of the Petition

SECTION 4 The Significance of Filing a Petition

A. Possession and Control of Property of the Estate / 321

B. Operation of the Debtor's Business / 321

C. Exemptions / 321

SECTION 5 Appointment and Duties of a Chapter 13 Trustee

SECTION 6 Motions and Complaints after the Order for Relief

A. Motions / 323

B. Complaints / 325

SECTION 7 The Clerk's Notice

SECTION 8 Meeting of Creditors (The Section 341 Meeting)

SECTION 9 Hearing on Confirmation of the Plan

SECTION 10 Trustee's Distribution of Payments under the Plan

SECTION 11 Modification of the Plan after Confirmation

SECTION 12 Revocation of Order of Confirmation

SECTION 13 Discharge

SECTION 14 Revocation of the Discharge

SECTION 15 Closing the Case and Proceedings after the Case Is Closed

CHAPTER 7

The Chapter 12 Bankruptcy (Adjustment of Debts of a Family Farmer with Regular Annual Income) 344

SECTION 1 The Initiation of a Chapter 12 Case

SECTION 2 The Chapter 12 Plan

A. Contents of a Chapter 12 Plan / 357
  1. Mandatory Provisions / 357
  2. Permissive Provisions / 358
  3. A Sample Chapter 12 Plan / 358
B. The Debtor's Payments under the Plan / 358
C. Modification of the Plan before Confirmation / 363

SECTION 3 The Filing of the Petition

SECTION 4 The Significance of Filing a Petition

A. Possession and Control of Property of the Estate: The Debtor in Possession / 368
B. Operation of the Debtor's Business / 368
C. Exemptions / 369

SECTION 5 Appointment and Duties of a Chapter 12 Trustee

SECTION 6 Motions and Complaints after the Order for Relief

A. Motions / 371
B. Complaints / 374

SECTION 7 The Clerk's Notice

SECTION 8 Meeting of Creditors (The Section 341 Meeting)

SECTION 9 Hearing on Confirmation of the Plan

SECTION 10 Trustee's Distribution of Payments under the Plan

SECTION 11 Modification of the Plan after Confirmation

SECTION 12 Revocation of Order of Confirmation, Conversion, or Dismissal

SECTION 13 Discharge

SECTION 14 Revocation of the Discharge

SECTION 15 Closing the Case and Proceedings after the Case Is Closed

CHAPTER 8

The Voluntary Chapter 11 Bankruptcy (Reorganization) 388

SECTION 1 The Initiation of a Chapter 11 Case

SECTION 2 The Chapter 11 Petition and the Significance of Filing a Chapter 11 Petition

A. The Filing of the Chapter 11 Petition / 395
B. The Significance of Filing a Petition / 401
   1. Possession and Control of Property of the Estate / 401
   2. Operation of the Debtor's Business / 402
   3. Use of Cash Collateral / 402
   4. Adequate Protection / 402
   5. Employment of Professionals / 403
   6. Obtaining Credit / 403
   7. Utility Services / 404
   8. Shedding Burdensome Collective Bargaining Contracts / 404
   9. Dealing with Pending and Future Litigation / 404
C. Evidence of Debtor in Possession (DIP) Status / 405
D. Exemptions / 405

SECTION 3 The Chapter 11 Plan

A. Strategies Utilized in Reorganization Plans / 407
B. Contents of a Chapter 11 Plan / 413
   1. Mandatory Provisions / 413
   2. Permissive Provisions / 414
   3. A Sample Chapter 11 Plan / 415

C. Modification of a Chapter 11 Plan / 415
D. Chapter 11 Plan Filed by Parties Other Than the Debtor / 422

SECTION 4 A Disclosure Statement or Evidence Showing Compliance with 11 U.S.C.A. § 1126(b)

SECTION 5 Order and Notice of Chapter 11 Bankruptcy Filing, Meeting of Creditors, and Fixing of Dates

SECTION 6 Motions and Complaints
A. Motions / 435
B. Complaints / 435

SECTION 7 Appointment of a Committee of Unsecured Creditors and a Committee of Equity Security Holders

SECTION 8 Meeting of Creditors (The Section 341 Meeting) and Meeting of Equity Security Holders

SECTION 9 Hearing on the Disclosure Statement

SECTION 10 Hearing on Confirmation of the Plan

SECTION 11 Effect of Confirmation of the Plan

SECTION 12 Distribution under the Plan and Reporting by Debtor in Possession or Chapter 11 Trustee

SECTION 13 Revocation of an Order of Confirmation

SECTION 14 Final Report and Final Decree

CHAPTER 9

Selecting the Appropriate Type of Bankruptcy Filing 458

SECTION 1 Eligibility

SECTION 2 Selecting the Chapter If the Debtor Is Eligible under Multiple Chapters
A. The Business Debtor / 464
1. Choosing to Liquidate under Chapter 7 or Reorganize under Chapter 11 / 464
2. Choosing to Liquidate under Chapter 7 or Liquidate under Chapter 11 / 465
3. Choosing to Reorganize under Chapter 11 or Adjust Debt under Chapter 12 or 13 / 465

B. The Nonbusiness Debtor / 467
1. Choosing to Liquidate under Chapter 7 or Adjust Debt under Chapter 13 / 467
2. Choosing to Liquidate under Chapter 7 or Reorganize under Chapter 11 / 472
3. Choosing to Reorganize under Chapter 11 or Adjust Debt under Chapter 13 / 472

CHAPTER 10

The Involuntary Bankruptcy: Chapter 7 or Chapter 11 473

SECTION 1 Limitations on Filing an Involuntary Petition

A. Debtors Who May Be Subject to an Involuntary Petition / 474
B. Requirements of a Petitioning Creditor / 474

SECTION 2 Flow Chart for the Involuntary Petitions

SECTION 3 The Filing of the Creditors' Petition

SECTION 4 The Significance of Filing a Petition

A. The Order for Relief, the Bankruptcy Estate, and the Automatic Stay / 485
B. Appointment of a Trustee / 485
C. Gap Period Creditors / 485

SECTION 5 The Debtor's Answer

SECTION 6 Hearing and Disposition of an Involuntary Petition

A. The Order for Relief / 486
B. Dismissal of an Involuntary Petition / 490

APPENDIX A *Interview Questionnaire for the Debtor-Client* 493
APPENDIX B *Interview Questionnaire for the Creditor-Client* 538
APPENDIX C *Chapter 9—Debts of Municipalities* 540
Glossary 542
Index 550

TABLE OF EXHIBITS

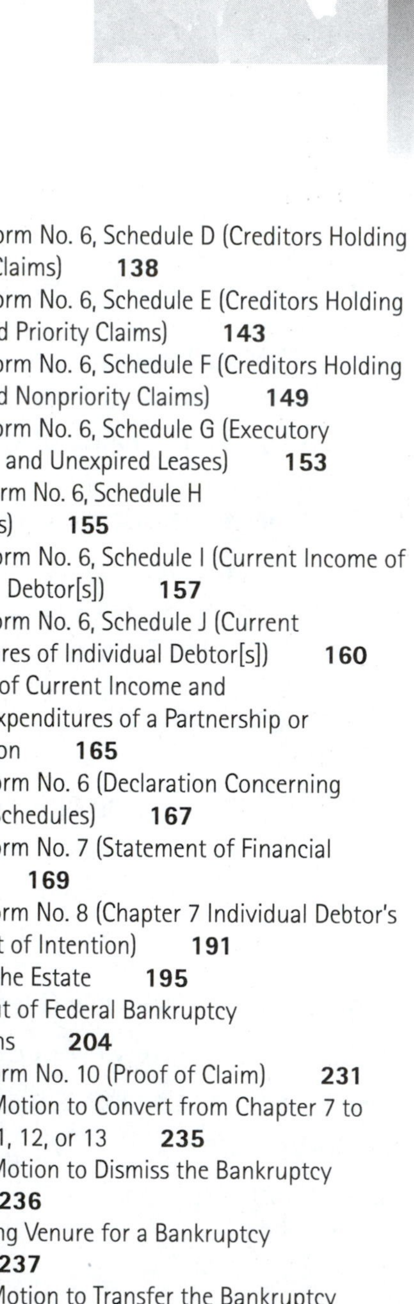

1.1 Adjustment of Dollar Amount (11 U.S.C.A. § 104) **6**
2.1 Federal Court Structure for Bankruptcy for Circuits with Bankruptcy Appellate Panels **23**
2.2 Federal Court Structure for Bankruptcy for Circuits without Bankruptcy Appellate Panels **23**
3.1 Real Estate Mortgage Transaction **34**
3.2 Secured Transaction **35**
3.3 Sale of Accounts or Chattel Paper **36**
3.4 Lease Transaction **40**
3.5 United States Trustees and Private Trustees **45**
4.1 Debtors and Operative Chapters of the Code **71**
5.1 Flow Chart for Chapter 7 **91**
5.2 Monthly Expenses for the McPhersons Assuming They Receive a Discharge under Chapter 7 **101**
5.3 Official Form No. 1 (The Debtor's Petition) **104**
5.4 Official Form No. 3 (Application to Pay Filing Fee in Installments) **113**
5.5 Procedural Form 201 (Clerk's Notice to Individual Consumer Debtor[s]) **116**
5.6 Corporate Resolution Authorizing Filing of a Chapter 7 Petition **117**
5.7 Procedural Form B 203 (Disclosure of Attorney's Compensation Statement) **119**
5.8 Official Form No. 6 (Summary of Schedules) **123**
5.9 Official Form No. 6, Schedule A (Real Property) **124**
5.10 Official Form No. 6, Schedule B (Personal Property) **126**
5.11 Official Form No. 6, Schedule C (Property Claimed as Exempt) **136**
5.12 Official Form No. 6, Schedule D (Creditors Holding Secured Claims) **138**
5.13 Official Form No. 6, Schedule E (Creditors Holding Unsecured Priority Claims) **143**
5.14 Official Form No. 6, Schedule F (Creditors Holding Unsecured Nonpriority Claims) **149**
5.15 Official Form No. 6, Schedule G (Executory Contracts and Unexpired Leases) **153**
5.16 Official Form No. 6, Schedule H (Codebtors) **155**
5.17 Official Form No. 6, Schedule I (Current Income of Individual Debtor[s]) **157**
5.18 Official Form No. 6, Schedule J (Current Expenditures of Individual Debtor[s]) **160**
5.19 Schedule of Current Income and Current Expenditures of a Partnership or Corporation **165**
5.20 Official Form No. 6 (Declaration Concerning Debtor's Schedules) **167**
5.21 Official Form No. 7 (Statement of Financial Affairs) **169**
5.22 Official Form No. 8 (Chapter 7 Individual Debtor's Statement of Intention) **191**
5.23 Creating the Estate **195**
5.24 Opting Out of Federal Bankruptcy Exemptions **204**
5.25 Official Form No. 10 (Proof of Claim) **231**
5.26 Debtor's Motion to Convert from Chapter 7 to Chapter 11, 12, or 13 **235**
5.27 Debtor's Motion to Dismiss the Bankruptcy Case **236**
5.28 Establishing Venure for a Bankruptcy Case **237**
5.29 Debtor's Motion to Transfer the Bankruptcy Case **238**
5.30 Motion to Avoid a Judicial Lien **239**

5.31 Party in Interest's Motion for Relief from the Automatic Stay **246**
5.32 Party in Interest's Motion to Dismiss the Bankruptcy Case **248**
5.33 Complaint Objecting to Debtor's Discharge **259**
5.34 Complaint Objecting to the Dischargeability of a Debt **261**
5.35 Official Form No. B 9A (Notice of Chapter 7 Bankruptcy Filing, Meeting of Creditors, and Fixing of Dates) (Chapter 7 Individual or Joint Debtor No Asset Case) **264**
5.36 Official Form No. B 9C (Notice of Chapter 7 Bankruptcy Filing, Meeting of Creditors, and Fixing of Dates) (Chapter 7 Individual or Joint Debtor Asset Case) **266**
5.37 Official Form No. B 9D (Notice of Chapter 7 Bankruptcy Filing, Meeting of Creditors, and Deadlines) (Chapter 7 Corporation/Partnership Asset Case) **268**
5.38 Procedural Form B 240 (Reaffirmation Agreement) **273**
5.39 Procedural Form 240M (Motion for Approval of Reaffirmation Agreement) **277**
5.40 Trustee's Final Report and Proposed Distribution **282**
5.41 Notice to Creditors and Other Parties in Interest Concerning the Trustee's Final Report and Proposed Distribution **291**
5.42 Trustee's Declaration That the Estate Has Been Fully Administered **292**
5.43 Trustee's Final Account after Distribution and Request for Discharge **293**
5.44 Final Decree **295**
6.1 Flow Chart for Chapter 13 **301**
6.2 Sample Chapter 13 Plan **310**
6.3 Motion of Debtors to Avoid Lien **315**
6.4 Official Form No. B9I (Notice of Chapter 13 Bankruptcy Case, Creditors, and Deadlines) **328**
6.5 Order Confirming Chapter 13 Plan **335**
7.1 Flow Chart for Chapter 12 **349**
7.2 The Chapter 12 Plan **359**
7.3 Official Form No. B9G (Notice of Chapter 12 Bankruptcy, Meeting of Creditors, & Deadlines) **375**
7.4 Official Form No. B9H (Notice of Chapter 12 Bankruptcy Case, Meeting of Creditors, & Deadlines) **377**
8.1 Flow Chart for Chapter 11 **391**
8.2 Official Form No. 1, Exhibit "A" (Exhibit "A" to the Voluntary Petition) **397**
8.3 Official Form No. 4 (List of Creditors Holding 20 Largest Unsecured Claims) **398**
8.4 List of Equity Security Holders **400**
8.5 Procedural Form B 207 (Certificate of Retention of Debtor in Possession) **406**
8.6 A Chapter 11 Plan **416**
8.7 A Chapter 11 Disclosure Statement **423**
8.8 Official Form No. 12 (Order and Notice for Hearing on Disclosure Statement) **441**
8.9 Official Form No. 13 (Order Approving Disclosure Statement and Fixing Time for Filing Acceptances or Rejections of Plan, Combined with Notice Thereof) **442**
8.10 Official Form No. 14 (Ballot for Accepting or Rejecting the Chapter 11 Plan) **452**
8.11 Official Form No. 15 (Order Confirming the Chapter 11 Plan) **454**
8.12 Sample Final Decree **456**
9.1 U.S. Bankruptcy Courts–Business and Nonbusiness Cases Commenced, by Chapter of the Bankruptcy Code, During the 12-month Period Ending September 30, 2002 **460**
9.2 Business Filings during Twelve Months Ending September 30, 2002 **463**
9.3 Nonbusiness Filings during Twelve Months Ending September 30, 2002 **464**
10.1 Flow Chart for the Involuntary Chapter 7 Case and the Chapter 11 Case **478**
10.2 Official Form No. 5 (Involuntary Case: Creditors Petition) **481**
10.3 Summons to Debtor in Involuntary Case **483**
10.4 Procedural Form B 253 (Order for Relief in an Involuntary Case) **489**

TABLE OF CASES

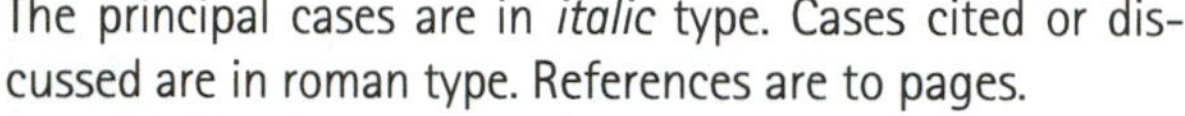

The principal cases are in *italic* type. Cases cited or discussed are in roman type. References are to pages.

American Card Co. v. H. M. H. Co., **11**
Casco, Bank & Trust Co. v. Cloutier, **11**
Cohen, In re, **252**
Conroe Forge & Manufacturing Corp. In re, **409**
Continental Airlines Corp., In re, **404**
Cooper (Chapter 7 liquidation), *In re,* **242**
Cooper (Chapter 11 liquidation), *In re,* **384**
Crater, In re, **206**
Damar Creative Group, Inc., In re, **220**
D. H. Overmyer Co. v. Frick Co., **82**
Dykstra, In re, **371**
Edgewater Motel, Inc., In re, **443**
Faberge Restaurant of Florida, Inc., In re, **475**
Flood v. Chrysler Financial Corp., **332**
Geen, In re, **249**
Grogan v. Garner, **255**
In re (see name of party)
Johns-Manville Corp., In re, **404**
Johnson v. Home State Bank, **470**
Keenan, In re, **255**
Kelly, In re, **249**
Kroskie, In re, **216**
Leibowitz v. Imsorn, **226**
Letsche, In re, **330**
Marathon (see Northern Pipe)
Mast, In re, **325**
Matter of (see name of party)
May, In re, **249**
Moog, In re, **11**
Mulliken, In re, **323**
Northern Pipeline Construction Co. v. Marathon Pipe Line Co., **10, 20**
Owens, In re, **223**
Palace Oriental Rugs, Inc., **487**
Porter, In re, **237**
Pulliam, In re, **209**
Richardson, In re, **338**
Runyon, In re, **489**
Scioto Valley Mortgage Co., In re, **437**
Smith, In re, **367**
Swanson, In re, **346**
Swarb v. Lennox, **82**
Thompson, In re, **294**
Toibb v. Radloff, **11, 73**
Traveler's Insurance Co. v. Bullington, **380**
United Savings Assoc. of Texas v. Timbers of Inwood Forest Associates, Ltd., **403**
Wamsganz v. Boatmen's Bank of De Soto, **11**

TABLE OF STATUTES AND RULES

Section 101, **16**
Section 101(5), **230**
Section 101(13), **30**
Section 101(14), **47, 403**
Section 101(16), **39, 399**
Section 101(17), **399**
Section 101(18), **74, 345**
Section 101(18)(A), **346**
Section 101(19), **345**
Section 101(21), **74**
Section 101(27), **15**
Section 101(28), **39**
Section 101(29), **39**
Section 101(31), **181, 396**
Section 101(36), **204**
Section 101(37), **204**
Section 101(40), **30**
Section 101(41), **30**
Section 101(51), **14**
Section 101(51)(B), **187**
Section 101(51)(C), **405, 437**
Section 101(51CV), **405**
Section 101(53), **39**
Section 102, **16**
Section 102(1), **16**
Section 102(3), **449**
Section 103, **16, 18**
Section 103(b)–(i), **18**
Section 103(e), **13**
Section 104, **6**
Section 104(b), **37, 75, 299**
Section 104(b)(1), **474**
Section 105(51C), **436, 437**
Section109, **6, 16, 30, 31, 71, 342**
Section 109(a), **30**
Section 109(b), **18, 99, 458, 463**
Section 109(b)(2), **31**
Section 109(b)–(f), **31**
Section 109(c), **73**
Section 109(d), **73**
Section 109(e), **99**
Section 109(f), **345**
Section 109(g), **31**
Section 110, **34**
Section 110(a), **33**
Section 110(a)(1), **111, 115**
Section 155(b), **42**
Section 158(c)(1), **22**
Section 301, **16, 108**
Section 302, **16, 53, 108**
Section 302(a), **108**
Section 303, **16**
Section 303(a), **84, 474**
Section 303(b), **6, 86**
Section 303(b)(1), **474**
Section 303(b)(2), **474**
Section 303(c), **474**
Section 303(e), **474**
Section 303(f), **485**
Section 303(g), **47, 485**
Section 303(h)(1), **486**
Section 303(h)(2), **486**
Section 303(i), **84**
Section 303(i)(1), **489**
Section 303(i)(2), **489**
Section 303(j), **489**
Section 305, **16, 86, 325, 373, 435**
Section 307, **46, 373**
Section 321(a)(1), **47**
Section 321(a)(2), **47**
Section 321–331, **16**
Section 322(c), **47**
Section 327(a), **403**
Section 329, **31, 118**

Section 329(a), **403**
Section 329(b), **118**
Section 329(c), **403**
Section 330, **363, 403**
Section 330(a)(4)(B), **319, 365**
Section 330(a)(5), **319, 365**
Section 341(b), **271**
Section 341(d), **270**
Section 341, **47**
Section 341–350, **16**
Section 342, **115**
Section 342(a), **327, 374, 434**
Section 342(b), **115, 129**
Section 342(c), **434**
Section 342(d), **115, 467**
Section 343, **270**
Section 348(f)(1), **321**
Section 348(f)(2), **321**
Section 350, **455**
Section 350(a), **343, 387**
Section 350(b), **343, 387**
Section 361, **369, 402**
Section 361(1), **410**
Section 361(2), **410**
Section 361(3), **410**
Section 362, **41**
Section 362–364, **19**
Section 362(a), **207, 242, 485**
Section 362(a)(1), **208, 367**
Section 362(a)(2), **208**
Section 362(a)(3), **317**
Section 362(a)(4), **208**
Section 362(a)(5), **314**
Section 362(a)(6), **208**
Section 362(a)(7), **208**
Section 362(a)(8), **208**
Section 362(b), **41, 209, 237**
Section 362(b)(1), **238**
Section 362(b)(3), **313**
Section 362(c)(1), **212**
Section 362(c)(2), **212**
Section 362(d), **325, 368, 373**
Section 362(d)(1), **242**
Section 362(e), **244**
Section 362(f), **244**
Section 362(g), **244**
Section 362(h), **209**
Section 363, **368**
Section 363(a), **402**
Section 363(b), **402**
Section 363(b)(1), **323**
Section 363(c), **326**
Section 363(c)(2), **371, 402, 435**
Section 363(d), **326**
Section 363(e), **402**
Section 363(f), **465**
Section 363(h), **233**
Section 363(l), **326**
Section 364, **368, 403**
Section 364(c), **403**
Section 364(d), **403**
Section 365, **368, 408**
Section 365(a), **215**
Section 365(d)(1), **215**
Section 365(d)(2), **415**
Section 366, **369**
Section 366(a), **404**
Section 501, **229**
Section 501–510, **17**
Section 501(b), **321**
Section 501(c), **321**
Section 502, **325, 373, 435**
Section 502(a), **229, 245**
Section 502(b), **245**
Section 502(b)(9), **317, 434**
Section 502(e), **221**
Section 502(f), **486**
Section 503(b), **278**
Section 503(b)(1), **403**
Section 503(b)(2), **403**
Section 504, **118**
Section 506, **413**
Section 506(a), **38, 205, 313, 316**
Section 506(b), **364**
Section 506(d), **121**
Section 507, **309, 413**
Section 507(a), **6, 309**
Section 507(a)(1), **37, 278**
Section 507(a)(1)–(9), **37**
Section 507(a)(2), **37, 278, 486**
Section 507(a)(3), **37, 278**
Section 507(a)(3)–(9), **142**
Section 507(a)(4), **37, 279**
Section 507(a)(5), **38**
Section 507(a)(5)(A), **279**
Section 507(a)(5)(B), **279**
Section 507(a)(6), **38, 279**
Section 507(a)(7), **38, 279**
Section 507(a)(8), **37, 38, 280**
Section 507(a)(8)(B), **38**
Section 507(a)(8)(C), **38**
Section 507(a)(8)(D), **38**

Section 507(a)(9), **38, 280**
Section 521(1), **121, 163**
Section 521(2)(A), **103, 190**
Section 521(2)(B), **190**
Section 521(2)(C), **192**
Section 521(3), **122**
Section 521–524, **17**
Section 522, **65, 201, 206**
Section 522(1), **135**
Section 522(a)(1), **202**
Section 522(a)(2), **202**
Section 522(b), **33, 202**
Section 522(b)(1), **201**
Section 522(b)(2), **135, 136**
Section 522(c), **203**
Section 522(d), **6, 201–203**
Section 522(d)(2), **137, 206**
Section 522(d)(3), **135**
Section 522(d)(7), **136**
Section 522(e), **206, 207**
Section 522(f), **207, 238, 323**
Section 522(f)(1), **204, 240**
Section 522(f)(1)(A), **204, 316, 323**
Section 52(f)(1)(B), **314, 323**
Section 522(f)(2)(B), **364**
Section 522(h), **326**
Section 523, **18, 255, 325**
Section 523(a), **255, 471**
Section 523(a)(2), **470**
Section 523(a)(3)(A), **296, 297**
Section 523(a)(3)(B), **296**
Section 523(a)(4), **470**
Section 523(a)(6), **470**
Section 523(a)(8), **316**
Section 523(a)(8)(A), **256, 257**
Section 523(a)(8)(B), **257, 258**
Section 523(a)(15), **376**
Section 523(c), **78**
Section 523(c)(1), **434**
Section 524, **17**
Section 524(c), **272**
Section 524(c)(6)(A), **272**
Section 524(c)(6)(B), **272**
Section 524(d), **272**
Section 524(f), **272**
Section 524(g), **405**
Section 525, **17**
Section 541, **65, 194, 200, 201**
Section 541(a), **194, 196**
Section 541(a)(4), **197**
Section 541(a)(5), **193, 197–199, 319, 366**
Section 541(a)(5)(A), **199**
Section 541(a)(5)(B), **199**
Section 541(a)(5)(C), **199**
Section 541(a)(6), **199**
Section 541(b), **194**
Section 541(b)(1), **197**
Section 541(b)(2), **197**
Section 541(b)(3), **197**
Section 541(c)(1)(B), **200**
Section 541(c)(2), **194, 197**
Section 542, **200, 213, 326, 374, 435**
Section 543, **200, 326, 374, 435**
Section 544, **435**
Section 544(a), **215, 262**
Section 544(b), **220**
Section 544–549, **322, 370**
Section 545, **222**
Section 546(a)(1), **370**
Section 546(a)(1)(A), **215, 322**
Section 546(a)(1)(B), **322**
Section 547, **222, 223, 262**
Section 547(b), **435**
Section 547(e)(3), **222**
Section 547(f), **222**
Section 548, **226, 262, 435**
Section 548(a)(1)(A), **226**
Section 548(a)(1)(B), **226**
Section 549(a), **228, 262**
Section 549(c), **229**
Section 553, **185, 196**
Section 554, **17, 246, 247**
Section 554(a), **213**
Section 554(b), **214, 233**
Section 554(c), **214**
Section 554(d), **214**
Section 586(e), **362**
Section 701, **48, 212**
Section 701(a)(1), **48**
Section 702, **402**
Section 702(b), **47, 270**
Section 702(d), **47, 270**
Section 704, **19, 47, 194**
Section 704(1), **278**
Section 704(8), **370**
Section 706(a), **234**
Section 707(a), **252**
Section 707(a)(1), **245**
Section 707(a)(3), **46, 247**
Section 707(b), **7, 100, 156, 159, 247, 249, 252, 467**
Section 722, **205, 271**
Section 726, **194, 278, 280**

Section 726(a)(4), **280**
Section 727, **18, 78, 271**
Section 727(a), **250, 435, 451**
Section 727(a)(2)(A), **259**
Section 727(a)(3), **164, 166, 254, 260**
Section 727(a)(4), **166, 254**
Section 727(a)(4)(A), **260**
Section 727(a)(5), **164, 166, 254, 260**
Section 727(a)(8), **470**
Section 727(a)(9), **65, 342, 386**
Section 727(c)(1), **46, 252, 262**
Section 727(d), **46, 272**
Section 727(e), **272**
Section 741–752, **73**
Section 742, **41**
Section 761–766, **73**
Section 901, **5, 13, 18**
Section 1101, **18**
Section 1101(1), **401**
Section 1101(2), **455**
Section 1102, **396, 399**
Section 1102(a)(1), **436**
Section 1102(a)(2), **436**
Section 1102(a)(3), **405, 436**
Section 1102(b)(1), **436**
Section 1103(a), **436**
Section 1103(b), **436**
Section 1104(a), **401, 435, 485**
Section 1104(a)(1), **435**
Section 1104(a)(2), **435**
Section 1104(b), **402**
Section 1104(c), **49, 402, 435**
Section 1106, **401**
Section 1106(a)(3), **232, 370, 401**
Section 1106(a)(4), **370, 401**
Section 1106(a)(4)(A), **323**
Section 1106(a)(7), **455**
Section 1107(a), **401**
Section 1108, **18, 402**
Section 1109(a), **41**
Section 1112(a), **435**
Section 1112(b), **435**
Section 1112(d), **435**
Section 1112(e), **435**
Section 1113, **408**
Section 1121(a), **407**
Section 1121(b), **407**
Section 1121(c), **407, 422**
Section 1121(c)(1)–(3), **422**
Section 1121(d), **407**
Section 1121(e), **18, 437**
Section 1122, **415, 421**
Section 1122(a), **413**
Section 1122(b), **413**
Section 1123, **415, 421**
Section 1123(a), **413**
Section 1123(a)(1), **413**
Section 1123(a)(2), **414**
Section 1123(a)(3), **414**
Section 1123(a)(4), **414**
Section 1123(a)(5), **414**
Section 1123(a)(5)(A)–(J), **414**
Section 1123(a)(6), **414**
Section 1123(a)(7), **414**
Section 1123(b), **413**
Section 1123(b)(1), **414**
Section 1123(b)(2), **415**
Section 1123(b)(3), **415**
Section 1123(b)(4), **408, 415, 465**
Section 1123(b)(5), **415**
Section 1123(b)(6), **415**
Section 1124, **414**
Section 1124(1), **414**
Section 1124(2), **414**
Section 1125, **408, 421, 422**
Section 1125(a), **434, 437**
Section 1125(a)(1), **422**
Section 1125(a)(2), **422**
Section 1125(b), **438**
Section 1125(c), **422**
Section 1125(e), **433**
Section 1125(f), **437**
Section 1126(b), **396**
Section 1126(b)(1), **434**
Section 1126(b)(2), **434**
Section 1126(B), **396**
Section 1126(f), **450**
Section 1127(a), **415**
Section 1127(b), **421**
Section 1127(c), **421**
Section 1127(d), **421**
Section 1128, **46**
Section 1128(b), **440**
Section 1129, **421, 440**
Section 1129(a)(6), **41**
Section 1129(a)(7), **433**
Section 1129(a)(7)(A), **449**
Section 1129(a)(7)(A)(i), **448**
Section 1129(a)(7)(A)(ii), **447**
Section 1129(a)(8), **449**
Section 1129(a)(9)(A), **403**
Section 1129(a)(11), **444, 448, 449**

Section 1129(b), **454**
Section 1129(b)(1), **440**
Section 1129(b)(2), **449**
Section 1129(b)(2)(A), **443**
Section 1129(b)(2)(A)(i), **447, 449**
Section 1129(b)(2)(A)(iii), **449**
Section 1129(b)(2)(B), **443**
Section 1129(b)(2)(C), **443**
Section 1141, **342**
Section 1141(a), **451**
Section 1141(b), **451**
Section 1141(d), **435, 451**
Section 1141(d)(3)(A), **18**
Section 1144, **455**
Section 1145, **408**
Section 1161–1174, **73**
Section 1201, **366**
Section 1201(a), **366**
Section 1201(b), **366**
Section 1201(c), **366**
Section 1201(d), **366**
Section 1202(a), **48, 369**
Section 1202(b), **48**
Section 1202(b)(1), **370**
Section 1202(b)(2), **370**
Section 1202(b)(3), **370**
Section 1202(b)(4), **370**
Section 1202(b)(5), **370**
Section 1202(5), **370**
Section 1203, **364, 368, 374**
Section 1204(a), **368**
Section 1204(b), **368**
Section 1205(a), **369**
Section 1205(b), **369**
Section 1205(b)(1), **369**
Section 1207, **366**
Section 1208, **373**
Section 1208(a), **18, 371, 373, 383**
Section 1208(b), **371, 383**
Section 1208(c), **373**
Section 1208(c)(3), **357**
Section 1208(c)(5), **383**
Section 1208(c)(7), **386**
Section 1208(d), **373, 386**
Section 1209(a)(7), **405**
Section 1221, **357, 366**
Section 1222, **357**
Section 1222(a), **357**
Section 1222(a)(1), **357**
Section 1222(a)(2), **357**
Section 1222(a)(3), **358**
Section 1122(a)(5)(A), **364**
Section 1122(a)(5)(B), **364**
Section 1222(b), **358**
Section 1222(b)(2), **364**
Section 1222(b)(5), **364**
Section 1222(b)(6), **360**
Section 1222(b)(8), **361**
Section 1222(b)(9), **358, 467**
Section 1222(c), **358**
Section 1222(d), **364**
Section 1223, **366**
Section 1223(a), **363**
Section 1223(a)(2), **363**
Section 1223(a)(3), **363**
Section 1223(b), **363**
Section 1223(c), **363**
Section 1224, **373, 379**
Section 1225, **379**
Section 1225(a)(1), **379**
Section 1225(a)(2), **379**
Section 1225(a)(3), **379**
Section 1225(a)(4), **364, 379**
Section 1225(a)(5), **379**
Section 1225(a)(5)(A), **364**
Section 1225(a)(5)(B), **364**
Section 1225(a)(5)(B)(i), **381**
Section 1225(a)(5)(B)(ii), **379**
Section 1225(a)(5)(C), **381**
Section 1225(a)(6), **380**
Section 1225(b)(1), **379**
Section 1225(b)(2), **359**
Section 1226(a), **358, 383**
Section 1227(a), **383**
Section 1227(b), **383**
Section 1227(c), **383**
Section 1228, **342**
Section 1228(a), **386**
Section 1228(b), **386**
Section 1228(c), **386**
Section 1228(d), **386**
Section 1229, **362, 385**
Section 1229(a), **383**
Section 1229(b)(1), **385**
Section 1230(a), **386**
Section 1230(b), **386**
Section 1301, **314, 320, 470**
Section 1301(a), **320**
Section 1301(b), **320**
Section 1301(c), **320, 325**
Section 1301(d), **320**
Section 1301–1330, **326**

Section 1302(a), **48, 322**
Section 1302(b), **48**
Section 1302(b)(1), **322**
Section 1302(b)(2), **322**
Section 1302(c), **48, 323**
Section 1303, **323, 325**
Section 1304(b), **321**
Section 1306, **312**
Section 1306(a), **321**
Section 1306(a)(2), **320**
Section 1306(b), **19, 321**
Section 1307(a), **323, 334**
Section 1307(b), **323, 334**
Section 1307(c), **325**
Section 1307(c)(4), **318**
Section 1307(c)(5), **334**
Section 1307(c)(7), **325**
Section 1307(c)–(e), **325**
Section 1307(d), **325**
Section 1307(e), **323, 325**
Section 1321, **308**
Section 1322, **308**
Section 1322(a), **308**
Section 1322(a)(1), **309**
Section 1322(a)(2), **309**
Section 1322(a)(3), **309**
Section 1322(a)(5), **470**
Section 1322(b), **309**
Section 1322(b)(1), **314**
Section 1322(b)(2), **100, 314**
Section 1322(b)(2)(A), **309**
Section 1322(b)(4), **313**
Section 1322(b)(5), **314**
Section 1322(c), **314**
Section 1322(c)(1), **314**
Section 1322(d), **99, 306, 309**
Section 1322(e), **314, 470**
Section 1323(a), **318**
Section 1323(b), **318**
Section 1323(c), **318**
Section 1324, **46, 325, 327**
Section 1325, **327**
Section 1325(a), **334**
Section 1325(a)(1), **327**
Section 1325(a)(2), **327**
Section 1325(a)(3), **330, 468**
Section 1325(a)(4), **316, 322, 330, 468**
Section 1325(a)(5), **330**
Section 1325(a)(5)(B), **469, 471**
Section 1325(a)(5)(B)(i), **372, 373**
Section 1325(a)(5)(C), **314, 369**
Section 1325(a)(6), **330, 334**
Section 1325(b)(1), **332**
Section 1325(b)(1)(B), **99, 306, 316**
Section 1325(b)(2), **306**
Section 1326, **314, 422**
Section 1326(a)(1), **318**
Section 1326(a)(2), **318**
Section 1326(c), **314**
Section 1327(a), **334**
Section 1327(a)(2), **338**
Section 1327(b), **317, 334**
Section 1327(c), **334**
Section 1328, **342**
Section 1328(a), **316, 341, 470**
Section 1328(a)(2), **341, 471**
Section 1328(b), **342, 471**
Section 1328(c), **342**
Section 1328(e), **342**
Section 1329, **340**
Section 1329(a), **338**
Section 1330(a), **341**
Section 1330(b), **341**

FEDERAL RULES OF BANKRUPTCY PROCEDURE

Rule 365(a), **214**
Rule 521(i), **214**
Rule 524(d), **214**
Rule 554(b), **214**
Rule 554(c), **214**
Rule 1002(a), **103**
Rule 1003(b), **474, 486**
Rule 1006(a), **112**
Rule 1006(b), **112**
Rule 1006(b)(3), **112**
Rule 1007(3), **399**
Rule 1007(a)(1), **121**
Rule 1007(b)(1), **152, 163**
Rule 1007(c), **107, 319**
Rule 1007(d), **396**
Rule 1007(h), **193, 199, 319, 366, 396**
Rule 1008, **193**
Rule 1009, **365**
Rule 1009(a), **193, 319, 396**
Rule 1009(b), **190**
Rule 1010, **477**
Rule 1011(a), **486**
Rule 1011(b), **486**
Rule 1011(d), **486**

Rule 1013(a), **486**
Rule 1013(b), **486**
Rule 1014, **325, 371, 373**
Rule 1014(a)(1), **245**
Rule 1017, **252, 323, 371, 435**
Rule 1017(a), **245**
Rule 1107(b)(2), **190**
Rule 1930(a)(1), **263**
Rule 2000(k), **46**
Rule 2002, **374, 434**
Rule 2002(a), **234, 263**
Rule 2002(l), **263**
Rule 2003, **327, 374**
Rule 2003(a), **270**
Rule 2003(b)(2), **271**
Rule 2003(c), **270**
Rule 2003(e), **270**
Rule 2004, **245, 325, 371, 373, 435, 325, 371, 373, 435**
Rule 2004(b), **247, 270**
Rule 2008, **47**
Rule 2011, **405**
Rule 2014(a), **403**
Rule 2015(a)(5), **401**
Rule 2015(c)(1), **321**
Rule 2016, **31**
Rule 2016(b), **118, 403**
Rule 2017, **233**
Rule 3002, **368**
Rule 3002(c), **338, 383**
Rule 300(c)(5), **230**
Rule 3004, **321, 368**
Rule 3005, **321**
Rule 3013, **413**
Rule 3015, **308**
Rule 3015(b), **319**
Rule 3017(a), **437**
Rule 3019, **421**
Rule 3022, **455**
Rule 4001, **325, 373, 435**
Rule 4001(a), **234**
Rule 4001(d), **315**
Rule 4003(a), **135**
Rule 4003(b), **206, 263, 315**
Rule 4003(d), **314, 364, 371**
Rule 4004(a), **78, 252, 262**
Rule 4007, **435**
Rule 4007(a), **255, 325**
Rule 4007(c), **78, 434, 435**
Rule 4008, **451**
Rule 5001(a), **44**
Rule 5001(c), **44**
Rule 5003, **43**
Rule 5003(c), **43**
Rule 5003(d), **44**
Rule 5003(e), **44**
Rule 5006, **44**
Rule 5007(a), **43**
Rule 5009, **343, 387**
Rule 6002, **435**
Rule 6004, **323**
Rule 6007(b), **214**
Rule 6008, **271**
Rule 7001, **233, 245, 252, 255, 262, 325, 326, 455**
Rule 7002–7087, **233**
Rule 7004, **477**
Rule 7004(h), **364**
Rule 7052, **368**
Rule 9006(a), **44**
Rule 9006(f), **315**
Rule 9014, **233, 373, 435**
Rule 9016, **245**
Rule 9028, **42**
Rule 9034, **46**

28 U.S.C.A.—JUDICIARY AND JUDICIAL PROCEDURE

Section 148(a)(2), **407**
Section 151, **42**
Section 152(a), **42**
Section 152(a)(1), **42**
Section 152(a)(3), **42**
Section 152(b)(1), **42**
Section 152(c), **42**
Section 152(d), **42**
Section 153(a), **42**
Section 153(b), **42**
Section 153(e), **42**
Section 155(a), **42**
Section 156(b), **44**
Section 156(e), **43**
Section 156(f), **44**
Section 157, **261**
Section 157(a), **235**
Section 157(2)(A), **437**
Section 157(b)(1), **437**
Section 157(b)(2)(F), **223**
Section 157(b)(2)(L), **443**
Section 158(b), **26**
Section 305, **245**

Section 523(a)(3), **59**
Section 581(a), **46**
Section 581(b), **46**
Section 581(c), **46**
Section 581–589a, **5, 46**
Section 586, **46**
Section 586(a)(1), **46**
Section 586(a)(3)(A), **118**
Section 1334, **233, 261**
Section 1334(a), **234**
Section 1334(c), **245**
Section 1334(e), **198**
Section 1408, **235, 237**
Section 1408(1), **235**
Section 1409, **237**
Section 1412, **237, 245, 435**
Section 1452, **233**
Section 1475, **55**
Section 1746, **166**
Section 1930(a)(6), **401, 455**
Section 1930(b), **44**
Section 1961(a), **447**
Section 2075, **20**

UNIFORM COMMERCIAL CODE

Section 1–201(b)(35), **40**
Section 2–702, **81**
Section 9–102(a)(12), **35**
Section 9–102(a)(12)(B), **36**
Section 9–102(a)(28), **35**
Section 9–102(a)(28)(B), **36**
Section 9–102(a)(41), **35, 36**
Section 9–102(a)(52)(C), **215**
Section 9–102(a)(72), **35**
Section 9–102(a)(72)(D), **36**
Section 9–102(a)(73), **35**
Section 9–103, **205**
Section 9–109(a)(1), **35**
Section 9–202, **35**
Section 9–315(a)(1), **36**
Section 9–317(a)(2)(A) **215**
Section 9–317(b), (e), **36**
Section 9–320(a), **36**
Section 9–609, **82**
Section 9–610(a), **82**
Section 9–620(a), **82**

PREFACE

Bankruptcy is in the public eye, now more than ever, due to the headline-grabbing filings by large corporations such as Enron, K-Mart, United Airlines, Global Crossing, and WorldCom; the ever-increasing number of bankruptcy filings generally (more than 1,500,000 in 2002); and the controversy over Congress's attempt to pass bankruptcy reform legislation to curb the perceived abuse in consumer bankruptcies. This includes a highly controversial new provision to be codified as 11 U.S.C.A. § 523(a)(20) to prevent the discharge of debt arising from the intentional acts of a debtor by force or threat of force or by physical obstruction that interferes with one's efforts to provide goods or services (which could include providing abortion services). Consequently, bankruptcy is a very dynamic area of the law, thereby necessitating this fourth edition of our text, accompanying Instructor's Manual and On-Line Companion. We make a brief reference to the bankruptcy reform bills that were passed by each house of Congress in 2001 but have not yet been reconciled. It is difficult to know as we complete this text if, when, and in what form this bankruptcy reform legislation—presently known as the Bankruptcy Abuse Prevention and Consumer Protection Act of 2002—will become law. The Conference Committee of the House and Senate in the 107th Congress had reached an agreement on many of the differences between their respective versions. A summary of the Conference Report, issued as H.R. 333, can be found at http://www.abiworld.org.

CHANGES TO THIS EDITION

This edition includes relevant changes to the Bankruptcy Code, the Federal Rules of Bankruptcy Procedure, and the Official Forms. At times, more recent cases have replaced older cases, although the emphasis remains on text, examples, and problems.

On a more practical level, Chapter Four has been revised to emphasize information gathering including client interviews and the paralegal's role in this process. Also, the discussion concerning the eligibility of debtors under various chapters of the Bankruptcy Code has been deleted from Chapter Four and now appears in its own chapter, Chapter Nine of this text. We also introduce the McPhersons—hypothetical debtors whose bankruptcy case is followed and explained from beginning to end—in the hope of giving the student a clear idea of how a bankruptcy case really works. In Chapter Four, we explain how the attorney and paralegal gather facts from the McPhersons so a decision can be made as to whether or not to file bankruptcy. In addition, we analyze under what chapter of the Bankruptcy Code the bankruptcy should be filed if a decision is made to file.

The text develops nonbankruptcy as well as bankruptcy solutions. Not all clients with financial problems will want or need to file bankruptcy. This text includes alternatives to filing bankruptcy to aid the paralegal in working with an attorney who has clients in this situation.

Chapter Five, dealing with Chapter 7 liquidation, has been changed substantially to better reflect how a typical (if there is such a thing) Chapter 7 bankruptcy case might proceed. In this regard, the new flow chart emphasizes the two tracks in bankruptcy for an individual debtor, the administration of the estate and the debtor's discharge. The theme of Chapter Four, the information gathering process, is further refined for a Chapter 7 filing. The McPhersons from Chapter Four now find themselves in a Chapter 7 bankruptcy. We retain the discussion about how to complete the documents necessary for a Chapter 7 filing, although the official forms have been updated and emphasize on-line filing rather than hard-copy filing.

Chapter Six of the text, the Chapter 13 bankruptcy, has been expanded with a new flow chart and a new Chapter 13 plan. The plan shows how a Chapter 13 plan benefits the debtor concerning various types of debt. The McPhersons from Chapters Four and Five now find themselves in a Chapter 13 bankruptcy to enable the reader to more clearly understand the distinction between a Chapter 7 bankruptcy and a Chapter 13 bankruptcy.

Chapter Seven, the Chapter 12 bankruptcy, has been revised with an emphasis on information gathering and a Chapter 12 plan that explores the differences between a Chapter 13 and a Chapter 12 plan.

As noted in the third edition, the paralegal plays an increasingly important role in the bankruptcy process of many law firms. Duties may include interviewing clients, drafting and on-line filing of the necessary documents in a bankruptcy case, and legal research. With this in mind, we have included a detailed questionnaire on the On-line Companion that the paralegal can use when interviewing a client and step-by-step guides for preparing the forms for filing a bankruptcy. Although we emphasize Chapter 7 because it comprises the bulk of cases filed in the bankruptcy court, illustrative Chapter 11, 12, and 13 plans are included and discussed.

We provide many examples and problems in this text to help the reader understand how the bankruptcy process works. Our goal is to provide a text for those new to the bankruptcy field and not a text by bankruptcy experts for bankruptcy experts.

We believe this text will stimulate discussion in the classroom and provide the reader with a solid foundation in the field of bankruptcy. We welcome your comments and hope that you will find the following materials informative and challenging.

SUPPLEMENTAL TEACHING MATERIALS

- The **Instructor's Manual** is available on-line at *www.westlegalstudies.com* in the Instructor's Lounge under Resource. Written by the authors of the text, the *Instructor's Manual* contains the following:
    - Chapter Outlines
    - Answers to the Problems within the Text
    - Test Bank

- **On-line Companion™**—The On-line Companion™ Web site can be found at *www.westlegalstudies.com* in the resource section of the Web site.
- **Web page**—Come visit our Web site at *www.westlegalstudies.com,* where you will find valuable information such as hot links and sample materials to download, as well as other West Legal Studies products.
- **Westlaw®**—West's on-line computerized legal research system offers students "hands-on" experience with a system commonly used in law offices. Qualified adopters can receive ten free hours of Westlaw®. Westlaw® can be accessed with Macintosh and IBM PC and compatibles. A modem is required.
- **Survival Guide for Paralegal Students,** a pamphlet by Kathleen Mercer Reed and Bradene Moore covers practical and basic information to help students make the most of their paralegal courses. Topics covered include choosing courses of study and note-taking skills.

- **West's Paralegal Video Library**—West Legal Studies is pleased to offer the following videos at no charge to qualified adopters:
  - *The Drama of the Law II: Paralegal Issues Video*
    ISBN: 0-314-07088-5
  - *The Making of a Case Video*
    ISBN: 0-314-07300-0
  - *ABA Mock Trial Video-Product Liability*
    ISBN: 0-314-07342-6
  - *Arguments to the United States Supreme Court Video*
    ISBN: 0-314-07070-2
- **Court TV Videos**—West Legal Studies is pleased to offer the following videos from Court TV for a minimal fee while supplies last.
  - *New York v. Ferguson—Murder on the 5:33: The Trial of Colin Ferguson*
    ISBN: 0-7668-1098-4
  - *Ohio v. Alfieri*
    ISBN: 0-7668-1099-2
  - *Flynn v. Goldman Sachs—Fired on Wall Street: A Case of Sex Discrimination?*
    ISBN: 0-7668-1096-8
  - *Dodd v. Dodd—Religion and Child Custody in Conflict*
    ISBN: 0-7668-1094-1
  - *In Re Custody of Baby Girl Clausen—Child of Mine: The Fight for Baby Jessica*
    ISBN: 0-7668-1097-6
  - *Fentress v. Eli Lilly & Co., et al—Prozac on Trial*
    ISBN: 0-7668-1095-x
  - *Garcia v. Garcia—Fighting over Jerry's Money*
    ISBN: 0-7668-0264-7
  - *Hall v. Hall—Irretrievably Broken—A Divorce Lawyer Goes to Court*
    ISBN: 0-7668-0196-9
  - *Maglica v. Maglica—Broken Hearts, Broken Commitments*
    ISBN: 0-7668-0867-x
  - *Northside Partners v. Page and New Kids on the Block—New Kids in Court: Is Their Hit Song a Copy?*
    ISBN: 0-7668-9426-7

Please note the internet resources are of a time-sensitive nature and URL addresses may often change or be deleted.

Contact us at westlegalstudies@delmar.com

ACKNOWLEDGMENTS

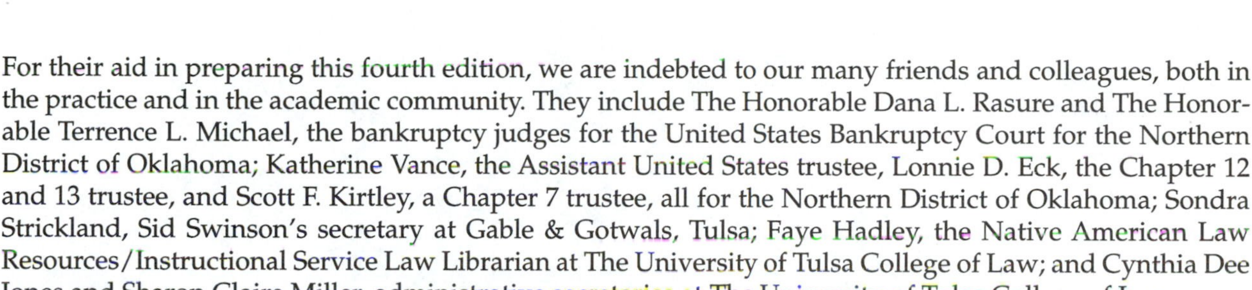

For their aid in preparing this fourth edition, we are indebted to our many friends and colleagues, both in the practice and in the academic community. They include The Honorable Dana L. Rasure and The Honorable Terrence L. Michael, the bankruptcy judges for the United States Bankruptcy Court for the Northern District of Oklahoma; Katherine Vance, the Assistant United States trustee, Lonnie D. Eck, the Chapter 12 and 13 trustee, and Scott F. Kirtley, a Chapter 7 trustee, all for the Northern District of Oklahoma; Sondra Strickland, Sid Swinson's secretary at Gable & Gotwals, Tulsa; Faye Hadley, the Native American Law Resources/Instructional Service Law Librarian at The University of Tulsa College of Law; and Cynthia Dee Jones and Sharon Claire Miller, administrative secretaries at The University of Tulsa College of Law.

We wish to thank our friends at Thomson–Delmar Learning for working with us on this project. Special thanks to Pamela Fuller, our Acquisitions Editor; Melissa Riveglia, our Developmental Editor; Sarah Duncan, our Editorial Assistant; and all those who worked to transform the manuscript into this book.

Finally, Phyllis and I would like to welcome Sid Swinson as our third author. Sid replaces our late friend and colleague, Warren L. McConnico, who was our co-author when we developed the first edition of the text. Sid brings a wealth of bankruptcy experience to this text. In addition to his many years of practice in the field of bankruptcy, Sid is a Chapter 7 trustee for the Northern and Eastern Districts of Oklahoma, an Adjunct Professor at The University of Tulsa College of Law, an Adjunct Settlement Judge for both the United States Bankruptcy and District Courts for the Northern District of Oklahoma, and a member of the American Bankruptcy Institute.

M.A.F.
P.H.F.
S.K.S

CHAPTER 1

The Evolution of Bankruptcy Law

CHAPTER OUTLINE

SECTION 1
BRIEF HISTORY OF MODERN BANKRUPTCY LAW
A. The Appearance of Bankruptcy in Early English Law
B. Treatment of Bankruptcy in the United States Constitution
C. Early American Bankruptcy Statutes
D. The Bankruptcy Act of 1898
E. The Bankruptcy Reform Act of 1978
F. Amendments to the Bankruptcy Reform Act of 1978
G. Future Bankruptcy Reform

SECTION 2
THE DUAL NATURE OF BANKRUPTCY AS A REMEDY FOR BOTH CREDITORS AND DEBTORS

Debt collection has come a long way since the days of the Romans. Although Roman creditors were allowed by law to physically divide the debtor's body proportionately among themselves, there is no record of this ever having been done and it would hardly have helped the creditors to recover their losses. Selling the debtor as a slave was a common practice, however, and did produce some revenue. The threat of imprisonment or exile also stimulated some debt repayment. Under Roman law, debtors were obligated to pay their debts, and if their estates were sold by creditors, the debtors received no discharge from any unpaid balance.

SECTION 1
BRIEF HISTORY OF MODERN BANKRUPTCY LAW

The word "bankruptcy" has its origin in the commercial practices of early Italian merchants, traders, and moneylenders, who transacted their business from benches in central town markets. When a merchant was unable to pay his debts, it was common practice for his creditors to break his bench as a symbol of financial failure. This practice led to the phrase "banca rotta," which is derived from the Italian *banca* (bench) and *rotta* (break). English merchants became familiar with the Italian practice and changed "banca rotta" to the English "bankrupt."

A. THE APPEARANCE OF BANKRUPTCY IN EARLY ENGLISH LAW

The earliest English bankruptcy laws, from which American law was derived, were creditors' remedies only and were quite punitive. Prior to the late 1700s, failure to pay debts was viewed as an immoral act and the debtor often faced imprisonment.

Conditions of imprisonment in the debtors' prisons of London varied considerably. Debtors lived in the prisons with their families and were not forced to work. People not even connected with the prison could rent apartments or rooms there. The truly poor debtors lived in crowded wards. It was their living conditions that brought about reform. In 1829, approximately 7,000 debtors were imprisoned in London, and as late as 1921, about 400 debtors were in London prisons.

The concept of discharge of indebtedness first appeared in English law in 1705 in a bankruptcy law available only to the commercial debtor. At this time, debtors could not bring actions to discharge indebtedness. The actions were brought by creditors to collect indebtedness, and the debtors responded by requesting discharge of their indebtedness. The commercial debtors were allowed an exemption for necessary family wearing apparel. They were also allowed an exemption of 5 percent of the estate (up to £200) if they could pay a certain dividend to their creditors.

The bankruptcy law passed in England in 1849 classified the bankrupt's discharge certificate based on fault. There were three types of discharge certificates. A first-class discharge certificate was issued if the debtor was without fault. A second-class discharge certificate was issued if the debtor had some fault, such as carelessness, but was not dishonest. A third-class discharge certificate was issued if the debtor was totally at fault due to dishonesty.

B. TREATMENT OF BANKRUPTCY IN THE UNITED STATES CONSTITUTION

During colonial days, the English colonies in North America naturally followed English law. After the American Revolution, the Articles of Confederation were passed by the Continental Congress and ratified by the 13 original states. The Articles became effective on March 1, 1781. The Articles continued to recognize the Congress as the central government of the Confederation but severely limited its powers. For example, Congress had to rely on the states for money and an army. The Articles contained no reference to bankruptcy, which meant that all bankruptcy law during this period was left to the states.

In 1789, the Articles of Confederation were superseded by the United States Constitution. Article I, Section 8, of the Constitution grants Congress power to act in enumerated areas. Article I, Section 8, Clause 4, gives Congress the power to enact uniform bankruptcy laws.

> Section 8. The Congress shall have the power . . .
>
> 4. To establish a uniform rule of naturalization, and uniform laws on the subject of bankruptcy throughout the United States.

Although the Constitution gave Congress the power to enact bankruptcy laws in 1789, it did not require the enactment of such laws. The first federal bankruptcy law was not enacted until 1800.

C. EARLY AMERICAN BANKRUPTCY STATUTES

1. The Bankruptcy Act of 1800

The Bankruptcy Act of 1800 was enacted in response to the financial panics of 1792 and 1797, which were caused by speculation in land, stock, and government scrip. Scrip was paper money issued in the United States in amounts of less than a dollar. These panics resulted in the imprisonment of many debtors, some of whom were quite prominent.

For instance, two signers of the Constitution had serious debt problems at this time. One signer named Robert Morris, a financier who supervised the finances of the revolutionary war from 1781 to 1784, had established the Bank of North America in Philadelphia in 1781. He lost his money in land speculation and was in a debtors' prison when the Bankruptcy Act of 1800 was passed. Morris spent three years in prison and was released after obtaining a discharge under the Act. The other, James Wilson, had a distinguished career as a revolutionary patriot, lawyer, and member of Congress. He was one of the drafters of the Pennsylvania Constitution and the first professor of law at the College of Pennsylvania, which is now the University of Pennsylvania. Wilson was appointed to the United States Supreme Court in 1789. In 1798, he fled Pennsylvania to avoid debtors' prison and died a short time later in North Carolina.

Not all debtors were prominent persons by any standard. In the generation after the Revolution, about 60 percent of the people in debtors' prison owed $10 or less. Imprisonment for debt was, however, the exception rather than the rule at this time. Even though debtors were likely to be arrested, most were not imprisoned; those who were imprisoned were generally free again in a short time.

The Bankruptcy Act of 1800, which applied only to merchants, was a temporary measure designed to expire in 1805. It was repealed in 1803. For the next 38 years, the country operated without federal bankruptcy legislation.

2. The Bankruptcy Act of 1841

The Bankruptcy Act of 1841, the second federal bankruptcy act, became effective in 1842 in response to poor economic conditions brought about by the panic of 1837. The years prior to 1837 were a "get-rich-quick" time nationally. The Bankruptcy Act of 1841 is important historically because it provided for the initiation of bankruptcy proceedings by the nonmerchant debtor who had total debts of less than $2,000. The exemption provisions of this Act were also more favorable to the debtor. For example, clothing, furniture, and other "necessaries" not to exceed $300 in value were allowed as exempt property.

The Bankruptcy Act of 1841 lasted less than two years. For the next 25 years, the country again operated without federal bankruptcy legislation.

3. The Bankruptcy Act of 1867

The Bankruptcy Act of 1867, the third federal bankruptcy act, was enacted after the Civil War in response to another economic crisis. It was the first bankruptcy legislation designed to be permanent. This bankruptcy law allowed the filing of both voluntary and involuntary petitions for merchants, nonmerchants, and corporate debtors. An involuntary petition is one filed by the debtor's creditors, rather than by the debtor.

The Bankruptcy Act of 1867 provided for an assignee, who was elected by creditors at the first meeting after notice of the bankruptcy petition. The assignee performed the same basic duties as today's trustee. The assignee gathered up the property of the debtor, with the exception of exempt property, and held it for distribution to creditors. Discharge would be denied for dishonest acts by the debtor.

A debtor had to have debts of more than $300 to qualify for bankruptcy under this Act. Exemptions were expanded to $500 and included necessary household and kitchen furniture, wearing apparel for the debtor and his wife and children, and other necessaries designated by the assignee, as well as property exempted by both federal nonbankruptcy law and the debtor's state law.

The Bankruptcy Act of 1867 was not repealed until 1878. For the next 20 years, the country again operated without federal bankruptcy legislation. This was the last period in American history without federal bankruptcy law.

D. THE BANKRUPTCY ACT OF 1898

The Bankruptcy Act of 1898 was the fourth federal bankruptcy act. It was divided into 14 chapters, numbered consecutively, using Roman numerals, from I through XIV.

Chapter I	Definitions
Chapter II	Courts of Bankruptcy
Chapter III	Bankrupts
Chapter IV	Courts and Procedure Therein
Chapter V	Officers, Their Duties and Compensation
Chapter VI	Creditors
Chapter VII	Estates
Chapter VIII	Provisions for the Relief of Debtors
Chapter IX	Readjustment of Debts of Agencies or Instrumentalities (muncipal corporations)
Chapter X	Corporate Reorganizations
Chapter XI	Arrangements
Chapter XII	Real Property Arrangements by Persons Other Than Corporations
Chapter XIII	Wage Earners' Plans
Chapter XIV	Maritime Commission Liens

Voluntary initiation of proceedings by the nonmerchant debtor, a concept initiated in the Bankruptcy Act of 1841, was incorporated into the Bankruptcy Act of 1898. The Bankruptcy Act of 1898 also enhanced the debtor's relief by eliminating creditor consent to discharge in liquidation cases. Involuntary proceedings were also retained. Although the 1898 Act did not provide the debtor with federal exemptions, it did adopt state exemptions.

Under the Bankruptcy Act of 1898, bankruptcy courts were created as a part of the United States district courts. This gave district court judges primary responsibility over bankruptcy cases. The district court judges delegated the administration of bankruptcy cases, on a case by case basis, to "referees." These quasi-judicial officials performed both the administrative and judicial functions associated with bankruptcy cases. Over the years, referees evolved into judges and actually became bankruptcy judges under the 1973 Bankruptcy Rules.

The Bankruptcy Act of 1898 used the term "trustee" to describe the elected representative of the creditors. The Act also provided that the trustee was to be paid out of the assets of the estate.

Although the 1898 Act was substantially amended over the years, it remained in effect as the national bankruptcy law for 81 years. It was superseded by the Bankruptcy Reform Act of 1978, which became effective on October 1, 1979.

E. THE BANKRUPTCY REFORM ACT OF 1978

As the years passed, the Bankruptcy Act of 1898 became obsolete. It was not a true codification of bankruptcy law but merely a collection of bankruptcy enactments and amendments. The language was outdated, and the organization was poor. Perhaps the most objectionable features of the Bankruptcy Act of 1898 were the dual responsibilities of the office of the bankruptcy judge. The judicial function of resolving disputes was inconsistent with the administrative duties performed by the bankruptcy judge. Administrative functions usually involved contact with the litigants on an ex-parte basis, which was unavoidable and even encouraged by the administrative duties imposed upon the bankruptcy judge. Even if no impropriety existed, the administrative duties performed by the bankruptcy judge created the appearance of a bias in favor of the estate because its representatives had frequent contact with the judge.

On November 8, 1978, President Jimmy Carter signed into law the Bankruptcy Reform Act of 1978. This Act, commonly referred to as the **Bankruptcy Code** or the **Code** (not to be confused with the Bankruptcy Act of 1898, which is commonly referred to as the "Bankruptcy Act" or the "Act"), became effective on October 1, 1979, and represented the first overall reenactment of the bankruptcy laws since 1898.

The Code was originally divided into eight chapters. The chapters were numbered consecutively, using Arabic numbers, from 1 to 15, not from 1 to 8, using only the odd numbers. The even numbers were reserved for later additions. The original chapters of the Code were

Chapter 1	General Provisions
Chapter 3	Case Administration
Chapter 5	Creditors, Debtor, and the Estate
Chapter 7	Liquidation
Chapter 9	Adjustment of Debts of a Municipality
Chapter 11	Reorganization
Chapter 13	Adjustment of Debts of an Individual with Regular Income
Chapter 15	United States Trustee

Chapters 1, 3, and 5 deal with administration, priorities, and **exemptions** and apply to all the chapters. These three chapters are known as the **universal chapters.** Only selected sections of Chapter 3 and Chapter 5, however, apply to a case under Chapter 9. 11 U.S.C.A. § 901.

Chapters 7, 9, 11, and 13 are mutually exclusive chapters; each deals with a different type of bankruptcy case. These four chapters are known as the **operative chapters.** Selected sections of Chapter 11 are, however, applicable in a Chapter 9 case.

Chapter 7 deals with liquidation bankruptcy. The Chapter 7 trustee converts the debtor's estate into money and distributes it to the debtor's creditors. Chapter 7 may be used by individuals, partnerships, and corporations.

Chapter 9, a rarely used chapter, applies to financially troubled municipalities. A "municipality" is defined as a "political subdivision or public agency or instrumentality of a State." 11 U.S.C.A. § 101(40). The Chapter 9 bankruptcy has a history of its own, apart from the rest of the Code. A short discussion of Chapter 9 can be found in Appendix C.

Chapter 11 generally deals with **reorganization,** usually business reorganizations. Unlike the Chapter 7 liquidation, a Chapter 11 bankruptcy is designed for filing a reorganization plan to keep a business going. In reorganization cases, creditors are usually repaid through the plan as the debtor continues its operation and not through liquidation of the debtor's estate. However, Chapter 11 cases may, by design or by circumstances, become liquidation cases.

Chapter 13 is similar to Chapter 11 in that the estate of the debtor is not liquidated. Chapter 13 deals with debt adjustment for individuals with regular income. It permits debtors to repay all or part of their debts over a three- to five-year period with their disposable income.

The final original chapter of the Code, Chapter 15, initially established a pilot **United States trustee** program in 18 judicial districts. Chapter 15 had a sunset provision for automatic repeal on September 30, 1986. When the United States trustee program ceased being experimental and became a permanent part of the bankruptcy process, Chapter 15 of the Bankruptcy Code was repealed and the United States trustee system was moved to Title 28 of the United States Code. 28 U.S.C.A. §§ 581–589a.

F. AMENDMENTS TO THE BANKRUPTCY REFORM ACT OF 1978

During the years since its enactment, there have been a number of changes in the Bankruptcy Reform Act of 1978. These changes include

1. The Bankruptcy Amendments and Federal Judgeship Act of 1984
2. The Bankruptcy Judges, United States Trustees, and Family Farmer Bankruptcy Act of 1986
3. The 1990 amendments, consisting of four separate statutes: The Omnibus Reconciliation Act of 1990; The Criminal Victims Protection Act (the MADD law); The Crime Control Act; and The Judicial Improvements Act

4. The 1991 Revision of the Bankruptcy Rules and Official Forms
5. The Bankruptcy Reform Act of 1994 (which also brought about changes in the Official Bankruptcy Forms and the Procedural Bankruptcy Forms)

As authorized by 11 U.S.C.A. § 104, the Judicial Conference of the United States adjusts the dollar amounts every three years for Chapter 13 eligibility (11 U.S.C.A. § 109(e)), minimum aggregate claims needed to commence an involuntary bankruptcy (11 U.S.C.A. § 303(b)), certain priority claims (11 U.S.C.A. § 507(a)), and the value of property exemptions allowed to the debtor (11 U.S.C.A. § 522(d)). This text uses the dollar amounts as adjusted on April 1, 2004. The next adjustment is scheduled for April 1, 2007. A table of adjustment of dollar amounts is Exhibit 1–1.

EXHIBIT 1–1 Adjustment of Dollar Amount—11 U.S.C.A. § 104.

	1979	**1994**	**April 1, 1998**	**April 1, 2001**	**April 1, 2004**
11 U.S.C.A. § 109(e)—allowable debt limits for filing under Chapter 13					
	100,000	250,000	269,250	290,525	307,675
	350,000	750,000	807,750	871,550	922,975
11 U.S.C.A. § 303(b)—minimum aggregate claims needed for the commencement of an involuntary bankruptcy					
¶(1)	5,000	10,000	10,775	11,625	12,300
¶(2)	5,000	10,000	10,775	11,625	12,300
11 U.S.C.A. § 507(a)—priority claims					
¶(3)	2,000	4,000	4,300	4,650	4,925
¶(4)(B)(i)	2,000	4,000	4,300	4,650	4,925
¶(5)	2,000	4,000	4,300	4,650	4,925
¶(6)	900	1,800	1,950	2,100	2,225
11 U.S.C.A. § 522(d)—value of property exemptions allowed to the debtor					
¶(1)	7,500	15,000	16,150	17,425	18,450
¶(2)	1,200	2,400	2,575	2,775	2,950
¶(3)	200	400	425	450	475
	4,000	8,000	8,625	9,300	9,850
¶(4)	500	1,000	1,075	1,150	1,225
¶(5)	400	800	850	925	975
	3,750	7,500	8,075	8,725	9,250
¶(6)	750	1,500	1,625	1,750	1,850
¶(8)	4,000	8,000	8,625	9,300	9,850
¶(11)(D)	7,500	15,000	16,150	17,425	18,450
11 U.S.C.A. § 523(a)(2)(C)—"luxury goods and services" or cash advances obtained by the consumer debtor within 60 days before the filing of a bankruptcy petition, which are considered nondischargeable					
	500	1,000	1,075	1,150	1,225

G. FUTURE BANKRUPTCY REFORM

The Bankruptcy Reform Act of 1978 has been criticized for being too debtor-friendly, thereby allowing individual consumer debtors to discharge debt they could otherwise repay. For several years, bankruptcy reform legislation has been proposed in Congress but none of the bills has become law. As recently as 2000, Congress passed a bankruptcy reform bill, but that bill was vetoed by President Clinton. Other legislation has since been proposed, including the Bankruptcy Abuse Prevention and Consumer Protection Act of 2002. Although it is unclear when and to what extent bankruptcy reform will occur, it is likely that some legislation will be enacted to address the perceived need for substantial changes to the Bankruptcy Code.

SECTION 2
THE DUAL NATURE OF BANKRUPTCY AS A REMEDY FOR BOTH CREDITORS AND DEBTORS

The Bankruptcy Reform Act of 1978 was viewed as highly favorable to debtors. American bankruptcy law, at least from 1978 up to the enactment of the 1984 amendments, appears to have adopted the philosophy of bankruptcy on demand. There are no provisions suggesting that it is morally wrong for a debtor to file for bankruptcy, and there is no requirement that the debtor be **insolvent** to file a **voluntary petition** under any chapter of the Code.

Two of the 1984 amendments, however, began to push back the idea of "bankruptcy on demand." One of these amendments required an attorney to certify that the prospective debtor whose debts were primarily **consumer debts** had been informed of the differences between a Chapter 13 case ("Adjustment of Debts of an Individual with Regular Income") and a Chapter 7 case ("Liquidation"). The other amendment allowed a bankruptcy court to dismiss on its own motion a case for substantial abuse of the provisions of Chapter 7.

Another adjustment in the balance between creditors and debtors occurred when Congress amended 11 U.S.C.A. § 707(b) in 1986 to allow the United States trustee to file a motion to dismiss. The amendment provides that

> (b) After notice and a hearing, the court, on its own motion or on a motion by the United States trustee, but not at the request or suggestion of any party in interest, may dismiss a case filed by an individual debtor under this chapter whose debts are primarily consumer debts if it finds that the granting of relief would be a substantial abuse of the provisions of this chapter. There shall be a presumption in favor of granting the relief requested by the debtor.

It has been suggested that 11 U.S.C.A. § 707(b) represents a substantial shift of the balance between creditors and debtors back to the creditors' side. There is, however, no suggestion that a shift has occurred back toward the connection of moral implications to the mere filing of a bankruptcy case.

Although modern bankruptcy law originated in creditor-oriented proceedings, bankruptcy in the United States, from a public policy point of view, now has two purposes:

1. To give honest debtors a fresh start to assure their return to full productivity, relieved from burdensome and unmanageable debt
2. To promote the **best interests of creditors** by providing them with an equitable distribution equal to the liquidation value of the debtor's nonexempt assets

The debtor in bankruptcy has two objectives:

1. To be **discharged** from as many of its debts as possible
2. To preserve ownership of as much property as free from debt as may be possible

The trustee and the creditors also have two objectives:

1. To maximize distribution to creditors, either in property or in money
2. To assure that the debtor does not receive a discharge unless one is justified and that the debts that are **nondischargeable** according to law are not discharged through the bankruptcy proceeding

Public policy seeks to balance the interests of debtors and creditors. A constant tension exists in the bankruptcy court process and in the legislative and rule-making processes related to bankruptcy. The dual nature of bankruptcy law as a remedy for both creditors and debtors has prevailed. Although this balancing of interests between the contending parties shifts from time to time, it is continually being adjusted by legislation and judicial decisions.

KEY TERMS

bankruptcy code (the code)
best interests of creditors
consumer debts
discharge
exemptions
insolvent
operative chapters
reorganization
United States trustee
universal chapters
voluntary petition

CHAPTER 2

Bankruptcy Law and Where to Find It

CHAPTER OUTLINE

SECTION 1
THE BANKRUPTCY CODE
A. The Universal Chapters
B. The Operative Chapters

SECTION 2
THE FEDERAL RULES OF BANKRUPTCY PROCEDURE AND OFFICIAL FORMS
A. The Federal Rules of Bankruptcy Procedure and Official Forms
B. The Local Rules

SECTION 3
BANKRUPTCY LAW CASES

SECTION 4
SECONDARY AUTHORITY
A. Legislative History
B. Digests
C. Loose-Leaf Services
D. Treatises
E. Legal Periodicals
F. American Law Reports
G. Legal Encyclopedias
H. Internet Resources

Legal authority may be primary or secondary. Primary authority is found in the Constitution, statutes, rules and administrative regulations issued pursuant to statutory authority, and case law. Primary authority may be mandatory or persuasive. Mandatory authority is law or reasoning that a court must follow. Persuasive authority is law or reasoning that a court may follow but is not bound to follow.

Secondary authority is found in all other written expressions of the law, such as legislative history, treatises, periodicals, and form books. Secondary authority is useful in understanding primary authority.

The United States Constitution is mandatory primary authority. Article I, Section 8, Clause 4, of the Constitution gives Congress the power to act in certain enumerated areas. One of these enumerated areas is bankruptcy:

> Section 8. The Congress shall have the power . . .
>
> 4. To establish an uniform Rule of Naturalization, and uniform Laws on the subject of Bankruptcies throughout the United States.

Article I, Section 8, Clause 18, gives Congress the power to enact laws that are "necessary and proper" to implement the power that has been previously enumerated.

18. To make all Laws which shall be necessary and proper for carrying into Execution the foregoing Powers, and all other Powers vested by this Constitution in the Government of the United States, or in any Department or Officer thereof.

Federal legislation is mandatory primary authority. In some areas, the power conferred to Congress is exclusive. Therefore, regardless of whether Congress acts, it is the only governmental body that can act in these areas. Congressional power preempts these areas, and the states may not legislate on them.

EXAMPLE

Article I, Section 8, Clause 4, gives Congress the power to establish "uniform Laws on the subject of Bankruptcies throughout the United States." Congress, acting through its necessary and proper clause, enacted the Bankruptcy Code. The United States Bankruptcy Code is mandatory primary authority and must be followed by all states. The power to establish bankruptcy laws is also exclusive, so the states are preempted from the field. Therefore, if either State A or State B chooses to enact bankruptcy legislation, that legislation will be unconstitutional.

The holding and rationale of a United States Supreme Court opinion is mandatory primary authority.

EXAMPLE

When enacting the Bankruptcy Reform Act of 1978, Congress conferred Article III judicial power on bankruptcy court judges who were not given the life tenure and protection against salary decreases required for Article III judges. The lack of life tenure and protection against salary decreases meant that the judges were really only Article I judges. The United States Supreme Court, in *Northern Pipeline Construction Co. v. Marathon Pipe Line Co.*, 458 U.S. 50 (1982), held that this section of the Act violated Article III of the Constitution.

Article I judges could not be given the broad judicial power authorized by the Act. Congress was thus forced to restructure the bankruptcy court system to make it constitutional. Congress could either give the judges Article III status and continue the broad designation of power or give the judges Article I status and reduce their power. In either event, Congress was obligated to comply with the holding and rationale of the Supreme Court because the Court had mandatory primary authority over this issue.

State legislation is mandatory primary authority for transactions covered by state statute.

EXAMPLE

When the various states enacted the 2001 version of article 9 (Secured Transactions) of the **Uniform Commercial Code (UCC),** each adopted the general language of section 9-501 as written by the drafters—the American Law Institute and the National Conference of Commissioners on Uniform State Laws—and each designated the appropriate filing office for their state. The State of Washington enacted the following:

WA Stat. § 62A.9A-501. Filing Office

(a) Filing offices. Except as otherwise provided in subsection (b) of this section, if the local law of this state governs perfection of a **security interest** or agricultural lien, the office in which to file a financing statement to perfect the security interest or agricultural lien is:
   (1) The office designated for the filing or recording of a record of a mortgage on the related real property, if:
      (A) The **collateral** is as-extracted collateral or timber to be cut; or
      (B) The financing statement is filed as a fixture filing and the collateral is goods that are or are to become fixtures; or
   (2) The department of licensing, in all other cases, including a case in which the collateral is goods that are, or are to become, fixtures and the financing statement is not filed as a fixture filing.

(b) Filing office for transmitting utilities. The office in which to file a financing statement to perfect a security interest in collateral, including fixtures, of a transmitting utility is the department of licensing. The financing statement also constitutes a fixture filing as to the collateral indicated in the financing statement which is or is to become fixtures.

Thus the general rule in the State of Washington is to file a financing statement, if a financing statement is the appropriate method of perfection, in the department of licensing. WA Stat. § 62A.9A-501(a)(2).

PROBLEM 2.1 Check your state's version of the section 9-501 of the 2001 Uniform Commercial Code. Where must a financing statement be filed in your state to perfect a security interest? Would this be the same office if filing were required in the State of Washington?

The holding and rationale of a United States bankruptcy court, a United States district court, or a United States circuit court opinion interpreting a *federal statute* is mandatory primary authority for transactions within the jurisdictional boundaries of the decision making court. It need not be followed by all courts nationwide, as a United States Supreme Court opinion must be followed.

EXAMPLE

In 1985, the United States Circuit Court for the Eleventh Circuit held that Chapter 11 is available to individuals who are not engaged in business. *In re Moog,* 774 F.2d 1073 (11th Cir. 1985). One year later, the Eighth Circuit held that Chapter 11 is not available to individuals who are not engaged in business. *Wamsganz v. Boatmen's Bank of De Soto,* 804 F.2d 503 (8th Cir. 1986). The Eleventh Circuit decision, even though primary authority, need not be followed in the Eighth Circuit because it is not mandatory authority beyond the jurisdictional boundaries of the Eleventh Circuit, which is the decision-making court.

In 1991, the United States Supreme Court held that an individual debtor not engaged in business is eligible to reorganize under Chapter 11. *Toibb v. Radloff,* 501 U.S. 157 (1991). This decision is mandatory primary authority and must be followed by all United States courts.

The holding and rationale of a United States bankruptcy court, district court, or circuit court or a state court opinion interpreting a *state statute* is mandatory primary authority for transactions within the jurisdictional boundaries of the decision making court. It need not be followed by courts beyond the decision making court's jurisdictional boundaries.

EXAMPLE

The Grand Old Theatre, located in Rhode Island, purchased theater seats from the Plush Furniture Company for $200,000. Plush, also located in Rhode Island, orally agreed to finance the sale if Grand would give Plush a security interest in the seats. Grand signed a promissory note for $200,000 and a financing statement but did not sign a written security agreement.

After paying $50,000, Grand defaulted on the note and filed for bankruptcy under Chapter 7 (liquidation). Both the trustee in bankruptcy and Plush claimed the theater seats. The trustee claimed that Plush was unsecured because it did not have a security agreement signed by the debtor, Grand Old Theatre, as required by RI Stat. § 6A-9-203(b)(3)(i). Plush claimed that it was secured because the financing statement coupled with the promissory note satisfied the "authenticated" security agreement requirement of § 9-203(b)(3)(i).

Rhode Island's version of UCC § 9-203(b)(3)(i) states the following:

6A-9-203. Attachment and Enforceability of Security Interest; Proceeds; Supporting Obligations; Formal Requisites.

(a) Attachment. A security interest attaches to collateral when it becomes enforceable against the debtor with respect to the collateral, unless an agreement expressly postpones the time of attachment.

(b) Enforceability. Except as otherwise provided in subsections (c) through (i), a security interest is enforceable against the debtor and third parties with respect to the collateral only if:

   (1) Value has been given;

   (2) The debtor has rights in the collateral or the power to transfer rights in the collateral to a secured party; and

   (3) One of the following conditions is met:

      (i) The debtor has authenticated a **security agreement** that provides a description of the collateral and, if the security interest covers timber to be cut, a description of the land concerned. . . .

A "security agreement" is defined in UCC § 9-102(a)(73) as meaning "an agreement that creates or provides for a security interest."

In *American Card Co. v. H.M.H. Co.,* 196 A.2d 150 (R.I. 1963), the Rhode Island Supreme Court held that a financing statement could not operate as a security agreement because there was no language granting a security interest to a creditor. Implicit in UCC § 9-203 is the "creation" language of UCC § 9-102. Therefore, because *American Card* is mandatory primary authority in Rhode Island, the Bankruptcy Court for the United States District Court for the District of Rhode Island was required to follow *American Card* and hold Plush unsecured.

If Grand and Plush were both located in Maine, the answer would have been different. The Supreme Court of Maine, in *Casco Bank & Trust Co. v. Cloutier,* 398 A.2d 1224 (Me. 1979), held that a financing statement coupled with a promissory note could constitute the security agreement. Implicit in the *Casco Bank* opinion was that express "creation" language was not required for a security agreement to exist. Therefore, if the case had been before the Bankruptcy Court for the United States District Court for the District of Maine, Plush would have been secured. Because Plush filed a financing statement to become a perfected secured party (rather than remaining an unperfected secured party), Plush would have had priority over the trustee in bankruptcy (a lien creditor). The negative inference is derived from UCC § 9-317(a)(2)(A).

PROBLEM 2.2 Assume that Grand and Plush are located in Gary, Indiana. Indiana has enacted sections 9–102(a)(73) and 9–203(b)(3)(i) of the UCC without variance from the official text. Assume that this is a case of first impression before the United States Bankruptcy Court for Indiana. Also assume that no other court having jurisdiction over cases arising in Gary, Indiana, has ruled on the issue of whether a financing statement coupled with a promissory note would satisfy the writing requirement under 9–203(b)(3)(i).

Should Plush or the trustee in bankruptcy prevail as to the seats? Is either *American Card* or *Casco Bank* primary authority? Is either mandatory primary authority in Indiana? Could either be persuasive primary authority in Indiana?

Judicial decisions from one federal court need not be followed in another federal court on the same level (i.e., two bankruptcy courts or two district courts), even though both courts are in the same circuit.

PROBLEM 2.3 Create an example to demonstrate the principle outlined in the previous paragraph. Use the Ninth Circuit as your circuit. This circuit includes the states of Alaska, Arizona, California, Hawaii, Idaho, Montana, Nevada, Oregon, and Washington, as well as Guam and the Northern Mariana Islands.

Primary authority in the field of bankruptcy (statutes, rules, and cases) will be covered in Sections 1, 2, and 3, respectively, of this chapter. Secondary authority (legislative history, treatises, periodicals, and form books and how they can be used in understanding the law of bankruptcy) will be covered in Section 4.

SECTION 1 THE BANKRUPTCY CODE

The Bankruptcy Reform Act of 1978, Public Law 95–598, is known as the Bankruptcy Code, or just the Code. Public Law 95–598, in its original form, can be found in the United States Statutes at Large. The designation "public law" distinguishes this bill from a "private law." A public law affects the nation as a whole or deals with individuals as a class and relates to public matters. A private law benefits only a specific individual or class of individuals and does not relate to public matters. The numbers before the dash (in this case,"95") refer to the number of the Congress. This bill came out of the 95th Congress. The numbers after the dash (in this case, "598") mean that this was the 598th bill passed by this Congress. Because the bills are arranged in the United States Statutes at Large in chronological order, rather than by subject, an amendment to this bill might not be found near 95–598.

The public laws found in the Statutes at Large are incorporated into the **United States Code** (U.S.C.). The United States Code is updated annually with cumulative supplements. It is printed and sold by the U.S. Government Printing Office and is the official edition of federal statutes. U.S.C. is organized by title and section. The citation "11 U.S.C. § 301" would mean section 301 (not page 301) of Title 11 (not volume 11) of the United States Code.

Since the U.S. Government Printing Office was slow to publish U.S.C., West Group Publishing Company created the series United States Code Annotated. This series, abbreviated U.S.C.A., is also organized by title and section. A statute cited as 11 U.S.C. § 301 would appear in the United States Code Annotated as 11 U.S.C.A. § 301. United States Code Annotated has several features not found in the United States Code. For example, if a Code section has been cited and discussed in a court opinion, an annotation of that opinion is included following the Code section discussed. Lexis Publishing Co. publishes the United States Code Service (U.S.C.S.) that is similar to United States Code Annotated (U.S.C.A.), published by West Group. Both services reference American Law Reports, American Jurisprudence, Corpus Juris Secundum, and Bankruptcy Reporter.

Although 11 U.S.C. (the codification of bankruptcy law) and 28 U.S.C. (the provisions relating to the structure and jurisdiction of bankruptcy courts) are the substantive and procedural laws of bankruptcy, not a great deal of the "how to do it" procedural law is contained in either title of the Code. Instead, Congress decided to leave procedural matters primarily as a part of the rule making function of the United States Supreme Court. The bankruptcy rules are discussed in Section 2 of this chapter.

The provisions in 28 U.S.C. relating to bankruptcy have undergone considerable change since the enactment of the Bankruptcy Reform Act of 1978. Title 28 provisions relate to the jurisdiction of the bankruptcy court, **venue** of cases and proceedings under Title 11, removal of cases to the bankruptcy court, the structure of the court, and the appointment of bankruptcy judges. Matters pertaining to appeals in bankruptcy cases and the regulation of the United States trustees are also found in Title 28 provisions.

As pointed out in Chapter One, the drafters wrote the Code using only odd-numbered chapters: 1, 3, 5, 7, 9, 11, 13, 15. The even numbers were reserved for later additions to the Code. Chapter 15, which pertains to the pilot program for U.S. trustees, was repealed on October 27, 1986, thereby reducing the number of chapters from 1 through 15 to 1 through 13. Although Chapter 15 was repealed, the United States trustee concept was not discarded but was made a permanent part of bankruptcy law applicable to most bankruptcy courts. Pub. L. 99–554. The United States trustee chapter was not included in the 1986 version of the Bankruptcy Code (i.e., 11 U.S.C.) but became Chapter 39 of Title 28 of the United States Code (i.e., 28 U.S.C.).

Public Law 99–554 also includes the Family Farmer Bankruptcy Act of 1986. This added Chapter 12, entitled "Adjustment of Debts of a Family Farmer with Regular Annual Income," to the Code. Chapter 12 was tailored for family farmers whose needs are not met by Chapter 11 or Chapter 13. The current Code chapters are

Chapter 1	General Provisions
Chapter 3	Case Administration
Chapter 5	Creditors, Debtor, and the Estate
Chapter 7	Liquidation
Chapter 9	Adjustment of Debts of a Municipality
Chapter 11	Reorganization
Chapter 12	Adjustment of Debts of a Family Farmer with Regular Annual Income
Chapter 13	Adjustment of Debts of an Individual with Regular Income

The chapters of the Code, are readily divided into two groups. Chapter 1, Chapter 3, and Chapter 5 are the universal chapters. Chapter 7, Chapter 9, Chapter 11, Chapter 12, and Chapter 13 are the operative chapters.

If the section number has three digits, the first digit designates the chapter. If the section number has four digits, the first two digits designate the chapter.

EXAMPLES

Section 101 is in Chapter 1.
Section 547 is in Chapter 5.
Section 1107 is in Chapter 11.

PROBLEM 2.4 In which chapter of the Bankruptcy Code is each of the following sections found?

Section 1324
Section 324
Section 1112
Section 501

A. THE UNIVERSAL CHAPTERS

The universal chapters of the Code (1, 3, and 5) contain important definitional and administrative provisions that generally apply to all operative chapters of the Code. Only a few of the sections of Chapter 3 and Chapter 5, however, apply to Chapter 9. 11 U.S.C.A. §§ 103(e), 901.

EXAMPLE

Jane Dillon filed for bankruptcy under Chapter 7 of the Code. The provisions of Chapter 7, rather than the provisions of Chapter 9, 11, 12, or 13, will apply to Jane's case. The provisions of the universal chapters (1, 3, and 5) will also apply to Jane's case.

Richard Ramirez filed for reorganization under Chapter 11 of the Code. The provisions of Chapter 11, rather than the provisions of Chapter 7, 9, 12, or 13, will apply to Richard's case. The provisions of the universal chapters (1, 3, and 5) will also apply to Richard's case.

1. Chapter 1—General Provisions

The Bankruptcy Code contains its own set of definitions, and they are found in Chapter 1. If a term used in the Bankruptcy Code is defined in the Bankruptcy Code, then the Bankruptcy Code definition applies and any non-Bankruptcy Code definition is inapplicable.

EXAMPLE

The Bankruptcy Code defines *debtor* as a "person or municipality concerning which a case under this title has been commenced." 11 U.S.C.A. § 101(13). Article 9 of the Uniform Commercial Code defines *debtor* as "a person having an interest, other than a security interest or other lien, in collateral." UCC § 9-102(b)(28).

If the case is a bankruptcy case, the Bankruptcy Code definition of debtor will apply, rather than the UCC definition.

PROBLEM 2.5 Compare the Bankruptcy Code definition of "security interest" with the Uniform Commercial Code definition; i.e., compare 11 U.S.C.A. § 101(51) with UCC § 1–201(b)(35). Does each cover real estate mortgages?

Section 101 of Chapter 1 provides an extensive list of definitions. The definitions found in section 101 apply to *all* other Bankruptcy Code sections, whether the section is found in Chapter 1 or in Chapter 3, 5, 7, 9, 11, 12, or 13. The terms defined in section 101 are arranged alphabetically.

PROBLEM 2.6 How does the Bankruptcy Code define the term "creditor"?

PROBLEM 2.7 Are the following "entities" under the Bankruptcy Code?

1. a relative who lent the debtor money
2. a partnership that sold the debtor goods on credit
3. a corporation that sold the debtor goods on credit
4. an estate that sold the debtor heirlooms on credit
5. a trust fund that owed the debtor wages for services
6. a school district that owed the debtor money for services
7. the United States trustee

A term found in a Bankruptcy Code section may itself contain terms that need to be defined. In this case, the process of using the Code to define the term continues until all the terms are defined.

EXAMPLE

A debtor under Chapter 7 may convert the case from Chapter 7 to another chapter.

> (a) The debtor may convert a case under this chapter to a case under chapter 11, 12, or 13 of this title at any time, if the case has not been converted under section 1112, 1208, or 1307 of this title. Any waiver of the right to convert a case under this subsection is unenforceable. 11 U.S.C.A. § 706(a).

The term *debtor* is defined in 11 U.S.C.A. § 101(13) as

> [a] person or municipality concerning which a case under this title has been commenced.

The term ***person*** in section 101(13) is defined in section 101(41) to include

> individual, partnership, and corporation, but does not include governmental unit, except that a governmental unit that–
>
> (A) acquires an asset from a person–
>
> (i) as a result of the operation of a loan guarantee agreement; or
>
> (ii) as receiver or liquidating agent of a person;
>
> (B) is a guarantor of a pension benefit payable by or on behalf of the debtor or an affiliate of the debtor; or
>
> (C) is the legal or beneficial owner of an asset of–
>
> (i) an employee pension benefit plan that is a governmental plan, as defined in section 414(d) of the Internal Revenue Code of 1986; or
>
> (ii) an eligible deferred compensation plan, as defined in section 457(b) of the Internal Revenue Code of 1986;
>
> shall be considered, for purposes of section 1102 of this title, to be a person with respect to such asset or such benefit.

The term *governmental unit* is defined in section 101(27) to mean

> United States; State; Commonwealth; District; Territory; municipality; foreign state; department, agency, or instrumentality of the United States (but not a United States trustee while serving as a trustee in a case under this title), a State, a Commonwealth, a District, a Territory, a municipality, or a foreign state; or other foreign or domestic government.

PROBLEM 2.8 Which terms in the following section, 11 U.S.C.A. § 545, statutory liens, are defined in section 101?

> The trustee may avoid the fixing of a statutory lien on property of the debtor to the extent that such lien—
>
> (1) first becomes effective against the debtor—
>
> (A) when a case under this title concerning the debtor is commenced;
>
> (B) when an insolvency proceeding other than under this title concerning the debtor is commenced;
>
> (C) when a custodian is appointed or authorized to take or takes possession;
>
> (D) when the debtor becomes insolvent;
>
> (E) when the debtor's financial condition fails to meet a specified standard; or
>
> (F) at the time of an execution against property of the debtor levied at the instance of an entity other than the holder of such statutory lien;
>
> (2) is not perfected or enforceable at the time of the commencement of the case against a bona fide purchaser that purchases such property at the time of the commencement of the case, whether or not such a purchaser exists;
>
> (3) is for rent; or
>
> (4) is a lien of distress for rent.

It should be noted that not all Code definitions are found in section 101. Various chapters and subchapters of the Code also contain definitions. If, however, a definition is contained in an operative chapter rather than in Chapter 1, the definition will apply only to the chapter in which it is found and not to all other chapters.

EXAMPLE

Section 741 defines nine terms for use in Subchapter III (Stockbroker Liquidation) of Chapter 7:

1. Commission
2. Customer
3. Customer name security
4. Customer property
5. Margin payment
6. Net equity
7. Securities contract
8. Settlement payment
9. SIPC

Section 1101 defines two terms for use in Chapter 11 (Reorganization):

1. Debtor in possession
2. Substantial consummation

Not all terms are defined in the Code. When this occurs, a definition can sometimes be gleaned from the term's usage in the Code, from case law, or from common usage in the bankruptcy court.

PROBLEM 2.9 Is the term "party [or parties] in interest" defined in the Code? Does **party in interest** include the trustee, examiners, U.S. trustee, indenture trustee, creditors, and equity security holders? Are other entities of the U.S. government or state government, who do not hold a claim or have regulatory duties, parties in interest? See 11 U.S.C.A. §§ 101, 102(1).

In addition to the general definitions provided in Chapter 1, a few other highlights are worth a brief mention. Chapter 1 defines the concept of "after notice and a hearing."

> The concept is central to the bill and to the separation of the administrative and judicial functions of bankruptcy judges. The phrase means after such notice as is appropriate in the particular circumstances (to be prescribed by either the Rules of Bankruptcy Procedure or by the court in individual circumstances that the Rules do not cover. In many cases, the Rules provide for combined notice of several proceedings), and such opportunity for a hearing as is appropriate in the particular circumstances. Thus, a hearing will not be necessary in every instance. If there is no objection to the proposed action, the action may go ahead without court action. This is a significant change from present law [the Bankruptcy Act of 1898], which requires the affirmative approval of the bankruptcy judge for almost every action. The change will permit the bankruptcy judge to stay removed from the administration of the bankruptcy or reorganization case, and to become involved only when there is a dispute about a proposed action, that is, only when there is an objection. The phrase "such opportunity for a hearing as is appropriate in the particular circumstances" is designed to permit the Rules and the courts to expedite or dispose with hearings when speed is essential. 11 U.S.C.A. § 102, Notes of Committee on the Judiciary, Senate Report No. 95–989.

Chapter 1 describes who may be a debtor and under which chapters a particular debtor may file a petition. 11 U.S.C.A. § 109. Chapter 1 also sets forth which chapters are applicable to a particular case under Title 11. 11 U.S.C.A. § 103.

2. Chapter 3—Case Administration

Chapter 3 is a very important chapter of Title 11 in terms of the progress of a case through the bankruptcy court. Chapter 3 is divided into four subchapters:

Subchapter I Commencement of a Case
Subchapter II Officers
Subchapter III Administration
Subchapter IV Administrative Powers

Subchapter I (Commencement of a Case) provides for the voluntary or involuntary commencement of a case. 11 U.S.C.A. §§ 301, 303. It also authorizes an individual debtor to file a joint case with his or her spouse. 11 U.S.C.A. § 302. The court has the power to dismiss a case or to suspend all proceedings in a case. 11 U.S.C.A. § 305.

Subchapter II (Officers) covers the eligibility and qualifications of a trustee in bankruptcy, the role and capacity of the trustee, and provisions relating to compensation of trustees and professional persons employed in the administration of bankruptcy estates. 11 U.S.C.A. §§ 321–331.

Subchapter III (Administration) focuses on such topics as the meeting of creditors and equity security holders (commonly known as "the 341 meeting"), notice, examination of the debtor, self-incrimination and immunity, effect of conversion, effect of dismissal, and the closing and reopening of the case. 11 U.S.C.A. §§ 341–350.

Subchapter IV (Administrative Powers) imposes an **automatic stay** on actions against the debtor or his or her estate and authorizes the trustee to use, sell, or lease collateral in the debtor's business and to obtain credit. 11 U.S.C.A. §§ 362–364. Utilities are prohibited from altering, refraining, or discontinuing service because of nonpayment of a bill or because the debtor has filed a petition in bankruptcy. 11 U.S.C.A. § 366. If the entity affected is not afforded **adequate protection,** relief from the automatic stay will be granted or the trustee's proposed use, sale, lease, or borrowing against collateral will be prohibited. 11 U.S.C.A. § 361. Adequate protection may include cash payments, additional collateral, or replacement collateral. The trustee may assume or reject any **executory contract** or **unexpired lease** of the debtor. 11 U.S.C.A. § 365.

3. Chapter 5—Creditors, Debtor, and the Estate

Chapter 5 is divided into three subchapters:

Subchapter I Creditors and Claims
Subchapter II Debtor's Duties and Benefits
Subchapter III The Estate

Subchapter I (Creditors and Claims) regulates the filing of **proofs of claim** or **proofs of interest,** the allowance of claims or interests, the allowance of administrative expenses, the determination of secured status, and priorities. 11 U.S.C.A. §§ 501–510. The section entitled "Determination of Secured Status" is generally regarded as one of the most important sections of Chapter 5. 11 U.S.C.A. § 506. The "Priorities" section sets forth which expenses and claims have priority and in what order. 11 U.S.C.A. § 507.

Subchapter II (Debtor's Duties and Benefits) describes the debtor's duties, provides the debtor with a choice between state and federal exemptions (unless the debtor's state has opted out of the federal exemptions), and states the effect of discharge. 11 U.S.C.A. §§ 521–524. The Code prevents discriminatory treatment of debtors. 11 U.S.C.A. § 525. This is the codification of the "fresh-start" policy, which allows the debtor to begin a new fiscal life.

The discharge provisions (11 U.S.C.A. §§ 523, 524) are of critical importance and must be read in conjunction with related provisions in the operative chapters. In Chapter 7, they are read in conjunction with section 727 (discharge); in Chapter 9, with section 944 (effect of confirmation); in Chapter 11, with section 1141 (effect of confirmation); in Chapter 12, with section 1228 (discharge); and in Chapter 13, with section 1328 (discharge).

The filing of a bankruptcy petition creates a bankruptcy estate. Subchapter III (The Estate) focuses on what the **estate** consists of and on how it is collected by the trustee. 11 U.S.C.A. §§ 541, 543. Under this subchapter, the trustee has the power to avoid unperfected liens, the fixing of a statutory lien, and preferences and fraudulent conveyances. 11 U.S.C.A. §§ 544–549. This authority furnishes the trustee with powerful means by which to collect the **property of the estate** for distribution to creditors or to preserve the property of the estate so the plan for reorganization can be successful. The trustee also has the power to remove property from the estate if it is burdensome or of inconsequential value and benefit to the estate. 11 U.S.C.A. § 554.

B. THE OPERATIVE CHAPTERS

The Code has five operative chapters—Chapters 7, 9, 11, 12, and 13:

Chapter 7 Liquidation
Chapter 9 Adjustment of Debts of a Municipality
Chapter 11 Reorganization
Chapter 12 Adjustment of Debts of a Family Farmer with Regular Annual Income
Chapter 13 Adjustment of Debts of an Individual with Regular Income

Each operative chapter generally relates only to cases being administered under that particular chapter. Some Chapter 11 sections, however, apply to Chapter 9, and some Chapter 7 sections apply to Chapter 11. 11 U.S.C.A. §§ 103(b)–(i), 901, 1106.

1. Chapter 7—Liquidation

Of the five operative chapters, only one—Chapter 7—deals with **liquidation,** the distribution of the debtor's estate to his or her creditors, as its only option. The other four operative chapters—Chapters 9, 11, 12, and 13—deal with restructuring the debt.

Liquidation under Chapter 7 is available to all persons who may be debtors under this chapter, whether they are individuals, partnerships, or corporations. Railroads, insurance companies, and certain banking institutions may not be debtors under Chapter 7. A debtor need not be insolvent to take advantage of Chapter 7 liquidation. 11 U.S.C.A. § 109(b).

Chapter 7 deals specifically with the liquidation bankruptcy in which a trustee gathers up the debtor's non-exempt assets, sells them, and generally makes a one-time distribution to creditors. In some cases, there may be more than one distribution. Chapter 7 cases constitute the bulk of original bankruptcy filings. In addition to the cases originally filed as liquidation cases, many Chapter 11 and Chapter 13 filings will eventually convert to Chapter 7 filings. 11 U.S.C.A. §§ 1112, 1307(a). The Chapter 12 debtor may also convert to Chapter 7. 11 U.S.C.A. § 1208(a).

Two particularly significant sections in Chapter 7 are sections 707 and 727. Section 707 provides for dismissal of a case for dilatory tactics, nonpayment of fees, and substantial abuse of Chapter 7. The presumption, however, is in favor of the debtor. Section 727 (discharge) is the *raison d'être* of a bankruptcy filing. In order for a debtor to obtain a discharge, he or she must meet the Chapter 7 criteria for discharge as read in conjunction with the exceptions to discharge found in Chapter 5. 11 U.S.C.A. §§ 523, 727.

2. Chapter 9—Adjustment of Debts of a Municipality

Chapter 9 is the least used operative chapter of the Code because the debtor must be a municipality to qualify for this chapter. If a paralegal is employed by an attorney representing either the debtor or the creditor in a municipal bankruptcy, sections 103 and 901 would be the point of embarkation. These sections list which sections in Chapters 1, 3, 5, and 11 will apply to a Chapter 9 case. 11 U.S.C.A. §§ 103, 901.

3. Chapter 11—Reorganization

Chapter 11—the only chapter entitled "Reorganization" (although Chapters 9, 12, and 13 also involve restructuring of debt)—begins with the definition of **debtor in possession:** a debtor in a Chapter 11 case in which no trustee has been appointed. 11 U.S.C.A. § 1101. In the practice of law, debtor in possession is often abbreviated as: DIP and pronounced as initials: D I P.

Chapter 11 is the chapter of choice for many businesses, large and small, filing for relief under the Code. This chapter has become an even more practical choice for the small business, given the "fast track" provision in the Code. 11 U.S.C.A. § 1121(e). The **order for relief** in a Chapter 11 case offers a respite from the demands of creditors and affords an opportunity for the beleaguered business to resolve its difficulties. The ability to remain in operation enables the DIP to preserve ongoing relationships with both suppliers and customers as well as to keep employees on the job. 11 U.S.C.A. § 1108. The assets of some debtors may be liquidated, however, under a Chapter 11 liquidation plan. 11 U.S.C.A. § 1141(d)(3)(A).

4. Chapter 12—Adjustment of Debts of a Family Farmer with Regular Annual Income

Chapter 12 applies only to a special category of debtor. For Chapter 12 to apply, the debtor must be a **family farmer** with **regular annual income.** The definition of "family farmer," found in section 101(18), is long and complicated.

> (18) "family farmer" means—
>
> (A) individual or individual and spouse engaged in a farming operation whose aggregate debts do not exceed $1,500,000 and not less than 80 percent of whose aggregate noncontingent, liquidated debts (excluding a debt for the principal residence of such individual or such individual and spouse unless such debt arises out of a farming operation), on the date the case is filed, arise out of a farming operation owned or operated by such individual or such individual and spouse, and such individual or such individual and spouse receive from such farming operation more than 50 percent of such individual's or such individual and spouse's gross income for the taxable year preceding the taxable year in which the case concerning such individual or such individual and spouse was filed; or
>
> (B) corporation or partnership in which more than 50 percent of the outstanding stock or equity is held by one family, or by one family and the relatives of the members of such family, and such family or such relatives conduct the farming operation; and
>
> (i) more than 80 percent of the value of its assets consist of assets related to the farming operation;
>
> (ii) its aggregate debts do not exceed $1,500,000 and not less than 80 percent of its aggregate noncontingent, liquidated debts (excluding a debt for one dwelling which is owned by such corporation or partnership and which a shareholder or partner maintains as a principal residence, unless such debt arises out of a farming operation), on the date the case is filed, arise out of the farming operation owned or operated by such corporation or such partnership; and
>
> (iii) if such corporation issues stock, such stock is not publicly traded.

PROBLEM 2.10 Farmer Brown wants to file for bankruptcy under Chapter 12. Her aggregate debt totals $1,345,000. Of that debt, 85 percent arises from a farming operation. Of her gross income for the taxable year last year, 60 percent was derived from farming. Is Farmer Brown a "family farmer" and therefore eligible for Chapter 12?

5. Chapter 13—Adjustment of Debts of an Individual with Regular Income

Chapter 13, like Chapter 12, applies only to a special category of debtor. For Chapter 13 to apply, the debtor must be an individual with regular income. Therefore, corporations and partnerships are not eligible for protection under Chapter 13. It is important to note that only a debtor may file a Chapter 13 petition. This means that creditors cannot force a debtor into bankruptcy under Chapter 13.

PROBLEM 2.11 Michael Gelt has never worked at a paying job. He lives on the regular income from a trust set up for his benefit by his grandmother. Michael has expensive tastes and is in debt for clothing, airfare, hotels, and restaurants. Is Michael eligible to file a petition under Chapter 13?

In a Chapter 13 case, the debtor retains possession of property of the estate. 11 U.S.C.A. § 1306(b). This is in contrast to a Chapter 7 case, in which the trustee is required to "collect and reduce to money the property of the estate." 11 U.S.C.A. § 704. This means that creditors in a Chapter 7 case will be paid by the trustee after he or she has collected and sold the nonexempt property of the estate, but creditors in a Chapter 13 case will be paid by the trustee with money earned by the debtor after the filing of the petition.

SECTION 2 THE FEDERAL RULES OF BANKRUPTCY PROCEDURE AND OFFICIAL FORMS

The provision of the judiciary code relating to rules of the bankruptcy courts is found at 28 U.S.C.A. § 2075. This provision gives the United States Supreme Court the power to prescribe by general rules the forms of process, writs, pleadings and motions, and the practice and procedure in cases under Title 11. This provision requires that such rules shall not abridge, enlarge, or modify any substantive right; accordingly, the bankruptcy rules may relate only to procedural law and not to substantive law. Rules prescribed by the United States Supreme Court under this section generally take effect 90 days after they have been reported to Congress by the chief justice.

A. THE FEDERAL RULES OF BANKRUPTCY PROCEDURE AND OFFICIAL FORMS

The early predecessors of the Federal Rules of Bankruptcy Procedure were the general orders in bankruptcy adopted by the United States Supreme Court in 1898 pursuant to the authority of section 30 of the Bankruptcy Act, which was enacted in the same year. The general orders themselves provided for a set of official forms. The Federal Rules of Civil Procedure also had limited applicability.

Under the rule-making authority of 28 U.S.C.A. § 2075, the Supreme Court, commencing in 1973, issued Rules of Bankruptcy Procedure for general application in the bankruptcy courts. New rules were necessitated by the passage of the Bankruptcy Reform Act of 1978. New rules of practice and procedure applicable to the bankruptcy courts were adopted and became effective August 1, 1983, and were known as the Rules of Bankruptcy Procedure. Further changes were necessitated by the ruling of the Supreme Court in *Northern Pipeline Construction Co. v. Marathon Pipe Line Co.*, 458 U.S. 50 (1982). These rules were submitted to Congress by the Supreme Court on March 30, 1987, and became effective August 1, 1987.

On August 1, 1991, the Federal Rules of Bankruptcy Procedure replaced the Bankruptcy Rules. Although the new rules did not radically change the substance of many of the old rules, the new rules updated the rules to correspond with the 1986 Amendments to the Bankruptcy Code and integrated the former U.S. Trustee Rules and former Interim Chapter 12 Rules into the new rules.

The Federal Rules of Bankruptcy Procedure is subdivided into nine parts:

Part I	Commencement of Case; Proceedings Relating to Petition and Order for Relief
Part II	Officers and Administration; Notices; Meetings; Examinations; Elections; Attorneys and Accountants
Part III	Claims and Distribution to Creditors and Equity Interest Holders; Plans
Part IV	The Debtor: Duties and Benefits
Part V	Courts and Clerks
Part VI	Collection and Liquidation of the Estate
Part VII	Adversary Proceedings
Part VIII	Appeals to District Court or Bankruptcy Appellate Panel
Part IX	General Provisions

Part I of the Federal Rules of Bankruptcy Procedure deals with the commencement of cases and with proceedings related to the petition and order for relief in both voluntary and involuntary cases. Part I also contains the rules governing proceedings initiated by such involuntary petitions.

Part II sets forth the rules pertaining to the court's officers and administration, together with notices, meetings, examinations, and elections of trustees. Part II also treats the important subject of the appointment and employment of attorneys, accountants, and other professionals for trustees and debtors in possession.

Part III handles the claims and distribution to creditors and equity interest holders. Part III also covers the filing and confirmation of plans in Chapter 9, 11, 12, and 13 cases.

Part IV considers the duties of the debtor and the important benefits to the debtor, including the right to the defense of the automatic stay, claim of exemptions, proceedings dealing with the determination of dischargeability of a debt, and proceedings relating to discharge and reaffirmation hearings.

Part V provides for the operation of the court and the court clerk's office. Part V also covers record keeping, the handling of funds of bankruptcy estates, and the closing and reopening of cases. Rule 5011 deals with the matter of withdrawal of reference of a case or proceeding and abstention of the bankruptcy court from hearing a proceeding.

Part VI governs the collection and liquidation of the estate and covers such things as disbursement of money of the estate; the use, sale, or lease of property; and use of auctioneers and appraisers. Part VI also deals with the important matters of assumption, rejection and assignment of executory contracts, and abandonment or other disposition of property, together with redemption of property from a lien.

Part VII, which governs adversary proceedings, basically tracks the Federal Rules of Civil Procedure. Some Part VII rules apply to contested matters.

Part VIII provides for appeals of decisions of the bankruptcy courts to the district court or bankruptcy appellate panel.

Part IX is a collection of general provisions, including definitions and regulations of notices. Rule 9014 sets the procedures for contested matters.

Appended to the Federal Rules of Bankruptcy Procedure is a set of 19 official forms. The official forms may also be found and downloaded at http://www.uscourts.gov. Select U.S. Bankruptcy Courts, then Official Bankruptcy Forms. These forms include the schedules and statement of affairs that are filed as an important part of each bankruptcy case. Their detailed format should prove very helpful to the paralegal. Commercially prepared forms are available from a number of sources nationally and may also be available locally. For the student who would like to see some forms at this point, Chapter 7 forms are found in Chapter Five of this text.

The Bankruptcy Code, Federal Rules of Bankruptcy Procedure, and official forms are printed by several publishers in paperback format and are updated annually. An example is *Bankruptcy Code, Rules and Forms* by West Group Publishing Company. Several bankruptcy filing programs are available for the computer user.

The U.S. Government Printing Office reproduces some forms for the bankruptcy practitioner. They are available from the office of the clerk of the bankruptcy court. Many are standard required forms and are available from commercial sources as well. The office of the clerk of the bankruptcy court will also have copies of local court rules and various printed handouts related to filing requirements.

A major development is West's Bankruptcy Library, PREMISE® CD-ROM ed. This computer database contains bankruptcy cases (1979 to date); the *Bankruptcy Annotated Code, Rules, and Forms; West's® Bankruptcy Digest; Norton Bankruptcy Law and Practice* 2d; and Russell, *Bankruptcy Evidence Manual.*

B. THE LOCAL RULES

District courts and bankruptcy courts write their own rules to implement the Bankruptcy Code and supplement the Federal Rules of Bankruptcy Procedure. Both sets of court rules must be consulted in bankruptcy matters.

1. District Court Rules

Many district courts have adopted local rules concerning bankruptcy cases and proceedings. These rules deal with the reference of cases and proceedings from the district court to the bankruptcy court and the withdrawal of such references back to the district court. These district court rules also deal with review of bankruptcy court decisions and appeals of the decisions of bankruptcy judges. Copies of the local district court rules may be obtained from the office of the clerk of the United States district court. Local district court rules may also be found on the Web at http://www.uscourt.gov. Select "links to United States District Court Web Sites," then select your United States district court, and finally select "Rules and General Orders."

2. Bankruptcy Court Rules

Each bankruptcy court has adopted a set of local rules. The rules adopted by the bankruptcy court must not be inconsistent with the bankruptcy rules emanating from either the district court or the United States Supreme Court. Copies of the local bankruptcy court rules may be obtained from the office of the clerk of the bankruptcy court. Local bankruptcy court rules may also be found on the Web at http://www.uscourt.gov. Select "links to United States District Court Web Sites," then select your United States bankruptcy court, and finally select "Rules and General Orders."

SECTION 3 BANKRUPTCY LAW CASES

Although a few state court cases find their way into the law of bankruptcy, most cases are from the federal courts. As Exhibits 2–1 and 2–2 illustrate, the federal court structure for bankruptcy has four tiers: United States Bankruptcy Court, United States District Court or Bankruptcy Appellate Panel (BAP), United States Court of Appeals, and the United States Supreme Court.

A petition in bankruptcy is initiated in a United States bankruptcy court. Each of the 94 federal districts has a United States bankruptcy court. After litigation of an issue in bankruptcy court, the judge may decide to write an opinion. The judge will decide whether the opinion will be published or will remain unpublished. These opinions appear in the *Bankruptcy Reporter,* published by West Group Publishing Co. and cited B.R. or Bankr.; *Bankruptcy Court Decisions,* published by CRR Publishing Co. and cited B.C.D. or Bankr.Ct.Dec. (CCR); *Collier's Bankruptcy Cases,* published by Matthew Bender and cited C.B.C.2d (MB); and *Bankruptcy Law Reporter,* published by Commerce Clearing House and cited Bankr.L.Rep. (CCH).

If, however, a bankruptcy proceeding only involves rights created by the Constitution, by state law, or even by common law (as distinguished from congressionally created rights), the proceeding must be initiated in a United States district court or a state court rather than in a United States bankruptcy court. The district court judge may decide to write an opinion and that opinion may be published or may remain unpublished. If published, these opinions appear in the *Federal Supplement,* published by West Group Publishing Co. and cited F.Supp., as well as in the *Bankruptcy Reporter, Bankruptcy Court Decisions, Collier's Bankruptcy Cases,* and *Bankruptcy Law Reporter.*

If an order or judgment is appealed from the bankruptcy court, the direction of its appeal may depend on whether the circuit has established bankruptcy appellate panels (BAP). As of September 2002, five circuits—the First, Sixth, Eighth, Ninth, and Tenth—had bankruptcy appellate panels. The Second Circuit's bankruptcy appellate panels ended operations on July 1, 2000. Each BAP panel consists of three judges, none of whom is from the district from which the appeal originated.

If a circuit has bankruptcy appellate panels, the appeal from the bankruptcy court is taken to the BAP unless "the appellant elects at the time of the appeal" or "any other party elects, not later than 30 days after service of notice of appeal," to have the appeal heard by the United States District Court. 11 U.S.C.A. § 158(c)(1). If a circuit does not have bankruptcy appellate panels, the appeal is to the United States District Court.

If an issue is appealed from the district court or a BAP, it will be appealed to a United States circuit court. The 94 districts are allocated among 12 circuits. The opinions from the circuits are printed

EXHIBIT 2–1 Federal Court Structure for Bankruptcy for Circuits with Bankruptcy Appellate Panels

United States Supreme Court
Certiorari
United States Courts of Appeals
Appeal
Bankruptcy Appellate Panels unless the appellant elects to appeal to the United States District Court at the time of the appeal or the appellee elects, not later than 30 days after service of notice of the appeal, to have the United States District Court hear the appeal
United States District Courts hear the appeal if the appellant elects to appeal to the District Court at the time of the appeal or the appellee elects, not later than 30 days after service of notice of the appeal, to have the District Court hear the appeal
Appeal
United States Bankruptcy Courts

United States Supreme Court
Certiorari
United States Courts of Appeals
Appeal
United States District Courts
Appeal
United States Bankruptcy Courts

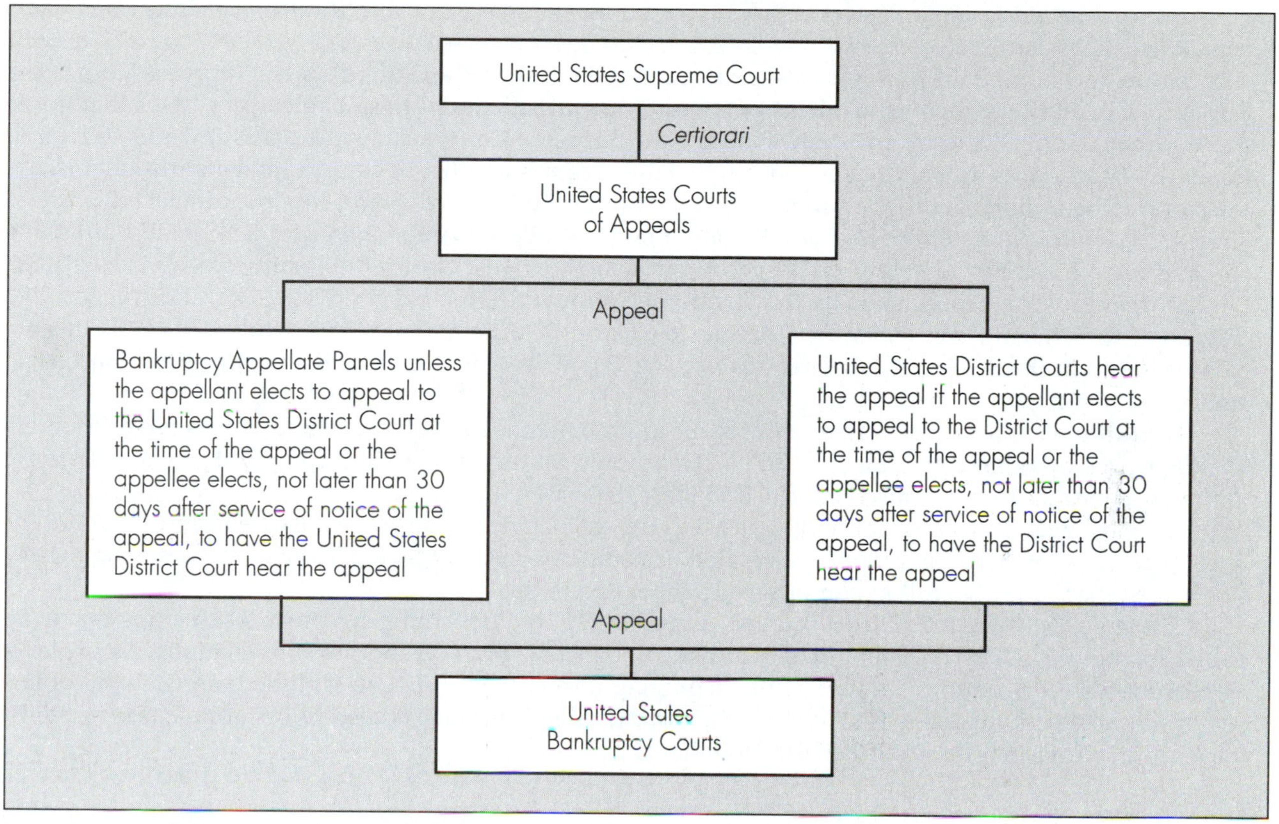

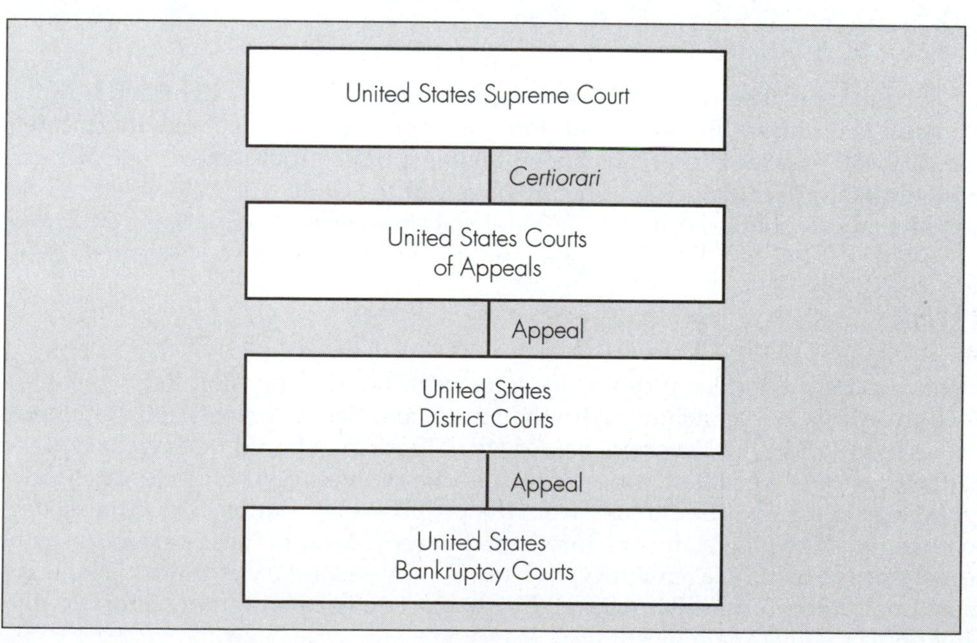

EXHIBIT 2–2 Federal Court Structure for Bankruptcy for Circuits without Bankruptcy Appellate Panels

in the *Federal Reporter*, published by West Group Publishing Co. and cited F.2d or F.3d. They may also be found in the *Bankruptcy Reporter, Bankruptcy Court Decisions, Collier's Bankruptcy Cases,* and *Bankruptcy Law Reporter.*

More and more bankruptcy cases are finding their way to the United States Supreme Court. The Supreme Court, the highest court, is a court of limited jurisdiction. Those bankruptcy cases that get to the Supreme Court do so by *certiorari.* Because the Supreme Court selects the cases it wants to hear, it generally hears cases in which decisions of the circuit courts conflict or important constitutional issues are raised. The opinions of the Supreme Court are published in *United States Reports,* official edition and cited U.S.; *United States Supreme Court Reports,* Lawyers' Edition, published by LEXIS Law Publishing Co. and cited L.Ed.2d; *Supreme Court Reporter,* published by West Group Publishing Co. and cited S.Ct.; *United States Law Week,* published by the Bureau of National Affairs and cited U.S.L.W.; and *United States Supreme Court Bulletin,* published by Commerce Clearing House and cited S.Ct.Bull. (CCH). They may also be found in the *Bankruptcy Reporter, Bankruptcy Court Decisions, Collier's Bankruptcy Cases,* and *Bankruptcy Law Reporter.*

In addition to the standard hard copy, bankruptcy opinions from all the federal courts can be found in the databases of WESTLAW; LEXIS; West's Bankruptcy Library, PREMISE® CD-ROM ed.; and Loislaw. Some unreported cases may also be located in these databases.

Shepardizing is an essential part of any legal research. Once an appropriate case has been found, the current status of that case must be investigated. Has the case been appealed, overruled, or distinguished? Are there other cases that follow the principles discussed in this case?

Shepard's Bankruptcy Citations, published by LEXIS Law Publishing Co. provides this up-to-date information on the history and treatment of a case through a system of elaborate abbreviations. An explanation of the use of *Shepard's* is found at the beginning of each volume. Also included are citations of law reviews and *American Law Reports (ALR). Shepard's Bankruptcy Citations* also lists statute citations to the bankruptcy provisions of the United States Code.

SECTION 4 SECONDARY AUTHORITY

In the field of bankruptcy, secondary authority provides an insight into the Bankruptcy Code and how it is or ought to be applied to specific problems. Secondary authority may give a paralegal the drafters' intent when the Code was drafted, a lead to cases interpreting and applying specific provisions of the Code, or a legal scholar's interpretations and applications of specific provisions of the Code. The following is a brief introduction to some of the secondary sources that may aid paralegals in their research.

A. LEGISLATIVE HISTORY

The legislative history concerning the Bankruptcy Code begins with the Commission Report, continues with the congressional hearings, and concludes with the House and Senate reports and statements concerning compromise as reported in the *Congressional Record.* Great care should be exercised when using legislative history because the legislative process itself is one of evolution. The legislation ultimately enacted and signed into law may differ greatly from the proposed legislation. The ultimate legislation may have been changed so the legislative history is no longer relevant. These changes may be obvious or subtle. Also, legislative history, even when relevant, is only secondary authority. The legislation itself is the primary, mandatory authority. A court, however, may use legislative history to give the legislation a meaning other than its plain meaning.

B. DIGESTS

As discussed earlier in this chapter, past cases may be helpful in determining how a court will interpret and apply the Bankruptcy Code and other federal and state statutes. The following digests, published by West Group Publishing Co., are helpful in the bankruptcy field:

- *Federal Practice Digest* 3d
- *Federal Practice Digest* 4th
- *West's Bankruptcy Digest*

These digests abstract a one-sentence explanation of a topic in a case and provide the name and citation of the case. To find appropriate cases, the descriptive word index is used to identify a West digest topic and key number. Once an appropriate topic and key number are found, the West digests can be used to locate cases on that subject.

C. LOOSE-LEAF SERVICES

Loose-leaf services help keep legal professionals updated in a specialized area. Recent developments in a given field are updated weekly, biweekly, or monthly, and information is provided on recent cases, statutes, regulations, and current developments in the law. Loose-leaf services cover all jurisdictions and often report relevant lower court decisions that are not available in other case reports.

Loose-leaf services vary in format. Some have a "how-to-use" section, which is usually located at the beginning of the first volume. This section will explain what the treatise contains, how the particular treatise is organized, and how the needed information can be found. If a loose-leaf service does not contain a how-to-use section, the index or index volume can provide similar information.

Some well-known bankruptcy loose-leaf services are

- Aaron, *Bankruptcy Law Fundamentals* (West Group Publishing Co.)
- *Bankruptcy Law Reporter* (Commerce Clearing House)
- *Bankruptcy Service,* Lawyers' Edition (West Group Publishing Co.)
- Boelter, *Representing the Bankrupt Taxpayer* (West Group Publishing Co.)
- *Collier on Bankruptcy* (15th ed., rev., LEXIS Law Publishing Co.)
- Drake, *Bankruptcy Practice for the General Practitioner* (3d ed., rev., West Group Publishing Co.)
- *Herzog's Bankruptcy Forms and Practice* (8th ed., West Group Publishing Co.)
- Murphy, *Creditors' Rights in Bankruptcy* (Shepard's/McGraw-Hill)
- McQueen & Williams, *Tax Aspects of Bankruptcy Law and Practice* (3d ed., West Group Publishing Co.)
- Norton, *Bankruptcy Code and Rules: including bankruptcy code, related statutes, bankruptcy rules (with related civil procedure rules), federal rules of evidence* (West Group Publishing Co.)
- Resnick, *Bankruptcy Law Manual* (5th ed., West Group Publishing Co.)
- Snyder & Ponoroff, *Commercial Bankruptcy Litigation* (West Group Publishing Co.)
- Williams, *Bankruptcy Practice Handbook* (2d ed., West Group Publishing Co.)

D. TREATISES

A treatise is a book by a legal expert that covers a particular legal subject in depth. Treatises are useful as a starting point for background research and as a way of later refining the point of research. Published as a single volume or as a multiple-volume series, treatises offer interpretation and analysis of the law pertaining to a particular subject, as well as the author's opinion on how the law should be interpreted and applied. The authors often cite helpful cases and other sources.

Some well known bankruptcy treatises are

- Anderson, *Chapter 11 Reorganizations* (2d ed., West Group Publishing Co., 1998)
- Baird, *The Elements of Bankruptcy* (3d ed., Foundation Press, 2001)
- Bienenstock, *Bankruptcy Reorganization* (Practicing Law Institute, 1987)
- Cowans, *Bankruptcy Law and Practice* (7th ed., West Group Publishing Co.)
- *Epstein, Nickles and White's Hornbook on Bankruptcy* (West Group Publishing Co., 1993)
- Jackson, *The Logic and Limits of Bankruptcy Law* (Harvard University Press, 1986)
- Lopucki, *Strategies for Creditors in Bankruptcy Proceedings* (3d ed., Aspen Law & Business, 1997)
- Tabb's *The Law of Bankruptcy* (University Textbook Series, Foundation Press, 1997)

Most of these treatises have some form of periodic supplementation.

E. LEGAL PERIODICALS

Legal periodicals include law school publications (the law reviews and law journals), bar association publications, special subject periodicals, and legal newspapers. Law reviews publish leading articles written by law professors, judges, and practitioners, and student written articles, notes, and comments. Law reviews are an excellent source of information concerning a specific topic.

A number of state, county, and local bar associations publish periodicals. Some bar association publications publish articles that are often more practice oriented than the articles that appear in the law reviews.

Subject journals focus on one area of law. *American Bankruptcy Law Journal* (Am.Bankr.L.J.) is a subject journal published by the National Conference of Referees in Bankruptcy.

Following are some well-known law reviews and legal periodicals that address bankruptcy issues:

- *ABI Journal*, published 10 times a year by the American Bankruptcy Institute.
- *ABI Law Review*, published twice a year by the St. John's University School of Law.
- *Bankruptcy Developments Journal*, Emory University School of Law, published twice a year (Fall & Spring).
- *Journal of Bankruptcy Law and Practice*, published bi-monthly.
- *Journal of the National Conference of Referees in Bankruptcy*, 1966–1970, published quarterly and continued by the *American Bankruptcy Law Journal* (Am. Bankr. L.J.), published quarterly beginning in 1971 with volume 45.

Legal articles can be located through the following sources:

- *Current Law Index, 1980–present, (Information Access Corp.)*. Current Law Index (CLI) published by the Information Access Corp. in cooperation with the American Association of Law Libraries, is a printed index issued monthly, with quarterly and annual cumulations. It contains a subject index, an author/title index, a table of cases, and a table of statutes.
- *Index to Legal Periodicals and Books, 1908–present, (H. W. Wilson Co.)*. Index to Legal Periodicals and Books, published by H. W. Wilson Co., is a printed index issued monthly, with quarterly, annual and multi-year cumulations. It contains an author/subject index, a table of cases commented upon, a table of statutes commented upon, and a book review index.
- *Index to Legal Periodicals and Books, 1981–present, (WilsonWeb)* http://wilsonweb2.hwwilson.com. WilsonWeb is H. W. Wilson's subscription-based information retrieval system for the World Wide Web. This service provides several search tools for easy access to Wilson's renowned databases. The user

can search for references pertaining to a topic of interest; display details (including the full text of a document in full-text databases) about that reference; and print, save, and e-mail that information.

- *LegalTrac/InfoTrac, 1980–present, (Gale Group)* http://infotrac.galegroup.com. Use this database to find articles in all major law reviews, law journals, specialty law and bar association journals, and legal newspapers. Included are articles on federal and state cases, laws and regulations, legal practice, and taxation. Also included are British Commonwealth, European Union, and international law.

F. AMERICAN LAW REPORTS

American Law Reports, published by West Group Publishing Co., is currently in its Fifth Series (A.L.R. 5th) (1992–date). A companion set, *American Law Reports, Federal* (A.L.R.Fed.) (1969–date), covers federal statutes and cases. A.L.R.5th does not replace the prior four series. A.L.R. annotations are extensive and provide a rich source of case decisions on a topic. Cases are cited from all jurisdictions; both majority and minority viewpoints are given. Each annotation cross-references other West publications that contain discussions on the subject. A.L.R. is supplemented with pocket parts, so that annotations remain current.

An A.L.R. annotation can be found through the multi-volume Index to Annotations, which covers A.L.R.2d, A.L.R.3d, A.L.R.4th, A.L.R.5th, and A.L.R.Fed. Each volume has a cumulative pocket supplement inside its back cover. These volumes also contain an annotation history table and a table of the laws, rules, and regulations. A.L.R. annotations may also be found through *Shepard's* and the *American Jurisprudence* series.

G. LEGAL ENCYCLOPEDIAS

The legal encyclopedias, *American Jurisprudence 2d,* published by West Group Publishing Co., and cited Am.Jur.2d, *Corpus Juris Secundum,* published by West Group Publishing Co., and cited C.J.S., are organized alphabetically and contain discussions on a large variety of legal subjects. These encyclopedias have a table of contents for each topic as well as a multi-volume index for the complete set.

Am.Jur.2d does not attempt to cite all reported cases but only selected decisions. It cites relevant A.L.R. annotations.

C.J.S. attempts to cite all reported cases. It also refers to relevant West digest topics and key numbers, thus facilitating access to the American Digest System.

H. INTERNET RESOURCES

The Internet provides a rich source of resources that includes the following:

- ABI World, The premier site for Bankruptcy information on the Web: http://www.abiworld.org/.
- American Bankruptcy Institute "Cracking the Code": http://www.abiworld.org/
- InterNet Bankruptcy Library: http://bankrupt.com. Sponsored by Peter A. Chapman, Bankruptcy Creditors' Service, Inc. & Christopher Beard, Beard Group, Inc.
- World Internet Insolvency & Bankruptcy Resources, United States of America: http://www.insolvency.com.

Two general law-related Web sites have subject specialties focusing on bankruptcy:

- FindLaw for Legal Professionals: http://www.findlaw.com. Located under FindLaw > Legal Subjects > Bankruptcy Law.
- Washburn University School of Law Web Page/Washlaw: http://www.washlaw.edu.

National Bankruptcy Web Sites is a project sponsored by the Topeka Area Bankruptcy Council, in cooperation with the Washburn University School of Law Library, and the U.S. Bankruptcy Court for the

District of Kansas. It provides a good list, with descriptions, of legal Web sites that pertain to bankruptcy, and also includes a link to Bankruptcy Forms (in PDF format).

Be careful when using Internet resources. Here are some guidelines to help evaluate the information you find on the Internet:

- Is the site trustworthy? Be aware of who is putting the information on the Web. What is their point of view? Are they a reputable source for the information presented? Is it a governmental source, a law firm, or a private group with its own agenda? Are sources of information stated? Can the author or webmaster be contacted for clarification?
- How current is the information? Look for an indication of how often the information on the Web site is updated. How much confidence can you place in a Web site that says it has the "latest developments" on an issue, if the last time it was updated was six months ago?
- How reliable is the information? Is the information complete or edited? Can you tell from the Web site if the information has been abstracted or summarized from another source? Is there enough information for you to find the original source for comparison purposes?

KEY TERMS

adequate protection
automatic stay
collateral
debtor in possession (DIP)
estate
executory contract
family farmer
liquidation
order for relief
party in interest
proof of claim
proof of interest
property of the estate
regular annual income
security agreement
security interest
unexpired lease
Uniform Commercial Code (UCC)
United States Code (U.S.C.)
venue

CHAPTER 3

The Cast of Characters and Their Roles in the Bankruptcy Process

CHAPTER OUTLINE

SECTION 1
THE DEBTOR, THE DEBTOR'S ATTORNEY, AND THE PARALEGAL
A. The Debtor
B. The Debtor's Attorney
C. The Paralegal

SECTION 2
THE BANKRUPTCY PETITION PREPARER

SECTION 3
THE CREDITORS AND OTHER PARTIES IN INTEREST
A. Creditors
B. Other Parties in Interest

SECTION 4
THE ADMINISTRATIVE OFFICE OF THE UNITED STATES COURTS

SECTION 5
THE BANKRUPTCY JUDGE AND STAFF
A. The Bankruptcy Judge
B. The Judge's Law Clerk, Judicial Assistant, and Courtroom Deputy
C. The Court Reporter

SECTION 6
THE OFFICE OF THE CLERK OF THE BANKRUPTCY COURT
A. The Bankruptcy Court Clerk
B. The Deputy Clerks

SECTION 7
THE UNITED STATES TRUSTEES, PRIVATE TRUSTEES, AND EXAMINERS
A. The United States Trustees
B. Private Trustees
C. Examiners

The bankruptcy process vitally influences the lives of great numbers of people. In addition to debtors and creditors, the bankruptcy process annually affects the employment of thousands of people, involves billions of dollars in assets, and, to a great extent, concerns the public interest. The debtors range from individuals to giant corporations. The bankruptcy process has been used by a number of major publicly held companies, including Adelphia Communications, Conseco, Enron, Federal-Mogul, FINOVA Group, Global Crossing, Kmart, Mirant, Montgomery Ward, NTL, Pacific Gas & Electric, Reliance Group Holdings, United Airlines, and Worldcom.

The bankruptcy process can be characterized as a stage upon which a large cast of characters play out their respective roles. The Bankruptcy Reform Act of 1978, with its subsequent amendments, provides a script for the performance. It attempts to balance the interests among these various actors and to provide the mechanism through which each can pursue his or her own interests.

The cast of characters in the bankruptcy process can be classified into the following basic groups:

1. the debtor, the debtor's attorney, and the paralegal;
2. the bankruptcy petition preparer;
3. the creditors and other parties in interest;
4. the Administrative Office of the United States Courts;
5. the bankruptcy judge and staff;
6. the office of the clerk of the bankruptcy court; and
7. the United States trustee, private trustees, and examiners.

SECTION 1 THE DEBTOR, THE DEBTOR'S ATTORNEY, AND THE PARALEGAL

The central player, the debtor, is supported by his or her attorney and the attorney's paralegal.

A. THE DEBTOR

The bankruptcy process naturally focuses on the debtor. The Bankruptcy Reform Act of 1978 selected the terminology "debtor," rather than "bankrupt," in part to remove some of the stigma from the filing of a bankruptcy case.

The Bankruptcy Reform Act of 1978 defines "debtor" as a "person or municipality concerning which a case under this title has been commenced." 11 U.S.C.A. § 101(13). The definition of "debtor" uses both the terms "person" and "municipality," since they are mutually exclusive. "Person" includes "individual, partnership, and corporation, but does not include governmental unit." 11 U.S.C.A. § 101(41). A "municipality" is a "political subdivision or public agency or instrumentality of a State." 11 U.S.C.A. § 101(40). Thus, by definition, a "person" would not include a "municipality" and a "municipality" would not include a "person."

The Code specifies who is eligible to be a debtor under bankruptcy law. 11 U.S.C.A. § 109. All persons may become debtors under the Code with three limitations. First, the person seeking to become a debtor must be a person who resides or has a domicile, a place of business, or property in the United States. 11 U.S.C.A. § 109(a).

PROBLEM 3.1 Stephanie Simpson, a reporter for a major newspaper, has been assigned for the past three years to London. Other than the condo she owns in New York City, all of her property is with her in London. Over the past few years, Stephanie has spent faster than she has earned, and she now finds herself unable to keep up with her creditors.

Is Stephanie eligible to be a debtor under the Code? Does it matter whether Stephanie is a citizen of the United States?

PROBLEM 3.2 The facts are the same as in Problem 3.1 except that Stephanie sold her condo in New York City six months ago. Is she eligible to be a debtor under the Code?

Second, an individual or family farmer may not be a debtor under the Code if he or she has been a debtor in a case pending under the Code at any time in the preceding 180 days if: (1) the case was dismissed by the court for willful failure of the debtor to abide by orders of the court or to appear before the court in proper prosecution of the case; or (2) if the debtor requested and obtained the voluntary dismissal of the case following the filing of a request for relief from the automatic stay. 11 U.S.C.A. § 109(g).

PROBLEM 3.3 On June 1, Clarence Collier filed a petition for bankruptcy under Chapter 7. On June 15, First National Bank filed a motion for relief from the automatic stay. On June 20, Clarence filed a motion requesting dismissal of his case. The case was dismissed on July 1.

Could Clarence file a new petition in bankruptcy under Chapter 7 on November 15, November 28, or December 15? Rule 9006 may provide some assistance on whether the date of the filing of the first petition should count toward the 180 days.

In addition to defining in general terms who may be a debtor under the Code, the Code defines who may be a debtor under each of the operative chapters of the Code. 11 U.S.C.A. §§ 109(b)–(f). The Bankruptcy Reform Act of 1994 makes two amendments to 11 U.S.C.A. § 109. The selection of the appropriate operative chapter will be discussed in Chapter Nine.

B. THE DEBTOR'S ATTORNEY

The attorney who represents the debtor in bankruptcy may be representing an established client he or she has represented in other matters, a client referred by another attorney, a client referred by a lawyer referral service, a client who learned about this attorney through a former client, or, if the attorney advertises as a bankruptcy practitioner, a client who has seen an advertisement. If the debtor is an established client, the attorney may be aware of the client's financial problems and the two of them may start to consider bankruptcy as an option weeks before the filing of the petition. The attorney who practices bankruptcy law extensively will probably receive a number of referrals from other attorneys who do not practice bankruptcy law. A client who has gone through bankruptcy and is satisfied with an attorney's handling of the case will often speak favorably to family, friends, and neighbors, leading them to seek out this attorney if they encounter financial difficulties. Advertising in the bankruptcy area appears to be successful. The attorney who advertises will probably acquire a number of clients in this manner.

Every client who goes to an attorney with financial problems will not file bankruptcy. One of the attorney's services will be to determine whether alternatives to bankruptcy are viable for a particular client and so advise the client. Presuming there is no viable alternative, the attorney, after so advising the client, will begin the process of gathering information from the client for preparation of the bankruptcy filing. The attorney will supervise the paralegal in the preparation of pleadings, file any necessary motions, and represent the client at the meeting of creditors and at any bankruptcy court or appellate court proceedings in the case.

The length of time in which an attorney is involved in a bankruptcy case varies. A routine Chapter 7 case will be quickly finished, but a complex Chapter 11 case may take several years.

The attorney's compensation is regulated by the Code and the Federal Rules of Bankruptcy Procedure. 11 U.S.C.A. § 329; Fed. R. Bank. P. 2016.

C. THE PARALEGAL

The paralegal's role in aiding the attorney will depend on the law firm, the training and experience of the paralegal, and the type of client involved. Bankruptcy practice is handled by a number of different types of firms:

1. A small firm could consist of one attorney who may or may not specialize in bankruptcy, one paralegal, and one secretary.
2. A larger firm could consist of several attorneys who may or may not specialize in bankruptcy, several paralegals, and several secretaries.
3. A very large firm may have a bankruptcy department with a number of paralegals and secretaries.

Naturally, a paralegal who has studied bankruptcy and has extensive experience will be given more responsibility than one who is new to the bankruptcy area. The needs of a Chapter 7 debtor with few assets will be quite different from those of a large corporate client. The attorney charged with handling the case must determine the role of the paralegal and closely supervise his or her activities in every case, regardless of the size of the case or its relative importance to the firm.

A paralegal in the bankruptcy field performs a number of activities that relate to the practice of law but does not advise clients or represent clients in judicial proceedings. Paralegal activities include, but are not limited to, client interviews, investigation, legal research, and document drafting. Not all paralegals will perform all these activities. The activities performed will depend on the supervising attorney. The relationship between attorney and paralegal is constantly evolving. As the relationship grows, the range of activities the attorney assigns to the paralegal becomes broader and more complex. The following discussion touches only on some of the activities to which a paralegal could be assigned. Other activities exist as well.

At the initial interview, the paralegal may meet with the client to review an extensive questionnaire on the debtor's assets and liabilities and to help the debtor create a plan for acquiring the information necessary to complete the questionnaire. At subsequent meetings, the paralegal will review and organize the information gathered by the debtor and identify additional information needed to complete the various schedules, lists, and statements.

In addition to working with the debtor to develop the information necessary to complete the documents to be filed, the paralegal will investigate the completeness and accuracy of the information gathered by the debtor. The amounts of various debts must be confirmed, and the paralegal must determine whether these debts are secured or unsecured. Record offices should be checked for UCC filings and real estate recordings. Tax offices should be checked for unpaid taxes and whether unpaid taxes have led to tax liens. The location of the debtor's property should be determined.

The paralegal will open a bankruptcy file and prepare the inventories of the debtor's assets and liabilities. Ultimately, these inventories will become a part of Official Form No. 6 (Schedules). As part of this process, the paralegal begins the identification and classification of property that the debtor will claim as exempt. This information will be incorporated into Official Form No. 6, Schedule C (Property Claimed as Exempt). The paralegal may be responsible for arranging to have some assets appraised to establish their value.

As the information gathering stage continues, the paralegal plays an important role in maintaining contact with the debtor, asking the debtor for more information, and keeping the debtor current on the status of the case. The paralegal performs a liaison role, communicating with the client for the attorney and with the attorney for the client.

After the essential information has been gathered and verified, the paralegal begins drafting the documents needed to file the case. The first document is the **voluntary petition** in bankruptcy, Official Form No. 1. Depending on which chapter the case is being filed under, a number of schedules, lists, and statements must be completed as well. If the case requires an attorney's fee application, the paralegal will prepare it for the attorney's approval. After these documents have been prepared in rough draft form, the paralegal supervises the clerical staff finalizing the documents. The attorney reviews the final documents with the paralegal for accuracy and completeness.

The paralegal files the necessary documents at the office of the clerk of the bankruptcy court and works with the clerk's office personnel and the judge's staff on behalf of the supervising attorney for the case.

The paralegal will do legal research on specific issues raised by the attorney. This research could be required before the petition and schedules are filed, or it could be necessary for a motion or complaint that the debtor's attorney may file during the progress of the case through the court. If the bankruptcy judge's decision on a motion or a complaint is appealed, the paralegal could play an important role in the research and preparation of the appellate brief.

The duties of a paralegal can extend beyond a given case to the function of keeping the attorney current on recent developments in the bankruptcy field. The paralegal may also be responsible for developing new office procedures to streamline the processing of bankruptcy cases, including devising a new calendar system, reorganizing work flow, determining better use of existing equipment, or purchasing more sophisticated hardware and software.

SECTION 2 THE BANKRUPTCY PETITION PREPARER

The cast of characters in the bankruptcy process has been expanded to include the bankruptcy petition preparer. 11 U.S.C.A. § 110(a). A bankruptcy petition preparer is defined as a "person, other than an attorney or an employee of an attorney, who prepares for compensation a document for filing." According to the legislative history, this section was added to Chapter 1 of the Code to create standards and penalties for what have been termed non-lawyer bankruptcy mills.

The petition preparer may perform typing services only and may not attempt to provide legal advice or legal service to the debtor. The bankruptcy petition preparer must

1. print his or her name and address on any document for filing;
2. place an identifying number (last four digits of social security number) on any document for filing;
3. furnish the debtor a copy of the document for filing at the time it is presented for the debtor's signature;
4. not execute a document on behalf of the debtor;
5. not use the word "legal" or any similar term in advertisements; and
6. not collect or receive any payment from the debtor or from anyone else on behalf of the debtor for court filing fees.

The bankruptcy petition preparer who fails to comply with these requirements may be fined not more than $500 for each violation.

The petition preparer shall file, within 10 days after the petition is filed, a declaration disclosing any fee from the debtor or on behalf of the debtor received within 12 months prior to the filing, as well as any unpaid fee charged to the debtor. Any fee found to be excessive by the court will be disallowed and turned over to the bankruptcy trustee. The individual debtor will be allowed to exempt the funds recovered. 11 U.S.C.A. § 522(b).

The penalties become even steeper if a case is dismissed because of the preparer's failure to file papers, negligence, or intentional disregard. On the motion of a debtor, trustee, or creditor, the petition preparer shall be ordered to pay

1. the debtor's actual damages;
2. $2,000 or double the amount, whichever is greater, paid by the debtor to the preparer;
3. reasonable attorney's fees and costs.

An extra $1,000 shall be ordered paid if the movant is a trustee or creditor.

The petition preparer may be enjoined from preparing petitions for violation of the provisions of 11 U.S.C.A. § 110. The petition preparer may even face imprisonment of not more than one year or a fine, or both, for a knowing attempt to disregard the Bankruptcy Code or Federal Rules of Bankruptcy Procedure, which results in the dismissal of the bankruptcy case or related proceeding. 18 U.S.C.A. § 156.

The paralegal, as an employee of an attorney, will not be affected by 11 U.S.C.A. § 110 because he or she does not fit the definition of a bankruptcy petition preparer. A paralegal works for an attorney and under the supervision of that attorney. Any person with paralegal training who chooses to prepare bankruptcy petitions outside employment by, and supervision of, an attorney is subject to the standards and penalties set forth in the Code.

SECTION 3
THE CREDITORS AND OTHER PARTIES IN INTEREST

Creditors hold three basic types of claims: priority, secured, and unsecured. **Priority claims** include claims by employees for employee compensation, claims for alimony, maintenance, or support, claims by the Internal Revenue Service, and claims by the state tax commission. **Secured claims** are secured by real estate, fixtures, or personal property. The real estate, fixtures, or personal property that secures a claim is known as **collateral** and may be taken (repossessed) by the creditor if the debtor does not fulfill his or her obligation to pay the debt. **Unsecured claims** are not secured by collateral.

Creditors are **parties in interest.** Other parties in interest include equity security holders, indenture trustees, statutory lienholders, lessors, and governmental regulatory authorities. The United States trustee and private trustees, also parties in interest, are discussed in Section 7 of this chapter.

A. CREDITORS

Creditors include creditors holding secured claims, creditors holding priority claims, and creditors holding unsecured claims. The emphasis is on the claim and not on the creditor. Therefore, reference is to a creditor holding a secured claim, rather than to a secured creditor.

1. Creditors Holding Secured Claims

Creditors holding secured claims may have a security interest in real property, personal property, or fixtures. A real estate mortgagee has an interest in real estate that secures payment or performance of an obligation. If the mortgagor defaults as to his or her obligation, the mortgagee can repossess the real estate. (See Exhibit 3–1.)

EXHIBIT 3–1 Real Estate Mortgage Transaction

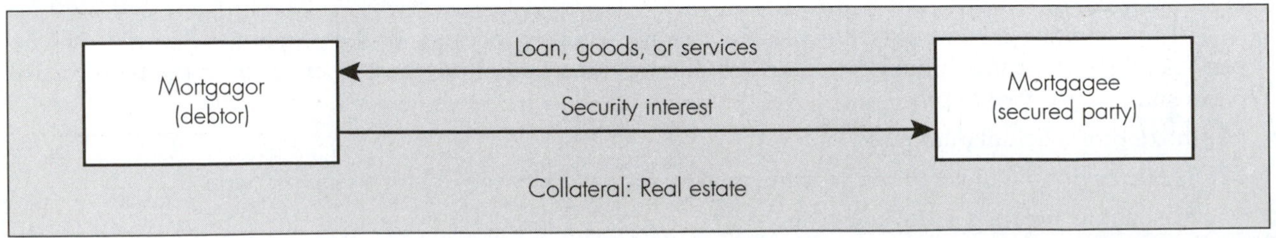

PROBLEM 3.4 Franklin and Sylvia Richardson purchased a house from Anthony and Gloria Woodberry for $175,000. The Richardsons paid the Woodberrys by withdrawing $17,500 from their savings account and borrowing $157,500 from the Gotham Savings and Loan Association. The Richardsons gave Gotham Savings a mortgage on the house.

Who is the mortgagor and who is the mortgagee? What is the collateral for the mortgage?

Three years after the sale, the Richardsons found themselves in financial difficulties and ceased paying Gotham Savings on the mortgage. Gotham Savings repossessed the house and sold it.

If Gotham sells the house for more than the mortgage balance, who receives the surplus? If Gotham sells the house for less than the mortgage balance, do the Richardsons still owe Gotham the difference? Is the difference a secured or an unsecured claim?

Fixtures are "goods that have become so related to particular real property that an interest in them arises under state real property law." UCC § 9–102(a)(41). Therefore, whether something is a fixture depends on state real estate law. Fixture claimants may claim through their interest in the real estate. Thus, the mortgagor may, in a real estate mortgage, give the mortgagee more than just an interest in the real estate. The mortgagor may also give the mortgagee an interest in fixtures.

EXAMPLE

John and Martha Wright borrowed $100,000 from Credit Union to purchase a house. The Wrights gave Credit Union a mortgage on their house and the "fixtures therein." Credit Union's fixture claimant status derives from its interest in the real estate.

A **secured party** under Article 9 of the Uniform Commercial Code is "a person in whose favor a security interest is created or provided for under a security agreement." UCC § 9–102(a)(72). A **security interest** is "an interest in personal property or fixtures which secured payment or performance of an obligation." UCC § 1–201(b)(35). The person who has "an interest other than a security interest or other lien, in the collateral" is known as the debtor. UCC § 9–102(a)(28). The collateral is "the property that is subject to a security interest." UCC § 9–102(a)(12). The agreement that "creates or provides for a security interest" is known as the security agreement. UCC § 9–102(a)(73). The code term "security agreement" replaces all previously used terms such as assignment, chattel mortgage, chattel trust, conditional sale, equipment trust, factor's lien, pledge, trust deed, trust receipt, and other lien or title retention contract intended to create a security interest (the right to repossess the collateral in the event of default) in the collateral. See UCC §§ 9–109(a)(1), 9–202. (See Exhibit 3–2.)

PROBLEM 3.5 Ronald purchased a winter coat from Baldwin's Men's Shop for $500. Ronald charged the coat on his Baldwin's credit card. Since buying the coat, Ronald has lost his job and cannot pay for the coat.

Now that Ronald is in default as to the purchase price, can Baldwin's repossess the coat? At the time of the purchase, did Ronald give Baldwin's a security interest in the coat, making Baldwin's a secured party?

EXHIBIT 3–2 Secured Transaction

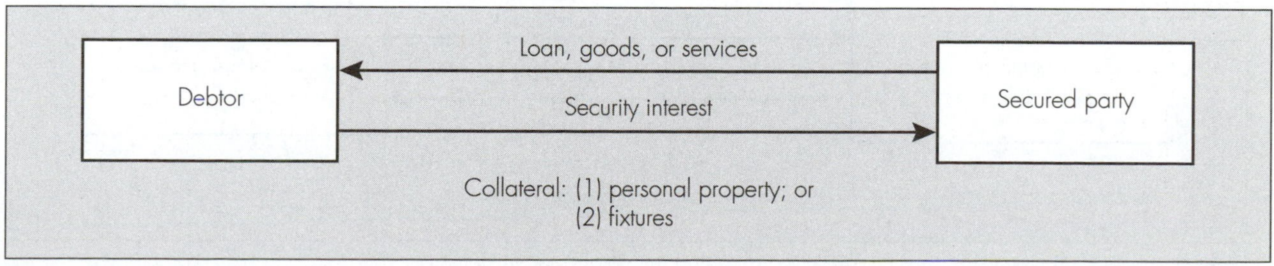

PROBLEM 3.6 Ronald purchased a winter coat for his girlfriend, Janet, from Ms. Smythe's Fine Fashions for $1,000. Ronald charged the coat on his Ms. Smythe's credit card and gave Ms. Smythe's a security interest in the coat. Ronald took the coat home and hung it in a closet until he could give it to Janet for her birthday. After he bought the coat but before he could give it to Janet, Ronald lost his job and now cannot pay for the coat.

Since Ronald is in default as to the purchase price, can Ms. Smythe's repossess the coat from him?

PROBLEM 3.7 Assume the same facts as in Problem 3.6, except that Ronald gave the coat to Janet for her birthday before he lost his job and defaulted on his obligation to pay.

Now that Ronald is in default as to the purchase price, can Ms. Smythe's repossess the coat from Janet? Does it make any difference whether the secured party seeks to repossess from the debtor or from someone to whom the debtor has given the collateral? See UCC §§ 9–315(a)(1); 9–317(b), (e); 9–320(a).

As previously stated, fixtures are goods that become so related to the real property that an interest in them arises under state real estate law. UCC § 9–102(a)(41). Therefore, whether something is a fixture depends on state law. Fixture claimants may claim through their interest in the real estate. Fixture claimants may also be personal property claimants and claim through their interest in goods, not through an interest in real estate. Thus, a debtor may, in a UCC Article 9 security agreement, give a party an interest in goods that are fixtures or are to become fixtures. The secured party then has a security interest in fixtures.

EXAMPLE

John and Martha Wright borrowed $100,000 from Credit Union to purchase a house. The Wrights gave Credit Union a mortgage on their house and the "fixtures therein." Credit Union's fixture claimant status derives from its interest in the real estate.

John and Martha borrowed $2,000 from First Bank to purchase a new furnace for their house. The Wrights gave First Bank a security interest in the furnace. Under state law, the furnace, once installed, became a fixture. First Bank's fixture claimant status derives from its interest in the goods that became fixtures.

PROBLEM 3.8 John and Martha Wright purchased a new patio door from Quality Patio Doors, Inc. Quality financed the sale, and the Wrights gave Quality a security interest in the patio door. The Wrights installed the door in their house. How is Quality's fixture claimant status established?

The term "secured party" also includes "a person to which accounts or **chattel paper,** payment intangibles, or promissory notes have been sold." UCC § 9–102(a)(72)(D). The "seller of accounts or chattel paper" is also known as the "debtor." UCC § 9–102(a)(28)(B). The collateral is the accounts or chattel paper that have been sold. UCC § 9–102(a)(12)(B). (See Exhibit 3–3.)

The following two examples illustrate accounts and chattel paper, respectively, as collateral.

EXHIBIT 3–3 Sale of Accounts or Chattel Paper

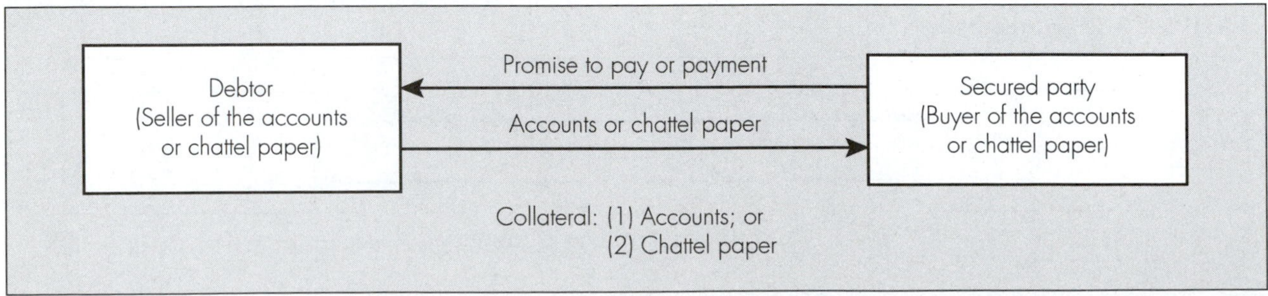

EXAMPLE

The Big Apple Office Supply Company sells office equipment and supplies on a cash or credit basis. Many large customers charge their purchases and are billed at the end of the month. If a bill is not paid in full within 30 days, a 1.5 percent finance charge is added on the next month's statement. Such obligations to pay are known as "accounts" or "accounts receivable."

The Big Apple was in need of cash, so it sold its accounts to First Bank. Even though First Bank is the buyer of the accounts, the UCC defines First Bank as a party holding a security interest in the accounts.

EXAMPLE

The Southpark Office Machine Company sold a photocopy machine on credit to the Newtown Pharmacy. Rather than just take Newtown's promise to pay, Southpark had Newtown sign a security agreement giving Southpark a security interest in the photocopy machine. The security agreement also contained Newtown's promise to pay.

Southpark sold Newtown's security agreement to Friendly Finance. Even though Friendly Finance is the buyer of the security agreement, the UCC defines Friendly as a party holding a security interest in Newtown's security agreement. Newtown's security agreement is chattel paper because it is a writing which evidences both a monetary obligation and a security interest in specific goods. The monetary obligation is Newtown's promise to pay. The security interest in specific goods is the security interest in the photocopy machine.

2. Creditors Holding Unsecured Priority Claims

The nine categories of creditors holding unsecured priority claims are listed in 11 U.S.C.A. § 507(a)(1)–(9). The dollar amounts for certain of these priority claims are adjusted every three years. 11 U.S.C.A. § 104(b). Future adjustment dates will be April 1, 2007 and April 1, 2010.

(1) Administrative fees. **Administrative expenses** include costs and expenses of preserving the estate (wages, salaries, and commissions for services rendered after the commencement of the case), taxes incurred by the estate other than those given priority status in 11 U.S.C.A. § 507(a)(8), and compensation for professional services rendered by an attorney or an accountant. 11 U.S.C.A. § 507(a)(1).

(2) Extensions of credit in an involuntary case. Claims that arose in the ordinary course of the debtor's business or financial affairs after the commencement of an involuntary case but before either the trustee was appointed or the order for relief issued are unsecured priority claims. 11 U.S.C.A. § 507(a)(2).

(3) Wages, salaries, and commissions. Employees can claim wages, salaries, and commissions, including vacation, severance, and sick leave pay, and independent sales representatives can claim commissions up to $4,925 per person earned within 90 days immediately preceding the filing of the original petition, or the cessation of business, whichever occurs first, to the extent provided in 11 U.S.C.A. § 507(a)(3).

PROBLEM 3.9 Mary Malone was the personal administrative assistant to the president of Quality Office Supply Co., a wholesale and retail office supply company. Mary's salary was $6,000 per month. For the four months before Quality filed for bankruptcy under Chapter 7, Mary had been receiving $2,300 per month.

Does Mary hold a priority claim and, if so, for how much?

(4) Contributions to employee benefit plans. An employee benefit plan can claim for money owed to the plan for services rendered within 180 days immediately preceding the filing of the original petition, or the cessation of business, whichever occurred first. For each plan, the amount is limited to $4,925 times the number of employees covered by the plan less the aggregate amount paid to each employee as a priority claim for wages, salaries, or commissions, plus the aggregate amount paid by the estate on behalf of these employees to any other employee benefit plan. These claims are not paid directly to the employee but rather to the benefit plan. 11 U.S.C.A. § 507(a)(4).

PROBLEM 3.10 Prior to its petition in bankruptcy, Quality Office Supply had 50 employees, including Mary Malone. During each of the seven months prior to the filing of the petition, Quality failed to contribute $750 per month for each employee to the employee benefit plan. Each of 20 employees was entitled to a priority claim for unpaid wages of $700. Twenty employees were entitled to a priority claim for unpaid wages of $1,500 each. Ten employees were entitled to a priority claim for unpaid wages of $4,925 each. The estate has not paid any other employee benefit plan on behalf of Quality's employees.

Does Mary hold a priority claim for unpaid contributions to her employee benefit plan? If so, for how much?

Does the plan itself hold a priority claim for unpaid contributions to the employee benefit plan? If so, for how much?

(5) Certain farmers and fishermen. Farmers who have unsecured claims against grain storage facilities for grain or the proceeds of grain and United States fishermen who have unsecured claims against fish produce storage or processing facilities can claim up to $4,925 per farmer or fisherman. 11 U.S.C.A. § 507(a)(5).

(6) Deposits by individuals. Consumers who have made unsecured money deposits in connection with the purchase, lease, or rental of property or services that were not delivered or provided have an unsecured priority claim. Each consumer is limited to a priority claim of $2,225. 11 U.S.C.A. § 507(a)(6).

PROBLEM 3.11 Cindy Shephard began her Christmas shopping in July. She selected a number of items from People's Department Store and had them put on layaway. At the time of purchase, Cindy paid $250 of the total bill of $4,000. On the first of each month, Cindy sent People's a check for $750. On November 15, People's filed a petition for bankruptcy under Chapter 7.

Does Cindy hold a priority claim? If so, for how much?

(7) Alimony, maintenance, or support. The debtor's spouse, former spouse, or child can have an unsecured priority claim for alimony, maintenance, or support, to the extent provided in 11 U.S.C.A. § 507(a)(7).

(8) Taxes and certain other debts owed to governmental units. Federal, state, and local governmental units have an unsecured priority claim for taxes, customs duties, and penalties as set forth in 11 U.S.C.A. § 507(a)(8). Included in this priority are property taxes assessed before the filing of a petition in bankruptcy and last payable without penalty after one year before the date of the filing of the petition. 11 U.S.C.A. § 507(a)(8)(B). If the debtor is an employer, taxes required to be collected and withheld and for which the debtor is liable and employment taxes on wages, salary, or commission are priority claims. 11 U.S.C.A. §§ 507(a)(8)(C), (D).

(9) Commitments to maintain the capital of an insured depository institution. The FDIC, RTC, Director of the Office of Thrift Supervision, Comptroller of the Currency, or Board of Governors of the Federal Reserve System, or their predecessors or successors, have unsecured priority claims based on the debtor's commitments to maintain the capital of an insured depository institution. 11 U.S.C.A. § 507(a)(9).

3. Creditors Holding Unsecured Nonpriority Claims

All of the debtor's creditors who have no special interest in property of the debtor's estate hold unsecured claims. Creditors holding unsecured nonpriority claims have loaned the debtor money, performed services for the debtor, or sold the debtor merchandise *without* demanding collateral to secure the debtor's promise to pay.

EXAMPLE

Allison Smiley borrowed $1,000 from Friendly Finance. Friendly did not require collateral to secure Allison's promise to pay. Friendly Finance is a creditor holding an unsecured claim until Allison pays in full. Friendly has an unsecured claim if Allison files a petition in bankruptcy.

EXAMPLE

Allison Smiley purchased a VCR from Neighborhood Electronics for $600. Neighborhood did not take a security interest in the VCR. Allison paid $150 down and agreed to pay the balance in three equal installments, each spaced one month apart. Once the VCR is delivered to Allison, Neighborhood's interest in the VCR ceases. Until Allison pays in full, Neighborhood holds an unsecured claim.

Also included in the category of creditors with unsecured claims are those parties with secured claims who are owed more than the collateral is worth. These parties hold unsecured claims for the amounts for which they are undercollateralized. 11 U.S.C.A. § 506(a).

EXAMPLE

Anna Holmes purchased a TV from Quality Electronics for $700. She paid $50 down and promised to pay $50 each month for 13 months. Anna gave Quality a security interest in the TV.

Because the TV is now used, it has a resale value of $400. Quality has a secured claim for $400 and an unsecured claim for $250.

B. OTHER PARTIES IN INTEREST

Creditors are not the only parties in interest. Also included in this category are equity security holders, indenture trustees, statutory lienholders, lessors, and governmental regulatory authorities.

1. Equity Security Holders

An *equity security holder* is one who holds an equity security of the debtor.

> "[E]quity security" means—
> (A) share in a corporation, whether or not transferable or denominated "stock," or similar security;
> (B) interest of a limited partner in a limited partnership; or
> (C) warrant or right, other than a right to convert, to purchase, sell, or subscribe to a share, security, or interest of a kind specified in subparagraph (A) or (B) of this paragraph. 11 U.S.C.A. § 101(16).

EXAMPLE

Daniel Drummond owns 100 shares of common stock in the Timber Toothpick Co. Timber filed for bankruptcy under Chapter 7. Drummond is an equity security holder.

PROBLEM 3.12 Ted, Alice, Bob, and Carol formed a partnership for the sale of hot tubs. Under the partnership, Ted and Alice were to manage the business. Bob and Carol were silent partners. They contributed most of the money for start-up costs. The partnership agreement provided that all profits would be divided equally among the four.

Within six months, the business failed and the partnership filed for bankruptcy under Chapter 7. Are Ted, Alice, Bob, and Carol equity security holders?

2. Indenture Trustees

An **indenture trustee** is a "trustee under an indenture." 11 U.S.C.A. § 101(29). An "indenture" is a "mortgage, deed of trust, or indenture, under which there is outstanding a security . . . constituting a claim against the debtor, a claim secured by a lien on any of the debtor's property, or an equity security of the debtor." 11 U.S.C.A. § 101(28). To qualify as an indenture under this Bankruptcy Code definition, the mortgage, deed of trust, or indenture must have outstanding a security other than a voting trust certificate.

3. Statutory Lienholders

When a person in the ordinary course of his or her business furnishes services or materials with respect to real estate, state statute or case law may give this person a lien on the real estate. This person is called a statutory lienholder. See 11 U.S.C.A. § 101(53).

EXAMPLE

Quality Roofing Co. put a new roof on Sally Mead's home. Sally agreed to pay for the roof over a period of one year. Under state statute, a person who repairs another's real estate is entitled to file a lien on the real estate in the office of real estate records. The lien gives Quality an interest in Sally's real estate for the price of the services until the lien is satisfied.

When a person in the ordinary course of his or her business furnishes services or materials with respect to the debtor's goods, state statute or case law may give this person a lien on the goods in his or her possession. See 11 U.S.C.A. § 101(53).

EXAMPLE

Phil was involved in an automobile accident, and his car sustained $1,500 in damage. Adam's Garage repaired Phil's automobile, but Phil was unable to pay the bill. Under state law, Adam's Garage may be able to retain possession of the automobile and to impose a mechanic's lien on Phil's automobile until Phil pays.

4. Lessors

Rather than purchasing property, the "buyer" may only wish to acquire the use of the property for a period of time. This transaction is known as a lease. The lessee acquires the exclusive right to use the property for the lease term. On completion of the lease term, the property is returned to the lessor, unless a new arrangement is made. (See Exhibit 3–4.)

EXAMPLE

Sally and Jonathan MacMillion signed an agreement with Sleepy Hollow for the rental of a two bedroom apartment for $900 a month for a period of one year. This transaction is a lease. Sally and Jonathan are the lessees, and Sleepy Hollow is the lessor. The subject of the lease is real estate (the apartment).

EXAMPLE

When Bill Bailey was building a patio in his backyard, he rented a portable cement mixer from E-Z Rentals for a month. This transaction is a lease. Bill Bailey is the lessee, and E-Z Rentals is the lessor. The subject of the lease is personal property (the cement mixer).

At times, the distinction between a lease and a security agreement is not clear. If the transaction is a lease, the goods will be the property of the estate for only the lease term or until the lease has been breached. At the end of the lease term or after the lease has been breached, the lessor will be entitled to the goods leased. If, however, the transaction is not a lease but is actually a security agreement, the "lessor" will not be entitled to the goods, which will remain property of the estate. The UCC addresses this problem when it defines a security interest. UCC § 1–201(b)(35).

A debtor in bankruptcy may be either a lessee or lessor. If the debtor is the lessee, then another party will claim to be the lessor of property that the debtor has in his or her possession at the time of filing the petition in bankruptcy. If the debtor is the lessor, then the debtor will have an ownership interest in property in the possession of another at the time of filing the petition in bankruptcy.

EXAMPLE

On January 1, Raymond rented a computer from ABC Computer Company for one year. On May 1, Raymond filed a petition in bankruptcy under Chapter 7. Raymond's bankruptcy estate includes a lease interest in the computer for the balance of the lease term. ABC has an ownership interest in the computer and has a right to its return at the end of the lease period.

EXAMPLE

On January 1, Raymond leased his typewriter to Oscar for one year. On May 1, Raymond filed a petition in bankruptcy under Chapter 7. Oscar has a lease interest in the typewriter for the balance of the lease term. Raymond's bankruptcy estate includes an ownership interest in the typewriter and has a right to its return at the end of the lease period.

EXHIBIT 3–4 Lease Transaction

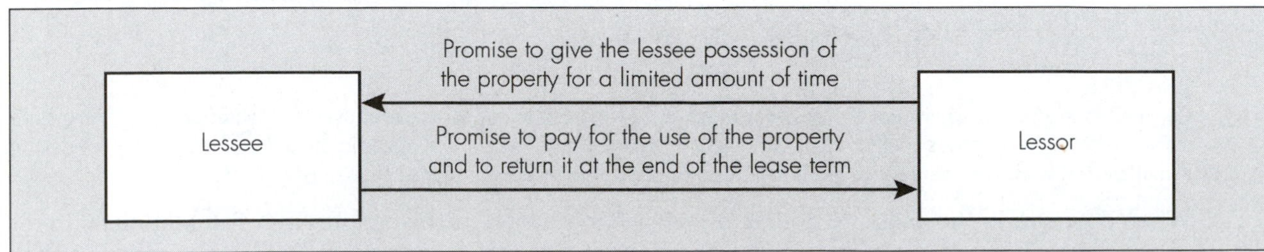

5. Governmental Regulatory Authorities

In addition to the various types of creditors who are owed money by a debtor filing a bankruptcy case, other interested parties in both the federal government and the state government may have regulatory responsibilities in connection with the debtor. Government involvement may be quite important to the outcome of a case. For example, any rate change provided for in a reorganization plan must be approved by the regulatory commission with jurisdiction in order for the plan to be confirmed. 11 U.S.C.A. § 1129(a)(6).

The Securities Investor Protection Corporation (SIPC) and the Securities and Exchange Commission (SEC) both have an interest in stockbroker liquidation cases filed under Subchapter III of Chapter 7 of the Bankruptcy Code. The SEC may raise, appear, and be heard on any issue in a Chapter 11 case but may not appeal from any judgment, order, or decree entered in the case. 11 U.S.C.A. § 1109(a). The SIPC may, in effect, "take over" a stockbroker liquidation case because the automatic stay provided for by 11 U.S.C.A. § 362 does not prevent the SIPC from filing an application for a protective decree under the Securities Investor Protection Act of 1970. This protective decree suspends all proceedings, except as provided by 11 U.S.C.A. § 362(b), until the SIPC has completed its action in the case. This may even mean total liquidation of the debtor by the SIPC, after which the bankruptcy case is dismissed. 11 U.S.C.A. § 742.

The state securities commission will have an interest in stockbroker liquidation cases on the state level, just as the SEC and the SIPC have an interest on the federal level.

The Commodity Futures Trading Commission has an interest in commodity broker liquidation cases filed under Subchapter IV of Chapter 7 of the Bankruptcy Code.

SECTION 4
THE ADMINISTRATIVE OFFICE OF THE UNITED STATES COURTS

Although the public has no relationship with the Administrative Office of the United States Courts, this office plays a critical role in the bankruptcy process. Generally, only the bankruptcy judge and the clerk of the bankruptcy court have a relationship with the Administrative Office (AO). The AO controls the size of the staff at the clerk's office, the salaries (to some extent), the quarters for the court and the clerk's office, and the rank of each employee. The AO serves as a resource on technical issues for bankruptcy courts throughout the nation. It also provides the bankruptcy courts with statistics and forms and examines the operations of each court and clerk's office. Statistics may be found at http://www.uscourts.gov under U.S. Bankruptcy Courts > Judicial Business of the United States Courts. Forms may be found at http://www.uscourts.gov under U.S. Bankruptcy Courts as well. A description of the Administrative Office is also found under http://www.uscourts.gov.

SECTION 5
THE BANKRUPTCY JUDGE AND STAFF

Considering the number of cases filed in each jurisdiction every year, each bankruptcy judge is supported by a relatively small staff, which includes the judge's law clerk or law clerks, the judge's judicial assistant, the courtroom deputy, and the court reporter.

A. THE BANKRUPTCY JUDGE

The bankruptcy judges in each judicial district are a unit of the United States district court. This unit is known as the bankruptcy court for that district. 28 U.S.C.A. § 151. Bankruptcy judges are appointed by the United States circuit court of appeals after recommendations of the Judicial Conference of the United States are considered. If a majority of the judges of that court cannot agree on the appointment, the chief judge of any such court of appeals shall make the appointment of a bankruptcy judge. 28 U.S.C.A. § 152(a)(3).

The official duty stations of bankruptcy judges and the places of holding court are determined by the Judicial Conference after recommendations of the director of the Administrative Office of the United States Courts are considered. The recommendations of the director are formulated by consultation with the judicial council of the circuit involved. This chain of consultation and recommendation ensures that the needs of the circuit are determined by the circuit rather than by an individual or group far removed from the situation. 28 U.S.C.A. § 152(b)(1). If the business of the court necessitates holding court in places within the judicial district other than the official duty station, a bankruptcy judge may hold court at such places. 28 U.S.C.A. § 152(c). A bankruptcy judge may also be designated to serve in any district adjacent to or near the district for which he or she has been appointed. Such designation requires approval of the Judicial Conference and of the judicial councils involved. 28 U.S.C.A. § 152(d). A bankruptcy judge may even be transferred temporarily to serve in any judicial district. Such a transfer requires approval of the judicial councils of the circuits involved. 28 U.S.C.A. § 155(a).

A bankruptcy judge is appointed for 14 years. 28 U.S.C.A. § 152(a)(1). He or she serves on a full-time basis and "may not engage in the practice of law or any other practice, business, occupation or employment" that would be "inconsistent with the expeditious, proper and impartial performance" of the judge's duties. 28 U.S.C.A. §§ 153(a), (b).

Persons appointed as bankruptcy judges are required to take the following oath or affirmation before performance of judicial duties:

> I, ______________ ______________, do solemnly swear (or affirm) that I will administer justice without respect to persons, and do equal right to the poor and to the rich, and that I will faithfully and impartially discharge and perform all the duties incumbent upon me as ____________________ according to the best of my abilities and understanding, agreeably to the Constitution and laws of the United States. So help me God.

In a bankruptcy court where more than one judge presides, the division of cases and other matters among the judges will be determined by rules promulgated by majority vote of the court.

The district court judges designate one judge to serve as chief judge of the bankruptcy court in a bankruptcy court having more than one judge. The chief judge of the district court will make the designation if the majority of the judges of the district court cannot agree.

A bankruptcy judge may be removed during the term of appointment only by the judicial council of the circuit in which the judge's official duty station is located. Removal requires concurrence in the order of removal by a majority of all the judges of the judicial council. A bankruptcy judge must be furnished a full specification of charges and must have an opportunity to be heard on the charges. Grounds for removal are incompetence, misconduct, neglect of duty, or physical or mental disability. 28 U.S.C.A. § 153(e).

If a judge dies or becomes disabled after an action has been tried and is unable to perform the duties required by the court at that point, any other judge who regularly sits in that court or is assigned to that court may perform these duties. This second judge has discretion to grant a new trial if this judge feels incapable of performing the necessary duties because he or she did not preside at the original trial or for any other reason. Fed. R. Bank. P. 9028; Fed. R. Civ. P. 63.

A retired bankruptcy judge may consent to be recalled to serve in any judicial district. The judicial council of the circuit within which the district is located would recall the judge. 28 U.S.C.A. § 155(b).

B. THE JUDGE'S LAW CLERK, JUDICIAL ASSISTANT, AND COURTROOM DEPUTY

A bankruptcy judge normally has three staff members—a law clerk, a judicial assistant, and a courtroom deputy. The courtroom deputy is a member of the office of the clerk of the court and is an assistant bankruptcy court clerk, although assigned to a bankruptcy judge. Some judges use the courtroom deputy as their judicial assistant, thus adding a second law clerk.

The law clerk in a bankruptcy court has the same duties as a law clerk in any other court. His or her main duty is to research questions raised before the court in disputed matters and write legal memos to the judge. The law clerk also drafts orders for the judge to sign.

The judicial assistant performs the usual duties of any administrative assistant, such as screening telephone calls and performing word processing, but the function most likely to be of interest to the paralegal is that of keeping the judge's calendar. The coordination of the judge's in-court and out-of-court schedules is vital to a smoothly run court. It will be helpful to the paralegal to become acquainted with the judicial assistant.

The courtroom deputy manages the judge's calendar. If a motion is filed and there is an objection, the courtroom deputy consults the judge's calendar and sets the date for the hearing. The courtroom deputy also attends the court hearings so, as issues arise that require a court date, the courtroom deputy can set the hearing date.

C. THE COURT REPORTER

A court reporter will make a verbatim record of any proceeding in which he or she is utilized. A certified copy of the transcript of a proceeding must be filed by the court reporter with the bankruptcy court clerk. Fed. R. Bank. P. 5007(a).

SECTION 6
THE OFFICE OF THE CLERK OF THE BANKRUPTCY COURT

The office of the clerk of the bankruptcy court is comprised of the clerk and the deputy clerks. The clerk's office is the administrative center for bankruptcy cases. Cases are not only filed in this office but are also physically maintained here. Any activity that takes place in a case will be recorded in this office.

A. THE BANKRUPTCY COURT CLERK

The bankruptcy court clerk is the official custodian of the records and dockets of the court. 28 U.S.C.A. § 156(e). Records to be kept by the clerk are enumerated under Fed. R. Bank. P. 5003. A bankruptcy docket is to be kept in each and every case under the Code. Each judgment, order, and activity in the case is entered and dated on the docket. A claims register is not kept in all cases but is necessary if it appears that a distribution may be made to creditors holding unsecured claims. This claims register consists of a list of claims filed in such a case.

The clerk must keep "a correct copy of every final judgment or order affecting title to or lien on real property or for the recovery of money or property." Fed. R. Bank. P. 5003(c). On request of the prevailing party, a correct copy of every such judgment or order must be kept and indexed with the civil judgments of the district court. The court may also direct any other order to be kept. The form and manner of such copies are prescribed by the director of the Administrative Office of the United States Courts. The clerk must keep an index of all cases and a separate index of adversary proceedings in a manner also prescribed by the director of the Administrative Office. A search of these indices and certification of whether a case or proceeding has been filed in the court or transferred to the court or whether a discharge has been entered must be made by the clerk upon request. Fed. R. Bank. P. 5003(d). The director of the Administrative Office may require the clerk to keep other books and records in addition to those listed here. Fed. R. Bank. P. 5003(e).

The clerk is accountable for all fees, costs, and other monies collected and makes returns of these monies to the director of the Administrative Office of the United States Courts and the director of the Executive Office for United States Trustees. 28 U.S.C.A. § 156(f).

Rule 5001(a) provides that "[t]he courts shall be deemed always open for the purpose of filing any pleading or other proper paper, issuing and returning process, and filing, making, or entering motions, orders and rules." Rule 5001(c), however, sets forth regular hours for the clerk's office: "The clerk's office with the clerk or a deputy in attendance shall be open during business hours on all days except Saturdays, Sundays and the legal holidays listed in Rule 9006(a)." There have been instances in which a bankruptcy petition has been accepted for filing after regular hours by the bankruptcy court judge at his or her residence. The clerk might also accept such filings.

The clerk is charged with issuing "a certified copy of the record of any proceeding in a case under the Code or of any paper filed with the clerk on payment of any prescribed fee." Fed. R. Bank. P. 5006. Fees for certification and for copying are fixed by the Judicial Conference. 28 U.S.C.A. § 1930(b).

As this summary of the clerk's duties and responsibilities indicates, the bankruptcy court clerk occupies an administrative position of great importance to the smooth operation of the court.

B. THE DEPUTY CLERKS

Deputy clerks are appointed by the clerk of the bankruptcy court subject to the approval of the court. 28 U.S.C.A. § 156(b). They may be removed from office in the same manner.

The duties of the deputy clerks are many and varied, ranging from the word processing inherent in any clerical position to answering inquiries from attorneys, paralegals, administrative assistants, debtors, and creditors by telephone or in the clerk's office. The deputy clerks are the front line soldiers in the bankruptcy court and, as such, are the members of the court personnel that paralegals most often encounter. Deputy clerks process the cases that paralegals bring in to file or explain why a particular document does not meet filing requirements. Well trained, experienced deputy clerks are of inestimable aid to the paralegal. Some deputy clerks are themselves paralegals.

The record keeping required by the clerk of the court under Rule 5003 is performed by the various deputy clerks under the clerk's supervision. Thus, the docket sheets will be more familiar to the particular deputy who maintains them whereas a question regarding claims will probably be answered by the deputy in charge of the claims registers.

There may or may not be a supervisor of deputies who can help with questions beyond the knowledge or authority of the deputies. If there is no supervisor or if the supervisor is unable to assist the paralegal, the clerk will be called.

From the beginning of the paralegal's career, a good working relationship should be established with all members of the clerk's office. A professional manner on the part of the paralegal ensures that he or she will receive all the services that the clerk's staff is trained to provide.

SECTION 7
THE UNITED STATES TRUSTEES, PRIVATE TRUSTEES, AND EXAMINERS

The two basic categories of trustees are United States trustees and private trustees. United States trustees are appointed by the Attorney General of the United States. Private trustees include members of the trustee panel, standing trustees for Chapter 12 and Chapter 13 cases, and other trustees, such as those who serve in Chapter 11 cases. The category of other trustees includes those who have been serving in a case before the order for relief or those who are appointed or elected to serve in a case after the order for relief. The U.S. trustee appoints private trustees. Creditors in Chapter 7 cases may, however, elect a trustee to replace the interim trustee appointed by the U.S. trustee from the trustee panel. (See Exhibit 3–5.)

A. THE UNITED STATES TRUSTEES

Prior to the Bankruptcy Reform Act, some kind of supervision over trustees in the private trustee system was felt to be needed. The lack of such supervision was at the heart of one of the more substantive problems of the old system. The United States Trustee Pilot Program began on October 1, 1979, under former Chapter 15, when the Code went into effect in 18 judicial districts under the supervision of the United States Attorney

EXHIBIT 3–5 United States Trustees and Private Trustees

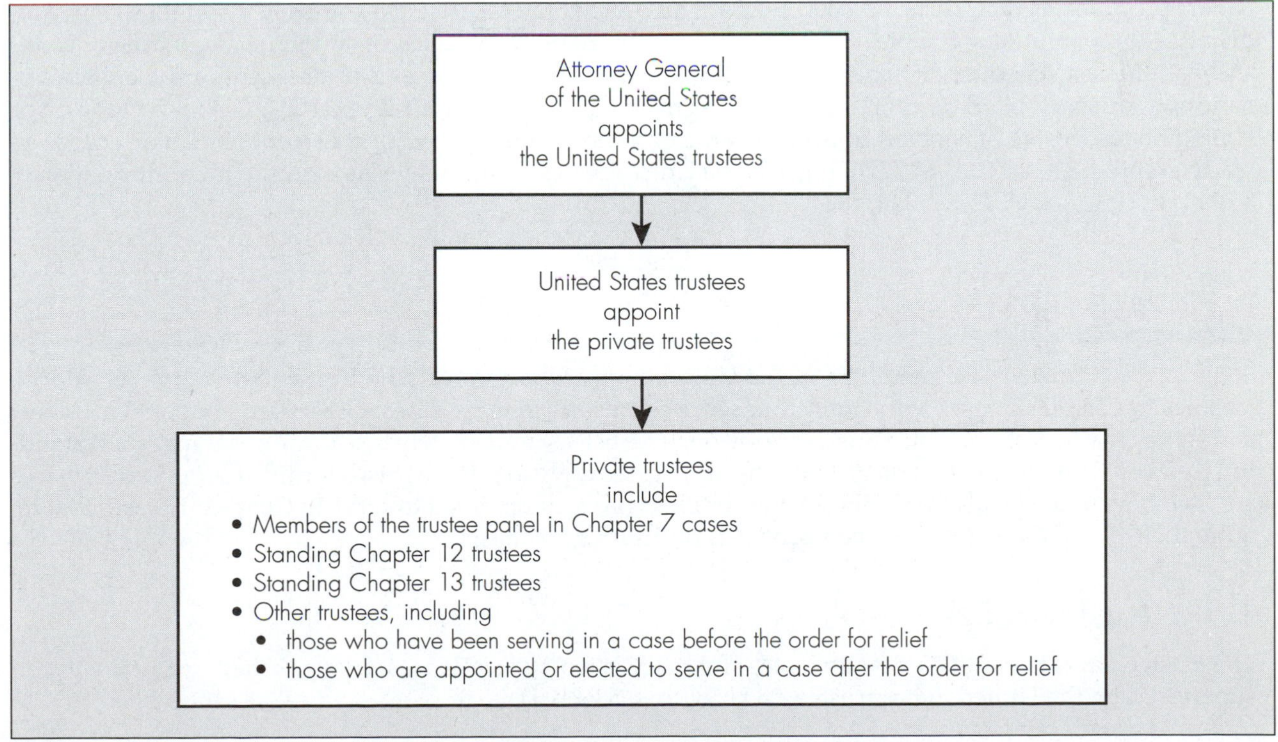

General. The program was structured to follow the United States attorney system, so that **United States trustees** could serve in the same federal judicial districts as United States attorneys. It was contemplated in the Bankruptcy Reform Act that the system would be applied in all judicial districts if it was successful in the original 18 districts. Unless continued by Congress, the system would meet its end on April 1, 1984, according to its own sunset provisions. The Bankruptcy Amendments Act of 1984 extended the pilot program until September 30, 1986. This Act was followed by the Bankruptcy Judges, United States Trustees, and Family Farmer Bankruptcy Act of 1986, which not only expanded the pilot program from the original 18 judicial districts to the entire nation but also made it a permanent part of bankruptcy law. 28 U.S.C.A. §§ 581–589a.

According to 28 U.S.C.A. § 581, the attorney general appoints one United States trustee for each of the 21 regions composed of one or more federal judicial districts.

The United States Code provides that a United States trustee will be appointed for a term of five years and shall continue to serve until a successor is appointed and qualifies. 28 U.S.C.A. § 581(b). The United States trustee serves at the pleasure of the attorney general. The United States Code states that such trustee shall be appointed by the attorney general and provides for removal of trustees by the attorney general. 28 U.S.C.A. §§ 581(a), (c).

The duties of the United States trustee are set forth in the United States Code. 28 U.S.C.A. § 586. These duties include the establishment, maintenance, and supervision of a panel of private trustees to serve in Chapter 7 cases. The United States trustee may also be required to serve as trustee in certain cases. The United States trustee monitors applications for compensation and reimbursement and may file comments with the court regarding such applications. Plans filed in Chapters 11, 12, and 13 are monitored as are disclosure statements in Chapter 11 cases. Creditors' committees in Chapter 11 cases are appointed and supervised by the United States trustee. The United States trustee is to prevent undue delays in bankruptcy cases by monitoring the progress of cases and taking action whenever deemed necessary.

The United States trustee has been made a party in interest under the Code. 11 U.S.C.A. § 307. The Federal Rules of Bankruptcy Procedure require that he or she receive notice of practically all matters in every bankruptcy case. Fed. R. Bank. P. 2000(k), 9034. The United States trustee has the exclusive right to move for dismissal of a voluntary Chapter 7 case when the debtor fails to file a list of creditors, a schedule of assets and liabilities, a schedule of current income and current expenditures, and a statement of the debtor's financial affairs within 15 days or such period as the court has fixed for filing. 11 U.S.C.A. § 707(a)(3). The United States trustee may object to the discharge of a debtor and may request revocation of a discharge already granted. 11 U.S.C.A. §§ 727(c)(1), (d). The United States trustee may also object to the confirmation of a plan. 11 U.S.C.A. §§ 1128, 1224, 1324.

B. PRIVATE TRUSTEES

Some private trustees are members of the trustee panel who receive appointments to serve as **interim trustees** in Chapter 7 cases and continue to serve as trustees in those cases. Others are not panel members and serve only in cases in which they were serving as trustees immediately before the order for relief. **Standing trustees** who serve in Chapter 12 or Chapter 13 cases are also private trustees. Still other private trustees are members of the legal and business communities who are appointed to serve in Chapter 11 cases that require their particular expertise. Their service is on an irregular basis.

1. The Trustee Panel

The trustee panel, a panel of private trustees that serves in Chapter 7 cases, is established, maintained, and supervised by the United States trustee. 28 U.S.C.A. § 586(a)(1).

a. Eligibility to Serve as a Trustee. To be eligible for the trustee panel, a prospective panel member must be eligible to serve as a trustee. The Chapter 7 trustee panel member may be an individual who is competent to perform the duties of a trustee and who resides or has an office either in the judicial district in which the case is pending or in an adjacent district. 11 U.S.C.A. § 321(a)(1). The Chapter 7 trustee panel member may also be a corporation, rather than an individual, if authorized by the corporation charter or bylaws to act as a trustee. The corporation must have an office either in the judicial district in which the case is pending or in an adjacent district. 11 U.S.C.A. § 321(a)(2).

b. Selection and Qualification. It is the duty of the United States trustee to appoint "a disinterested person" that is a panel trustee as interim trustee promptly after the order for relief in all Chapter 7 cases. A "disinterested person" is defined by the Code. 11 U.S.C.A. § 101(14). The interim trustee almost always continues as trustee for a particular case after the meeting of creditors, generally called the 341 meeting, because it is provided for by section 341 of the Code. 11 U.S.C.A. § 341. Election of a trustee by creditors is possible under the Code, but it rarely occurs. 11 U.S.C.A. § 702(b). The interim trustee continues to serve as trustee if no election takes place. 11 U.S.C.A. § 702(d). The elected trustee need not be a member of the trustee panel. If no member of the panel is willing to serve as interim trustee in a case, the U.S. trustee may serve in this capacity.

A panel trustee may also be appointed as interim trustee in a Chapter 7 involuntary case *before* the order for relief has been entered. The court may order the U.S. trustee, on request of a party in interest and after notice to the debtor and a hearing, to appoint an interim trustee to preserve the property of the estate or to prevent loss to the estate. 11 U.S.C.A. § 303(g).

After a person has been selected to serve as trustee in any case, the clerk must immediately notify this person about how to qualify. A person selected to serve in a case as interim trustee or trustee must qualify within five days after selection and before beginning official duties by filing a bond in favor of the United States. The bond is a faithful performance bond, which covers the honesty of the trustee while the duties required in a case are performed. The trustee has no personal liability for forfeiture of the debtor. 11 U.S.C.A. § 322(c).

A trustee serving as a member of the panel may be authorized by the U.S. trustee to file a blanket bond with the court. A blanket bond is a bond that covers the trustee in most cases. In cases in which assets exceed the blanket coverage, it will be necessary for the trustee to increase the bond. A trustee with a blanket bond selected to serve in a Chapter 7 or Chapter 13 case shall be deemed to have accepted appointment in the case unless the court has been notified in writing of rejection within five days after the trustee's receipt of notification of selection. A person without a blanket bond must notify the court in writing of acceptance within five days after receipt of notice of selection. Otherwise, this person shall be deemed to have rejected the office of trustee in this particular case. Fed. R. Bank. P. 2008.

The duties of a Chapter 7 trustee are enumerated in 11 U.S.C.A. § 704.

The trustee shall—

(1) collect and reduce to money the property of the estate for which such trustee serves, and close such estate as expeditiously as is compatible with the best interests of parties in interest;
(2) be accountable for all property received;
(3) ensure that the debtor shall perform his intention as specified in section 521(2)(B) of this title;
(4) investigate the financial affairs of the debtor;
(5) if a purpose would be served, examine proofs of claims and object to the allowance of any claim that is improper;
(6) if advisable, oppose the discharge of the debtor;
(7) unless the court orders otherwise, furnish such information concerning the estate and the estate's administration as is requested by a party in interest;
(8) if the business of the debtor is authorized to be operated, file with the court, with the United States trustee, and with any government unit charged with responsibility for collection or determination of any tax arising out of such operation, periodic reports and summaries of the operation of such business, including a statement of receipts and disbursements, and such other information as the United States trustee or the court requires; and
(9) make a final report and file a final account of the administration of the estate with the court and with the United States trustee.

2. Standing Trustees

A standing trustee is one appointed by the U.S. trustee to serve in any case filed under Chapter 12 or Chapter 13. 11 U.S.C.A. §§ 1202(a), 1302(a).

The duties of a Chapter 12 trustee are enumerated in 11 U.S.C.A. § 1202(b).

> (b) The trustee shall—
> (1) perform the duties specified in sections 704(2), 704(3), 704(5), 704(6), 704(7) and 704(9) of this title;
> (2) perform the duties specified in sections 1106(a)(3) and 1106(a)(4) of this title if the court, for cause and on request of a party in interest, the trustee, or the United States trustee, so orders;
> (3) appear and be heard at any hearing that concerns—
> (A) the value of property subject to a lien;
> (B) confirmation of a plan;
> (C) modification of the plan after confirmation; or
> (D) the sale of property of the estate;
> (4) ensure that the debtor commences making timely payments required by a confirmed plan; and
> (5) if the debtor ceases to be a debtor in possession, perform the duties specified in sections 704(8), 1106(a)(1), 1106(a)(2), 1106(a)(6), 1106(a)(7), and 1203.

The duties of a Chapter 13 trustee are enumerated in 11 U.S.C.A. §§ 1302(b) and (c).

> (b) The trustee shall—
> (1) perform the duties specified in sections 704(2), 704(3), 704(4), 704(5), 704(6), 704(7), and 704(9) of this title;
> (2) appear and be heard at any hearing that concerns—
> (A) the value of property subject to a lien;
> (B) confirmation of a plan; or
> (C) modification of the plan after confirmation;
> (3) dispose of, under regulations issued by the Director of the Administrative Office of the United States Courts, moneys received or to be received in a case under chapter XIII of the Bankruptcy Act; and
> (4) advise, other than on legal matters, and assist the debtor in performance under the plan; and
> (5) ensure that the debtor commences making timely payments under section 1326 of this title.
> (c) If the debtor is engaged in business, then in addition to the duties specified in subsection (b) of this section, the trustee shall perform the duties specified in sections 1106(a)(3) and 1106(a)(4) of this title.

The U.S. trustee is not required to appoint a standing trustee for Chapter 12 and Chapter 13 cases. A disinterested person may be appointed, or the U.S. trustee may serve if necessary. 11 U.S.C.A. §§ 1202(a), 1302(a).

3. Other Trustees

A private trustee, other than a panel trustee, is only called upon to serve as an interim trustee in a Chapter 7 case in which this person has been serving as trustee in the case immediately before the order for relief in Chapter 7. 11 U.S.C.A. § 701(a)(1). This generally occurs when a case is converted from Chapter 11 to Chapter 7.

Private trustees who are not members of the panel are more likely to serve in Chapter 11 cases. Chapter 11 reorganizations sometimes require expertise in a particular area to preserve an ongoing business and successfully reorganize it when the debtor in possession is unable to do so.

4. Paralegals

Paralegals may work for someone on the Chapter 7 trustee panel (usually an attorney or an accountant), for a Standing Chapter 12 or 13 trustee (again, usually an attorney or an accountant), or even for a Chapter 11 trustee (who is probably managing the debtor's business). Because the function of bankruptcy cases differs depending upon the chapter the case is being administered under, the role of the paralegal may vary dramatically from case to case.

Working for a Chapter 7 panel trustee, for instance, a paralegal will review the case files as they are received to identify whether the Schedules and Statement of Financial Affairs have been filled out completely and accurately, determine whether any action needs to be taken in the case before the meeting of creditors, identify issues to be addressed at the meeting of creditors, correspond with the debtor about documentation to be brought by the debtors to the meeting of creditors, correspond with creditors about their claims, prepare pleadings to hire professionals to be employed by the trustee in the case, prepare reports to the court as prescribed by the United States trustee, review proofs of claim and prepare objections as appropriate, assist the trustee and professionals with filing fee applications, and if there are assets in the estate for administration, prepare the final report.

A paralegal who works for a standing Chapter 12 or 13 trustee may initially review the Schedules and Statement of Financial Affairs to determine if they have been filled out completely and accurately and identify issues to be addressed at the meeting of creditors. He or she may then review the plan to determine whether it is feasible and whether there is enough disposable income to be contributed under the plan to pay all priority claims and secured claims and to meet the best interests test. Once the plan is confirmed, the paralegal can monitor the cases to make sure that each debtor performs under the plan.

Since the nature of each Chapter 11 case differs so much from case to case, the role of a paralegal in a Chapter 11 case is less uniform. In many instances, much of the work in a Chapter 11 case that is suitable for a paralegal will likely be performed by a paralegal in the offices of the accountant or attorney hired by the Chapter 11 trustee. Nevertheless, one role a paralegal can perform for a Chapter 11 trustee is to maintain the file (which can be voluminous) and maintain the trustee's calendar in the case for deadlines, meetings, and court hearings.

C. EXAMINERS

After notice and a hearing, an **examiner** may be appointed by the court upon request of a party in interest or the United States trustee. Such an appointment occurs only in a Chapter 11 case in which no trustee has been appointed and in which no plan has been confirmed. An examiner is charged with conducting an investigation of the debtor. This investigation includes allegations of fraud, dishonesty, incompetence, mismanagement, or irregularity in the management of the affairs of the debtor.

An examiner is appointed only if it is in the interests of creditors, equity security holders (if any), and other interests of the estate or if the debtor's fixed, liquidated unsecured debts exceed $5,000,000. Debts owed to an insider and debts for goods, services, or taxes are not included in the $5,000,000. As Chapter 11 cases have increased in number and size, there has been a corresponding increase in the appointment of examiners. 11 U.S.C.A. § 1104(c).

KEY TERMS

administrative expenses
chattel paper
collateral
examiner
fixtures
indenture trustee
interim trustee
parties in interest
priority claim
secured claim
secured party
security interest
standing trustee
United States trustee
unsecured claim
voluntary petition

CHAPTER 4

Information Gathering, Analysis, Counseling, and Drafting

CHAPTER OUTLINE

SECTION 1
THE DEBTOR-CLIENT
A. Information Gathering
B. Analysis: Nonbankruptcy or Bankruptcy?
C. Counseling
D. Drafting of Bankruptcy Forms

SECTION 2
THE CREDITOR-CLIENT
A. The Causes of the Creditor's Distress
B. Information Gathering
C. Analysis: If the Debtor Has Filed Bankruptcy
D. Analysis: Alternatives If the Debtor Has Not Filed Bankruptcy
E. Counseling

SECTION 3
THE DEBTOR-CLIENT IN AN INVOLUNTARY BANKRUPTCY
A. Information Gathering
B. Analysis
C. Counseling

Not all clients are debtors; some may be creditors. This chapter discusses both the debtor-client and the creditor-client. Once it becomes apparent whether the client is a debtor or a creditor, the attorney will evaluate the client's options, advise the client of the options, and draft the necessary documents with the aid of the paralegal.

SECTION 1 THE DEBTOR-CLIENT

The initiation of a bankruptcy case for the debtor involves four steps:

1. information gathering;
2. analysis;

3. counseling; and
4. drafting.

Every attorney has his or her own style when it comes to information gathering, analysis, counseling, and drafting. Some attorneys become involved with the debtor at the earliest stages of information gathering. They conduct the initial interview with the debtor to solicit basic information about the debtor and the debtor's financial problems; they conduct a second meeting to advise the debtor whether to pursue a bankruptcy or nonbankruptcy solution and instruct the debtor in terms of what information should be gathered; they conduct a third meeting to initiate the drafting process; and they conduct additional meetings to complete the drafting in more complicated cases. The paralegal provides a support role for the attorney and has little involvement with the debtor at the various meetings in the initiation of a bankruptcy case.

Other attorneys do not interview the debtor until the debtor has completed a questionnaire and has provided substantial financial information. The paralegal has the initial contact with the debtor and works with the debtor in gathering information through the questionnaire and document gathering step of the process. When the attorney first meets the debtor, it is to advise the debtor whether to pursue a bankruptcy or nonbankruptcy solution. If bankruptcy is recommended, the attorney advises the debtor under which chapter the case should be filed and proceeds to draft the various documents required for filing with the office of the clerk of the bankruptcy court. The paralegal may or may not assist the attorney in drafting these documents.

This text describes a process somewhere between the one in which the attorney takes a very early active role in the information gathering and one in which the attorney takes little or no role in that step but first meets the client to advise the client as to bankruptcy or nonbankruptcy and, if bankruptcy, which chapter. In the process described here, the attorney and paralegal work as a team. For example, an attorney may employ the following procedure:

- After the debtor has initiated contact with the attorney's firm, the paralegal sets up the client file, acquires a list of the debtor's creditors, and initiates a conflict of interest check.
- Once the conflict of interest check has been completed, the paralegal gives the debtor a questionnaire (worksheets) that will help the debtor itemize his or her assets and liabilities, as well as monthly income and monthly expenses.
- The paralegal requires the debtor to provide copies of relevant documents such as real estate deeds and mortgages, loan agreements, security agreements, vehicle titles, and tax returns.
- The debtor completes the questionnaire and returns it to the paralegal along with the documents requested.
- The paralegal meets with the debtor and reviews the questionnaire to insure that it is completed fully and accurately and to identify any emergencies that may require the attorney's immediate attention.
- The attorney and paralegal meet with the debtor, and the attorney discusses the questionnaire adding, deleting, modifying, and verifying the debtor's entries.
- The attorney advises the debtor whether bankruptcy is the appropriate course of action and, if so, whether the case should be filed under Chapter 7, Chapter 11, Chapter 12, or Chapter 13. The attorney will explain the bankruptcy process to the debtor and will discuss attorney fees and other aspects of the attorney/client contract for services.
- The attorney completes the petition, the list of creditors, the disclosure of attorney's compensation statement, the schedules and the statement of financial affairs, or asks the paralegal to complete these documents under supervision. If the relief selected is a Chapter 13 bankruptcy, the attorney or an experienced paralegal, under the attorney's supervision, drafts the Chapter 13 plan.
- The attorney and paralegal meet with the debtor, review the completed documents, receive the debtor's approval and signature, and discuss the next steps in the process.

- The paralegal files the documents to initiate the bankruptcy process with the office of the clerk of the bankruptcy court.

When appropriate, these steps may be telescoped. For example, during the information gathering step with the attorney, it may be obvious to the attorney that the debtor has little choice but to file bankruptcy and the debtor is prepared to proceed immediately. In such cases, the drafting of the documents may begin at this meeting.

Sometimes the filing of the petition in bankruptcy is an emergency because essential property will be lost if the petition is not filed immediately. This type of situation requires that drafting of at least the petition, clerk's notice (in the case of an individual consumer debtor), statement of attorney's compensation, and list of creditors be done at the first meeting. The schedules and statement of financial affairs are then filed within 15 days of the petition.

EXAMPLE

The day before a foreclosure sale, Andrew Augustine visited an attorney for the first time to discuss bankruptcy. Shortly into the interview, it became clear to the attorney that Augustine's only option was to file a Chapter 11 or Chapter 13 petition to invoke the automatic stay and forestall a foreclosure sale. The attorney filed the petition prior to the foreclosure sale to avoid having to revoke the sale.

Although one debtor, such as Mr. Augustine, will see an attorney for the first time just prior to foreclosure, another may have made long-term advance plans to file bankruptcy in the event that all other efforts failed to prevent foreclosure.

EXAMPLE

PRINCE ALBERT POLO CLUB FILES BANKRUPTCY
FORECLOSURE SALE AVOIDED

The Prince Albert Polo Club, Inc., paid $9 million to build the Prince Albert Race Track. The track operated for one racing season and then was idled due to financial and regulatory problems.

The Club negotiated with Friendly Bank, the Club's largest creditor, to forestall a foreclosure sale. After negotiations failed and only one hour before Friendly Bank's foreclosure sale, the Club filed a Chapter 11 bankruptcy petition, thus protecting the track from the foreclosure sale. At the time of the filing, the Club listed $8.5 million in assets and $7.1 million in liabilities. Had the Club not filed for the bankruptcy court's protection, it would have lost the opportunity to operate the track.

Timing for filing the bankruptcy petition and schedules can be critical to preserve the assets of the case. Therefore, in an emergency situation, the law provides for the filing of a "barebones" case. For a Chapter 7, this consists of the petition, clerk's notice (in the case of an individual consumer debtor), statement of attorney's compensation, and list of creditors. The schedules and statements of financial affairs are due within 15 days of the filing of the petition unless the court grants an extension for cause. Although granting an extension for cause is fairly routine in larger cases, it is preferable to file all the documents of the case at the same time. It is particularly good practice to file all documents together in a Chapter 7 case as there may be assets in the estate that need the trustee's immediate attention. Lack of attention could cause a problem, for example, with perishable goods in a grocery store that files a Chapter 7. If the schedules have not been filed with the petition, the trustee has no information to prevent loss.

A. INFORMATION GATHERING

During the information gathering stage of the process the attorney or paralegal elicits information from the debtor and gives the debtor basic information. The attorney is seeking information to determine whether to recommend a nonbankruptcy or bankruptcy solution and if bankruptcy is the solution, under which chapter of the Bankruptcy Code the case should be filed. The debtor, of course, is seeking a viable solution to his or her financial difficulties.

One of the most important things the attorney or paralegal does at the first meeting is to put the debtor at ease. This will be the first contact with the legal world for many debtors. Many are apprehensive not only about their financial situation but may be even more apprehensive about being in an attorney's office. Some will be embarrassed about discussing their finances and the causes of their financial dilemma. The attorney or paralegal who is sensitive to these matters will be able to allay the debtor's fears and get the necessary information in a more timely manner. The attorney or paralegal should always explain to the debtor what is needed and why it is needed in terms the debtor can understand. Although many debtors intentionally withhold vital information, others do so because they fail to understand what is required. The success of the recommended solution for a particular debtor's problems will hinge upon full knowledge of the debtor's situation. The groundwork for this success is laid at the initial interview.

The attorney and paralegal should formulate their own information gathering materials. The questionnaire can be maintained in a computer database, ready to print when the need arises. Experience will suggest additions and modifications in the format.

When assembling information for the questionnaire the official bankruptcy forms, which are a part of the Federal Rules of Bankruptcy Procedure, are helpful because they suggest much of the needed information. At almost every point in the information gathering process, the placing of one item of information on the questionnaire will suggest the need for other information. The following information discusses some main points for a questionnaire.

Identity of the Debtor

Who is the debtor? Complete information is necessary regarding the identity of the debtor and related entities. A debtor may be an individual, a partnership, or a corporation.

If an individual debtor is married, the name of the debtor's spouse and information about him or her similar to that gathered about the debtor will be important. A married debtor immediately raises the question of the necessity or the desirability of filing on behalf of both the debtor and the debtor's spouse. If the filing is for an individual and his or her spouse, the case is filed as a joint case. 11 U.S.C.A. § 302. No other combination of entities may file a joint case.

The name of an individual is incomplete for bankruptcy purposes unless the full first, middle, and last names are given. "Jr." and "III" must be included when applicable. Also, all other names used by the debtor or his or her spouse during the previous six years are essential. This enables creditors who receive notice of the bankruptcy and a copy of the petition to compare the names on its accounts with all the names of the debtor and his or her spouse since the last time the debtor could have received a Chapter 7 discharge.

With regard to the precise and exact identification of the entity to be involved in the bankruptcy case, the debtor must be apprised that if an individual case is filed, all of that debtor's individually owned enterprises will be affected and cannot be divided so that only the personal debts or only the debts of one particular business enterprise are included in the bankruptcy case. The person who owns more than one individual proprietorship business will find that all of his or her debts (both business and personal) and all of his or her assets (both business and personal) will be affected by an individual bankruptcy filing.

EXAMPLE

A debtor, Joe Smith, may say something like "Joe's Grocery & Market is doing just fine and I don't want to put that business in bankruptcy. It is Joe's Service Station that has caused me all this trouble and I want to file for that business only." The debtor will discover, however, that the grocery store must be included in the bankruptcy filing.

If a filing is contemplated on behalf of either a partnership or a corporation, the attorney's and paralegal's job becomes more complex and further information concerning the identity of such an entity will be required. A *partnership* is a business organization involving two or more persons. Although originally a common law form of business entity, the partnership concept was codified by the Uniform Partnership Act and enacted in virtually all states. A general partnership may be formed orally or by written agreement. In a general partnership, the partners share the right to manage and share equally in the right to participate in the partnership's profits and losses, unless their partnership agreement provides otherwise. Each partner is personally liable, jointly and severally, for partnership debts. If a partner is compelled to satisfy a partnership debt, the partner is entitled to indemnification from the partnership, if the partnership has assets from which to indemnify.

A variation of partnership is the **limited partnership.** Unlike the general partnership where all partners are general partners and share the right to manage, in a limited partnership two classes of partners exist: general partner(s) and limited partner(s). The limited partners do not have the general right to manage the partnership or provide services—only very limited rights to participate in management decisions. Limited partners generally contribute money or other property to the partnership. General partners are personally liable for the debts of the partnership; limited partners are not. The limited partnership was created by the Uniform Limited Partnership Act and is enacted in various forms in all jurisdictions. A limited partnership is created by filing a document or certification with the office designated by the statute.

A variation of the limited partnership is the limited liability partnership (LLP), an entity created for "professionals," such as attorneys, accountants, and doctors. In this relatively new form of entity, partners can render services (and thus participate in management decisions) but limit their personal liability. Depending on the state, a limited liability partner may not limit personal liability when they themselves have committed malpractice or negligence or oversee partners who have committed malpractice or negligence. A general partnership may become a limited liability partnership by filing an appropriate statement with the office designated by the statute.

What are the bankruptcy ramifications of filing as a partnership versus filing as an individual? If the case is filed as a partnership, the partnership entity is the debtor and not the individuals who make up the partnership. Therefore, the case is filed in the name of the partnership rather than in the names of the partners. The debts are the partnership debts, not individual debts.

Sometimes it is necessary to file for individuals along with the bankruptcy filing of a partnership owned by them. In the case of the filing of a partnership bankruptcy, it is necessary to establish the precise identity of the partnership and to refer carefully to the documents under which the partnership was created. The names of each of the general and limited partners and the respective interest of each in the partnership are required information. The attorney and paralegal must, of course, be dealing with either the controlling parties or parties who have the right, under the bankruptcy law, to file the bankruptcy case on behalf of the partnership.

A corporation is an "artificial entity" created when one or more persons file articles of incorporation with the appropriate state official. A corporation is independent of who the current owners or investors are, can exist in perpetuity, and is managed by a board of directors elected by the shareholders. The shareholders may sell or transfer their ownership interests without approval or consent of the corporation or the other shareholders. Corporations may be large, publicly held corporations or small, privately held corporations. Corporations may be Chapter C or Chapter S corporations for tax purposes. Corporate stockholders have no personal liability in the debts of the corporation.

A variation of the corporation is the limited liability company (LLC). An LLC is created by filing articles of incorporation with the appropriate state official. In an LLC, the stockholders participate in the management of the corporation without being personally liable for the corporation's debts.

In many cases, it is necessary to file either an individual or a joint case and then to simultaneously file the case of a corporation owned by such individual or individual and spouse, because both will have financial problems. Such persons may have guaranteed corporate debts and would not be protected from creditors under the automatic stay that applies only to the debts of the corporation. The same careful analysis required for the individuals constituting a partnership must be done for individuals operating a corporation. An attorney must exercise care in conferring with and representing both the owners of a corporation and the corporation itself in a Chapter 11 case. The attorney for the debtor in possession must be approved by the court in a Chapter 11 case, and it is required that an attorney not represent conflicting interests. The dual representation of a Chapter 11 debtor-corporation and its stockholders in a Chapter 11 case raises serious conflict of interest issues.

Debtor's Address

Where is the debtor currently living? A permanent mailing address, if the debtor has one, that will be good for some time into the future is required. Does the debtor plan to move in the near future? Some debtors will be in the process of moving out of a foreclosed house or mobile home. It is important to know how long the debtor has lived at that address to determine venue.

Where is the debtor's place of business? The location of the debtor is more than just an address. It is impossible to even determine the venue of a case without information about the legal residence and place of business of a debtor. Once venue has been determined, it may be desirable or even necessary to refer the case to counsel in another district. Perhaps the case will be filed in a district other than the one in which the debtor contemplates the case will be filed. All of this must be explained to the debtor after a thorough analysis has taken place and a decision has been made concerning where to file the case based upon the location, or situs information. If a debtor is a wage earner and has a fixed residence address, it is a simple matter to note the address of the debtor for bankruptcy filing information. In some instances, however, a partnership or a corporation will have several places of business, or its primary property will be in a district other than the place where its main office is located. There will be instances where more than one place is "a proper venue," and the court of the district in which the case is filed may transfer the case to another district for the convenience of the parties. On occasion, this will allow a debtor to do some degree of "forum shopping."

PROBLEM 4.1 Several months ago, AmTex, Inc., a Delaware corporation with its principal place of business and principal corporate offices in Denver, Colorado, filed a Chapter 7 bankruptcy petition in the United States Bankruptcy Court for the District of New Mexico.

AmTex has ten secured creditors, seven in Colorado and three in New Mexico. The seven in Colorado hold more than 50 percent of AmTex's debt. The largest secured creditor, Denver National Bank, holds 20 percent of AmTex's debt and is located in Denver. The second largest secured creditor, Albuquerque National Bank, is located in Albuquerque and holds 15 percent of AmTex's debt. AmTex has 400 unsecured creditors, 40 percent are in Colorado, 30 percent are in New Mexico, and 30 percent are in Texas.

AmTex's major stockholders live in Denver, Albuquerque, and Dallas. The corporate officers lived in Denver before the company filed for Chapter 7 protection and have now begun moving to other employment out of state.

Most of AmTex's inventory and equipment are in Denver, although it holds accounts receivable from buyers across the nation and has bank deposits in Albuquerque, Dallas, and Denver.

Over the years, AmTex has paid 85 percent of its taxes to Colorado and 15 percent to New Mexico.

Denver National Bank has moved for a change of venue to Colorado. Albuquerque National Bank has objected.

A change of venue is authorized in 28 U.S.C.A. § 1475 "in the interest of justice and for the convenience of the parties." Federal Rules of Bankruptcy Procedure 1014(a)(1) provides:

> If a petition is filed in a proper district, on timely motion of a party in interest, and after hearing on notice to the petitioners and to other persons as directed by the court, the case may be transferred to any other district if the Court determines that the transfer is for the convenience of the parties and witnesses in the interest of justice.

The terms "in the interest of justice" and "for the convenience of the parties" has been interpreted to include five factors:

1. proximity of creditors of every kind to the court;
2. proximity of the debtor to the court;
3. proximity of witnesses necessary to the administration of the estate;
4. location of assets; and
5. economic administration of the estate.

Denver National Bank has the burden of overcoming the presumption that AmTex is entitled to file and maintain its case in the venue in which it is filed.

Should the court grant the Denver National Bank's motion?

Debtor's Employment Situation

What is the debtor's situation? How long has the debtor been employed on his or her present job, and how stable does the job situation look? If the debtor is unemployed, a petition in bankruptcy may not be appropriate, no matter what the debt is. The unemployed individual is not eligible to file a Chapter 13 case which requires regular income. Even if the debts currently owed were to be discharged under a Chapter 7 case, more debts would be swiftly amassed that the debtor would not be able to pay. If the debtor is a wage earner, the attorney needs to obtain information to evaluate whether the debtor is a candidate for a Chapter 13.

An individual who is self-employed or who is a commissioned salesperson may not have regular stable income to support a Chapter 13 plan. More often than not the individual who files under Chapter 13 is employed by someone else because the amount of the monthly check is stable and known.

What are the debtor's attitudes about Chapter 7 and Chapter 13, if he or she is an individual wage earner? Sometimes the debtor has a choice. Sometimes, the debtor's attitude determines which chapter will be selected. Would the debtor rather dump the whole mess or fight with it for three years? The attorney may conclude that the debtor is just not able to make a Chapter 13, because he or she does not have the staying power to carry through with the plan, or that the debt structure would be too much to meet under a Chapter 13 plan. The debt structure might be such that the debtor would have to struggle to pay off a minimal amount of the debt.

Causes for the Debtor's Financial Difficulties

What caused the debtor to be in this financial condition? Although debtors very often cite an inappropriate reason for their bankruptcy, it is still necessary to have the debtor discuss the cause of his or her financial problems. Many debtors will be very anxious to reveal these matters at the earliest possible opportunity. Of course, a single triggering catastrophe, such as a long continuing illness or a lengthy period of unemployment, may reveal the fundamental cause of the financial problem. Many debtors, especially in small businesses, may be unaware of or may not want to admit the real cause of the financial problems and will simply say that they had a "cash flow" problem. The hallmark of consumer debtor and small business bankruptcies is the lack of money, but this may not be the fundamental cause. The real cause will be discovered as the debtor's case proceeds.

What are the stated causes for the debtor's financial predicament? It has been customary to attribute the causes of bankruptcy to various factors, such as economic conditions, the inability to manage financial affairs, or some catastrophe beyond the control of the future debtor in bankruptcy.

What are the real causes of the debtor's financial predicament? The answers to this question will have some bearing on the selection of a nonbankruptcy or bankruptcy solution.

A major difficulty in dealing with the causes of bankruptcy is that the party most immediately involved, the debtor in bankruptcy, very often does not state the ultimate cause of bankruptcy filing and may cite some more immediate situation. A consumer debtor may very well believe that the cause of the bankruptcy filing is a garnishment against his or her paycheck, but the objective observer sees that the actual cause behind the bankruptcy filing and the garnishment itself was the unwise use of credit. The debtor might have gone along indefinitely juggling his or her debts on a salary inadequate to cover living expenses and pay all debts, but the garnishment forced a different solution to the problem.

PROBLEM 4.2 Judy Rogers earns $400 a week as a secretary. After taxes, social security withholding, and insurance, Judy takes home $1,000 a month. Each month she pays $400 for rent, $200 for car payments, and $350 for living expenses.

Last year Judy was involved in an automobile accident (which was her fault) and spent several weeks in the hospital. Although her medical insurance covered most of her hospital and medical bills, she still owed the hospital $1,000 and the doctor $1,500. For the past year, Judy has been sending $25 a month to the hospital and $25 to the doctor.

The hospital became dissatisfied with Judy's low payments and obtained a judgment against her. The hospital then had the court enter a garnishment decree for $200 a month from Judy's wages. Because of the garnishment, Judy now has only $800 a month in take-home pay and no longer has enough money to pay $400 for rent, $200 for car payments, $350 for living expenses, and $25 toward her doctor's bill.

What caused Judy's current problem, and what are Judy's options?

Evaluate each option.

A small business owner is very often apt to describe the cause of bankruptcy as a "cash flow" problem when the real cause of the bankruptcy filing may very well be lack of sufficient business because of poor management or improper selection of a business site.

PROBLEM 4.3 Tom's Hamburger Stand has been in business for 15 years. A year ago, a national fast-food chain opened a restaurant within a block of Tom's. Naturally, the fast-food restaurant diverted customers from the hamburger stand. During the past six months, Tom's has been unable to generate enough money to pay all of its bills.

What caused Tom's current problem, and what are the options?

Evaluate each option.

When dealing with the intake of a bankruptcy case, the attorney and the paralegal must ferret out both the immediate and ultimate causes of the bankruptcy. The results of this investigation will enhance the possibility of selecting the proper alternative to follow either in taking some nonbankruptcy course of action or, if filing a bankruptcy case, in selecting the chapter of the Bankruptcy Code under which the case should be filed. Determining the causes of bankruptcy is also important in that if the proper cause is ascertained, investigation of the actual facts of the case will be facilitated. The attorney and the paralegal will know precisely what to look for to avoid any surprises and to prepare thoroughly before the case is filed in bankruptcy court.

In dealing with consumer bankruptcies, the bankruptcy population must be compared with the nonbankruptcy population. This could very well lead to the conclusion that one theory is simply, "some do, some don't." An examination of indebtedness and other factors might reveal that many indebted persons do not file bankruptcy. Their economic conditions may actually be much worse than many of those who do file bankruptcy. Many people who do file bankruptcy might have found an acceptable alternative but have, in fact, taken what they regard to be the easy way out. Although recent amendments have attempted to deal with the "easy way out" filing, this problem still does exist.

There are a number of generally accepted reasons for bankruptcy filings. One of the basic causes, especially of business bankruptcies, is economic conditions on a national or a regional level. A general recession on a national level can be an ultimate cause of bankruptcy filings, and an increase in the number of bankruptcy filings can be expected in such times. On a regional level, a particular area of the country that is especially impacted by a recession or that is in a regional recession (for example, states with economies that depend heavily on the oil industry) can expect an increase in bankruptcy filings. Such economic conditions can be given as causes of bankruptcy filings because they do, of course, lead to higher unemployment and business failures.

A reason often cited for bankruptcy filings, particularly by persons other than the debtor in the case, is the lack of ability to manage either personal or business finances. In dealing with this cause, the attorney or the paralegal must be particularly careful to note which party is giving information. A creditor often cites lack of management ability as a reason or cause of bankruptcy, but the debtor who goes into bankruptcy seldom mentions this as a factor.

Illnesses of debtors and catastrophic losses are related because either will deplete the debtors' assets. Prolonged illness, especially involving persons without health insurance, is a common cause of bankruptcy filing, as is the occurrence of some catastrophic casualty for which the debtor has no insurance protection.

Sustained periods of unemployment by the debtor often result in a bankruptcy filing. Few people have the necessary financial cushion to meet even ordinary living expenses while unemployed, particularly if they have no source of regular income such as unemployment insurance.

Some comments should be made about the question of whether or not the enactment of the Bankruptcy Reform Act of 1978 caused an increase in the number of bankruptcy filings. There is a difference of opinion on this subject, and a person's outlook is probably influenced by his or her position as a creditor or a debtor in the bankruptcy process.

The Bankruptcy Reform Act of 1978 received substantial publicity directed both to the public and to attorneys. This information may have generated more awareness of bankruptcy as an option in the would-be debtor and in the attorney counseling a client having financial difficulties. Economic conditions since the effective date of the new law have probably had as important an impact as the law itself although, admittedly, it would be difficult to separate out these factors. Consumer debt has risen to an unprecedented level in the last several years. As it continues to rise, neither debtors nor creditors seem able to say no to further indebtedness.

Another factor that has made an answer to the question of the cause of the increase in bankruptcies more difficult is that the effective date of the new law coincided with the beginning of heavy advertising by attorneys. This increased advertising in the bankruptcy area by attorneys may have actually created additional demand for legal services in debt situations. Advertising appears to be especially effective in the bankruptcy area of the law. Many debtors have never used the services of an attorney. Their creditors may be pressing them for payment when they notice an advertisement for bankruptcy services on television or in the TV section of their local newspaper. The debtor who is accustomed to using the yellow pages of the telephone directory for various types of services may seek legal help there when faced with garnishment or foreclosure.

PROBLEM 4.4 Check the yellow pages of your local telephone directory and the TV section of your local newspaper. Find several advertisements concerning bankruptcy services and other services offered by attorneys. Compare attorney advertising in the area of bankruptcy with attorney advertising in other areas.

General Nature of the Debtor's Financial Condition

What is the debtor's financial condition? The general nature of the debtor's financial situation should be ascertained at the first opportunity. An outline of the debtor's primary assets, together with their collective value, and a rather close estimate of the debtor's total debts should be made.

If the debtor is an individual, then in addition to assets and liabilities, a complete overview of the debtor's current income and expenses is necessary. This overview should include the estimated average monthly income of the debtor and his or her spouse, if married, and the estimated average current monthly expenses of the debtor and his or her family.

The debts should be categorized as secured (noting the property by which they are secured) and as unsecured. Eventually, it will be necessary to make a precise check of assets against liabilities for liens and encumbrances, but it will be satisfactory initially to get the overall picture. The general trend of the debtor's financial situation over the past several years should be examined. This investigation may be hampered by the fact that the debtor has not kept accurate financial records, particularly if the debtor is not engaged in business. Even the debtor engaged in a small business often has inadequate records.

At this point it is not necessary to look for insolvency. In a voluntary bankruptcy situation under any chapter under the present law, insolvency is not a prerequisite to the filing of a bankruptcy petition. In fact, in many cases, the debtor's estimation of the value of assets will far exceed the amount of liabilities.

The attorney must know (the debtor should always inform the attorney immediately) of any impending threat to the debtor's assets or financial situation. It is not unusual for an attorney to receive a panicky telephone call from a debtor just before noon on Thursday advising that help is needed because a foreclosure is to take place on the debtor's principal residence or on his or her business assets on Friday morning (the next day) at 10:00 A.M.

Identification and Location of the Debtor's Assets

What are the debtor's assets, and where are they located? The identification of the debtor's assets affects whether an individual debtor files for bankruptcy relief under Chapter 7 or Chapter 13.

EXAMPLE

Sharon Williams has been collecting antique glass bottles since she was twelve. Naturally she would like to avoid giving up her collection when she files for bankruptcy, if at all possible. As a nonexempt asset, the bottle collection would be sold by the trustee if Sharon were to file under Chapter 7 and the proceeds would be distributed to her creditors. Although the bottle collection would still be a nonexempt asset if she were to file under Chapter 13, she would be able to retain her collection and pay her creditors with her future earnings.

It is important that the attorney and the paralegal for the debtor obtain the best information available concerning the identification and location of the collateral. Information on the status of that collateral—whether it is still owned by the debtor or it has been totally expended or utilized—should be obtained.

The location of the debtor's assets not only affects venue but also is of vital concern for administration of the estate.

Identification and Location of the Creditors

The attorney or the paralegal should carefully review the creditor lists for proper and complete addresses (including zip codes) and question the debtor about any address that does not appear to be valid. The debtor should provide account numbers for all creditors who use them. Each creditor must be properly identified by the correct name of the entity involved, and the debtor should give information about the debt.

One point of critical importance is that the client should be responsible for listing all debts and assets in his or her own handwriting. An attorney or a paralegal who takes such information orally is running an unnecessary risk.

Failing to schedule a creditor may have postbankruptcy ramifications for an individual debtor. If the debtor files for bankruptcy under Chapter 7 and has no assets, the unscheduled debt is discharged because with a no-asset case, no deadline has been established for filing proofs of claim. See 11 U.S.C.A. § 523(a)(3). Not listing a creditor, however, creates a problem for the debtor because the creditor may sue the debtor on the debt and the debtor will be required to defend. Therefore, it is essential that the schedules be complete.

All creditors must be listed regardless of whether the *debtor believes that the debt will be satisfied by other means.* If the debt ultimately is not satisfied by other means and the creditor has not received notice of the bankruptcy, the debt will not be discharged.

EXAMPLE

Jim Olson, a building contractor, entered into a contract to build an office building for the Utopia Fitness Center. Olson contracted with a number of suppliers. After the building was completed, Olson was not paid by the fitness center. Olson, in turn, did not pay his suppliers. This compounded Olson's financial problems, which were already numerous. Olson sought legal assistance.

When Olson was completing his questionnaire for the initial interview, he left out a number of debts that he had incurred with various suppliers. He rationalized that these debts would be taken care of by the court because the suppliers had filed liens against the real estate.

When the real estate was liquidated, the proceeds were inadequate to satisfy the debts of all of the suppliers. Those debts not satisfied were not discharged by the bankruptcy proceeding.

All creditors must be listed, regardless of what the *debtor plans to do about a particular debt.*

The debtor cannot have bankruptcy *a la carte.* The debtor must schedule every creditor. If the debtor wants to pay the debt, the debtor could reaffirm the debt. If the debt is discharged in bankruptcy, the debtor could pay the debt postbankruptcy. Debtors need to understand that when they sign their bankruptcy schedules, they sign under penalty of perjury (the unsworn declaration that is a part of the bankruptcy filing). In addition to committing a crime, they also assume the risk of not receiving a discharge. A discharge may be denied if the bankruptcy schedules are not inclusive. While there is a distinction between an honest mistake and fraud, the more incomplete the schedules, the more the debtor places himself or herself in jeopardy for not receiving a discharge.

EXAMPLE

Agnes Milbrook borrowed $500 from her sister Flo. When Agnes completed her questionnaire, she left out her debt to Flo on the ground that she intended to pay Flo after she received her discharge in bankruptcy. Regardless of Agnes's intentions, her debt to Flo should have been listed on the questionnaire.

All creditors must be listed, regardless of what the *creditor plans to do about a particular debt.* If a creditor has not received notice of the bankruptcy, the debt will not be discharged.

EXAMPLE

Simon Smith borrowed $2,000 from his mother. When Smith developed financial problems, his mother told him to forget the debt. Unknown to Smith's mother, Smith filed for bankruptcy. Believing that his mother had forgiven the debt, he did not list this debt on his schedules. Shortly after the bankruptcy, his mother died and her executor attempted to collect the debt. Regardless of whether Smith's mother told him to forget the debt, the debt should have been listed on the questionnaire.

Status of the Creditors as to Collateral and Relative Priorities

Who are the creditors, and how much is each creditor owed? Does the creditor hold an unsecured priority claim; a secured claim; or an unsecured nonpriority claim? The status of the creditor's claim as to collateral must be viewed from the debtor's perspective.

EXAMPLE

Juan Gomez borrowed $10,000 from First Bank. Before First Bank would make the loan, the bank required Juan to have a guarantor and for the guarantor to give the bank a security interest in some of the guarantor's property. Juan asked his girlfriend, Carlotta Montoya, to act as his guarantor. Carlotta signed Juan's note and gave the bank a security interest in her automobile.

If Juan were to file for bankruptcy under Chapter 7, the bank would hold an unsecured claim because the collateral, the automobile, belongs to Carlotta, a nondebtor. If Carlotta were to file for bankruptcy under Chapter 7, the bank would hold a secured claim in the automobile.

The unsecured priority claimants must be identified. These include employees with wage claims or unpaid benefit plans and government taxing authorities owed taxes.

Secured or unsecured creditors must also be distinguished. A major concern is whether the creditor holding a secured claim has properly perfected a security interest. This will have a great effect on the ability of the debtor to reaffirm a debt in many cases and of course will affect the debtor's right to effectively claim and fully utilize an exemption.

The amount of each debt must be determined. Some debtors can give the attorney or the paralegal accurate and up-to-date information on their creditors and loans; others have little or no information to provide.

Debtor's Attempts to Effect a Nonbankruptcy Solution

What has the debtor done to attempt to effect a workout? Has the debtor talked to his or her creditors? If so, what is the status of these discussions or what resulted from them? What is the name of the creditor or the creditor's representative with whom the debtor has been dealing, and what is his or her telephone number and address? Some debtors never try to deal with any creditors at all. Some are trying to deal with every

creditor. Some are dealing successfully with some of their creditors and unsuccessfully with the others. Some debtors are dealing with their secured creditors and ignoring their unsecured creditors; others are dealing with their unsecured creditors and ignoring their secured creditors.

Identification of Pending Lawsuits

Is the debtor the subject of a pending lawsuit or lawsuits? What is the status of this suit or suits? Some lawsuits may be on the verge of a judgment. Upon judgment, the prevailing party may seek garnishment, which should be avoided if possible. A number of debtors do not recognize a lawsuit when they see it. A debtor may mistake a summons for a letter or a collection letter for a summons or complaint. The attorney must see all letters and documents regarding financial matters pertaining to the debtor.

If the bankruptcy is complex at all or the attorney or paralegal has reason to doubt the debtor's memory, the courthouse records should be checked to determine whether any lawsuits are pending against the debtor. With the computerization of courthouse records, whether the debtor is a defendant in a lawsuit might be checked online.

EXAMPLE

The DeMarcos have filed for bankruptcy under Chapter 7. They own a home with Sunbelt Bank being the mortgagee. They want to keep their home and reaffirm their debt with the bank.

In the state in which the DeMarcos live, a judgment lien can attach to a homestead, although the creditor cannot foreclose on the lien. The creditor must wait until the debtor either sells the homestead or refinances the mortgage on the homestead. Bankruptcy is the only way the debtor has to avoid that lien. A check of the courthouse records reveals that Quality Roofing Company has placed a lien on the DeMarco home. Having this information, the attorney could help the DeMarcos avoid the lien using 11 U.S.C.A. § 522(f).

Determination of Whether the Debts are the Debtor's Debts

Whose debts are they? Are the debts the debtor's or those of another party? If the debtors are husband and wife, the debts may be only the husband's or only the wife's. If the debtor is a partner in a partnership, the debts may be partnership debts and not personal debts. If the debtor is the president of a closely held corporation, the debts may be corporate debts and not individual debts, or individual debts and not corporate debts.

Debtor's Expectations

What are the debtor's expectations and goals? What does the debtor expect to get out of his or her meeting with an attorney or a paralegal, and where is the debtor ultimately going financially?

The debtor will need to know which debts are dischargeable through the bankruptcy process and which are not. If a significant amount of debt is nondischargeable, then bankruptcy may not meet the debtor's expectations.

The debtor will need to know which debts can be reaffirmed and which cannot be reaffirmed because even if the debtor wishes to reaffirm a debt that is in default, the creditor may not be inclined to reaffirm the debt. Also, the debtor will need to know whether a secured debt is perfected because if the security interest has not been perfected, the Chapter 7 trustee will avoid the security interest and the collateral will be sold and the proceeds distributed to the debtor's creditors. Therefore, the debtor will lose the collateral that he or she is seeking to retain even if the debt is reaffirmed.

What are the debtor's attitudes about nonbankruptcy and bankruptcy, and what would need to be done to effect a successful nonbankruptcy solution? Some debtors will not do what is necessary to achieve a successful nonbankruptcy solution. For example, some debtors who could avoid bankruptcy by executing a deed in lieu of foreclosure to the holder of the mortgage on their house, will refuse to use this procedure.

Fees

A full discussion of fees and how they will be paid should take place at the initial interview. Many attorneys do not charge the debtor for the first interview. This gives the attorney flexibility in his or her decision to take or not take the case. It also gives the debtor the opportunity to go elsewhere. The attorney will discuss what fees would be if the case is not to be taken through bankruptcy or if the case is to be taken through bankruptcy. If the case is not to be taken through bankruptcy, the attorney may charge an hourly fee. If the case is to be taken through bankruptcy, the attorney may charge a minimum fee for the routine filing, the lien avoidances, reaffirmations, and the basic walk through. Services beyond these basics may be billed at an hourly rate. Such services would include the defense of an adversary proceeding to deny a discharge or to determine the dischargeability of a debt or litigation concerning exemptions. The discussion of fees should be followed by a written contract for services, which would be a part of the next interview when the decision on how to proceed is recommended.

Although the statement of attorney's compensation, which is filed with the petition, could serve as the contract for services, better practice mandates a written contract devoted to services and fees. In a written contract, the debtor's attorney can specifically exclude certain services. Thus, if specified in the written contract, the attorney could charge separately for adversaries as to dischargeability, reaffirmation agreements, and motions to avoid liens.

EXAMPLE

At the time of entering into the attorney/client relationship, the attorney discussed with the client that her flat fee for filing a Chapter 7 bankruptcy petition was $800 and that this fee did not include defending the debtor if a creditor objected to the dischargeability of a debt. This agreement was reduced to writing and both the debtor and the attorney signed.

Subsequently a creditor objected to the dischargeability of its debt. The attorney defended the debtor and sought additional compensation from the debtor. The debtor asserts that the attorney's services were covered by the $800 fee, but the attorney can point to the written contract and say—no, the $800 did not cover creditors' objections.

Although it is not possible to make a hard and fast rule about whether the debtor should pay the fees in advance, the attorney may try to get everything paid up front. Some attorneys are not willing to take a bankruptcy case without full payment in advance. Others may be willing to permit the debtor to pay as the case progresses. Most attorneys understand that many debtors will not pay the attorney's fees after the case is finished. Fees under this arrangement are hard to collect. The biggest problem is that many debtors are very optimistic about what this bankruptcy will do for them. They very quickly find out that just making bare living expenses from a paycheck is difficult and that little will be left over to pay an attorney. For this reason, it is best to get the fees in advance. (All of the fees for Chapter 13 cases may not be paid in advance. Some could be taken out of the retainer paid by the client up front and the balance paid out under the plan.) Most debtors will somehow come up with the money for fees. If they do not have it, they will find it. If fees are on credit, many debtors will never find the money to pay the fees for services rendered.

The attorney should remember to

1. discuss the amount of fees at the first interview;
2. set out the fee arrangement in writing;
3. know where the money for fees is coming from; and
4. get paid before the case is filed, if at all possible and if permitted by the Code.

The questionnaire in Appendix A organizes these general themes into a concrete list. The questionnaire is designed for both the debtor engaged in business and the debtor not engaged in business.

PROBLEM 4.5 For the purpose of illustrating Chapter 7 and Chapter 13 bankruptcy, the text will follow Jennifer E. and Eric R. McPherson, husband and wife, as they try to untangle their financial dilemma. The McPhersons have contacted a law office and have spoken with the paralegal who works under the supervision of the bankruptcy attorney. After obtaining general information about the McPhersons, the paralegal asks the McPhersons to submit a list of their creditors so the firm can initiate a conflict of interest check and decide whether it can take the case. The paralegal informs the McPhersons that once the conflicts check has been completed, and if the firm has no conflict, the McPhersons will be required to complete a questionnaire concerning their assets and liabilities. The paralegal describes the procedure that the office will follow in preparing for their bankruptcy filing.

The McPhersons deliver the list of their creditors to the firm, and the paralegal conducts a conflict of interest check. Finding no conflict, the paralegal sends the McPhersons the questionnaire that they must complete for the process to go forward.

The following is the McPhersons' personal history from which they will complete their questionnaire.

Jennifer McPherson is a licensed practical nurse (LPN) and works for the Highland Medical Clinic, which is located in your city. Jennifer received her medical training at a local community college. She has been working at the clinic for the past three years.

Eric McPherson is a teacher and assistant football coach at a local high school. Eric earned his B.A. and M.A. from a state university in your state. He began working at the local high school this past fall. Prior to that time, Eric was unable to find a teaching position, so he and a friend formed Premier Painting Company.

This is the second marriage for both. Jennifer was previously married to Bobby Baxter and has a four-year-old daughter, Irene Baxter, from that marriage. Eric has an 18-year-old son, Eric McPherson, Jr., and an eight-year-old daughter, Bethany McPherson, from his previous marriage to Sarah Jane Smith. Bethany lives with her mother who has sole custody.

Jennifer McPherson's Social Security number is 445-74-2787. Eric McPherson's Social Security number is 403-54-1277. Because both are employees, neither has an employer's identification number.

The McPhersons live at 8110 South Windsor Drive in your city, county, and state. They have lived at this address since they were married two years ago. Prior to that time, Jennifer lived at 542 Evergreen Lane in your city, county, and state. She had lived at that address for one year between her previous marriage and her marriage to Eric. During her previous marriage to Bobby Baxter, Jennifer lived at 3120 East Avenue in your city, county, and state.

Jennifer, as a salaried employee, earns $24,000 a year. Her monthly check is reduced by $500 for FICA, Medicare, and payroll taxes, and $250 for her 401(k) plan with Acme Insurance Company. She has $6,000 in her 401(k). She pays $240 a year for her state license and $300 for professional books, journals, and continuing education.

Eric earns $36,000 a year at the high school as a biology teacher and assistant football coach. He is paid on a 12-month basis. His monthly check is currently reduced by $700 for FICA, Medicare, and payroll taxes; $150 for medical and dental insurance; and $150 for his state teachers' retirement plan. His retirement plan is currently worth $1,250.

At times during the summer, Eric may earn up to $500 teaching at football camps. Generally, these earnings are spent on extra child care and family vacations.

Prior to receiving his teaching position, Eric earned $20,000 in the year before joining the high school's staff and $9,000 as a painter during the first eight months before joining the high school's staff. After receiving his teaching position and closing the painting company, Eric leased storage space from Eastside Mini Storage to store his painting equipment. The lease was for one year and cost Eric $100 a month.

Eric pays his first wife, Sarah Jane Smith, $400 a month for child support for Bethany. Sarah Jane has remarried. Sarah Jane claims that Eric is in arrears in his alimony and child support by $1,000 and $400, respectively. Eric believes Sarah Jane has not given him credit for all of his past payments and he is current in both alimony and child support.

The South Windsor Drive house was purchased for $80,000 and is now valued at $90,000. At the time of purchase, Eric and Jennifer paid $20,000 and took a $62,000 mortgage from First Mortgage Company at 8 percent. Their mortgage payment is $500 a month. The outstanding balance is $60,000. They are $1,575 in arrears. The mortgage payment includes home insurance and real estate taxes.

Because the house is aging, maintenance has increased. They owe the Jiffy Plumbing Company $600 and the Rockwell Construction Company $2,500.

The house has an electric air conditioning system, and electricity has averaged $75 a month. The house is heated by natural gas, and the gas bill averages $100 a month. The water bill is generally about $25 a month. The telephone bill (including long distance) averages $50 a month. Neither Jennifer nor Eric has a mobile phone.

Last year the McPhersons took a second mortgage from Second Mortgage Company on their South Windsor Drive house. The second mortgage was for $7,000 at 10 percent. In addition to the house, the McPhersons gave Second Mortgage Company a security interest in all of their household furniture (valued at $5,000). They still owe Second Mortgage $6,000 and pay $125 a month. They are current in their payments but they are struggling to make the payments.

The McPherson family usually spends about $1,000 a month on food. This includes about $500 in groceries and $500 for lunches and dinners at restaurants. They also spend about $800 a month on clothing and $400 a month on entertainment. Their main source of entertainment is their Boomer bass boat that they purchased for $19,000 several years ago. It currently is worth $16,000. Last summer Eric gave his brother, Robert McPherson, a 75 HP Evinrude® Motor worth $1,250.

The McPhersons spend about $75 a week on laundry and dry cleaning. The remainder of their laundry is done at home. Recently, their washer broke and they purchased a Kenmore® washer and dryer from Sears for $1,200, and gave Sears a purchase-money security interest in the items. The value of the washer and dryer is now $500, although they still owe $850. Payments are $32 a month at an interest rate of 21 percent.

The McPhersons receive home delivery of their local newspaper, which costs $10 a month.

Most medical and dental bills are covered by insurance. Although insurance covers most of the prescribed medications, the insured must pay $2 per prescription. All members of the family suffer from allergies and take prescribed medications for this condition. The monthly medical bills average $40, which includes the deductible. Eric carries a $500,000 term life insurance policy to which he pays $75 a month.

Both Eric and Jennifer have automobiles. Eric drives a Chevrolet Blazer that is four years old. Jennifer drives a Buick Regal that is six years old. Eric's Blazer is financed by Auto Finance Company. He still owes Auto Finance $12,000 (at 14 percent) although the current value of the vehicle is $8,000. He makes payments of $310 a month and is current in his payments. Jennifer's Buick has a current value of $3,000 with an outstanding debt of $7,000 with Capital Finance Company. The finance charge is 12 percent. She pays $170 a month. Their automobile insurance premiums on two vehicles total $400 per quarter. The Buick is, however, no longer in Jennifer's possession. It was repossessed by Maple Street Garage on behalf of Capital Finance a few days before Christmas because she had defaulted in her payments. Capital Finance has not yet sold the vehicle.

Irene attends a private preschool program. This costs $1,800 a year in tuition. Because the preschool program is only for half a day, Jennifer has made arrangements for a child care center to pick up Irene at the preschool program and care for her for the remainder of the day. The child care center charges $65 a week.

Eric, Jr. attends a state university. His tuition, room, and board cost $4,800 for the year. Eric, Sr. pays his son's tuition, room, and board and gives Eric, Jr. a $300 a month allowance.

The McPhersons have pledged $45 a month for four years to their church for its building fund. They have not made a payment for the last three months. They also contribute $100 a month to their church.

Jennifer has $3,000 in non-exempt U.S. Savings Bonds that have matured but have not been cashed in. They are in the family safe deposit box at First Bank. The annual rental for the safe deposit box is $60.

Jennifer received $400 a month in alimony when she was divorced, but those payments have ceased since she remarried. She receives $500 a month from Bobby Baxter, her former husband, for child support for Irene. Bobby Baxter is behind in his child support payments. Last year Jennifer sued

Bobby and recovered a judgment. She has not attempted to execute her judgment since Bobby is unemployed and has few assets.

The McPhersons have $450 in a joint checking account at Second Bank that has earned $5 interest this past year. Between the two, they have about $75 in cash.

Jennifer pays a cleaning service $50 a week to clean the house. Eric pays a yard service $45 a week to mow the grass, rake the leaves, and tend to the flower gardens.

Over the years, both Jennifer and Eric have overcharged on their credit cards. They owe National Bank VISA® $2,500, Discover Card® $25,000, and American Express® $10,000. Each charges 1.5 percent interest per month on the unpaid balance. They have not paid any of these credit cards for the last three months.

Last summer Premier Painting Company procured two contracts, expecting to make $5,000 on each. Anticipating this additional income, the McPhersons took an early summer cruise to the Caribbean, charging $5,000 on their Discover Card®. After the cruise, Eric McPherson learned that due to the economic slump, both painting jobs were cancelled and his painting company was unable to find other jobs to fill the void.

Last summer the McPhersons borrowed $1,500 from Friendly Finance at an annual rate of 15 percent. Eric's father, Benjamin Franklin McPherson, cosigned for the loan. Monthly payments are $100 a month. Friendly Finance has not been paid for four months. The outstanding balance is still $1,500.

A year ago Christmas, Jennifer borrowed $450 from her sister, Janet Tompkins. A month before this past Christmas, Jennifer paid her sister the $450 she had borrowed.

The McPhersons also owe back taxes from the gain they realized last year from the sale of a lake lot. They owe the Internal Revenue Service $8,000 and their state's tax commission $3,500.

The final outstanding obligation is to Thrifty Credit Union. This involves a government-insured educational loan made to Jennifer while she was attending nursing school. The outstanding balance is $35,000. The interest rate is 12 percent a year. Monthly payments are scheduled at $400. Thrifty has not been paid for the past six months.

Based on this information, begin to complete the questionnaire in Appendix A. You may download the questionnaire from the Web site for this text. As you progress through the questionnaire, you will discover that you have incomplete information. Make a list of additional information you need from the McPhersons.

B. ANALYSIS: NONBANKRUPTCY OR BANKRUPTCY

The analysis step is the point at which the attorney evaluates the information gathered and formulates a course of action. The attorney must recommend to the client whether or not to file. If the recommendation is to file, then the attorney must inform the client under which chapters of the Bankruptcy Code the case could be filed. The attorney must also help the client to evaluate the choices so that the appropriate chapter can be selected. This responsibility is substantial and cannot be taken lightly for at least two reasons. First, a debtor taken through a Chapter 7 liquidation will suffer the loss of all nonexempt assets that are not recovered under reaffirmation agreements. 11 U.S.C.A. §§ 522, 541. The attorney must evaluate whether this loss may be avoidable and, if so, determine what strategy could be used to avoid it. Second, a debtor can receive a discharge in a Chapter 7 bankruptcy case only once every six years. 11 U.S.C.A. § 727(a)(9). The attorney must determine whether the filing of a bankruptcy petition at this time is premature and would make bankruptcy unavailable if the debtor has a greater need to file at a later date.

EXAMPLE

Jason Browning was diagnosed with lymphoma and was undergoing chemotherapy when his group insurance medical benefits ran out. Unable to continue to pay his medical bills and having exhausted his savings, Jason visited an attorney to investigate filing for bankruptcy.

The attorney advised Jason that he might want to delay filing because otherwise, the debt for his post-filing treatment would not be dischargeable.

EXAMPLE

Meridith McDonald has substantial credit card debt and is considering filing for bankruptcy. She also owns an expensive sailboat that was given to her as a graduation present by her great aunt. She rents an apartment along with several of her friends but has been considering purchasing a modest home if she only had the down payment.

Meridith's attorney has advised her to sell the sailboat and use that money in a down payment for a home. While the sailboat would be nonexempt property and would be sold by the Chapter 7 trustee and the proceeds paid to her creditors, the home would be her homestead and would be exempt under the law of her state.

EXAMPLE

Millie Wong borrowed $30,000 from her uncle, Charles Wong, to attend college. After graduation, Millie was hired by an advertising agency. Having a good job, Millie overcharged on her credit cards. After six months and before she was laid off due to hard economic times, Millie was able to save $20,000.

Millie is considering bankruptcy. She has been advised that if she pays Uncle Charles now and waits for at least 90 days, she could be discharged from her credit card debt (and the balance that she owes to Uncle Charles). If she files now, Uncle Charles and the credit card companies would both be treated as creditors holding unsecured nonpriority claims and Uncle Charles would be lucky to see even a small percentage of the $20,000 that she has saved.

The information obtained at the initial interview must be sufficient to enable the attorney to determine what, if any, action is necessary. If the attorney decides that some action is needed, the next step is to determine whether such action will involve bankruptcy relief or perhaps some other course of action. At times, the attorney may only need to calm the debtor and discuss nonbankruptcy strategies.

1. Alternatives to a Bankruptcy Filing

After the interview, the attorney and the debtor should carefully consider alternatives to proceeding in the bankruptcy court. Nonbankruptcy alternatives will probably be less expensive and better received by the creditors. Furthermore, nonbankruptcy solutions do not carry the stigma of a bankruptcy filing. All debtors should not be taken through bankruptcy.

If the case is a consumer case and the matter is inappropriate for a bankruptcy remedy, the attorney might not handle the case at all. In a consumer situation, it is often more practical to refer the client to a credit counseling center for assistance. On the other hand, the business client will generally be facing a situation that requires an attorney's involvement.

Private nonbankruptcy alternatives available to the debtor are negotiation with creditors, consolidation loans, credit counseling, assignments for the benefit of creditors, and defending an action brought on a debt.

a. Negotiation. Negotiation may involve discussion and agreement between the debtor and a creditor whereby the creditor agrees to terms different from those originally agreed to with the debtor. Such relief may be feasible and will not require the protection of the bankruptcy court. As a result of negotiation, the debtor may receive an extension of time in which to pay the debt, a reduction in the amount of the debt, or a combination of the two. Negotiation depends on the cooperation of the creditor. For negotiation to be successful, the debtor must be able to make some payment toward the debt.

The negotiated agreement is governed by contract law. The debtor must promise to perform an act or omission in exchange for the creditor's promise to perform an act or omission. The creditor's promise is the consideration for the debtor's promise. Also, the creditor must promise to perform an act or omission in exchange for the debtor's promise to perform an act or omission. The debtor's promise is the consideration for the creditor's promise. If the debtor promises to pay the creditor what the debtor already has a duty to pay the creditor, the debtor's promise will not be consideration for the creditor's promise to accept less than what the debtor owes or to accept what the debtor owes over a longer period. The creditor is only seeking what the debtor already had a preexisting duty to do. The creditor's promise lacks consideration, and it cannot be either an offer or an acceptance. Without either an offer or an acceptance, there can be no contract.

EXAMPLE

Patsie Wilburn borrowed $1,500 from her sister Tina and promised to pay $100 a month until the loan was repaid. After Patsie became delinquent in her payments, she renegotiated the contract to reduce her payments to $75 a month.

In the original contract, the offer was Tina's promise to loan Patsie $1,500 in exchange for Patsie's promise to repay $1,500 in $100 a month installments. Patsie accepted Tina's offer by promising to pay $1,500 in installments of $100 a month in exchange for Tina's promise to loan her $1,500. Patsie's promise to repay $1,500 in monthly installments of $100 was the consideration that Tina requested for her promise to loan Patsie $1,500. Tina's promise to loan $1,500 was the consideration that Patsie requested for her promise to repay $1,500 in monthly installments of $100. Because there was consideration for both Patsie's promise and Tina's promise, there was an offer and an acceptance and thus a contract.

Patsie renegotiated the contract to reduce the monthly payments from $100 to $75. After Patsie made three $75 payments, Tina demanded that she begin paying $100 a month. When Patsie refused, Tina brought action for breach of contract, claiming that the renegotiated contract was not a contract because it lacked consideration for her promise to take less per month. When Patsie promised to pay in $75 a month installments, she promised to do what she had a preexisting duty to do (albeit less). The renegotiation is not a contract, and the original contract is enforceable.

If Patsie seeks to renegotiate her contract with Tina, she needs to offer Tina something other than what she is already obligated to do. For example, she could offer to pay interest.

EXAMPLE

Belinda Richards owns a small business in partnership with her twin sister, Delinda. Belinda borrowed $30,000 from United Bank for improvements for her business and gave United a security interest in her present and after-acquired inventory. At the time the loan was made, United Bank did not ask Belinda whether she owned the business as an individual or as a partner in a partnership. United Bank attempted to perfect by filing a financing statement under the name of Belinda Richards rather than under the name of the partnership, Richards Cosmetics.

In recent months Richards Cosmetics has been losing money. If the partnership files for bankruptcy, United Bank will be treated as an unsecured creditor because it does not have a perfected security interest. It will join the pool of other unsecured creditors and will probably receive only a small payoff when the assets are liquidated. If Belinda could effect a workout with United Bank to avoid having the partnership file for bankruptcy, the bank might gain a larger payoff and the partnership could continue in business.

If the attorney determines that the debtor has nonexempt property that he or she cannot afford to jeopardize, a solution might be available to utilize the nonexempt property to keep the debtor out of bankruptcy.

EXAMPLE

Charlene Brown, age 30, owes $10,000 in medical bills from a prolonged illness. Her doctors and hospital have become impatient and have refused to wait for payment. They have threatened to sue. Charlene wants to file a Chapter 7.

Charlene has accumulated $5,000 in a 401(k). If she files for bankruptcy under Chapter 7, the 401(k) is nonexempt property and would be distributed among her creditors. She would also have the stigma of bankruptcy if she files a Chapter 7.

Charlene could save her 401(k) if a nonbankruptcy solution could be arranged. If Charlene could use the 401(k) as collateral for a $4,000 loan and if she could negotiate a settlement with her doctors and hospital to pay 40 cents on the dollar, she could pay them off. She could then repay the $4,000 loan over a period of time. After paying the loan, Charlene would still have her 401(k) for retirement.

If a negotiated agreement involves a debtor and two or more creditors, it is an extension or a composition, or both. If the debtor and the creditors agree to permit the debtor additional time to pay the debt, the agreement is called an extension. If the debtor and the creditors agree to permit the debtor to satisfy the debt by paying less than the full amount, the agreement is called a **composition.**

The consideration problem present in a negotiation between a debtor and one creditor (preexisting duty) may not exist in an extension or a composition. The fact that only two parties were in the original transaction but three or more parties are in the new transaction permits promises to be made between parties who were not parties in the original contract and thus eliminates the preexisting duty problem.

An extension allows a debtor additional time to pay his or her debts. Creditors will usually agree to an extension if it is justified. They base their decision on the past payment record of the debtor and on the debtor's future prospects. Extensions offer an advantage to both creditors and debtor; the creditors get all the money owed to them and the debtor stays out of bankruptcy court. The problems with an extension are that all creditors may not agree to it and that the debts may be so large that it is not feasible for the debtor to pay them.

EXAMPLE

Arnold Everett borrowed $5,000 against each of his three credit cards. When he was unable to pay his minimum monthly payments, he negotiated an agreement with two of the credit card companies. Under the agreement, Arnold returned the credit cards to the issuers (and thereby accrued no new charges) and promised to pay half of his minimum monthly payments until each balance was reduced to zero. The unpaid balance would continue to accrue interest at the normal rate.

After Arnold sent the three credit card companies half of their minimum monthly payment, the company that did not participate in the extension sued Arnold for breach of contract. Because this company was not a party to the extension, it was not bound by the contract.

In a composition the creditors agree to accept a reduced amount in satisfaction of the debts. It may be necessary to deal with only one or a few of the creditors. A remedy may be worked out with multiple creditors on a collective basis if they are all willing to work together, perhaps under the leadership of one of the creditors or one of the creditors with the assistance of the debtor's attorney. A composition is especially beneficial to the debtor because it discharges a portion of the debt without having to go through bankruptcy proceedings. Composition, however, should not be considered unless the debtor has the money to pay off the reduced debt immediately or is prepared to file for bankruptcy and has made the creditor aware of this. If the debtor files for bankruptcy, the creditor may receive nothing, so the threat of bankruptcy on the part of the debtor may make the creditor more amenable to a composition agreement. A composition poses the same problem that an extension does: some creditors may not agree to it. For a creditor to agree to a composition, he or she has to be assured of receipt of the promised payment from the debtor or at least receipt of more than if a bankruptcy claim was filed. Compositions are used by businesses more often than by individuals and are often arranged by workout departments in many banks. Some law firms have gained considerable expertise in nonjudicial workouts.

EXAMPLE

John and Alice Washington owned the majority interest in a partnership in a restaurant. The restaurant was profitable, but John and Alice had problems with their personal expenses. The monthly mortgage payments on their house coupled with debts from living beyond their means raised serious problems with personal, rather than business, debts.

If John and Alice filed bankruptcy, their partnership interest in the restaurant would be an asset of the estate and would be distributed to creditors. If John and Alice did not file bankruptcy, they could try to effectuate a workout on a piecemeal basis.

John and Alice restructured their business by selling a further interest in the partnership to one of their partners. This raised money to pay their creditors. John and Alice sought a composition with their creditors to satisfy their unsecured debts. They also conveyed their house by deed in lieu of foreclosure to the bank that held the mortgage. This got them out from under the monthly mortgage payments that they were unable to maintain. This solution gave John and Alice the relief they needed from their debts and did not jeopardize their interest in the restaurant.

At times, it may be beneficial for the debtor to give up a part of his or her property that would be nonexempt in bankruptcy in return for being able to keep the remainder.

EXAMPLE

James and Rachael McArthur own a number of heirlooms that were left to Rachael by her grandmother when she died. Their value is $100,000. Rachael has a deep attachment to this property. The McArthurs owe unsecured creditors $150,000.

The McArthurs know that Rachael's heirlooms are nonexempt and would become an asset of the estate for distribution among creditors if they file for bankruptcy under Chapter 7. If the McArthurs could arrange a composition with their creditors for 50 cents on the dollar, then Rachael could select the heirlooms she wants to keep and sell the remainder to raise $75,000 to pay the creditors.

If the debtor has only nondischargeable debts, then a negotiated settlement, rather than bankruptcy, may be the more appropriate solution to the debtor's problem.

EXAMPLE

Aaron Stevenson recently graduated from college and went to work for a radio station as a disc jockey. During college, Aaron accumulated $50,000 in college loans. The student loans are nondischargeable. Therefore, bankruptcy under Chapter 7 will not provide him with the relief that he seeks. Aaron negotiates to pay the loans off over a longer period of time.

b. Consolidation Loan. A **consolidation loan** allows a debtor to obtain one loan large enough to pay off all of his or her debts. A consolidation loan does not lower the total amount the debtor owes; it does, however, reduce the number of payments the debtor must make a month. If the debtor obtains a consolidated loan to pay off a number of creditors, and if the interest rate for the consolidated loan is the same as the interest rates on the prior debts, and if the time to pay off the consolidated loan is the same as the time to pay off the prior debts, the monthly consolidated loan payment will equal the sum of the prior monthly payments.

EXAMPLE

Ethel and Fred Kurtz owed five creditors $2,000 each. The interest rate for each was 5 percent per annum. Each creditor was paid $200 a month.

Ethel and Fred obtained a consolidated loan for $10,000 at 5 percent interest per annum. Their monthly payments were $1,000 a month.

The total amount paid under the consolidation loan will be the same as if Ethel and Fred had paid each creditor $200 a month.

The consolidation loan may require the debtor to pay a higher interest rate than the debtor was previously paying and to pay the debt over a longer period.

EXAMPLE

Ethel and Fred Kurtz owed five creditors $2,000 each. The interest rate for each was 5 percent per annum. Each creditor was paid $200 a month.

Ethel and Fred obtained a consolidated loan for $10,000 at 10 percent interest per annum. Their monthly payments were $750 a month.

Although their monthly payment will be smaller, Ethel and Fred will pay more under the consolidation loan because the interest rate is higher and the number of monthly payments will be greater.

A debtor considering a consolidation loan must be aware of the actual cost of the loan, especially the finance charges and interest rates. There can be a big difference in the cost of the loan, depending on whether interest is charged only on the unpaid balance or on the total amount to be paid in a fixed number of installments. It is always advisable for a debtor to consult an attorney about any consolidation loan to prevent problems such as usury, which may cost the debtor a great deal more in the long run than the original debts.

If the consolidation loan is secured by collateral, it is important that the debtor thoroughly understand the security agreement. A consolidation loan security agreement may cover exempt and nonexempt property. In the event a debtor must file bankruptcy after having tried a consolidation loan, he or she may lose both exempt and nonexempt property. In bankruptcy, the debtor will keep exempt property and has an option to keep some nonexempt property through reaffirmation agreements.

EXAMPLE

After several months, the Kurtzes found that the $750 monthly payment on the consolidation loan exceeded their ability to pay and they defaulted on the consolidation loan. Since the loan was secured, the lender repossessed all of the Kurtzes' property.

Had the Kurtzes filed bankruptcy under Chapter 7, rather than obtaining a consolidation loan, they would have been able to retain their house and car as well as other exempt and some nonexempt property.

c. Credit Counseling. Some debtors should go to **credit counseling** rather than file for bankruptcy. If a Chapter 7 bankruptcy is filed on their behalf and their financial problems are temporarily solved, the debtors will not be able to discharge their debts under Chapter 7 again for another six years. In the event of a catastrophic situation such as unemployment, an uninsured loss, or large medical bills prior to the expiration of the six year period, debtors have no bankruptcy solution unless they fit within Chapter 13, and Chapter 13 solves only a limited number of cases.

Many debtors owe a relatively small amount of debt but have financial problems because of their spending habits. Such debtors need education and should be referred to credit counseling. If the educational process is ignored, these debtors will continue to have financial problems. Credit Counseling Centers are licensed and bonded. They analyze the debtor's obligations and negotiate with creditors for the repayment of the debtor's bills on a schedule the agency feels the debtor can manage. These agencies do not lend money. They only distribute the debtor's money to the debtor's creditors. Creditor participation is totally voluntary. Credit Counseling Centers offer no protection to the debtor if the creditor decides to initiate a suit for the debtor's default.

Providing credit counseling services for a fee is illegal in the majority of states, but nonfee services are located in many states as a community service. Credit Counseling Centers are often supported by community charity campaigns such as United Way and by the nominal fee charged the creditor.

EXAMPLE

Terry Kelly earns $15,000 a year as a legal secretary. He has outstanding unsecured debts of $5,000. If he files for bankruptcy under Chapter 7, his $5,000 in debts will be discharged. He will, however, preclude himself from filing another Chapter 7 petition for six years. During that period he could lose his job, have an accident on his motorcycle, or accumulate medical bills far beyond his ability to pay. If he loses his job, he cannot consider Chapter 13 because he will have no regular income to support a Chapter 13 plan. Therefore, arranging the payment of his debts through a Credit Counseling Center will preserve Terry's opportunity to file a Chapter 7 case in the future if the need arises.

d. Assignments for the Benefit of Creditors. **Assignments for the benefit of creditors** involve the transfer of the debtor's assets to a third party to ensure the payment of the debtor's obligations. Assignments for the benefit of creditors are used almost exclusively by business debtors. In an assignment for the benefit of creditors, a business debtor liquidates its assets and distributes the proceeds to its creditors. In the case of an ongoing business, particularly the small retail establishment, perhaps the key creditor, either a wholesaler or a lender, can assist in finding a buyer who believes that a turnaround is possible under new management. The liquidation is carried out by an assignee appointed by the creditor. The assignee acts as a trustee and is regulated by the principles of trust law.

Advantages of an assignment for the benefit of creditors include the time and money saved over the cost of bankruptcy and the fact that higher prices are often obtained in this type of liquidation than might be realized in a bankruptcy liquidation, thereby enabling the creditors to realize a higher return on their claims. An assignment for the benefit of creditors is covered by state statute in the majority of states and is a voluntary act on the part of the debtor.

2. Bankruptcy Choices

If it is decided that the debtor should file for bankruptcy, the attorney must work with the debtor to decide if the bankruptcy filing will be as an individual, a partnership, or a corporation, or possibly as an individual and a partnership or as an individual and a corporation.

The married debtor has a choice between filing as an individual or filing a joint petition with his or her spouse. The decision is made on the basis of who owes the debts. Do both spouses owe the debts or does only one owe the debts? Does one spouse have separate property that is not subject to the other's debts? Attorneys occasionally erroneously assume that both spouses owe the debts. It is important to investigate who owes the debts before the decision is made to file an individual or a joint petition.

EXAMPLE

After John and Alice were married, John moved into Alice's house. Alice owned her own business, a consignment shop, and kept her own records. John owned his own business, a print shop, and kept his own records. Both maintained their own business and personal charge accounts and checking accounts.

John overextended his credit on both the print shop and his personal charge accounts. Alice's business is thriving and she is able to pay both her business and personal debts.

If John and Alice decide on bankruptcy, John should file as an individual because all of the problem debts are his. The case should not be filed as a joint petition because Alice's credit is not overextended. If a joint petition is filed, Alice's assets will be used to pay John's creditors.

A choice must also be made regarding which bankruptcy chapter will best suit the debtor's needs. Section 109 may be treated as the "scope" provision for each of the operative chapters of the Bankruptcy Code. 11 U.S.C.A. § 109. The different operative chapters (7, 9, 11, 12, and 13) apply to different classifications of debtors. Exhibit 4–1 presents an overview of who may be a debtor under which operative chapter.

The operative chapters follow two distinct drafting patterns. Chapters 7 and 11 apply to all debtors, subject to express exclusions. Chapters 9, 12, and 13 apply only to specifically enumerated debtors.

a. Chapter 7—Liquidation A Chapter 7 case should generally be filed only as a last resort. It should not be filed until absolutely necessary or until it is definitely ready for filing. The proper approach to a Chapter 7 filing is to be deliberate. There should be no rush jobs unless it is truly an emergency and there is no other course. Therefore, in preparing to file a Chapter 7, the attorney should answer the following questions:

1. What kind of a client is involved?
2. How ready is the client for the bankruptcy case?

EXHIBIT 4–1 Debtors and Operative Chapters of the Code

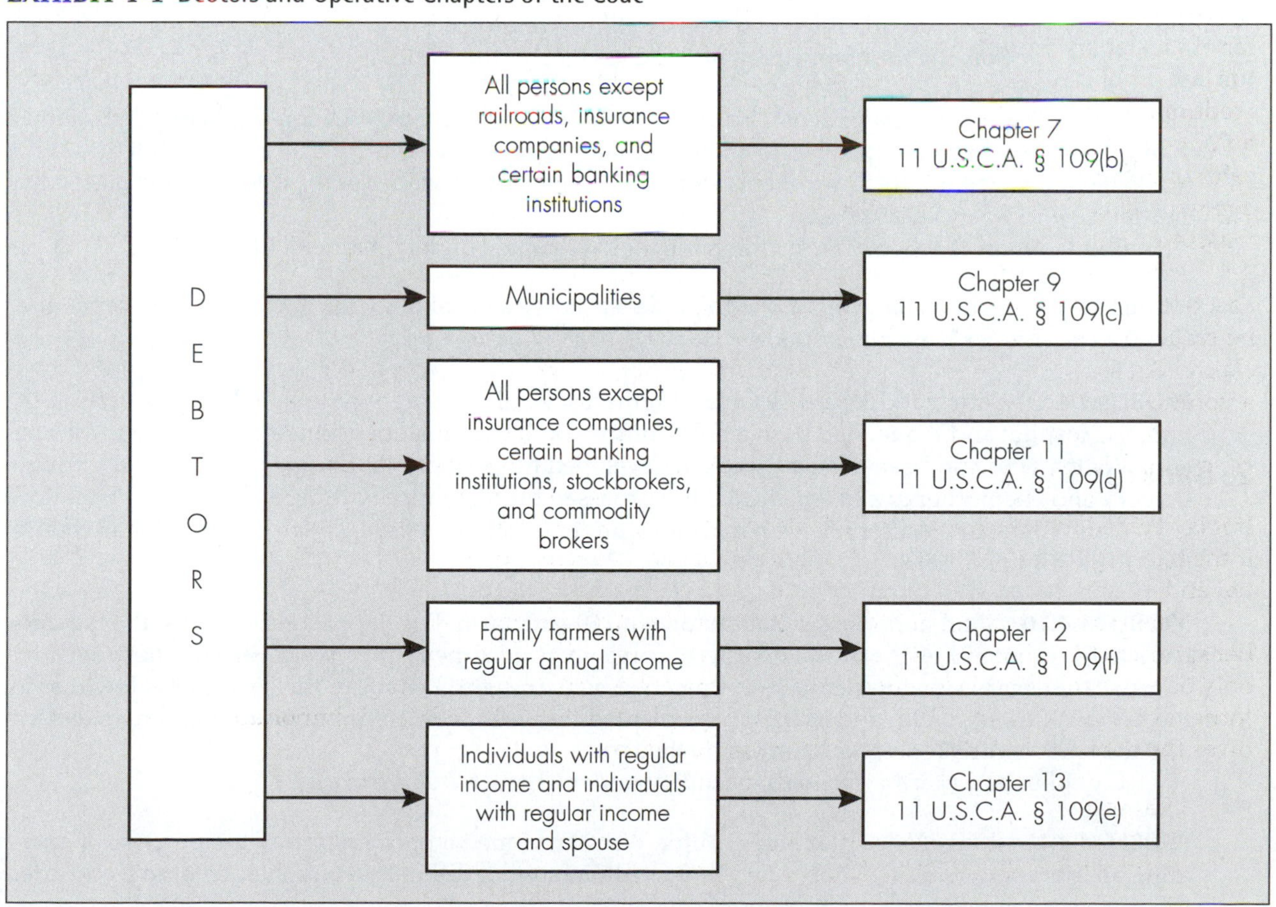

3. How much interviewing is needed to satisfy the attorney and the paralegal that they have all the necessary information?

Section 109(b) defines eligibility for liquidation under Chapter 7. All persons are eligible except railroads, insurance companies, and certain banking institutions.

> (b) A person may be a debtor under chapter 7 of this title only if such person is not—
> (1) a railroad;
> (2) a domestic insurance company, bank, savings bank, cooperative bank, savings and loan association, building and loan association, homestead association, a new Markets Venture Capital company as defined in section 351 of the Small Business Investment Act of 1958, a small business investment company licensed by the Small Business Administration under subsection (c) or (d) of section 301 of the Small Business Investment Act of 1958, credit union, or industrial bank or similar institution which is an insured bank as defined in section 3(h) of the Federal Deposit Insurance Act, except . . . ; or
> (3) a foreign insurance company, bank, savings bank, cooperative bank, savings and loan association, building and loan association, homestead association, or credit union, engaged in such business in the United States.

Banking institutions and insurance companies engaged in business in the United States are excluded from liquidation under the bankruptcy laws because they are covered for insolvency and receivership purposes under other state and federal legislation. When a foreign bank or insurance company is not engaged in the banking or insurance business in the United States, these regulatory laws are inapplicable and the bankruptcy laws are the only laws available for administration of any assets found in the United States.

PROBLEM 4.6 The Lone Star Railroad Company has been in financial difficulties for several years. The company would like to cease doing business and divide its assets among its many creditors. Unfortunately, the assets are insufficient to satisfy all the creditors.

Can Lone Star file for bankruptcy under Chapter 7 of the Code?

PROBLEM 4.7 Over the past several years, the Gotham Teachers Credit Union has loaned substantial sums of money to oil well speculators without obtaining adequate security. The glut of oil on the world market led to substantially lower oil prices and to default on a number of these loans. This placed the credit union in financial difficulty.

Can Gotham Teachers Credit Union file for bankruptcy under Chapter 7 of the Code?

PROBLEM 4.8 Charles Smithfield, a fifth grade teacher, was unable to pay his bills as they came due. Can Charles file for bankruptcy under Chapter 7 of the Code?

PROBLEM 4.9 Wilma and Walter O'Connor retired several years ago. Wilma had been a nurse at St. Francis Hospital and Walter had been a police officer. Both had small pensions and social security benefits. Walter, who had been a heavy smoker, developed lung cancer. Although Walter pulled through surgery and chemotherapy, his medical bills surpassed his insurance coverage.

Can Wilma and Walter file for bankruptcy under Chapter 7 of the Code? If they can file, should they file a joint petition?

PROBLEM 4.10 John and Martha Babbitt own a 160-acre farm. For the past three years, the Babbitts have had to contend with natural disasters. Three years ago, their crops were partially destroyed by locusts. Two years ago, their crops were parched by a drought. Last year, their yield was low due to the floods. Although John and Martha have planted this year, their creditors are demanding payment and the bank is threatening to foreclose on the farm.

Can John and Martha file for bankruptcy under Chapter 7 of the Code?

PROBLEM 4.11 Mary Valesquez and Cynthia Webster formed a partnership for the purpose of operating an interior decorating shop. Mary and Cynthia found it difficult to pay their creditors, and after the first year in business, the shop closed.

Can Mary and Cynthia file for bankruptcy under Chapter 7 of the Code? If they can file, should they file as a partnership or as individuals? Can they file a joint petition?

PROBLEM 4.12 The Waterfront Fish Market was incorporated under the laws of Delaware. For many years the market was able to show a small profit. About a year ago, a new fish market opened nearby and the Waterfront Fish Market lost some of its customers. For the past several months, the market has been unable to pay its creditors.

Can the Waterfront Fish Market file for bankruptcy under Chapter 7 of the Code?

PROBLEM 4.13 Since the federal government deregulated the airlines, Blue Sky Airlines, a major commercial passenger carrier, has been losing money. The airlines has cut back on its routes and has sold some of its equipment.

Can Blue Sky Airlines file for bankruptcy under Chapter 7 of the Code?

b. Chapter 9—Municipalities. Chapter 9 is a specialized chapter for municipalities only. A municipality seeking relief under Chapter 9 must be specifically authorized to be a debtor under Chapter 9 by state law or authorized by a governmental officer or organization empowered by state law to authorize such entity to be a debtor under Chapter 9. The municipality must be insolvent (unable to meet its debts as they mature) and must meet the other requirements of 11 U.S.C.A. § 109(c). Because Chapter 9 has limited application, it will not be covered here. A short discussion of Chapter 9 can be found in Appendix C.

c. Chapter 11—Reorganization. Persons who may be debtors under Chapter 7, with the exception of stockbrokers or commodity brokers, may be debtors under Chapter 11. Although the courts were divided over whether the debtor needed a business objective or a business purpose to file under Chapter 11, the issue was resolved by the United States Supreme Court in 1991, when it held that an individual debtor not engaged in business was eligible to reorganize under Chapter 11. *Toibb v. Radloff*, 501 U.S. 157 (1991).

Stockbrokers and commodity brokers are eligible for relief only under specially tailored provisions found in Chapter 7. 11 U.S.C.A. §§ 741–752 (stockbroker liquidation) and 11 U.S.C.A. §§ 761–766 (commodity broker liquidation). Railroads, excluded under Chapter 7, may be debtors under special provisions in Chapter 11. 11 U.S.C.A. §§ 1161–1174 (railroad reorganization). Insurance companies and certain banking institutions—debtors expressly excluded from Chapter 7—are also excluded from Chapter 11 because, unlike railroads, they are not expressly included in Chapter 11. 11 U.S.C.A. § 109(d).

> (d) Only a railroad, a person that may be a debtor under chapter 7 of this title (except a stockbroker or a commodity broker), and an uninsured State member bank . . . may be a debtor under chapter 11 of this title.

PROBLEM 4.14 Can the Lone Star Railroad Company in Problem 4.6 file for bankruptcy under Chapter 11 of the Code?

PROBLEM 4.15 Can the Gotham Teachers Credit Union in Problem 4.7 file for bankruptcy under Chapter 11 of the Code?

PROBLEM 4.16 Can Charles Smithfield in Problem 4.8 file for bankruptcy under Chapter 11 of the Code?

PROBLEM 4.17 Can Wilma and Walter O'Connor in Problem 4.9 file for bankruptcy under Chapter 11 of the Code? If they can file, should they file a joint petition?

PROBLEM 4.18 Can John and Martha Babbitt in Problem 4.10 file for bankruptcy under Chapter 11 of the Code?

PROBLEM 4.19 Can Mary Valesquez and Cynthia Webster in Problem 4.11 file for bankruptcy under Chapter 11 of the Code? If they can file, should they file as a partnership or as individuals? Can they file a joint petition?

PROBLEM 4.20 Can the Waterfront Fish Market in Problem 4.12 file for bankruptcy under Chapter 11 of the Code?

PROBLEM 4.21 Can Blue Sky Airlines in Problem 4.13 file for bankruptcy under Chapter 11 of the Code?

d. Chapter 12—Adjustment of Debts of a Family Farmer with Regular Annual Income The new Chapter 12 is available only to family farmers, as defined in section 101(18) of the Code, who have regular annual income. Section 101 of the Bankruptcy Code defines **family farmer with regular annual income.**

> (19) "family farmer with regular annual income" means family farmer whose annual income is sufficiently stable and regular to enable such family farmer to make payments under a plan under chapter 12 of this title. 11 U.S.C.A. § 101(19).

Because this definition is worded in terms of a family farmer with regular annual income, it becomes necessary to consult the definition of family farmer, which is also found in section 101.

> (18) "family farmer" means—
> (A) individual or individual and spouse engaged in a farming operation whose aggregate debts do not exceed $1,500,000 and not less than 80 percent of whose aggregate noncontingent, liquidated debts (excluding a debt for the principal residence of such individual or such individual and spouse unless such debt arises out of a farming operation), on the date the case is filed, arise out of a farming operation owned or operated by such individual or such individual and spouse, and such individual or such individual and spouse receive from such farming operation more than 50 percent of such individual's or such individual and spouse's gross income for the taxable year preceding the taxable year in which the case concerning such individual or such individual and spouse was filed; or
> (B) corporation or partnership in which more than 50 percent of the outstanding stock or equity is held by one family, or by one family and the relatives of the members of such family, and such family or such relatives conduct the farming operation; and
> (i) more than 80 percent of the value of its assets consists of assets related to the farming operation;
> (ii) its aggregate debts do not exceed $1,500,000 and not less than 80 percent of its aggregate noncontingent, liquidated debts (excluding a debt for one dwelling which is owned by such corporation or partnership and which a shareholder or partner maintains as a principal residence, unless such debt arises out of a farming operation), on the date the case is filed, arise out of the farming operation owned or operated by such corporation or such partnership; and
> (iii) if such corporation issues stock, such stock is not publicly traded. 11 U.S.C.A. § 101(18).

Since the definition of family farmer includes the term farming operation, it becomes necessary to consider the definition of farming operation. This term is also defined in section 101.

> (21) "farming operation" includes farming, tillage of the soil, dairy farming, ranching, production or raising of crops, poultry, or livestock, and production of poultry or livestock products in an unmanufactured state. 11 U.S.C.A. § 101(21).

PROBLEM 4.22 Can the Lone Star Railroad Company in Problem 4.6 file for bankruptcy under Chapter 12 of the Code?

PROBLEM 4.23 Can the Gotham Teachers Credit Union in Problem 4.7 file for bankruptcy under Chapter 12 of the Code?

PROBLEM 4.24 Can Charles Smithfield in Problem 4.8 file for bankruptcy under Chapter 12 of the Code?

PROBLEM 4.25 Can Wilma and Walter O'Connor in Problem 4.9 file for bankruptcy under Chapter 12 of the Code? If they can file, should they file a joint petition?

PROBLEM 4.26 Can John and Martha Babbitt in Problem 4.10 file for bankruptcy under Chapter 12 of the Code?

PROBLEM 4.27 Can Mary Valesquez and Cynthia Webster in Problem 4.11 file for bankruptcy under Chapter 12 of the Code? If they can file, should they file as a partnership or as individuals? Can they file a joint petition?

PROBLEM 4.28 Can the Waterfront Fish Market in Problem 4.12 file for bankruptcy under Chapter 12 of the Code?

PROBLEM 4.29 Can Blue Sky Airlines in Problem 4.13 file for bankruptcy under Chapter 12 of the Code?

e. Chapter 13—Adjustment of Debts of an Individual with Regular Income. Chapter 13 is available only to individuals with regular income who owe debts of less than $307,675 unsecured and $922,975 secured.

> (e) Only an individual with regular income that owes, on the date of the filing of the petition, noncontingent, liquidated, unsecured debts of less than $307,675 and noncontingent, liquidated, secured debts of less than $922,975, or an individual with regular income and such individual's spouse, except a stockbroker or a commodity broker, that owe, on the date of the filing of the petition, noncontingent, liquidated, unsecured debts that aggregate less than $307,675 and noncontingent, liquidated, secured debts of less than $922,975 may be a debtor under chapter 13 of this title. 11 U.S.C.A. § 109(e).

The dollar amounts for a Chapter 13 are adjusted every three years. 11 U.S.C.A. § 104(b). Future adjustment dates will be April 1, 2007 and April 1, 2010.

PROBLEM 4.30 Can the Lone Star Railroad Company in Problem 4.6 file for bankruptcy under Chapter 13 of the Code?

PROBLEM 4.31 Can the Gotham Teachers Credit Union in Problem 4.7 file for bankruptcy under Chapter 13 of the Code?

PROBLEM 4.32 Can Charles Smithfield in Problem 4.8 file for bankruptcy under Chapter 13 of the Code?

PROBLEM 4.33 Can Wilma and Walter O'Connor in Problem 4.9 file for bankruptcy under Chapter 13 of the Code? If they can file, should they file a joint petition?

PROBLEM 4.34 Can John and Martha Babbitt in Problem 4.10 file for bankruptcy under Chapter 13 of the Code?

PROBLEM 4.35 Can Mary Valesquez and Cynthia Webster in Problem 4.11 file for bankruptcy under Chapter 13 of the Code? If they can file, should they file as a partnership or as individuals? Can they file a joint petition?

PROBLEM 4.36 Can the Waterfront Fish Market in Problem 4.12 file for bankruptcy under Chapter 13 of the Code?

PROBLEM 4.37 Can Blue Sky Airlines in Problem 4.13 file for bankruptcy under Chapter 13 of the Code?

C. COUNSELING

The attorney will review the information received, give his or her recommendation, and gain the debtor's assent to the recommendation during the counseling session. This is also the time to gather more information if necessary. Often, the attorney will not begin to draft the bankruptcy documents at this point. Instead, he or she will request that the debtor come in three or four more times before the drafting. This is done to determine that the client is ready to file bankruptcy—that he or she knows it is the last resort and inevitable. Several meetings will also provide enough information for the attorney and the paralegal to prepare everything that is needed for filing.

Substantial discussion may be necessary before filing a case to determine that a debtor who wants to retain an item of property will be able to do so from the standpoint of exemption and encumbrance. Retention will depend on the debtor's ability to pay for the item and to make a reaffirmation, as well as on whether he or she is in arrears. It will also depend on who has a security interest in the item and if the security interest is perfected. In other words, is the debtor really going to be able to keep a particular item of property? Does the debtor understand what can be kept and what cannot be kept and the conditions for each item? If there is any question involved, does the debtor understand how that question can be resolved and that it may go for or against the debtor? There should be no surprises.

After the attorney and the debtor discuss the various solutions available to the debtor, fees should be discussed again. This discussion should culminate in a written document to avoid any misunderstanding. If a decision to file bankruptcy has been made, the Administrative Office's form for disclosure of attorney's compensation will provide the necessary information. The document should be signed by the debtor and can be used as the written contract for services. If an alternative other than bankruptcy has been selected, the attorney will need to draft his or her own contract.

D. DRAFTING OF BANKRUPTCY FORMS

The attorney or the paralegal is ready for drafting when a clear understanding has been reached regarding the property of the debtor. A simple case may be drafted in an hour and a little more difficult one in two hours; a complex case may be drafted over several days. Even a simpler case may take longer to complete if there is not enough information and the debtor must be contacted to provide it. A paralegal trained in this field could sit down with the information and draft a total filing set. Some attorneys do it that way and some do not. One attorney may want to do all the drafting, while another may turn over part or all of the drafting to a paralegal.

The debtor should be present when the forms are drafted to avoid errors in the final form. The drafting should go smoothly if a questionnaire has been used. The drafting of the necessary forms in a Chapter 7 case will be discussed in detail, line by line, in Chapter Five of this text.

SECTION 2
THE CREDITOR-CLIENT

The attorney representing the creditor-client may be operating in a nonbankruptcy situation, a voluntary bankruptcy situation, or an involuntary bankruptcy situation. In a nonbankruptcy situation, the creditor may work with the debtor toward a solution to the problem through the use of a private alternative to bankruptcy or through a state court alternative such as garnishment of wages. If the debtor files a voluntary bankruptcy petition, the attorney for the creditor may, among other things, attend the meeting of creditors and file a proof of claim. If the debtor does not file a voluntary bankruptcy petition, the creditor-client and his or her attorney may decide it is necessary to file an involuntary bankruptcy petition against the debtor to protect the creditor's interests.

A. THE CAUSES OF THE CREDITOR'S DISTRESS

The creditor is distressed because he or she is losing present dollars. These are the dollars currently loaned to the debtor. The creditor also may be losing future dollars if the debtor has been a regular customer and their relationship has suddenly been jeopardized or terminated by the insolvency or bankruptcy of the debtor.

Creditors who are regulated by state or federal agencies face periodic audits. Those who are faced with regulatory examinations are concerned because they may have made a very bad loan to begin with and the examiner may express concern. This may lead to additional regulatory scrutiny, sanctions, and loss of control over the institution.

A loss may be large enough to jeopardize a small institution's capital and its own financial stability. A loss of half a million dollars may throw the small lending institution into insolvency.

A director or officer of a lending institution will be concerned about impairment of his or her own financial position. An officer or director often is a stockholder or has options and other valuable rights, and his or her whole future will be jeopardized by a large loss.

Credit problems certainly add administrative costs through attorney fees to creditors. They also cost substantial staff time, especially if the debtor wants to do a workout and the creditors want to do a part of the work themselves. Costs will be involved if the creditors want to follow the workout and analyze it closely as it progresses. Creditors may become apprehensive enough to neglect other work that they should be doing.

Creditor problems may have a bad psychological effect on the creditor's staff. Lending officers may become too conservative when making loans and may pass up good opportunities because they have been burned in the past.

B. INFORMATION GATHERING

Information gathering with the creditor-client may be very different from that with the debtor-client. The creditor-client often has a long-standing relationship with an attorney, and the steps necessary for the debtor-client may not be necessary for the creditor-client. Many times the creditor does not need to meet with his or her attorney. All that needs to be done is for the attorney to receive necessary papers and instructions specific to the case at hand. The attorney will generally know what to do, how to do it, and when to do it in representing a long-standing client. Certain basic information will, of course, be necessary for representation of the creditor-client. This information may be obtained by mail, telephone or facsimile in many cases. At least one meeting will be necessary in others. The attorney and the paralegal should make sure they are furnished all necessary information by the creditor. Some creditor-clients will know exactly what information the attorney needs and will provide this information without the necessity of a formal request by the attorney or the paralegal. Other clients will have the information but may not provide it to the attorney or the paralegal except on request.

The attorney may have an arrangement in advance with the creditor on how much to bill for services if the creditor is a regular client. If no prior fee arrangement has been made with the creditor, it will be necessary for the attorney to get an agreement in writing at the beginning of his or her representation of the creditor. Often attorneys doing collections will provide the services on a flat rate basis, a percentage of collection basis, a straight hourly fee, or a combination. Generally banks, credit unions, and savings and loan associations will pay fees on an hourly basis.

For a sample interview questionnaire for the creditor-client, see Appendix B.

C. ANALYSIS: IF THE DEBTOR HAS FILED BANKRUPTCY

This subsection sets forth the steps an attorney should take on behalf of a creditor-client if the debtor has filed bankruptcy. First, the creditor must determine whether its claim is secured or unsecured. Second, the creditor must determine whether the debtor has filed for bankruptcy under Chapter 7, 11, 12, or 13.

1. If the Debtor Has Filed a Chapter 7 Case

If the debtor has filed a Chapter 7 case and the creditor holds a secured claim, the creditor should

1. review the debtor's statement of financial affairs and schedules;
2. check the debtor's statement of intention to see what the debtor's intention is regarding the collateral;
3. determine the value of the collateral;
4. file a proof of claim and attach to the proof of claim documentation to substantiate the lien or security interest and that it is perfected;
5. get the debtor to sign a reaffirmation agreement if the debtor indicated in the Statement of Intention a desire to reaffirm on terms which are acceptable to the creditor; or file a motion for relief for the automatic stay and for an order of abandonment so the collateral can be repossessed and the security interest or lien can be foreclosed;
6. decide if client or attorney, or both, should attend the meeting of creditors; and
7. investigate whether there is any basis for objecting to the dischargeability of the debt.

If any portion of the creditor's claim is unsecured, the creditor should

1. review the debtor's statement of financial affairs and schedules;
2. file a proof of claim unless notified that the case is a no-asset case;
3. pursue any co-obligors or guarantors on the creditor's claim against the debtor (unless they also have filed bankruptcy);
4. decide if client or attorney, or both, should attend the meeting of creditors;
5. report to the trustee any evidence or even suspicion that the debtor is concealing or disposing of assets; and
6. investigate the possibility of objecting to the debtor's discharge or to the dischargeability of the creditor's claim.

If the debtor seeks to discharge the creditor's debt, the creditor must file a complaint under 11 U.S.C.A. § 523(c) to object to the dischargeability of the debt or object to the debtor's discharge under 11 U.S.C.A. § 727. The deadline for filing such a complaint is 60 days after the first date set for the meeting of creditors under section 341. Fed. R. Bank. P. 4007(c) and 4004(a), respectively.

The creditor or the attorney will attend the meeting of creditors only if the creditor needs information from the debtor. If the creditor holds a secured claim, the creditor may attend the meeting of creditors to arrange for repossessing the collateral when the stay is lifted, to verify that the debtor has insurance on the collateral, or to have the opportunity to get a reaffirmation agreement signed.

If the creditor holds an unsecured claim, the creditor may attend the meeting of creditors to get information to determine whether there is a basis upon which to object to the dischargeability of the debt.

EXAMPLE

When the creditor reads the debtor's schedules, the creditor is surprised to find that the collateral that secured its loan is not listed. The creditor would attend the meeting of creditors to ask the debtor, "Where is my collateral?" The debtor might respond "I forgot to tell you the collateral was stolen."

2. If the Debtor Has Filed a Chapter 11 Case

If the debtor has filed a Chapter 11 case and the creditor holds a secured claim, the creditor should

1. if the debtor in possession or trustee proposes to use cash collateral, make sure that a satisfactory cash collateral order is first entered by the court;
2. file a motion for adequate protection or motion to modify stay if the creditor's interest in the collateral being used by the debtor in possession or trustee is not adequately protected;
3. determine the value of the collateral securing the creditor's claim;

4. review the monthly operating reports;
5. if cause exists, move to convert case to Chapter 7 or to dismiss it;
6. if cause exists, request the appointment of a trustee;
7. review the disclosure statement to make sure it contains adequate information; and
8. review the plan to determine if the plan is generally confirmable and to make sure the proposed treatment of the secured claim is either satisfactory to the creditor or meets the requirements for confirmation.

If any portion of the creditor's claim is unsecured, the creditor should consider

1. filing a proof of claim;
2. if eligible, electing whether to be a member of the committee of unsecured creditors;
3. reviewing the monthly operating reports;
4. if cause exists, requesting the appointment of a trustee;
5. if cause exists, requesting the conversion of the case to Chapter 7 or to dismiss the case;
6. reviewing the disclosure statement to make sure it contains adequate information; and
7. reviewing the plan to make sure that the confirmation requirements are met, that is, that it meets the best interests of creditors test, that it is feasible, that it is proposed in good faith, and whether it can be confirmed by cramdown without the consent of the class of unsecured creditors.

3. If the Debtor Has Filed a Chapter 12 Case

If the debtor has filed a Chapter 12 case and the creditor holds a secured claim, the creditor should

1. understand that the automatic stay may, if it is a consumer debt, protect both the debtor and any co-debtor;
2. determine if the debtor has possession of the creditor's collateral and, if so, the condition and value of the collateral;
3. file a proof of claim and send a copy to the Chapter 12 trustee;
4. review the Chapter 12 plan to see how the debtor proposes to treat the secured claim;
5. object to the plan, if necessary; and
6. if the creditor's interest in the collateral is not adequately protected, file a motion to modify stay.

If the creditor holds an unsecured claim, the creditor should:

1. file a proof of claim;
2. examine the debtor's Schedules I and J to verify the amount of the debtor's disposable income;
3. check whether the amount to be paid to the creditors holding unsecured claims under the plan is not less than the amount creditors would receive under Chapter 7 (i.e., whether the plan meets the best interests of creditors test);
4. determine whether the plan provides that all the debtor's disposable income will be made available under the plan; and
5. object to confirmation of the plan if the plan is proposed in bad faith (i.e., whether a minimal amount will be paid to unsecured creditors and a substantial portion of the debt would be non-dischargeable in a case under Chapter 7).

4. If the Debtor Has Filed a Chapter 13 Case

If the debtor has filed a Chapter 13 case and the creditor holds a secured claim, the creditor should

1. understand that the automatic stay may, if it is a consumer debt, protect both the debtor and any co-debtor;
2. file a proof of claim and send a copy to the Chapter 13 trustee;

3. review the Chapter 13 plan to see how the debtor proposes to treat the secured claim;
4. object to the plan, if necessary; and
5. if the creditor's interest in the collateral is not adequately protected, file a motion to modify stay.

If the creditor holds an unsecured claim, the creditor should

1. file a proof of claim;
2. examine the debtor's Schedules I and J to verify the amount of the debtor's disposable income;
3. check whether the amount to be paid to the creditors holding unsecured claims under the plan is not less than the amount creditors would receive under Chapter 7 (i.e., whether the plan meets the best interests of creditors test);
4. determine whether the plan provides that all the debtor's disposable income will be made available under the plan; and object to confirmation of the plan if the plan is proposed in bad faith (i.e., whether a minimal amount will be paid to unsecured creditors and a substantial portion of the debt would be nondischargeable in a case under Chapter 7).

D. ANALYSIS: ALTERNATIVES IF THE DEBTOR HAS NOT FILED BANKRUPTCY

The creditor may pursue a number of alternatives if the debtor has not filed a voluntary bankruptcy petition. The creditor may pursue private alternatives by working directly with the debtor. State court remedies are also available to the creditor. In particular, the creditor holding a secured claim has several options in state court. If none of the private or state court alternatives work for the creditor, it is possible to file an involuntary bankruptcy petition against the debtor in some instances.

1. Private Alternative

A creditor can work individually with the debtor to solve the creditor's problems and to help the debtor's position or, if more than one creditor is involved, a creditor can try to get all the creditors to work together to find a remedy. A creditor is required to act in good faith toward the debtor and may be subject to bad faith claims. A creditor must also closely monitor the security and resources of the debtor without becoming so involved with the debtor's situation that the creditor becomes liable to other creditors. The creditor should consider the following when making a decision about working with the debtor:

1. Does the debtor have reason to think that the relationship between the debtor and the creditor will continue?
2. Has the debtor been given adequate notice that the obligation has been called in to allow time to work something out?
3. Should an attorney be consulted concerning the creditor's proper course of action?

If a creditor does decide to work with the debtor, the creditor has the options of totally forgiving the debt or providing temporary relief until the debtor resolves his or her problems. Because few creditors are likely to forgive a debt, that leaves the option of providing temporary relief. Temporary relief involves negotiations, extensions, and compositions, all of which have been discussed under the debtor's remedies.

2. State Court Alternatives

Legal remedies vary depending on whether the creditor holds an unsecured or secured claim and whether the remedy is a prejudgment or postjudgment remedy. A creditor holding an unsecured claim has few remedies available. Usually, a creditor holding an unsecured claim can only file a claim, obtain a judgment, and then execute the judgment against the property of the debtor. The majority of states permit prejudgment garnishment and attachment of a debtor's property when a creditor files suit, so that the property is secured if the creditor prevails on the claim. Caution should be exercised, however, in order to comply strictly with statutes that protect the debtor's due process rights.

a. Prejudgment Garnishment. **Garnishment** is the taking of the debtor's property, in the control of a third party, to satisfy the debtor's obligation to the creditor. Property garnished is usually in the form of bank accounts or wages of the debtor. A creditor may have to post a bond when garnishment proceedings are initiated. Garnishment of wages is not allowed in all states. A creditor may be liable to a debtor if the debtor prevails on a claim of wrongful garnishment.

b. Attachment. **Attachment** is the process of taking another person's property as the result of a judicial order. The sheriff is sent out to seize the property. The property is then sold at a public sale. Attachment can be used to secure any judgment that may be rendered in the future against the debtor. Attachment proceedings are governed by state statute and vary from state to state. Federal courts follow the applicable state statute.

Attachment is not always available and can only be used in certain situations listed in the statutes. Attachment can generally be used when the creditor cannot reach the debtor because he or she cannot be found or is residing in another state; when the creditor can claim fraud or other extenuating circumstances; or when the debtor is preparing to conceal or assign the property to defraud the creditor. Most statutes require that a bond be posted in the event the creditor does not prevail against the debtor. Some statutes also require notice and a hearing be given the debtor before property is seized.

To obtain an attachment, the creditor usually has to file a complaint. After the complaint is filed, the creditor must file an affidavit, bond, and writ of attachment. If an order of attachment is obtained, it is given to the county sheriff who will seize the property.

Attachment has several advantages. It keeps the debtor from transferring or disposing of the property. If the debtor is in default to other creditors, the attachment serves as a priority lien over the other creditors. Attachment gives the creditor an advantage over the debtor. Seizure of the debtor's property may result in the debtor paying off the obligation.

Attachment has disadvantages as well. It can be expensive. A bond is required and fees must be paid to the attorney and the sheriff. If a creditor does not obtain judgment against the debtor, the creditor is liable to the debtor for any damages the debtor incurs as a result of the loss of property. If a debtor files for bankruptcy within 90 days of the attachment, the attachment is invalid. A debtor may post a bond that results in termination of the attachment.

c. Receivership. A **receivership** is an equitable remedy whereby a receiver is appointed to protect the debtor's assets and to satisfy the claims of creditors. Receivership is usually a postjudgment remedy and therefore is only a last resort in prejudgment situations. All other remedies must be exhausted before receivership is allowed. The powers of the receiver are given by the court or by statute. The receiver has possession of the debtor's property but does not have title. In a prejudgment receivership, a receiver does little more than hold the property pending outcome of the judgment. Receivership does not give a creditor any advantage over other creditors; any existing liens on the property are still valid.

d. UCC § 2–702. Section 2–702 of the Uniform Commercial Code allows an additional remedy to a creditor holding an unsecured claim who is a seller of goods. A seller of goods to an insolvent buyer may refuse to deliver goods unless paid in cash and may also stop delivery of goods that have already been shipped. If the insolvent buyer has already received the goods, the seller can reclaim the goods on demand if demand is made within 10 days of receipt. The 10-day limit does not apply if the seller was led to believe the buyer was solvent by a written statement to that effect made by the buyer within three months previous to delivery.

A creditor holding a secured claim has all the remedies available to a creditor holding an unsecured claim, plus some additional remedies: replevin, self-help repossession, disposition of the collateral, and retention of the collateral.

e. Replevin. **Replevin** is an action similar to attachment but is limited to personal property to which the creditor has title or a lien. In an action of replevin, the sheriff seizes the applicable piece of property and gives it to the creditor until title to the property is decided. The debtor may countermand this action with a delivery bond.

f. Self-Help Repossession. **Self-help repossession** is governed by UCC § 9–609, which allows the creditor to take possession of collateral upon default of the debtor. A limitation on self-help repossession is that it cannot be done if it will breach the peace. This is a problem area because the UCC does not define what constitutes a breach of the peace.

The creditor can either sell or retain the repossessed collateral. When repossessing collateral, the creditor must be careful to take only the property that is collateral, must avoid any damage to the property, and should have a witness to the repossession in case problems arise later.

One of the immediate problems a creditor faces is the administration of repossessed collateral. Repossession often is a last resort because lending institutions do not really want to own oil wells or fleets of automobiles and trucks. Mobile home dealers do not want to own lots filled with used mobile homes. The lender may be frustrated by repossession because he or she may not want to take collateral back.

One solution for the creditor is to write off bad debts and take a corresponding loss on taxes. Internal Revenue Code § 166 allows a bad debt to be written off when it is uncollectible. The loan then changes from an asset to an expense on the balance sheet, which lowers the year-to-date earnings of the creditor.

g. Disposition of Collateral. A creditor who decides to dispose of collateral of which he or she has obtained possession is governed by UCC § 9–610(a). Section 9–610(b) allows a creditor to sell the collateral at a public or private sale provided notice of the sale is given to the debtor. Notice must be given within a reasonable time so that the debtor has time to remedy the situation or participate in the sale. Sale of collateral has the effect of discharging the security interest or lien of the creditor.

h. Retention of Collateral. UCC § 9–620(a) authorizes a creditor to keep the collateral and, by doing so, to discharge the debt. Retention usually occurs when the value of the collateral is greater than the debt or when it may be difficult to sell the collateral. Written notice must be provided by the creditor to the debtor that the creditor intends to keep the collateral and that the debtor's obligation is discharged. Other requirements apply to whether the collateral involves consumer goods and whether the debtor has paid a certain percentage of the obligation.

i. Cognovit Judgment. One other prejudgment creditor remedy that deserves mention is the cognovit judgment (judgment by confession). In a **cognovit judgment,** the debtor and the creditor agree at the time the debtor-creditor relationship is created that if the debtor defaults, the creditor can obtain a judgment without any notice to the debtor or a hearing. Upon default, the creditor's attorney makes a court appearance to confess judgment against the debtor for any unpaid obligation and for fees and charges. Because the debtor has probably not received service of process, the debtor will not be prepared to contest the creditor's confession of judgment.

Although the cognovit judgment has survived (although not unscathed) constitutional attack, most states have either eliminated the cognovit judgment or have severely restricted its application. See *D.H. Overmyer Co. v. Frick Co.,* 405 U.S. 174 (1972); *Swarb v. Lennox,* 405 U.S. 191 (1972).

PROBLEM 4.38 Check the current status of the cognovit judgment (judgment by confession) in your state. Check both statute and case law.

j. Judgment Lien. A judgment lien is a statutory measure providing that a judgment entered against a debtor becomes a lien on the debtor's property. A judgment lien is general. It does not relate to a specific piece of property but to all the property of the debtor, including any property obtained after the judgment lien is created. The judgment lien does not solve all the creditor's problems. It merely gives the creditor the right to levy on the debtor's property. Most states have a statute of limitations on judgment liens that dissolves the lien if the creditor does not act within a specified time.

k. Execution Lien. **Execution liens** are regulated by statute and provide for a writ of execution, which allows the creditor to seize the debtor's property and have it sold to satisfy the creditor's judgment against the debtor. An execution lien can usually be applied to both real and personal property. The writ of execution is carried out by the county sheriff rather than by the creditor. Problems with writs of execution are the possibility of liability for improper seizure and the possibility that the debtor's property was purchased by a third party before seizure but after the writ of execution was given. Execution liens are subject to a statute of limitations.

l. Execution Sale. An **execution sale** is the actual sale of the debtor's property to satisfy the creditor's lien or judgment. Proceeds from an execution sale go to satisfy the creditor first. Anything left over goes to the debtor. Execution sales are governed by statute and differ from a judicial sale in that they do not deal with specific property. Any property of the debtor can be sold under an execution sale.

m. Creditor's Bill. A **creditor's bill** is an equitable remedy allowing for a lien to be instituted against nonexempt property that is alienable or assignable under state law. A creditor's bill can be used as a bankruptcy alternative allowing all the debtor's creditors to join together. If a creditor's bill is for the benefit of only one creditor, then that creditor has priority over others. A creditor's bill allows for court discovery of a debtor's property. After discovery an injunction is issued against the debtor to prevent transfer of the property, and a receiver may also be appointed. Since the creditor's bill is an equitable remedy, it cannot be used if a legal remedy is available.

n. Supplementary Proceedings. Supplementary proceedings are proceedings supplementary to execution. They are used as a discovery mechanism for the debtor's property in the event an execution has not been satisfied. Supplementary proceedings are similar to a creditor's bill because they provide for discovery, injunction, receivership, and sale of property. Supplementary proceedings are not available when a third party has an interest in the debtor's property.

o. Postjudgment Garnishment. Postjudgment garnishment is similar to prejudgment garnishment, which was discussed earlier.

p. Fraudulent Conveyance. A fraudulent conveyance is one in which a debtor transfers his or her interest in property to friends or relatives to avoid the creditor's claims but still uses the property. Under the Uniform Fraudulent Conveyances Act, a creditor can recover property if he or she can prove it was fraudulently conveyed.

q. Consensual Lien. A **consensual lien** is an agreement entered into by the creditor and the debtor that gives the creditor a lien on specific property of the debtor, such as a car or a house. A consensual lien conveys added rights to a creditor, including foreclosure and priority over other creditors. Consensual liens in personal property and fixtures are governed by Article 9 of the Uniform Commercial Code. Consensual liens in real property, known as real estate mortgages, are governed by the real property laws of the state. A real estate mortgage can also include an interest in fixtures.

r. Equitable Lien. An **equitable lien** is given when a consensual lien was intended but never created or when failure to give the lien would result in unjust enrichment. Under an equitable lien, the property of the debtor can be sold to satisfy the creditor's claim.

In addition to the remedies just listed, state and federal statutes have instituted a number of other liens that may provide a benefit to a debtor or a creditor. Examples of these liens are materialmen's and mechanic's liens, tax liens, employee's liens, and landlord's liens.

3. Involuntary Bankruptcy Choices

The filing of an involuntary petition should be carefully considered as a last resort for the creditor seeking a solution to problems with a debtor engaged in business. An involuntary bankruptcy is an extraordinary action. It is extraordinary because it affects the race to the courthouse. As a general rule, the first to the courthouse is the first to get paid. The only time an involuntary bankruptcy makes sense is if the creditor feels the debtor is dishonest and the only way to get paid anything would be to put the debtor under the jurisdiction of the bankruptcy court. The debtor loses access to the estate because of the independent trustee. The creditor must feel that the bankruptcy court can better deal with a dishonest debtor than can the state courts.

There are limitations regarding which debtors may be filed against.

> (a) An involuntary case may be commenced only under chapter 7 or 11 of this title, and only against a person, except a farmer, family farmer, or a corporation that is not a moneyed business, or commercial corporation, that may be a debtor under the chapter under which such case is commenced. 11 U.S.C.A. § 303(a).

In addition to the limitation on the types of debtors who may be filed against, there can be substantial penalties for the creditor if the involuntary case is dismissed.

> (i) If the court dismisses a petition under this section other than on consent of all petitioners and the debtor, and if the debtor does not waive the right to judgment under this subsection, the court may grant judgment—
> (1) against the petitioners and in favor of the debtor for—
> (A) costs; or
> (B) a reasonable attorney's fee; or
> (2) against any petitioner that filed the petition in bad faith, for—
> (A) any damages proximately caused by such filing; or
> (B) punitive damages. 11 U.S.C.A. § 303(i).

Even though the debtor may file a voluntary petition in bankruptcy if he or she knows the creditor is considering filing an involuntary petition, the creditor must be careful not to threaten the debtor. This could prove costly to the creditor, especially if the involuntary petition is dismissed.

Except for the gap between the filing date and the order for relief, an involuntary case will proceed in the same manner as a voluntary case. The involuntary filing creates an estate and invokes the automatic stay. This protects the creditor not only by preventing the debtor from disposing of the assets but also by preventing other creditors from seizing the assets. It also protects the debtor by keeping the creditors at arm's length.

Only about 1 percent of all bankruptcies filed are involuntary cases. For this reason, the coverage of involuntary cases will not be extensive in this text.

a. Involuntary Chapter 7—Liquidation. The involuntary Chapter 7 is filed against the debtor who appears to the petitioning creditors to have no prospect for reorganization. The creditors in this type of case just want to see the debtor liquidated before all assets are dissipated. This may be their only hope of collecting anything on what is owed them.

b. Involuntary Chapter 11—Reorganization. Creditors usually file an involuntary Chapter 11 petition against a debtor when they have evidence of either dishonesty or incompetence in the operation of the debtor's business. By filing an involuntary Chapter 11 reorganization petition, the creditors may be able to maintain the debtor's assets in a more valuable state for creditors. Property may be deteriorating or disappearing through seizure by other creditors, or the debtor may be concealing or transferring property to avoid paying creditors. In this type of situation, the petitioning creditors should move to have a trustee appointed. The incompetent or dishonest debtor should not remain in control of the assets to the extent allowed the debtor in possession under a Chapter 11.

E. COUNSELING

A second meeting may be necessary in some cases. At this session, the attorney will counsel the creditor-client and draft the necessary documents.

1. Counseling the Creditor-Client

If a second meeting is necessary, the attorney will review the information received from the creditor-client, discuss the available alternatives, make a recommendation concerning how to proceed to protect the creditor's interests, and gain the assent of the creditor to proceed.

The attorney and the paralegal should keep creditor-clients fully informed at each step of the process. Creditor-clients should be allowed to participate to the extent that they are able and want to participate. Their direct participation at hearings, depositions, meetings, and conferences should be encouraged. The attorney and the paralegal should get direct and, at times, written approval from the client before taking any substantial steps. This permits the client to consent to or disagree with the strategy suggested by the attorney at each juncture of the process. Creditor-clients will often be knowledgeable about the bankruptcy process and have their own thoughts on how the attorney should proceed. If several choices exist, the creditor-client should be consulted and his or her consent should be secured.

The creditor-client can be an excellent resource in matters such as obtaining an expert witness and should be utilized by the attorney and the paralegal.

If necessary, fee arrangements should be finalized and the contract for services should be signed at the second meeting.

2. Drafting Bankruptcy Forms

The creditor's attorney should send the creditor a copy of everything that is filed as soon as it is filed. This apprises the creditor of what the attorney is doing. The attorney does not need to tell the creditor what was filed, the creditor can read the documents. Sending the creditor copies of the filed documents helps the attorney get paid because the creditor can see the quality of the attorney's work and will not object to paying the attorney's fee. The drafting of the necessary forms in a Chapter 7 case will be discussed in Chapter Five of this text.

SECTION 3
THE DEBTOR-CLIENT IN AN INVOLUNTARY BANKRUPTCY

Representing the debtor-client in an involuntary bankruptcy can be very much the same as representing the debtor in a voluntary bankruptcy if the debtor decides not to defend against the insolvency filing. The involuntary petition will result in either the issuance of an order for relief or a dismissal. If an order for relief is entered, the attorney and the paralegal will proceed with the preparation of the necessary forms. If, however, the debtor decides to defend against the involuntary filing, the work of the attorney and the paralegal will be substantially different.

A. INFORMATION GATHERING

In the initial interview with the debtor-client against whom an involuntary bankruptcy petition has been filed, the attorney and the paralegal will attempt to obtain as much pertinent information as possible. The attorney may also explain the options available to the debtor. What the debtor needs to do may be obvious at this point, or the course of action may require further analysis by the attorney.

There should always be a discussion of fees at the first interview. Involuntary cases will probably be handled on an hourly fee basis, unless the debtor concedes to the involuntary filing. If the case has been filed in Chapter 7 and remains in Chapter 7 or is converted to Chapter 13, the attorney often charges a standard fee for these bankruptcy chapters. A written contract should be prepared setting forth the fee agreement.

B. ANALYSIS

The attorney representing the debtor-client in an involuntary bankruptcy will have three basic options to consider:

1. the debtor may concede the petition and allow the order for relief to go forward;
2. the debtor may concede the petition and allow the order for relief to be entered but convert to another chapter; or
3. the debtor may assert the various defenses available.

An involuntary filing will generally involve a business debtor. The filing will be Chapter 7 or Chapter 11. If the filing began as a Chapter 11, the debtor will be more likely to concede and remain in that chapter. A Chapter 11 reorganization is no longer considered a fatal blow to a business by many in the business community. It is being used routinely and voluntarily by many corporations.

Many times creditors will file an involuntary case as a Chapter 7 because they have no confidence in the debtor's ability to reorganize. Some debtors who realize they have little hope of reorganization will concede and remain in the Chapter 7. An individual debtor engaged in a small business can either convert to Chapter 13 to avoid the cumbersome procedures of the traditional Chapter 11 or utilize the fast track procedures established by the new small business Chapter 11.

The debtor who is totally opposed to bankruptcy in any form or who believes the involuntary filing is unwarranted may choose to defend. The debtor's first line of defense is to ask the bankruptcy court to abstain from exercising jurisdiction. 11 U.S.C.A. § 305. The debtor may assert that the court lacks jurisdiction or venue. If that does not work, the debtor can attack the merits of the petition, asserting that debts are being paid or that no custodian has been appointed. The debtor may question the claims of the petitioning creditors. Perhaps the amount owed is not as much as is required by the Code or some of the claims are contingent. 11 U.S.C.A. § 303(b). The debtor may attempt to get an indemnity bond furnished by the petitioning creditors before the case is allowed to go forward. The purpose of such a bond would be to protect the debtor against losses that might be incurred because of the involuntary filing.

C. COUNSELING

During the counseling session, the attorney will explain fully the options available to the debtor, make a recommendation on which option will best preserve the debtor's assets, and gain the assent of the debtor to proceed. If more information was needed following the initial interview, the paralegal will have obtained it.

If the contract for fees was not signed at the first interview, it should be handled at this time.

KEY TERMS

assignments for the benefit of creditors
attachment
cognovit judgment
composition
consensual lien
consolidation loan
credit counseling
creditor's bill
equitable lien
execution lien
execution sale
family farmer with regular annual income
garnishment
limited partnership
receivership
replevin
self-help repossession

CHAPTER 5

The Voluntary Chapter 7 Bankruptcy (Liquidation)

CHAPTER OUTLINE

SECTION 1
THE INITIATION OF A CHAPTER 7 CASE

SECTION 2
THE FILING OF THE PETITION

A. The Debtor's Petition (Official Form No. 1)
B. The Filing Fee
C. The Clerk's Notice
D. Corporate Resolution Authorizing Filing of Chapter 7
E. Disclosure of Attorney's Compensation Statement
F. The List of Creditors
G. Schedules (Official Form No. 6)
H. Statement of Financial Affairs
I. Statement of Intention If the Debtor Is an Individual with Consumer Debts
J. Debtor's Duty to Supplement the Schedules
K. Debtor's Right to Amend the Petition, Lists, Schedules, and Statements

SECTION 3
THE SIGNIFICANCE OF FILING A PETITION

A. The Order for Relief
B. The Estate Is Created
C. Exemptions
D. The Automatic Stay

SECTION 4
THE APPOINTMENT AND POWERS OF AN INTERIM TRUSTEE

A. Abandon Property of the Estate
B. Assume or Reject Executory Contracts
C. Avoiding Transfers

SECTION 5
PROOFS OF CLAIM AND PROOFS OF INTEREST

A. Creditors' and Indenture Trustees' Proofs of Claim
B. Equity Security Holders' Proofs of Interest

SECTION 6
MOTIONS AND COMPLAINTS AFTER THE ORDER FOR RELIEF

A. Motions
B. Complaints

SECTION 7
ORDER AND NOTICE OF CHAPTER 7 BANKRUPTCY FILING, MEETING OF CREDITORS, AND FIXING OF DATES

SECTION 8
OBJECTIONS BY A PARTY IN INTEREST TO DEBTOR'S CLAIM OF EXEMPTIONS

SECTION 9
MEETING OF CREDITORS (THE SECTION 341 MEETING) AND MEETING OF EQUITY SECURITY HOLDERS
A. The Meeting of Creditors
B. The Meeting of Equity Security Holders

SECTION 10
REDEMPTION, DISCHARGE AND REAFFIRMATION
A. Redemption
B. Discharge and Reaffirmation
C. Revocation of Discharge

SECTION 11
DISTRIBUTION OF THE PROPERTY OF THE ESTATE
A. Priority Claims
B. Nonpriority Claims

SECTION 12
CLOSING THE CASE
A. Trustee's Final Report and Proposed Distribution
B. Trustee's Final Account after Distribution and Request for Discharge
C. Closing the Case

SECTION 13
AFTER THE CASE IS CLOSED
A. Amending the Case without Reopening the Case
B. Reopening a Closed Case

This chapter is devoted exclusively to voluntary Chapter 7 bankruptcy, commonly known as **liquidation.** A Chapter 7 case is developed in chronological order, beginning when a potential client approaches the law office for advice and continuing to the closing of the case. Therefore, this chapter includes

- the initiation of the attorney/client relationship;
- the filing of the Chapter 7 petition, the clerk's notice, the disclosure of attorney's compensation statement, the list of creditors, the schedules, the statement of financial affairs, and the individual debtor's statement of intention;
- the significance of the filing;
  - the order for relief
  - the creation of the estate and what the estate encompasses
  - the automatic stay that protects the estate from dismemberment while the estate is being administered by the trustee and the debtor from collection procedures pending the entry of the discharge
- the appointment of the trustee, including the interim trustee, and the power of the trustee to abandon property of the estate, to assume or reject executory contracts and unexpired leases, to avoid certain transfers of property of the estate as voidable preferences, fraudulent transfers, or postpetition transfers, and to avoid unperfected security interests;
- proofs of claim and proofs of interest;
- the difference between contested matters and adversary proceedings and the motions and complaints used for each;
- the bankruptcy court's order and the clerk's notice to the trustee, all creditors, indenture trustees, and the U.S. trustee of the bankruptcy filing, the meeting of creditors, and the various important dates in the case;

- the creditors' meeting, commonly known as the "341 meeting";
- the discharge hearing and discharge if the debtor is an individual (partnerships and corporations are not discharged from their debts under Chapter 7);
- the distribution and liquidation of property of the estate, if property of the estate exists;
- the trustee's final account;
- approval of the trustee's final account by the U.S. trustee;
- discharge of the trustee;
- the closing of the case;
- further action on the case after it is closed.

For those readers who like information presented in chart form, a flow chart for the Chapter 7 bankruptcy case follows. Exhibit 5–1 provides a quick overview of the textual material. It is also useful as a checklist for taking a Chapter 7 case through the bankruptcy court from filing through closing and beyond closing, if that should ever become necessary. As readers progress through this chapter, periodic reference to this flow chart may be helpful.

SECTION 1
THE INITIATION OF A CHAPTER 7 CASE

As was set forth in Chapter 4 of this text, all attorneys have their own way of allocating responsibility to their paralegals and for dealing with debtor-clients. Some attorneys effectively use their paralegals by significantly involving them in the process. For example, an attorney may employ the following procedure:

- After the debtor has initiated contact with the attorney's firm, the paralegal sets up the client file, acquires a list of the debtor's creditors, and initiates a conflict of interest check.
- The paralegal gives the debtor a questionnaire (worksheets) that will help the debtor itemize his or her assets and liabilities as well as monthly income and monthly expenses.
- The paralegal requires the debtor to provide copies of relevant documents such as real estate deeds and mortgages, loan agreements, security agreements, vehicle titles, and tax returns.
- The debtor completes the questionnaire and returns it to the paralegal along with the documents requested by the paralegal.
- The paralegal meets with the debtor and reviews the questionnaire to insure that it is completed fully and accurately and to identify any emergencies that may require the attorney's immediate attention.
- The attorney and paralegal meet with the debtor, and the attorney discusses the questionnaire adding, deleting, modifying, and verifying the debtor's entries.
- The attorney advises the debtor whether bankruptcy is the appropriate course of action and, if so, whether the case should be filed under Chapter 7, Chapter 11, Chapter 12, or Chapter 13. The attorney explains the bankruptcy process to the debtor and discusses attorney fees and other aspects of the attorney/client contract for services.
- The paralegal, under the attorney's supervision, completes the petition, the list of creditors, the disclosure of attorney's compensation statement, the schedules, and the statement of financial affairs.
- The attorney and paralegal meet with the debtor so the debtor can review and sign the documents.

EXHIBIT 5–1 Flow Chart for Chapter 7

Filing the Voluntary Chapter 7 Petition

The debtor files with the bankruptcy court clerk's office:
1. Filing fee
2. Voluntary petition, including Exhibit B, if the debtor is an individual whose debts are primarily consumer debts, and Exhibit C, if debtor has some connection to hazardous waste
3. Clerk's notice (if an individual consumer debtor), if required by the court
4. Corporate resolution authorizing the filing of the Chapter 7 petition (if the debtor is a corporation)
5. Disclosure of attorney's compensation statement or disclosure of compensation statement by a non-attorney bankruptcy petition preparer
6. List of creditors
7. Schedules
    a. Summary of schedules
    b. Schedule A. Real property
    c. Schedule B. Personal property
    d. Schedule C. Property claimed as exempt
    e. Schedule D. Creditors holding secured claims
    f. Schedule E. Creditors holding unsecured priority claims
    g. Schedule F. Creditors holding unsecured nonpriority claims
    h. Schedule G. Executory contracts and unexpired leases
    i. Schedule H. Codebtors
    j. Schedule I. Current income of individual debtor(s)
    k. Schedule J. Current expenditures of individual debtor(s)
    l. Schedule of income and expenditures of a partnership or a corporation
8. Statement of financial affairs

If the petition is accompanied by the list of creditors, the debtor has up to 15 days to file items 7 and 8

9. An individual debtor with consumer debts is secured by property of the estate must file a statement of intention within 30 days after the filing of the petition or by the date of the meetings of creditors, whichever is earlier

Upon filing of the voluntary petition, which constitutes an order for relief, an estate is created and the automatic stay goes into effect, protecting the estate from dismemberment and the debtor from collection procedures

---

The U.S. trustee appoints an interim trustee

The clerk of the bankruptcy court mails to the debtor, the debtor's attorney, the trustee, all creditors, indenture trustees, and the U.S. trustee:
1. notice of the filing of the Chapter 7 bankruptcy case
2. an explanation of the automatic stay
3. the date, time, and place of the meeting of creditors
4. the dealines for filing objections to the discharge of the debtor or the dischargeability of a debt
5. the time fixed for filing proofs of claims or the fact that insufficient assets presently exist to pay claims, and
6. the time for filing objections to the debtor's claim of exemptions

---

An eligible debtor may convert the case to Chapter 11, 12, or 13

The debtor may move:
1. to dismiss the case
2. for a change of venue

(continued)

EXHIBIT 5–1 Filing the Voluntary Chapter 7 Petition, Continued

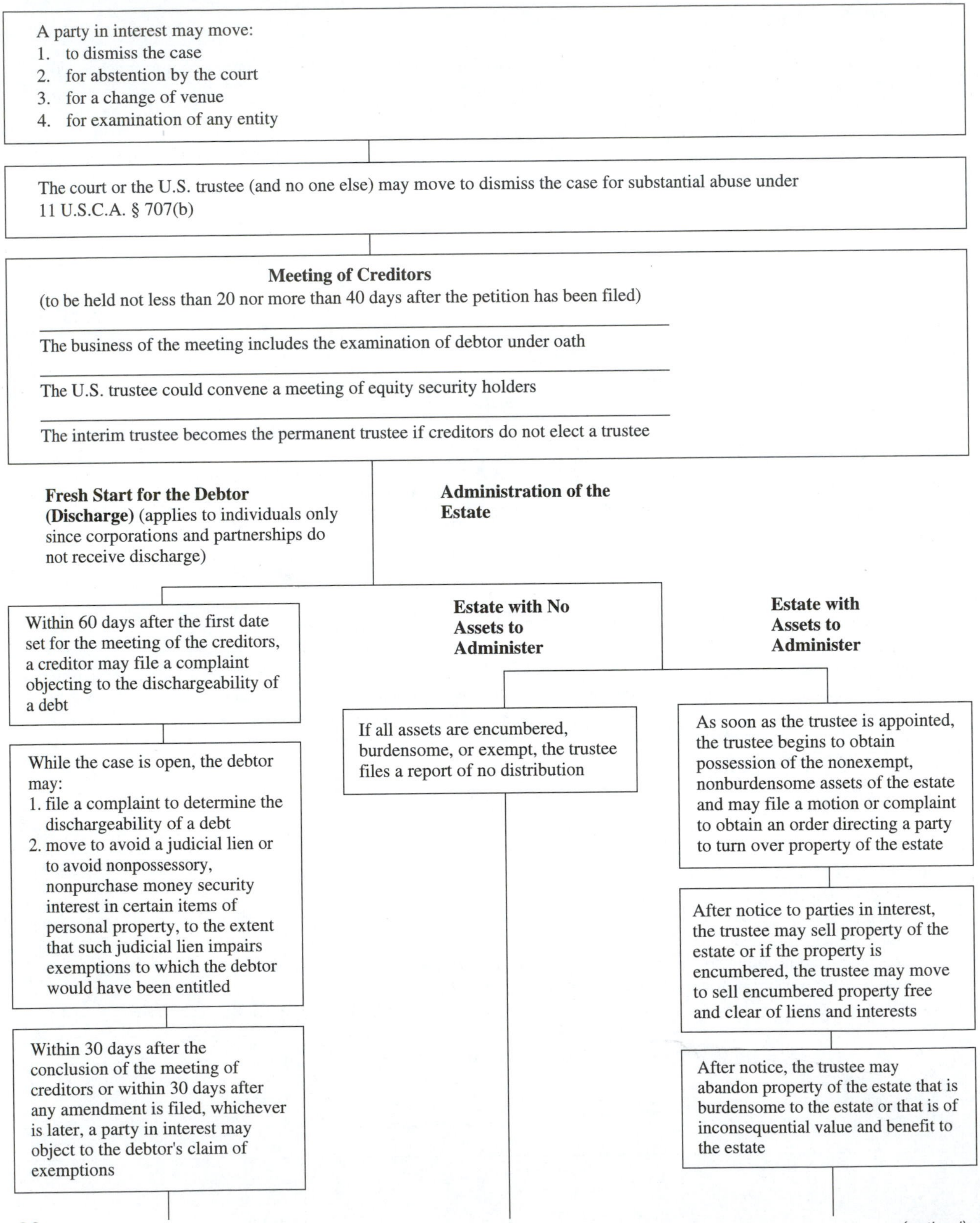

A party in interest may move:
1. to dismiss the case
2. for abstention by the court
3. for a change of venue
4. for examination of any entity

The court or the U.S. trustee (and no one else) may move to dismiss the case for substantial abuse under 11 U.S.C.A. § 707(b)

Meeting of Creditors
(to be held not less than 20 nor more than 40 days after the petition has been filed)

The business of the meeting includes the examination of debtor under oath

The U.S. trustee could convene a meeting of equity security holders

The interim trustee becomes the permanent trustee if creditors do not elect a trustee

Fresh Start for the Debtor (Discharge) (applies to individuals only since corporations and partnerships do not receive discharge)

Within 60 days after the first date set for the meeting of the creditors, a creditor may file a complaint objecting to the dischargeability of a debt

While the case is open, the debtor may:
1. file a complaint to determine the dischargeability of a debt
2. move to avoid a judicial lien or to avoid nonpossessory, nonpurchase money security interest in certain items of personal property, to the extent that such judicial lien impairs exemptions to which the debtor would have been entitled

Within 30 days after the conclusion of the meeting of creditors or within 30 days after any amendment is filed, whichever is later, a party in interest may object to the debtor's claim of exemptions

Administration of the Estate

Estate with No Assets to Administer

If all assets are encumbered, burdensome, or exempt, the trustee files a report of no distribution

Estate with Assets to Administer

As soon as the trustee is appointed, the trustee begins to obtain possession of the nonexempt, nonburdensome assets of the estate and may file a motion or complaint to obtain an order directing a party to turn over property of the estate

After notice to parties in interest, the trustee may sell property of the estate or if the property is encumbered, the trustee may move to sell encumbered property free and clear of liens and interests

After notice, the trustee may abandon property of the estate that is burdensome to the estate or that is of inconsequential value and benefit to the estate

(continued)

EXHIBIT 5–1 Filing the Voluntary Chapter 7 Petition, Continued

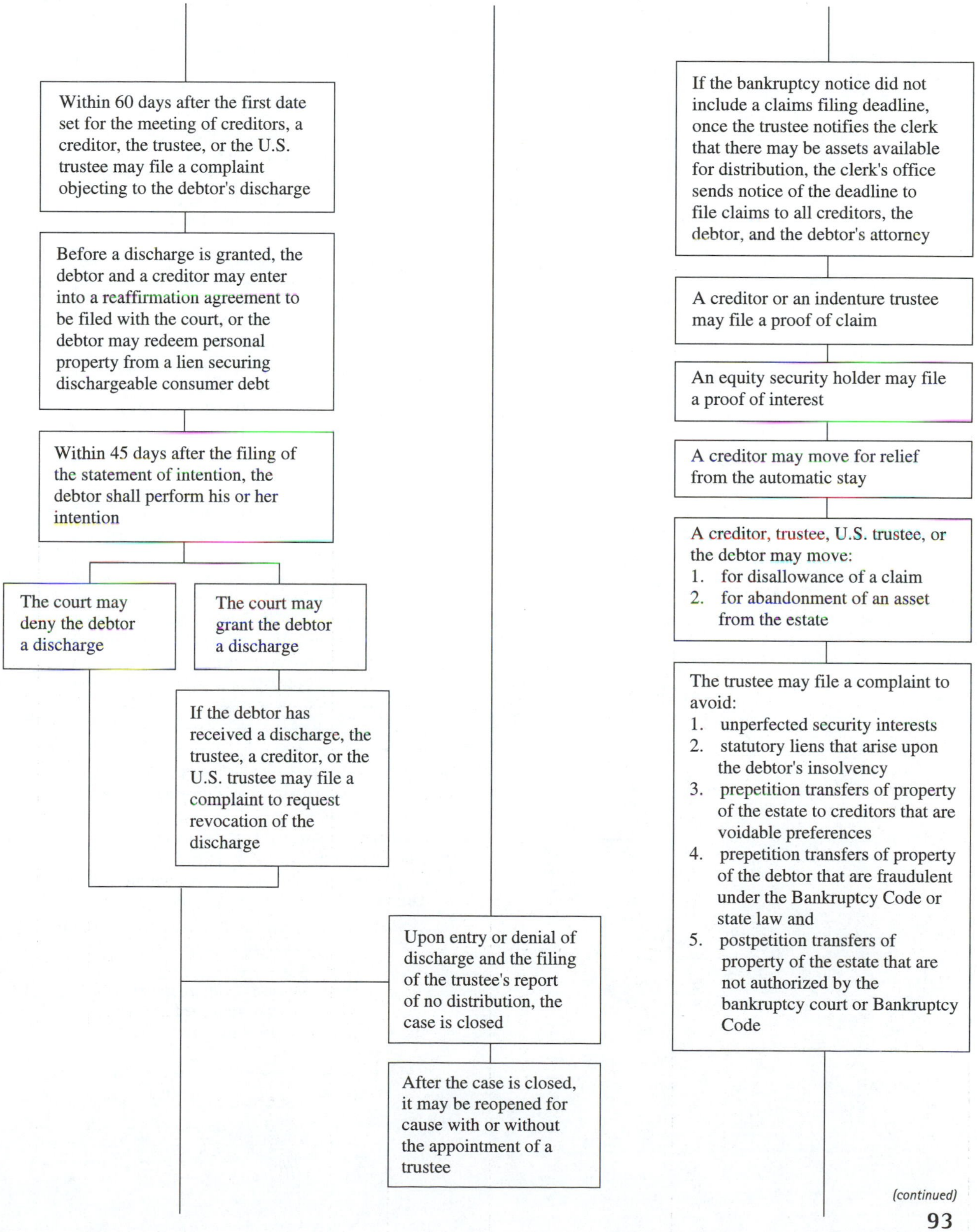

Within 60 days after the first date set for the meeting of creditors, a creditor, the trustee, or the U.S. trustee may file a complaint objecting to the debtor's discharge

Before a discharge is granted, the debtor and a creditor may enter into a reaffirmation agreement to be filed with the court, or the debtor may redeem personal property from a lien securing dischargeable consumer debt

Within 45 days after the filing of the statement of intention, the debtor shall perform his or her intention

The court may deny the debtor a discharge

The court may grant the debtor a discharge

If the debtor has received a discharge, the trustee, a creditor, or the U.S. trustee may file a complaint to request revocation of the discharge

Upon entry or denial of discharge and the filing of the trustee's report of no distribution, the case is closed

After the case is closed, it may be reopened for cause with or without the appointment of a trustee

If the bankruptcy notice did not include a claims filing deadline, once the trustee notifies the clerk that there may be assets available for distribution, the clerk's office sends notice of the deadline to file claims to all creditors, the debtor, and the debtor's attorney

A creditor or an indenture trustee may file a proof of claim

An equity security holder may file a proof of interest

A creditor may move for relief from the automatic stay

A creditor, trustee, U.S. trustee, or the debtor may move:
1. for disallowance of a claim
2. for abandonment of an asset from the estate

The trustee may file a complaint to avoid:
1. unperfected security interests
2. statutory liens that arise upon the debtor's insolvency
3. prepetition transfers of property of the estate to creditors that are voidable preferences
4. prepetition transfers of property of the debtor that are fraudulent under the Bankruptcy Code or state law and
5. postpetition transfers of property of the estate that are not authorized by the bankruptcy court or Bankruptcy Code

(continued)

EXHIBIT 5–1 Filing the Voluntary Chapter 7 Petition, Continued

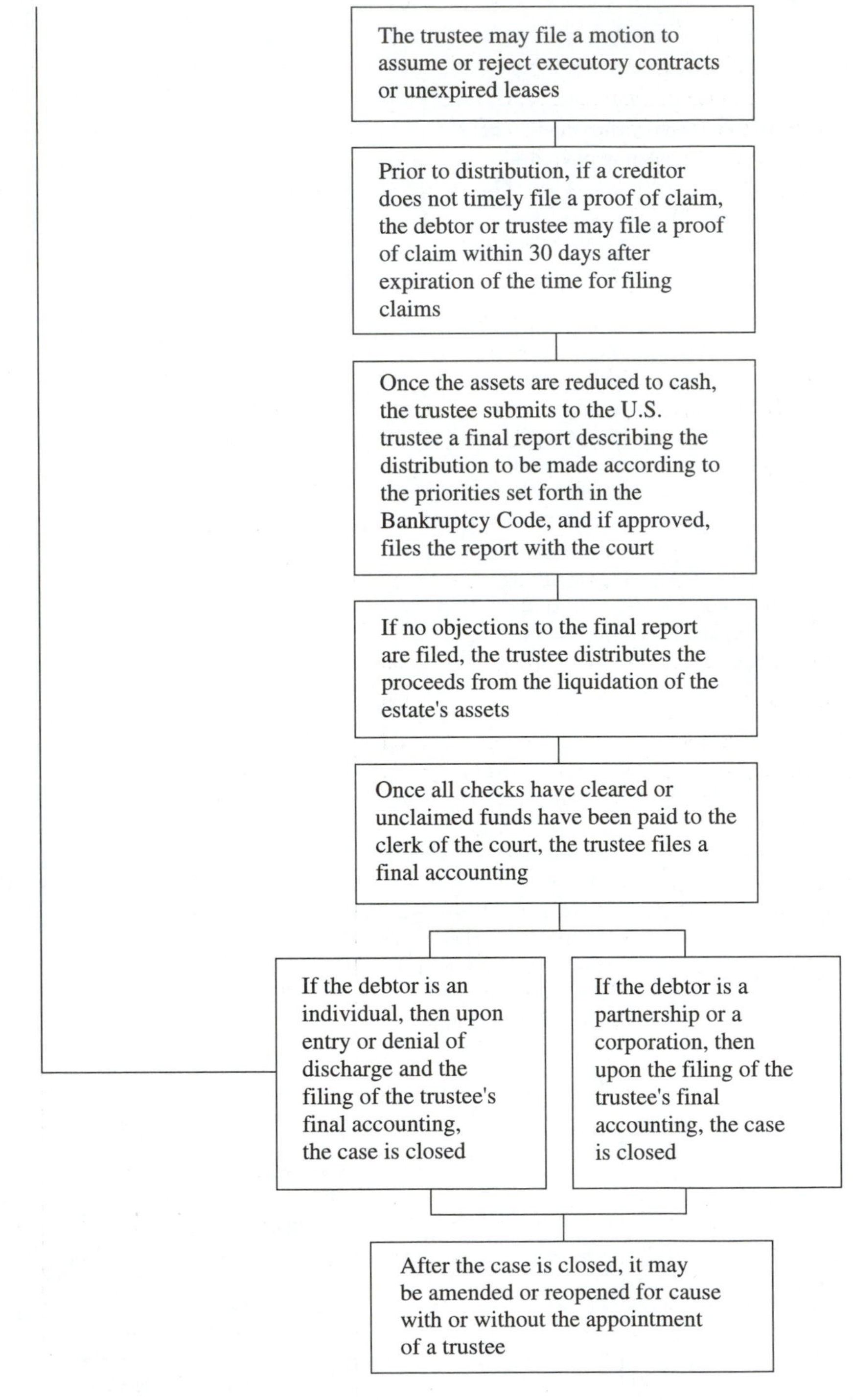

- The paralegal then files the petition and accompanying list of creditors, disclosure of attorney's compensation statement, schedules, and statement of financial affairs in the office of the clerk of the bankruptcy court.

To illustrate a Chapter 7 bankruptcy, the text will follow Jennifer and Eric McPherson, the husband and wife who appeared in Problem 4.5 in Chapter 4 of this text. In that problem, the McPhersons contacted a law office and spoke with the paralegal who worked under the supervision of the bankruptcy attorney. After obtaining general information about the McPhersons, the paralegal asked the McPhersons to submit a list of their creditors so the firm could initiate a conflict of interest check and decide whether the firm could take the case. The paralegal informed the McPhersons that once the conflicts check had been completed, and if the firm had no conflict, the McPhersons would be required to complete a questionnaire concerning their assets and liabilities. The paralegal described the procedure that the office would follow in preparing for the McPhersons' bankruptcy filing, if a filing were to occur.

The McPhersons delivered the list of their creditors to the firm and the paralegal conducted a conflict of interest check. Finding no conflicts, the paralegal sent the McPhersons the questionnaire, which they completed and returned.

The following information summarizes the McPhersons' completed questionnaire.

Assets			
House (equity)	value	=	$30,000
Checking account	value	=	450
Bass boat	value	=	16,000
U.S. Savings Bonds	value	=	3,000
Jennifer's 401(k)	value	=	6,000
Eric's State Teachers' Retirement Plan	value	=	1,250
Cash	value	=	75
Liabilities			
First Mortgage Co.			
(home)	value	=	$90,000
	owe	=	60,000
	payment	=	500 per month
	interest	=	8%
	arrearage	=	1,575
Second Mortgage Co.			
(home)	value	=	$90,000
(household furniture)	value	=	5,000
	owe	=	6,000
	payment	=	125 per month
	interest	=	10%

(continued)

Liabilities			
Auto Finance Co.			
(4-year old	value	=	$8,000
Chevrolet Blazer)	owe	=	12,000
	payment	=	310 per month
	interest	=	14%
Capital Finance Co.			
(6-year-old	value	=	$3,000.00
Buick Regal)	owe	=	7,000.00
	payment	=	170.00 per month
	interest	=	12.0%
Sears			
(washer and dryer)	value	=	$500
	owe	=	850
	payment	=	32 per month
	interest	=	21%
Friendly Finance Co.	owe	=	$1,500
(signature loan,	payment	=	100 per month
father co-signed)	interest	=	15%
Jiffy Plumbing Co.	owe	=	$600
Rockwell Construction	owe	=	$2,500
National Bank VISA®	owe	=	$2,500
	interest		1.5% per month
Discover Card®	owe	=	$25,000
	interest		1.5% per month
American Express®	owe	=	$10,000
	interest		1.5% per month
Thrifty Credit Union	owe	=	$35,000
(educational loan)	payment	=	$400 per month
	interest	=	12%
Internal Revenue Service	owe	=	$8,000
State Tax Commission	owe	=	$3,500
Child support	arrearage	=	$400 (disputed)
Alimony	arrearage	=	$1,000 (disputed)

Income	
Jennifer	
Salary	$24,000 per year
Child support (for Irene)	$500 per month

(continued)

Eric	
Salary (teaching)	$36,000 per year
Salary (football camps)	up to $500 per summer
Expenses	
Jennifer	
Payroll deductions	
FICA, Medicare, Payroll Tax	$500 per month
401(k) (Acme Insurance)	$250 per month
State license (LPN)	$240 per year
Books, journals, continuing education	$300 per year
Expenses	
Eric	
Payroll deductions	
FICA, Medicare, Payroll Taxes	$700 per month
Medical & dental insurance	$150 per month
State teachers' retirement plan	$150 per month
Child support (Bethany)	$400 per month
House Payments (First Mortgage Company)	$500 per month
Eric Jr.'s allowance	$300 per month
Eric Jr.'s tuition	$4,800 per year
Irene's tuition	$1,800 per year
Irene's day care	$65 per week
Irene's day care (additional during summer)	varies
Electricity	$75 per month
Natural gas	$100 per month
Water	$25 per month
Telephone	$50 per month
Food	$1,000 per month
Clothing	$800 per month
Entertainment	$400 per month
Laundry and dry cleaning	$75 per week
Newspaper	$10 per month
Medical bills	$40 per month
Prescriptions	$2 per prescription
Automobile insurance (2 cars)	$400 per quarter
Church pledge (building fund)	$45 per month
Church contributions	$100 per month

(continued)

Expenses	
Safe deposit box	$60 per year
Eastside Mini Storage	$100 per month
Life Insurance (Eric)	$75 per month
Cleaning service	$50 per week
Yard service	$45 per week
Thrifty Credit Union (student loans)	$400 per month
Second Mortgage Company	$125 per month
Auto Finance Company (Blazer)	$310 per month
Capital Finance Company (Regal)	$170 per month
Friendly Finance Company	$100 per month
Sears	$32 per month

This list does not include the IRS ($8,000), the State Tax Commission ($3,500), Jiffy Plumbing Company ($600), Rockwell Construction Company ($2,500), the arrearage for First Mortgage Company ($1,575), National Bank VISA® ($2,500), Discover Card® ($25,000), and American Express® ($10,000), all of which have not been paid.

Our discussion now picks up with the paralegal's meeting with the McPhersons for the purpose of reviewing the completed questionnaire to insure that it has been completed accurately and to identify any emergencies that would require the attorney's immediate attention.

The paralegal notes that the McPhersons have not included any routine repairs to their home. The McPhersons state that they spend an average of $1,200 a year on such repairs and these repairs were not reflected in their answers to the questionnaire.

The paralegal notes that the McPhersons have not included any routine repairs or fuel for their two vehicles. The McPhersons say that they spend an average of $3,000 a year on repairs and fuel and that this was not reflected in their answers to the questionnaire.

The paralegal inquires whether insurance and taxes on the home were included in their monthly mortgage payment and the paralegal is assured that they were.

PROBLEM 5.1 Some of the McPhersons' expenses were given as weekly, monthly, quarterly, or yearly. Convert the McPhersons' list of expenses so they are all on a monthly basis. Add to this list the additional expenses raised by the paralegal. What is the total of the McPhersons' monthly expenses?

The McPhersons now meet with the attorney and the paralegal to discuss their answers to the questionnaire. The attorney verifies the McPhersons' answers, and adds, deletes, and modifies where necessary.

The attorney inquires when the debt to Rockwell Construction Company became due and whether Rockwell has filed a lien against the McPhersons' home. In doing so, the attorney is checking whether the grace period for filing has expired or whether the filing of the lien is still a possibility (which it is).

The McPhersons state that their tax liability came as a shock to them. The attorney asks whether either the IRS or the state tax commission has filed a lien on any of the McPhersons' property. The attorney discovers that neither has filed. The attorney asks whether the McPhersons have tried to work out a payment arrangement with either the IRS or the state tax commission, particularly with the continuing accrual of interest and penalties. The McPhersons explain that they have tried but have been unsuccessful.

The McPhersons explain to the attorney that they are desperate to keep their bass boat because it is the only form of recreation they can afford that the whole family enjoys.

The attorney then discusses the attorney/client contract with the McPhersons. The attorney notes that since all of their assets, other than the savings bonds, bass boat, and checking account, are either exempt or fully encumbered by liens and that they have regular income, bankruptcy would appear to be their best option. The attorney cautions that bankruptcy would not be a panacea for all of the McPhersons financial problems. First, a discharge in bankruptcy would discharge them from their dischargeable debts only, so the government guaranteed student loan, which is a nondischargeable obligation, would remain after their discharge by the bankruptcy court. Also, even after a bankruptcy discharge, their expenses substantially outpace their income and therefore adjustments to their expenses would need to be addressed.

This latter point, income vs. expenses, is relevant if the McPhersons were to file for bankruptcy. They would need to file either under Chapter 7 or Chapter 13 of the United States Bankruptcy Code. The attorney explained that if they filed under Chapter 7, a Chapter 7 trustee would be appointed and the trustee would sell all of the McPhersons' nonexempt property, thus converting the property into money. The trustee would then distribute this money to the McPhersons' creditors.

If the McPhersons were to file under Chapter 13, they would retain all of their assets (exempt and nonexempt), but they would need to reduce their monthly expenses to substantially less than their monthly income. The difference between monthly income and monthly expenses is known in the bankruptcy court as disposable income and would be paid to the Chapter 13 trustee. When filing for Chapter 13 relief, the McPhersons would be required to submit a plan to the court outlining how their various creditors would be paid. The plan could last from 36 months to 60 months. At the end of the plan, they would receive a discharge from those debts that were not paid, with the exception of their nondischargeable government-guaranteed student loan.

The attorney explains to the McPhersons that even if they decide to file for Chapter 7 protection, they must still file a statement of income and a statement of expenses as part of their filing package. The bankruptcy judge will evaluate their statement of expenses to determine whether they could reduce their expenses to the point that the difference between monthly income and monthly expenses would finance a Chapter 13 plan. Therefore, regardless of whether a Chapter 7 petition or a Chapter 13 petition is filed, the same documents will need to be filed for both, with the exception of the Chapter 13 plan. The attorney explains that it will be imperative that they work together to determine what would be reasonable monthly expenses for the McPhersons.

The attorney then informs the McPhersons that they could expect attorney fees, trustee fees, and court costs for filing their Chapter 7 or Chapter 13 bankruptcy. The attorney discusses the difference in fees and costs depending on whether the case is filed as a Chapter 7 or a Chapter 13 and how they would be paid under each type of filing.

PROBLEM 5.2 Based on the facts in Problem 4.5 and the summary of information gathered from the McPhersons' questionnaire, are the McPhersons eligible to file a Chapter 7 petition? See 11 U.S.C.A. § 109(b).

Are they eligible to file a Chapter 13 petition? See 11 U.S.C.A. § 109(e).

The attorney notes that a Chapter 13 filing requires that a Chapter 13 plan be submitted to and confirmed by the court. The Chapter 13 plan term may be as short as three years or, with the court's approval, as long as five years. 11 U.S.C.A. § 1322(d). During the life of the plan, the McPhersons' disposable income will be paid to the Chapter 13 trustee. 11 U.S.C.A. § 1325(b)(1)(B). Therefore, under the plan the McPhersons will be on a strict budget and the difference between their income and their budget will be considered disposable income (11 U.S.C.A. § 1322(b)(2)) and will be distributed by the Chapter 13 trustee to their creditors under the terms of a confirmed plan. As an initial impression, the attorney notes that to be in good faith and to have enough disposable income to fund the plan, the McPhersons will need to cut back spending. For example, they have been spending $1,000 on food a month and this will need to be trimmed to about $600. The $800 a month for clothing will need to be reduced to about $500. The $400 a month on entertainment will need to be reduced to about $150. Contributions to the church may need to be reduced or eliminated, but they can discuss this as the plan develops. Dry cleaning will be reduced from $300 a month to about $35. Eric, Jr. may need to take out student loans or find alternative avenues for financing his education (his allowance will be eliminated) and Irene may need to attend public school rather than the private school she now attends. The attorney also explains that the yard and cleaning services may need to be cancelled for the plan to be confirmed. The McPhersons' failure to make these concessions might prevent their plan from being confirmed due to an absence of good faith and their failure to meet the best interests test. Also the McPhersons' failure to make these concessions might result in a dismissal of their case if they file under a Chapter 7. 11 U.S.C.A. § 707(b). The McPhersons agree to proceed with either a Chapter 7 or Chapter 13 filing and to work with the attorney in structuring a reasonable monthly budget.

After this meeting, the attorney and paralegal devise a monthly budget for the McPhersons.

> **PROBLEM 5.3** Based on the categories listed in Exhibit 5–2, complete a monthly budget for the McPhersons, assuming they receive a discharge under Chapter 7 from their dischargeable debts. Assume their combined monthly income will be $3,750. Reduce their monthly expenses so they will live within their means. What did you reduce and why? Note that taxes, alimony, and support are nondischargeable debts and therefore will remain after their Chapter 7 discharge. Omit from their monthly expenses all payments past due. Make a separate list for payments past due. You may download Exhibit 5–2, the outline for monthly expenses, from the Web site for this text.

After completing the monthly budget, the paralegal, under the attorney's supervision, completes the voluntary Chapter 7 petition, the disclosure of attorney's compensation statement, the list of creditors, the schedules, and the statement of financial affairs.

SECTION 2
THE FILING OF THE PETITION

Once the client has been properly interviewed and the necessary information has been gathered, the preparation of the petition and supporting documents can begin. The preparation for filing must be done carefully, and all documents must be completed in accordance with the Bankruptcy Code, the Federal Rules of Bankruptcy Procedure, and local court rules. Even if the case appears to be a walk-through, it is best not to regard any bankruptcy case as simple or routine. If difficulties with the court, the office of the court clerk, the trustee in bankruptcy assigned to this case, the creditors, and the office of the U.S. trustee are to be avoided, the appropriate forms must be properly completed.

In a voluntary Chapter 7, the debtor must file a number of documents:

1. Filing fee;
2. Voluntary Petition (Official Form No. 1);
3. The clerk's notice if the debtor is an individual consumer debtor and if required by the court;

EXHIBIT 5–2 Monthly Expenses for the McPhersons Assuming They Receive a Discharge under Chapter 7

Rent or home mortgage payment	
(first mortgage)	$________
(second mortgage)	$________
Automobile ________________	$________
Automobile ________________	$________
Household appliances	
(specify) ________________	$________
(specify) ________________	$________
Utilities:	
Electricity and heating fuel	$________
Water and sewer	$________
Telephone	$________
Others ________________	$________
Home maintenance (repairs and upkeep)	$________
Food	$________
Clothing	$________
Laundry and dry cleaning	$________
Medical and dental expenses	$________
Transportation (not including car payments)	$________
Recreation, clubs, entertainment, newspapers, magazines, etc.	$________
Charitable contribution	$________
Insurance (not deducted from wages or included in home mortgage payments)	
Homeowner's or renter's insurance	$________
Life insurance	$________
Health insurance	$________
Automobile insurance	$________
Other insurance ________________	$________
Taxes (taxes owed) if debtor has a monthly payment plan with the taxing authority	
IRS	$________
State	$________
Other (specify) ________________	$________
Taxes (not deducted from wages or included in home mortgage payments)	
(specify) ________________	$________
Alimony, maintenance, and support paid to others	$________
Payments for support of additional dependents not living at your home	$________

(continued)

EXHIBIT 5–2 Monthly Expenses for the McPhersons Assuming They Receive a Discharge under Chapter 7, Continued

Regular expenses from operation of business, profession, or farm	$__________
Loans (secured)	
(specify) ____________________	$__________
(specify) ____________________	$__________
Other expenses	
Safe deposit box	$__________
Professional license	$__________
Professional books, journals	$__________
(specify) ____________________	$__________
(specify) ____________________	$__________
TOTAL MONTHLY EXPENSES	$__________
PAYMENTS PAST DUE	
Alimony ____________________	$__________
Support ____________________	$__________
Home mortgage (arrearage)	$__________
Home repairs	
(specify) ____________________	$__________
(specify) ____________________	$__________
(specify) ____________________	$__________
Credit cards	
(specify) ____________________	$__________
(specify) ____________________	$__________
(specify) ____________________	$__________
(specify) ____________________	$__________
Loans (amount past due)	
(specify) ____________________	$__________
(specify) ____________________	$__________
(specify) ____________________	$__________
(specify) ____________________	$__________
Taxes	
IRS	$__________
State Tax Commission ____________________	$__________
Other taxes ____________________	$__________
Others	
(specify) ____________________	$__________
(specify) ____________________	$__________

4. Corporate resolution authorizing the filing of a Chapter 7 petition (if the debtor is a corporation);
5. Disclosure of attorney's compensation statement or disclosure of compensation statement by a non-attorney bankruptcy petition preparer;
6. List of creditors;
7. Schedules (Official Form No. 6)
   a. Summary of Schedules
   b. Schedule A: Real Property
   c. Schedule B: Personal Property
   d. Schedule C: Property Claimed as Exempt
   e. Schedule D: Creditors Holding Secured Claims
   f. Schedule E: Creditors Holding Unsecured Priority Claims
   g. Schedule F: Creditors Holding Unsecured Nonpriority Claims
   h. Schedule G: Executory Contracts and Unexpired Leases
   i. Schedule H: Codebtors
   j. Schedule I: Current Income of Individual Debtor(s)
   k. Schedule J: Current Expenditures of Individual Debtor(s)
   l. Schedule of Income and Expenditures of a Partnership or a Corporation;
8. Statement of Financial Affairs (Official Form No. 7);
9. Statement of Intention (Official Form No. 8) (if the debtor is an individual debtor with consumer debts).

The official bankruptcy forms may be downloaded from http://www.uscourts.gov > U.S. Bankruptcy Courts > Official Bankruptcy Forms.

Good practice mandates that the petition, list of creditors, schedules, and statements be filed at one time. If, however, the petition is accompanied by the list of all creditors, the debtor has up to 15 days after the date of filing to file the schedules and the statement of financial affairs. Fed. R. Bank. P. 1007(c). If an individual debtor has consumer debts that are secured by property of the estate, the debtor has 30 days after the filing of a petition or until the meeting of creditors, whichever is earlier, or until the time set by the court for cause, which is between the 30 days and the meeting of creditors, to file a statement of his or her intention to redeem or reaffirm debts secured by property of the estate. 11 U.S.C.A. § 521(2)(A). These grace periods should be used only in emergency situations and should not be a common practice.

The documents filed for a Chapter 7 case are filed with the clerk of the bankruptcy court. Fed. R. Bank. P. 1002(a). They are to be printed on one side of the paper only. Commercial bankruptcy filing programs significantly simplify preparation of the necessary documents.

The filing consists of handing the documents and the filing fee to a deputy clerk in the office of the clerk. The deputy clerk places the appropriate stamps on the petition to indicate the court, date, and time of receipt.

A. THE DEBTOR'S PETITION (OFFICIAL FORM NO. 1)

The debtor's petition to commence a voluntary Chapter 7 must substantially conform to Official Form No. 1. Fed. R. Bank. P. 1002(a). This form is found in any printed set of bankruptcy forms and computer bankruptcy filing programs. By filing the voluntary petition, the debtor actually initiates the case. (See Exhibit 5–3.)

EXHIBIT 5–3 Official Form No. 1 (The Debtor's Petition)

(Official Form 1) (12/03)

FORM B1 A **United States Bankruptcy Court**
______________________**District of**______________________

Voluntary Petition

Name of Debtor (if individual, enter Last, First, Middle): B	Name of Joint Debtor (Spouse) (Last, First, Middle): B
All Other Names used by the Debtor in the last 6 years (include married, maiden, and trade names): C	All Other Names used by the Joint Debtor in the last 6 years (include married, maiden, and trade names): C
Last four digits of Soc. Sec. No./Complete EIN or other Tax I.D. No. (if more than one, state all): D	Last four digits of Soc. Sec.No./Complete EIN or other Tax I.D. No. (if more than one, state all): D
Street Address of Debtor (No. & Street, City, State & Zip Code):	Street Address of Joint Debtor (No. & Street, City, State & Zip Code):
County of Residence or of the Principal Place of Business:	County of Residence or of the Principal Place of Business:
Mailing Address of Debtor (if different from street address):	Mailing Address of Joint Debtor (if different from street address):

Location of Principal Assets of Business Debtor
(if different from street address above):

Information Regarding the Debtor (Check the Applicable Boxes) E

Venue (Check any applicable box)

☐ Debtor has been domiciled or has had a residence, principal place of business, or principal assets in this District for 180 days immediately preceding the date of this petition or for a longer part of such 180 days than in any other District.

☐ There is a bankruptcy case concerning debtor's affiliate, general partner, or partnership pending in this District.

Type of Debtor (Check all boxes that apply) F

☐ Individual(s) ☐ Railroad
☐ Corporation ☐ Stockbroker
☐ Partnership ☐ Commodity Broker
☐ Other ____________ ☐ Clearing Bank

Chapter or Section of Bankruptcy Code Under Which the Petition is Filed (Check one box) H

☐ Chapter 7 ☐ Chapter 11 ☐ Chapter 13
☐ Chapter 9 ☐ Chapter 12
☐ Sec. 304 - Case ancillary to foreign proceeding

Nature of Debts (Check one box) G

☐ Consumer/Non-Business ☐ Business

Filing Fee (Check one box) I

☐ Full Filing Fee attached
☐ Filing Fee to be paid in installments (Applicable to individuals only) Must attach signed application for the court's consideration certifying that the debtor is unable to pay fee except in installments. Rule 1006(b). See Official Form No. 3.

Chapter 11 Small Business (Check all boxes that apply)

☐ Debtor is a small business as defined in 11 U.S.C. § 101
☐ Debtor is and elects to be considered a small business under 11 U.S.C. § 1121(e) (Optional)

Statistical/Administrative Information (Estimates only) J

☐ Debtor estimates that funds will be available for distribution to unsecured creditors.
☐ Debtor estimates that, after any exempt property is excluded and administrative expenses paid, there will be no funds available for distribution to unsecured creditors.

THIS SPACE IS FOR COURT USE ONLY

Estimated Number of Creditors	1-15	16-49	50-99	100-199	200-999	1000-over
	☐	☐	☐	☐	☐	☐

Estimated Assets

$0 to $50,000	$50,001 to $100,000	$100,001 to $500,000	$500,001 to $1 million	$1,000,001 to $10 million	$10,000,001 to $50 million	$50,000,001 to $100 million	More than $100 million
☐	☐	☐	☐	☐	☐	☐	☐

Estimated Debts

$0 to $50,000	$50,001 to $100,000	$100,001 to $500,000	$500,001 to $1 million	$1,000,001 to $10 million	$10,000,001 to $50 million	$50,000,001 to $100 million	More than $100 million
☐	☐	☐	☐	☐	☐	☐	☐

(continued)

EXHIBIT 5–3 Official Form No. 1 (The Debtor's Petition), Continued

(Official Form 1) (12/03) FORM B1, Page 2

Voluntary Petition
(This page must be completed and filed in every case)

Name of Debtor(s): K

Prior Bankruptcy Case Filed Within Last 6 Years (If more than one, attach additional sheet)

Location Where Filed: L

Case Number:

Date Filed:

Pending Bankruptcy Case Filed by any Spouse, Partner or Affiliate of this Debtor (If more than one, attach additional sheet)

Name of Debtor: M

Case Number:

Date Filed:

District:

Relationship:

Judge:

Signatures

Signature(s) of Debtor(s) (Individual/Joint)

I declare under penalty of perjury that the information provided in this petition is true and correct.

[If petitioner is an individual whose debts are primarily consumer debts and has chosen to file under chapter 7] I am aware that I may proceed under chapter 7, 11, 12 or 13 of title 11, United States Code, understand the relief available under each such chapter, and choose to proceed under chapter 7.

I request relief in accordance with the chapter of title 11, United States Code, specified in this petition.

X ______________________ N

Signature of Debtor

X ______________________

Signature of Joint Debtor

____

Telephone Number (If not represented by attorney)

____

Date

Signature of Attorney

X ______________________

Signature of Attorney for Debtor(s)

O ______________________

Printed Name of Attorney for Debtor(s)

____

Firm Name

____

Address

____

____

Telephone Number

____

Date

Signature of Debtor (Corporation/Partnership)

I declare under penalty of perjury that the information provided in this petition is true and correct, and that I have been authorized to file this petition on behalf of the debtor.

The debtor requests relief in accordance with the chapter of title 11, United States Code, specified in this petition.

X ______________________ P

Signature of Authorized Individual

____

Printed Name of Authorized Individual

____

Title of Authorized Individual

____

Date

Exhibit A

(To be completed if debtor is required to file periodic reports (e.g., forms 10K and 10Q) with the Securities and Exchange Commission pursuant to Section 13 or 15(d) of the Securities Exchange Act of 1934 and is requesting relief under chapter 11)

☐ Exhibit A is attached and made a part of this petition.

Exhibit B Q

(To be completed if debtor is an individual whose debts are primarily consumer debts)

I, the attorney for the petitioner named in the foregoing petition, declare that I have informed the petitioner that [he or she] may proceed under chapter 7, 11, 12, or 13 of title 11, United States Code, and have explained the relief available under each such chapter.

X ______________________

Signature of Attorney for Debtor(s) Date

Exhibit C R

Does the debtor own or have possession of any property that poses or is alleged to pose a threat of imminent and identifiable harm to public health or safety?

☐ Yes, and Exhibit C is attached and made a part of this petition.

☐ No

Signature of Non-Attorney Petition Preparer S

I certify that I am a bankruptcy petition preparer as defined in 11 U.S.C. § 110, that I prepared this document for compensation, and that I have provided the debtor with a copy of this document.

____

Printed Name of Bankruptcy Petition Preparer

____

Social Security Number (Required by 11 U.S.C.§ 110(c).)

____

Address

____

Names and Social Security numbers of all other individuals who prepared or assisted in preparing this document:

If more than one person prepared this document, attach additional sheets conforming to the appropriate official form for each person.

X ______________________

Signature of Bankruptcy Petition Preparer

____

Date

A bankruptcy petition preparerís failure to comply with the provisions of title 11 and the Federal Rules of Bankruptcy Procedure may result in fines or imprisonment or both 11 U.S.C. §110; 18 U.S.C. §156.

(continued)

Form B1, Exh.A (9/97)

Exhibit "A"

[If debtor is required to file periodic reports (*e.g.*, forms 10K and 10Q) with the Securities and Exchange Commission pursuant to Section 13 or 15(d) of the Securities Exchange Act of 1934 and is requesting relief under chapter 11 of the Bankruptcy Code, this Exhibit "A" shall be completed and attached to the petition.]

United States Bankruptcy Court

_______________ District Of _______________

In re ______________________________,
Debtor

Case No. ______________________

Chapter ______________

Exhibit "A" to Voluntary Petition

1. If any of the debtor's securities are registered under Section 12 of the Securities Exchange Act of 1934, the SEC file number is _______________.

2. The following financial data is the latest available information and refers to the debtor's condition on _____________.

a.	Total assets			$ ______________________	
b.	Total debts (including debts listed in 2.c., below)			$ ______________________	
c.	Debt securities held by more than 500 holders.				Approximate number of holders
	secured / /	unsecured / /	subordinated / /	$ ______________________	____________
	secured / /	unsecured / /	subordinated / /	$ ______________________	____________
	secured / /	unsecured / /	subordinated / /	$ ______________________	____________
	secured / /	unsecured / /	subordinated / /	$ ______________________	____________
	secured / /	unsecured / /	subordinated / /	$ ______________________	____________
d.	Number of shares of preferred stock			______________________	____________
e.	Number of shares common stock			______________________	____________

Comments, if any: ____
____
____

3. Brief description of debtor's business: ____
____
____

4. List the names of any person who directly or indirectly owns, controls, or holds, with power to vote, 5% or more of the voting securities of debtor:
____
____
____

(continued)

Form B1, Exhibit C
(9/01)

Exhibit "C"

[If, to the best of the debtor's knowledge, the debtor owns or has possession of property that poses or is alleged to pose a threat of imminent and identifiable harm to the public health or safety, attach this Exhibit "C" to the petition.]

United States Bankruptcy Court

_______________ District Of _______________

Exhibit "C" to Voluntary Petition

1. Identify and briefly describe all real or personal property owned by or in possession of the debtor that, to the best of the debtor's knowledge, poses or is alleged to pose a threat of imminent and identifiable harm to the public health or safety (attach additional sheets if necessary):

....

....

....

....

2. With respect to each parcel of real property or item of personal property identified in question 1, describe the nature and location of the dangerous condition, whether environmental or otherwise, that poses or is alleged to pose a threat of imminent and identifiable harm to the public health or safety (attach additional sheets if necessary):

....

....

....

The petition may be filed by a person who may be a debtor under Chapter 7, such as an individual debtor or joint debtors. 11 U.S.C.A. §§ 301, 302. Only an individual debtor and his or her spouse may be joint debtors. 11 U.S.C.A. § 302(a). Unmarried couples cannot file a joint case. The joint case permits a husband and wife, who hold most of their property jointly and who are liable on their debts jointly, to consolidate their estates and thus benefit both themselves and their creditors by reducing costs. The joint case also reduces the cost of filing to one filing fee.

The petition (Official Form No. 1)—a two-page form—should not be confused with the entire filing package. The filing package includes the schedules and the statement of financial affairs. In practice, it is customary to refer to the package as "the petition," even though technically only the two-page Official Form No. 1 is the petition.

Instructions for Completing Official Form No. 1 (The Debtor's Petition)

A Complete the name of the bankruptcy court in which the petition is filed. 28 U.S.C.A. § 152 lists the bankruptcy courts located within a state.

Examples: For a state that has more than one federal district, indicate the district and the state: United States Bankruptcy Court for the Northern District of Oklahoma.

For a state that has only one federal district, indicate only the state: United States Bankruptcy Court for the District of Vermont.

B Complete the name of the debtor.

Examples: For an individual debtor . . .

If the debtor is an individual, the debtor's name must appear in the following order: last name, first name, middle name. The complete middle name in full, rather than an initial, must be used:

Jones, James Wesley

Brown, John William, Jr.

Delany, Donald Douglas III

If the debtor does not have a middle name, so indicate by NMN:

Mead, Joan (NMN)

If the debtor has four names, include all four:

Taft, John William Howard

If the debtor uses a hyphenated name, use the hyphenated name:

Holland-Smyth, Mary Agnes

If the debtor is a medical doctor or a dentist, M.D. and D.D.S. are optional:

Brown, John William, M.D., or Brown, John William

Walsh, Jane Sampson, D.D.S., or Walsh, Jane Sampson

If the debtor is an attorney or has a doctorate degree, do not include Esq. or Ph.D.

Examples: For a partnership debtor . . .

Use the name of the partnership and not the names of the partners:

Mary and Joe's Dinette

The Rainbow Inn

John Winkler & Associates

Roy Frazier & Daughter

Examples: For a corporate debtor . . .

Use the official name of the corporation and not its trade name:

The Whitehouse Restaurant, Inc.

Ricky Pratt & Son, Co., Inc.

Ms. Judy's School of Dance, Inc.

C List all other names used by the debtor(s) during the six years prior to the filing of the petition. Include maiden names, married names, aka's (also known as), fka's (formerly known as), and dba's (doing business as). If more space is needed, type the names on a separate page as an addendum to the petition. At the top of each addendum page, include the debtor's full name as it appears on the petition, the case number, the chapter under which the case was filed, and the title of the document. The purpose of this listing is to enable creditors to identify the debtor with whom they have accounts.

Examples: For an individual debtor . . .

If the debtor is an unmarried woman filing as an individual and she has used two additional names during the previous six years:

Joan Ann Mead, aka Sue Lynn Mead, Jean Ann Mead

If the debtor is an unmarried woman filing as an individual and she has been married and divorced during the previous six years:

Joan Ann Mead, fka Joan Mead Reynolds

If the debtor is an unmarried woman filing as an individual and she has been married and divorced twice during the previous six years:

Joan Ann Mead, fka Joan Mead Reynolds, Joan Mead Washburn

If the debtor is a married woman filing as an individual and she was married during the previous six years:

Joan Mead Reynolds, fka Joan Ann Mead

If the debtor is a transsexual and was a man during the previous six years:

Roberta Ann Mead, fka Robert Albert Mead

If the debtor has a business:

Joan Ann Mead, dba Honest Joan's Loan, Gun and Pawn Shoppe

Examples: For a partnership debtor . . .

If the partnership is known by a trade name or has changed names within the past six years:

Mary and Joe's Dinette, aka M & J's Dinette, fka The Route 66 Dinette

The Rainbow Inn, aka The Rainbow Club, fka Eric's Bar and Grill

John Winkler & Associates, aka The Fireworks Man, fka John Winkler

Roy Frazier & Daughters, aka Frazier's Doughnut Delight, fka Roy Frazier & Daughter

Examples: For a corporate debtor . . .

If the corporation is known by a trade name or has changed names within the past six years:

The Whitehouse Restaurant, Inc., aka Mel's Place, fka Mel's Restaurant

Ricky Pratt & Son, Co., Inc., aka The Quality Fur Salon

Ms. Judy's School of Dance, Inc., fka East Ridge School of Dance

D List the last four digits of the debtor's social security number and the full employer's tax identification number, if one is applicable.

Fed. R. Bank. P. 1005 was amended in 2003 so the Chapter 7 petition would contain only the last four digits of the debtor's social security number rather than the debtor's full nine-digit social security number. The change was made in response to identify theft and privacy protection issues. The debtors, however, must submit with their petition a statement setting out their full social security number. The clerk of the bankruptcy court will include these numbers on the notice of the 341 meeting of creditors. This change does not affect the requirement of the full employer identification number, if one is available.

Federal law requires every employer to have an employer's tax identification number, which is secured from the Social Security Administration (Form SS-4). This number is generally two digits followed by seven digits (73-5467821). If the debtor should have an employer's tax identification number but does not, the answer should be "none."

The last four digits of the debtor's social security number or the full employer's tax ID number (employer's taxpayer identification number) will be used to assure accurate identification and recording of the debtor's case, to assure that papers pertaining to the debtor's case will be filed under the appropriate case, and to facilitate the sending of accurate notice to debtors.

The employer's tax ID number must be included if the debtor is a corporation, partnership, or individual who is doing business.

E Check one box. The information in these boxes establishes whether the petition has been filed in a bankruptcy court that has jurisdiction.

F The petition may be filed by a person who may be a debtor under Chapter 7, such as an individual debtor or joint debtors. 11 U.S.C.A. §§ 301, 302. Only an individual debtor and his or her spouse may be joint debtors. 11 U.S.C.A. § 302(a). Unmarried couples cannot file a joint case. The joint case permits a husband and a wife, who hold most of their property jointly and who are liable on their debts jointly, to consolidate their estates and thus benefit both themselves and their creditors by reducing the cost of administration. The joint case also reduces the cost of filing to one filing fee.

G If the debtor is an individual whose debts are primarily consumer debt, select the Non-Business/Consumer category.

If the debtor is a business enterprise or if most of the debts of an individual arose from the operation of a business or self-employment, "Business" should be selected.

H Select Chapter 7.

I Payment of the filing fee in installments is applicable only to individual debtor(s). If the filing fee is to be paid in installments, Official Form No. 3 must be completed and attached to the petition. In Official Form No. 3, the debtor's application to the court, the debtor must certify that he or she is unable to pay the filing fee except in installments. Fed. R. Bank. P. 1006(b).

J This estimate should correspond to the information appearing in the debtor's schedules. The estimate should be the debtor's best estimate and need not be exact.

K The name of the debtor should be the full name of the debtor (last name, first name, full middle name) as it appears on the first page of Official Form No. 1.

L These questions are answered only if the debtor has filed a prior bankruptcy case within the last six years. If there was more than one bankruptcy case filed by the debtor during the past six years, attach an additional page and provide the requested information.

The client should be questioned about prior bankruptcies. The client may have previously filed a petition in bankruptcy without understanding what he or she did.

The paralegal or the attorney must understand where and when the debtor has filed prior bankruptcy petitions. Therefore, the information is available if it subsequently becomes necessary to look up the prior bankruptcies. Sometimes, in prior bankruptcies, it is important to know what happened and when it happened. Debtors may be in error about what type of case the prior bankruptcy was, or may lose track of the actual date of a prior bankruptcy and be in error by several years, or may be in error as to the disposition of the previous bankruptcy.

M These questions are answered only if there is a pending bankruptcy case filed by any spouse, partner, or affiliate of the debtor. If there is more than one pending case, attach an additional page and provide the requested information.

If there is a related bankruptcy case, complete the name of the debtor as it appears on that petition (last name, first name, full middle name).

Example: John files for bankruptcy. One of John's loans is guaranteed by Alice, his wife. Six months later Alice files for bankruptcy. Alice's case is a related case and should be before the same bankruptcy judge.

Example: XYZ Corporation, a closely held corporation, files for bankruptcy and the owner of XYZ also files for bankruptcy. The XYZ Corporation's bankruptcy and the owner's bankruptcy are related cases.

Because entities may be interlocked in one way or another and various bankruptcy petitions may be filed in relation to the various entities, all related bankruptcy cases must be referenced, one to another. The court may ultimately consider joint administration or consolidation.

The case number is the number assigned to the case by the deputy clerk.

N After the petition has been completed, the debtor must sign the petition. The debtor signs for two purposes: (1) to declare that the petition's information is true; and (2) to affirm his or her choice of Chapter 7.

The debtor must sign his or her name in the following order: first name, middle name, last name. The debtor must sign his or her complete middle name in full, rather than use an initial, regardless of the fact that the debtor normally signs an initial in place of his or her middle name. If the debtor has been known by more than one name, the debtor must sign the first name that appears in "B." This is the name under which the case is docketed.

If a joint petition is filed, both debtors must sign their full names as they appear in "B." The debtors must sign their complete middle names in full.

O If the attorney is a member of a law firm, use the law firm's name.

Example: Savage, O'Donnell, Scott, McNulty, Affeldt, and Genges, rather than Warren L. McConnico

If the attorney is a solo practitioner, use the attorney's name.

Example: John T. Mortimer

If the debtor has no attorney and is filing pro se, write "none" under "name of law firm or attorney."

Include the area code.

Example: (918) 599-9000

Include the name of the attorney and his or her bar membership number.

Example: Warren L. McConnico, #5907

If the debtor has no attorney and is filing pro se, write "none" above printed "name of attorney for debtor(s)."

P If the petition is filed by a partnership, one of the partners of the partnership must sign on behalf of the partnership.

Example: The Mellon Shop, by James Earl Quackenbush, partner

If the petition is filed by a corporation, an authorized officer of the corporation must sign on behalf of the corporation and his or her corporate position must be indicated.

Example: The Snidley Gas and Oil Exploration Corporation, by Elmer J. Snidley, Jr., President

After the petition is signed by the debtor(s), the date on which the debtor(s) signed the petition is added by the debtor(s). The date must include the month, day, and year.

Examples: July 1, 2004

7/1/04

1 July 2004

Some bankruptcy courts, by local rule, require the petition to be filed within ten days of the debtor's signature. Otherwise, there must be a separate verification that the debtor's signature is still active.

Example: The debtor signs the petition and the attorney waits to file the petition until the debtor comes up with the filing fee. When the petition is filed, the attorney discovers the petition is stale.

Q To complete Exhibit "B," the debtor's attorney must declare that he or she has informed the debtor that the debtor could proceed under Chapter 7, 11, 12, or 13 and has explained the relief available under each chapter. The signature of the debtor's attorney must correspond to the attorney's name as it appears on page one of the petition. The attorney must also indicate the date of his or her signature. The signature of the debtor's attorney and the date signed are entered here. If the debtor is not represented by an attorney, then this line is left blank.

R By checking the "Yes" box, the debtor indicates that it owns or possesses property that poses a threat of imminent and identifiable harm to public health or safety. If the debtor checks the "Yes" box, the debtor must complete Exhibit "C" and identify and describe the property that possesses such a threat and describe the nature and location of the dangerous condition.

S This section applies to the "non-attorney bankruptcy preparer," who is defined in 11 U.S.C.A. § 110(a)(1) as "a person, other than an attorney or an employee of an attorney, who prepares for compensation a document for filing." If a non-attorney bankruptcy preparer prepares a document to be filed in a bankruptcy case, he or she must, in addition to signing the document, include his or her name, address, and social security number. 11 U.S.C.A. § 110. Otherwise, this section should be left blank.

PROBLEM 5.4 The following case will be filed in the United States bankruptcy court in the district in which you reside. The date is the current date.

The debtors are Jennifer and Eric McPherson from Problem 4.5.

You and your instructor are members of a major law firm in your city, and you both specialize in bankruptcy law. You have interviewed the McPhersons and reviewed their questionnaire. After discussing this case with you, your instructor has decided that the McPhersons should file a chapter 7 petition and has recommended this to the clients; they have concurred. It is now your responsibility to complete the petition (Official Form No. 1) and Exhibit "B," if appropriate. Complete these forms for your instructor's review and for the McPhersons' signatures. You can download your Official Bankruptcy Forms from http://www.uscourts.gov > U.S. Bankruptcy Courts > Official Bankruptcy Forms.

B. THE FILING FEE

Every petition must be accompanied by the filing fee, except when the payment of the filing fee is in installments. Fed. R. Bank. P. 1006(a). The filing fee must be paid in full before the debtor can pay an attorney or any other person for services in connection with the case. Fed. R. Bank. P. 1006(b)(3). The filing fee for a voluntary Chapter 7 is found in 28 U.S.C.A. § 1930(a)(1). The debtor may pay the filing fee by cash, cashier's check, or money order. If the debtor's attorney is paying the filing fee on behalf of the debtor, the fee may be paid by the law firm's check that need not be certified. Some courts accept a law firm's credit card. The method of payment is governed by local rule. The checks and money orders are drawn to the order of "United States Bankruptcy Court" or to the order of the specific United States bankruptcy court in which the case is filed.

EXAMPLES

United States Bankruptcy Court
U.S. Bankruptcy Court
United States Bankruptcy Court
for the Southern District of New York

Paying the filing fee in installments, while rare, is permissible.

(b) Payment of Filing Fee in Installments.

(1) *Application for Permission to Pay Filing Fee in Installments.* A voluntary petition by an individual shall be accepted for filing if accompanied by the debtor's signed application stating that the debtor is unable to pay the filing fee except in installments. The application shall state the proposed terms of the installment payments and that the applicant has neither paid any money nor transferred any property to an attorney for services in connection with the case.

(2) *Action on Application.* Prior to the meeting of creditors, the court may order the filing fee paid to the clerk or grant leave to pay in installments and fix the number, amount and dates of payment. The number of installments shall not exceed four, and the final installment shall be payable not later than 120 days after filing the petition. For cause shown, the court may extend the time of any installment, provided the last installment is paid not later than 180 days after filing the petition. Fed. R. Bank P. 1006(b).

The application and order to pay the filing fee in installments is Official Form No. 3. (See Exhibit 5–4.) Although Official Form No. 3 is designed for an individual debtor, it may be revised for use by individual debtors filing a joint petition by changing the term "debtor" to "debtors" and by making other appropriate changes.

Instructions for Completing Official Form No. 3 (Application to Pay Filing Fee in Installments)

A Complete the name of the court in which the petition is filed. See Official Form No. 1.

B Complete the name of the debtor as it appears on the bankruptcy petition.

C Complete the case number by inserting the bankruptcy case number assigned by the court at the time the petition is filed.

D Complete the payment schedule. The number of installments cannot exceed four and the final installment must be paid no later than 120 days after the filing of the petition.
Before completing the payment schedule, a paralegal should check with his or her local bankruptcy court clerk's office for information concerning the amount that must be paid when the petition is filed and the amount that must be paid in each installment.

The court, for cause, can extend the time for paying the last installment from 120 to 180 days after the filing of the petition.

EXHIBIT 5–4 Official Form No. 3 (Application to Pay Filing Fee in Installments)

Form 3
(12/03)

UNITED STATES BANKRUPTCY COURT
__________________ DISTRICT OF __________________ **A**

In re ____________________________ **B** Case No.

____________________________ Chapter ______________ **C**

Debtor

APPLICATION TO PAY FILING FEE IN INSTALLMENTS

1. In accordance with Fed. R. Bankr. P. 1006, I apply for permission to pay the Filing Fee amounting to $__________ in installments.

2. I certify that I am unable to pay the Filing Fee except in installments.

3. I further certify that I have not paid any money or transferred any property to an attorney for services in connection with this case and that I will neither make any payment nor transfer any property for services in connection with this case until the filing fee is paid in full.

4. I propose the following terms for the payment of the Filing Fee.*

$ ________ **D** ________ Check one ☐ With the filing of the petition, or
☐ On or before __________

$ ________________ on or before ________________________

$ ________________ on or before ________________________

$ ________________ on or before ________________________

* The number of installments proposed shall not exceed four (4), and the final installment shall be payable not later than 120 days after filing the petition. For cause shown, the court may extend the time of any installment, provided the last installment is paid not later than 180 days after filing the petition. Fed. R. Bankr. P. 1006(b)(2).

5. I understand that if I fail to pay any installment when due my bankruptcy case may be dismissed and I may not receive a discharge of my debts.

____________________________ ____________________________
Signature of Attorney Date **E** Signature of Debtor Date
(In a joint case, both spouses must sign.)

____
Name of Attorney

____
Signature of Joint Debtor (if any) Date

CERTIFICATION AND SIGNATURE OF NON-ATTORNEY BANKRUPTCY PETITION (See 11 U.S.C. § 110)

I certify that I am a bankruptcy petition preparer as defined in 11 U.S.C. § 110, that I prepared this document for compensation, and that I have provided the debtor with a copy of this document. I also certify that I will not accept money or any other property from the debtor before the filing fee is paid in full.

____________________________ ________________
Printed or Typed Name of Bankruptcy Petition Preparer **F** Social Security No.

____

____
Address

Names and Social Security numbers of all other individuals who prepared or assisted in preparing this document:

If more than one person prepared this document, attach additional signed sheets conforming to the appropriate Official Form for each person.

x____________________________ ________________
Signature of Bankruptcy Petition Preparer Date

A bankruptcy petition preparer's failure to comply with the provisions of title 11 and the Federal Rules of Bankruptcy Procedure may result in fines or imprisonment or both. 11 U.S.C. § 110; 18 U.S.C. § 156.

(continued)

EXHIBIT 5–4 Official Form No. 3 (Application to Pay Filing Fee in Installments), Continued

Form 3
(9/97)

UNITED STATES BANKRUPTCY COURT
____________________ DISTRICT OF ____________________

In re ______________________________,
Debtor

Case No. _______________

Chapter _______________

ORDER APPROVING PAYMENT OF FILING FEE IN INSTALLMENTS

IT IS ORDERED that the debtor(s) may pay the filing fee in installments on the terms proposed in the foregoing application.

IT IS FURTHER ORDERED that until the filing fee is paid in full the debtor shall not pay any money for services in connection with this case, and the debtor shall not relinquish any property as payment for services in connection with this case.

BY THE COURT

Date: _______________

____
United States Bankruptcy Judge

E Complete the date, signature, and address of the debtor(s). The name(s) of the debtor(s) and address must correspond to the name(s) and address found on the petition (and on this form under "B"). The debtor must sign his or her name in the following order: first name, middle name, last name. The debtor must sign his or her complete middle name, rather than use an initial, regardless of the fact that the debtor normally signs an initial in place of his or her middle name.
The date should be the date signed by the debtor(s) and need not be the date the petition is filed.
The debtor's attorney must also sign and date.

F This section applies to the "non-attorney bankruptcy petition preparer," who is defined in 11 U.S.C.A. § 110(a)(1) as "a person, other than an attorney or an employee of an attorney, who prepares for compensation a document for filing." This section should be left blank.

PROBLEM 5.5 Using the information in Problem 4.5 and the following information, decide whether the McPhersons should apply to pay their filing fee in installments. If you decide that they should so apply, complete Official Form No. 3—Application to Pay Filing Fees in Installments.

The McPhersons have little cash on hand. Jennifer expects to be paid at the end of the month. Eric could borrow the filing fee from his father, although he would be embarrassed to do so. They could reduce some expenses by driving only one car. This would also save about $50 a month on gasoline and about $50 a month on maintenance.

C. THE CLERK'S NOTICE

If the debtor is an individual and the debts are primarily consumer debts, then the **clerk's notice** must be completed if required by the court. Exhibit "B" in the petition (Official Form No. 1) is a statement by the debtor's attorney that he or she has informed the debtor that he or she may proceed under Chapter 7, 11, 12, or 13 of Title 11 of the Bankruptcy Code and has explained the relief available under each such chapter to the debtor. The Bankruptcy Code, however, in 11 U.S.C.A. § 342(b), requires the clerk to give written notice to the debtor as to each operative chapter of the Bankruptcy Code under which the debtor could proceed and makes no mention of the debtor's attorney giving the notice.

In practice, B 201, although not an official form, was issued by the Administrative Office of the United States Courts for use in compliance with 11 U.S.C.A. § 342. As a practical matter, the bankruptcy filing program prints B 201 for the debtor's attorney, who in turn explains the various chapters of the Bankruptcy Code to the debtor and obtains the debtor's signature. Attorneys or debtors who are filing *pro se* may obtain copies of B 201 at their Bankruptcy Court Clerk's Office. Some courts by local rule require B 201 to be filed along with the petition. Others do not.

The following forms are the notice to the individual consumer debtor and the affirmation by the debtor that he or she has been notified. (See Exhibit 5–5.)

Instructions for Completing the Clerk's Notice to Individual Consumer Debtor(s)

A Complete the date and signature of the debtor(s). The name(s) of the debtor(s) must correspond to the name(s) found on the petition. The debtor must sign his or her name in the following order: first name, middle name, last name. The debtor must sign his or her complete middle name, rather than use an initial, regardless of the fact that the debtor normally signs an initial in place of his or her middle name. If the debtor has been known under more than one name, the debtor must sign the name under which the case is docketed.

The date should be the date signed by the debtor(s) and need not be the date the petition is filed.

EXHIBIT 5–5 Procedural Form 201 (Clerk's Notice to Individual Consumer Debtor[s])

B 201 (11/03)

UNITED STATES BANKRUPTCY COURT

NOTICE TO INDIVIDUAL CONSUMER DEBTOR

The purpose of this notice is to acquaint you with the four chapters of the federal Bankruptcy Code under which you may file a bankruptcy petition. The bankruptcy law is complicated and not easily described. Therefore, you should seek the advice of an attorney to learn of your rights and responsibilities under the law should you decide to file a petition with the court. Court employees are prohibited from giving you legal advice.

Chapter 7: Liquidation ($155 filing fee plus $39 administrative fee plus $15 trustee surcharge)

1. Chapter 7 is designed for debtors in financial difficulty who do not have the ability to pay their existing debts.

2. Under chapter 7 a trustee takes possession of all your property. You may claim certain of your property as exempt under governing law. The trustee then liquidates the property and uses the proceeds to pay your creditors according to priorities of the Bankruptcy Code.

3. The purpose of filing a chapter 7 case is to obtain a discharge of your existing debts. If, however, you are found to have committed certain kinds of improper conduct described in the Bankruptcy Code, your discharge may be denied by the court, and the purpose for which you filed the bankruptcy petition will be defeated.

4. Even if you receive a discharge, there are some debts that are not discharged under the law. Therefore, you may still be responsible for such debts as certain taxes and student loans, alimony and support payments, criminal restitution, and debts for death or personal injury caused by driving while intoxicated from alcohol or drugs.

5. Under certain circumstances you may keep property that you have purchased subject to valid security interest. Your attorney can explain the options that are available to you.

Chapter 13: Repayment of All or Part of the Debts of an Individual with Regular Income ($155 filing fee plus $39 administrative fee)

1. Chapter 13 is designed for individuals with regular income who are temporarily unable to pay their debts but would like to pay them in installments over a period of time. You are only eligible for chapter 13 if your debts do not exceed certain dollar amounts set forth in the Bankruptcy Code.

2. Under chapter 13 you must file a plan with the court to repay your creditors all or part of the money that you owe them, using your future earnings. Usually, the period allowed by the court to repay your debts is three years, but no more than five years. Your plan must be approved by the court before it can take effect.

3. Under chapter 13, unlike chapter 7, you may keep all your property, both exempt and non-exempt, as long as you continue to make payments under the plan.

4. After completion of payments under your plan, your debts are discharged except alimony and support payments, student loans, certain debts including criminal fines and restitution and debts for death or personal injury caused by driving while intoxicated from alcohol or drugs, and long term secured obligations.

Chapter 11: Reorganization ($800 filing fee plus $39 administrative fee)

Chapter 11 is designed for the reorganization of a business but is also available to consumer debtors. Its provisions are quite complicated, and any decision by an individual to file a chapter 11 petition should be reviewed with an attorney.

Chapter 12: Family Farmer ($200 filing fee plus $39 administrative fee)

Chapter 12 designed to permit family farmers to repay their debts over a period of time from future earnings and is in many ways similar to chapter 13. The eligibility requirements are restrictive, limiting its use to those whose income arises primarily from a family-owned farm.

I, the debtor, affirm that I have read this notice.

A

Date	Signature of Debtor	Case Number

WHITE - DEBTOR COPY **PINK - COURT COPY**

D. CORPORATE RESOLUTION AUTHORIZING FILING OF CHAPTER 7

The corporate resolution gives the person filing the Chapter 7 case authority to file the case and to engage and reimburse any attorney or accountant whose services are necessary in the case. The corporate resolution must be consistent with the corporate charter and state law. (See Exhibit 5–6.)

EXHIBIT 5–6 Corporate Resolution Authorizing Filing of a Chapter 7 Petition

RESOLUTION OF THE BOARD OF DIRECTORS
OF [DEBTOR'S NAME]

Special Meeting of [SPECIAL MEETING DATE]

The Board of Directors met at this special meeting to discuss the financial condition of the corporation. After discussion a motion was made and seconded to adopt the following resolution:

Whereas the affairs of the business of this corporation have not been successfully conducted for several months,

Be it therefore resolved that this corporation file its voluntary Petition for relief under Chapter 7 of Title 11 of the United States Code in the United States Bankruptcy Court and

Be it further resolved that [PETITION AUTHORITY] is hereby authorized to prepare the necessary Petition for relief and by that person's single signature execute all necessary documents and bind this corporation thereby and

Be it further resolved that [REPRESENTATIVE AUTHORITY] is hereby authorized to engage the services of any attorney or accountant or both as shall appear necessary to assist in this matter and to reimburse any attorney or accountant so engaged out of the assets of the corporation.

The motion was adopted by a vote of [VOTES FOR] to [VOTES AGAINST] .

There being no further business to come before this meeting, a motion to adjourn was made and seconded and the meeting was adjourned.

____
Chair

____
Secretary to the Board of Directors

Affix the corporate seal

E. DISCLOSURE OF ATTORNEY'S COMPENSATION STATEMENT

The Code requires any attorney representing a debtor in a case under the Bankruptcy Code to file with the court a statement of the compensation paid or agreed to be paid for services connected with the bankruptcy case and the source of the compensation. 11 U.S.C.A. § 329. This disclosure of attorney's compensation statement must be completed regardless of whether the attorney applies to the court for compensation. The Federal Rules of Bankruptcy Procedure also require the debtor's attorney to transmit the statement of compensation to the United States trustee. Fed. R. Bank. P. 2016(b). (See Exhibit 5–7.)

This reporting requirement serves two functions:

1. It permits the court to determine whether the compensation exceeds the reasonable value of the services rendered. 11 U.S.C.A. § 329. See also 28 U.S.C.A. § 586(a)(3)(A). If the court determines that the compensation exceeds the reasonable value of the services rendered, it may deny compensation to the attorney, cancel the agreement to pay compensation, or order the return of compensation paid. 11 U.S.C.A. § 329(b); 28 U.S.C.A. § 586(a)(3)(A).
2. The disclosure permits the court to determine whether the attorney has made an agreement to share compensation. The Code prohibits the debtor's attorney from sharing or agreeing to share with another person any compensation or reimbursement received by either the attorney for the debtor or the other person. This prohibits fee splitting among attorneys, other professionals, or trustees. The debtor's attorney is, however, permitted to share compensation with partners or associates in his or her professional association, partnership, or corporation. 11 U.S.C.A. § 504.

The disclosure of attorney's compensation statement must be filed with the court and transmitted to the United States trustee within 15 days after the petition has been filed or by another date set by the court. Fed. R. Bank. P. 2016(b).

Because the statement specifies the services the attorney will provide the client and the compensation the client will provide the attorney, it can also serve as the written contract between attorney and client. A copy of the statement should be signed by the client for the attorney's records. The client could also be provided a copy for his or her records.

Instructions for Completing the Disclosure of Attorney's Compensation Statement

The disclosure of attorney's compensation statement is completed and signed by the debtor's attorney. Although the statement is self-explanatory, the following tips may be helpful.

A Complete the name of the court in which the petition is filed. See Official Form No. 1.

B Complete the name of the debtor as it appears on the bankruptcy petition.

C Complete the case number by inserting the bankruptcy case number assigned by the court at the time the petition was filed. Since the petition has not been filed at this time, there will not be an assigned number so case number should be left blank.

D Insert "Chapter 7."

E State the dollar amount of the agreed upon legal fees, the dollar amount that the attorney has already received, and the balance due.

If a fixed fee will be charged for the basic filing and an hourly fee will be charged for enumerated services, so indicate.

If more than one attorney or one or more paralegals will be working on the case, itemize the hourly rates for each attorney or paralegal.

Example: a) Attorney $ _____/hour
b) Attorney $ _____/hour
c) Paralegal $ _____/hour

The amount to be deducted from the total fee is not only the amount received prior to the completion of the disclosure of compensation statement but also the amount that will be received prior to the filing of the disclosure statement. Therefore, include any fee that will be paid prior to the filing of the petition.

EXHIBIT 5–7 Procedural Form B 203 (Disclosure of Attorney's Compensation Statement)

B 203
(12 / 94)

United States Bankruptcy Court

_______________ District Of ____A____

In re

Case No. ____C____

Debtor B

Chapter ____D____

DISCLOSURE OF COMPENSATION OF ATTORNEY FOR DEBTOR

1. Pursuant to 11 U.S.C. § 329(a) and Fed. Bankr. P. 2016(b), I certify that I am the attorney for the above-named debtor(s) and that compensation paid to me within one year before the filing of the petition in bankruptcy, or agreed to be paid to me, for services rendered or to be rendered on behalf of the debtor(s) in contemplation of or in connection with the bankruptcy case is as follows:

   For legal services, I have agreed to accept . . . . $____E____

   Prior to the filing of this statement I have received . . . . $__________

   Balance Due . . . . $__________

2. The source of the compensation paid to me was:

   ☐ Debtor ☐ Other (specify) F

3. The source of compensation to be paid to me is:

   ☐ Debtor ☐ Other (specify) G

4. ☐ I have not agreed to share the above-disclosed compensation with any other person unless they are members and associates of my law firm. H

   ☐ I have agreed to share the above-disclosed compensation with a other person or persons who are not members or associates of my law firm. A copy of the agreement, together with a list of the names of the people sharing in the compensation, is attached.

5. In return for the above-disclosed fee, I have agreed to render legal service for all aspects of the bankruptcy case, including: I

   a. Analysis of the debtor's financial situation, and rendering advice to the debtor in determining whether to file a petition in bankruptcy;

   b. Preparation and filing of any petition, schedules, statements of affairs and plan which may be required;

   c. Representation of the debtor at the meeting of creditors and confirmation hearing, and any adjourned hearings thereof;

(continued)

EXHIBIT 5–7 Procedural Form B 203 (Disclosure of Attorney's Compensation Statement), Continued

DISCLOSURE OF COMPENSATION OF ATTORNEY FOR DEBTOR (Continued)

d. Representation of the debtor in adversary proceedings and other contested bankruptcy matters;

e. [Other provisions as needed]

6. By agreement with the debtor(s), the above-disclosed fee does not include the following services:

J

CERTIFICATION

I certify that the foregoing is a complete statement of any agreement or arrangement for payment to me for representation of the debtor(s) in this bankruptcy proceedings.

K

_______________ Date

_______________ *Signature of Attorney*

_______________ *Name of law firm*

F Check the box to indicate the source of the compensation already paid. If the source is "Other," specify the source. If the source is from the debtor and others, indicate both sources.

G Check the box to indicate the source of the compensation to be paid in the future. If the source is "Other," specify the source. If the source is from the debtor and others, indicate both sources.

H Check whether the attorney has agreed or has not agreed to share the compensation with a person other than a member or associate of his or her law firm. If the attorney has agreed to share the compensation with such a person, a copy of the agreement and the names of those who will share in the compensation must be attached. Remember to label those attachments with the name of the debtor, last name first, and the debtor's social security number.

I Write "NA" by any services listed in question 5 that will not be provided. Especially note 5(d), "Representation of the debtor in adversary proceedings and other contested bankruptcy matters." Leaving these services in as a part of the fixed fee may be damaging to an attorney if the attorney is later required to represent the client at no extra charge at such matters as an objection to discharge or an objection to dischargeability. Defending an objection to discharge could cost several thousand dollars and the attorney would not want to include these services in his or her fixed fee.

Complete question 5(e) in detail. Specify other services to be rendered. Use additional pages, if necessary, and attach them to this form.

Example: e.

1. negotiation and preparation of reaffirmation agreements;
2. preparation and filing of pleadings and representation of the debtor in all proceedings relating to:
   a) the use of cash collateral;
   b) the modification or enforcement of the automatic stay;
   c) the rejection, assumption, assignment of executory contracts;
3. representation of the debtor in motions as necessary and proper to avoid liens pursuant to 11 U.S.C.A. §§ 522(f), 506(d); and
4. representation of the debtor at any reaffirmation or discharge hearing

If no other services, then state "none" or "NA."

J Complete question 6 in detail. Specify services that will not be rendered. Use additional pages, if necessary, and attach them to this form.

Example:

6. Notwithstanding 5(d) above:
   a. representation of the debtor in adversary proceedings and other contested bankruptcy matters (e.g., contest of exemption claims, objection to discharge or dischargeability of a claim, redemption of real or personal property, and motions to dismiss);
   b. representation of the debtor in any state court matter;
   c. representation of the debtor in any criminal matter; and
   d. examination of any person pursuant to Federal Rules of Bankruptcy Procedure 2004

K This section is self-explanatory. The address and telephone number of the attorney or the firm should not be included.

PROBLEM 5.6 Using the information in Problem 4.5 and in Problem 5.1, complete the disclosure of attorney's compensation statement.

F. THE LIST OF CREDITORS

The debtor is required to file with the petition a list containing the name and address of each creditor. 11 U.S.C.A. § 521(1); Fed. R. Bank. P. 1007(a)(1). This list gives the clerk's office information necessary for the mailing of the notice of the meeting of creditors and the order for relief.

Once the information concerning creditors is entered into the bankruptcy filing program, the program will generate the **list of creditors** in triple column, the format appropriate for filing with the Office of the Bankruptcy Clerk.

G. SCHEDULES (OFFICIAL FORM NO. 6)

The Summary of Schedules (Official Form No. 6) is a listing of all of the debtor's real and personal property, claimed exemptions, creditors, executory contracts and unexpired leases, codebtors, and the current income and current expenditures for an individual debtor or husband and wife filing a joint petition. (See Exhibit 5–8.) The Schedules A–J form the heart of the Chapter 7 bankruptcy filing. The debtor is required to sign an unsworn declaration under penalty of perjury to the Summary and Schedules. The form for the unsworn declaration appears at the end of Official Form No. 6.

Schedule A is the listing of all real property with the exception of interests in executory contracts and unexpired leases. This schedule shows the current market value of the debtor's interest with no deductions for secured claims or exemptions. Section 521(3) of the Bankruptcy Code requires the debtor to cooperate with the trustee. This cooperation may take the form of furnishing documents required by the trustee to enable the trustee to perform his or her duties in effective administration of the bankruptcy estate. The description of property, for example, might be inaccurate on the schedules, leading the trustee to ask for a copy of the deed to the property in question.

Schedule B is the listing of all personal property with the exception of interests in executory contracts and unexpired leases. The debtor is required to cooperate with requests made by the trustee for copies of documents relating to the debtor's personal property in order to facilitate administration of the estate.

Schedule C is a listing of the property that the debtor claims as exempt.

Schedules D, E, and F classify the creditors into creditors holding secured claims (Schedule D), creditors holding unsecured priority claims (Schedule E), and creditors holding unsecured nonpriority claims (Schedule F). Schedules D, E, and F are designed so that claims need to be listed only once.

Schedule G is a listing of executory contracts and unexpired leases.

Schedule H is a listing of the codebtors.

Schedules I (Current Income) and J (Current Expenditures) are applicable only to an individual debtor or to a husband and wife filing a joint petition.

Although the Summary of Schedules appears before Schedules A–J, it is compiled from the totals that are generated on all the other schedules.

1. Schedule A: Real Property

Schedule A (see Exhibit 5–9) is used to report all of the debtor's interests in real property except executory contracts and unexpired leases, which are to be listed in Schedule G.

Schedule A requires five items of information for each item of real property:

1. a description and location of all real property in which the debtor has an interest (the interest may be present or future, legal or equitable, entire or partial);
2. the nature of the debtor's interest;
3. if the debtor is married, an indication of who owns the property (husband, wife, joint, or community);
4. the current market value of the debtor's interest in the property without deducting for secured claims or exemptions; and
5. the amount of any secured claim on that property.

Requiring the married debtor to indicate who owns the property is designed to minimize the potential for concealment of assets. The trustee can request copies of any documents concerning the debtor's property necessary to the administration of the estate.

EXHIBIT 5–8 Official Form No. 6 (Summary of Schedules)

FORM B6-Cont.
(6/90)

UNITED STATES BANKRUPTCY COURT

________________District of ________________

In re ______________________________, Case No. ________________
Debtor (If known)

SUMMARY OF SCHEDULES

Indicate as to each schedule whether that schedule is attached and state the number of pages in each. Report the totals from Schedules A, B, D, E, F, G, H, I, and J in the boxes provided. Add the amounts from Schedules A and B to determine the total amount of the debtor's assets. Add the amounts from Schedules D, E, and F to determine the total amount of the debtor's liabilities.

NAME OF SCHEDULE	ATTACHED (YES/NO)	NO. OF SHEETS	AMOUNTS SCHEDULED ASSETS	LIABILITIES	OTHER
A - Real Property			$		
B - Personal Property			$		
C - Property Claimed as Exempt					
D - Creditors Holding Secured Claims				$	
E - Creditors Holding Unsecured Priority Claims				$	
F - Creditors Holding Unsecured Nonpriority Claims				$	
G - Executory Contracts and Unexpired Leases					
H - Codebtors					
I - Current Income of Individual Debtor(s)					$
J - Current Expenditures of Individual Debtor(s)					$
	Total Number of Sheets of ALL Schedules ➤				
		Total Assets ➤	$		
			Total Liabilities ➤	$	

EXHIBIT 5–9 Official Form No. 6, Schedule A (Real Property)

FORM B6A
(6/90)

In re ______________________________, Case No. ______________________
Debtor (If known)

SCHEDULE A - REAL PROPERTY

Except as directed below, list all real property in which the debtor has any legal, equitable, or future interest, including all property owned as a co-tenant , community property, or in which the debtor has a life estate. Include any property in which the debtor holds rights and powers exercisable for the debtor's own benefit. If the debtor is married, state whether husband, wife, or both own the property by placing an "H," "W," "J," or "C" in the column labeled "Husband, Wife, Joint, or Community." If the debtor holds no interest in real property, write "None" under "Description and Location of Property."

Do not include interests in executory contracts and unexpired leases on this schedule. List them in Schedule G - Executory Contracts and Unexpired Leases.

If an entity claims to have a lien or hold a secured interest in any property, state the amount of the secured claim. See Schedule D. If no entity claims to hold a secured interest in the property, write "None" in the column labeled "Amount of Secured Claim."

If the debtor is an individual or if a joint petition is filed, state the amount of any exemption claimed in the property only in Schedule C - Property Claimed as Exempt.

DESCRIPTION AND LOCATION OF PROPERTY	NATURE OF DEBTOR'S INTEREST IN PROPERTY	HUSBAND, WIFE, JOINT, OR COMMUNITY	CURRENT MARKET VALUE OF DEBTOR'S INTEREST IN PROPERTY, WITHOUT DEDUCTING ANY SECURED CLAIM OR EXEMPTION	AMOUNT OF SECURED CLAIM
A B	C	D	E	F
		Total➤	G	

(Report also on Summary of Schedules.)

Instructions for Completing Official Form No. 6, Schedule A (Real Property)

A List by legal description (e.g., lot number, block number, addition, city, county, and state) all real property in which the debtor has a legal, equitable, or future interest.

Example: Lot 2, Block 2, Brookwood Addition
Tulsa, Tulsa County, Oklahoma

Do not include interests in executory contracts (e.g., one-year lease on residential or business property) and unexpired leases. They will be listed in Schedule G.

List any property in which the debtor holds rights and powers exercisable for the debtor's own benefit.

If the debtor does not hold any interest in real property, state "none."

B In addition to the legal description, provide the mailing address (street, city, state, zip code) for all real property.

Example: 3214 Beaver Creek Lane
Northbrook, IL 62105

C State the nature of the debtor's interest in the property.

Examples: fee simple
option to purchase
life estate
contract for deed

D If the debtor is married, state whether the property is owned by the husband, wife, jointly, or as community property. Use the initials H, W, J, and C. If the debtor is not married, leave this column blank.

E State the current market value of the debtor's interest in the property. Do not deduct any secured claim or exemption.

Example:	current market value	$40,000
	secured claim	$20,000
	exemption	$ 8,000
	List $40,000, the current market value.	

Appraisals are not required for the schedules. The current market value for scheduling purposes is established by the debtor's best judgment. The debtor may use whatever source he or she wishes.

F If the real property has a secured claim, state the amount of that claim.

List the amount of the secured claim even though it may exceed the current market value of the property.

Example:	current market value	$40,000
	amount of the indebtedness	$50,000
	List $50,000 as the secured claim.	

G Total the amounts of all interests of real property. Report the total on the Summary of Schedules.

PROBLEM 5.7 Using the information in Problem 4.5, complete Schedule A of Official Form No. 6 for the McPhersons.

2. Schedule B: Personal Property

Schedule B (see Exhibit 5–10) is used to report all of the debtor's interests in personal property except executory contracts and unexpired leases, which are to be listed in Schedule G.

Schedule B categorizes personal property into 33 types of property. Three items of information are required for each type of personal property that the debtor owns:

1. a description and location of the various items of property;
2. if the debtor is married, an indication of who owns the property; and
3. the current market value of the debtor's interest in the property, without deducting for secured claims or exemptions.

EXHIBIT 5–10 Official Form No. 6, Schedule B (Personal Property)

Form B6B
(10/89)

In re ______________________________________, **Case No.** ____________________
Debtor **(If known)**

SCHEDULE B - PERSONAL PROPERTY

Except as directed below, list all personal property of the debtor of whatever kind. If the debtor has no property in one or more of the categories, place an "x" in the appropriate position in the column labeled "None." If additional space is needed in any category, attach a separate sheet properly identified with the case name, case number, and the number of the category. If the debtor is married, state whether husband, wife, or both own the property by placing an "H," "W," "J," or "C" in the column labeled "Husband, Wife, Joint, or Community." If the debtor is an individual or a joint petition is filed, state the amount of any exemptions claimed only in Schedule C - Property Claimed as Exempt.

Do not list interests in executory contracts and unexpired leases on this schedule. List them in Schedule G - Executory Contracts and Unexpired Leases.

If the property is being held for the debtor by someone else, state that person's name and address under "Description and Location of Property."

TYPE OF PROPERTY	NONE	DESCRIPTION AND LOCATION OF PROPERTY	HUSBAND, WIFE, JOINT, OR COMMUNITY	CURRENT MARKET VALUE OF DEBTOR'S INTEREST IN PROPERTY, WITHOUT DEDUCTING ANY SECURED CLAIM OR EXEMPTION
1. Cash on hand.		A		
2. Checking, savings or other financial accounts, certificates of deposit, or shares in banks, savings and loan, thrift, building and loan, and homestead associations, or credit unions, brokerage houses, or cooperatives.		B		
3. Security deposits with public utilities, telephone companies, landlords, and others.		C		
4. Household goods and furnishings, including audio, video, and computer equipment.		D		
5. Books; pictures and other art objects; antiques; stamp, coin, record, tape, compact disc, and other collections or collectibles.		E		
6. Wearing apparel.		F		
7. Furs and jewelry.		G		
8. Firearms and sports, photographic, and other hobby equipment.		H		
9. Interests in insurance policies. Name insurance company of each policy and itemize surrender or refund value of each.		I		
10. Annuities. Itemize and name each issuer.		J		

(continued)

EXHIBIT 5–10 Official Form No. 6, Schedule B (Personal Property), Continued

Form B6B-Cont.
(10/89)

In re ______________________________, **Case No.** ______________________
Debtor **(If known)**

SCHEDULE B - PERSONAL PROPERTY

(Continuation Sheet)

TYPE OF PROPERTY	NONE	DESCRIPTION AND LOCATION OF PROPERTY	HUSBAND, WIFE, JOINT, OR COMMUNITY	CURRENT MARKET VALUE OF DEBTOR'S INTEREST IN PROPERTY, WITHOUT DEDUCTING ANY SECURED CLAIM OR EXEMPTION
11. Interests in IRA, ERISA, Keogh, or other pension or profit sharing plans. Itemize.		K		
12. Stock and interests in incorporated and unincorporated businesses. Itemize.		L		
13. Interests in partnerships or joint ventures. Itemize.		M		
14. Government and corporate bonds and other negotiable and non-negotiable instruments.		N		
15. Accounts receivable.		O		
16. Alimony, maintenance, support, and property settlements to which the debtor is or may be entitled. Give particulars.		P		
17. Other liquidated debts owing debtor including tax refunds. Give particulars.		Q		
18. Equitable or future interests, life estates, and rights or powers exercisable for the benefit of the debtor other than those listed in Schedule of Real Property.		R		
19. Contingent and noncontingent interests in estate of a decedent, death benefit plan, life insurance policy, or trust.		S		
20. Other contingent and unliquidated claims of every nature, including tax refunds, counterclaims of the debtor, and rights to setoff claims. Give estimated value of each.		T		
21. Patents, copyrights, and other intellectual property. Give particulars.		U		
22. Licenses, franchises, and other general intangibles. Give particulars.		V		

(continued)

EXHIBIT 5–10 Official Form No. 6, Schedule B (Personal Property), Continued

Form B6B-cont.
(10/89)

In re ____, **Case No.** ____________________
Debtor **(If known)**

SCHEDULE B -PERSONAL PROPERTY

(Continuation Sheet)

TYPE OF PROPERTY	NONE	DESCRIPTION AND LOCATION OF PROPERTY	HUSBAND, WIFE, JOINT, OR COMMUNITY	CURRENT MARKET VALUE OF DEBTOR'S INTEREST IN PROPERTY, WITH-OUT DEDUCTING ANY SECURED CLAIM OR EXEMPTION
23. Automobiles, trucks, trailers, and other vehicles and accessories.		**W**		
24. Boats, motors, and accessories.		**X**		
25. Aircraft and accessories.		**Y**		
26. Office equipment, furnishings, and supplies.		**Z**		
27. Machinery, fixtures, equipment, and supplies used in business.		**AA**		
28. Inventory.		**BB**		
29. Animals.		**CC**		
30. Crops - growing or harvested. Give particulars.		**DD**		
31. Farming equipment and implements.		**EE**		
32. Farm supplies, chemicals, and feed.		**FF**		
33. Other personal property of any kind not already listed. Itemize.		**GG**		

_________continuation sheets attached Total $ **HH**

(Include amounts from any continuation sheets attached. Report total also on Summary of Schedules.)

Instructions for Completing Official Form No. 6, Schedule B (Personal Property)

Among the most common questions asked by a debtor as schedule B is being completed is, "I don't know what the property is worth. What do I put down? Do I put down what I paid for it? Do I put down how much it would cost me if I had to replace it?" The answer might be phrased—"What if you had a garage sale and sold everything that you own. What price would you tag the various items? That is the market value of what you have and that is what should be listed on Schedule B." Therefore the debtor should use common sense—what could a trustee or anyone sell the items for if they had to be sold?

Property that will be administered by the bankruptcy trustee must be valued more carefully than property that the debtor will retain because it is exempt. If the exemption is not by kind but rather by dollar, the value must be more accurate. For example: if the exemption is one car, the value need not be as accurate as if the exemption were $3,000 in one car.

One way to place a value on a car is to take it to a used car dealership and see what the dealer would pay for it. There is a great deal of subjectivity here. Another method is to check the Kelley Blue Book, NABA book, black book, or one of several others. It may be prudent to look at several of these and compare values. Some of these books may be found on the Internet (e.g., http://www.NABA.com). They are also available at a public library.

To what extent must property be itemized? Be reasonable and use good judgment. If a group of items is exempt, such as furniture, itemization by piece is unnecessary (i.e., sofa, kitchen table, four kitchen chairs). On the other hand, if the group is jewelry or furs and several items are expensive, each piece must be itemized.

If the debtor does not hold any interest in a type of personal property, state "none" for that type.

A Cash on hand

Example: currency and coin

If the cash is kept at a business location, state the address (including the zip code) of the business.

If the cash is kept at a private residence, state the address (including the zip code) of the residence.

If property is being held for the debtor by someone else, state that person's name and address.

State the current market value of the debtor's interest in the cash on hand, without deducting any secured claim or exemption. The amount of any exemption will be claimed in Schedule C—Property Claimed as Exempt.

B Checking, savings, or other financial accounts; certificates of deposit, or shares in banks, savings and loan, thrift, building and loan, and homestead associations; or credit unions, brokerage houses, or cooperatives

Examples: checking account
Account No. 343721-6
Pioneer National Bank
savings account
Account No. 44510-7
Peoples State Bank

State the address (including zip code) of the financial institution.

The current market value of shares of stock can be ascertained from a stockbroker or ticker tape.

The amount of any exemption will be claimed in Schedule C—Property Claimed as Exempt.

C Security deposits with public utilities, telephone companies, landlords, and others

State the entity holding the security deposit.

Example: Public Service Co.

State the address (including the zip code) of the entity holding the security deposit.

D Household goods and furnishings, including audio, video, and computer equipment

Examples: general household goods
IBM PS2/50 computer

State the address (including zip code) of the residence where the household goods and furnishings are generally located.

Current market value is the debtor's best estimate. The amount of any exemption will be claimed in Schedule C—Property Claimed as Exempt.

E Books, pictures and other art objects, antiques, stamp, coin, record, tape, compact disc, and other collections or collectibles

Examples: books
records
paintings
stamp collection
butterfly collection

State the address (including zip code) of the residence where the books, pictures, and other collections or collectibles are generally located.

The current market value is the debtor's best estimate. The amount of any exemption will be claimed in Schedule C—Property Claimed as Exempt.

F Wearing apparel

Example: personal clothing

State the address (including zip code) of the residence where the wearing apparel is generally located.

The current market value is the debtor's best estimate. The amount of any exemption will be claimed in Schedule C—Property Claimed as Exempt.

G Furs and jewelry

Examples: mink coat
Rolex watch

If furs are in storage, state the address (including zip code) of the furrier or other entity where the furs are stored.

If jewelry is in a safe deposit box, state the address (including zip code) of the institution where the box is located.

State the address (including zip code) of the residence where the furs or jewelry are generally located.

The current market value is the debtor's best estimate. The amount of any exemption will be claimed in Schedule C—Property Claimed as Exempt.

H Firearms and sports, photographic, and other equipment

Examples: 357 Magnum
sports equipment

State the address (including zip code) of the residence where the equipment is generally located.

The current market value is the debtor's best estimate. The amount of any exemption will be claimed in Schedule C—Property Claimed as Exempt.

I Interests in insurance policies

For each policy that has a surrender or refund value, describe the type of insurance, name and address of the insurance company, and the policy number.

List only the insurance policies that have a cash value. Do not list term insurance.

Examples: cash surrender value
life insurance on life of debtor
with Met Life, One Madison Ave., New York, NY 10010
Policy No. 594819 658A
Issued 1-10-54
refund of premium from auto insurance
on vehicle that will be sold
State Farm, Bloomington, IL 61710
Policy No. 7 0963-F01-54A

State the address (including zip code) where the policies are generally kept (e.g., home, safe deposit box, office).

A statement in writing of the cash surrender value or refund due on the premiums should be obtained from the agent servicing each policy. The amount of any exemption will be claimed in Schedule C—Property Claimed as Exempt.

J Annuities

Itemize and name each issuer.

List all annuities, whether or not the debtor is currently receiving payments.

Example: retirement annuity
Florida Teachers Retirement Fund

State the address (including zip code) where the certificate is generally kept (e.g., home, safe deposit box, office).

Use the current value of the fund as of the date of the filing of the petition. The amount of any exemption will be claimed in Schedule C—Property Claimed as Exempt.

K Interests in IRA, ERISA, Keogh, or other pension or profit-sharing plans

List each interest separately.

Example: IRA
Friendly Federal Savings

State the address (including zip code) where the institution is located.

The current market value is the balance in the plan. The amount of any exemption will be claimed in Schedule C—Property Claimed as Exempt.

L Stock and interests in incorporated and unincorporated businesses

List each holding separately.

Example: 15 common shares of General Toaster

State the address (including zip code) where the stock certificates are kept.

The current market value is the debtor's best estimate as determined by the sources available to the debtor (e.g., the debtor's stockbroker)

M Interests in partnerships or joint ventures

List each interest separately.

Example: ¼ limited partnership interest in Omni Toy Company

If the debtor has a document, then state the address where the document is kept.
If the debtor has no document, then state the address (including zip code) of the entity.

The current market value is the debtor's best estimate as determined by the sources available to the debtor.

N Government and corporate bonds and other negotiable and non-negotiable instruments

Examples: T-Bill matures 7-1-08, discount 8.32
checks
note from J. Smith, 6504 N. Fourth Place, Avon, OH

State the address (including zip code) where the certificate is kept.

The current market value is determined by the market on which they are commonly traded. The amount of any exemption will be claimed in Schedule C—Property Claimed as Exempt.

O Accounts receivable

Include the name of the account debtor and when the account first became due.

Example: Accounts Receivable
Mary L. Wentworth
due 12/5/04

State the address (including zip code) of the account debtor.

The current market value is the amount due.

P Alimony, maintenance, support, and property settlements to which the debtor is or may be entitled

Include what the obligation is based on, the name of the person who owes the obligation, the recipient of the obligation, the court issuing the decree, and the date of the decree.

Example: alimony due from Jack Williamson (former spouse)
for Jackie Williamson
Cherokee County Court
Idabelle, NC
12/24/04

State the address (including zip code) of the person who owes the obligation.

The current market value is either the total amount due or the amount of the monthly payments and the length of time over which they are to be paid, depending on the arrangement. The amount of any exemption will be claimed in Schedule C—Property Claimed as Exempt.

Q Other liquidated debts owing debtor, including tax refunds

Examples: Federal Tax refund on 1040 for 2004
due from U.S. Treasury
State Tax refund for 2004
due from Oklahoma Tax Commission
Ad valorem tax refund for 2004
due from Beaver County Treasurer

State the address (including zip code) of the person or entity who owes the obligation.

The current market value is the amount due. The amount of any exemption will be claimed in Schedule C—Property Claimed as Exempt.

R Equitable or future interests, life estates, and rights or powers exercisable for the benefit of the debtor other than those listed in Schedule A—Real Property

Example: life estate
Walker Trust Fund

State the address (including zip code) of the trustee, if one exists.

The current market value is the debtor's best judgment. The amount of any exemption will be claimed in Schedule C—Property Claimed as Exempt.

S Contingent and noncontingent interests in estate of a decedent, death benefit plan, life insurance policy, or trust

Example: TIAA/CREF
contingent interest in annuity
of Agnes Adams, deceased

State the address (including zip code) of the person who will administer the estate or trust.

The current market value is the face value shown on the document. The amount of any exemption will be claimed in Schedule C—Property Claimed as Exempt.

T Other contingent and unliquidated claims of every nature, including tax refunds, counterclaims of the debtor, and rights to setoff claims

Examples: Jones v. Smyth
action for damages
for breach of contract
Jones v. Everton Press
workers' compensation claim

State the address (including zip code) of the defendant.

The current market value is the debtor's best estimate of what the claims are worth. The amount of any exemption will be claimed in Schedule C—Property Claimed as Exempt.

U Patents, copyrights, and other intellectual property

Examples: patent on submersible pump
U.S. Patent #10,239,341
(copy of U.S. Patent in debtor's possession)
Patent Application Serial #876,923
filed 1/4/03
(copy of patent application in debtor's possession)
1,325,004 for the trademark "Wong's Wok"
(copy of trademark registration in debtor's possession)
Copyright G 104,995—copyright for
"Exploring Outer Space"
(copy of copyright certificate attached)

State the address (including zip code) where the documentation is generally kept.

The current market value is the debtor's best estimate of what the property interest is worth.

V Licenses, franchises, and other general intangibles

Example: franchise for MacDougal's Restaurant

State the address (including zip code) where the documentation is generally kept.

The current market value is the debtor's best estimate based on whatever sources are available.

W Automobiles, trucks, trailers, and other vehicles and accessories

Include serial number or vehicle identification number (VIN), if the vehicle has one.

Examples: 2002 Ford Mustang
6F02Y122713
1999 Mercury Grand Marquis
IMEBP92F6FH656643
2002 Kawasaki Voyager XII
1985 29-ft. Elandan II Winnebago

State the address (including zip code) where the vehicle is generally parked.

The current market value is the debtor's best estimate, which may be determined from bluebook or other sources (including the debtor's opinion). The amount of any exemption will be claimed in Schedule C—Property Claimed as Exempt.

X Boats, motors, and accessories

Include serial number or VIN, if one applies.

Examples: Sea Bass Boat
Johnson 75 hp motor
Dilly Trailer

State the address (including zip code) where the boats, motors, and accessories are generally kept (e.g., home, marina, storage facility).

The current market value is the debtor's best estimate, which may be determined from bluebook or other sources (including the debtor's opinion). The amount of any exemption will be claimed in Schedule C—Property Claimed as Exempt.

Y Aircraft and accessories

Include serial number or VIN, if one applies.

Example: 1985 Cessna TT

State the address (including zip code) where the aircraft and accessories are generally hangared.

The current market value is the debtor's best estimate, which may be determined from various sources, including the debtor's opinion.

Z Office equipment, furnishings, and supplies

Examples: desk

Power Mac 65

State the address (including zip code) of the office where the equipment, furnishings, and supplies can be found.

The current market value is the debtor's best estimate. The amount of any exemption will be claimed in Schedule C—Property Claimed as Exempt.

AA Machinery, fixtures, equipment, and supplies used in business

Examples: cement mixer

compressor

2 bags cement

State the address (including zip code) of the business where the machinery, fixtures, equipment, and supplies can be found.

The current market value is the debtor's best estimate. The amount of any exemption will be claimed in Schedule C—Property Claimed as Exempt.

BB Inventory

Example: stock of groceries

State the address (including zip code) where the inventory is physically located (e.g., factory, warehouse).

For the current market value, use cost basis or accrual method, depending on the accounting method used in the Schedule of Current Income and Current Expenditures for a Partnership or Corporation.

CC Animals

Examples: 93 head Holstein milk cows

100 chickens

registered German Shepherd (female)

Myna bird

State the address (including zip code) where the animals are physically located.

If a market exists, use the established market for the current market value. If no established market exists, use the debtor's best estimate. The amount of any exemption will be claimed in Schedule C—Property Claimed as Exempt.

DD Crops—growing or harvested

Example: 180 acres of cotton in the field

State the address (including zip code) where the crops are physically located.

The current market value is the debtor's best estimate, which may be based on an established market, if one exists. The amount of any exemption will be claimed in Schedule C—Property Claimed as Exempt.

EE Farming equipment and implements

Include serial number or VIN, if applicable.

Examples: Case tractor

Deere plow

State the address (including zip code) where the farming equipment or implements are physically located.

The current market value is the debtor's best estimate. The amount of any exemption will be claimed in Schedule C—Property Claimed as Exempt.

FF Farm supplies, chemicals, and feed

Example: 80 gal. of Malathion

State the address (including zip code) where the farm supplies, chemicals, and feed are physically located.

For the current market value, use cost basis or accrual method, depending on the accounting method used in the Schedule of Current Income and Current Expenditures for a Partnership or Corporation. The amount of any exemption will be claimed in Schedule C—Property Claimed as Exempt.

GG Other personal property of any kind not already listed

The amount of any exemption will be claimed in Schedule C—Property Claimed as Exempt.

HH Total the amounts of all items of personal property. Report the total on the Summary of Schedules.

PROBLEM 5.8 Using the information in Problem 4.5 complete Schedule B of Official Form No. 6 for the McPhersons.

3. Schedule C: Property Claimed as Exempt

The Code requires the debtor to file a list of property that he or she claims as exempt property from the property of the estate. 11 U.S.C.A. § 522 (1); Fed. R. Bank. P. 4003(a). If a debtor fails to file a list to claim the exemptions, then a dependent of the debtor ("dependent," by definition, includes the spouse of the debtor, whether or not the spouse is actually dependent) may file the list of property. Absent an objection to the list by a party in interest, the property claimed on the list as exempt is exempt. Rule 1007(c) requires the schedules to be filed within 15 days after the order for relief, unless the court extends the time.

Schedule C of Official Form No. 6 (see Exhibit 5–11) is a list of property claimed as exempt. Local court rules may affect the exact method for claiming exempt property including the time and place for claiming exemptions and the manner of indicating what property is claimed as exempt. Whether a debtor may claim specific items of real and personal property as exempt will be explored in detail later in this chapter.

To claim an exemption, the debtor must provide the following information:

1. a description of property;
2. the statute creating the exemption;
3. the value claimed as exempt; and
4. the current market value of the property without the deduction of the exemption.

The current market value of the property without the deduction of the exemption should correspond to the current market value as indicated in Schedules A and B.

Instructions for Completing Official Form No. 6, Schedule C (Property Claimed as Exempt)

A The debtor must elect either the federal exemptions or the state exemptions. Whether this choice exists will depend on whether the debtor's state has opted out of the federal exemptions. Thirty-four states have chosen to "opt out" of the federal bankruptcy exemption alternative. Opting out will be discussed in detail later in this chapter. If the debtor's state has opted out of the federal bankruptcy exemptions, check the box for 11 U.S.C.A. § 522(b)(2). If the debtor's state has not opted out of the federal bankruptcy exemptions but the debtor has elected to claim state exemptions, also check the box for 11 U.S.C.A. § 522(b)(2).

If the debtor's state has not opted out of the federal bankruptcy exemptions and the debtor has elected the federal bankruptcy exemptions, then check the box for 11 U.S.C.A. § 522(b)(1).

By checking the first box, the debtor has chosen the federal bankruptcy exemptions. By checking the second box, the debtor has chosen the state exemptions and the federal nonbankruptcy exemptions.

B Since the property claimed as exempt has already been listed and described either on Schedule A—Real Property or on Schedule B—Personal Property, the same description should be entered on Schedule C.

List the property in the order in which it appears on Schedule A and Schedule B.

C Specify the law that provides the exemption.

Examples: OK Stat. Ann. tit. 31, § 2 (2001)

11 U.S.C.A. § 522(d)(3)

42 U.S.C.A. § 407

EXHIBIT 5–11 Official Form No. 6, Schedule C (Property Claimed as Exempt)

FORM B6C
(6/90)

In re ______________________________,
Debtor

Case No. ______________________
(If known)

SCHEDULE C - PROPERTY CLAIMED AS EXEMPT

Debtor elects the exemptions to which debtor is entitled under:
(Check one box)

A
☐ 11 U.S.C. § 522(b)(1): Exemptions provided in 11 U.S.C. § 522(d). **Note: These exemptions are available only in certain states.**

☐ 11 U.S.C. § 522(b)(2): Exemptions available under applicable nonbankruptcy federal laws, state or local law where the debtor's domicile has been located for the 180 days immediately preceding the filing of the petition, or for a longer portion of the 180-day period than in any other place, and the debtor's interest as a tenant by the entirety or joint tenant to the extent the interest is exempt from process under applicable nonbankruptcy law.

DESCRIPTION OF PROPERTY	SPECIFY LAW PROVIDING EACH EXEMPTION	VALUE OF CLAIMED EXEMPTION	CURRENT MARKET VALUE OF PROPERTY WITHOUT DEDUCTING EXEMPTION
B	C	D	E

D State the value of the claimed exemption.

For statutes carrying value limitations, use the value limitation, unless the statutory exemption exceeds the market value of the property. In that event, only the market value of the property can be claimed as the exemption.

Example: "The debtor's interest, not to exceed $2,950 in value, in one motor vehicle." 11 U.S.C.A. § 522(d)(2).

For statutes not carrying value limitations, use the current market value of the property.

Example: "Any unmatured life insurance contract owned by the debtor, other than a credit life insurance contract." 11 U.S.C.A. § 522(d)(7).

E State the current market value of the property without deducting the exemption.

The current market value should correspond to the current market value given for the property when it was listed on either Schedule A or Schedule B.

Example: If the current market value reported on Schedule B is $40,000 and the exemption is $8,000, report $40,000.

PROBLEM 5.9 Using the information in Problem 4.5, complete Schedule C of Official Form No. 6 for the McPhersons.

Check to see if your state has opted out of the federal exemptions before you begin this problem.

4. Schedule D: Creditors Holding Secured Claims

Official Form No. 6, Schedule D (see Exhibit 5–12) lists all entities holding claims secured by property of the debtor as of the date of the filing of the petition. Included are judgment liens, garnishments, statutory liens, mortgages, deeds of trust, and other security interests.

Schedule D requires the following information for each **creditor holding a secured claim:**

1. the creditor's name, mailing address (including zip code), and account number, if any;
2. whether a codebtor exists (other than a spouse in a joint case) who is liable on a claim;
3. if the debtor is married, whether the property is held by the husband, wife, jointly, or as community property;
4. the date when the claim was incurred by the debtor, the nature of the lien, and a description and the market value of the property subject to the lien;
5. an indication if the claim is contingent, unliquidated, or disputed;
6. the amount of the claim without deducting the value of the collateral; and
7. the amount of the unsecured portion of the claim, if any.

Instructions for Completing Official Form No. 6, Schedule D (Creditors Holding Secured Claims)

Problems will be minimized if a bankruptcy filing program is used because once a value of an item is entered, the listing of the item and its value will be consistent throughout the schedules. If forms are completed manually, sometimes an item or its value is not listed consistently. When data is manually entered in schedule D, it must be consistent with schedule B.

A Does the debtor have creditors holding secured claims to report on Schedule D?

The following are secured claims that must be listed on Schedule D:

judgment lien
garnishment
statutory lien
mortgage
deed of trust
contract for deed
security agreement
retail installment contract
any other security agreement

EXHIBIT 5–12 Official Form No. 6, Schedule D (Creditors Holding Secured Claims)

Form B6D
(12/03)

In re ______________________________, **Case No.** ______________________
Debtor **(If known)**

SCHEDULE D - CREDITORS HOLDING SECURED CLAIMS

State the name, mailing address, including zip code and last four digits of any account number of all entities holding claims secured by property of the debtor as of the date of filing of the petition. The complete account number of any account the debtor has with the creditor is useful to the trustee and the creditor and may be provided if the debtor chooses to do so. List creditors holding all types of secured interests such as judgment liens, garnishments, statutory liens, mortgages, deeds of trust, and other security interests. List creditors in alphabetical order to the extent practicable. If all secured creditors will not fit on this page, use the continuation sheet provided.

If any entity other than a spouse in a joint case may be jointly liable on a claim, place an "X" in the column labeled "Codebtor," include the entity on the appropriate schedule of creditors, and complete Schedule H - Codebtors. If a joint petition is filed, state whether husband, wife, both of them, or the marital community may be liable on each claim by placing an "H," "W," "J," or "C" in the column labeled "Husband, Wife, Joint, or Community."

If the claim is contingent, place an "X" in the column labeled "Contingent." If the claim is unliquidated, place an "X" in the column labeled "Unliquidated." If the claim is disputed, place an "X" in the column labeled "Disputed." (You may need to place an "X" in more than one of these three columns.)

Report the total of all claims listed on this schedule in the box labeled "Total" on the last sheet of the completed schedule. Report this total also on the Summary of Schedules.

A ☐ Check this box if debtor has no creditors holding secured claims to report on this Schedule D.

CREDITORíS NAME, MAILING ADDRESS INCLUDING ZIP CODE, AND ACCOUNT NUMBER (See instructions above.)	CODEBTOR	HUSBAND, WIFE, JOINT, OR COMMUNITY	DATE CLAIM WAS INCURRED, NATURE OF LIEN, AND DESCRIPTION AND MARKET VALUE OF PROPERTY SUBJECT TO LIEN	CONTINGENT	UNLIQUIDATED	DISPUTED	AMOUNT OF CLAIM WITHOUT DEDUCTING VALUE OF COLLATERAL	UNSECURED PORTION, IF ANY
ACCOUNT NO. **B**	**C**	**D**	**EFG** VALUE $		**H**		**I**	**J**
ACCOUNT NO.			VALUE $					
ACCOUNT NO.			VALUE $					
ACCOUNT NO.			VALUE $					

_______continuation sheets attached

Subtotal➤ (Total of this page)	$
Total➤ (Use only on last page)	$ **K**

(Report total also on Summary of Schedules)

(continued)

EXHIBIT 5–12 Official Form No. 6, Schedule D (Creditors Holding Secured Claims), Continued

Form B6D - Cont.
(12/03)

In re ______________________________, **Case No.** ______________________
Debtor **(If known)**

SCHEDULE D - CREDITORS HOLDING SECURED CLAIMS

(Continuation Sheet)

CREDITORíS NAME, MAILING ADDRESS INCLUDING ZIP CODE AND ACCOUNT NUMBER (See instructions.)	CODEBTOR	HUSBAND, WIFE, JOINT, OR COMMUNITY	DATE CLAIM WAS INCURRED, NATURE OF LIEN, AND DESCRIPTION AND MARKET VALUE OF PROPERTY SUBJECT TO LIEN	CONTINGENT	UNLIQUIDATED	DISPUTED	AMOUNT OF CLAIM WITHOUT DEDUCTING VALUE OF COLLATERAL	UNSECURED PORTION, IF ANY
ACCOUNT NO.			VALUE $					
ACCOUNT NO.			VALUE $					
ACCOUNT NO.			VALUE $					
ACCOUNT NO.			VALUE $					
ACCOUNT NO.			VALUE $					

Sheet no. ___ of ___continuation sheets attached to Schedule of Creditors Holding Secured Claims Subtotal➤ (Total of this page) $

Total➤ (Use only on last page) $

(Report total also on Summary of Schedules)

A creditor's claim should be listed only once even if the claim is secured in part. The remainder of the claim should be treated as a general unsecured claim. A partially secured claim should be listed on Schedule D. The unsecured portion of the claim should *not* be listed on Schedule F.

A creditor is a secured creditor in Schedule D only if the collateral is still in existence. If the asset does not show up on Schedule A or B, the claim should not be shown as a secured claim.

Example: Debtor purchased a set of tires and gave the seller a security interest in the tires. After the tires wore out and before the debt was fully paid, debtor filed for bankruptcy. The seller is not listed as a secured creditor because the collateral (the tires) no longer exists.

Even if there is no equity in the collateral upon which to secure the claim, the claim still goes in Schedule D.

Example: $100,000 market value of the property

60,000 first mortgage holder's claim

70,000 second mortgage holder's claim

50,000 third mortgage holder's claim

Third mortgage holder is still listed on Schedule D and not on Schedule F.

If the debtor has no creditors holding secured claims, then this box should be checked and the total, "–0–," should be entered on the Summary of Schedules. This completes Schedule D.

B Creditor's account number, name, and mailing address

Creditors should be listed in alphabetical order to the extent practicable.

If the account number is unknown, state "unknown." If the claim does not have an account number, state "none."

If the creditor is represented by a collection agency or an attorney, list the name of the collection agency or the attorney. Indicate that the collection agency or the attorney is the representative for the creditor. The collection agency or the attorney should be listed among the creditors in alphabetical order.

If the creditor is represented by a collection agency or an attorney, state the mailing address of the collection agency or the attorney.

C Codebtors (other than a spouse in a joint petition)

If any entity, other than a spouse in a joint petition, may be jointly liable on the claim, indicate "yes" by placing an "X" in the Codebtor column. If no entities are jointly liable on the claim, leave the Codebtor column blank. If there is a codebtor, then complete Schedule H—Codebtors.

D When a joint petition is filed, the debtors must indicate who is liable on each claim by the first letter of the designation:

Example:

	husband	H
	wife	W
	jointly	J
	marital community	C

If the petition is not joint, leave this column blank.

E The nature of the lien

Examples:

judgment lien

garnishment

mechanic's lien

real estate mortgage

deed of trust

UCC article 9 security interest

F A description of the property subject to the lien

Examples: *judgment lien:* List every item of property of the judgment debtor that is subject to the lien. Use the description from Schedule A or Schedule B.

garnishment: State the source of the judgment debtor's wages:

Ajax Manufacturing Co. wages garnished from debtor's employer.

mechanic's lien: Describe the property that is subject to the lien. Use the description from Schedule B.

real estate mortgage: Use the legal description as it appears in Schedule A, rather than the mailing address:

2d mortgage on homestead

Lot 2, Block 2, Brookwood Addition

Tulsa, Tulsa County, OK

deed of trust: Describe the property that is subject to the deed of trust. Use the description from Schedule A or Schedule B.

UCC article 9 security interest: Describe the collateral that is subject to the security interest. Use the description from Schedule B.

G The market value of the property subject to the lien

For the market value of the property of the debtor that is subject to the lien, use the current market value stated in Schedule A or Schedule B.

Examples: If the property has a market value of $75,000 with a lien of $100,000, the market value of property subject to the lien is $75,000.

If the property has a market value of $125,000 with a lien of $100,000, the market value of the property subject to the lien is $125,000.

For garnishment, use the amount of the judgment but no more than the amount subject to garnishment under the law.

H Indicate whether the claim is contingent, unliquidated or disputed. Since a claim may qualify under more than one category (i.e., a claim may be contingent and unliquidated, contingent and disputed, unliquidated and disputed, or contingent, unliquidated and disputed), indicate each category.

1. *Contingent:* A **contingent claim** is dependent on some future event that may or may not take place.

   Example: Before Janice's mother filed for bankruptcy under Chapter 7, Janice borrowed $1,000 from First Bank and signed a promissory note. Before First Bank would loan Janice the money, the Bank required Janice to have her mother sign a security agreement giving the bank a security interest in a diamond bracelet. The security agreement provided that if Janice did not pay the note when due, Janice's mother would either pay Janice's obligation or permit the bank to repossess the bracelet. First Bank's claim against Janice's mother is a contingent claim.

   If the claim is contingent, place an "X" in the Contingent column. If the claim is not contingent, leave the Contingent column blank.

2. *Unliquidated:* An **unliquidated claim** is a claim the amount of which is uncertain.

   Example: The Flower Market hired the Metro Agency to design an advertising campaign. The compensation was set as "a reasonable fee." Metro designed the campaign but has not sent a bill to the Flower Market.

   The Metro Agency borrowed $10,000 from Gotham Bank and gave Gotham a security interest in its accounts receivable, including the Flower Market's promise to pay "a reasonable fee." Subsequently, the Metro Agency filed a petition in bankruptcy under Chapter 7. Gotham's claim as to the Flower Market account receivable is unliquidated.

   If the claim is unliquidated, place an "×" in the column labeled "Unliquidated."

   If the claim is not unliquidated, leave the Unliquidated column blank.

3. *Disputed:* A **disputed claim** is a claim contested by the debtor.

   Example: Ethel and Roland Charles, husband and wife, owned a tractor. Roland borrowed $5,000 from People's Bank and gave People's a security interest in the tractor. When signing the security agreement, Roland signed his own name and Ethel's name. When Roland died, Ethel inherited Roland's interest in the tractor. Ethel refused to pay the loan, claiming that her signature was a forgery. Ethel filed for bankruptcy under Chapter 7. The bank's claim as to the tractor is disputed.

   If the claim is disputed, place an "×" in the column labeled "Disputed." If the claim is not disputed, leave the Disputed column blank.

4. *Disputed and Unliquidated:* A disputed and unliquidated claim is contested by the debtor and the amount of the claim is uncertain.

Example: Geraldine is involved in an automobile accident and is sued by the driver of the other vehicle for $50,000. Geraldine claims that the accident was the fault of the other driver and that even if it were her fault, she would not owe $50,000. The claim is contested and therefore disputed. The amount of the claim is also uncertain and therefore unliquidated.

I State the amount of the claim secured by property of the debtor without deducting the value of the collateral.

To the extent that it is possible, state the amount of the claim as of the date of the bankruptcy filing. If the claim is a secured claim, the claim is the payoff amount. The debtor may be able find the payoff amount by accessing the account over the Internet or by telephoning the lender.

J State the amount of the unsecured portion of the claim, if any.

The claim secured by the property of the debtor (the lien) is the amount of the claim not to exceed the value of the property.

$100,000	market value of the property
60,000	first mortgage holder
70,000	second mortgage holder
20,000	third mortgage holder

The first mortgage holder has no unsecured claim. The second mortgage holder has an unsecured claim of $30,000. The third mortgage holder has an unsecured claim of $20,000. See 11 U.S.C.A. § 506(a).

K Total the amount of the claims without deducting the value of the collateral. Report the total on the Summary of Schedules.

PROBLEM 5.10 Using the information in Problem 4.5, complete Schedule D of Official Form No. 6 for the McPhersons.

5. Schedule E: Creditors Holding Unsecured Priority Claims

The categories of creditors having priority status in a voluntary Chapter 7 case are listed in the Bankruptcy Code. See 11 U.S.C.A. §§ 507(a)(3)–(9). Official Form No. 6, Schedule E (see Exhibit 5–13) summarizes these categories and requires the debtor to indicate claims for each category.

A claim that is entitled to priority in whole or in part should be listed on Schedule E only. Whether the claim is listed on Schedule E will not determine the rights among the parties or how the property will ultimately be distributed. Each creditor will file a proof of claim that will determine if, and how, the claim will be paid.

Schedule E requires the following information for each creditor holding an unsecured priority claim:

1. the creditor's name, mailing address (including zip code), and account number, if any;
2. whether a codebtor exists (other than a spouse in a joint case) who is liable on a claim;
3. if the debtor is married, whether the property is held by the husband, wife, jointly, or as community property;
4. the date when the claim was incurred and the consideration for the claim;
5. an indication if the claim is contingent, unliquidated, or disputed;
6. the total amount of the claim; and
7. the amount entitled to priority.

Requests for information concerning judgments and negotiable instruments have been deleted from the schedules. Such requests are left to the trustee's inquiries.

EXHIBIT 5–13 Official Form No. 6, Schedule E (Creditors Holding Unsecured Priority Claims)

Form B6E
(04/04)

In re ______________________________,
Debtor

Case No.______________________
(if known)

SCHEDULE E - CREDITORS HOLDING UNSECURED PRIORITY CLAIMS

A complete list of claims entitled to priority, listed separately by type of priority, is to be set forth on the sheets provided. Only holders of unsecured claims entitled to priority should be listed in this schedule. In the boxes provided on the attached sheets, state the name, mailing address, including zip code, and last four digits of the account number, if any, of all entities holding priority claims against the debtor or the property of the debtor, as of the date of the filing of the petition. The complete account number of any account the debtor has with the creditor is useful to the trustee and the creditor and may be provided if the debtor chooses to do so.

If any entity other than a spouse in a joint case may be jointly liable on a claim, place an "X" in the column labeled "Codebtor," include the entity on the appropriate schedule of creditors, and complete Schedule H-Codebtors. If a joint petition is filed, state whether husband, wife, both of them or the marital community may be liable on each claim by placing an "H,""W,""J," or "C" in the column labeled "Husband, Wife, Joint, or Community."

If the claim is contingent, place an "X" in the column labeled "Contingent." If the claim is unliquidated, place an "X" in the column labeled "Unliquidated." If the claim is disputed, place an "X" in the column labeled "Disputed." (You may need to place an "X" in more than one of these three columns.)

Report the total of claims listed on each sheet in the box labeled "Subtotal" on each sheet. Report the total of all claims listed on this Schedule E in the box labeled "Total" on the last sheet of the completed schedule. Repeat this total also on the Summary of Schedules.

☐ Check this box if debtor has no creditors holding unsecured priority claims to report on this Schedule E.

TYPES OF PRIORITY CLAIMS (Check the appropriate box(es) below if claims in that category are listed on the attached sheets)

☐ **Extensions of credit in an involuntary case**

Claims arising in the ordinary course of the debtor's business or financial affairs after the commencement of the case but before the earlier of the appointment of a trustee or the order for relief. 11 U.S.C. § 507(a)(2).

☐ **Wages, salaries, and commissions**

Wages, salaries, and commissions, including vacation, severance, and sick leave pay owing to employees and commissions owing to qualifying independent sales representatives up to $4,925* per person earned within 90 days immediately preceding the filing of the original petition, or the cessation of business, whichever occurred first, to the extent provided in 11 U.S.C. § 507(a)(3).

☐ **Contributions to employee benefit plans**

Money owed to employee benefit plans for services rendered within 180 days immediately preceding the filing of the original petition, or the cessation of business, whichever occurred first, to the extent provided in 11 U.S.C. § 507(a)(4).

☐ **Certain farmers and fishermen**

Claims of certain farmers and fishermen, up to $4,925* per farmer or fisherman, against the debtor, as provided in 11 U.S.C. § 507(a)(5).

☐ **Deposits by individuals**

Claims of individuals up to $2,225* for deposits for the purchase, lease, or rental of property or services for personal, family, or household use, that were not delivered or provided. 11 U.S.C. § 507(a)(6).

(continued)

Form B6E
(04/04)

In re ______________________________________, Debtor — Case No.______________________ (if known)

☐ **Alimony, Maintenance, or Support**

Claims of a spouse, former spouse, or child of the debtor for alimony, maintenance, or support, to the extent provided in 11 U.S.C. § 507(a)(7).

☐ **Taxes and Certain Other Debts Owed to Governmental Units**

Taxes, customs duties, and penalties owing to federal, state, and local governmental units as set forth in 11 U.S.C. § 507(a)(8).

☐ **Commitments to Maintain the Capital of an Insured Depository Institution**

Claims based on commitments to the FDIC, RTC, Director of the Office of Thrift Supervision, Comptroller of the Currency, or Board of Governors of the Federal Reserve System, or their predecessors or successors, to maintain the capital of an insured depository institution. 11 U.S.C. § 507 (a)(9).

* Amounts are subject to adjustment on April 1, 2007, and every three years thereafter with respect to cases commenced on or after the date of adjustment.

____ continuation sheets attached

(continued)

EXHIBIT 5–13 Official Form No. 6, Schedule E (Creditors Holding Unsecured Priority Claims), Continued

Form B6E - Cont.
(04/04)

In re ________________________, **Case No.** ________________
Debtor **(If known)**

SCHEDULE E - CREDITORS HOLDING UNSECURED PRIORITY CLAIMS

(Continuation Sheet)

____
TYPE OF PRIORITY

CREDITORíS NAME, MAILING ADDRESS INCLUDING ZIP CODE, AND ACCOUNT NUMBER (See instructions.)	CODEBTOR	HUSBAND, WIFE, JOINT, OR COMMUNITY	DATE CLAIM WAS INCURRED AND CONSIDERATION FOR CLAIM	CONTINGENT	UNLIQUIDATED	DISPUTED	AMOUNT OF CLAIM	AMOUNT ENTITLED TO PRIORITY
ACCOUNT NO.								
ACCOUNT NO.								
ACCOUNT NO.								
ACCOUNT NO.								
ACCOUNT NO.								

Sheet no. ___ of ___ sheets attached to Schedule of Creditors Holding Priority Claims

Subtotal➤ (Total of this page) $

Total➤ (Use only on last page of the completed Schedule E.) (Report total also on Summary of Schedules) $

Instructions for Completing Official Form No. 6, Schedule E (Creditors Holding Unsecured Priority Claims)

The dollar amounts were adjusted on April 1, 2007, and will be adjusted again on April 1, 2010. Check 11 U.S.C.A. § 104 and comments.

A If, after answering "no" to the questions in "B" (i.e., Does the debtor have a creditor holding an unsecured priority claim?), there is no claim to report on Schedule E, then this box should be checked and "-0-" entered on the Summary of Schedules. This completes Schedule E.

The first type of priority claim listed in Schedule E applies only to an insolvency case. There will be no creditors in this category for the voluntary Chapter 7 case. Therefore, either state "none" or leave the box blank.

B A creditor holding an unsecured priority claim in a voluntary Chapter 7 case may be classified under one of seven categories.

1. Does the debtor have a creditor holding an unsecured claim for wages, salaries, and commissions?

   This claim is for wages, salaries, and commissions, including vacation, severance, and sick-leave pay owing to employees, up to a maximum of $4,925 per employee, earned within 90 days immediately preceding the filing of the original petition, or the cessation of business, whichever occurred first, to the extent provided in 11 U.S.C.A. § 507(a)(3).

   If there is no creditor in this category, either state "none" or leave the box blank.

2. Does the debtor have a creditor holding an unsecured claim for contributions to employee benefit plans?

   This claim arises due to money owed to employee benefit plans for services rendered within 180 days immediately preceding the filing of the original petition, or the cessation of business, whichever occurred first, to the extent provided in 11 U.S.C.A. § 507(a)(4).

   Example: retirement funds

   If there is no creditor in this category, either state "none" or leave the box blank.

3. Does the debtor have a creditor holding an unsecured claim of certain farmers and fishermen?

   This claim arises from unsecured claims of certain farmers and fishermen, up to a maximum of $4,925 per farmer or fisherman, against the debtor, as provided in 11 U.S.C.A. § 507(a)(5).

   Examples: A farmer has left grain with a grain elevator, and the elevator files for bankruptcy before paying for the grain.

   A fisherman has left a fish catch with a cannery, and the cannery files for bankruptcy before paying for the catch.

   If there is no creditor in this category, either state "none" or leave the box blank.

4. Does the debtor have a creditor holding an unsecured claim of an individual arising from deposits?

   These claims are unsecured claims of individuals up to a maximum of $2,225 for deposits for the purchase, lease, or rental of property or services for personal, family, or household use, that were not delivered or provided. 11 U.S.C.A. § 507(a)(6).

   Examples: layaways

   deposits for concert tickets

   If there is no creditor in this category, either state "none" or leave the box blank.

5. Does the debtor have a creditor holding an unsecured claim for alimony, maintenance, or support for a spouse, former spouse, or child of the debtor?

   These claims arise in connection with a separation agreement, divorce decree, or other order of the court. 11 U.S.C.A. § 507(a)(7).

   If there is no creditor in this category, either state "none" or leave the box blank.

6. Does the debtor have a creditor holding an unsecured claim of governmental units for taxes and certain other debts owed?

   These claims arise from taxes, customs duties, and penalties owing to federal, state, and local governmental units as set forth in 11 U.S.C.A. § 507(a)(8).

Examples: income tax
payroll tax
social security tax
excise tax
sales tax
corporate tax

If there is no creditor in this category, either state "none" or leave the box blank.

7. Does the debtor have a creditor holding an unsecured claim based on a commitment to an authority to maintain the capital of an insured depository institution?

   These unsecured claims are based on any commitment by the debtor to the Federal Deposit Insurance Corporation (FDIC), the Resolution Trust Corporation (RTC), the Director of the Office of Thrift Supervision, the Comptroller of the Currency, or the Board of Governors of the Federal Reserve System, or their predecessors or successors, to maintain the capital of an insured depository institution. 11 U.S.C.A. § 507(a)(9).

   If there is no creditor in this category, either state "none" or leave the box blank.

   If the debtor has answered one or more of the above questions "yes," then each type of priority must be listed on a separate "continuation sheet." (Note the "Type of Priority" line in the upper right portion of the Schedule E form.)

C For each claim, provide the following information.

1. The debtor's account number assigned by the creditor, the creditor's name, and mailing address. Creditors should be listed in alphabetical order to the extent practicable. A creditor's claim should be listed only once, even if the claim is entitled only in part to priority under 11 U.S.C.A. § 507(a), with the remainder of the claim to be treated as a general unsecured claim. A claim entitled only in part to priority should be listed on Schedule E. The portion of the claim not entitled to priority should not be listed on Schedule F.

   Example: For an unsecured claim for contributions to an employee benefit plan, the nature of the claim would be "retirement fund" and the name of the creditor would be the name of the fund itself.

   If the account number is unknown, state "unknown." If the claim does not have an account number, state "none."

2. If there is a codebtor other than a spouse in a joint case (i.e., an entity jointly liable on the claim), place an "X" in the column labeled "Codebtor." If there are no entities jointly liable on the claim, leave the Codebtor column blank.

   If there is a codebtor, then complete Schedule H—Codebtors.

3. If a joint petition is filed, indicate whether the debt is owed by the husband (H), wife (W), jointly (J), or as community property (C). If the petition is not joint, leave this column blank.

   When a joint petition is filed, the debtors must indicate who is liable on each claim.

4. Provide the following information:

   a. the date the claim was incurred by the debtor

   b. the consideration for the claim

      Examples: wages
      vacation pay
      severance pay
      sick leave

5. Indicate whether the claim is contingent, unliquidated, or disputed.

   a. *Contingent:* A claim is contingent if it is dependent on some future event that may or may not take place.

      Example: A wage claim to which the debtor is a guarantor.

      If the claim is contingent place an "×" in the Contingent column. If the claim is not contingent, leave the Contingent column blank.

   b. *Unliquidated:* A claim is unliquidated if the amount of the claim is uncertain.

      If the claim is unliquidated, place an "×" in the column labeled "Unliquidated." If the claim is not unliquidated, leave the Unliquidated column blank.

Example: A tax claim is unliquidated if, at the time of bankruptcy, it is uncertain as to the amount due.

c. *Disputed:* A claim by a creditor is disputed when the debtor contests the claim.

If the claim is disputed, place an "X" in the column labeled "Disputed." If the claim is not disputed, leave the Disputed column blank.

6. State the total amount of the claim as of the date of the bankruptcy petition.
7. State the amount entitled to priority.

D Total the amount of the claims. Report the total on the Summary of Schedules.

PROBLEM 5.11 Using the information in Problem 4.5, complete Schedule E for the McPhersons.

6. Schedule F: Creditors Holding Unsecured Nonpriority Claims

Schedule F (see Exhibit 5–14) is for creditors holding unsecured nonpriority claims. If a claim is partially secured or entitled in part to priority, it should be listed on Schedule D or Schedule E, respectively, and not on Schedule F.

Schedule F requires the following information for each creditor holding an unsecured nonpriority claim:

1. the creditor's name, mailing address (including zip code), and account number, if any;
2. whether a codebtor exists (other than a spouse in a joint case) who is liable on a claim;
3. if the debtor is married, whether the debt is owed by the husband, wife, jointly, or as community property;
4. the date when the claim was incurred by the debtor, the consideration for the claim, and whether the claim is subject to a setoff;
5. an indication if the claim is contingent, unliquidated, or disputed; and
6. the total amount of the claim.

Instructions for Completing Official Form No. 6, Schedule F (Creditors Holding Unsecured Nonpriority Claims)

A A creditor's claim should be listed only once even if the claim is secured in part. The remainder of the claim should be treated as a general unsecured claim. A partially secured claim should be listed on Schedule D. A claim entitled to priority in part under 11 U.S.C.A. § 507(a) should be listed on Schedule E. The unsecured portion of either claim should not be listed on Schedule F.

A creditor's claim should be listed only once if the claim is an unsecured priority claim in part. The unsecured priority claim is listed in Schedule E. If the claim exceeds the statutory priority amount, the excess should not be included in Schedule F. In Schedule E, the amount of the claim is listed as well as the total amount entitled to priority. Therefore, the distinction between what is an unsecured priority claim and an unsecured nonpriority claim has already been made.

If the debtor has no creditors holding unsecured nonpriority claims, then this box should be checked and "-0-" should be entered on the Summary of Schedules. This completes Schedule F.

B The debtor's account number assigned by the creditor, the creditor's name, and mailing address

Creditors should be listed in alphabetical order to the extent practicable.

If the account number is unknown, state "unknown." If the claim does not have an account number, state "none."

If the creditor is represented by a collection agency or an attorney, list the name of the collection agency or the attorney. Indicate that the collection agency or the attorney is the representative for the creditor. The collection agency or the attorney should be listed among the creditors in alphabetical order.

If the creditor is represented by a collection agency or an attorney, state the mailing address of the collection agency or the attorney.

EXHIBIT 5–14 Official Form No. 6, Schedule F (Creditors Holding Unsecured Nonpriority Claims)

Form B6F (12/03)

In re ______________________________, **Case No.** ______________________
Debtor **(If known)**

SCHEDULE F- CREDITORS HOLDING UNSECURED NONPRIORITY CLAIMS

State the name, mailing address, including zip code, and last four digits of any account number, of all entities holding unsecured claims without priority against the debtor or the property of the debtor, as of the date of filing of the petition. The complete account number of any account the debtor has with the creditor is useful to the trustee and the creditor and may be provided if the debtor chooses to do so. Do not include claims listed in Schedules D and E. If all creditors will not fit on this page, use the continuation sheet provided.

If any entity other than a spouse in a joint case may be jointly liable on a claim, place an "X" in the column labeled "Codebtor," include the entity on the appropriate schedule of creditors, and complete Schedule H - Codebtors. If a joint petition is filed, state whether husband, wife, both of them, or the marital community maybe liable on each claim by placing an "H," "W," "J," or "C" in the column labeled "Husband, Wife, Joint, or Community."

If the claim is contingent, place an "X" in the column labeled "Contingent." If the claim is unliquidated, place an "X" in the column labeled "Unliquidated." If the claim is disputed, place an "X" in the column labeled "Disputed." (You may need to place an "X" in more than one of these three columns.)

Report total of all claims listed on this schedule in the box labeled "Total" on the last sheet of the completed schedule. Report this total also on the Summary of Schedules.

A ☐ Check this box if debtor has no creditors holding unsecured claims to report on this Schedule F.

CREDITOR'S NAME, MAILING ADDRESS INCLUDING ZIP CODE, AND ACCOUNT NUMBER (See instructions above.)	CODEBTOR	HUSBAND, WIFE, JOINT, OR COMMUNITY	DATE CLAIM WAS INCURRED AND CONSIDERATION FOR CLAIM. IF CLAIM IS SUBJECT TO SETOFF, SO STATE.	CONTINGENT	UNLIQUIDATED	DISPUTED	AMOUNT OF CLAIM
ACCOUNT NO. B	C	D	E	F			G
ACCOUNT NO.							
ACCOUNT NO.							
ACCOUNT NO.							

_____continuation sheets attached

Subtotal ➤ $
Total ➤ $ H
(Report also on Summary of Schedules)

(continued)

EXHIBIT 5–14 Official Form No. 6, Schedule F (Creditors Holding Unsecured Nonpriority Claims), Continued

FORM B6F - Cont.
(12/03)

In re ______________________________, Debtor

Case No. ______________________________ (If known)

SCHEDULE F - CREDITORS HOLDING UNSECURED NONPRIORITY CLAIMS

(Continuation Sheet)

CREDITOR'S NAME AND MAILING ADDRESS INCLUDING ZIP CODE	CODEBTOR	HUSBAND, WIFE, JOINT, OR COMMUNITY	DATE CLAIM WAS INCURRED, AND CONSIDERATION FOR CLAIM. IF CLAIM IS SUBJECT TO SETOFF, SO STATE.	CONTINGENT	UNLIQUIDATED	DISPUTED	AMOUNT OF CLAIM
ACCOUNT NO.							
ACCOUNT NO.							
ACCOUNT NO.							
ACCOUNT NO.							
ACCOUNT NO.							

Sheet no. ___ of ___sheets attached to Schedule of Creditors Holding Unsecured Nonpriority Claims

Subtotal ➤ $
(Total of this page)

Total ➤ $
(Use only on last page of the completed Schedule E.)
(Report total also on Summary of Schedules)

C Codebtors (other than a spouse in a joint petition)

If any entity, other than a spouse in a joint petition, may be jointly liable on the claim, indicate "yes" by placing an "X" in the Codebtor column. If no entities are jointly liable on the claim, leave the Codebtor column blank. If there is a codebtor, then complete Schedule H—Codebtors.

D When a joint petition is filed, the debtors must indicate who is liable on each claim by the first letter of the designation:

Examples:	husband	H
	wife	W
	jointly	J
	marital community	C

If the petition is not joint, then leave this column blank.

E Provide the following information:

1. The date the claim was incurred by the debtor
2. The consideration for the claim

   Examples: services
   merchandise
   loan

3. If the claim is subject to a setoff, state "Claim is subject to a setoff."

   A **setoff** is the crediting of one claim against another without an actual exchange of money between the parties.

   Example: Agnes owes her doctor $100 for medical services. Her doctor owes Agnes $80 for bookkeeping. The $80 claim can be credited against the $100 claim.

F Indicate whether the claim is contingent, unliquidated, or disputed. Since a claim may qualify under more than one category (i.e., a claim may be contingent and unliquidated, contingent and disputed, unliquidated and disputed, or contingent, unliquidated, and disputed), indicate each category.

1. *Contingent:* A claim is contingent if it is dependent on some future event that may or may not take place.

   Example: Janice borrowed $1,000 from First Bank and signed a promissory note. Before First Bank would loan Janice the money, the Bank required Janice to have her mother sign the promissory note as an accommodation maker. Janice's mother signed as co-maker with the notation "collection guaranteed." By adding "collection guaranteed," Janice's mother promised that if the note is not paid by Janice when due, she will pay the note, but only after First Bank has reduced its claim against Janice to judgment and execution on the judgment has been returned unsatisfied, or after Janice has become insolvent or it is otherwise apparent that it is useless to proceed against her. First Bank's claim against Janice's mother is a contingent claim.

   If the claim is contingent, place an "×" in the Contingent column. If the claim is not contingent, leave the Contingent column blank.

2. *Unliquidated:* A claim is unliquidated if the amount of the claim is uncertain.

   Example: The Flower Market hired the Metro Agency to design an advertising campaign. The compensation was set as "a reasonable fee." Metro designed the campaign and presented its bill for $5,000. Flower Market refused to pay the bill, claiming that it should be $2,000. Because the contract stated that the fee would be a "reasonable fee," Metro's claim is unliquidated.

   If the claim is unliquidated, place an "×" in the column labeled "Unliquidated." If the claim is not unliquidated, leave the Unliquidated column blank.

3. *Disputed:* A claim by a creditor is disputed if the debtor contests the claim.

   Example: Alexander Wiggins and Vanessa Gray were involved in an automobile accident. Both Alexander and Vanessa claim to have had the right of way, and neither admits to being at fault. Each claim is disputed.

   If the claim is disputed, place an "×" in the column labeled "Disputed." If the claim is not disputed, leave the Disputed column blank.

G State the amount of the claim as of the date of the filing of the bankruptcy petition.

The amount of a contingent or unliquidated claim is the debtor's best estimate, considering all of the factors involved, of what will be due on the claim.

The amount of the claim, if disputed, is the debtor's best estimate of what the claimant may recover.

If the claim is not contingent, unliquidated, or disputed, the amount of the claim is the debtor's best estimate of how much is owed on the debt.

The debtor's best estimate may be zero. The amount listed will be the amount discharged.

If the creditor is represented by a collection agency or an attorney, the amount of the claim should be listed as zero with the representative's name since the amount of the claim has been listed with the creditor's name.

H Total the amount of the claims. Report the total on the Summary of Schedules.

PROBLEM 5.12 Using the information in Problem 4.5, complete Schedule F for the McPhersons.

7. Schedule G: Executory Contracts and Unexpired Leases

Rule 1007(b)(1) requires the debtor to file a schedule of **executory contracts** and **unexpired leases,** unless the court orders otherwise. In bankruptcy, a contract is executory if it remains unexecuted on both sides (i.e., not fully performed on either side). If the contract is executory, both parties to the contract continue to have a duty to perform. A contract is nonexecutory when one or both parties have fully performed their contractual duties.

EXAMPLE

Mary enters into a brokerage arrangement with Neighborhood Realtors for the sale of her house. During the term of the brokerage contract and before the house is sold, Mary files for bankruptcy under Chapter 7. Since both Mary and Neighborhood Realtors have duties under the contract, the contract is still an executory contract.

EXAMPLE

Jorge's leases a store in Greenacres Shopping Center for 36 months. Six months into the lease period, Jorge's files a petition for bankruptcy. The lease is unexpired because there are 30 months still remaining on the lease period. The lease is also an executory contract since both parties continue to have duties.

EXAMPLE

Ted and Carol enter into a timeshare arrangement for a Florida condo with six other families. When Ted and Carol file for bankruptcy, their timeshare interest in the condo is an executory contract.

Schedule G—Executory Contracts and Unexpired Leases (see Exhibit 5–15), provides the vehicle for listing contracts that have performance remaining by both contracting parties as of the date of the filing of the petition in bankruptcy. Schedule G also requires a listing of all unexpired leases of real or personal property, including timeshare interests.

Schedule G requires the following information:

1. the names and the mailing addresses (including zip codes) of the other parties to the executory contract or unexpired lease; and
2. a description of the executory contract or unexpired lease, and the nature of the debtor's interest.

Instructions for Completing Official Form No. 6, Schedule G (Executory Contracts and Unexpired Leases)

A If the debtor has no executory contracts or unexpired leases, then check this box. This completes Schedule G.

B State the names and the mailing addresses (including zip codes) of other parties to the executory contract or unexpired lease.

EXHIBIT 5–15 Official Form No. 6, Schedule G (Executory Contracts and Unexpired Leases)

B6G
(10/89)

In re ______________________________,
Debtor

Case No.______________________
(if known)

SCHEDULE G - EXECUTORY CONTRACTS AND UNEXPIRED LEASES

Describe all executory contracts of any nature and all unexpired leases of real or personal property. Include any timeshare interests.

State nature of debtor's interest in contract, i.e., "Purchaser," "Agent," etc. State whether debtor is the lessor or lessee of a lease.

Provide the names and complete mailing addresses of all other parties to each lease or contract described.

NOTE: A party listed on this schedule will not receive notice of the filing of this case unless the party is also scheduled in the appropriate schedule of creditors.

A ☐ Check this box if debtor has no executory contracts or unexpired leases.

NAME AND MAILING ADDRESS, INCLUDING ZIP CODE, OF OTHER PARTIES TO LEASE OR CONTRACT.	DESCRIPTION OF CONTRACT OR LEASE AND NATURE OF DEBTOR'S INTEREST. STATE WHETHER LEASE IS FOR NONRESIDENTIAL REAL PROPERTY. STATE CONTRACT NUMBER OF ANY GOVERNMENT CONTRACT.
B	C

C For each executory contract and unexpired lease, provide the following information:

1. Description of the contract or lease

   Examples: dance lessons
   6 lessons
   exterminator
   4 months
   apartment lease
   9 months
   office lease
   35 months
   equipment lease
   48 months

   If an executory contract does not have a set term, but is month to month, then list one month.

2. The nature of the debtor's interest

   Examples: executory contract
   purchaser
   agent
   broker
   unexpired lease
   lessor
   lessee

3. If the lease is for nonresidential real property, state "nonresidential real property."
4. If a government contract is involved, state the contract number.

PROBLEM 5.13 Using the information in Problem 4.5, complete Schedule G for the McPhersons.

8. Schedule H: Codebtors

Schedule H (see Exhibit 5–16) must be completed when a codebtor is indicated in Schedule D—Creditors Holding Secured Claims, Schedule E—Creditors Holding Unsecured Priority Claims, or Schedule F—Creditors Holding Unsecured Nonpriority Claims.

Schedule H is designed to provide the trustee and the creditors with information about codebtors who are nondebtors in this case. A **codebtor** is a person or entity also liable on any debt listed by the debtor in the schedules of creditors. Since a spouse in a **joint case** is a debtor, a spouse in a joint case will not be listed in Schedule H. Codebtors include guarantors and cosigners.

In a **community property state,** a married debtor not filing a joint case should report the name and the address of the nondebtor spouse on this schedule. All names used by the nondebtor spouse during the six years immediately preceding the commencement of this case should be included.

Schedule H requires the following information:

1. the name and address of the codebtor; and
2. the name and address of the creditor.

Instructions for Completing Official Form No. 6, Schedule H (Codebtors)

A A codebtor is a person or entity also liable on any debt listed by the debtor in the schedules of creditors. Codebtors are also creditors of the debtor because of the debtor's underlying obligation to his or her comakers or guarantors. All codebtors indicated on Schedules D, E, and F must be listed on Schedule H.

EXHIBIT 5–16 Official Form No. 6, Schedule H (Codebtors)

B6H
(6/90)

In re ______________________________,
Debtor

Case No. ______________________
(if known)

SCHEDULE H - CODEBTORS

Provide the information requested concerning any person or entity, other than a spouse in a joint case, that is also liable on any debts listed by debtor in the schedules of creditors. Include all guarantors and co-signers. In community property states, a married debtor not filing a joint case should report the name and address of the nondebtor spouse on this schedule. Include all names used by the nondebtor spouse during the six years immediately preceding the commencement of this case.

A ☐ Check this box if debtor has no codebtors.

NAME AND ADDRESS OF CODEBTOR	NAME AND ADDRESS OF CREDITOR
B	C

In a joint case: A spouse in a joint case will not be listed in Schedule H.

Example: Gerald and Sydney, husband and wife, have filed a joint petition for bankruptcy under Chapter 7. Neither Sydney nor Gerald is a codebtor for the purposes of Schedule H.

For an individual not filing a joint case: A married debtor not filing a joint case should report the name and the address of the nondebtor spouse on Schedule H if that person is also liable on the debt.

Example: Gerald and Sydney are husband and wife. Sydney files as an individual for bankruptcy under Chapter 7. Gerald is a codebtor on their home mortgage and is therefore a codebtor for the purposes of Schedule H.

If the debtor has no codebtors, then check this box. This completes Schedule H.

B State the name and the complete mailing address (including zip code) of the codebtor.

List all the names used by the nondebtor spouse during the six years immediately preceding the commencement of this case.

C State the name and the complete mailing address (including zip code) of the creditor.

PROBLEM 5.14 Using the information in Problem 4.5, complete Schedule H for the McPhersons.

9. Schedule I: Current Income of Individual Debtor(s)

Official Form No. 6, Schedule I (see Exhibit 5–17), is a comprehensive statement of the total current monthly income of an individual debtor or a husband and wife filing a joint petition. Schedule I is designed only for an individual debtor or for a husband and wife filing a joint petition. Schedule I is keyed to the bankruptcy court's power to dismiss a case if substantial abuse of Chapter 7 is determined to exist in a case. 11 U.S.C.A. § 707(b).

Instructions for Completing Official Form No. 6, Schedule I (Current Income of Individual Debtor(s))

All questions on Schedule I must be answered. A spouse's income must be reflected in Schedule I even if the spouse is not filing for bankruptcy with the debtor. If a question seeks descriptive information that does not apply to the debtor, indicate "not applicable." If a question seeks numerical information and the debtor's response is zero, indicate "–0–."

A Indicate the debtor's marital status.

Examples: married
single
divorced
widowed
separated

B State the full names of the debtor's dependents—first name, middle name (no middle initial), last name—including the debtor's spouse. Give the age of each and the relationship (son, daughter, stepson, granddaughter, mother).

Examples:	Agatha Anne Wilson	spouse	43
	Mary Jo Wilson	daughter	16
	Billy Joe Short	stepson	15
	Anna Wilson Smith	mother	82

C If the debtor is currently employed outside the home, state the debtor's occupation and the name of the debtor's employer. State how long the debtor has been employed with this employer and the employer's address. If the debtor has recently changed jobs, list the current employment.

If the debtor is currently self-employed, state the debtor's occupation, the name of the debtor's business, how long the debtor has been self-employed in that business, and the address of the debtor's place of business, including zip code.

EXHIBIT 5–17 Official Form No. 6, Schedule I (Current Income of Individual Debtor(s))

FORM B6I
(12/03)

In re ______________________________, Debtor

Case No. ______________________ (if known)

SCHEDULE I - CURRENT INCOME OF INDIVIDUAL DEBTOR(S)

The column labeled "Spouse" must be completed in all cases filed by joint debtors and by a married debtor in a chapter 12 or 13 case whether or not a joint petition is filed, unless the spouses are separated and a joint petition is not filed.

Debtor's Marital Status:	DEPENDENTS OF DEBTOR AND SPOUSE		
	NAMES	AGE	RELATIONSHIP
A	B		

Employment:	DEBTOR	SPOUSE
Occupation		
Name of Employer	C	
How long employed		
Address of Employer		

Income: (Estimate of average monthly income) D	DEBTOR	SPOUSE
Current monthly gross wages, salary, and commissions (pro rate if not paid monthly.)	$	$
Estimated monthly overtime	$	$
SUBTOTAL	$	$
LESS PAYROLL DEDUCTIONS		
a. Payroll taxes and social security	$	$
b. Insurance	$	$
c. Union dues	$	$
d. Other (Specify: ____________)	$	$
SUBTOTAL OF PAYROLL DEDUCTIONS	$	$
TOTAL NET MONTHLY TAKE HOME PAY	$	$
Regular income from operation of business or profession or farm (attach detailed statement)	$	$
Income from real property	$	$
Interest and dividends	$	$
Alimony, maintenance or support payments payable to the debtor for the debtor's use or that of dependents listed above.	$	$
Social security or other government assistance (Specify) ____________	$	$
Pension or retirement income	$	$
Other monthly income	$	$
(Specify) ____________	$	$
____________	$	$
TOTAL MONTHLY INCOME	$	$

TOTAL COMBINED MONTHLY INCOME $__________ (Report also on Summary of Schedules)

Describe any increase or decrease of more than 10% in any of the above categories anticipated to occur within the year following the filing of this document:

E

Example: florist
Fred's Floral Arrangements
3 years
86 East Fourth Avenue
Oklahoma City, OK 73149

If the debtor is not currently employed outside the home, state the debtor's status in lieu of an occupation.

Examples: homemaker
retired
unemployed
medical leave
disabled

If the debtor is married, complete this information for the debtor's spouse, regardless of whether the debtor is filing as an individual or with the spouse in a joint petition.

D The schedule of current income has a double column for current income, one for the debtor and the other for the debtor's spouse. If the debtor is married, complete an income statement for the debtor and for the debtor's spouse, even if the debtor contemplates filing as an individual rather than with his or her spouse in a joint petition.

Note that these figures represent the debtor's estimated average monthly income. If income fluctuates over several months or over the year, average the income for the months of that period.

If the debtor ceased employment several months ago and currently has no take-home pay, the current income should be shown rather than what the debtor earned while employed.

Remember that this form will be used to determine whether the debtor has disposable income sufficient to support a Chapter 13 plan. This may determine whether the debtor should file a Chapter 13 rather than a Chapter 7.

The following information lists and explains possible sources of income. Some of this information can be obtained from the debtor's tax return.

1. Gross monthly take-home pay
   a. Current monthly gross wages, salary, and commissions

      If the debtor is paid by tips, the amount should be the actual amount the debtor receives in tips and not an arbitrary number set by the government for tax withholding purposes.

      Include bonuses, prizes, and awards if they occur on a regular basis. Omit bonuses, prizes, and awards if their incidence is unpredictable and may or may not occur again.

      If the debtor is a commission salesperson, deduct all of the debtor's business expenses: e.g., hotels and motels, mileage or gasoline, other expenses for operating his or her business vehicle, installment payments on the vehicle (or some calculation for replacement), and auto insurance. Therefore, the take-home pay of a commission salesperson will be similar to a debtor with a paycheck after taxes. If the debtor's expenses are not taken off here, the income statement will be distorted. The debtor's food expense will not be deducted under "other" because the debtor would need to eat whether or not he or she was on the road.
   b. Estimated monthly overtime
2. Payroll deductions

   The debtor's take-home pay is calculated by taking the debtor's gross pay and subtracting all deductions. The deductions include

   a. payroll taxes and social security
   b. insurance
   c. union dues

   For many debtors, gross wages and take-home pay can be calculated directly from the debtor's pay stub. Care should be taken, however, when dealing with deductions on pay stubs for installment loans and garnishments. For example, installment payments may be directly deducted for automobile payments made to a credit union. This amount should be added back into gross wages and take-home pay and should appear as an expense under Schedule J—Current Expenditures of Individual Debtor(s).

3. Regular income from the operation of a business, profession, or farm

   Indicate the net income, rather than the gross income, for operating a business, profession, or farm. To arrive at regular income, subtract all business expenses.

4. Income from real property
5. Interest and dividends
6. Alimony, maintenance, or support payments

   Include

   a. Payments payable to the debtor for the debtor's use
   b. Payments payable to the debtor for the support of another, such as child support

      The name, age, and relationship of the person for whose benefit the payments are made should be listed at the beginning of this schedule.

7. Social Security or other government assistance (specify the type of assistance)

   Examples: Supplemental Security Income (SSI)
food stamps

8. Pension or retirement income
9. Other monthly income

   Examples: income from personal property
other investment income
royalties

E Within the year following the filing of this document, does the debtor anticipate an increase or a decrease of more than 10 percent in any of the above categories?

State, in an addendum, whatever it is that will affect income the debtor knows about. This could include seasonal layoffs or seasonal overtime, if the debtor could reasonably forecast that the event will occur. Describe the change and its impact on current income.

Example: Debtor is expecting a baby in July and anticipates taking three months of unpaid maternity leave. Therefore, the debtor's total net monthly take-home pay will be reduced to zero for that period.

Also, the debtor anticipates receiving additional income on other than a monthly basis in the next year (such as an income tax refund), use an addendum to describe the nature of the income, when it is expected, and the amount.

10. Schedule J: Current Expenditures of Individual Debtor(s)

Official Form No. 6, Schedule J (see Exhibit 5–18), is a comprehensive list of the total *current monthly expenditures of the debtor* and the debtor's family. Schedule J is designed for use by an individual debtor or a husband and wife filing a joint petition. It is keyed to the bankruptcy court's power to dismiss a case if substantial abuse of Chapter 7 is determined to exist in a case. 11 U.S.C.A. § 707(b).

Instructions for Completing Official Form No. 6, Schedule J (Current Expenditures of Individual Debtor(s))

All questions on Schedule J must be answered. If a question seeks descriptive information but does not apply to the debtor, indicate "not applicable." If a question seeks numerical information and the debtor's response is zero, indicate "–0–."

A Complete the expenses statement, giving estimated average current monthly expenses of the debtor and the debtor's family. LIST ONLY EXPENSES THAT THE DEBTOR WOULD BE PAYING IF HE OR SHE WERE TO RECEIVE A DISCHARGE UNDER CHAPTER 7. Therefore, do not list expenses based on debts that will be discharged. Do include obligations the debtor intends to reaffirm.

EXHIBIT 5–18 Official Form No. 6, Schedule J (Current Expenditures of Individual Debtor(s))

FORM B6J
(6/90)

In re ______________________________, Case No.______________________
Debtor (If known)

SCHEDULE J - CURRENT EXPENDITURES OF INDIVIDUAL DEBTOR(S)

Complete this schedule by estimating the average monthly expenses of the debtor and the debtor's family. Pro rate any payments made bi-weekly, quarterly, semi-annually, or annually to show monthly rate. A

B ☐ Check this box if a joint petition is filed and debtor's spouse maintains a separate household. Complete a separate schedule of expenditures labeled "Spouse."

Rent or home mortgage payment (include lot rented for mobile home) C $ ________

Are real estate taxes included? Yes ________ No ________

Is property insurance included? Yes ________ No ________

Utilities Electricity and heating fuel $ ________

Water and sewer $ ________

Telephone $ ________

Other ______________________________ $ ________

Home maintenance (repairs and upkeep) $ ________

Food $ ________

Clothing $ ________

Laundry and dry cleaning $ ________

Medical and dental expenses $ ________

Transportation (not including car payments) $ ________

Recreation, clubs and entertainment, newspapers, magazines, etc. $ ________

Charitable contributions $ ________

Insurance (not deducted from wages or included in home mortgage payments)

Homeowner's or renter's $ ________

Life $ ________

Health $ ________

Auto $ ________

Other ______________________________ $ ________

Taxes (not deducted from wages or included in home mortgage payments)
(Specify) ______________________________ $ ________

Installment payments: (In chapter 12 and 13 cases, do not list payments to be included in the plan)

Auto $ ________

Other ______________________________ $ ________

Other ______________________________ $ ________

Alimony, maintenance, and support paid to others $ ________

Payments for support of additional dependents not living at your home $ ________

Regular expenses from operation of business, profession, or farm (attach detailed statement) $ ________

Other ______________________________ $ ________

TOTAL MONTHLY EXPENSES (Report also on Summary of Schedules) $ ________

[FOR CHAPTER 12 AND 13 DEBTORS ONLY]
Provide the information requested below, including whether plan payments are to be made bi-weekly, monthly, annually, or at some other regular interval.

A. Total projected monthly income $ ________

B. Total projected monthly expenses $ ________

C. Excess income (A minus B) $ ________

D. Total amount to be paid into plan each ______________________________ $ ________
(interval)

Example: At the time of completing the current expenditures schedule, the Alexanders own two automobiles, a Buick and a Ford, both of which were subject to security interests. The Alexanders intend to reaffirm their obligation on the Ford but not on the Buick. Therefore, the Buick will be repossessed. The payments on the Buick should not appear as an expense because if the Alexanders were to receive a discharge under Chapter 7, that debt would be discharged and they would make no further payments.

B If the debtor and his or her spouse maintain separate households, the debtor must check the box and complete a separate schedule of expenditures for his or her spouse. Label the spouse's schedule of expenditures "Spouse."

C The expenses are the total family expenses and not the expenses of an individual debtor. Therefore, it is critical to show the expenses of the debtor and the expenses of the debtor's spouse, whether the case will be filed as an individual or a joint case. The following information lists and explains types of expenses.

1. Rent or home mortgage payment
   a. Home mortgage payment
   b. Rent, if debtor does not own a home
   c. Condominium fees
   d. Lot rental for mobile home

   If real estate taxes are included under rent or home mortgage payments, they cannot be included as current expenditures under the heading of taxes.

   If property insurance is included under rent or home mortgage payments, it cannot be included as current expenditures under the heading of insurance.

   If mortgage insurance is included under rent or home mortgage payments, it cannot be included as current expenditures under the heading of insurance.
2. Utilities (average expenses over the year)
   a. Electricity
   b. Heating fuel (e.g., coal, gas, oil)
   c. Water
   d. Sewer
   e. Telephone
   f. Other

      Examples: trash and garbage removal
      cable TV
3. Home maintenance (repairs and upkeep)

   Include installment payments for home repairs, such as a new roof, fence, driveway, or foundation restoration. The payments could be made to the contractor or to a lending institution.

   Also estimate home maintenance expenses for a one-year period and divide by 12.
4. Food

   Include: groceries
   restaurants
   school lunches

   If the debtor has a dependent not living at home, the food for that dependent could be included here or under the category "Payments for support of additional dependents not living at your home."

   Include the food for a salesperson on commission here, since this amount was not deducted from take-home pay under income on the income statement.
5. Clothing

   Include: uniforms
6. Laundry and dry cleaning

7. Medical and dental expenses

   Include: medicines

   Include only the amount not covered by insurance

8. Transportation (not including car payments)

   Do not include installment payments on automobiles, trucks, and other vehicles used for transportation. They will be included under "Installment payments."

   Include: gasoline
   maintenance
   taxi fares (including tips)
   bus fares
   train fares
   air fares

9. Recreation, clubs and entertainment, newspapers, magazines

   Include: admission fees for movies and sporting events
   home video rentals
   night clubs
   health clubs (e.g., exercise club memberships, tennis clubs, swim clubs)
   country club membership
   lodge and fraternal order memberships

10. Charitable contributions

    Include: churches
    Salvation Army
    Red Cross
    CARE
    Goodwill Industries
    United Way
    Boy Scouts
    Girl Scouts of the U.S.A.
    Boys Club of America
    veterans' and certain cultural groups
    nonprofit schools and hospitals
    public parks and recreational facilities

11. Insurance (not deducted from wages or included in home mortgage payments)

    a. Homeowner's or renter's insurance
    b. Life insurance
    c. Health insurance
    d. Auto insurance

       If the debtor is a salesperson on commission and has deducted automobile insurance from his or her gross wages, salary, or commission on the income statement, that automobile insurance should not be shown here.

    e. Other insurance (specify the type of insurance)

       Under "Other insurance" include home mortgage insurance.

12. Taxes (not deducted from wages or not included in home mortgage payments)

    The taxes must be specified.

    Include: real estate taxes
    sales tax
    excise taxes

13. Installment payments

Installment payments must be specified to the extent they are obligations the debtor intends to reaffirm.

Include: automobiles
trucks
recreational vehicles
boats
airplanes
consumer goods (e.g., refrigerator, washer, dryer, freezer, TV, VCR, computer equipment, typewriter, stereo, exercise machine, bicycle, clothing, jewelry)

If the debtor is a salesperson on commission who has deducted installment payments on a business vehicle in his or her income statement, then installment payments on that vehicle should *not* be shown here. They have already been taken into account.

14. Alimony, maintenance, and support paid to others

List the name, age, and relationship to the debtor of each recipient of payments.

15. Payments for support of additional dependents not living at your home

If the debtor is supporting a child living away at school, include tuition, room, board, laundry, books and supplies, vehicle costs, transportation, and additional spending money. The name of the child should be listed as a dependent in the family status section of Schedule I—Current Income.

Also include other payments for support of dependents not living at home and not at school.

If the debtor is supporting a parent who is not living with the debtor, include payments made by the debtor on a regular basis. This would include any money sent by the debtor to his or her parent or paid to a nursing facility on a monthly basis. The name of the parent should be listed as a dependent in the family status section of Schedule I—Current Income.

16. Regular expenses from operation of business, profession, or farm

To claim these expenses, a detailed statement of these expenses must be included.

17. Other

Specify the expenses.

Include: child-care expenses
education costs not previously claimed (e.g., tuition, school books)

If there is something extraordinary about the debtor's case, the attorney and paralegal should not hesitate to explain an unusual situation.

Example: The debtor has a son who has severe mental problems. When the son became violent, he would trash his parent's home. Periodically, the debtor had to spend substantial sums to repair the damage done to the home. This was home maintenance of an astronomical amount. Just listing the amount as an expense without an explanation would raise questions by the U.S. trustee.

PROBLEM 5.15 Using the information in Problem 4.5, complete Official Form No. 6, Schedules I and J, for the McPhersons.

11. The Schedule of Current Income and Current Expenditures of a Partnership or Corporation

When the Bankruptcy Code mandates that the debtor must file a schedule of current income and current expenditures, the mandate is not limited to individual debtors. See 11 U.S.C.A. § 521(1); Fed. R. Bank. P. 1007(b)(1). The mandate also applies to partnership and corporate debtors. Official Form No. 6, Schedule J, however, applies only to an individual debtor or to a husband and wife filing a joint petition. No official form has been drafted for the partnership or corporate debtor. In practice, partnership and corporate debtors file a schedule of current income and current expenditures, unless waived by the court.

Since no official form has been created, the schedule filed with the court need only be in substantial compliance with the rules. An illustration of a Schedule of Current Income and Current Expenditures of a Partnership or Corporation appears in Exhibit 5–19. A debtor may choose to file a more elaborate schedule, i.e., one with printouts and attachments.

Instructions for Completing the Schedule of Current Income and Current Expenditures of a Partnership or Corporation

A Check whether the debtor's accounting records are kept on a cash basis or accrual method.

Records kept on a *cash basis* will report revenues and expenses in the year in which the revenues were received or the expenses were paid. Under the cash basis, revenues are not allocated to the year in which they were earned nor are expenses allocated to the year in which they were incurred.

Records kept on an *accrual method* will allocate revenues to the year in which they were earned and allocate expenses to the year in which they were incurred. Under the accrual method, revenues are not allocated to the year in which they were received unless that also was the year in which they were earned. Likewise, expenses are not allocated to the year in which they were paid unless that also was the year in which they were incurred.

Example: The Sunshine Bake Shoppe supplies the New York Delicatessen with all of its bakery products. Rather than require cash as each daily delivery is made, Sunshine sends the delicatessen a bill at the first of each week for bakery products delivered the previous week. Payment is due by the following Friday. Under this system, bakery products delivered during the last week of a month are paid for in the following month. Bakery products delivered during the last week of the year are paid for in the following year.

Under the cash basis of accounting, the date Sunshine receives payment is the date the revenue is indicated on Sunshine's ledger. For products delivered during the last week of the year, the payment would not appear until the following year.

Under an accrual method of accounting, the date the income is earned is the date the revenue is indicated on Sunshine's ledger. For products delivered during the last week of the year, income would be shown for that week even though the actual payment will not be received until the following year.

B Cash basis: Complete this question if the debtor's accounting records are kept on a cash basis. If the debtor's accounting records are kept on an accrual method, indicate "not applicable."

Summarize the debtor's cash flow during a 90- to 120-day period, the end date being no more than 30 days before the commencement of the case.

Complete questions (a)–(f) concerning the debtor's cash flow.

a. Beginning date

   Example: If the case will be filed on July 15, the last day of the period can be no earlier than June 16. The period should begin no sooner than 90 days and no later than 120 days before the end date. Therefore, if the end date is selected as June 30, the period should begin between March 3 and April 2.

b. Ending date

c. Cash balance at the beginning date

   The cash balance at the beginning date can be found in the debtor's financial statement.

d. Cash receipts during this period

   The cash receipts during this period can be calculated by adding the various entries found in the debtor's accounting records.

   If the debtor has not kept accurate records of cash receipts, a best estimate should be used. If accurate records have not been kept, a creditor may object to discharge based on the debtor's failure to explain satisfactorily any loss of assets or deficiency of assets to meet the debtor's liability or based on the debtor's failure to keep books or records. 11 U.S.C.A. §§ 727(a)(3), (5).

EXHIBIT 5–19 Schedule of Current Income and Current Expenditures of a Partnership or Corporation

IN THE UNITED STATES BANKRUPTCY COURT FOR THE
_______________ DISTRICT OF _______________

In re ________________________________,
Debtor

Case No. _____________

Chapter _____________

SCHEDULE OF CURRENT INCOME AND CURRENT EXPENDITURES OF A PARTNERSHIP OR CORPORATION

1. The debtor's accounting records are kept on a cash basis ___A___ or accrual method _______ .

   Complete question 2 if the debtor's accounting records are kept on a cash basis or question 3 if the debtor's accounting records are kept on an accrual method.

2. Cash basis: Summarize the debtor's cash flow for a period ending no more than 30 days prior to the commencement of this case. The summary period shall be not less than 90 nor more than 120 days in duration.

   a. Beginning date _______________
   b. Ending date _______________ **B**
   c. Cash balance at the beginning date $ ______
   d. Cash receipts during this period $ ______
   e. Cash disbursements during this period $ ______
   f. Cash balance at the ending date $ ______

3. Accrual method: Summarize the debtor's revenue and expenses on an accrual method for a period ending no more than 30 days prior to the commencement of this case. The summary period shall be not less than 90 or more than 120 days in duration.

   a. Beginning date _______________
   b. Ending date _______________ **C**
   c. Revenue during this period $ ______
   d. Expenses during this period $ ______
   e. Net gain or (loss) during this period $ ______

4. Attach a copy of the most recent financial statement (audited or unaudited) which has been prepared by or for the debtor.

D

e. State the cash disbursements during this period

The cash disbursements during this period can be calculated by adding the various entries found in the debtor's accounting records.

If the debtor has not kept accurate records of disbursements, a best estimate should be used. If accurate records have not been kept, a creditor may object to discharge based on the debtor's failure to explain satisfactorily any loss of assets or deficiency of assets to meet the debtor's liability or based on the debtor's failure to keep books or records. 11 U.S.C.A. §§ 727(a)(3), (5).

f. State the cash balance at the ending date

The cash balance at the ending date can be found in the debtor's financial statement.

C Accrual method: Complete this question if the debtor's accounting records are kept on an accrual method. If the debtor's accounting records are kept on a cash basis, indicate "not applicable."

Summarize the debtor's revenue and expenses on an accrual method during a 90- to 120-day period, the end date being no more than 30 days before the commencement of the case.

Complete questions (a)–(e) concerning the debtor's cash flow.

a. Beginning date

The beginning date can be determined by identifying the end date for the summary period (which must be not more than 30 days from the commencement of the case) and counting back from that date no more than 120 or less than 90 days.

b. Ending date

The summary period cannot end more than 30 days prior to the commencement of this case and must be not less than 90 or more than 120 days in duration.

c. Revenue during this period

This information can be found in the debtor's financial statement.

d. Expenses during this period

This information can be found in the debtor's financial statement.

e. Net gain or (loss) during this period

This information can be found in the debtor's financial statement.

D Attach a copy of the debtor's most recent financial statement. Indicate in the top left corner the name of the debtor (as it appears on the petition) and the debtor's employer's tax identification number. Although either an audited or unaudited financial statement is acceptable, an audited statement should be submitted if available.

12. Declaration Concerning Debtor's Schedules

The Declaration Concerning Debtor's Schedules (see Exhibit 5–20) is the signature page for the schedules. The declaration has three parts: one for the individual debtor, one for the nonattorney bankruptcy petition preparer, and one for a corporation or partnership. The Declaration Concerning Debtor's Schedules follows the requirement set forth in 28 U.S.C.A. § 1746.

Instructions for Completing the Declaration Concerning Debtor's Schedules

If the debtor is an individual or a husband and wife filing a joint petition:

A Enter the total number of pages. This is the number of pages as shown on the summary page plus one.

B Before the debtor signs his or her name, each entry on the schedules should be carefully reviewed with the debtor. The debtor must be sure the information is correct. The declaration should then be read to the debtor. If the debtor assents, the debtor should sign his or her full name (as it appears on the petition) and date the declaration. The date is the date the debtor signs the declaration and not the date the petition is filed. If a joint petition is being filed, these steps should be taken for both debtors.

An individual debtor who knowingly and fraudulently makes a false oath is subject to a fine, imprisonment of not more than five years, or both. 18 U.S.C.A. § 152. An individual debtor may also forfeit his or her right to a discharge. 11 U.S.C.A. § 727(a)(4).

EXHIBIT 5–20 Official Form 6 (Declaration Concerning Debtor's Schedules)

Official Form 6-Cont.
(12/03)

In re ______________________________, Case No. ______________________
Debtor (If known)

DECLARATION CONCERNING DEBTOR'S SCHEDULES

DECLARATION UNDER PENALTY OF PERJURY BY INDIVIDUAL DEBTOR

I declare under penalty of perjury that I have read the foregoing summary and schedules, consisting of ______A______ *(Total shown on summary page plus 1.)* sheets, and that they are true and correct to the best of my knowledge, information, and belief.

Date ______________________ **B** Signature: ______________________
Debtor

Date ______________________ Signature: ______________________
(Joint Debtor, if any)

[If joint case, both spouses must sign.]

CERTIFICATION AND SIGNATURE OF NON-ATTORNEY BANKRUPTCY PETITION PREPARER (See 11 U.S.C. § 110)

I certify that I am a bankruptcy petition preparer as defined in 11 U.S.C. § 110, that I prepared this document for compensation, and that I have provided the debtor with a copy of this document.

______________________ ______________________
Printed or Typed Name of Bankruptcy Petition Preparer Social Security No.
(Required by 11 U.S.C. § 110(c).)

____

____
Address

Names and Social Security numbers of all other individuals who prepared or assisted in preparing this document:

If more than one person prepared this document, attach additional signed sheets conforming to the appropriate Official Form for each person.

X______________________ ______________________
Signature of Bankruptcy Petition Preparer Date

A bankruptcy petition preparer's failure to comply with the provisions of title 11 and the Federal Rules of Bankruptcy Procedure may result in fines or imprisonment or both. 11 U.S.C. § 110; 18 U.S.C. § 156.

DECLARATION UNDER PENALTY OF PERJURY ON BEHALF OF A CORPORATION OR PARTNERSHIP

I, the ______C______ [the president or other officer or an authorized agent of the corporation or a member or an authorized agent of the partnership] of the ______D______ [corporation or partnership] named as debtor in this case, declare under penalty of perjury that I have read the foregoing summary and schedules, consisting of ______E______ sheets, and that they are true and correct to the best of my knowledge, information, and belief. *(Total shown on summary page plus 1.)*

Date ______________________ Signature: ______G______

______F______
[Print or type name of individual signing on behalf of debtor.]

[An individual signing on behalf of a partnership or corporation must indicate position or relationship to debtor.]

Penalty for making a false statement or concealing property: Fine of up to $500,000 or imprisonment for up to 5 years or both. 18 U.S.C. §§ 152 and 3571.

If the debtor is a partnership or a corporation:

C State the title of the person signing the declaration or in what capacity the declarant is signing.

Examples: If a corporation, use "President."

If a partnership, use "Partner."

D State the name of the entity filing the petition. State the name as it appears on the petition.

E Enter the total number of pages. This is the number of pages as shown on the summary page plus one.

F Type or print the name of the individual who will be signing on behalf of the partnership or corporation. The name typed or printed should be the same as it will appear in the signature.

G Before the individual signing on behalf of the partnership or corporation signs his or her name, each entry on the schedules should be carefully reviewed with that individual. The individual must be sure the information is correct. The declaration should then be read to that individual. If the individual assents, have him or her sign his or her name as it appears on the typed line and date the declaration. The date is the date the individual signs the declaration and not the date the petition is filed.

An individual who knowingly and fraudulently makes a false oath is subject to a fine, imprisonment of not more than five years, or both. 18 U.S.C.A. § 152.

H. STATEMENT OF FINANCIAL AFFAIRS

The debtor's statement of financial affairs, Official Form No. 7 (see Exhibit 5–21), must be completed by all debtors. Spouses filing a joint petition may file a single statement on which the information for both spouses is combined. An individual debtor in business as a sole proprietor, partner, family farmer, or self-employed professional must provide the information requested on this statement concerning all business activities as well as the debtor's personal affairs.

Questions 1–18 must be completed by all debtors. Debtors that are or have been "in business" also must complete Questions 19–25. A debtor is "in business" for the purpose of this form if the debtor is

1. a corporation
2. a partnership
3. an individual who is or has been within the six years immediately preceding the filing of this bankruptcy case
   a. an officer, director, managing executive, owner of 5 percent or more of the voting or equity securities of the corporation.
   b. a partner, other than a limited partner, of a partnership
   c. a sole proprietor or self-employed

Prior to completing the statement of financial affairs, it is of critical importance for the paralegal or the attorney to understand what the debtor means by being in business. What is important is not the debtor's perception of whether he or she was in business but whether the debtor fits within the definition of "in business" as stated in Official Form No. 7. In some cases, the question may be whether the debtor is a sole proprietor or otherwise self-employed (and therefore in business) or an employee (and therefore not in business).

PROBLEM 5.16 Dr. Montoya, a neurological surgeon, was a shareholder in a professional association (P.A.) that specialized in neurological problems. Several years ago, Dr. Montoya sold his interest in the professional association at fair market value to the remaining shareholders. After the sale, Dr. Montoya retained no ownership interest in the P.A. or in its accounts, although he did remain as an associate with the P.A. under a document entitled "Employment Agreement."

Dr. Montoya has now filed for bankruptcy under Chapter 7 of the Bankruptcy Code. Must he complete questions 19–25 of the Statement of Financial Affairs?

EXHIBIT 5–21 Official Form No. 7 (Statement of Financial Affairs)

Form 7
(12/03)

UNITED STATES BANKRUPTCY COURT

______________________________ **DISTRICT OF** ______________________________

In re: ______________________________, Case No. ______________________________
(Name) (if known)
Debtor

STATEMENT OF FINANCIAL AFFAIRS

This statement is to be completed by every debtor. Spouses filing a joint petition may file a single statement on which the information for both spouses is combined. If the case is filed under chapter 12 or chapter 13, a married debtor must furnish information for both spouses whether or not a joint petition is filed, unless the spouses are separated and a joint petition is not filed. An individual debtor engaged in business as a sole proprietor, partner, family farmer, or self-employed professional, should provide the information requested on this statement concerning all such activities as well as the individual's personal affairs.

Questions 1 - 18 are to be completed by all debtors. Debtors that are or have been in business, as defined below, also must complete Questions 19 - 25. **If the answer to an applicable question is "None," mark the box labeled "None."** If additional space is needed for the answer to any question, use and attach a separate sheet properly identified with the case name, case number (if known), and the number of the question.

DEFINITIONS

"In business." A debtor is "in business" for the purpose of this form if the debtor is a corporation or partnership. An individual debtor is "in business" for the purpose of this form if the debtor is or has been, within the six years immediately preceding the filing of this bankruptcy case, any of the following: an officer, director, managing executive, or owner of 5 percent or more of the voting or equity securities of a corporation; a partner, other than a limited partner, of a partnership; a sole proprietor or self-employed.

"Insider." The term "insider" includes but is not limited to: relatives of the debtor; general partners of the debtor and their relatives; corporations of which the debtor is an officer, director, or person in control; officers, directors, and any owner of 5 percent or more of the voting or equity securities of a corporate debtor and their relatives; affiliates of the debtor and insiders of such affiliates; any managing agent of the debtor. 11 U.S.C. §101.

A

1. Income from employment or operation of business

None ☐

State the gross amount of income the debtor has received from employment, trade, or profession, or from operation of the debtor's business from the beginning of this calendar year to the date this case was commenced. State also the gross amounts received during the **two years** immediately preceding this calendar year. (A debtor that maintains, or has maintained, financial records on the basis of a fiscal rather than a calendar year may report fiscal year income. Identify the beginning and ending dates of the debtor's fiscal year.) If a joint petition is filed, state income for each spouse separately. (Married debtors filing under chapter 12 or chapter 13 must state income of both spouses whether or not a joint petition is filed, unless the spouses are separated and a joint petition is not filed.)

AMOUNT SOURCE (if more than one)

(continued)

B

None ☐

2. Income other than from employment or operation of business

State the amount of income received by the debtor other than from employment, trade, profession, or operation of the debtor's business during the **two years** immediately preceding the commencement of this case. Give particulars. If a joint petition is filed, state income for each spouse separately. (Married debtors filing under chapter 12 or chapter 13 must state income for each spouse whether or not a joint petition is filed, unless the spouses are separated and a joint petition is not filed.)

AMOUNT	SOURCE

C

3. Payments to creditors

None ☐

a. List all payments on loans, installment purchases of goods or services, and other debts, aggregating more than $600 to any creditor, made within **90 days** immediately preceding the commencement of this case. (Married debtors filing under chapter 12 or chapter 13 must include payments by either or both spouses whether or not a joint petition is filed, unless the spouses are separated and a joint petition is not filed.)

NAME AND ADDRESS OF CREDITOR	DATES OF PAYMENTS	AMOUNT PAID	AMOUNT STILL OWING

None ☐

b. List all payments made within **one year** immediately preceding the commencement of this case to or for the benefit of creditors who are or were insiders. (Married debtors filing under chapter 12 or chapter 13 must include payments by either or both spouses whether or not a joint petition is filed, unless the spouses are separated and a joint petition is not filed.)

NAME AND ADDRESS OF CREDITOR AND RELATIONSHIP TO DEBTOR	DATE OF PAYMENT	AMOUNT PAID	AMOUNT STILL OWING

4. Suits and administrative proceedings, executions, garnishments and attachments

D

None ☐

a. List all suits and administrative proceedings to which the debtor is or was a party within **one year** immediately preceding the filing of this bankruptcy case. (Married debtors filing under chapter 12 or chapter 13 must include information concerning either or both spouses whether or not a joint petition is filed, unless the spouses are separated and a joint petition is not filed.)

CAPTION OF SUIT AND CASE NUMBER	NATURE OF PROCEEDING	COURT OR AGENCY AND LOCATION	STATUS OR DISPOSITION

(continued)

EXHIBIT 5–21 Official Form No. 7 (Statement of Financial Affairs), Continued

None ☐ b. Describe all property that has been attached, garnished or seized under any legal or equitable process within **one year** immediately preceding the commencement of this case. (Married debtors filing under chapter 12 or chapter 13 must include information concerning property of either or both spouses whether or not a joint petition is filed, unless the spouses are separated and a joint petition is not filed.)

NAME AND ADDRESS OF PERSON FOR WHOSE BENEFIT PROPERTY WAS SEIZED	DATE OF SEIZURE	DESCRIPTION AND VALUE OF PROPERTY

E

5. Repossessions, foreclosures and returns

None ☐ List all property that has been repossessed by a creditor, sold at a foreclosure sale, transferred through a deed in lieu of foreclosure or returned to the seller, within **one year** immediately preceding the commencement of this case. (Married debtors filing under chapter 12 or chapter 13 must include information concerning property of either or both spouses whether or not a joint petition is filed, unless the spouses are separated and a joint petition is not filed.)

NAME AND ADDRESS OF CREDITOR OR SELLER	DATE OF REPOSSESSION, FORECLOSURE SALE, TRANSFER OR RETURN	DESCRIPTION AND VALUE OF PROPERTY

F

6. Assignments and receiverships

None ☐ a. Describe any assignment of property for the benefit of creditors made within **120 days** immediately preceding the commencement of this case. (Married debtors filing under chapter 12 or chapter 13 must include any assignment by either or both spouses whether or not a joint petition is filed, unless the spouses are separated and a joint petition is not filed.)

NAME AND ADDRESS OF ASSIGNEE	DATE OF ASSIGNMENT	TERMS OF ASSIGNMENT OR SETTLEMENT

None ☐ b. List all property which has been in the hands of a custodian, receiver, or court-appointed official within **one year** immediately preceding the commencement of this case. (Married debtors filing under chapter 12 or chapter 13 must include information concerning property of either or both spouses whether or not a joint petition is filed, unless the spouses are separated and a joint petition is not filed.)

NAME AND ADDRESS OF CUSTODIAN	NAME AND LOCATION OF COURT CASE TITLE & NUMBER	DATE OF ORDER	DESCRIPTION AND VALUE OF PROPERTY

(continued)

G

7. Gifts

None ☐

List all gifts or charitable contributions made within **one year** immediately preceding the commencement of this case except ordinary and usual gifts to family members aggregating less than $200 in value per individual family member and charitable contributions aggregating less than $100 per recipient. (Married debtors filing under chapter 12 or chapter 13 must include gifts or contributions by either or both spouses whether or not a joint petition is filed, unless the spouses are separated and a joint petition is not filed.)

NAME AND ADDRESS OF PERSON OR ORGANIZATION	RELATIONSHIP TO DEBTOR, IF ANY	DATE OF GIFT	DESCRIPTION AND VALUE OF GIFT

H

8. Losses

None ☐

List all losses from fire, theft, other casualty or gambling within **one year** immediately preceding the commencement of this case **or since the commencement of this case**. (Married debtors filing under chapter 12 or chapter 13 must include losses by either or both spouses whether or not a joint petition is filed, unless the spouses are separated and a joint petition is not filed.)

DESCRIPTION AND VALUE OF PROPERTY	DESCRIPTION OF CIRCUMSTANCES AND, IF LOSS WAS COVERED IN WHOLE OR IN PART BY INSURANCE, GIVE PARTICULARS	DATE OF LOSS

I

9. Payments related to debt counseling or bankruptcy

None ☐

List all payments made or property transferred by or on behalf of the debtor to any persons, including attorneys, for consultation concerning debt consolidation, relief under the bankruptcy law or preparation of a petition in bankruptcy within **one year** immediately preceding the commencement of this case.

NAME AND ADDRESS OF PAYEE	DATE OF PAYMENT, NAME OF PAYOR IF OTHER THAN DEBTOR	AMOUNT OF MONEY OR DESCRIPTION AND VALUE OF PROPERTY

J

10. Other transfers

None ☐

List all other property, other than property transferred in the ordinary course of the business or financial affairs of the debtor, transferred either absolutely or as security within **one year** immediately preceding the commencement of this case. (Married debtors filing under chapter 12 or chapter 13 must include transfers by either or both spouses whether or not a joint petition is filed, unless the spouses are separated and a joint petition is not filed.)

NAME AND ADDRESS OF TRANSFEREE, RELATIONSHIP TO DEBTOR	DATE	DESCRIBE PROPERTY TRANSFERRED AND VALUE RECEIVED

(continued)

EXHIBIT 5–21 Official Form No. 7 (Statement of Financial Affairs), Continued

K **11. Closed financial accounts**

None ☐

List all financial accounts and instruments held in the name of the debtor or for the benefit of the debtor which were closed, sold, or otherwise transferred within **one year** immediately preceding the commencement of this case. Include checking, savings, or other financial accounts, certificates of deposit, or other instruments; shares and share accounts held in banks, credit unions, pension funds, cooperatives, associations, brokerage houses and other financial institutions. (Married debtors filing under chapter 12 or chapter 13 must include information concerning accounts or instruments held by or for either or both spouses whether or not a joint petition is filed, unless the spouses are separated and a joint petition is not filed.)

NAME AND ADDRESS OF INSTITUTION	TYPE OF ACCOUNT, LAST FOUR DIGITS OF ACCOUNT NUMBER, AND AMOUNT OF FINAL BALANCE	AMOUNT AND DATE OF SALE OR CLOSING

L **12. Safe deposit boxes**

None ☐

List each safe deposit or other box or depository in which the debtor has or had securities, cash, or other valuables within **one year** immediately preceding the commencement of this case. (Married debtors filing under chapter 12 or chapter 13 must include boxes or depositories of either or both spouses whether or not a joint petition is filed, unless the spouses are separated and a joint petition is not filed.)

NAME AND ADDRESS OF BANK OR OTHER DEPOSITORY	NAMES AND ADDRESSES OF THOSE WITH ACCESS TO BOX OR DEPOSITORY	DESCRIPTION OF CONTENTS	DATE OF TRANSFER OR SURRENDER, IF ANY

M **13. Setoffs**

None ☐

List all setoffs made by any creditor, including a bank, against a debt or deposit of the debtor within **90 days** preceding the commencement of this case. (Married debtors filing under chapter 12 or chapter 13 must include information concerning either or both spouses whether or not a joint petition is filed, unless the spouses are separated and a joint petition is not filed.)

NAME AND ADDRESS OF CREDITOR	DATE OF SETOFF	AMOUNT OF SETOFF

N **14. Property held for another person**

None ☐

List all property owned by another person that the debtor holds or controls.

NAME AND ADDRESS OF OWNER	DESCRIPTION AND VALUE OF PROPERTY	LOCATION OF PROPERTY

(continued)

O **15. Prior address of debtor**

None ☐

If the debtor has moved within the **two years** immediately preceding the commencement of this case, list all premises which the debtor occupied during that period and vacated prior to the commencement of this case. If a joint petition is filed, report also any separate address of either spouse.

ADDRESS	NAME USED	DATES OF OCCUPANCY

P **16. Spouses and Former Spouses**

None ☐

If the debtor resides or resided in a community property state, commonwealth, or territory (including Alaska, Arizona, California, Idaho, Louisiana, Nevada, New Mexico, Puerto Rico, Texas, Washington, or Wisconsin) within the **six-year period** immediately preceding the commencement of the case, identify the name of the debtorís spouse and of any former spouse who resides or resided with the debtor in the community property state.

NAME

Q **17. Environmental Information.**

For the purpose of this question, the following definitions apply:

"Environmental Law" means any federal, state, or local statute or regulation regulating pollution, contamination, releases of hazardous or toxic substances, wastes or material into the air, land, soil, surface water, groundwater, or other medium, including, but not limited to, statutes or regulations regulating the cleanup of these substances, wastes, or material.

"Site" means any location, facility, or property as defined under any Environmental Law, whether or not presently or formerly owned or operated by the debtor, including, but not limited to, disposal sites.

"Hazardous Material" means anything defined as a hazardous waste, hazardous substance, toxic substance, hazardous material, pollutant, or contaminant or similar term under an Environmental Law

None ☐

a. List the name and address of every site for which the debtor has received notice in writing by a governmental unit that it may be liable or potentially liable under or in violation of an Environmental Law. Indicate the governmental unit, the date of the notice, and, if known, the Environmental Law:

SITE NAME AND ADDRESS	NAME AND ADDRESS OF GOVERNMENTAL UNIT	DATE OF NOTICE	ENVIRONMENTAL LAW

None ☐

b. List the name and address of every site for which the debtor provided notice to a governmental unit of a release of Hazardous Material. Indicate the governmental unit to which the notice was sent and the date of the notice.

SITE NAME AND ADDRESS	NAME AND ADDRESS OF GOVERNMENTAL UNIT	DATE OF NOTICE	ENVIRONMENTAL LAW

(continued)

None ☐ c. List all judicial or administrative proceedings, including settlements or orders, under any Environmental Law with respect to which the debtor is or was a party. Indicate the name and address of the governmental unit that is or was a party to the proceeding, and the docket number.

NAME AND ADDRESS OF GOVERNMENTAL UNIT	DOCKET NUMBER	STATUS OR DISPOSITION

R **18 . Nature, location and name of business**

None ☐ a. If the debtor is an individual, list the names, addresses, taxpayer identification numbers, nature of the businesses, and beginning and ending dates of all businesses in which the debtor was an officer, director, partner, or managing executive of a corporation, partnership, sole proprietorship, or was a self-employed professional within the **six years** immediately preceding the commencement of this case, or in which the debtor owned 5 percent or more of the voting or equity securities within the **six years** immediately preceding the commencement of this case.

If the debtor is a partnership, list the names, addresses, taxpayer identification numbers, nature of the businesses, and beginning and ending dates of all businesses in which the debtor was a partner or owned 5 percent or more of the voting or equity securities, within the **six years** immediately preceding the commencement of this case.

If the debtor is a corporation, list the names, addresses, taxpayer identification numbers, nature of the businesses, and beginning and ending dates of all businesses in which the debtor was a partner or owned 5 percent or more of the voting or equity securities within the **six years** immediately preceding the commencement of this case.

NAME	TAXPAYER I.D. NO. (EIN)	ADDRESS	NATURE OF BUSINESS	BEGINNING AND ENDING DATES

None ☐ b. Identify any business listed in response to subdivision a., above, that is "single asset real estate" as defined in 11 U.S.C. § 101.

NAME	ADDRESS

The following questions are to be completed by every debtor that is a corporation or partnership and by any individual debtor who is or has been, within the **six years** immediately preceding the commencement of this case, any of the following: an officer, director, managing executive, or owner of more than 5 percent of the voting or equity securities of a corporation; a partner, other than a limited partner, of a partnership; a sole proprietor or otherwise self-employed.

(An individual or joint debtor should complete this portion of the statement ***only*** *if the debtor is or has been in business, as defined above, within the six years immediately preceding the commencement of this case. A debtor who has not been in business within those six years should go directly to the signature page.)*

(continued)

S **19. Books, records and financial statements**

None ☐ a. List all bookkeepers and accountants who within the **two years** immediately preceding the filing of this bankruptcy case kept or supervised the keeping of books of account and records of the debtor.

NAME AND ADDRESS | DATES SERVICES RENDERED

None ☐ b. List all firms or individuals who within the **two years** immediately preceding the filing of this bankruptcy case have audited the books of account and records, or prepared a financial statement of the debtor.

NAME | ADDRESS | DATES SERVICES RENDERED

None ☐ c. List all firms or individuals who at the time of the commencement of this case were in possession of the books of account and records of the debtor. If any of the books of account and records are not available, explain.

NAME | ADDRESS

None ☐ d. List all financial institutions, creditors and other parties, including mercantile and trade agencies, to whom a financial statement was issued within the **two years** immediately preceding the commencement of this case by the debtor.

NAME AND ADDRESS | DATE ISSUED

T **20. Inventories**

None ☐ a. List the dates of the last two inventories taken of your property, the name of the person who supervised the taking of each inventory, and the dollar amount and basis of each inventory.

DATE OF INVENTORY | INVENTORY SUPERVISOR | DOLLAR AMOUNT OF INVENTORY (Specify cost, market or other basis)

None ☐ b. List the name and address of the person having possession of the records of each of the two inventories reported in a., above.

DATE OF INVENTORY | NAME AND ADDRESSES OF CUSTODIAN OF INVENTORY RECORDS

(continued)

EXHIBIT 5–21 Official Form No. 7 (Statement of Financial Affairs), Continued

U **21 . Current Partners, Officers, Directors and Shareholders**

None ☐ a. If the debtor is a partnership, list the nature and percentage of partnership interest of each member of the partnership.

NAME AND ADDRESS	NATURE OF INTEREST	PERCENTAGE OF INTEREST

None ☐ b. If the debtor is a corporation, list all officers and directors of the corporation, and each stockholder who directly or indirectly owns, controls, or holds 5 percent or more of the voting or equity securities of the corporation.

NAME AND ADDRESS	TITLE	NATURE AND PERCENTAGE OF STOCK OWNERSHIP

V **22 . Former partners, officers, directors and shareholders**

None ☐ a. If the debtor is a partnership, list each member who withdrew from the partnership within **one year** immediately preceding the commencement of this case.

NAME	ADDRESS	DATE OF WITHDRAWAL

None ☐ b. If the debtor is a corporation, list all officers, or directors whose relationship with the corporation terminated within **one year** immediately preceding the commencement of this case.

NAME AND ADDRESS	TITLE	DATE OF TERMINATION

W **23 . Withdrawals from a partnership or distributions by a corporation**

None ☐ If the debtor is a partnership or corporation, list all withdrawals or distributions credited or given to an insider, including compensation in any form, bonuses, loans, stock redemptions, options exercised and any other perquisite during **one year** immediately preceding the commencement of this case.

NAME & ADDRESS OF RECIPIENT, RELATIONSHIP TO DEBTOR	DATE AND PURPOSE OF WITHDRAWAL	AMOUNT OF MONEY OR DESCRIPTION AND VALUE OF PROPERTY

(continued)

EXHIBIT 5–21 Official Form No. 7 (Statement of Financial Affairs), Continued

X **24. Tax Consolidation Group.**

None ☐ If the debtor is a corporation, list the name and federal taxpayer identification number of the parent corporation of any consolidated group for tax purposes of which the debtor has been a member at any time within the **six-year period** immediately preceding the commencement of the case.

NAME OF PARENT CORPORATION	TAXPAYER IDENTIFICATION NUMBER (EIN)

Y **25. Pension Funds.**

None ☐ If the debtor is not an individual, list the name and federal taxpayer identification number of any pension fund to which the debtor, as an employer, has been responsible for contributing at any time within the **six-year period** immediately receding the commencement of the case.

NAME OF PENSION FUND	TAXPAYER IDENTIFICATION NUMBER (EIN)

* * * * * *

(continued)

Z *[If completed by an individual or individual and spouse]*

I declare under penalty of perjury that I have read the answers contained in the foregoing statement of financial affairs and any attachments thereto and that they are true and correct.

Date ______________________ Signature of Debtor ______________________________

Date ______________________ Signature of Joint Debtor (if any) ______________________________

[If completed on behalf of a partnership or corporation]

I declare under penalty of perjury that I have read the answers contained in the foregoing statement of financial affairs and any attachments thereto and that they are true and correct to the best of my knowledge, information and belief.

Date ______________________ Signature ______________________________

____
Print Name and Title

[An individual signing on behalf of a partnership or corporation must indicate position or relationship to debtor.]

____ continuation sheets attached

Penalty for making a false statement: Fine of up to $500,000 or imprisonment for up to 5 years, or both. 18 U.S.C. § 152 and 3571

CERTIFICATION AND SIGNATURE OF NON-ATTORNEY BANKRUPTCY PETITION PREPARER (See 11 U.S.C. § 110)

I certify that I am a bankruptcy petition preparer as defined in 11 U.S.C. § 110, that I prepared this document for compensation, and that I have provided the debtor with a copy of this document.

____
Printed or Typed Name of Bankruptcy Petition Preparer

____
Social Security No.
(Required by 11 U.S.C. § 110(c).)

____

____
Address

Names and Social Security numbers of all other individuals who prepared or assisted in preparing this document:

If more than one person prepared this document, attach additional signed sheets conforming to the appropriate Official Form for each person.

X ______________________________
Signature of Bankruptcy Petition Preparer

____
Date

A bankruptcy petition preparer's failure to comply with the provisions of title 11 and the Federal Rules of Bankruptcy Procedure may result in fines or imprisonment or both. 18 U.S.C. § 156.

Official Form No. 7, the **Statement of Financial Affairs** (see Exhibit 5–21), contains questions concerning the source of the debtor's income; payments to creditors; lawsuits, executions, garnishments, and attachments; transfers of property prior to the filing of the petition in bankruptcy; casualty or gambling losses; the location of safe deposit boxes; setoffs; property of others held by the debtor; and previous addresses of the debtor. In addition to these questions, a debtor "in business" must provide information concerning the books, records, and financial statements of the business; the last two inventories; current and former partners, officers, directors, and shareholders; and withdrawals from a partnership or distributions by a corporation.

After the statement of financial affairs has been completed, the debtor (in the case of an individual debtor) or the debtors (in the case of a husband and wife filing a joint petition) must complete the unsworn declaration. The debtor must declare under penalty of perjury that he or she has read the answers contained in the statement of financial affairs and any attachments and that they are true and correct. For a partnership or a corporation, the person with authority to represent the debtor must declare under penalty of perjury that he or she has read the answers contained in the statement of financial affairs and any attachments and that they are true and correct to the best of his or her knowledge.

Instructions for Completing Official Form No. 7 (Statement of Financial Affairs)

The questions on Official Form No. 7 track the questions on the debtor-client questionnaire. (See Appendix A.) The debtor's answers to the questionnaire should be used as an aid in filling out this statement of financial affairs. The paralegal or the attorney should proceed through the questions on the statement of financial affairs very carefully with the debtor-client, using the previously prepared questionnaire as a starting point. The debtor's answers on the questionnaire are often incomplete and may suggest further questions that the paralegal or the attorney must follow up with the debtor.

A Income from employment or operation of business

See client's answers to Debtor-Client Questionnaire, Part VII, Question 1.

From the beginning of this calendar year to the date this case was commenced, state the gross amount of income the debtor has received from employment, trade, or profession or from operation of the debtor's business. Also state the sources of this income.

If the debtor's financial records are maintained on a fiscal-year basis, report fiscal-year rather than calendar-year income. Identify the beginning and ending dates of the debtor's fiscal year.

For the two years immediately preceding this calendar or fiscal year, state the gross amounts received from employment, trade, or profession, or from operation of the debtor's business. Also state the sources of this income.

If a husband and wife have filed a joint petition, state the income for each spouse separately.

If the debtor has had no income from employment or the operation of a business during either of these periods, check the "none" box for question 1.

B Income other than from employment or operation of business

See client's answers to Debtor-Client Questionnaire, Part VII, Question 2.

For the two years immediately preceding the commencement of this case, state the amount of income received by the debtor other than from employment, trade, profession, or operation of the debtor's business. Also state the sources of this income.

If a joint petition is filed, state the amount of income and its sources for each spouse separately.

If the debtor has had no other income during this period, check the "none" box for question 2.

C Payments to creditors

See client's answers to Debtor-Client Questionnaire, Part VII, Question 3.

a. Payments made within 90 days

For the 90 days immediately preceding the commencement of this case, list all payments of loans, installment purchases of goods or services, and other debts aggregating more than $600 to any creditor.

For each creditor, include the following:

1) the name and address of the creditor
2) the dates of payments
3) the amount paid
4) the amount still owing

If the debtor has made no payment during this period, check the "none" box for question 3.a.

This question relates to the 90-day preference. See 11 U.S.C.A. § 547.

b. Payments made within one year to insiders

For the one-year period immediately preceding the commencement of this case, list all payments made to or for the benefit of creditors who are or were insiders. For each creditor, include the name and address of the creditor and the relationship to the debtor, the date of payment, the amount paid, and the amount still owing.

If the debtor has made no payment during this period to an insider, check the "none" box for question 3.b.

The term "insider" includes but is not limited to

1) relatives of the debtor;
2) general partners of the debtor and their relatives;
3) corporations of which the debtor is an officer, director, or person in control;
4) officers, directors, and any person in control of a corporate debtor and their relatives;
5) affiliates of the debtor and insiders of such affiliates; and
6) any managing agent of the debtor. 11 U.S.C.A. § 101(31).

This question relates to the one-year preference period for payments to an insider. See 11 U.S.C.A. § 547.

D Suits and administrative proceedings, executions, garnishments, and attachments

See client's answers to Debtor-Client Questionnaire, Part VII, Question 4.

a. Lawsuits

For the one-year period immediately preceding the filing of this bankruptcy case, list all suits to which the debtor is or was a party. Include the following information:

1) the caption of the lawsuit and the case number
2) the nature of the lawsuit
3) the court in which the lawsuit was filed and court's location
4) the current status or disposition of the lawsuit

Repeat until all lawsuits have been listed.

The paralegal or the attorney may need to conduct a personal investigation regarding lawsuits against the debtor. The courthouse records may be searched on-line using the debtor's name. This information must be accurate. Some debtors do not understand why they have been summoned and the significance of the summons. Sometimes a debtor does not realize he or she has been sued. For example, divorces are also lawsuits.

If the debtor has not been a party to a lawsuit during this period, check the "none" box for question 4.a.

b. Attachments, seizures, and garnishments

For the one-year period immediately preceding the commencement of this case, provide the following information as to property attached, seized, or garnished under any legal or equitable process:

1) the name of the person for whose benefit the property was attached or seized
2) the address of the person for whose benefit the property was attached or seized
3) the date of attachment or seizure
4) a description of the property
5) the value of the property

Repeat until all attachments, seizures, and garnishments have been listed.

If a garnishment, execution, or attachment is underway which would constitute a judicial lien, it may be subject to avoidance by the debtor to the extent that the lien impairs an exemption to which the debtor would be entitled under 11 U.S.C.A. § 522(b). 11 U.S.C.A. § 522(f).

If the debtor has not had property attached, seized, or garnished during this period, check the "none" box for question 4.b.

E Repossessions, foreclosures, and returns

See client's answers to Debtor-Client Questionnaire, Part VII, Question 5.

For the one-year period immediately preceding the commencement of this case, provide the following information for each repossession, foreclosure, or return:

1) the name of the creditor or seller
2) the address of the creditor or seller
3) the date of repossession, foreclosure sale, transfer, or return
4) a description of the property
5) the value of the property

If there has been no repossession, foreclosure, or return during this period, check the "none" box for question 5.

F Assignments and receiverships

See client's answers to Debtor-Client Questionnaire, Part VII, Question 6.

a. Assignments

For the 120 days immediately preceding the commencement of this case, provide the following information for each assignment of property for the benefit of creditors:

1) the name of the assignee
2) the assignee's address
3) the date of the assignment
4) the terms of the assignment or settlement

If there has been no assignment of property for the benefit of creditors during this period, check the "none" box for question 6.a.

b. Receiverships

For the one-year period immediately preceding the commencement of this case, provide the following information for any property which has been in the hands of a custodian, receiver, or court-appointed official:

1) the name of the custodian
2) the address of the custodian
3) the name of the court
4) the location of the court
5) the case title
6) the case number
7) the date of the order
8) a description of the property
9) the value of the property

If there has been no property in the hands of a custodian, receiver, or court-appointed official during this period, check the "none" box for question 6.b.

G Gifts

See client's answers to Debtor-Client Questionnaire, Part VII, Question 7.

For the one-year period immediately preceding the commencement of this case, provide the following information for all gifts or charitable contributions, except ordinary and usual gifts made to family members aggregating less than $200 in value per individual family member and charitable contributions aggregating less than $100 per recipient:

1) the name of the person or organization receiving the gift
2) the address of the person or organization receiving the gift
3) the relationship of the recipient to the debtor, if any
4) the date of the gift
5) a description of the gift
6) the value of the gift

If no such gifts were made, check the "none" box for question 7.

Question 7 relates to preferences (11 U.S.C.A. § 547), fraudulent transfers (11 U.S.C.A. § 548), and voidable transfers under the Uniform Fraudulent Conveyances Act, the Uniform Fraudulent Transfer Act, and other state laws. 11 U.S.C.A. § 544(b).

H Losses

See client's answers to Debtor-Client Questionnaire, Part VII, Question 8.

For the one-year period immediately preceding the commencement of this case or since the commencement of this case, provide the following information for all losses from fire, theft, other casualty, or gambling:

1) a description of the property
2) the value of the property
3) a description of the circumstances surrounding the loss
4) if the loss was covered in whole or in part by insurance, the particulars of the insurance coverage
5) the date of the loss

If the debtor suffered no losses from fire, theft, other casualty, or gambling during this period, check the "none" box for question 8.

I Payments related to debt counseling or bankruptcy

See client's answers to Debtor-Client Questionnaire, Part VII, Question 9.

a. Payments

For the one-year period immediately preceding the commencement of this case, provide the following information for all payments made by or on behalf of the debtor to any person, including attorneys, for consultation concerning debt consolidation, relief under the bankruptcy law, or preparation of a petition in bankruptcy:

1) the name of the payee
2) the address of the payee
3) the date of the payment
4) the name of the payor, if other than the debtor
5) the amount of money paid

b. Transfers

For the one-year period immediately preceding the commencement of this case, provide the following information for all property transferred by or on behalf of the debtor to any person, including attorneys, for consultation concerning debt consolidation, relief under the bankruptcy law, or preparation of a petition in bankruptcy:

1) the name of the transferee
2) the address of the transferee
3) the date of the transfer
4) the name of the transferor, if other than the debtor
5) a description and the value of the property transferred

If no payments were made or no property was transferred during this period, check the "none" box for question 9.

J Other transfers

See client's answers to Debtor-Client Questionnaire, Part VII, Question 10.

For the one-year period immediately preceding the commencement of this case, provide the following information for all other property, other than property transferred in the ordinary course of the business or financial affairs of the debtor, transferred either absolutely or as security:

1) the name of the transferee
2) the address of the transferee
3) the relationship of the transferee to the debtor
4) the date of the transfer
5) a description of the property transferred
6) the value received for the property

These questions relate to fraudulent transfers (11 U.S.C.A. § 548), and voidable transfers under applicable law (11 U.S.C.A § 544(b)).

The debtor may not fully comprehend what constitutes a transfer. Some debtors do not understand that a sale is a transfer. They may believe that only gifts are transfers.

Some debtors believe that only a sale is a transfer. Therefore, a debtor may not have stated that she gave a car to her son because the car was not sold but was given as a gift.

Some debtors believe that only the transfer of property that is collateral for a security interest is a transfer of property. Therefore, a debtor may not have stated that she gave a car to her son because the car was hers when she gave it to him.

Some debtors believe that transfer of property refers only to real property. Therefore, a debtor may not have stated that he gave a car to his daughter because it was not real property.

If no other property was transferred absolutely or as security within this period, other than property transferred in the ordinary course of the business or financial affairs of the debtor, check the "none" box for question 10.

K Closed financial accounts

See client's answers to Debtor-Client Questionnaire, Part VII, Question 11.

For the one-year period immediately preceding the commencement of this case, provide the following information for all financial accounts and instruments (including checking accounts, savings accounts, other financial accounts, certificates of deposit, shares and share accounts held in banks, credit unions, pension funds, cooperatives, associations, brokerage houses, and other financial institutions) held in the name of the debtor or for the benefit of the debtor which were closed, sold, or otherwise transferred:

1) the name of the institution
2) the address of the institution
3) the name under which the account was carried
4) the type of account and the account number
5) the amount of the final balance
6) the amount and the date of the sale or closing

If the debtor had the ability to sign on the account, the account must be listed.

If no financial accounts or instruments were closed, sold, or otherwise transferred during this period, check the "none" box for question 11.

L Safe deposit boxes

See client's answers to Debtor-Client Questionnaire, Part VII, Question 12.

For the one-year period immediately preceding the commencement of this case, list each safe deposit box or other box or depository in which the debtor has or had securities, cash, or other valuables. For each box or depository, provide the following information:

1) the name of the bank or other depository
2) the address of the bank or other depository

3) the name of every person who had the right of access to the box or depository

4) the address of every person who had the right of access to the box or depository

5) a brief description of the contents

6) if the box or other depository has been transferred, state the transfer date

7) if the box or other depository has been surrendered, state the date of surrender

If the debtor did not have a safe deposit box or other box or depository which has or had securities, cash, or other valuables during this period, check the "none" box for question 12.

M Setoffs

See client's answers to Debtor-Client Questionnaire, Part VII, Question 13.

For the 90 days preceding the commencement of the case, list all setoffs made by any creditor, including a bank, against a debtor or a deposit of the debtor. If there has been such a setoff, provide the following information:

1) the name of the creditor

2) the address of the creditor

3) the date of the setoff

4) the amount of the debt owed to the creditor

5) the amount of the setoff.

See 11 U.S.C.A. § 553 for the right of setoff.

If no setoffs were made during this period, check the "none" box for question 13.

N Property held for another person

See client's answers to Debtor-Client Questionnaire, Part VII, Question 14.

List all property owned by another person that the debtor holds or controls. For each item of property held or controlled by the debtor, provide the following information:

1) the name of the owner

2) the address of the owner

3) the description of the property

4) the value of the property

5) the location of the property

If the debtor does not hold or control any property owned by another person, check the "none" box for question 14.

O Prior address of debtor

See client's answers to Debtor-Client Questionnaire, Part VII, Question 15.

If the debtor has moved within the two years immediately preceding the commencement of this case, list all premises which the debtor occupied during that period and vacated prior to the commencement of this case. For each such address of the debtor, provide the following information:

1) the former address

2) the name under which the premises were occupied

3) the dates of occupancy

If a joint petition, also state any separate address of the debtor's spouse during this period. For each separate address of the debtor's spouse, provide the following information:

1) the former address

2) the name under which the premises were occupied

3) the dates of occupancy

If the debtor or, in the case of a joint petition, the debtor and his or her spouse have not moved within this period, or the debtor's spouse has not had a separate address, check the "none" box for question 15.

P Spouse and Former Spouses

See client's answers to Debtor-Client Questionnaire, Part VII, Question 16.

If the debtor resided in a community property state within the six-year period immediately preceding the commencement of this bankruptcy case, name the debtor's spouse or former spouses who resided with the debtor in that state.

Q Environmental Information

See client's answers to Debtor-Client Questionnaire, Part VII, Question 17.

a. If the debtor has received a written notice by a governmental unit that the debtor may be liable or potentially liable for an environmental law violation, list the site name and address, the name and address of the governmental unit, the date of the notice, and the environmental law cited in the notice. If the debtor has not received such a notice, check the "none" box.

b. If the debtor has received a written notice by a governmental unit that the debtor has released hazardous material, list the site name and address, the name and address of the governmental unit, the date of the notice, and the environmental law cited in the notice. If the debtor has not received such a notice, check the "none" box.

c. If the debtor is or was a party to any judicial or administrative proceedings, including settlements or orders, under any environmental law, list the name and address of the governmental unit, the docket number, and the status or disposition of the proceeding. If the debtor has never been a party, check the "none" box.

R Nature, location, and name of business

See client's answers to Debtor-Client Questionnaire, Part VII, Question 18.

a. Individual, partnership, or corporation

1) Answer this question if the debtor is filing as an individual. If question 18.a. does not apply to the debtor, check the "none" box.

a) For the two years immediately preceding the commencement of this case, list all businesses in which the debtor was an

(1) officer

(2) director

(3) partner

(4) managing executive of a

(a) corporation

(b) partnership

(c) sole proprietorship

b) For the two years immediately preceding the commencement of this case, list all businesses in which the debtor was a self-employed professional.

c) For the two years immediately preceding the commencement of this case, list all businesses in which the debtor owned 5 percent or more of the voting or equity securities.

For each operation, provide the following information:

a) the name

b) the address

c) the nature of the business

d) the beginning date of operation

e) the ending date of operation

2) Answer this question if the debtor is filing as a partnership. For the two years immediately preceding the commencement of this case, list all businesses in which the debtor was

a) a partner

b) owned 5 percent or more of the voting securities

For each business, provide the following information:

a) the name
b) the address
c) the nature of the business
d) the beginning date of operation
e) the ending date of operation

If the debtor has nothing to report for question 18.a., check the "none" box.

3) Answer this question if the debtor is filing as a corporation. If question 18.b. does not apply to the debtor, check the "none" box.

For the two years immediately preceding the commencement of this case, list all businesses in which the debtor was

a) a partner
b) owned 5 percent or more of the voting securities

For each business, provide the following information:

1) the name
2) the address
3) the nature of the business
4) the beginning date of operation
5) the ending date of operation

If the debtor has nothing to report for question 18.b., check the "none" box.

b. If a business was listed in 18.a., then identify any "single asset real estate" as defined in 11 U.S.C.A. § 101(51B) by name and address. A "single asset real estate" is one real property or project, excluding residential real property of less than four residential units, that generates substantially all of the debtor's gross income and on which the debtor does not conduct a substantial business other than the business of operating the property or activities incidental to operating the property and having aggregate noncontingent, liquidated secured debts of no more than $4,000,000.

Complete questions 19–25 if the answer to question 18.a. is not "none." If your answer is "none," the Statement of Financial Affairs is now complete except for the unsworn declaration that follows question 25.

S Books, records, and financial statements

See client's answers to Debtor-Client Questionnaire, Part VII, Question 19.

a. Bookkeepers and accountants

For the two years immediately preceding the filing of this bankruptcy case, list all bookkeepers and accountants who kept or supervised the keeping of the debtor's account books and records. For any such bookkeeper or accountant, provide the following information:

1) the name of the bookkeeper or accountant
2) the address of the bookkeeper or accountant
3) the dates the services were rendered

If there were no bookkeepers or accountants who kept or supervised the keeping of the debtor's books of account and records during this period, check the "none" box for question 19.a.

b. Audits and preparation of financial statements

For the two years immediately preceding the filing of this bankruptcy case, list the firms or individuals who audited the books of account and records or prepared a financial statement of the debtor. For any such services, provide the following information:

1) the name of the firm or individual
2) the address of the firm or individual
3) the dates the services were rendered

If no firm or individual audited the debtor's books of account and records or prepared a financial statement of the debtor, check "none" for question 19.b.

c. Possession of books and records

Provide the following information concerning the firms or individuals who currently have possession of the debtor's books of account or records:

1) the name of the firm or individual who currently has possession of the debtor's books of account or records

2) the address of the firm or individual

If any of these books or records are unavailable, explain the circumstances surrounding the unavailability of these books or records. See 11 U.S.C.A. § 727(a)(3) concerning the relationship between the failure to preserve books and records and discharge of the debtor.

If no firm or individual was in possession of the debtor's books of account or records at the time of the commencement of this case, check the "none" box for question 19.c.

d. Financial statements

List all financial institutions, creditors and other parties (including mercantile and trade agencies) to whom a financial statement was issued within the two years immediately preceding the commencement of this case by the debtor. For each, provide the following information:

1) the name of the person receiving the written financial statement

2) the address of the person receiving the written financial statement

3) the date the financial statement was issued

If no financial statement was issued during this period, check the "none" box for question 19.d.

T Inventories

See client's answers to Debtor-Client Questionnaire, Part VII, Question 20.

a. The last two inventories

For the last two inventories of the debtor's property, provide the following information:

1) the date the inventory of the debtor's property was taken

2) the name of the person under whose supervision the inventory was taken

3) the dollar amount of the inventory

4) whether the inventory was taken at cost, market, or other basis

If an inventory of the debtor's property has not been taken, check the "none" box for question 20.a.

b. Custodian of the inventory records

State the following information concerning the custodian of the inventory records for the last two inventories:

1) the date of the inventory

2) the name of the custodian of the records

3) the address of the custodian of the records

If an inventory has not been taken or if no one has possession of the records of the inventory, check the "none" box for question 20.b.

U Current partners, officers, directors, and shareholders

See client's answers to Debtor-Client Questionnaire, Part VII, Question 21.

a. Answer this question if the debtor is filing as a partnership. If this question is not applicable to the debtor, check the "none" box for question 21.a.

For each member of the partnership, provide the following information:

1) the name of the partner

2) the address of the partner

3) the nature of the partner's interest

4) the percentage of the partnership interest

b. Answer this question if the debtor is filing as a corporation. If this question is not applicable to the debtor, check the "none" box for question 21.b.

For each officer or director of the corporation and each stockholder who directly or indirectly owns, controls, or holds 5 percent or more of the voting securities of the corporation, provide the following information:

1) the name of the officer, director, or stockholder
2) the address of the officer, director, or stockholder
3) the title of the party
4) the nature of stock ownership
5) the percentage of stock ownership

V Former partners, officers, directors, and shareholders

See client's answers to Debtor-Client Questionnaire, Part VII, Question 22.

a. Answer this question if the debtor is filing as a partnership. If this question is not applicable to the debtor, check the "none" box for question 22.a.

For each member of the partnership who withdrew from the partnership within one year immediately preceding the commencement of this case, provide the following information:

1) the name of the former partner
2) the address of the former partner
3) the date of withdrawal from the partnership

If no member withdrew from the partnership within one year immediately preceding the commencement of this case, check the "none" box for question 22.a.

b. Answer this question if the debtor is filing as a corporation. If this question is not applicable to the debtor, check the "none" box for question 22.b.

For each officer or director of the corporation whose relationship with the corporation terminated within one year immediately preceding the commencement of this case, provide the following information:

1) the name of the officer or director
2) the address of the officer or director
3) the title of the officer or director
4) the date of termination of the relationship with the corporation

If no officer's or director's relationship with the corporation terminated within one year immediately preceding the commencement of this case, check the "none" box for question 22.b.

W Withdrawals from a partnership or distributions by a corporation

See client's answers to Debtor-Client Questionnaire, Part VII, Question 23.

Answer this question if the debtor is filing as a partnership or as a corporation.

For the one-year period immediately preceding the commencement of the case, list all withdrawals or distributions credited or given to an insider (including compensation in any form, bonuses, loans, stock redemptions, options exercised, or any other perquisite). For each insider recipient, provide the following information:

1) the name of the recipient
2) the address of the recipient
3) the recipient's relationship to the debtor
4) the date of the withdrawal
5) the purpose of the withdrawal
6) the amount of money withdrawn or a description of and the value of the property distributed

Question 23 relates to preferences, 11 U.S.C.A. § 547.

If there were no withdrawals or distributions credited or given to an insider during this period, check the "none" box for question 23.

The Statement of Financial Affairs is now complete except for the unsworn declaration.

X Tax Consolidation Group

If the debtor is a corporation and has been a member of a consolidated group for tax purposes within the past six years, give the name of the parent corporation and its taxpayer identification number. If the debtor has not participated in such a group, check the "none" box.

Y Pension Funds

If the debtor is an employer and has been responsible for contributing to a pension fund within the past six years, list the name of the pension fund(s) and the fund's federal taxpayer identification number. If there have been no contributions, check the "none" box.

Z Complete the unsworn declaration

a. If the debtor is an individual or a husband and wife filing a joint petition, complete the first unsworn declaration. Review the completed Statement of Financial Affairs with the debtor or with the joint debtors if a husband and wife are filing a joint petition. Read the declaration to the debtor(s) prior to the signing. After the unsworn declaration has been signed, have the declarant(s) date the declaration with the date the declaration was signed (not the date the petition or statement will be filed or was filed).

b. If the debtor is a partnership or a corporation, the party signing on behalf of the partnership or the corporation must complete the second unsworn declaration. Type or print the name and title of the party signing on behalf of the debtor. Review the completed Statement of Financial Affairs with the party who will sign on behalf of the debtor. Read the declaration to the party signing prior to his or her signing. After the unsworn declaration has been signed, have the declarant date the declaration with the date the declaration was signed (not the date the petition or statement will be filed or was filed).

PROBLEM 5.17 Using the information in Problem 4.5, complete the Statement of Financial Affairs for the McPhersons.

I. STATEMENT OF INTENTION IF THE DEBTOR IS AN INDIVIDUAL WITH CONSUMER DEBTS

An individual debtor whose schedule of assets and liabilities includes consumer debts secured by property of the estate must file with the bankruptcy court clerk a **statement of intention** with respect to the retention or surrender of the property. (See Exhibit 5–22.) If this property is claimed as exempt, the debtor must state whether he or she intends to redeem the property or to reaffirm debts secured by the property. 11 U.S.C.A. § 521(2)(A).

On or before the filing of the statement, a copy must be served on the trustee and named creditors. Fed. R. Bank. P. 1107(b)(2). The debtor must carry out his or her intention with respect to the property in question within 45 days after filing the statement of intention. The court, for cause, may (within the 45-day period) allow additional time for the debtor to perform his or her intention. 11 U.S.C.A. § 521(2)(B).

The debtor may amend his or her statement of intention at any time before the expiration of the 45-day period (or longer period allowed by the court) for carrying out his or her intention. If the debtor wishes to amend the statement of intention, he or she must give notice of the amendment to the trustee and to any party affected by the amendment. Fed. R. Bank. P. 1009(b).

The debtor who seeks to amend his or her statement of intention may be saved from a harsh application of the 45-day limitation (or longer time limitation at the court's discretion) of Fed. R. Bank. P. 1009(b).

EXHIBIT 5–22 Official Form No. 8 (Chapter 7 Individual Debtor's Statement of Intention)

Official Form 8
(12/03)

United States Bankruptcy Court

________________ District Of ________________

In re __________________________,
Debtor

Case No. ____________

Chapter 7

CHAPTER 7 INDIVIDUAL DEBTOR'S STATEMENT OF INTENTION

1. I have filed a schedule of assets and liabilities which includes consumer debts secured by property of the estate.

2. I intend to do the following with respect to the property of the estate which secures those consumer debts:

a. *Property to Be Surrendered.*

Description of Property A **Creditor's name**

b. *Property to Be Retained* *[Check any applicable statement.]*

Description of Property	Creditor's Name	Property is claimed as exempt	Property will be redeemed pursuant to 11 U.S.C. § 722	Debt will be reaffirmed pursuant to 11 U.S.C. § 524(c)
	B		C	

Date: ____________ D

____
Signature of Debtor

CERTIFICATION OF NON-ATTORNEY BANKRUPTCY PETITION PREPARER (See 11 U.S.C. § 110)

I certify that I am a bankruptcy petition preparer as defined in 11 U.S.C. § 110, that I prepared this document for compensation, and that I have provided the debtor with a copy of this document.

____
Printed or Typed Name of Bankruptcy Petition Preparer

____
Social Security No.
(Required by 11 U.S.C. § 110(c).)

____

____
Address

Names and Social Security Numbers of all other individuals who prepared or assisted in preparing this document.

If more than one person prepared this document, attach additional signed sheets conforming to the appropriate Official Form for each person.

X________________________
Signature of Bankruptcy Petition Preparer

____
Date

A bankruptcy petition preparer's failure to comply with the provisions of title 11 and the Federal Rules of Bankruptcy Procedure may result in fines or imprisonment or both. 11 U.S.C. § 110; 18 U.S.C. § 156.

The debtor shall—

. . .

(2) if an individual debtor's schedule of assets and liabilities includes consumer debts which are secured by property of the estate—

. . .

(C) nothing in subparagraphs (A) and (B) of this paragraph shall alter the debtor's or the trustee's rights with regard to such property under this title; . . . . 11 U.S.C.A. § 521(2)(C).

The Statement of Intention, Official Form No. 8—need only be completed by an individual debtor or by individual debtors (husband and wife) filing a joint petition. In the case of individual debtors filing a joint petition:

1. if the property and debts of the debtors are the same, each debtor must sign Official Form No. 8;
2. if the debts of the debtors are separate, each debtor must use a separate Official Form No. 8.

Instructions for Completing Official Form No. 8 (Chapter 7 Individual Debtor's Statement of Intention)

A Describe the property to be surrendered. Use the description as it appears in Schedule A or Schedule B. State the creditor's name as it appears in Schedule A or Schedule B.

B Describe the property to be retained. Use the description as it appears in Schedule A or Schedule B. State the creditor's name as it appears in Schedule A or Schedule B.

C Select the applicable statement of the debtor's intention by placing a check mark under the selected statement:

1. the debt will be reaffirmed pursuant to 11 U.S.C.A. § 524(c);
2. the Property is claimed as exempt and will be redeemed pursuant to 11 U.S.C.A. § 722;
3. the lien will be avoided pursuant to 11 U.S.C.A. § 522(f) and property will be claimed as exempt.

D The debtor signs his or her name as it appears on the petition. The debtor also dates the statement of intention.

PROBLEM 5.18 Complete the statement of intention for the McPhersons using the information found in Problem 4.5.

J. DEBTOR'S DUTY TO SUPPLEMENT THE SCHEDULES

The commencement of the case under Chapter 7 creates the estate, which consists of all property owned by the debtor as of the date of the filing of the petition. The Code provides that in some instances, although the frequency of occurrence is small, property acquired by the debtor after the filing of the petition may also become property of the estate.

(a) The commencement of a case under section 301, 302, or 303 of this title creates an estate. Such estate is comprised of all the following property, wherever located and by whomever held:

. . .

> (5) Any interest in property that would have been property of the estate if such interest had been an interest of the debtor on the date of the filing of the petition, and that the debtor acquires or becomes entitled to acquire within 180 days after such date—
> (A) by bequest, devise, or inheritance;
> (B) as a result of a property settlement agreement with the debtor's spouse, or of an interlocutory or final divorce decree; or
> (C) as a beneficiary of a life insurance policy or of a death benefit plan. 11 U.S.C.A. § 541(a)(5).

If the debtor acquires this property after the schedule of assets has been filed, the debtor must file a supplemental schedule listing the after-acquired property. This supplemental schedule must be filed "within 10 days after the information comes to the debtor's knowledge or within such further time as the court may allow. . . . If any of the property required to be reported under this subdivision is claimed by the debtor as exempt, the debtor shall claim the exemptions in the supplemental schedule." Fed. R. Bank. P. 1007(h).

The debtor's duty to file a supplemental schedule continues even though the case has been closed if the debtor's duty to file arose before the case was closed, and the case was closed before the duty was or could be performed. Fed. R. Bank. P. 1007(h).

K. DEBTOR'S RIGHT TO AMEND THE PETITION, LISTS, SCHEDULES, AND STATEMENTS

A problem more common than after-acquired property involves errors in the documents filed. The errors may involve property or obligations that existed at the time of filing the petition that should have been listed on the various lists, schedules, or statements. The debtor may have forgotten about certain assets or debts or may have misunderstood the attorney's or the paralegal's instructions about what should be included in the lists, schedules, or statements. The attorney or the paralegal may have misunderstood the debtor when the lists, schedules, and statements were being prepared.

The Federal Rules of Bankruptcy Procedure authorize the debtor to amend.

> A voluntary petition, list, schedule, or statement may be amended by the debtor as a matter of course at any time before the case is closed. The debtor shall give notice of the amendment to the trustee and to any entity affected thereby. . . . Fed. R. Bank. P. 1009(a).

Any amendment must be verified or contain an unsworn declaration. Fed. R. Bank. P. 1008. A bankruptcy filing program contains a form for amending schedules, along with a verification form.

If a creditor's schedule is amended, the amended schedule must be served on the affected creditor, otherwise the creditor does not receive notice of the bankruptcy. The list of creditors must also be amended. The attorney and paralegal may, as good practice, send the creditor the amended schedule and a copy of the original bankruptcy notice along with a certificate of service to verify that the creditor has received notice.

After the notice has been given, if parties affected by the amendment do not challenge the debtor's right to make the amendment or do not bring a motion for disallowance of a claimed exemption, the petition, lists, schedules, or statements will stand as amended. If, however, the amendment would prejudice a party in interest, the court may refuse to let the debtor amend.

SECTION 3
THE SIGNIFICANCE OF FILING A PETITION

Once the petition for bankruptcy has been filed and the bankruptcy estate is created, the debtor's interest in the property ceases. Therefore, if the debtor dies while the case is pending, only property exempted from the bankruptcy estate, abandoned by the trustee, or acquired after commencement of the case (and not included as property of the estate) will be available to the representative of the debtor's probate estate. The bankruptcy proceeding will continue as it relates to the property of the bankruptcy estate. 11 U.S.C.A. § 541.

PROBLEM 5.19 On March 1, Donald Duncan filed a petition under Chapter 7 of the Bankruptcy Code. Two months later, Donald died intestate, leaving a wife and two children.

Will the property of Donald's bankruptcy estate be divided among his creditors or among his widow and children?

In a Chapter 7 case, the trustee in bankruptcy collects and sells the "property of the estate." 11 U.S.C.A. § 704. The trustee then distributes the proceeds from the sale among the creditors. 11 U.S.C.A. § 726. The larger the estate, the more the debtor gives up and the more the trustee sells. The more the trustee sells, the more there is to divide among the creditors. The debtor may be discharged from his or her outstanding obligations and receive a "fresh start" *during* this process of "reallocation of wealth."

A. THE ORDER FOR RELIEF

The commencement of a voluntary case under Chapter 7 by a single debtor or by joint debtors (i.e., the filing of the petition with the bankruptcy court) constitutes an **order for relief** under Chapter 7. 11 U.S.C.A. §§ 301, 302. The clerk will affix a filing stamp showing the date and time filed and the court in which the petition was filed. The petition is stamped with a case number at this time.

B. THE ESTATE IS CREATED

Upon the filing of a bankruptcy petition, an **estate in bankruptcy (bankruptcy estate)** is automatically created. 11 U.S.C.A. § 541(a). This estate includes all legal and equitable interests of the debtor, with minor exceptions. 11 U.S.C.A. §§ 541(b), (c)(2). The debtor may claim certain property of the estate as exempt. This exempt property is then removed from the bankruptcy estate. Other items of property of the estate may be abandoned by the trustee in bankruptcy. The remaining assets of the estate will be subject to administration by the bankruptcy trustee for the benefit of creditors. (See Exhibit 5–23.)

1. Property of the Estate

Property is generally defined as those things capable of being the subject of ownership. Ownership is the right of a person to possess and use a thing to the exclusion of others.

Property is generally classified as being either real or personal. Real property is land and those things that are permanently affixed to land. Personal property is all property not classified as real property and may be tangible or intangible.

EXHIBIT 5–23 Creating the Estate

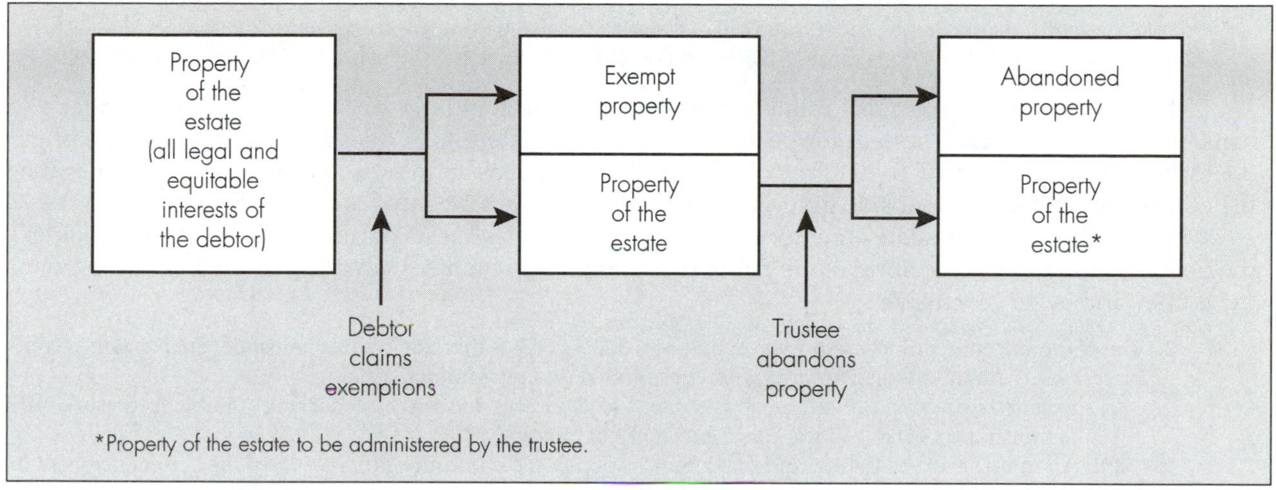

EXAMPLE

Jane wrote a song and went through the copyright process. Jane owns both the physical paper on which the song is written and the copyright. The paper on which the song is written is tangible property. The copyright is intangible property.

PROBLEM 5.20 Craig, a building contractor, remodeled Matthew's house. On completion of the work, Craig presented Matthew with a bill for $2,500. Is this account receivable tangible or intangible property?

An interest in property may be a present or a future interest. A present interest entitles the owner to an immediate right to possess the property. A future interest entitles the owner to a right to possess the property at some future time.

EXAMPLE

William promised his sister Alice that if she would promise to live in his house and care for him for the remainder of his life, he would give her the house in fee simple. If Alice promises William, a contract is formed. Alice has a future interest in William's house. Alice may not claim William's house until William dies.

PROBLEM 5.21 Martha has three daughters named Amanda, Beth, and Carrie. Each would like to use Martha's beach house in Hawaii. Each daughter has a large family and does not want to share the beach house with her sisters. Martha decided that she would allow each daughter to use the beach house for four months during the year. The dates were allocated by lot. Amanda drew January through April. Beth drew May through August. Carrie drew September through December.

The date is today's date. Who has a present interest and who has a future interest? Assume that this arrangement is to continue for five years.

EXAMPLE

Catherine owns Greenacre which she has leased to Donald for 10 years. Both Catherine and Donald have an interest in Greenacre. Catherine has a fee simple interest subject to Donald's 10-year lease. Donald's 10-year lease interest is a present possessory interest. Catherine has a present ownership interest. Catherine's right to possession is a future interest.

An interest in property may be entire or concurrent. Concurrent owners share ownership of the same interest in property.

EXAMPLE

Charles and Agnes, husband and wife, purchased Blackacre "as joint tenants and not as tenants in common, together with the right of survivorship." During their lives, both Charles and Agnes own Blackacre. If Charles dies first, Agnes is freed from Charles's claim and continues in her full ownership capacity. During the lives of the joint tenants, their interests in Blackacre are concurrent.

The property of a bankruptcy estate may include both real and personal property. Although federal bankruptcy law provides a system for dealing with property interests, it does not define the nature of the debtor's interest in property. To determine whether the debtor has an interest in property, the paralegal or the attorney must look at nonbankruptcy law which is primarily state law.

The "property of the estate" includes all legal or equitable interests of the debtor in property held by the debtor at the time of the filing of the petition. Section 541(a) itemizes what is included as "property of the estate" and is very inclusive.

(a) The commencement of a case under section 301, 302, or 303 of this title creates an estate. Such estate is comprised of all the following property, wherever located and by whomever held:
  (1) Except as provided in subsections (b) and (c)(2) of this section, all legal or equitable interests of the debtor in property as of the commencement of the case.
  (2) All interests of the debtor and the debtor's spouse in community property as of the commencement of the case that is—
    (A)under the sole, equal, or joint management and control of the debtor; or
    (B)liable for an allowable claim against the debtor, or for both an allowable claim against the debtor and an allowable claim against the debtor's spouse, to the extent that such interest is so liable.
  (3) Any interest in property that the trustee recovers under section 329(b), 363(n), 543, 550, 553, or 723 of this title.
  (4) Any interest in property preserved for the benefit of or ordered transferred to the estate under section 510(c) or 551 of this title.
  (5) Any interest in property that would have been property of the estate if such interest had been an interest of the debtor on the date of the filing of the petition, and that the debtor acquires or becomes entitled to acquire within 180 days after such date—
    (A)by bequest, devise, or inheritance;
    (B)as a result of a property settlement agreement with the debtor's spouse, or of an interlocutory or final divorce decree; or
    (C)as a beneficiary of a life insurance policy or of a death benefit plan.
  (6) Proceeds, product, offspring, rents, or profits of or from property of the estate, except such as are earnings from services performed by an individual debtor after the commencement of the case.
  (7) Any interest in property that the estate acquires after the commencement of the case.

(b) Property of the estate does not include—
  (1) any power that the debtor may exercise solely for the benefit of an entity other than the debtor;
  (2) any interest of the debtor as a lessee under a lease of nonresidential real property that has terminated at the expiration of the stated term of such lease before the commencement of the case under this title, and ceases to include any interest of the debtor as a lessee under a lease of nonresidential real property that has terminated at the expiration of the stated term of such lease during the case;
  (3) any eligibility of the debtor to participate in programs authorized under the Higher Education Act of 1965 (20 U.S.C. 1001 et seq.; 42 U.S.C. 2751 et seq.), or any accreditation status or State licensure of the debtor as an educational institution;
  (4) any interest of the debtor in liquid or gaseous hydrocarbons to the extent that—
    (A) (i) the debtor has transferred or has agreed to transfer such interest pursuant to a farmout agreement or any written agreement directly related to a farmout agreement; and
      (ii) but for the operation of this paragraph, the estate could include the interest referred to in clause (i) only by virtue of section 365 or 544(a)(3) of this title; or
    (B) (i) the debtor has transferred such interest pursuant to a written conveyance of a production payment to an entity that does not participate in the operation of the property from which such production payment is transferred; and
      (ii) but for the operation of this paragraph, the estate could include the interest referred to in clause (i) only by virtue of section 542 of this title; or

(5) any interest in cash or cash equivalents that constitute proceeds of a sale by the debtor of a money order that is made—
(A)on or after the date that is 14 days prior to the date on which the petition if filed; and
(B)under an agreement with a money order issuer that prohibits the commingling of such proceeds with property of the debtor (notwithstanding that, contrary to the agreement, the proceeds may have been commingled with property of the debtor),

Paragraph (4) shall not be construed to exclude from the estate any consideration the debtor retains, receives, or is entitled to receive for transferring an interest in liquid or gaseous hydrocarbons pursuant to a farmout agreement; or unless the money order issuer had not taken action, prior to the filing of the petition, to require compliance with the prohibition.

(c) (1) Except as provided in paragraph (2) of this subsection, an interest of the debtor in property becomes property of the estate under subsection (a)(1), (a)(2), or (a)(5) of this section notwithstanding any provision in an agreement, transfer instrument, or applicable nonbankruptcy law—
(A)that restricts or conditions transfer of such interest by the debtor; or
(B)that is conditioned on the insolvency or financial condition of the debtor, on the commencement of a case under this title, or on the appointment of or taking possession by a trustee in a case under this title or a custodian before such commencement and that effects or gives an option to effect a forfeiture, modification, or termination of the debtor's interest in property.
(2) A restriction on the transfer of a beneficial interest of the debtor in a trust that is enforceable under applicable nonbankruptcy law is enforceable in a case under this title.

(d) Property in which the debtor holds, as of the commencement of the case, only legal title and not an equitable interest, such as a mortgage secured by real property, or an interest in such a mortgage, sold by the debtor but as to which the debtor retains legal title to service or supervise the servicing of such mortgage or interest, becomes property of the estate under subsection (a)(1) or (2) of this section only to the extent of the debtor's legal title to such property, but not to the extent of any equitable interest in such property that the debtor does not hold. 11 U.S.C.A. § 541.

Only six very limited classes of property do not become property of the estate. The first is "any power that the debtor may exercise solely for the benefit of an entity other than the debtor." 11 U.S.C.A. § 541(b)(1).

PROBLEM 5.22 Brenda Cherry filed a petition for bankruptcy under Chapter 7 listing as one of her assets the premises located at 5035 Green Street, Philadelphia, Pennsylvania. The title to this property, however, was in the name of Brenda Cherry as "Executrix of the Estate of Virginia Cherry, deceased."

Is this realty the property of Brenda Cherry's estate?

The second is "any interest of the debtor as a lessee under a lease of nonresidential real property that has terminated at the expiration of the stated term of such lease before the commencement of the case." 11 U.S.C.A. § 541(b)(2). Because the property of the estate will be liquidated, this limitation seldom occurs in a Chapter 7 case.

The third is "any eligibility of the debtor to participate in programs authorized under the Higher Education Act of 1965 (20 U.S.C.A. § 1001; 42 U.S.C.A. § 2751), or any accreditation status or State licensure of the debtor as an educational institution." 11 U.S.C.A. § 541(b)(3).

The fourth is "any interest of the debtor in liquid or gaseous hydrocarbons" within the limitations set forth in the section. 11 U.S.C.A. § 541(a)(4).

The fifth is "any interest in cash or cash equivalents that constitute proceeds of a sale by the debtor of a money order that is made" under certain circumstances. 11 U.S.C.A. § 541(a)(5).

The sixth is "[a] restriction on the transfer of a beneficial interest of the debtor in a trust that is enforceable under applicable nonbankruptcy law." 11 U.S.C.A. § 541(c)(2).

EXAMPLE

When Horace Hemphill died testate, he left his entire estate to his only child, Maxwell. Because Horace was concerned that Maxwell would squander his inheritance, Horace did not give his estate to Maxwell outright but created a spendthrift trust instead. Under the terms of the trust, the trustee would determine how much money Maxwell should receive from the interest and principal and when he should receive it.

Shortly after Horace's death, Maxwell filed a petition in bankruptcy. Under 11 U.S.C.A. § 541(c)(2), the spendthrift trust was not property of the estate. The restriction on the transfer of Maxwell's interest in the trust, which was enforceable under state law was also enforceable under bankruptcy law. The spendthrift trust therefore continues even though Maxwell has filed a petition in bankruptcy.

PROBLEM 5.23 Janet Westbrook was employed for more than 30 years by Bank First. Westbrook and the other Bank First employees participated in the Bank First Pension Plan. The plan satisfied all applicable requirements of the Employee Retirement Income Security Act of 1974 (ERISA) and qualified for favorable tax treatment under the Internal Revenue Code. In particular, the plan contained the necessary antialienation provision required for qualification under section 206(d)(1) of ERISA ("Each pension plan shall provide that benefits provided under the plan may not be assigned or alienated"). Westbrook's interest in the plan was valued at $250,000.

Westbrook filed for bankruptcy under Chapter 7. Is her Bank First Pension Plan property of the estate?

2. LOCATION OF PROPERTY

The United States bankruptcy court in which a bankruptcy case is filed has exclusive jurisdiction over the property of the debtor, regardless of where the property is located.

> (e) The district court in which a case under title 11 is commenced or is pending shall have exclusive jurisdiction of all of the property, wherever located, of the debtor as of the commencement of such case, and of property of the estate. 28 U.S.C.A. § 1334(e).

EXAMPLE

Darla Ravenswood, whose domicile is Nashville, Tennessee, filed a petition in bankruptcy in the United States Bankruptcy Court for the Middle District of Tennessee. Darla owns property in Nashville and Chattanooga, Tennessee, and in Florida, California, and New York. Nashville and Chattanooga are located in the Middle and Eastern Districts of Tennessee, respectively. The United States Bankruptcy Court for the Middle District of Tennessee has exclusive jurisdiction over Darla's property, regardless of whether it is located in the Middle or Eastern Districts of Tennessee or in Florida, California, or New York.

PROBLEM 5.24 Delores Montague, whose domicile is Denver, Colorado, has property in Denver and in Melbourne, Australia. Delores files her petition in bankruptcy in the United States Bankruptcy Court for the District of Colorado.

Is Delores's property in Melbourne property of the estate?

Does the United States Bankruptcy Court for the District of Colorado have jurisdiction over Delores's property in Melbourne?

3. Property Acquired after Filing the Petition

In addition to the property in which the debtor owns an interest at the time of the filing of the bankruptcy petition, the estate of the debtor includes

> (5) Any interest in property that would have been property of the estate if such interest had been an interest of the debtor on the date of the filing of the petition, and that the debtor acquires or becomes entitled to acquire within 180 days after such date—
> (A) by bequest, devise, or inheritance;
> (B) as a result of a property settlement agreement with the debtor's spouse, or of an interlocutory or final divorce decree; or
> (C) as a beneficiary of a life insurance policy or of a death benefit plan. 11 U.S.C.A. § 541(a)(5).

Federal Rules of Bankruptcy Procedure 1007(h) implements 11 U.S.C.A. § 541(a)(5) by requiring the debtor to file a supplemental schedule.

> (h) **Interests Acquired or Arising After Petition.** If, as provided by § 541(a)(5) of the Code, the debtor acquires or becomes entitled to acquire any interest in property, the debtor shall within 10 days after the information comes to the debtor's knowledge or within such further time the court may allow, file a supplemental schedule in the chapter 7 liquidation case. . . . If any of the property required to be reported under this subdivision is claimed by the debtor as exempt, the debtor shall claim the exemptions in the supplemental schedule. The duty to file a supplemental schedule in accordance with this subdivision continues notwithstanding the closing of the case. . . .

EXAMPLE

On June 1, the debtor files for bankruptcy under Chapter 7. On July 1, the debtor's father dies and leaves his son $100,000 in his will.

Because the debtor acquired his interest in the $100,000 by devise within 180 days of his filing the bankruptcy petition, the $100,000 becomes property of the estate and the debtor is required to file a supplemental schedule. 11 U.S.C.A. § 541(a)(5)(A); Fed. R. Bank. P. 1007(h).

PROBLEM 5.25 Would the $100,000 in this example still be property of the estate if the estate were not probated on December 15?

Would the $100,000 in this example still be property of the estate if the debtor filed for bankruptcy under Chapter 7 on June 1 but his father did not die until December 15?

EXAMPLE

On February 1, the debtor and his spouse were divorced. The divorce decree provides that the debtor and his former spouse will equally divide the proceeds from the sale of their home. On June 1, the debtor filed for bankruptcy under Chapter 7. On July 1, the house was sold for $150,000.

Because the debtor acquired his interest in the $75,000 as a result of the property settlement agreement within 180 days of his filing the bankruptcy petition, the $75,000 becomes property of the estate and the debtor is required to file a supplemental schedule. 11 U.S.C.A. § 541(a)(5)(B); Fed. R. Bank. P. 1007(h).

EXAMPLE

On June 1, the debtor filed for bankruptcy under Chapter 7. On August 1, the debtor's mother died and named him as the sole beneficiary under her $40,000 life insurance policy.

Because the debtor acquired his interest in the $40,000 as a result of being the beneficiary of his mother's life insurance policy and this interest arose within 180 days of his filing the bankruptcy petition, the $40,000 becomes property of the estate and the debtor is required to file a supplemental schedule. 11 U.S.C.A. § 541(a)(5)(C); Fed. R. Bank. P. 1007(h).

Consistent with the idea of a fresh start, earnings from services performed by an individual debtor after the commencement of the case are excluded from the bankruptcy estate.

> (a) The commencement of a case under section 301, 302, or 303 of this title creates an estate. Such estate is comprised of all the following property, wherever located and by whomever held:
>
> . . . .
>
> (6) Proceeds, product, offspring, rents, or profits of or from property of the estate, except such as are earnings from services performed by an individual debtor after the commencement of the case. 11 U.S.C.A. § 541(a)(6).

EXAMPLE

Dawn Darling, a professional singer, filed a petition in bankruptcy on Friday, January 16. During February, Dawn worked at the Pink Kitty Kat Lounge and earned $6,000. These earnings are excluded from the bankruptcy estate.

PROBLEM 5.26 Dawn's previous job began on Friday, January 2, and ended on Thursday, January 29. She earned $6,000 which was paid in one lump sum when she completed her last performance on January 29.

Are all or some of these earnings excluded from the bankruptcy estate?

4. Contractual Provisions Limiting Transferability of Property

At times a contract may attempt to place a restriction on the transferability of property if a bankruptcy petition is filed. According to the terms of the contract, the debtor's property interest in the contract is forfeited upon the filing of the bankruptcy petition.

EXAMPLE

An illustration of the type of provisions often found in franchise agreements follows:

Unless the Company promptly after discovery of the relevant facts notifies Franchisee to the contrary in writing, the Franchise will immediately terminate without notice (or at the earliest time permitted by applicable law) if

(1) Franchisee becomes insolvent or is unable to pay its debts as they become due, Franchisee is adjudicated bankrupt, or files a petition or pleading under the federal bankruptcy law or under any other state or federal bankruptcy or insolvency laws, or an involuntary petition is filed with respect to Franchisee under any such laws and is not dismissed within 60 days after it is filed, or a permanent or temporary receiver or trustee for the Company or all or substantially all of Franchisee's property is appointed by any court, or any such appointment is acquiesced in, consented to, or not opposed through legal action, by Franchisee, or Franchisee makes a general assignment for the benefit of creditors or makes a written statement to the effect that Franchisee is unable to pay its debts as they become due, or a levy, execution, or attachment remains on all or a substantial part of the Company or of Franchisee's assets for 30 days, or Franchisee fails, within 60 days of the entry of a final judgment against Franchisee in any amount exceeding $50,000, to discharge, vacate or reverse the judgment, or to stay execution of it, or if appealed, to discharge the judgment within 30 days after a final adverse decision in the appeal.

EXAMPLE

Debbie Foy owns and operates Sunshine Burgers, a fast-food restaurant, under a franchise agreement with the parent company, Sunshine Burgers, Inc. The franchise agreement contains a provision rendering the agreement nontransferable and terminating the franchise in the event Debbie files a bankruptcy petition or a bankruptcy petition is filed against Debbie.

The purpose for this restriction is to prevent third parties from dictating what property will or will not go into a bankruptcy estate and thereby be subject to bankruptcy protection and administration. Section 541 curtails the effectiveness of such a restriction on the transferability of property and negates the effect of any forfeiture provided for in this clause.

(c)(1) . . . an interest of the debtor in property becomes property of the estate . . . notwithstanding any provision in an agreement . . .

(B) that is conditioned on the insolvency or financial condition of the debtor, on the commencement of a case under this title, or on the appointment of or taking possession by a trustee in a case under this title or a custodian before such commencement and that effects or gives an option to effect a forfeiture, modification, or termination of the debtor's interest in property. 11 U.S.C.A. § 541(c)(1)(B).

Section 541(c)(1)(B), in effect, eliminates the clause restricting the transferability of the property from the contract. The remainder of the contract is then enforceable.

PROBLEM 5.27 If Debbie Foy files a petition in bankruptcy, does her fast-food restaurant franchise become property of the estate?

5. Possession and Control of Property of the Estate

The Bankruptcy Code defines property of the estate without regard to possession. 11 U.S.C.A. § 541. It is, of course, essential that the trustee obtain possession and control of the property of the estate in order to properly administer the estate in liquidation cases. The trustee has the right to proceed in the bankruptcy case to recover the property of the estate from persons other than custodians. 11 U.S.C.A. § 542. In the event any property of the estate is in the possession of a custodian, the trustee has the right to recover that property as well. 11 U.S.C.A. § 543.

C. EXEMPTIONS

At the time of the filing of the petition in bankruptcy, the debtor's bankruptcy estate includes all the debtor's property, whether nonexempt or exempt. 11 U.S.C.A. § 541. The debtor, however, is permitted to exempt certain property from the property of the estate. 11 U.S.C.A. § 522. By permitting exemptions, the Bankruptcy Code enables the debtor to keep those assets needed for a fresh start. "Exempt property" refers to property protected from seizure by either a creditor or the trustee in bankruptcy.

1. Exemptions under the Bankruptcy Code: State vs. Federal Exemptions

The Bankruptcy Act of 1898 provided that the bankrupt was entitled to those exemptions authorized under the state law of his or her domicile and under nonbankruptcy federal law. There were no exemptions under the Bankruptcy Act itself. The policy supporting this scheme of exemptions drew substantial criticism, primarily on the basis that it had a tendency to render the bankruptcy law itself nonuniform and, in effect, gave a different meaning to "fresh start" depending on the domicile of the debtor. The lawmakers and writers felt that the policy of bankruptcy law as it related to a fresh start was rendered ineffective in those states with inadequate exemption laws. One proposal put forward in connection with the debates on the Bankruptcy Reform Act of 1978 urged a preemptive federal exemption law. The scheme of the old law, however, had substantial support. The legislation finally adopted in the Bankruptcy Code was a compromise.

The provision adopted relating to the debtor's exemptions, 11 U.S.C.A. § 522, gave the debtor a choice between the state exemption laws and the federal nonbankruptcy exemption laws on the one hand and a "laundry list" of federal bankruptcy exemptions on the other. A listing of some of the nonbankruptcy exemptions is found in the Historical and Revision Notes following 11 U.S.C.A. § 522.

All debtors, however, would not ultimately receive this choice. One important qualification in 11 U.S.C.A. § 522 permits individual states to "opt out" of the federal bankruptcy exemption alternative of 11 U.S.C.A. § 522(d). Any state legislature could, by the terms of 11 U.S.C.A. § 522(b)(1), forbid election of the exemptions available under 11 U.S.C.A. § 522(d) by its citizens.

EXAMPLE

The following Wyoming provision illustrates the statutory language one state used to "opt out."

> In accordance with section 522(b)(2) of the Bankruptcy Reform Act of 1978, 11 U.S.C. § 522(b)(1) [11 U.S.C. § 522(b)(2)], the exemptions from property of the estate in bankruptcy provided in 11 U.S.C. § 522(d) are not authorized in cases where Wyoming law is applicable on the date of the filing of the petition and the debtor's domicile has been located in Wyoming for the one hundred eighty (180) days immediately preceding the date of the filing of the petition or for a longer portion of the one hundred eighty (180) day period than in any other place. Wyoming Stat. Ann. 1-20-109 (2003 ed.).

Thirty-four states have chosen to opt out of the federal bankruptcy exemption alternative:

Alabama	Indiana	Montana	Oregon
Arizona	Iowa	Nebraska	South Carolina
California	Kansas	Nevada	South Dakota
Colorado	Kentucky	New York	Tennessee
Delaware	Louisiana	North Carolina	Utah
Florida	Maine	North Dakota	Virginia
Georgia	Maryland	Ohio	West Virginia
Idaho	Mississippi	Oklahoma	Wyoming
Illinois	Missouri		

In those states that have opted out, the debtor must depend on the generosity of the exemptions of the debtor's state of domicile and the federal nonbankruptcy exemptions.

EXAMPLE

Oklahoma and Missouri have opted out of federal bankruptcy exemptions. Under Oklahoma law, if the homestead is outside a city or town, the debtor may exempt a homestead of up to 160 acres, regardless of value. If, however, the homestead is inside a city or town, the debtor may exempt a homestead of up to 1 acre as long as 75 percent of the total square foot of the improvements is used as the principal residence. Okla. Stat. Ann. tit. 31, § 2 (West 1991, amended 1997). Under Missouri law, the debtor may exempt a homestead with an $15,000 value limitation. Vernon's Ann. Mo. Stat. § 513.475 (Supp. 1995, amended 2003).

If a husband and a wife file a joint case in a state that has *not* opted out of the federal bankruptcy exemptions (11 U.S.C.A. § 522(d)), both must elect the same option. A wife may not elect to exempt property under 522(d) if her husband elects to exempt property under the state exemptions, or vice versa. If the debtors cannot agree on the option to be elected, they will be deemed to have elected the federal bankruptcy exemptions. 11 U.S.C.A. § 522(b).

PROBLEM 5.28 Danielle and Donald Dailey of Santa Fe, New Mexico, filed a joint petition for bankruptcy under Chapter 7 of the Bankruptcy Code. New Mexico has not opted out of the federal bankruptcy exemptions. The debtors may elect to exempt property under 522(d) or under the New Mexico exemption laws. Danielle and Donald cannot agree on which set of exemptions to claim. Danielle wants to claim the federal bankruptcy exemptions while Donald wants to claim the New Mexico exemptions. If the parties cannot agree on which set of exemptions to elect, which exemptions will apply?

Could Danielle and Donald elect some exemptions from the New Mexico exemptions and some from 522(d)?

Would your answer to the original question be different if Danielle and Donald Dailey were domiciled in Omaha, Nebraska, rather than in Santa Fe, New Mexico?

If the federal bankruptcy exemptions apply, the term "dependent" used throughout section 522 is defined in 11 U.S.C.A. § 522(a)(1) as including the debtor's spouse, whether or not he or she is actually dependent. Also, the term "value" used throughout section 522 is defined in 11 U.S.C.A. § 522(a)(2) to mean the fair market value. The "value" is assessed as of the date the property becomes property of the estate, whether it is at the time the petition is filed or at a later date.

PROBLEM 5.29 Dorothy and Dennis Taylor have filed a joint petition in bankruptcy under Chapter 7. Their estate consists of the following items:

1. A homestead valued at $85,000 that has a $55,000 mortgage
2. A lake house valued at $65,000
3. Three motor vehicles (Dorothy's car valued at $7,000; Dennis's car valued at $4,000; and Dennis's truck valued at $3,500, which he uses for business)
4. A pet dog named Alphie valued at $400
5. Household items valued at $14,000
6. Clothing valued at $15,000
7. Dennis's trombone valued at $625
8. Dorothy's drums valued at $1,250
9. Household furniture valued at $15,000
10. Refrigerator valued at $250
11. Office furniture valued at $10,000

12. A diamond ring valued at $5,000
13. One man's and one woman's watch valued at $300 each
14. Tools of the trade valued at $2,500
15. $50,000 life insurance policy on Dorothy's life with loan value of $1,200
16. Dorothy's hearing aid valued at $350
17. Dennis's monthly check of $600 from his profit-sharing plan
18. Dorothy's personal injury claim against Ace Cleaners, Inc., which arose out of an automobile accident involving an Ace employee (claim includes compensatory damages as well as damages for pain and suffering)

Can Dorothy and Dennis claim any of these items and, if so, how much of each, under their 522(d) exemptions?

Property may be exempt even if it is subject to a lien or security interest, but only the unencumbered portion of the property can be counted as the "value" of the property for purposes of exemption. (This is significant only if the debtor is dealing with a value-type exemption and not an item-type exemption; e.g., $3,000 vs. 1/4 acre.)

EXAMPLE

Denny Vernon has filed a petition in bankruptcy under Chapter 7. Her residence, valued at $100,000, has a $95,000 mortgage. Under 522(d)(1), Denny is entitled to only $5,000 of the $18,450 exemption on her residence, the difference between its value and the mortgage.

PROBLEM 5.30 If the mortgage in the previous Example is only $75,000, how much is Denny's exemption under 522(d)(1)?

If a state has not opted out of the federal exemptions provided in 11 U.S.C.A. § 522(d) of the Bankruptcy Code, the debtor may choose these exemptions or the other federal law exemptions he or she is entitled to (exemptions found in U.S.C.A. sections other than 11 U.S.C.A. § 522(d) of the Bankruptcy Code) and the exemptions permitted under the laws of the state of his or her domicile. If the state has opted out of the federal Bankruptcy Code exemptions provided in 11 U.S.C.A. § 522(d), then this debtor has no choice and is entitled to only the other federal law exemptions and the exemptions permitted under the laws of the state of his or her domicile. (See Exhibit 5–24.)

In August 1976, the National Conference of Commissioners on Uniform State Laws promulgated the Uniform Exemptions Act. Only one state, Alaska, has enacted this act. Alaska Stat. 09.38.010–09.38.510.

PROBLEM 5.31 Compare the exemptions available in your state with the exemptions provided by 11 U.S.C.A. § 522(d). What are the similarities and the differences?

Although exempt property is protected from most prepetition claims, it is not shielded from all such claims. Under 11 U.S.C.A. § 522(c), exempt property is not protected from tax claims; valid liens; alimony, maintenance, or support claims that are excepted from discharge; and claims that are based on a commitment of the debtor to maintain the capital of an insured depository institution.

EXAMPLE

Charles Lincoln has a prepetition divorce decree that contains provisions for child support. Several months after the decree was entered, Charles filed a petition for bankruptcy under Chapter 7. His postpetition wages, which would normally be exempt, are not exempt as to the collection of the child support.

EXHIBIT 5–24 Opting Out of Federal Bankruptcy Exemptions

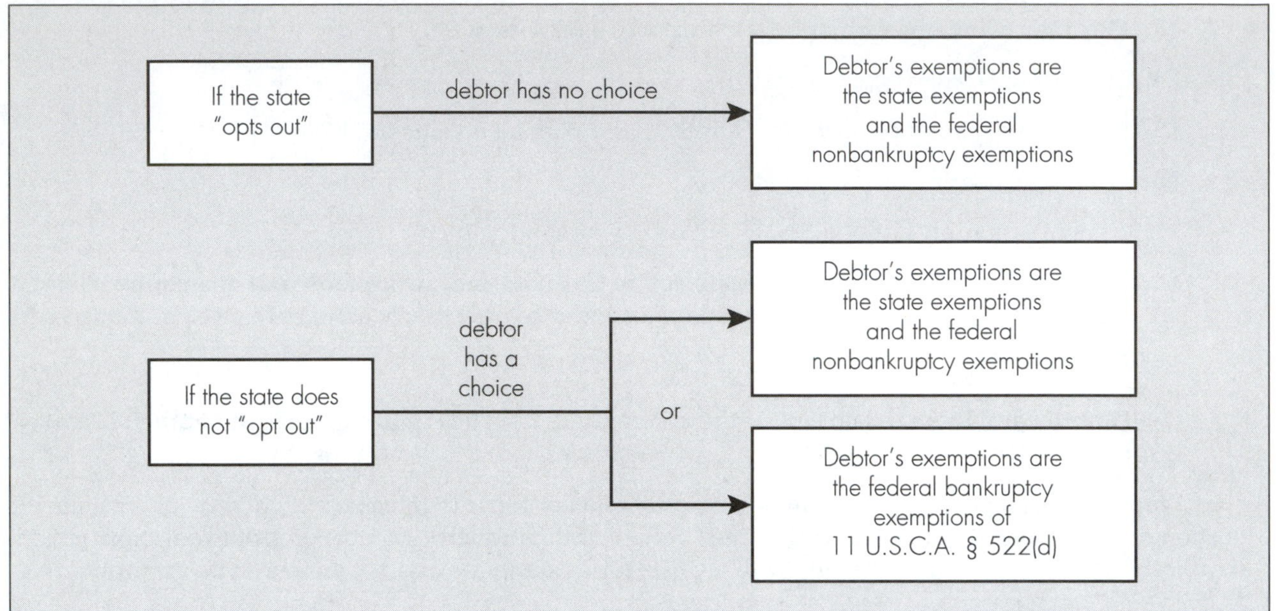

The Bankruptcy Code protects the debtor's exemptions by permitting the debtor to avoid certain liens on exempt property. The debtor may avoid a judicial lien on any property to the extent that the property could have been exempted in the absence of the lien.

> (f)(1) Notwithstanding any waiver of exemptions, but subject to paragraph (3), the debtor may avoid the fixing of a lien on an interest of the debtor in property to the extent that such lien impairs an exemption to which the debtor would have been entitled under subsection (b) of this section, if such lien is—
>
> (A) a judicial lien. . . . 11 U.S.C.A. § 522(f)(1)(A).

The debtor, however, may not avoid a judicial lien impairing an exemption for alimony, maintenance, or support secured by the lien. 11 U.S.C.A. § 522(f)(1)(A). "Lien" means charge against or interest in property to secure payment of a debt or performance of an obligation. 11 U.S.C.A. § 101(37). "Judicial lien" means lien obtained by judgment, levy, sequestration, or other legal or equitable process or proceeding. 11 U.S.C.A. § 101(36).

PROBLEM 5.32 Frank Farragut sued Shirley Yancy in state court for breach of contract and recovered a judgment. Farragut recorded the judgment in the land records in the county clerk's office. The judgment now appears against Yancy's homestead.

After learning about the recordation, Yancy can quiet title in state court because the recording of the judgment is not technically a lien against the homestead.

If Yancy files a petition in bankruptcy under Chapter 7, can she avoid the judicial lien under 11 U.S.C.A. § 522(f)(1)?

The debtor also may avoid a nonpossessory, nonpurchase money security interest in certain household and personal goods.

> (f)(1) Notwithstanding any waiver of exemptions, but subject to paragraph (3), the debtor may avoid the fixing of a lien on an interest of the debtor in property to the extent that such lien impairs an exemption to which the debtor would have been entitled under subsection (b) of this section, if such lien is—
>
> . . .

(B) a nonpossessory, nonpurchase money security interest in any—
   (i) household furnishings, household goods, wearing apparel, appliances, books, animals, crops, musical instruments, or jewelry that are held primarily for the personal, family, or household use of the debtor or a dependent of the debtor;
   (ii) implements, professional books, or tools, of the trade of the debtor or the trade of a dependent of the debtor; or
   (iii) professionally prescribed health aids for the debtor or a dependent of the debtor. 11 U.S.C.A. § 522(f)(1)(B).

A security interest is a purchase money security interest when it complies with the definition of "purchase money security interest in goods" under UCC § 9–103. Under this definition, the debtor either borrows money to purchase goods or buys goods on credit, using the goods as collateral for the loan or sale.

EXAMPLE

John and Agnes Anderson purchased a four-piece living room suite on credit from the Blue Sky Furniture Company. The Andersons gave Blue Sky a security interest in the living room suite. Blue Sky has a purchase money security interest in the living room suite under UCC § 9–103 because the seller (Blue Sky) took a security interest in the living room suite to secure at least a part of its purchase price.

EXAMPLE

John and Agnes Anderson purchased a four-piece living room suite from the Blue Sky Furniture Company. In order to finance the purchase, the Andersons obtained a loan from Friendly Finance Company. The Andersons gave Friendly Finance a security interest in the living room suite. Friendly Finance has a purchase money security interest in the living room suite under UCC § 9–103 because Friendly, by making the advance (the loan), has given the Andersons the money to enable them to purchase the living room suite from Blue Sky.

EXAMPLE

Allison Brown purchased a boat, motor, and trailer on credit from Speedway Boat Company. Allison gave Speedway a security interest in the boat, motor, and trailer. After making monthly payments for 24 months, Allison paid off her debt to Speedway.

Three months later, Allison borrowed $10,000 from the People's Credit Union and gave the credit union a security interest in the boat, motor, and trailer. The credit union's security interest is nonpurchase money (the credit union did not finance the purchase).

PROBLEM 5.33 Gerald Red Corn is employed by a major airlines as a mechanic. Gerald borrowed $2,000 from Elk City Finance and gave as security his toolbox (valued at $2,500).

If Gerald files a petition in bankruptcy under Chapter 7, can he avoid this security interest?

A related section provides that an individual debtor may redeem tangible personal property intended primarily for personal, family, or household use from a lien securing a dischargeable consumer debt if the personal property was exempted under section 522 or abandoned under section 554. 11 U.S.C.A. § 722. The debtor must pay the lienholder the amount of the allowed secured claim.

> An individual debtor may, whether or not the debtor has waived the right to redeem under this section, redeem tangible personal property intended primarily for personal, family, or household use, from a lien securing a dischargeable consumer debt, if such property is exempted under section 522 of this title or has been abandoned under section 554 of this title, by paying the holder of such lien the amount of the allowed secured claim of such holder that is secured by such lien. 11 U.S.C.A. § 722.

In this instance, the claim of the lienholder must be evaluated under 11 U.S.C.A. § 506(a) and the allowed amount of the secured claim determined. The property may then be redeemed by the debtor for the amount of the claim. The courts almost universally require this redemption to be done in a single, lump sum cash payment. Accordingly, it is not possible for the debtor to use a combination of reaffirmation and redemption to retain a single piece of property.

EXAMPLE

David Henry owns an old Cadillac worth $2,000. The Cadillac is subject to a $2,800 security interest (the lien) held by Friendly Finance. If David files his petition in bankruptcy under Chapter 7 in a state that has not opted out and he chooses the 522(d) exemptions, he is permitted a $2,950 exemption in his car. 11 U.S.C.A. § 522(d)(2). Under the redemption provision of section 722, David can pay $2,000 to Friendly Finance, the holder of the security interest, and redeem the entire Cadillac. The balance of the $2,800 debt ($800) will be an unsecured claim.

2. Converting Nonexempt Property to Exempt Property

Because the Bankruptcy Code permits the debtor to claim exemptions in order to retain assets necessary for a fresh start and because the property that can be claimed as exempt must be in an enumerated category, it is to the debtor's advantage to have as many assets as possible in exempt property categories prior to the filing of the petition in bankruptcy. The Bankruptcy Code is silent on the issue of whether a debtor can convert nonexempt property to exempt property prior to bankruptcy. The courts, however, have permitted the debtor to convert nonexempt property into exempt property if the conversion occurs before the filing of a bankruptcy petition. This practice, which permits the debtor to make full use of the exemptions to which he or she is entitled under the law, is not considered fraudulent per se. See 11 U.S.C.A. § 522, Historical and Revision Notes.

PROBLEM 5.34 Louis Bennasar's 2004 Ford was recently repossessed by the finance company because he could not make his payments. Louis traded his boat, motor, and boat trailer for a 1992 Ford, valued at $1,000, for needed transportation. This was an even trade since the boat, motor, and boat trailer were valued at $1,000. At the time of the trade, the boat, motor, and boat trailer were clear of any security interest.

A week later, Louis filed for bankruptcy under Chapter 7. Is this an acceptable practice?

The debtor's right to convert nonexempt property to exempt property on the eve of bankruptcy may be challenged by showing deception or concealment, an insider transaction, a fraudulent conveyance, a secretly retained possession or benefit, or the debtor explanation lacks credibility. See *In re* Crater, 286 B.R. 756 (Bankr. D. Ariz. 2002).

3. Waiver of Exemptions and Waiver of Avoidance Powers

Federal Rules of Bankruptcy Procedure 4003(b) provides that

> A party in interest may file an objection to the list of property claimed as exempt only within 30 days after the meeting of creditors held under § 341(a) is concluded or within 30 days after any amendment to the list or supplemental schedules is filed, whichever is later. The court may, for cause, extend the time for filing objections if, before the time to object expires, a party in interest files a request for an extension. Copies of the objections shall be delivered or mailed to the trustee, the person filing the list, and the attorney for that person.

If the debtor waives his or her right to claim an exemption, the property that would have been exempt will remain property of the estate. The Bankruptcy Code, however, protects the debtor from making a waiver in favor of a creditor who holds an unsecured claim by making such a waiver unenforceable.

> (e) A waiver of an exemption executed in favor of a creditor that holds an unsecured claim against the debtor is unenforceable in a case under this title with respect to such claim against property that the debtor may exempt under subsection (b) of this section. 11 U.S.C.A. § 522(e), sentence 1.

The debtor may be asked to waive his or her power to avoid certain liens and nonpurchase money security interests in certain household and personal goods or to exempt property that the trustee recovered under one of the trustee's **avoidance powers.** The Bankruptcy Code, however, protects the debtor from making a waiver of this power by making such a waiver unenforceable.

> A waiver by the debtor of a power under subsection (f) or (h) of this section to avoid a transfer, under subsection (g) or (i) of this section to exempt property, or under subsection (i) of this section to recover property or to preserve a transfer, is unenforceable in a case under this title. 11 U.S.C.A. § 522(e), sentence 2.

The Bankruptcy Code attempts to protect the debtor from improvident waiver of exemptions in certain consumer goods by giving the debtor the power to avoid nonpossessory, nonpurchase money security interests in these consumer goods and by making any attempted waiver unenforceable. See 11 U.S.C.A. §§ 522(e), (f).

EXAMPLE

Sarah Estrada borrowed $1,000 from Friendly Finance and gave Friendly a security interest in her TV, VCR, and compact disc player. When Sarah defaulted on her loan, Friendly threatened to repossess unless Sarah would sign a waiver of her exemptions as to these items if she subsequently filed for bankruptcy under Chapter 7. To replace these items would cost Sarah $1,800. If Friendly Finance repossessed these items and resold them, the items would bring $500.

This practice would give Friendly an unconscionable advantage over Sarah because Friendly's security interest in the goods would be much more valuable as leverage to coerce Sarah into repaying the loan. If Sarah files for bankruptcy under Chapter 7, she may avoid Friendly's lien because the waiver is unenforceable. 11 U.S.C.A. §§ 522(e), (f).

D. THE AUTOMATIC STAY

Immediately upon the filing of the case, the property of the estate comes under the protection of the **automatic stay.** 11 U.S.C.A. § 362(a).

> The automatic stay is one of the fundamental debtor protections provided by the bankruptcy laws. It gives the debtor a breathing spell from his creditors. It stops all collection efforts, all harassment, and all foreclosure actions. It permits the debtor to attempt a repayment or reorganization plan, or simply to be relieved of the financial pressures that drove him into bankruptcy. 11 U.S.C.A. § 362, Notes of Committee on the Judiciary, Senate Report No. 95-989.

The automatic stay is broad and inclusive. It protects both the debtor and the property of the estate.

> (a) Except as provided in subsection (b) of this section, a petition filed under section 301, 302, or 303 of this title . . . operates as a stay, applicable to all entities, of—
> (1) the commencement or continuation, including the issuance or employment of process, of a judicial, administrative, or other action or proceeding against the debtor that was or could have been commenced before the commencement of the case under this title, or to recover a claim against the debtor that arose before the commencement of the case under this title;
> (2) the enforcement, against the debtor or against property of the estate, of a judgment obtained before the commencement of the case under this title;
> (3) any act to obtain possession of property of the estate or of property from the estate or to exercise control over property of the estate;
> (4) any act to create, perfect, or enforce any lien against property of the estate;
> (5) any act to create, perfect, or enforce against property of the debtor any lien to the extent that such lien secures a claim that arose before the commencement of the case under this title;
> (6) any act to collect, assess, or recover a claim against the debtor that arose before the commencement of the case under this title;
> (7) the setoff of any debt owing to the debtor that arose before the commencement of the case under this title against any claim against the debtor; and
> (8) the commencement or continuation of a proceeding before the United States Tax Court concerning the debtor. 11 U.S.C.A. § 362(a).

EXAMPLE

On February 1, Ricardo Garcia was involved in an automobile accident while on his way to work. He was rendered unconscious by the impact and was taken to the emergency room at St. Mary's Hospital by paramedics. Dr. Ross provided medical services and billed Garcia $750. Garcia paid $150 and promised to pay the balance as soon as he could. The hospital sent Garcia a bill for $1,200, which he did not pay. The hospital then sued Garcia in small claims court and recovered a judgment for $1,200 plus attorney fees.

Shortly after the accident, Garcia purchased a new Mercury Grand Marquis from Green Country Ford & Mercury for $37,000. Garcia paid $2,000 down and financed the car with People's Credit Union. The payments were $1,000 a month for 36 months. Garcia gave People's Credit Union a purchase money security interest in the car. After making the first monthly payment, Garcia ceased paying.

On March 1, Garcia purchased a computer for his office from EXCEL Computer Store. Garcia gave EXCEL a purchase money security interest in the computer.

On March 5, Garcia hired the Bayshore Roofing Company to put a new roof on his house. The cost of the roof was $6,000. Garcia paid $2,500 and promised to pay $500 a month. Bayshore had a mechanic's and materialmen's lien put on the house. Garcia made only the April payment.

On March 15, Garcia went to Dr. Campbell, a dentist, for a root canal. Garcia paid $50 of the $400 bill. Dr. Campbell referred the bill to the Persistent Collection Agency. On April 1, the collection agency began its weekly telephone calls to Garcia.

On June 1, Garcia filed for bankruptcy under Chapter 7. Upon the filing of the petition, the automatic stay went into effect. After receiving notice of Garcia's bankruptcy, EXCEL discovered that it had not filed a financing statement to perfect its security interest in the computer. The IRS was scheduled to file its petition against Garcia in United States Tax Court on June 4 for failure to pay his previous year's income tax.

The stay prohibits

1. Dr. Ross from filing suit against Garcia for the balance owed for his services (11 U.S.C.A. § 362(a)(1));
2. St. Mary's Hospital from enforcing the judgment by garnishing Garcia's wages (11 U.S.C.A. § 362(a)(2));
3. People's Credit Union from filing a replevin action to recover the car (11 U.S.C.A. § 362(a)(3));
4. EXCEL from filing a financing statement to perfect its security interest in the computer (11 U.S.C.A. § 362(a)(4));
5. Bayshore Roofing Company from enforcing its lien (11 U.S.C.A. § 362(a)(5));
6. the Persistent Collection Agency from telephoning Garcia concerning Dr. Campbell's bill (11 U.S.C.A. § 362(a)(6));
7. People's Credit Union from setting off its claim against Garcia's balance in his checking account (11 U.S.C.A. § 362(a)(7)); and
8. the IRS from commencing an action against Garcia for nonpayment of his past year's income tax (11 U.S.C.A. § 362(a)(8)).

Exceptions to the automatic stay do exist.

(b) The filing of a petition under section 301 . . . does not operate as a stay—
- (1) under subsection (a) of this section, of the commencement or continuation of a criminal action or proceeding against the debtor;
- (2) under subsection (a) of this section—
  - (A) of the commencement or continuation of an action or proceeding for—
    - (i) the establishment of paternity; or
    - (ii) the establishment or modification of an order for alimony, maintenance, or support; or
  - (B) of the collection of alimony, maintenance, or support from property that is not property of the estate;
- (3) under subsection (a) of this section, of any act to perfect, or to maintain or continue the perfection of, an interest in property to the extent that the trustee's rights and powers are subject to such perfection under section 546(b) of this title or to the extent that such act is accomplished within the period provided under section 547(e)(2)(A) of this title;

. . .

- (9) under subsection (a), of—
  - (A) an audit by a governmental unit to determine tax liability;
  - (B) the issuance to the debtor by a governmental unit of a notice of tax deficiency;
  - (C) a demand for tax returns; or

(D) the making of an assessment for any tax and issuance of a notice and demand for payment of such an assessment (but any tax lien that would otherwise attach to property of the estate by reason of such an assessment shall not take effect unless such tax is a debt of the debtor that will not be discharged in the case and such property or its proceeds are transferred out of the estate to, or otherwise revested in, the debtor). 11 U.S.C.A. § 362(b).

Knowingly violating the automatic stay is contempt and could be punishable by the bankruptcy court.

EXAMPLE

Willy Walton was a tenant at the Silver Dollar Apartments. When Willy fell two months behind in his rent, the landlord procured a judgment in small claims court. The landlord then proceeded to tell Willy, "I don't care whether you file bankruptcy or not. I have a judgment, and I'm going to collect it." Upon hearing this, Willy filed a petition in bankruptcy under Chapter 7.

Before receiving notice of Willy's petition in bankruptcy, the landlord filed a forcible entry and detainer and had a summons served on Willy to evict him. The landlord's action would be a nullity but would not lead to contempt proceedings in the bankruptcy court.

The debtor may also seek damages and attorneys' fees against the creditor for violation of the automatic stay. The Code provides that the debtor may make such recovery.

(h) An individual injured by any willful violation of a stay provided by this section shall recover actual damages, including costs and attorneys' fees, and, in appropriate circumstances, may recover punitive damages. 11 U.S.C.A. § 362(h).

EXAMPLE

After receiving notice of Willy's petition in bankruptcy, the landlord, in violation of the stay, garnished Willy's bank account. The landlord's actions were an intentional and willful violation of the stay. The bankruptcy judge could assess actual damages, including attorneys' fees and costs, and punitive damages to the landlord.

In *In re Pulliam,* the Pulliams filed for bankruptcy under Chapter 7 and subsequently moved to have a judgment creditor held in contempt for violating the automatic stay when it refused to release a prepetition garnishment of Mr. Pulliam's salary.

In re Pulliam

262 B.R. 539 (Bankr. D. Kan. 2001)

ORDER GRANTING DEBTORS' MOTION TO SHOW CAUSE AND FOR SANCTIONS AND HOLDING LEWIS & WEST, INC., IN CONTEMPT FOR VIOLATION OF THE AUTOMATIC STAY UNDER § 362(A).
ROBERT E. NUGENT, Bankruptcy Judge.

This matter came before the Court for evidentiary hearing on April 17, 2001 concerning Debtors' Amended Motion To Show Cause And For Sanctions pursuant to Fed. R. Bankr. P. 9020(b). On November 30, 2000, Arthur and Jaime Pulliam, debtors, filed their Motion To Show Cause why Lewis & West, a creditor, was in contempt for violation of the automatic stay under § 362(a) which took effect on November 15, 2000, the date the Pulliams filed their Chapter 7 petition. In their motion, the Pulliams asserted that Lewis & West had continued to garnish Mr. Pulliam's wages pursuant to a garnishment order entered October 30, 2000, even after receiving notice of the pending case from the court and a request for release from the Pulliam's counsel. Thereafter, on December 11, 2000, the Pulliams filed an Amended Motion To Show Cause And For Sanctions claiming that Lewis & West had garnished another $506.47 since November 30, 2000. Lewis & West objected to the Motion to Show Cause and for Sanctions on December 21, 2000, stating that the garnishment entered on October 30, 2000 had been released and the garnishee had been notified of the release. On January 24, 2001, the Court ordered Lewis & West to appear and show cause why it should not be held in civil contempt for violation of § 362, Lewis & West objected, and the Court scheduled a contempt hearing. Arthur Pulliam, debtor, appeared in person and by counsel, David G. Arst. Lewis & West, Inc., appeared by Tim Connell. Following Mr. Pulliam's testimony and counsels' arguments, the Court took the matter under advisement and is ready to rule.

Prior to the hearing, the parties filed a partial stipulation of facts and several exhibits. The parties stipulated to the following facts. Lewis & West obtained a judgment against Mr. Pulliam on September 6, 2000 in the District Court of Butler County, Kansas, for $966.85 with interest at the rate of 1.75% per month from December 15, 1999, until paid in full; and for costs. Lewis & West filed a garnishment order on October 30, 2000, and served it on Timec Co., Mr. Pulliam's employer, the next day. On November 15, 2000, the Pulliams filed their Chapter 7 petition and mailed a Suggestion of Bankruptcy to Lewis & West along with a file-stamped copy of the petition. The Court sent notice to Lewis & West of the Pulliams' bankruptcy the following day. On November 22, 2000, Mr. Arst's assistant called Mr. Connell asking that the garnishment be released as to those funds obtained after the filing of the bankruptcy. Mr. Connell replied that he did not know what amounts those would be. Mr. Arst's assistant stated that she would discuss the matter with Mr. Arst. On November 30, 2000, the Pulliams filed the instant Motion and, on December 11, 2000, the Pulliams Amended that Motion alleging the further garnishment and attachment of some $506.74. On December 14, 2000, Lewis & West received a copy of the wage garnishment answer and filed a garnishment release that same day.

At trial, the Pulliams offered several additional exhibits. Exhibit 1 was a deduction report form Timec Company, showing the garnishment dates and amounts. Exhibit 2 was a check from Timec payable to Mr. Pulliam for $1,100, the total amount garnished; and exhibit 3 included Mr. Arst's time sheets and file notes. Lewis & West objected to the admission of debtors' exhibits 2 and 3 because they had not been supplied to the creditor in advance of trial. The Court sustained Lewis & West's objection to debtors' exhibits 2 and 3 and their contents are not a part of the record of these proceedings.

The Court heard undisputed testimony from Mr. Pulliam. Mr. Pulliam testified that he is employed at Timec Company in El Dorado, Kansas, and that shortly before filing his Chapter 7 petition, his wages were garnished and continued to be garnished after the bankruptcy was filed. Mr. Pulliam testified that $1,100 was withheld by Timec through December 24, 2000 because the garnishment was not released. Mr. Pulliam identified Exhibit 1, a compilation by Timec of the garnishments totaling $1,100. Lewis & West objected to admission of this exhibit, but the Court admitted Exhibit 1 for the limited purpose of showing the dates money was garnished from Mr. Pulliam's paycheck. Exhibit 1 clearly shows that funds were withheld from Pulliam's wages after the commencement of the case and after November 22, when creditor's counsel learned of the filing. Mr. Pulliam testified that the garnishment was finally released as of January 3, 2001. He further testified that he is compensated at $16.50 per hour. Mr. Pulliam contended on cross examination that money was garnished from his wages after Lewis & West's garnishment order was served, and continued even after he filed his case.

Debtors assert that § 362(a) required Lewis & West to immediately release the garnishment without awaiting an answer from Mr. Pulliam's employer.

Although debtors requested a prompt release of the garnishment, Lewis & West declined, preferring to wait until Timec had filed its garnishment answer so that it could determine how much was garnished prepetition and how much postpetition.

Lewis & West argues that it did not know what funds had been attached and could not determine how much to release. Lewis & West further contends that declining to dismiss the garnishment does not violate the automatic stay. Lewis & West also asserts that its only delay was in awaiting the paperwork to release (in other words, Timec's answer) and that Lewis & West released the garnishment the same day it received Timec's answer. In support of its position, Lewis & West cites two cases, *Carlsen v. Internal Revenue Service (In re Carlsen)*, 63 B.R., 706 (Bankr.C.D.Cal.1986) (requires garnishment be released within reasonable time), and *O'-Connor v. Methodist Hosp. of Jonesboro, Inc. (In re O'Connor)*, 42 B.R. 390 (Bankr.E.D.Ark.1984) (stay violation only because creditor received order to pay in and took possession of money). Lewis & West believes the issue to be one of whether the garnishment was released quickly enough, not whether it allowed attachment to remain in effect postpetition.

DISCUSSION

Section 362 of the Bankruptcy Code generally provides for the automatic stay of any and all proceedings against the debtor once a bankruptcy petition is filed. Pursuant to § 362(a),

> [e]xcept as provided in subsection (b) of this section, a petition filed under section 301, 302, 303 of this title . . . operates as a stay, applicable to all entitles of—

(1) the commencement or *continuation,* including the issuance of employment of process, of a judicial, administrative, or other action or proceeding against that debtor that was or could have been commenced before the commencement of the case under this title. . . ." (Italics added.)

The consequences of violating the automatic stay provisions are set forth in § 362(h), which provides that:

"[A]n individual injured by any willful violation of a stay provided by this section shall recover actual damages, including costs and attorney's fees, and in appropriate circumstances, may recover punitive damages."

Additionally, a party injured by a willful violation of the stay can seek sanctions for contempt of court under § 105(a). *See Mountain America Credit Union v. Skinner (In re Skinner),* 917 F.2d 444, 447 (10th Cir.1990).

Contrary to Lewis & West's argument, a garnishing creditor has an affirmative duty to release the garnishment of a debtor's wages as soon as it learns of the pending bankruptcy. To hold otherwise would be to eviscerate the power and purpose of the stay which is designed to protect debtors from collection activity during the pendency of a case in bankruptcy. This Court respectfully disagrees with the authority cited by Lewis & West that it did not violate the stay by waiting until Timec had filed its garnishment answer to release the garnishment. *See O'Connor,* 42 B.R. at 392 (Court does not believe it is necessary for creditor to dismiss the garnishment to avoid violating the automatic stay; to avoid violating the stay, creditor must not take any affirmative action towards proceeding with the garnishment).

A creditor who has initiated collection efforts without knowledge of a bankruptcy petition has an affirmative duty to restore the *status quo* without the debtor having to seek relief from the Bankruptcy Court.

In re Miller, 10 B.R. 778, 780 (Bankr.D.Md.1981); *aff'd* 22 B.R. 479 (D.Md.1982). This duty arises from the language of § 362(a) which stays the commencement or *continuation* of a judicial proceeding against the debtor. Courts presented with this issue have construed this language to mean, "[a]t whatever stage the garnishment is, the creditor's attorney must do everything he can to halt the proceeding." *Morris v. St. Joseph Med. Center, Inc. (In re Fisher),* 194 B.R. 525, 532 (Bankr.D.Kan.1996) (quotation omitted); *O'Connor,* 42 B.R. at 392; *In re Elder,* 12 B.R. 491, 494–495 (Bankr.M.D.Ga.1981); *In re Baum,* 15 B.R. 538, 541 (Bankr.E.D.Va.1981) ("It is the creditor's responsibility to stop the downhill snowballing of a continuing garnishment.") It has also been noted that a creditor's inaction can be as detrimental to a debtor as affirmative collection efforts. *See Elder,* 12 B.R. at 494; *Miller,* 10 B.R. at 778. Certainly, causing the withholding of over $1,000 of debtors' wages for a period of several months could work a detriment on the debtor and his family.

Lewis & West had an affirmative duty to release the garnishment of Mr. Pulliam's wages as soon as it learned of his pending bankruptcy. When Lewis & West refused to release the garnishment, claiming it could not file a release until Timec had filed its answer, Timec remained bound to withhold Mr. Pulliam's wages for any pay period ending during the 30 days following service of the order. *See* Kan. Stat. Ann. § 61–2005(c) (1999). This is precisely the "continuation" of process stayed by § 362(a). Lewis & West simply had no reason to delay releasing the garnishment. It is no excuse that Lewis & West did not know the exact amount of postpetition wages that had been garnished from Mr. Pulliam's paycheck. Wages that Mr. Pulliam earned prepetition were also property of the estate under § 541 in which the trustee could conceivably claim an interest. *See Fisher,* 194 B.R. at 529 ("The fact that St. Joseph obtained a prepetition garnishment lien does not preclude the Debtor's interest from becoming property of the estate.") The Court does not find that awaiting the employer's answer is the sort of "administrative delay" that some courts have found to excuse stay violations. *See Carlsen,* 63 B.R. at 709 (Court notes that some delays in releasing levies may be administrative, such as when paperwork makes "its way through channels.")

Therefore, the Court finds that Lewis & West willfully violated § 362(a).

In holding that Lewis & West violated the automatic stay, the Court must determine what damages Mr. Pulliam sustained. To prevail under § 362(h), Mr. Pulliam must prove that Lewis & West's action in failing to immediately release the garnishment was willful and that he incurred actual damages. The U.S. Court of Appeals for the Tenth Circuit has not defined "willful" for purposes of § 362(h), however, in *Diviney v. Nations Bank of Texas (In re Diviney),* 225 B.R. 762, 774 (10th Cir. BAP 1998), the U.S. Bankruptcy Appellate Panel for the Tenth Circuit adopted the majority definition outlined in *INSLAW, Inc. v. United States (In re INSLAW, Inc.),* 83 B.R. 89 (Bankr.D.D.C.1988):

A "willful violation" does not require a specific intent to violate the automatic stay. Rather, the statute provides for damages upon a finding that the defendant knew of the automatic stay and that the defendant's actions which violated the stay were intentional. Whether the party believes in good faith that it had a right to the property is not relevant to whether the act was "willful" or whether compensation must be awarded.

Other Kansas bankruptcy courts have adopted this definition of "willful" when the automatic stay has been violated. *See In re Fisher,* 194 B.R. at 542 (willful violation of automatic stay, as would allow award of costs and attorney's fees, occurs when creditor has knowledge of automatic stay yet intentionally takes actions which violate the stay). Even if the Court had not found Lewis & West in civil contempt, the Court could award attorney's fees and related costs to Mr. Pulliam. *See Bryant v. United States (In re Bryant),* 116 B.R. 272, 275 (Bankr.D.Kan.1990).

Here it is undisputed that the creditor knew of the inception of the stay and that the creditor intentionally allowed the garnishment to continue. The creditor's "good faith" belief in its entitlement to some of debtor's wages is not a defense to the creditor's stay violation. The Court finds that Mr. Pulliam has proven by a preponderance of the evidence that Lewis & West willfully violated the stay when notice of Mr. Pulliam's bankruptcy case was mailed to it around November 16, 2000, yet waited another month, until December 14, 2000, to file the release. *See TranSouth Fin. Corp. v. Sharon (In re Sharon),* 234 B.R. 676, 687 (6th Cir. BAP 1999); *Lamar v. Mitsubishi Motors Credit of America (In re Lamar),* 249 B.R. 822, 825 (Bankr. S.D.Ga.2000). For this violation, sanctions under § 362(h) are appropriate. The Court does note that Lewis & West never made any attempt to collect the monies garnished from Mr. Pulliam and the wages have been returned to Mr. Pulliam. Debtor's role in seeking only the release of postpetition garnished wages likely confused the matter further. Debtor presented no evidence concerning any actual damages it may have sustained by virtue of this creditor's stay violation. Weighing these factors, the Court finds that $300.00 in attorney's fees is a sufficient and appropriate remedial sanction to be imposed in this case. *See In re Bryant,* 116 B.R. 272, 275 (Bankr.D.Kan.1990) (citation omitted).

IT IS THEREFORE ORDERED THAT Lewis & West be held in contempt of court for violation of the automatic stay pursuant to 11 U.S.C. § 362(a) with sanctions awarded to debtor against Lewis & West in the amount of $300.00 attorney's fees.

If not modified by order of the court, the automatic stay will remain in effect until the property subject to the stay is no longer property of the estate. 11 U.S.C.A. § 362(c)(1).

EXAMPLE

The debtor's car is encumbered for $1,500 although its value is only $1,000. The debtor files a petition in bankruptcy under Chapter 7. If the debtor's trustee abandons the car, it will no longer be property of the estate. The stay no longer applies to the car.

The automatic stay will remain in effect as to any other act subject to the stay until the time the case is closed or dismissed, or a discharge is granted or denied, whichever is the earliest. 11 U.S.C.A. § 362(c)(2).

EXAMPLE

The debtor files for bankruptcy under Chapter 7 on June 1, and the automatic stay goes into effect. On June 25, the bankruptcy court sustains a creditor's complaint objecting to discharge. The denial of a discharge vacates the automatic stay. All the creditors now may attempt collection from the debtor's resources.

SECTION 4
THE APPOINTMENT AND POWERS OF AN INTERIM TRUSTEE

It is the duty of the United States trustee to appoint a panel trustee as **interim trustee** promptly after the order for relief in all Chapter 7 cases. 11 U.S.C.A. § 701(a)(1). If no panel member is willing to serve as interim trustee in a case, the U.S. trustee may serve in this capacity.

The primary role of the trustee is to administer the estate by reducing to cash the property of the estate that is not burdensome, exempt, or fully secured. The trustee has the power to expand the property being administered by obtaining a turnover of possession of property of the estate in the hands of a third person. 11 U.S.C.A. § 542. The trustee must address all the assets of the estate—all the assets that come into the estate must come out of the estate before the case can be closed. The assets come out of the estate either by the debtor's exemption being allowed or the property being abandoned (affirmative abandonment during the pendency of the case or the asset was scheduled by the debtor but did not get administered by the time the case was closed and thus by operation of the law was deemed abandoned), or by the property being sold. The cash is then distributed among the debtor's creditors.

The trustee's powers include the power to abandon property of the estate, to assume or reject executory contracts, to seek the disallowance of a creditor's claim as a secured claim, to avoid prepetition transfers that are voidable preferences or fraudulent, and to avoid certain postpetition transfers.

A. ABANDON PROPERTY OF THE ESTATE

Property of the estate that has not been claimed by the debtor as exempt may be abandoned in one of three ways. First, the trustee can make the affirmative act of abandonment. Second, a party in interest can force the trustee to abandon. Third, if the property is scheduled by the debtor but is not administered by the trustee before the case is closed, the property is abandoned. When property is abandoned, the title to the property goes back to where the title was before it became property of the estate; that is, the title of the property goes back to the debtor so the title to the property becomes property of the debtor.

1. Abandonment by the Trustee

The trustee may abandon property of the estate if the property is either burdensome to the estate or of inconsequential value and benefit to the estate. 11 U.S.C.A. § 554(a).

Property that is burdensome to the estate is property that will cost more to administer than its value or that is encumbered by a lien securing a debt for more than the value of the property plus the exemption amount.

PROBLEM 5.35 Mary Lou Williamson filed a petition for bankruptcy under Chapter 7. Mary Lou owned a Doberman. Mary Lou did not claim the Doberman as exempt.

Should the trustee abandon the Doberman?

Property of inconsequential value and benefit to the estate is property that is of insufficient value to justify administration by the trustee.

EXAMPLE

At the time of filing her petition in bankruptcy under Chapter 7, Georgia O'Riley, a single parent with a teen-age daughter, had two cars—a Thunderbird valued at $4,000 and an old Honda valued at $300.

Georgia owed Red Bud Valley Bank $3,000 on the Thunderbird, and she had given Red Bud Valley a security interest in that vehicle. The security interest appeared on the Thunderbird's certificate of title. Georgia reaffirmed her $3,000 obligation to Red Bud Valley and claimed the remaining $1,000 equity in the Thunderbird as exempt.

The trustee estimated that it would cost her $350 to administer the Honda as property of the estate. Because the estimated cost to administer this car exceeded its value, the Honda was burdensome to the estate.

Even if the Honda had been valued at $375, so its value exceeded the cost to administer by $25, it would have been of inconsequential value and benefit to the estate.

In either case, the trustee may abandon the Honda as property of the estate.

PROBLEM 5.36 During the spring, Georgia O'Riley purchased a sailboat from Surf & Sail for $7,500. She gave Surf & Sail $2,000 and a security interest in the sailboat. Surf & Sail perfected its security interest.

Georgia used the boat during the summer, did not make another payment, and filed for bankruptcy under Chapter 7 on October 1. The value of the sailboat on October 1 had decreased to $5,000.

May the trustee abandon the sailboat?

If the trustee does abandon the sailboat, is the sailboat property of the estate?

The procedure for abandonment by the trustee is provided in Fed. R. Bank P. 6007(a):

> (a) **Notice of Proposed Abandonment . . . ; Objections.** Unless otherwise directed by the court, the trustee . . . shall give notice of proposed abandonment . . . of property to the United States trustee [and] all creditors. . . . A party in interest may file and serve an objection within 15 days of the mailing of the notice, or within the time fixed by the court. If a timely objection is made, the court shall set a hearing on notice to the United States trustee and to other entities as the court may direct.

2. A Party in Interest Can Force the Trustee to Abandon

In the event the trustee neglects or declines to take the initiative on the matter of abandonment, a party in interest may move requiring the trustee to abandon any property of the estate that is either burdensome to the estate or of inconsequential value and benefit to the estate. Fed. R. Bank.P. 6007(b). The court, after notice and a hearing, may order the trustee to abandon the property. 11 U.S.C.A. § 554(b).

EXAMPLE

Using the facts in Problem 5.35, assume that the trustee declined to abandon the sailboat and that Surf & Sail moved the bankruptcy court to modify the stay and order the trustee to abandon the sailboat. After notice and a hearing, the court may order the trustee to abandon. Once abandoned, the sailboat is no longer property of the bankruptcy estate and Surf & Sail could then repossess it.

3. Abandoned by Being Scheduled but Not Administered

If property is scheduled by the debtor and not otherwise administered at the time of the closing of a case, such property is deemed abandoned. 11 U.S.C.A. § 554(c).

EXAMPLE

At the time of filing her petition in bankruptcy under Chapter 7, Georgia O'Riley owned a motorcycle valued at $250. The motorcycle was listed on her schedule of assets. The trustee took no action concerning the motorcycle, and the case was closed.

The motorcycle is considered abandoned, and Georgia does not lose her ownership interest.

PROBLEM 5.37 When completing her schedule of assets, Georgia O'Riley listed her home computer, TV, VCR, jewelry, and saxophone. She used her exemptions to claim other items of consumer goods but did not claim any of these items. After the estate was administered and the case was closed, Georgia still had possession of these items. What is the status of these items?

Property of the estate that is not duly scheduled by the debtor in accordance with 11 U.S.C.A. § 521(1) and that is not abandoned or otherwise dealt with in the administration remains property of the estate even after the closing of the case. 11 U.S.C.A. § 554(d).

PROBLEM 5.38 Now assume that when Georgia completed her schedule of assets, she did not list her home computer, TV, VCR, jewelry, and saxophone. After the estate was administered and the case was closed, Georgia still had possession of these items. What is the status of these items?

B. ASSUME OR REJECT EXECUTORY CONTRACTS

> [Subject to a number of exceptions], the trustee, subject to the court's approval, may assume or reject any executory contract or unexpired lease of the debtor. 11 U.S.C.A. § 365(a).

The provisions relating to executory contracts provide for the orderly adjustment of contractual rights that existed prior to the bankruptcy and give the trustee an opportunity to shed some of the contractual obligations of the debtor that may be too burdensome to allow the debtor a fresh start. The executory contract provisions are employed primarily in reorganization cases, but do arise occasionally in Chapter 7 cases.

EXAMPLE

Charles Bell had a contract to perform services for the United States Army. Prior to the beginning of performance of this contract, Charles filed for bankruptcy under Chapter 7. Charles listed his contract with the army on his schedules. He then asked the trustee to reject the executory contract, which the trustee did. Charles then renegotiated the contract with the army because he still wanted to perform the contract and the army still needed his services. Although the executory contract was an asset of the estate, it was of no value to the estate. Therefore, the trustee's rejection of the contract did not decrease the net worth of the estate. The renegotiated contract, which was made after the filing of the petition in bankruptcy, was not property of the estate.

If the trustee wants to assume the contract or unexpired lease under 11 U.S.C.A. § 365(a) and the contract or lease is in default, the trustee must cure the default, compensate the other party for the loss resulting from the default, and provide adequate assurance of future performance under the contract or lease. 11 U.S.C.A. § 365(b)(1). In the case of an executory contract or unexpired lease of residential real property or of personal property of the debtor, the trustee must assume the contract or lease within 60 days after the order for relief or within any additional time that the court allows or the lease is deemed rejected. 11 U.S.C.A. § 356(d)(1).

C. AVOIDING TRANSFERS

The avoidance powers given to the trustee are in support of the idea of equitable distribution, which means equal distribution or prorated distribution among the unsecured creditors. For an equitable distribution to occur, it is necessary to curb the tendency that creditors have to attempt to dismember the assets of an ailing entity prior to the filing of bankruptcy. The trustee may have to actually bring property back into the estate for the purpose of distribution if the property was seized by one creditor prior to the bankruptcy filing.

This policy of equitable distribution is supported by powers that the trustee has to avoid certain transfers. These avoidance powers apply to unperfected security interests, claims that an actual creditor could avoid under state law, statutory liens arising on the debtor's insolvency, prepetition transfers of property of the estate to creditors that are voidable preferences, prepetition transfers of property of the estate that are fraudulent under the Bankruptcy Code, and certain postpetition transfers of property of the estate unless they are authorized by the bankruptcy court or the Bankruptcy Code.

The Code imposes a two-year statute of limitations, running from the date of the order for relief, on the trustee's avoidance powers. 11 U.S.C.A. § 546(a)(1)(A).

1. Avoiding Unperfected Security Interests

The trustee has the rights of a hypothetical lien creditor as of the date of bankruptcy. 11 U.S.C.A. § 544(a). This power given under section 544(a) is known as the "strong-arm power" and enables the trustee to set aside unperfected security interests and certain other transfers that would be invalid against a creditor who levied under state law before the filing of a bankruptcy petition.

This strong-arm power operates in the following manner. The Uniform Commercial Code recognizes the trustee's status as a lien creditor, UCC §§ 9–102(a)(52)(C), and gives the lien creditor priority over an unperfected security interest, 9–317(a)(2)(A). The Bankruptcy Code, 11 U.S.C.A. § 544(a), goes one step further. Instead of just giving the trustee priority over unperfected security interests, the Bankruptcy Code gives the trustee the power to avoid these unperfected security interests.

EXAMPLE

Royal Cleaners purchased an automatic shirt-folding machine from United Laundry Equipment Company. United took a security interest in the machine but did not file a financing statement. United's security interest was therefore unperfected.

Royal filed a petition in bankruptcy under Chapter 7. Royal's trustee is a hypothetical lien creditor under 544(a) of the Bankruptcy Code and 9-102(a)(52)(C) of the Uniform Commercial Code. UCC § 9-317(a)(2)(A) gives Royal's trustee priority over United's unperfected security interest in the machine. 11 U.S.C.A. § 544(a) gives the trustee the power to avoid United's unperfected security interest in the machine so United becomes a creditor holding an unsecured claim.

Therefore, it is incumbent on the trustee to challenge claims asserted as perfected security interests. If the trustee can prevail in the challenge, the claim will be reduced to unsecured and the property will remain property of the estate. It will be liquidated, and the proceeds will be distributed prorata to unsecured creditors in the administration of the estate.

In *In re Kroskie,* the Kroskies, owners of a mobile home located on their own land, refinanced their real estate and mobile home by borrowing $80,000 from R-B Financial Mortgages, Inc. R-B Financial secured the debt by recording a traditional mortgage with the County Register of Deeds. The mortgage was then assigned to Chase Manhattan. Shortly thereafter the Kroskies filed for bankruptcy under Chapter 7 and the trustee moved to avoid the lien on the grounds the lien was unperfected at the time the bankruptcy petition was filed.

In re Kroskie

315 F.3d 644 (6th Cir. 2003)

Before: MERRITT and GILMAN, Circuit Judges; TARNOW, District Judge. [The Honorable Arthur J. Tarnow, United States District Judge for the Eastern District of Michigan, sitting by designation.]

GILMAN, J., delivered the opinion of the court, in which TARNOW, D. J., joined. MERRITT, J. delivered a separate dissenting opinion.

OPINION

GILMAN, Circuit Judge.

James W. Boyd, the Chapter 7 bankruptcy Trustee, filed a motion for summary judgment in the United States Bankruptcy Court for the Western District of Michigan that sought to avoid Chase Manhattan Mortgage Corporation's purported lien on a mobile home owned by the Debtors, Damon J. and Regina M. Kroskie. The bankruptcy court granted the Trustee's motion for summary judgment. This judgment was reversed on appeal by the United States District Court for the Western District of Michigan, which held that the bankruptcy court had erred in concluding that Chase Manhattan's lien was invalid and therefore avoidable by the Trustee. For the reasons set forth below, we REVERSE the judgment of the district court and REMAND the case with instructions that the judgment of the bankruptcy court be affirmed.

I. BACKGROUND

The Kroskies are the owners of a Four Seasons mobile home located on their own land. Approximately 10 months prior to filing for Chapter 7 bankruptcy on November 18, 1999, the Kroskies refinanced their real estate and mobile home by borrowing $80,000 from R-B Financial Mortgages, Inc. R-B Financial secured the debt by recording a traditional mortgage with the Wexford County Register of Deeds on January 21, 1999. Simultaneously, the mortgage was assigned to Chase Manhattan.

The bankruptcy court found that, at the time of the mortgage, the mobile home was situated on a full cement-block crawl-space foundation affixed to the land. In addition, the mobile home was connected to electrical lines, a private well, and a septic system. Both the bankruptcy court and the district court held, and the parties agree, that the mobile home was legally a fixture to the real estate. There is complete disagreement below, however, as to whether a mortgage recorded with the Register of Deeds perfects a security interest in an affixed mobile home under Michigan law.

The bankruptcy court held that Michigan's Mobile Home Commission Act (MHCA), MICH. COMP. LAWS §§ 125.2301-125.2350, provides the exclusive method for perfecting a security interest in mobile homes. It reached this conclusion based upon the MHCA provision that "[a]fter December 31, 1978, every mobile home located in this state shall be subject to the certificate of title provisions of this act," MICH. COMP. LAWS § 125.2330(1), and the requirement that "an owner named in a certificate of title . . . shall immediately execute an application in the form prescribed by the department showing the name and address of the holder of the security interest." MICH. COMP. LAWS § 125.2330d(1)(a). The MHCA created a Mobile Home Commission with whom all certificates of title and security interests are to be filed. MICH. COMP. LAWS § 125.2303.

Because neither R-B Financial nor Chase Manhattan filed anything with the Mobile Home Commission, the bankruptcy court concluded that Chase Manhattan was an unsecured creditor with regard to the Kroskies' mobile home. The bankruptcy court therefore granted the Trustee's motion for summary judgment. On appeal, the district court reversed the judgment of the bankruptcy court, holding that Chase Manhattan had perfected its security interest in the affixed mobile home when it recorded its mortgage with the Wexford County Register of Deeds. This appeal by the Trustee followed.

II. ANALYSIS

A. Standard of review

In considering the district court's reversal of the bankruptcy court's decision, we independently review the ruling of the bankruptcy court. *Longo v. McLaren (In re McLaren),* 3 F.3d 958, 961 (6th Cir.1993). The bankruptcy court's factual findings will not be set aside unless clearly erroneous, and its conclusions of law are reviewed *de novo. Rembert v. AT & T Universal Card Services Inc. (In re Rembert),* 141 F.3d 277, 280 (6th Cir.), *cert. denied,* 525 U.S. 978, 119 S.Ct. 438, 142 L.Ed.2d 357 (1998).

B. The MHCA provides the exclusive method for perfecting a security interest in a mobile home

Pursuant to the MHCA, a security interest in a mobile home may only be perfected by filing an application with the Mobile Home Commission. MICH. COMP. LAWS § 125.2330d. Chase Manhattan concedes that it did not comply with the MHCA's filing requirement. Instead, it recorded its mortgage with the Wexford County Register of Deeds, which under general real property principles would perfect its interest in all fixtures on the Kroskies' land. *Sequist v. Fabiano,* 274 Mich. 643, 265 N.W. 488, 489 (1936). This clash between the MHCA and Michigan's general real property law creates the precise issue to be resolved in the case before us.

1. Interpreting the Michigan statutes and real property law The bankruptcy court primarily relied on the fact that the filing requirement of the MHCA and Michigan real property law conflict when it comes to the matter of perfecting an interest in a mobile home affixed to real estate. This caused the bankruptcy court to look at principles of statutory construction regarding conflicting statutes. Invoking the principle that a specific statute trumps a more general one when statutes conflict, the bankruptcy court held that the MHCA was the sole method of perfecting a security interest in a mobile home, regardless of its fixture status. *In re Kroskie,* 258 B.R. 676, 679-80 (Bankr.W.D.Mich.2001) (*citing Frank v. William A. Kibbe & Assoc., Inc.,* 208 Mich.App. 346, 527 N.W.2d 82 (1995), for the proposition that a specific statute prevails over a more general one when statutes conflict).

Indeed, the MHCA specifically applies to mobile homes that are permanently affixed to real property. MICH. COMP. LAWS § 125.2302(g) (defining a mobile home as a structure "built on a chassis and designed to be used as a dwelling *with or without permanent foundation,* when connected to the required utilities") (emphasis added). This fact renders much of Chase Manhattan's argument about the fixture status of the Kroskies' mobile home irrelevant. Because the MHCA clearly applies to a permanently affixed mobile home, the bankruptcy court properly utilized the rule of construction pertaining to conflicting statutes. In other words, the general rule that a security interest in a fixture can be perfected through a properly recorded mortgage on real estate does not govern where, as here, there is a specific statute dealing with mobile home security interests.

Chase Manhattan, on the other hand, attempts to read parts of Michigan's Article 9 of the Uniform Commercial Code (UCC) dealing with fixtures as being in harmony with the MHCA's provisions. This attempt falters, however, because all security interests in fixtures do not have to be perfected under Article 9 as do all security interests in mobile homes under the MHCA. *Compare* MICH. COMP. LAWS § 440.9302(6) (amended 2000) *with* MICH. COMP. LAWS §§ 125.2330(1), 125.2330d, *and* § 440.9302(4) (amended 2000); *see also In re Bencker,* 122 B.R. 506, 511 (Bankr.W.D.Mich.1990) ("[T]he specific provisions of [the] Mobile Home Commission Act dictate how legal ownership is transferred, and it governs over the more general provisions of the Uniform Commercial Code."). For the bankruptcy court, this reasoning was persuasive and applicable to the perfection of security interests in mobile homes.

The district court, on the other hand, determined that the real question deals with the interplay between the general principles of real property law, the UCC, and the MHCA. In particular, the district court focused on the following sentence of the MHCA:

> The filing under this section or under section 30a of an application for a certificate of title showing the name and address of the holder of a security interest in a mobile home *is equivalent to the filing of a financing statement with respect to the security interest under article 9 of the uniform commercial code*... MICH. COMP. LAWS § 125.2330d(3) (emphasis added).

The district court reasoned that because the MHCA explicitly provides that a filing pursuant to its provisions is equivalent to the filing of a financing statement under the UCC, this means that alternative methods of perfecting security interests as recognized by the UCC are applicable to mobile homes. In other words, the district court concluded that just because filing under the MHCA was *sufficient* to perfect a security interest in a mobile home did not mean that it was the *exclusive* means of perfecting such an interest. Because the UCC recognizes that a security interest in a fixture can be perfected by a mortgage on the subject real estate in lieu of an Article 9 financing statement, MICH. COMP. LAWS § 440.9402(6) (amended 2000), the district court determined that this alternative is equally applicable to perfecting a security interest in a mobile home.

We disagree with the district court's conclusion for two reasons. First, it disregards the MHCA provision that mandates compliance with its terms in order to perfect a security interest in a mobile home. Mich. Comp. Laws § 125.2330d. Secondly, the key Article 9 provision as worded in 1999 expressly provided that "a security interest in property subject to the [MHCA] can be perfected ***only*** by compliance therewith. . . ." Mich. Comp. Laws § 440.9302(4) (amended 2000) (emphasis added). The UCC, therefore, expressly rules out the gateway to an alternative means of perfecting a security interest in a mobile home that is generally available to fixtures on real estate. Any other interpretation, including the attempts by both Chase Manhattan and the district court to explain away the unambiguous use of the word "only" in the above-quoted language, strikes us as strained and unpersuasive.

As a final argument, Chase Manhattan urges us to look to the UCC and general property law in cases such as the one before us where no mobile home creditor has made a filing under the MHCA. Adopting its reasoning, however, would give effect to an unauthorized method of perfecting security interests in a mobile home. Such a result would be at complete odds with the Michigan Legislature's clear intent to have the MHCA provide the exclusive method of perfecting such security interests, whether or not the mobile home is affixed to real estate. MICH. COMP. LAWS § 125.2302(g). We therefore find no merit in Chase Manhattan's argument.

2. The Trustee's interest as a judgment lien creditor trumps Chase Manhattan's unperfected security interest in the mobile home For all of the above reasons, we are persuaded that Chase Manhattan did not properly perfect its security interest in the Kroskies' mobile home. This raises the question of whether Chase Manhattan's unperfected interest is avoidable by the Trustee. We hold that Chase Manhattan's interest is avoidable because the Trustee's interest as a statutory judgment lien creditor is superior to that of an unperfected creditor. Mich. Comp. Laws § 440.9317(1)(b)(i) (providing that "[a] security interest or agricultural lien is subordinate to the rights of . . . a person that becomes a lien creditor before the . . . time the security interest or agricultural lien is perfected."); *Federal Land Bank of St. Paul v. Bay Park Place, Inc.*, 162 Mich.App. 1, 412 N.W.2d 222, 225 (1987) ("As noted by the circuit court, NBD's claim is unperfected and is thus defeated by the judicial liens of Federal Land Bank and Production Credit.").

As the Trustee has pointed out, the bankruptcy law gives him the status of a judicial lien creditor. Pursuant to Michigan law, an unperfected security interest like Chase Manhattan's is always subject to a judgment lien. MICH. COMP. LAWS § 440.9301(1)(b)(i) (amended 2000). Chase Manhattan did not disagree with this part of the Trustee's argument, instead contending that its interest is perfected. But as discussed above, such a contention requires a convoluted reading of the Michigan statutes that we believe is contrary to a proper analysis of the applicable provisions of both the MHCA and the UCC.

III. CONCLUSION

For all of the reasons set forth above, we REVERSE the decision of the district court and REMAND the case with instructions that the judgment of the bankruptcy court be affirmed.

DISSENT

MERRITT, Circuit Judge, dissenting.
I am persuaded that District Judge Hillman's opinion and reasoning is correct and should be affirmed. Here is the crux of his opinion which I would endorse:

> The parties agree that no Michigan case law precisely addresses the question before this court. *That question specifically is whether the procedures required under the MHCA preclude the securing of an interest in a mobile home as a fixture on real property through the recording of a mortgage.*
>
> . . . .

I see no conflict between the two provisions. The Mobile Home Commission Act itself does not purport to be the exclusive means of recording a security interest in a fixture on real property. Instead, it provides the means by which mobile home security interests are perfected, whether or not the mobile home is a fixture. No part of the statute suggests that it was intended to override ordinary real estate law, which permits the filing of mortgages to secure an interest in fixtures.

Appellee argues, however, that the exclusiveness of the MHCA is provided by Article 9 of the U.C.C., section 440.9302(4), which declares that financing statements must be filed in all cases except as provided in that section. Appellee contends that, since the filing of a mortgage is not a listed exception, whereas compliance with the MHCA is such exception, the recording of a mortgage is ineffective to provide a security interest.

I disagree. Section 440.9302 must be read in conjunction with the other provisions of Article 9 of the U.C.C.

First, as appellee notes, section 440.9302 does not include the filing of a mortgage on a fixture as one of the mentioned exceptions from the requirement of a financing statement. Nevertheless, section 440.9402(6) expressly permits the recording of a mortgage to serve as a financing statement. *See* MICH. COMP. LAWS 440.9402(6) ("A mortgage is effective as a financing statement filed as a fixture filing from the date of its recording if all of the following apply. . . ."). As a result, financing statements generally do not provide the exclusive means of perfecting a security interest in goods, including fixtures.

Second, the Mobile Home Commission Act itself provides only that a filing under the Act "is *equivalent* to the filing of a financing statement with respect to the security interest under article 9 of the uniform commercial code. . . ." MICH. COMP. LAWS § 125.2330d (emphasis added.) As previously stated, no dispute exists that under the terms of the U.C.C., the filing of a financial statement ordinarily is not exclusive of the filing of a mortgage and does not prevent creation of an encumbrance upon fixtures pursuant to real estate law. *See* MICH. COMP. LAWS §§ 440.9402(6); 440.9313(3). As a result, to conclude that the word "only" in section 440.9302(4) precludes the filing of a mortgage on a mobile home would give MICH. COMP. LAWS § 125.2330d broader effect than an Article 9 financing statement applicable to another sort of fixture. Such an interpretation directly conflicts with the limiting language contained in section 440.9302(4) as well as MICH. COMP. LAWS § 125.2330d, which both declare that application for title under MICH. COMP. LAWS § 125.2330d "is *equivalent* to the filing of a financing statement."

Third, other portions of Article 9 specifically declare that the article may not be interpreted in a manner that precludes the creation of a security interest through the recording of a mortgage. Under MICH. COMP. LAWS § 440.9313(3), the legislature specifically declares that "this article does not prevent creation of an encumbrance upon fixtures pursuant to real estate law." Appellee attempts to distinguish section 440.9313(3) by saying that the section applies only to priorities, not to the actual creation of security interests. However, MICH. COMP. LAWS § 440.9313(3) expressly states that it applies to the whole of Article 9 of the U.C.C.: "*This article* does not prevent the creation of an encumbrance upon fixtures pursuant to real estate law." Section 440.9302(4), upon which the bankruptcy court and appellee rely, is itself part of Article 9. As a result, section 9313(3) specifically states that section 9302(4) may not be construed as advocated by appellee.

Fourth, any other construction is at odds with the central premise of the U.C.C. The Uniform Commercial Code is designed to address secured transaction in goods and commercial paper. It does not provide the means for securing transactions in real property. Consequently, when the legislature equated an application for transfer of title under the Mobile Home Commission Act to a financing statement under Article 9 of the Uniform Commercial Code it must be deemed to have intended what it said—that MICH. COMP. LAWS § 125.2330d would do no more than any other financing statement under the U.C.C.

Fifth, even without the legislature's clearly declared limitation on the scope of MICH. COMP. LAWS § 125.2330d, this court would be obligated to presume that the legislature did not intend by adopting the MHCA to abrogate the entire body of real estate law regarding mortgages on fixtures. As the Michigan Supreme Court stated more than 100 years ago,

> The legislature should speak in no uncertain manner when it seeks to abrogate the plain and long-established rules of the common law. Courts should not be left to construction to sustain such bold innovations.

Bandfield v. Bandfield, 117 Mich. 80, 82, 75 N.W. 287 (1898), rev'd in part on other grounds. Hosko v. Hosko, 385 Mich. 39, 187 N.W.2d 236 (1971). See also Koenig v. City of South Haven, 460 Mich. 667, 677, 597 N.W.2d 99,

104 (1999); Rusinek v. Schultz, Snyder & Steele Lumber Co., 411 Mich. 502, 508, 309 N.W.2d 163 (1981).

Finally, I note that the bankruptcy judge's ruling intrudes upon Chase Manhattan's ability to preserve a precise mortgage value in the real property itself, not just in the mobile home fixture. Chase Manhattan, as mortgage holder, is left to the verbal assurances of counsel for appellee that the Trustee will exercise his discretion to determine an "equitable" amount attributable to the real estate. Chase Manhattan filed a mortgage on both the real estate and its fixtures in an amount that was not divisible under the mortgage terms. Invalidating the mortgage security at issue here deprives Chase Manhattan of its ordinary rights as a secured lender under the mortgage on the real property. Clearly the Mobile Home Commission Act does not apply or purport to apply to the real property on which the mobile home is situated.

2. Avoiding Claims That an Actual Creditor Can Avoid under State Law

The trustee may avoid transfers that an actual creditor with a provable claim could have avoided under state law, such as the Uniform Fraudulent Transfers Act. 11 U.S.C.A. § 544(b). Section 544(b) states that the trustee has the right to avoid any prepetition transfer that is "voidable under applicable law by a creditor holding an unsecured claim that is allowable." Thus, 544(b) gives the trustee the power to avoid transfers that are voidable under state fraudulent transfer and bulk sales laws. The transaction can be set aside for the benefit of all creditors.

EXAMPLE

Mom's & Pop's Corner Store purchased its inventory from a number of suppliers on credit. After a larger competitor opened down the block, Mom's & Pop's decided to close the store. Mom's & Pop's sold its inventory to the Dollar Store without notifying its creditors. Mom's & Pop's then filed for bankruptcy under Chapter 7. Because the sale to the Dollar Store violated the state bulk sales law, the Mom's & Pop's trustee could avoid this prepetition transfer.

In *In re Damar Creative Group, Inc.*, Damar Creative Group gave Daniel Ottow, its principal shareholder, officer, and director, a $225,050 bonus. Damar then filed for bankruptcy under Chapter 7. The trustee sought to use 544(b) and the state's fraudulent transfer act to avoid the transfer.

In re Damar Creative Group, Inc.

1995 WL 571374 (S.D. Ill. 1995)

MEMORANDUM OPINION AND ORDER
James H. Alesia,
District Judge

The matter now before the court is a bankruptcy appeal. Plaintiff-appellant, David R. Herzog, the trustee in bankruptcy, appeals from an order entered by the bankruptcy court on January 20, 1995, in favor of the defendant-appellee, Daniel Ottow ("Ottow"). In that order, the bankruptcy court dismissed the bankruptcy trustee's claim under 11 U.S.C. § 544(b) because the trustee lacked standing to bring an action under that section. The bankruptcy trustee has appealed to this court. For the reasons set forth below, this court reverses the bankruptcy court's order and remands this matter for further proceedings consistent with this opinion.

I. BACKGROUND

On January 21, 1992, the debtor, Damar Creative Group, Inc. ("debtor"), filed a petition for bankruptcy under Chapter 7 of the Bankruptcy Code, 11 U.S.C. § 701 et seq. ("the Code"). Thereafter, David R. Herzog was appointed as trustee in bankruptcy. In accordance with his duties as trustee, Herzog brought a two-count complaint against the defendant, Daniel Ottow, the principal shareholder, officer, and director of the debtor.

In Count I, the trustee alleged that a $37,355 bonus that Ottow received from the debtor within one year of the filing of the bankruptcy petition was a fraudulent conveyance under Section 548 of the Code. The parties have since settled with respect to this claim. In Count II, the trustee alleged that a $225,050 bonus that Ottow received from the debtor in June 1990 was a fraudulent transfer under Section 544 of the Code.

Ottow moved to dismiss Count II on the basis that the bankruptcy trustee had no standing to bring any action under Section 544 of the Code. His argument was based on his contention that in order to have standing under Section 544(b), a bankruptcy trustee must identify a specific unsecured creditor who existed at the time of the transfer. Since the parties had already stipulated that, at the time of the transfer, no such creditor existed, Ottow moved the bankruptcy court for dismissal of Count II. The court agreed, holding that "a trustee must first establish that at the time the transaction at issue occurred there was in fact a creditor in existence who had an unsecured claim allowable against the debtor's estate." *In re Damar Creative Group, Inc.*, No. 92 B 1225 (Bankr.N.D.Ill. January 20, 1995). Accordingly, the bankruptcy court dismissed Count II.

II. DISCUSSION

No issues of fact are raised on appeal by the trustee. Therefore, this court need only perform a de novo review of the challenged conclusion of law. *Matter of Yonikus*, 996 F.2d 866, 868 (7th Cir.1993).

The trustee's action, and the result here, depends on the court's interpretation of Section 544(b) of the Code. Section 544(b) provides:

> The trustee shall avoid any transfer of an interest of the debtor in property or any obligation incurred by the debtor that is voidable under applicable law by a creditor holding an unsecured claim that is allowable under section 502 of this title or that is not allowable only under section 502(e) of this title. 11 U.S.C. § 544(b).

For purposes of standing, Section 544(b) contains only one express restriction: the trustee must be able to assert the rights of at least one of the present unsecured creditors of the estate holding a claim that is either allowable under Section 502 or not allowable only under Section 502(e). 4 COLLIER ON BANKRUPTCY 544.03 (15th ed. 1988). Once the trustee overcomes this restriction, Section 544(b) gives him the power to avoid any of the debtor's transfers or obligations that are voidable for fraud or any other reason under applicable state or federal law. *Id.* Section 544(b) does not contain any substantive provisions to determine when and under what circumstances a particular transfer or obligation may be avoided; those circumstances are set by the applicable state or federal law affording grounds for avoidance. *Id.; In re Wedtech Corp.*, 88 B.R. 619, 622–23 (Bankr.S.D.N.Y. 1988); see also *In re Lico Mfg. Co., Inc.*, 201 F.Supp. 899, 903 (D.Conn.), aff'd, 323 F.2d 871 (2d Cir.1963) (no requirement that there be a creditor at the time of the transaction in former Section 70(e), the predecessor statute to Section 544(b); only applicable requirements are those contained in the state law giving rise to the cause of action).

Here, the bankruptcy court dismissed the trustee's claim because there was no unsecured creditor of the debtor's estate who existed at the time the debtor gave Ottow his bonus. From that, it is evident that the bankruptcy court has inserted an additional prerequisite that at least one unsecured creditor with an allowable claim exist at the time of the alleged transfer in order for a trustee to have standing under Section 544(b). However, the court sees no basis in the law for such a restriction. As stated above, for purposes of standing, the trustee must point to at least one of the present unsecured creditors holding an allowable claim. The bankruptcy court did not address this requirement in its order but this court finds no reason to dispute the trustee's assertion that there are at least thirty-two present unsecured claims allowable under Section 502.

Once the bankruptcy court is assured of that, it must look to the applicable state or federal law that the trustee has asserted in order to determine the circumstances in which a particular transfer may be avoided. The court notes that in many instances, the state fraudulent conveyance laws will not allow recovery for future creditors. R. GINSBERG AND R. MARTIN, BANKRUPTCY: TEXT, STATUTES, RULES, § 902(c) at p. 9–17 (3d ed.). If that were the case here, the bankruptcy court would have had every reason to dismiss the action. However, the Illinois statute which the trustee relied on, an adoption of the Uniform Fraudulent Transfer Act, does not limit recovery to creditors whose claims arose before the transfer. 740 ILCS 160/5. The statute states, in pertinent part:

> A transfer made or obligation incurred by a debtor is fraudulent as to a creditor, whether the

creditor's claim arose before or after the transfer was made or obligation was incurred, if . . . 740 ILCS 160/5 (emphasis added).

Therefore, since the applicable state law imposes no requirement that at least one unsecured creditor exist at the time of the alleged fraudulent transfer, the court finds no reason to dismiss the trustee for lack of standing.

Accordingly, this court reverses the Bankruptcy Court's order of January 20, 1995, and remands this case to the Bankruptcy Court for further proceedings consistent with this opinion. In doing so, this court expresses no opinion as to whether the alleged transfer was fraudulent under the Illinois statute; we merely remand this case to the Bankruptcy Court so that it can conduct further proceedings.

CONCLUSION

For the reasons outlined above, this court reverses the Bankruptcy Court's order of January 20, 1995, and remands this case to the Bankruptcy Court for further proceedings consistent with this opinion.

3. Avoiding Statutory Liens That Arise on the Debtor's Bankruptcy or Insolvency

Statutory liens that arise on the debtor's bankruptcy or insolvency can also be avoided. 11 U.S.C.A. § 545. This section prevents states from creating statutory liens that would circumvent the priority scheme of the Bankruptcy Code.

4. Avoiding Prepetition Transfers of Property of the Estate to Creditors That Are Voidable Preferences

The trustee's power to avoid preferential transfers by recovering for the estate money or property transferred is of great importance. Preferential transfers are avoidable under 11 U.S.C.A. § 547. Payment or transfer will be recoverable upon proof as follows:

1. the payment or transfer was to or for the benefit of a creditor;
2. the payment or transfer was on an account of an antecedent debt owed by the debtor before the transfer was made;
3. the transfer was made while the debtor was insolvent;
4. the payment or transfer was made within 90 days prior to the filing of a bankruptcy case or between 90 days and one year before the filing of the petition, if the creditor at the time of the transfer was an insider; and
5. the creditor received as the result of the transfer more than he or she would have received in a bankruptcy liquidation case under Chapter 7.

EXAMPLE

Alice borrowed $2,000 from First Bank for six months and gave First Bank a promissory note. When the note was due, Alice paid the Bank $2,000 plus interest. Two months later, Alice filed for bankruptcy under Chapter 7.

The trustee may avoid Alice's payment to the bank as a voidable preference under 11 U.S.C.A. § 547. The payment was for the loan, an antecedent debt, and the payment was made within 90 days prior to the filing of the Chapter 7 petition. Under 11 U.S.C.A. § 547(f) the debtor is presumed to have been insolvent during the 90-day period prior to filing its petition in bankruptcy. Finally, the Bank received full payment, which was more than it would have received as an unsecured creditor in Alice's Chapter 7 bankruptcy.

The concept of transfer is broadly construed and is not limited to the payment of money. The perfecting of a security interest in personal property is a transfer under 11 U.S.C.A. § 547. If the perfection of the security interest does not occur within ten days of the debt, the transfer is for an antecedent debt. 11 U.S.C.A. § 547(e)(3).

EXAMPLE

Alice borrowed $2,000 from First Bank for six months and gave First Bank a promissory note and a security interest in her equipment at her art studio. Two months later First Bank perfected its security interest in Alice's equipment by filing a financing statement. Two months later, Alice filed for bankruptcy under Chapter 7.

The trustee may avoid First Bank's perfected security interest since the filing of the financing statement constituted the transfer on account of an antecedent debt and therefore, by occurring within 90 days of the filing of the bankruptcy petition, was a voidable preference under 11 U.S.C.A. § 547. The perfection of the security interest did not occur within ten days of the debt and therefore is considered a transfer for an antecedent debt. Finally, by perfecting its security interest, First Bank would have had priority over the trustee under UCC § 9-317(a)(2)(A) and not be subject to the trustee's avoidance powers under 11 U.S.C.A. § 544(a).

PROBLEM 5.39 Alice borrowed $2,000 from First Bank for six months and gave First Bank a promissory note and a security interest in her equipment at her art studio. Two days later First Bank perfected its security interest in Alice's equipment by filing a financing statement. Two months later, Alice filed for bankruptcy under Chapter 7.

Could the trustee avoid First Bank's interest as a voidable preference under 11 U.S.C.A. § 547?

If Alice had filed for bankruptcy under Chapter 7 six months later rather than two, would First Bank have a voidable preference?

PROBLEM 5.40 Alice purchased equipment for her art studio from the Artist's Loft and paid Artist's Loft $2,000. Two months later, Alice filed for bankruptcy under Chapter 7.

Could the trustee avoid the $2,000 payment to Artist's Loft as a voidable preference under 11 U.S.C.A. § 547?

In *In re Owens,* the Owenses purchased a used automobile and gave the dealer a security interest in the automobile. The security interest was perfected but not in a timely manner (more than 20 days after the Owenses received possession of the vehicle). A short time later, the Owenses filed for bankruptcy under Chapter 7 and the trustee brought an adversary proceeding to avoid the dealer's security interest in the vehicle.

In re Owens

294 B.R. 289 (Bankr. S.D. Ohio 2003)

OPINION AND ORDER ON MOTION FOR SUMMARY JUDGMENT
DONALD E. CALHOUN, Jr., Bankruptcy Judge.

This matter comes before the Court upon Plaintiff's Motion for Summary Judgment Against Defendant, Defendant's Memorandum of Law in Opposition to Plaintiff's Motion for Summary Judgment, Affidavit of R. C. Mathews in Support of Memo Contra, Plaintiff's Reply to Defendants Memorandum in Opposition, and Memorandum of Law in Response to Plaintiff's Reply Memorandum.

I. STATEMENT OF JURISDICTION

The Court has jurisdiction over this matter pursuant to 28 U.S.C. § 1334 and the General Order of Reference entered in this district. This is a core proceeding under 28 U.S.C. § 157(b)(2)(F).

II. FACTS

Certain facts as alleged by Plaintiff and Defendant are undisputed. Those undisputed facts are as follows:

A. On April 25, 2002, a used 2001 Oldsmobile Alero automobile was purchased by the Debtors from Tom Peden Chevrolet-Olds-Pontiac-Buick Incorporated, a West Virginia dealer in new and used automobiles. At the time of the sale, the Debtors entered into a promissory note and security agreement with the dealer.

B. So far as alleged by the parties, the Debtors took possession of the automobile on the same date.

C. A master agreement existed between the Defendant and the dealer. Assuming the customer meets the Defendant's credit and other lending policy standards, the promissory note and security interest taken by the dealer at the time of sale is transferred to the Defendant, and the Defendant buys the customer's obligations from the dealer. Pursuant to the master agreement, the dealer is responsible for securing impressment of the lien on the certificate of title. The dealer had a department devoted to such work.

D. The dealer did not effect proper perfection of the security interest until May 21, 2002. Ohio Revised Code §§ 4505.06(A)(4) and (A)(5)(a)(1) require the dealer to submit an application for a certificate of title and payment of the applicable tax to the appropriate Court of Common Pleas of the State of Ohio within seven (7) business days after the date of delivery of the motor vehicle to the customer.

E. The Debtors filed their petition under Chapter 7 on August 6, 2002. Their petition date was seventy-seven (77) days after the May 21, 2002 date.

F. On November 7, 2002, the Chapter 7 Trustee filed a complaint to avoid preferential transfer. Within the adversary proceeding complaint, the Trustee alleged that the notation of the lien upon the memorandum title for the automobile constituted a transfer for or on an account of an antecedent debt owed by the Debtors before the transfer was made. The Trustee further alleged that the notation of the lien was made within ninety (90) days before the petition date. Pursuant to 11 U.S.C. § 547, the Trustee alleged that the Defendant's lien constituted an avoidable transfer and that he could recover the transfer or its equivalent pursuant to 11 U.S.C. § 550. The Trustee also alleged that Defendant's lien, once avoided, should be preserved for the benefit of the estate.

G. Defendant answered the adversary complaint on December 19, 2002. Defendant alleged that it had a valid and perfected first priority lien against the automobile and that the impressment of the lien did not constitute a preference.

H. On February 14, 2003, the Trustee filed his Motion. In the Motion, Trustee contends that there are no issues of material fact and that all elements of 11 U.S.C. § 547(b) have been established.

I. Defendant contends that Trustee is not entitled to judgment as a matter of law. Defendant contends that the law of the State of Ohio provides a "catch-all period of thirty days within which a person must apply for a motor vehicle certificate of title following delivery of the motor vehicle to the customer." Defendant contends that since the lien was impressed upon the certificate of title within the time prescribed by Ohio Revised Code § 4505.06(A)(5)(b), the lien should relate back to the date that the Debtors took possession.

III. SUMMARY JUDGMENT STANDARD

Rule 56(c) of the Federal Rules of Civil Procedure, incorporated by Bankruptcy Rule 7056 provides:

> [Summary judgment] . . . shall be rendered forthwith if the pleadings, depositions, answers to interrogatories, and admissions on file, together with the affidavits, if any, show that there is no genuine issue as to any material fact and that the moving party is entitled to a judgment as a matter of law.

The purpose of a motion for summary judgment is to determine if genuine issues of material fact exist to be tried. *Lashlee v. Sumner,* 570 F.2d 107, 111 (6th Cir.1978). The party seeking summary judgment bears the initial burden of asserting that the pleadings, depositions, answers to interrogatories, admissions and affidavits establish the absence of genuine issues of material fact. *Celotex Corp. v. Catrett,* 477 U.S. 317, 323, 106 S.Ct. 2548, 91 L.Ed.2d 265 (1986); *Street v. J.C. Bradford & Co.,* 886 F.2d 1472, 1479 (6th Cir.1989). The burden on the moving party is discharged by a "showing" that there is an absence of evidence to support a nonmoving party's case. Celotex Corp., 477 U.S. at 325, 106 S.Ct. 2548. Summary Judgment will be appropriate if the nonmoving party fails to establish the existence of an element essential to its case, and on which it will bear the burden of proof. Celotex Corp., 477 U.S. at 322, 106 S.Ct. 2548. Thus, the ultimate burden of demonstrating the existence of genuine issues of material fact lies with a nonmoving party. Lashlee, 570 F.2d at 110-111.

IV. DISCUSSION

A. Ohio Revised Code § 4505.06(A)(5)(b)

Ohio Revised Code § 4505.06(A)(5)(b) provides as follows:

> (b) In all cases of transfer of a motor vehicle, the application for certificate of title shall be filed within thirty days after the assignment or delivery of the motor vehicle. If an application for a certificate of title is not filed within the period specified in division (A)(5)(b) of this

section, the clerk shall collect a fee of five dollars for the issuance of the certificate, except that no such fee shall be required from a motor vehicle salvage dealer, as defined in division (A) of section 4738.01 of the Revised Code, who immediately surrenders the certificate of title for cancellation. The fee shall be in addition to all other fees established by this chapter, and shall be retained by the clerk. The registrar shall provide, on the certificate form prescribed by section 4505.07 of the Revised Code, language necessary to give evidence of the date on which the assignment or delivery of the motor vehicle was made.

B. 11 U.S.C. § 547(b).

Section 547(b) of the United States Code provides, in pertinent part, as follows:

> [T]he trustee may avoid any transfer of an interest of the debtor in property—
> (1) to or for the benefit of a creditor;
> (2) for or on account of an antecedent debt owed by the debtor before such transfer was made;
> (3) made while the debtor was insolvent;
> (4) made—
> (A) on or within 90 days before the date of the filing of the petition; or
> (B) between ninety days and one year before the date of the filing of the petition, if such creditor at the time of such transfer was an insider; and
> (5) that enables such creditor to receive more than such creditor would receive if—
> (A) this case were a case under chapter 7 of this title;
> (B) the transfer had not been made; and
> (C) such creditor received payment of such debt to the extent provided by the provisions of this title.
>
> 11 U.S.C. § 547(b).

C. APPLICATION OF O.R.C. § 4505.06(A)(5)(b) AND 11 U.S.C. § 547(b)

The United States Supreme Court already has determined that Congress intended to establish a uniform federal perfection period immune to alteration by state laws permitting relation back. Fidelity Financial Services, Inc. v. Fink, 522 U.S. 211, 220, 118 S.Ct. 651, 656, 139 L.Ed.2d 571 (1998). The Fidelity case facts are very similar to the facts in this case. In Fidelity, the Supreme Court reviewed a Missouri case where the debtor had purchased an automobile and had given Fidelity Financial Services, Inc. a promissory note for the purchase, secured by the automobile. Twenty-one days later, Fidelity Financial Services, Inc. mailed its application to perfect its security interest. Two months later, the debtor filed her Chapter 7 petition. After the bankruptcy proceeding was converted to one under Chapter 13, the trustee moved to set aside the security interest because the security interest had not been perfected within twenty (20) days after the debtor had received the automobile. Fidelity, 522 U.S. at 213, 118 S.Ct. 651. Fidelity Financial Services, Inc. argued that Missouri law allowed the lien to be treated as "perfected on the day of its creation because it delivered the papers within the 30 days allowed by the state law. . . ." Fidelity, 522 U.S. at 214, 215, 118 S.Ct. 651. The Supreme Court upheld the bankruptcy court's decision to set aside the lien as a voidable preference, holding that Missouri's relation back provision could not extend § 547(c)(3)(B)'s twenty (20) day perfection period. The conclusion in this case cannot be different.

Section 547(b) empowers the trustee to avoid any transfer of an interest in property that meets the requirements of the section. *Field v. Fifth Third Bank* (In re Nasr), 191 B.R. 689, 693 (Bankr.S.D.Ohio 1996). In this case, it is undisputed that the Debtors took possession of the vehicle on or before April 25, 2002. See, In re Nasr, 191 B.R. at 692 (citing In re Edney, 47 F.3d 1168 (full text not published) (6th Cir.1995)). See also Field v. Lebanon Citizens National Bank (In re Knee), 254 B.R. 710, 712 (Bankr.S.D.Ohio 2000). It is also undisputed that Defendant's lien was not noted on the certificate of title until May 21, 2002. Said notation of lien on the certificate of title was made to or for the benefit of the Defendant while Debtors were presumed to have been insolvent. Said transfer was made within ninety (90) days of Debtor's bankruptcy petition, and it enabled the Defendant to receive more than it would have received if the transfer had not been made. Based upon the foregoing, the Court finds and concludes that all elements of 11 U.S.C. § 547(b) have been established by the Plaintiff and that Plaintiff is entitled to judgment as a matter of law.

V. CONCLUSION

Based upon the foregoing, the Court hereby grants Plaintiff's Motion for Summary Judgment Against Defendant. A judgment entry in accordance with this Opinion and Order on Plaintiff's Motion for Summary Judgment Against Defendant will be entered separately.

IT IS SO ORDERED.

5. Avoiding Prepetition Transfers of Property of the Estate That Are Fraudulent under the Bankruptcy Code

Two types of fraudulent transfers are avoidable under 11 U.S.C.A. § 548. The first is a transfer where actual fraud is involved. 11 U.S.C.A. § 548(a)(1)(A). The second is a transfer considered constructively fraudulent. 11 U.S.C.A. § 548(a)(1)(B).

In *Leibowitz v. Imsorn,* Rungsarn sold a rental property and transferred $10,000 to his ex-wife and $10,000 to his daughter. Eight months later he filed for bankruptcy under Chapter 7. The trustee filed complaints against the ex-wife and daughter claiming the funds were transferred as fraudulent conveyances under 11 U.S.C.A. §§ 548(a)(1)(A) and (B).

Leibowitz v. Imsorn

2003 WL 21785620 (N.D. Ill. 2003)

OPINION
ZAGEL, J.

Appellant David P. Leibowitz, as Chapter 7 trustee for Rungsarn Imsorn ("Rungsarn"), filed two complaints in the United States Bankruptcy Court for the Northern District of Illinois against Rani Imsorn ("Rani") and Kovnvara Imsorn ("Kovnvara") to recover funds transferred to them by Rungsarn. Leibowitz claimed that the funds were transferred as either fraudulent conveyances or avoidable transfers under 11 U.S.C. §§ 548(a)(1)(A), 548(a)(1)(B), and 544 incorporating 740 ILCS 160/6. After a bench trial, the Court entered judgment in favor of Kovnvara and Rani, which Leibowitz appeals.

BACKGROUND

In December of 2000, approximately eight months before filing for bankruptcy, Rungsarn sold a rental piece of property from which he netted $96,558.48. He then transferred $10,000 to his ex-wife Rani and $10,000 to his daughter Kovnvara. Rungsarn claims he owed Rani $10,000 because she previously owned the property and executed a quitclaim deed during their divorce on the unwritten promise that he would pay her something from the sale of the property. As for his daughter, Rungsarn claims that he owed her $16,000 resulting from a loan she made to him in 1998 or 1999, and thus paid her $10,000 as partial payment. However, in his affirmative defenses in his answer to the complaint, Rungsarn stated that he gave her the $10,000 to pay for her wedding, which he reiterated at trial.

As to his personal financial situation, Rungsarn testified that he had a gambling problem and has lost over $50,000 each year for the past several years. On February 23, 2001, he was terminated from his full-time job at Jackson Park Hospital, where he had worked for 29 years. According to his testimony, his salary had been $2,200 per month (or $26,400 annually), although his Statement of Financial Affairs indicates he was making only $23,000 annually. After he lost his job, Rungsarn became depressed and gambled even more. With $950 per month of living expenses, a gambling problem, and no income except the proceeds from the sale of the building, Rungsarn ran out of money in August 2001. On August 23, 2001, he filed for Chapter 7 bankruptcy, and a trustee was assigned.

As part of his Chapter 7 bankruptcy, Rungsarn was required to file a Statement of Financial Affairs disclosing all transfers to insiders within one year of filing for bankruptcy. On his first schedule of affairs, he failed to list the transfers to Rani and Kovnvara. However, at the § 341 meeting on October 2, 2001, he acknowledged that he had transferred $10,000 to both of them. On October 31, 2001, he filed an Amended Schedule of Affairs including these transfers and an income and expense statement with copies of checks drawn showing how he spent the proceeds from the sale of the building.

Leibowitz subsequently filed adverse proceedings under 11 U.S.C. §§ 548(a)(1)(A), 548(a)(1)(B), and 544 incorporating 740 ILCS 160/6 (Illinois Uniform Fraudulent Transfer Act or "UFTA") against Rani and Kovnvara to recover the funds Rungsarn transferred to them.[i] After a bench trial, the Court ruled in favor of Rani and Kovnvara.

STANDARD OF REVIEW

Leibowitz now appeals: (1) the Court's finding that he failed to carry the burden of proving Rungsarn's insolvency; and (2) the Court's ruling as a matter of law that Rungsarn did not intend to defraud his creditors. I "review the courts' legal interpretations de novo; however, [I] review the bankruptcy court's findings of fact for clear error only." Union Planters Bank, N.A. v. Connors, 283 F.3d 896, 899 (7th Cir.2002).

ACTUAL FRAUD/FRAUD IN FACT

Leibowitz first claims that the Court improperly determined if there was actual fraud, a claim which I must review de novo. Actual fraud, or fraud in fact, requires Leibowitz to prove: (1) a transfer of an interest in property; (2) that the transfer of that property occurred within one year before the bankruptcy filing date; and (3) that the debtor had an actual intent to hinder, delay, or defraud his creditors. 11 U.S.C. § 548(a)(1)(A). The only element at issue here is whether Rungsarn had an actual intent to hinder, delay, or defraud his creditors. Because actual intent is often impractical to demonstrate, bankruptcy courts may use the circumstances surrounding the transfer to infer fraudulent intent. In re Chevrie, 2001 Bankr.LEXIS 97, at *27 (Bankr.N.D.Ill. Feb. 13, 2001) (citing Max Sugarman Funeral Home, Inc. v. A.D.B. Investors, 926 F.2d 1248, 1254 (1st Cir.1991)). These circumstances, or badges of fraud, may include: (1) whether the debtor was insolvent at the time of the transfer or became insolvent as a result of the transfer; (2) whether the debtor retained control of the asset; (3) whether the transfer was to a family member, In re Chevrie, 2001 Bankr.LEXIS 97, at *28; (4) whether the transfer was prior to debtor incurring a substantial debt; and (5) whether the transfer was substantially all of debtor's assets. In re Mussa, 215 B.R. 158, 168 (Bankr.N.D.Ill.1997). "Although the presence of a single badge of fraud . . . is insufficient to establish actual fraudulent intent, the confluence of several can constitute conclusive evidence of actual intent, absent significantly clear evidence of a legitimate supervening purpose for the transfer." In re Chevrie, 2001 Bankr.LEXIS 97, at *28. In other words, several badges of fraud may create a presumption of fraudulent intent, id., which "imposes on the party against whom it is directed the burden of going forward with evidence to rebut or meet the presumption, but does not shift to such party the burden of proof in the sense of the risk of nonpersuasion, which remains throughout the trial upon the party on whom it was originally cast," Fed.R.Evid. 301.

Leibowitz claims that three badges of fraud were sufficiently demonstrated at trial: (1) Rungsarn was insolvent or became insolvent as a result of the transfers; (2) the transfers were to family members; and (3) the transfers included substantially all of Rungsarn's assets. On this basis, Leibowitz claims he was entitled to but not given a presumption of Rungsarn's fraudulent intent. From its oral opinion, the Court stated that it did not believe Leibowitz carried his burden of proof on any count and that it did not "believe that [Rungsarn] intended to defraud his creditors," thus preventing Leibowitz from prevailing on his fraud in fact claim. As to the specific badges of fraud, the Court explicitly stated that Leibowitz did not carry the burden to prove Rungsarn was insolvent or became insolvent as a result of the transfer. Accordingly, I will review that finding for clear error only. However, because nothing in the record indicates whether the Court considered if the second or third badges of fraud (transfer to a family member or transfer of substantially all of debtor's assets) were present, I will review each badge de novo.

I will first address whether Leibowitz carried the burden to prove Rungsarn was insolvent or became insolvent as a result of the transfers to Rani and Kovnvara. "The UFTA defines insolvency as when 'the sum of the debtor's debts is greater than all of the debtor's assets at a fair valuation.' " In re Mussa, 215 B.R. at 169 (quoting 740 ILCS § 160/3(a)). Rungsarn admitted during the trial that at the time of the transfer to Rani and Kovnvara, he had unpaid debts. He also testified he had no other assets or income except the proceeds from the sale of his building and income from his job. While Rungsarn acknowledged he did not pay off all his debts, he never admitted he could not have paid off his debts. He netted almost $96,558.48 from the sale of the building. Between the sale of the building and the transfer to Rani and Kovnvara, he spent $6,710.70 of the proceeds on various expenses, leaving $89,847.78. Subtracting the $10,000 he transferred to both Rani and Kovnvara, Rungsarn still retained $69,847.78. Leibowitz presented no evidence at the trial that at the time he transferred the money to Rani and Kovnvara, his debts were greater than $89,847.78 or even $69,847.78. In fact, Leibowitz presented no evidence as to the amount of Rungsarn's outstanding debts at the time of the transfers. In addition, Rungsarn continued to pay various creditors after the transfers, such as $5,113 to Fleet, $5,000 to First USA Bank, $4,823 to First USA Bank, and $2,000 to Chase. Furthermore, after he lost his job and only source of income in February 2001, he increased his gambling and continued to lose money. Out of

45 withdrawals from his account between the time of the transfers and his filing for bankruptcy, only eight were to pay bills. The remaining transactions were to various casinos, to an unknown entity referred to as "H.C.B." or for cash, all of which arguably contributed to his insolvency. Therefore, the Court's finding that there was no evidence that Rungsarn was insolvent or became insolvent as a result of the transfers is not clearly erroneous.

As to whether the transfers in question went to a family member, Leibowitz is correct as to the existence of a badge of fraud on this basis. There is no dispute that Rungsarn made a transfer to his daughter and his ex-wife whom he continued to see socially. While transfers "between family members is not proof per se of fraudulent intent, a familial relationship is weighty proof of such intent," In re Chevrie, 2001 Bankr.LEXIS 97, at *28. Unfortunately for Leibowitz, however, the Court's failure to consider this badge of fraud is harmless error because Leibowitz did not sufficiently demonstrate the existence of a badge of fraud on the basis of Rungsarn's transfer of substantially all of his assets. At the time of the transfer, Rungsarn still retained $69,847.78 or nearly 75% from the sale of his building and was working full time. Therefore, he did not transfer "substantially" all of his assets. In sum, because Leibowitz demonstrated only one badge of fraud, he was not entitled to a presumption of fraud at trial. Accordingly, the Court did not commit error in finding that there was no fraudulent intent on the part of Rungsarn, thus sinking Leibowitz's actual fraud claim.

CONSTRUCTIVE FRAUD/FRAUD IN LAW

Leibowitz also challenges the Court's finding that his constructive fraud claim fails. To prove constructive fraud or fraud in law, Leibowitz must prove: (1) a transfer of an interest in property; (2) that the transfer of that property occurred within one year before the bankruptcy filing date; (3) that the debtor received less than equivalent value in exchange for the transfer; and (4) that the debtor was insolvent at the time of the transfer or became insolvent as a result of the transfer. 11 U.S.C. §§ 548(a)(1)(B)(i), 548(a)(1)(B)(ii)(I). For the reasons discussed above, the Court did not commit error in finding insufficient evidence proving that Rungsarn was insolvent at the time of the transfers or that Rungsarn became insolvent as a result of the transfers, thus sinking Leibowitz's constructive fraud claim.

For the reasons above, the bankruptcy court's judgment for both defendants is AFFIRMED.

---

[1]Because the state and federal statutes are functional equivalents, except for the statute of limitations, the analysis is the same. In re First Commercial Management Group, Inc., 279 B.R. 230, 240 (Bankr.N.D.Ill.2002) (citing In re Randy, 189 B.R., 425, 443 (Bankr.N.D.Ill.1995)).

6. Avoiding Postpetition Transfers of Property of the Estate Unless They Are Authorized by the Bankruptcy Code or by the Bankruptcy Court

Postpetition transfers may be avoided by the trustee unless they are authorized by the Bankruptcy Code or by the bankruptcy court. 11 U.S.C.A. § 549(a).

EXAMPLE

William Pratt filed a petition in bankruptcy under Chapter 7 on December 3. On December 4, Pratt sold his coin collection to Toni Rogers for $5,000. At the time of the filing of the petition, the coin collection was property of the estate. This postpetition transfer of property of the estate may be avoided by the trustee because it was authorized by neither the Bankruptcy Code nor the bankruptcy court.

PROBLEM 5.41 On June 1, William Pratt borrowed $10,000 from People's Bank. This loan was unsecured. On December 7, four days after filing his Chapter 7 petition, Pratt paid People's Bank $2,000.

Can Pratt's trustee recover the $2,000 from People's Bank?

The Bankruptcy Code protects some postpetition transfers of realty by the debtor from the trustee's avoidance powers. To be protected, the transfer must have occurred and be properly recorded before a copy of the bankruptcy petition is filed in the real estate records for the county where the real estate is located, and the transferee must be a good faith purchaser who has no knowledge of the bankruptcy petition and has paid present fair equivalent value. A good faith purchaser who meets all the requirements but has paid less than present fair equivalent value only has a lien on the property to the extent of present value given. 11 U.S.C.A. § 549(c).

PROBLEM 5.42 William Pratt filed a petition in bankruptcy under Chapter 7 on December 3. On December 4, Pratt sold his lakeshore home valued at $85,000 to Michelle Hodges for $85,000. She paid $10,000 down and took a $75,000 mortgage from First Bank. Hodges recorded her deed on December 5. On December 6, Pratt's petition in bankruptcy was filed in the office of the real estate records in the county where the lakeshore home was located. On December 7, Hodges learned of Pratt's bankruptcy.

Could Pratt's trustee in bankruptcy avoid the sale of the lakeshore home to Hodges?

PROBLEM 5.43 Assume the same facts as in Problem 5.42, except that Hodges paid $10,000 down and Pratt carried the mortgage.

Could Pratt's trustee in bankruptcy avoid the sale of the lakeshore home to Hodges?

SECTION 5
PROOFS OF CLAIM AND PROOFS OF INTEREST

Proofs of claim or proofs of interest filed under 11 U.S.C.A. § 501 are deemed allowed unless a party in interest objects. 11 U.S.C.A. § 502(a). A claim may be contingent, unliquidated, or disputed. A contingent claim depends on some future event that may or may not take place.

EXAMPLE

Janice borrowed $1,000 from First Bank and signed a promissory note. Before First Bank would loan Janice the money, the bank required Janice to have her mother sign the promissory note as an accommodation maker. Janice's mother signed as comaker with the notation "collection guaranteed." By adding "collection guaranteed," Janice's mother promised that if the note is not paid by Janice when due, she will pay it. Janice's mother, however, will pay the note only after First Bank has reduced its claim against Janice to judgment and execution on the judgment has been returned unsatisfied, or after Janice has become insolvent or it is otherwise apparent that it is useless to proceed against her. First Bank's claim against Janice's mother is a contingent claim.

The amount of the claim is uncertain in an unliquidated claim.

EXAMPLE

The Flower Market hired the Metro Agency to design an advertising campaign. The compensation was set as "a reasonable fee." Metro designed the campaign and presented its bill for $5,000. Flower Market refused to pay the bill, claiming that it should be $2,000. Because the contract stated that the fee would be "a reasonable fee," Metro's claim is unliquidated.

A disputed claim is a claim by a creditor that is contested by the debtor.

EXAMPLE

Alexander Wiggins and Vanessa Gray were involved in an automobile accident. Both Alexander and Vanessa claimed to have had the right of way and therefore neither admitted to being at fault. Each claim is disputed.

PROBLEM 5.44 Charles Rigby & Daughter, building contractors, contracted with Peaceful Valley Property Company to construct an apartment complex. Guaranty Surety Company issued a surety bond with Charles Rigby & Daughter as principal and Peaceful Valley as beneficiary. The bond provides that if the principal does not complete construction of the apartment complex, Guaranty will pay to complete the work.

Is Guaranty's liability contingent, unliquidated, or disputed?

A. CREDITORS' AND INDENTURE TRUSTEES' PROOFS OF CLAIM

When the debtor files a Chapter 7 petition, the debtor files Schedule D (Creditors Holding Secured Claims), Schedule E (Creditors Holding Unsecured Priority Claims), and Schedule F (Creditors Holding Unsecured Nonpriority Claims). When a trustee discovers that there may be assets available for administration, a notice of asset case form is filed with the Clerk of the Bankruptcy Court. That triggers the issuance of a second notice to creditors—a notice to file claims within 90 days after the mailing of the notice. Fed. R. Bank. P. 3002(c)(5).

A claim is a right to payment or a right to an equitable remedy for breach of performance if the breach gives rise to a right to payment. 11 U.S.C.A. § 101(5). Creditors (except for equity security holders) and indenture trustees file proofs of claim in a Chapter 7 case.

When filing a proof of claim, care must be taken to do the following:

1. complete the documents so they are legible;
2. state the amount of the claim that reflects the balance due on the petition date;
3. if the claim is filed as a secured claim, attach the documents that established the existence of the security interest, lien, or mortgage, and the documents that establish perfection;
4. if the claim is oversecured, include an addendum with a statement of the per diem interest because the oversecured claim will continue to accrue interest and, if applicable, attorney's fees, and the addendum will allow the trustee to quickly calculate the claim; and
5. mail a copy to the trustee because it is only the trustee who cares and who will challenge a claim as unsecured or unperfected.

If a creditor does not file a proof of claim on or before the first date set for the meeting of creditors, the debtor or the trustee may file it within 30 days following the deadline. Fed. R. Bank. P. 3004. An entity that is liable with the debtor to the creditor or that has secured the creditor may also file a proof of claim if the creditor does not timely file such proof. (See Exhibit 5–25.)

B. EQUITY SECURITY HOLDERS' PROOFS OF INTEREST

An interest can be the interest of a limited partner in a limited partnership. A share in a corporation is also an interest. These interests are called equity securities and are held by equity security holders. Equity security holders file proofs of interest in a Chapter 7 case.

SECTION 6
MOTIONS AND COMPLAINTS AFTER THE ORDER FOR RELIEF

Disputed matters in the bankruptcy process are designated as either contested matters or adversary proceedings. A **contested matter** is initiated by a motion. An adversary proceeding is initiated by a complaint.

The difference between raising an issue by motion or by complaint is very striking. If the issue is raised by a complaint, it becomes the basis of a federal court lawsuit. The complaint must be filed in the bankruptcy

EXHIBIT 5–25 Offical Form No. 10 (Proof of Claim)

FORM B10 (Official Form 10) (04/04)

INSTRUCTIONS FOR PROOF OF CLAIM FORM

The instructions and definitions below are general explanations of the law. In particular types of cases or circumstances, such as bankruptcy cases that are not filed voluntarily by a debtor, there may be exceptions to these general rules.

DEFINITIONS

Debtor

The person, corporation, or other entity that has filed a bankruptcy case is called the debtor.

Creditor

A creditor is any person, corporation, or other entity to whom the debtor owed a debt on the date that the bankruptcy case was filed.

Proof of Claim

A form telling the bankruptcy court how much the debtor owed a creditor at the time the bankruptcy case was filed (the amount of the creditor's claim). This form must be filed with the clerk of the bankruptcy court where the bankruptcy case was filed.

Secured Claim

A claim is a secured claim to the extent that the creditor has a lien on property of the debtor (collateral) that gives the creditor the right to be paid from that property before creditors who do not have liens on the property.

Examples of liens are a mortgage on real estate and a security interest in a car, truck, boat, television set, or other item of property. A lien may have been obtained through a court proceeding before the bankruptcy case began; in some states a court judgment is a lien. In addition, to the extent a creditor also owes money to the debtor (has a right of setoff), the creditor's claim may be a secured claim. (See also *Unsecured Claim.*)

Unsecured Claim

If a claim is not a secured claim it is an unsecured claim. A claim may be partly secured and partly unsecured if the property on which a creditor has a lien is not worth enough to pay the creditor in full.

Unsecured Priority Claim

Certain types of unsecured claims are given priority, so they are to be paid in bankruptcy cases before most other unsecured claims (if there is sufficient money or property available to pay these claims). The most common types of priority claims are listed on the proof of claim form. Unsecured claims that are not specifically given priority status by the bankruptcy laws are classified as *Unsecured Nonpriority Claims.*

Items to be completed in Proof of Claim form (if not already filled in)

Court, Name of Debtor, and Case Number:

Fill in the name of the federal judicial district where the bankruptcy case was filed (for example, Central District of California), the name of the debtor in the bankruptcy case, and the bankruptcy case number. If you received a notice of the case from the court, all of this information is near the top of the notice.

Information about Creditor:

Complete the section giving the name, address, and telephone number of the creditor to whom the debtor owes money or property, and the debtor's account number, if any. If anyone else has already filed a proof of claim relating to this debt, if you never received notices from the bankruptcy court about this case, if your address differs from that to which the court sent notice, or if this proof of claim replaces or changes a proof of claim that was already filed, check the appropriate box on the form.

1. Basis for Claim:

Check the type of debt for which the proof of claim is being filed. If the type of debt is not listed, check "Other" and briefly describe the type of debt. If you were an employee of the debtor, fill in the last four digits of your social security number and the dates of work for which you were not paid.

2. Date Debt Incurred:

Fill in the date when the debt first was owed by the debtor.

3. Court Judgments:

If you have a court judgment for this debt, state the date the court entered the judgment.

4. Total Amount of Claim at Time Case Filed:

Fill in the applicable amounts, including the total amount of the entire claim. If interest or other charges in addition to the principal amount of the claim are included, check the appropriate place on the form and attach an itemization of the interest and charges.

5. Secured Claim:

Check the appropriate place if the claim is a secured claim. You must state the type and value of property that is collateral for the claim, attach copies of the documentation of your lien, and state the amount past due on the claim as of the date the bankruptcy case was filed. A claim may be partly secured and partly unsecured. (See DEFINITIONS, above).

6. Unsecured Nonpriority Claim:

Check the appropriate place if you have an unsecured nonpriority claim, sometimes referred to as a "general unsecured claim". (See DEFINITIONS, above.) If your claim is partly secured and partly unsecured, state here the amount that is unsecured. If part of your claim is entitled to priority, state here the amount **not** entitled to priority.

7. Unsecured Priority Claim:

Check the appropriate place if you have an unsecured priority claim, and state the amount entitled to priority. (See DEFINITIONS, above). A claim may be partly priority and partly nonpriority if, for example, the claim is for more than the amount given priority by the law. Check the appropriate place to specify the type of priority claim.

8. Credits:

By signing this proof of claim, you are stating under oath that in calculating the amount of your claim you have given the debtor credit for all payments received from the debtor.

9. Supporting Documents:

You must attach to this proof of claim form copies of documents that show the debtor owes the debt claimed or, if the documents are too lengthy, a summary of those documents. If documents are not available, you must attach an explanation of why they are not available.

(continued)

EXHIBIT 5–25 Offical Form No. 10 (Proof of Claim), Continued

FORM B10 (Official Form 10) (04/04)

UNITED STATES BANKRUPTCY COURT ________________ DISTRICT OF ________________

PROOF OF CLAIM

Name of Debtor

Case Number

NOTE: This form should not be used to make a claim for an administrative expense arising after the commencement of the case. A "request" for payment of an administrative expense may be filed pursuant to 11 U.S.C. § 503.

Name of Creditor (The person or other entity to whom the debtor owes money or property):

Name and address where notices should be sent:

Telephone number:

☐ Check box if you are aware that anyone else has filed a proof of claim relating to your claim. Attach copy of statement giving particulars.

☐ Check box if you have never received any notices from the bankruptcy court in this case.

☐ Check box if the address differs from the address on the envelope sent to you by the court.

THIS SPACE IS FOR COURT USE ONLY

Account or other number by which creditor identifies debtor:

Check here if this claim ☐ replaces ☐ amends a previously filed claim, dated:__________

1. Basis for Claim

☐ Goods sold
☐ Services performed
☐ Money loaned
☐ Personal injury/wrongful death
☐ Taxes
☐ Other ______________________

☐ Retiree benefits as defined in 11 U.S.C. § 1114(a)
☐ Wages, salaries, and compensation (fill out below)
Last four digits of SS #: _______
Unpaid compensation for services performed
from ______________ to ______________
(date) (date)

2. Date debt was incurred:

3. If court judgment, date obtained:

4. Total Amount of Claim at Time Case Filed: $__________ (unsecured) __________ (secured) __________ (priority) __________ (Total)

If all or part of your claim is secured or entitled to priority, also complete Item 5 or 7 below.

☐ Check this box if claim includes interest or other charges in addition to the principal amount of the claim. Attach itemized statement of all interest or additional charges.

5. Secured Claim.

☐ Check this box if your claim is secured by collateral (including a right of setoff).

Brief Description of Collateral:

☐ Real Estate ☐ Motor Vehicle
☐ Other__________

Value of Collateral: $________________

Amount of arrearage and other charges at time case filed included in secured claim, if any: $______________

6. Unsecured Nonpriority Claim $______________

☐ Check this box if: a) there is no collateral or lien securing your claim, or b) your claim exceeds the value of the property securing it, or if c) none or only part of your claim is entitled to priority.

7. Unsecured Priority Claim.

☐ Check this box if you have an unsecured priority claim

Amount entitled to priority $___________

Specify the priority of the claim:

☐ Wages, salaries, or commissions (up to $4,925),* earned within 90 days before filing of the bankruptcy petition or cessation of the debtor's business, whichever is earlier - 11 U.S.C. § 507(a)(3).

☐ Contributions to an employee benefit plan - 11 U.S.C. § 507(a)(4).

☐ Up to $2,225* of deposits toward purchase, lease, or rental of property or services for personal, family, or household use - 11 U.S.C. § 507(a)(6).

☐ Alimony, maintenance, or support owed to a spouse, former spouse, or child - 11 U.S.C. § 507(a)(7).

☐ Taxes or penalties owed to governmental units-11 U.S.C. § 507(a)(8).

☐ Other - Specify applicable paragraph of 11 U.S.C. § 507(a)(____).

**Amounts are subject to adjustment on 4/1/07 and every 3 years thereafter with respect to cases commenced on or after the date of adjustment.*

8. Credits: The amount of all payments on this claim has been credited and deducted for the purpose of making this proof of claim.

9. Supporting Documents: *Attach copies of supporting documents,* such as promissory notes, purchase orders, invoices, itemized statements of running accounts, contracts, court judgments, mortgages, security agreements, and evidence of perfection of lien. DO NOT SEND ORIGINAL DOCUMENTS. If the documents are not available, explain. If the documents are voluminous, attach a summary.

10. Date-Stamped Copy: To receive an acknowledgment of the filing of your claim, enclose a stamped, self-addressed envelope and copy of this proof of claim

THIS SPACE IS FOR COURT USE ONLY

Date	Sign and print the name and title, if any, of the creditor or other person authorized to file this claim (attach copy of power of attorney, if any):

Penalty for presenting fraudulent claim: Fine of up to $500,000 or imprisonment for up to 5 years, or both. 18 U.S.C. §§ 152 and 3571.

court, a copy transmitted to the United States trustee, and the filing fee paid. The Federal Rules of Civil Procedure apply to the process for resolving the dispute, except as altered to meet the necessities of bankruptcy practice. See Fed. R. Bank. P. 7002–7087.

If an issue is raised by motion, the motion is filed with the bankruptcy court and a copy is transmitted to the United States trustee. No filing fee is paid. A motion results in a decision that is a judgment. That judgment is final for that particular issue, unless appealed.

The formalities of the adversary proceeding process and the time required to serve pleadings run counter to an expedited schedule. The motion practice, on the other hand, is better suited to an expedited schedule because it gives the bankruptcy court flexibility to fix hearing dates and other deadlines that are tailored to the case.

In bankruptcy practice, some judges allow a party to raise a disputed matter by motion, even though it should have been by complaint, if no one objects. If an objection is raised, the judge may require the disputed matter to be tried as an adversary proceeding. If a procedure for resolving a dispute should have been by complaint but was raised by motion and if the procedure was not challenged, the challenge to the procedure has been waived.

Whether an issue must be raised by motion or by complaint is governed by Federal Rules of Bankruptcy Procedure 9014 and 7001. Rule 7001 delineates those proceedings that must be brought under Part VII by a complaint and therefore are adversary proceedings:

(1) a proceeding to recover money or property, other than a proceeding to compel the debtor to deliver property to the trustee, or a proceeding under § 554(b) or § 725 of the Code, Rule 2017, or Rule 6002;
(2) a proceeding to determine the validity, priority, or extent of a lien or other interest in property, other than a proceeding under Rule 4003(d);
(3) a proceeding to obtain approval under § 363(h) for the sale of both the interest of the estate and of a co-owner in property;
(4) a proceeding to object to or revoke a discharge;
(5) . . . ;
(6) a proceeding to determine the dischargeability of a debt;
(7) a proceeding to obtain an injunction or other equitable relief, . . .
(8) a proceeding to subordinate any allowed claim or interest, except . . . ;
(9) a proceeding to obtain a declaratory judgment relating to any of the foregoing; or
(10) a proceeding to determine a claim or cause of action removed pursuant to 28 U.S.C. § 1452.

If a proceeding is not listed in Rule 7001, then it is raised by motion. Rule 9014, titled "Contested Matters," begins by stating:

(a) Motion. In a contested matter in a case under the Code not otherwise governed by these rules, relief shall be requested by motion. . . .

EXAMPLE

Title 11 U.S.C.A. § 522(f) states those instances in which the debtor may avoid a lien on his or her property to the extent that the lien impairs an exemption to which the debtor would have been entitled. This section of the Code does not state whether the debtor must seek to avoid the lien by filing a complaint or by filing a motion. Federal Rules of Bankruptcy Procedure 4003(d), however, states that the debtor's proceeding to avoid the lien is by motion in accordance with Rule 9014.

EXAMPLE

The Code does not state whether relief from the automatic stay is by motion or by complaint.

(d) *On request of a party in interest* and after notice and a hearing, the court shall grant relief from the stay provided under subsection (a) of this section, such as by terminating, annulling, modifying, or conditioning such stay—
  (1) for cause, including the lack of adequate protection of an interest in property of such party in interest;
  (2) with respect to a stay of an act against property under subsection (a) of this section, if—
    (A) the debtor does not have an equity in such property; . . . .
  (3) . . . .

11 U.S.C.A. § 362(d). (*Emphasis added.*)

Rule 4001(a), however, provides that a request for relief from an automatic stay must be made in accordance with Rule 9014, the rule authorizing motions. Therefore, requests for relief from an automatic stay do not commence with an adversary proceeding but rather with a motion.

A. MOTIONS

Motions may be made by the debtor, by a party in interest, by the United States trustee, and by the court.

1. Motions by the Debtor

The Chapter 7 debtor may move to convert the case to Chapter 11, 12, or 13, to dismiss the case, to change venue, or to avoid a judicial lien.

a. Motion to Convert to a Chapter 11, 12, or 13 Although a debtor who has filed a Chapter 7 case is authorized by the Code to convert the case to a Chapter 11, 12, or 13, the debtor rarely exercises this right. 11 U.S.C.A. § 706(a). In some jurisdictions, the debtor may convert a Chapter 7 case by notice, while in others a motion is required.

The filing of a Chapter 7 petition creates the estate and begins the process of liquidation, which depletes the assets that would be used in the Chapter 11, 12, or 13 plan. If the debtor changes his or her mind for some reason and decides to convert to another chapter, the conversion would have to take place before essential assets are liquidated to enable the debtor to prepare a viable plan.

The debtor may not convert a Chapter 7 case if the case has already been converted to a liquidation proceeding from Chapter 11, 12, or 13. 11 U.S.C.A. § 706(a). Also, the debtor may not waive the right to convert. An attempted waiver would be unenforceable. 11 U.S.C.A. § 706(a). See Exhibit 5–26 for a sample motion to convert the case.

b. Motion to Dismiss the Case Although the Bankruptcy Code does not state that a Chapter 7 debtor may move to dismiss the case, the debtor is required to file a list of all creditors' names and addresses within a time fixed by the court, unless a list was previously filed. Notice is sent by the office of the bankruptcy court clerk to all creditors and a hearing on the issue of dismissal is held. See Fed. R. Bank. P. 2002(a). The judge's decision whether to dismiss will be based on the best interest of the estate. The debtor does not have an automatic right to dismiss. See Exhibit 5–27 for a sample motion to dismiss the case.

EXAMPLE

On March 15, Sharon Sanders filed a petition in bankruptcy under Chapter 7. On April 1, she discovered that she would receive a $5,000 refund from the IRS as an overpayment on her last year's taxes. She also discovered that because she has filed a petition in bankruptcy, her tax refund will become property of the estate. Sanders may decide to file a motion to dismiss her case to retain the IRS refund.

PROBLEM 5.45 On July 1, Henry Hunter filed a petition in bankruptcy under Chapter 7. Shortly after filing, Hunter discovered that the security interest on his new Rolls Royce was unperfected by First Bank and that the exemption he could claim for the Rolls was limited to $2,950. Hunter had thought the security interest on the Rolls was perfected by First Bank and that he could enter a reaffirmation agreement with First Bank and thus retain the Rolls.

Hunter does not want to part with his Rolls. What should he do and why?

c. Motion for a Change of Venue The United States district courts "have original and exclusive jurisdiction of all cases under title 11." 28 U.S.C.A. § 1334(a). This jurisdictional grant is then passed on to the bankruptcy court. "Each district court may provide that any or all cases under title 11 and any or all proceedings arising under title 11 or arising in or related to a case under title 11 shall be referred to the bankruptcy judges

EXHIBIT 5–26 Debtor's Motion to Convert from Chapter 7 to Chapter 11, 12, or 13

UNITED STATES BANKRUPTCY COURT
____________________ DISTRICT OF ____________________

In re ________________________,
Debtor

Case No. ________________
Chapter 7

DEBTOR'S MOTION TO CONVERT FROM CHAPTER 7
TO CHAPTER 11, 12, or 13

______________________, debtor, moves the court:

1.

Debtor filed a petition under Chapter 7 of the Bankruptcy Code on ______________, 20 ____ .

2.

Debtor is eligible for relief under Chapter ____ of the Bankruptcy Code, having not previously converted this case from a case filed under Chapter 11, 12, or 13 of the Bankruptcy Code.

3.

Debtor moves the court to convert the Chapter 7 case to a case under Chapter ____ .

4.

A copy of debtor's proposed plan:
[ ] is attached; or
[ ] will be filed pursuant to Chapter ____ of the Bankruptcy Code.

WHEREFORE, debtor prays for an order for relief under Chapter ____ of the Bankruptcy Code.

Dated: __________________, 20____ ____________________
Attorney for the Debtor

for the district." 28 U.S.C.A. § 157(a). When a court has jurisdiction, it has the power to decide a case. Therefore, all United States bankruptcy courts have jurisdiction over all bankruptcy cases.

Venue is the location at which a particular case or issue in a particular case will be heard and decided. More than one United States bankruptcy court may have venue to hear a case or issue. 28 U.S.C.A. § 1408.

> Except as provided in section 1410 of this title, a case under title 11 may be commenced in the district court for the district—
>
> (1) in which the domicile, residence, principal place of business in the United States, or principal assets in the United States, of the person or entity that is the subject of such case have been located for the one hundred and eighty days immediately preceding such commencement, or for a longer portion of such one-hundred-and-eighty-day period than the domicile, residence, or principal place of business, in the United States, or principal assets in the United States, of such person were located in any other district . . . . 28 U.S.C.A. § 1408(1).

Exhibit 5–28 illustrates 28 U.S.C.A. § 1408(1).

EXHIBIT 5–27 Debtor's Motion to Dismiss the Bankruptcy Case

UNITED STATES BANKRUPTCY COURT
_______________ DISTRICT OF _______________

In re _______________,
Debtor

Case No. _______________
Chapter 7

DEBTOR'S MOTION TO DISMISS THE BANKRUPTCY CASE

_______________, debtor, moves the court:

1.

Debtor filed a petition under Chapter 7 of the Bankruptcy Code on _______________, 20 _____ .

2.

Debtor moves the court to dismiss this case.

3.

Debtor feels that he/she can resolve his/her financial affairs with creditors without the aid of proceedings under the Bankruptcy Code and that the best interests of debtor and his/her creditors are served by dismissal of this case.

WHEREFORE, debtor prays for an order dismissing this case.

Dated: _______________, 20_____ _______________
Attorney for the Debtor

EXAMPLE

For the 180 days immediately preceding the filing of a Chapter 7 petition in bankruptcy, the debtor's domicile was in the Eastern District of Tennessee, although her principal place of business was in the Middle District of Tennessee. The debtor has the option to file her Chapter 7 petition in either the Eastern or the Middle District.

PROBLEM 5.46 For the 180 days immediately preceding the filing of a Chapter 7 petition in bankruptcy, the debtor moved twice. She resided in the Eastern District of Tennessee for the first 80 days, in the Middle District of Tennessee for the next 55 days, and in the Western District of Tennessee for the final 45 days. During this time, the debtor's principal place of business was in the Eastern District of Tennessee for the first 80 days and in the Western District of Tennessee for the last 100 days.

Which district would have venue?

EXHIBIT 5–28 Establishing Venue for a Bankruptcy Case

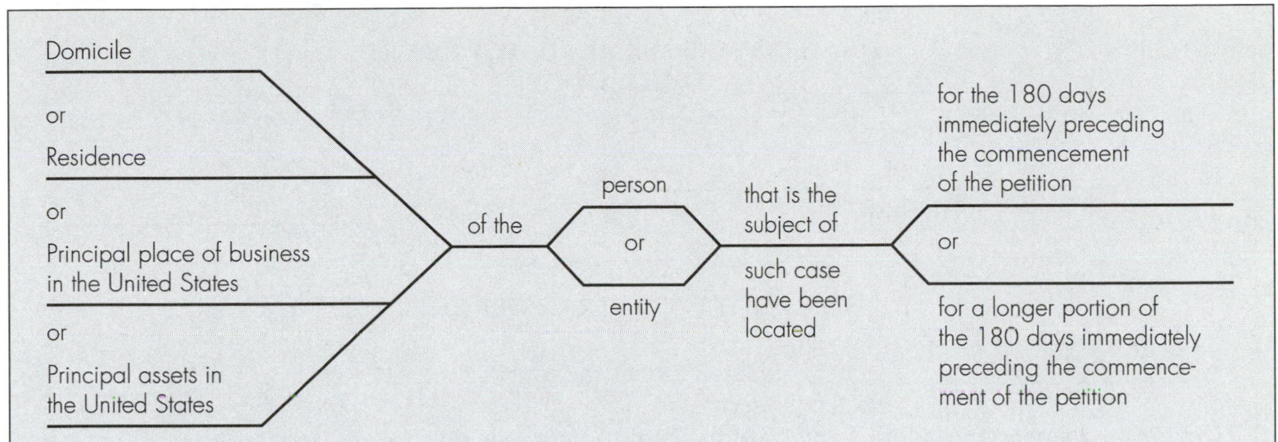

Could more than one district have venue?

A debtor may move to have the court transfer the case to another district if the transfer is "in the interest of justice or for the convenience of the parties." 28 U.S.C.A. § 1412. In a bankruptcy case, the proximity of the debtor, the creditors, and witnesses to the court; the location of assets; and the economic and efficient administration of the case are factors. See *In re Porter,* 276 B.R. 32 (Bankr. D. Mass. 2002). See Exhibit 5–29 for a sample motion to change venue.

PROBLEM 5.47 The debtor lived in the Eastern District of New York up until six months before she filed a petition in bankruptcy. When she left the Eastern District of New York for the District of Kansas, she left most of her assets in the Eastern District of New York. Two weeks after filing her petition in bankruptcy under Chapter 7 in the District of Kansas, the debtor was transferred back to the Eastern District of New York.

Should the debtor's case be transferred to the Eastern District of New York?

In addition to venue of the entire bankruptcy case, individual items of litigation are subject to venue. Contrast 28 U.S.C.A. § 1408 with 28 U.S.C.A. § 1409. The debtor may move to change venue of an individual item of litigation. 28 U.S.C.A. § 1412.

d. Motion to Enforce the Automatic Stay The automatic stay, although broad and inclusive, does not operate to stay a number of activities enumerated in 11 U.S.C.A. § 362(b). Parties in interest involved in an activity under 11 U.S.C.A. § 362(b) may move to modify the stay to clarify their rights. In practice, however, the parties in interest usually continue their activities, and it is the debtor who moves to enforce the stay. If the debtor moves to enforce the stay, the bankruptcy court must determine whether the party in interest's activity is within the exceptions of § 362(b).

EXAMPLE

On June 1, Oscar Moorehead purchased a TV from Pappy's Appliances and paid by check. On June 7, the check was dishonored by Moorehead's bank and returned to Pappy's Appliances for lack of sufficient funds. On June 12, Moorehead filed a petition in bankruptcy under Chapter 7. On June 15, Pappy's telephoned the county district attorney to file a complaint concerning the hot check.

On June 20, the district attorney filed charges on the hot check. Moorehead filed a motion in the bankruptcy court to stay the criminal proceedings in state court.

Most bankruptcy courts will not enjoin the county district attorney from prosecuting the debtor because the automatic stay does not operate to stay the commencement of a criminal action against the debtor. 11 U.S.C.A. § 362(b)(1).

EXHIBIT 5–29 Debtor's Motion to Transfer the Bankruptcy Case

UNITED STATES BANKRUPTCY COURT
______________ DISTRICT OF ______________

In re ______________________,
Debtor

Case No. ______________
Chapter 7

DEBTOR'S MOTION TO TRANSFER THE CASE

______________________, debtor, moves the court:

1.

Debtor filed a petition under Chapter 7 of the Bankruptcy Code on ______________, 20 ____.

2.

Debtor moves the court to transfer the case to the United States Bankruptcy Court for the __________ District of ______________.

3.

Debtor no longer has his/her residence or domicile in this district and the debtor has a substantial amount of his/her assets in the ______________ District of ______________.

WHEREFORE, debtor prays for an order transferring this case.

Dated: ______________, 20____ ______________________
Attorney for the Debtor

EXAMPLE

Assume the same facts as in the previous example except that on June 20 the district attorney wrote Moorehead the following letter: "If you do not pay this bad check within seven days, we will prosecute you." At the time of writing the letter, the district attorney knew that Moorehead had filed for bankruptcy. Moorehead did not respond to the letter, and the district attorney filed charges on the hot check. Moorehead filed a motion in the bankruptcy court to stay the criminal proceedings in state court.

Many bankruptcy courts will enjoin the county district attorney from prosecuting the debtor on the ground that the prosecution is being used as a collection device and not in a good faith effort to enforce the criminal laws. 11 U.S.C.A. § 362(b)(1).

e. Motion to Avoid a Judicial Lien Where a judgment lien impairs an exemption to which the debtor would otherwise be entitled, the debtor may move to avoid the judicial lien. 11 U.S.C.A. § 522(f).

EXAMPLE

Lisa MacDougal purchased an automobile from Friendly Motors for $20,000 and financed the sale with a loan for the full purchase price from People's Bank at 6 percent per annum. After making several payments, Lisa defaulted on her loan obligation and People's Bank reposed the automobile. The bank then sold the automobile in a commercially reasonable sale for $14,000. After subtracting the amount recovered from the sale and the administrative expenses from the outstanding balance of the loan, Lisa still owed the Bank $2,000. The Bank then sued Lisa on the deficiency and recovered a judgment. The Bank then filed a statement of judgment with the clerk of the county court and had a lien attached to Lisa's home.

Shortly thereafter, Lisa filed for bankruptcy under Chapter 7. She then moved to avoid the Bank's judicial lien that was attached to her homestead.

Since Lisa's homestead was exempt property under the exemptions laws of her state (Lisa's state had opted out of the federal bankruptcy exemptions), she could avoid the Bank's lien, thus reducing it to an unsecured claim.

A motion to avoid a judicial lien is shown in Exhibit 5–30.

EXHIBIT 5–30 Motion to Avoid a Judicial Lien

IN THE UNITED STATES BANKRUPTCY COURT

FOR THE ________________ DISTRICT OF _____________

IN RE:)
)
___________________________) Case No. _______________
SS# ***-**-****) Chapter 7
)
Debtor.)

MOTION OF _______________ TO AVOID JUDICIAL LIEN,
AND NOTICE OF OPPORTUNITY FOR HEARING

______________, for this Motion to Avoid Judicial Lien, and Notice of Opportunity for Hearing, states as follows:

1. _______________________ (the "Debtor") filed her Voluntary Petition For Relief under Chapter 7 of the United States Bankruptcy Code on ______________________.

2. This Court has jurisdiction over the parties and subject of this core proceeding pursuant to 28 U.S.C. SS 1334 and 157(b)(2)(K).

3. Included among the assets of the Debtor is the following-described property located in __________ County, ________________, claimed as exempt by the Debtor pursuant to _____________:

(continued)

An undivided half interest in the South forty (40) acres of the East Half of the Southeast Quarter (E/2 SE/4) of Section 30, Township 18 North, Range 15 East of the ______________________________

the "Subject Property." No objection to the exemption was timely filed. Therefore, the exemption is deemed allowed. 11 U.S.C.A. § 522(1).

4. On ________________________ the District Court of ______________ County, in Case No. ______________, entered judgment against ______________________ in favor of ________________________ in the amount of $________________. A Statement of Judgment was filed with the County Clerk of ______________ County, ________________, on ________________, in Book __, beginning at Page __. Pursuant to ________________, the judgment attached as a lien on the Subject Property.

5. The judgment lien impairs an exemption to which the Debtor would otherwise be entitled. Therefore, pursuant to 11 U.S.C.A. § 522(f)(1), the judgment lien is voidable.

Your rights may be affected. You should read this document carefully and consult your attorney about your rights and the effect of this document. If you do not want the Court to grant the requested relief, or if you wish to have your views considered, your must file a written response or objection to the requested relief, with the Clerk of the United States Bankruptcy Court for the ______________ District of ______________, ____ no

(continued)

later than fifteen (15) days from the date of filing of this request for relief. You should also mail a file-stamped copy of your response or objection to the undersigned movant's attorney [and others who are required to be served] and file a certificate of service with the Court. If no response or objection is timely filed, the Court may grant the requested relief without a hearing or further notice. The fifteen (15) day period includes the three (3) days allowed for mailing provided for in Rule 9006(f) Fed. R. Bankr. Proc.

THEREFORE, ________________ prays, in the absence of an objection or after a hearing on any objection, that the judgment lien of _________________________ be avoided.

DATED at __________________, this ____ day of ______________________.

Respectfully submitted,

____
Attorney for the debtor

CERTIFICATE OF SERVICE

I do hereby certify that on _______ day of ________________, a true, correct and exact copy of the above and foregoing document was served by placing same in the United States Mail, with proper postage thereon duly prepaid, addressed as follows:

____
Attorney for the debtor

2. Motions by a Party in Interest

A party in interest may move for relief from the automatic stay, to dismiss the case, for abstention by the court, to change venue, for disallowance of a claim, or for an examination of any entity.

a. Motion for Relief from the Automatic Stay The filing of a petition brings into effect an "order for relief" and invokes the automatic stay. 11 U.S.C.A. § 362(a). This, of course, gives complete and immediate protection to the debtor from the acts affected by the automatic stay, such as the collection of prebankruptcy debt and the dismemberment of the estate by a party in interest.

Upon the filing of the case, the debtor will not discontinue the use of property, and much of the property of the debtor that becomes a part of the debtor's estate will represent collateral secured by one or more secured creditors. This property may be of substantial value, depreciating with use, and subject to possible loss or damage incurred in the use.

Even if the property is subject to the automatic stay under 11 U.S.C.A. § 362(a), a party in interest may still repossess or foreclose. A party in interest must, however, move for a modification of the stay.

> (d) On request of a party in interest and after notice and a hearing, the court shall grant relief from the stay . . . such as by terminating, annulling, modifying, or conditioning such stay—
>
> (1) for cause, including the lack of adequate protection of an interest in property of such party in interest. . . . 11 U.S.C.A. § 362(d)(1).

Much bankruptcy litigation involves a party in interest's motion to modify the automatic stay.

In *In re Cooper,* Tidewater Finance, a secured debtor, moved for relief from the stay so it could repossess the Chapter 7 debtors' 1999 Chevrolet Cavalier. Tidewater Finance argued that the debtors have failed to adequately protect Tidewater's interest in the vehicle.

In re Cooper

296 B.R. 410
(Bankr. E.D. VA 2002)

MEMORANDUM OPINION
DOUGLAS O. TICE, Jr., Chief Judge.

Preliminary hearing was held February 27, 2002, on Tidewater Finance Company's motion to terminate automatic stay pursuant to 11 U.S.C.A § 362(d)(1). At conclusion of hearing, the court took the matter under advisement requesting that counsel for both plaintiff and defendants file briefs to support their position. Both sides filed their briefs on March 15, 2002. For the reasons stated herein, plaintiff's motion to terminate automatic stay is denied.

PROCEDURAL HISTORY

Debtors filed this chapter 7 bankruptcy petition on December 17, 2001. On February 6, 2002, Tidewater filed a motion to terminate automatic stay of 11 U.S.C.A. § 362(a) requesting permission to enforce its rights under a security interest in a 1999 Chevrolet Cavalier. Tidewater seeks relief pursuant to 11 U.S.C.A. § 362(d)(1), arguing that debtors have failed to adequately protect Tidewater's interest in the vehicle because: 1) debtors were in payment default under the contract on the filing date, 2) debtors remain in payment default under the contract, 3) the vehicle is depreciating, and 4) debtors have neither surrendered the vehicle to Tidewater, redeemed Tidewater's interest in the vehicle, nor reaffirmed the obligations under the contract.

On February 12, 2002, debtors filed a response, asserting that they are behind in payments by one month; however, they made a payment of $408.00 and intend to become current.

FINDINGS OF FACT

On October 31, 1998, debtors executed a simple interest motor vehicle contract and security agreement with Patrick Chevrolet, Inc.[1] Patrick Chevrolet assigned the contract to Tidewater.

Under the terms of the contract, the installments were due on the fifteenth day of each month beginning on December 15, 1998, with a seven day grace period. On the day of debtors' filing, December 17, 2001, debtors had not yet made their December 15, 2001, payment to Tidewater.[2] [As of the date of the instant preliminary hearing, debtors were current in their payments under the contract and the vehicle was covered by an insurance policy.]

Debtors filed their Statement of Intention under 11 U.S.C.A. § 521(2) of the United States Bankruptcy Code in which they indicate that their intention is to retain their 1999 Chevrolet Cavalier without reaffirming their debt under the contract or redeeming the vehicle under 11 U.S.C.A. § 722.

CONCLUSIONS OF LAW

In its motion filed on February 6, 2002, Tidewater asserts that it is entitled to relief from stay pursuant to 11 U.S.C.A, § 362(d)(1)[3] because 1) debtors have failed to adequately protect Tidewater's interest in the vehicle, and 2) debtors did not comply with 11 U.S.C.A. § 521(2)[4] because they did not surrender the vehicle, redeem the interest, or reaffirm the obligations.

There is a split among the Circuits regarding the correct interpretation of § 521(2). Some circuits have held that a debtor who desires to retain exempt or abandoned property has only two choices: redemption or reaffirmation. See, e.g., In re Johnson, 89 F.3d 249 (5th Cir.1996), In re Taylor, 3 F.3d 1512 (11th Cir.1993), In re Edwards, 901 F.2d 1383 (7th Cir.1990). Most courts have determined that relief from automatic stay should be denied and that creditors could not compel debtors to redeem the collateral or reaffirm the debt as long as debtors are current in their payments. Capital Comms. Fed. Credit Union v. Boodrow (In re Boodrow), 126 F.3d 43, 52-53 (2d Cir.1997); In re Belanger, 962 F.2d 345, 348–49 (4th Cir.1992); Lowry Fed. Credit Union v. West, 882 F.2d 1543, 1547 (10th Cir.1989); Sears Roebuck & Co. v. Lamirande, 199 B.R. 221, 224 (D.Mass.1996); In re Crouch, 104 B.R. 770, 772–73 (Bankr.S.D.W.Va.1989).

The Fourth Circuit, following the majority view, has decided that a debtor who is not in default can retain collateral after discharge without reaffirming, redeeming, or surrendering the collateral. In re Belanger, 962 F.2d at 346. The court determined that § 521(2)(A) is a procedural provision merely to inform the lien creditor of debtor's intention. Id. at 347. The court in Belanger did not specify from which date debtor's default is to be measured—filing date, date of creditor's motion, hearing date, or simply default at any time.

A creditor can obtain relief under § 362(d) for "cause."[5] Cause is not defined in the Code and a bankruptcy court has broad discretion to lift the stay in "appropriate circumstances." In re Holtkamp, 669 F.2d 505, 508 (7th Cir.1982). Usually, there must be a showing that continuation of the stay will cause some affirmative harm to the secured creditor. This burden is on the creditor, and the court "should deny relief from stay if the movant 'fails to make an initial showing of cause.' " In re Boodrow, 126 F.3d at 48 (2d Cir.1997) (quoting In re Sonnax Indus. Inc., 907 F.2d 1280, 1285 (2d Cir.1990)).

The court must exercise its discretion in determining whether to allow a debtor to retain collateral and keep making payments "by considering the debtor's 'previous payment record, a comparison of the value of the collateral and the amount of debt, and other relevant facts.' " Id. at 52 (quoting Capital Communications Federal Credit Union v. Boodrow, 197 B.R. 409, 412 (N.D.N.Y.1996)).

The United States District Court for the Western District of Virginia has determined that a defaulted debtor should be treated differently and that a debtor who defaults after filing does not have the option to retain the collateral, and must choose among the § 521(2)(A) options of surrender, redeem, or reaffirm. Am. Nat'l. Bank & Trust Co. v. DeJournette (In re DeJournette), 222 B.R. 86, 95 (W.D.Va.1998).[6] The court found that "where a debtor defaults after filing for bankruptcy the creditor's right to step in and repossess the collateral trumps any right of the debtor to retain the property under the terms of the original contract." Id. Similarly in Boodrow, the United States Court of Appeals for the Second Circuit determined that only non-defaulting debtors qualify for reinstatement. See In re Boodrow, 126 F.3d at 49 n. 6.

The situation in DeJournette can be distinguished from the case at hand. In DeJournette, debtors were delinquent at the date of filing their bankruptcy petition. As of the date of the hearing, the DeJournette debtors had paid payments to bring them current on their loan; however, debtors did not pay the late charges or legal fees and costs associated with their prior arrearage.

In this case, debtors were not in default when they filed their chapter 7 petition because they were within the contractual grace period, nor were they in default on February 27, the date of the preliminary hearing on relief from stay. While there was a time in between debtors' bankruptcy filing and the date of the hearing where debtors fell behind in their payments, they were current as of the hearing date.

Tidewater has failed to demonstrate any real harm or risk of financial loss resulting from continuation of the stay. Debtors are current in their monthly payments and have adequate insurance on the vehicle. Thus, allowing debtors to remain in possession of the vehicle in exchange for payment of the monthly installments places the parties in the same positions as they were in prior to debtors' filing.

Further, if debtors fail to remit their monthly payments, Tidewater can elect to repossess the vehicle. Because debtors were not in default at the time they filed their petition or at the date of relief from stay hearing, debtors are entitled to retain the collateral and continue to make payments pursuant to their contract. Tidewater's argument that it is not adequately protected is without merit.

A separate order consistent with this memorandum opinion will be entered.

---

[1]Under the contract, debtors purchased a 1999 Chevrolet Cavalier for $15,331.00 and a service contract for $900.00. Debtors financed $15,388.21 with interest at a rate of 18.5% per annum.

[2]Tidewater received its December installment on January 14, 2002, its January installment on February 12, 2002, and the February installment on February 25, 2002.

[3]Section 362(d)(1) states that relief shall be granted "for cause, including lack of adequate protection of an interest in property of such party in interest." 11 U.S.C.A. § 362(d)(1) (2002).

[4]The pertinent portions of § 521(2) provide that:

(2) If an individual debtor's schedule of assets and liabilities includes consumer debts which are secured by property of the estate

(A) within thirty days after the date of the filing of a petition under chapter 7 of this title or on or before the date of the meeting of creditors, whichever is earlier, or within such additional time as the court, for cause, within such period fixes, the debtor shall file with the clerk a statement of his intention with respect to the retention or surrender of such property and, if applicable, specifying that such property is claimed as exempt, that the debtor intends to redeem such property, or that the debtor intends to reaffirm debts secured by such property.

(B) within forty-five days after the filing of a notice of intent under this section, or within such additional time as the court, for cause, within such forty-five day period fixes, the debtor shall perform his intention with respect to such property, as specified by subparagraph (a) of this paragraph; . . . 11 U.S.C.A. §§ 521(2)(A), (B) (2002).

[5]The section provides, in part: "the court shall grant relief from the stay . . . (1) for cause." 11 U.S.C.A. § 362(d)(1) (2002).

[6]The court in DeJournette expressly disagreed with the Bankruptcy Court for the Western District of Virginia which held in First N. Am. Nat'l. Bank v. Doss that a debtor in default at the time of filing his or her petition could choose under § 521(2)(A) to retain the collateral, without redeeming or reaffirming. First N. Am. Nat'l. Bank v. Doss (In re Doss), 203 B.R. 57, 59 (Bankr.W.D.Va.1996). "the DeJournette court found this ruling too harsh for the creditor as the creditor would stand to lose the arrearages as the collateral depreciates, unless the debtor surrenders the property, reaffirms the obligation, or redeems the debt, and that the most appropriate remedy would be to permit modification of automatic stay. . . ." Am. Nat'l. Bank & Trust Co. v. DeJournette (In re DeJournette), 222 B.R. at 97.

The modification of the stay with respect to one act by a party in interest or item of property of the estate will not affect the applicability of the stay to other acts or other items of property.

When a party in interest files a motion to modify the stay, the Code mandates that the hearing be on an accelerated calendar. 11 U.S.C.A. § 362(e). The bankruptcy court has the power to grant a modification of the stay on the request of a party in interest without a hearing if necessary to prevent irreparable damage to that party's interest in the property. Such a modification of the stay will only be granted if the party's interest will suffer irreparable damage before there is an opportunity for notice and a hearing under 11 U.S.C.A. §§ 362(d) or (e). 11 U.S.C.A. § 362(f).

In any hearing concerning relief from the stay, the party requesting the relief has the burden of proof on the issue of the debtor's equity in property and the party opposing the relief has the burden of proof on all other issues. 11 U.S.C.A. § 362(g).

EXAMPLE

Mark Buffington, the owner of commercial real estate, financed his purchase of the real estate with Grand Avenue Bank. The real estate mortgage was substantial in light of the value of the real estate. Shortly after purchasing the property, Buffington defaulted on his mortgage payments and filed for bankruptcy under Chapter 7. Because the commercial real estate was property of the estate, it was subject to the automatic stay.

Grand Avenue Bank filed a motion to modify the stay so it could foreclose on the property and sell it. Grand Avenue Bank claimed that there was no equity in the property because the mortgage was larger than the value of the property.

In the hearing on the motion to modify the stay, Grand Avenue Bank, the party making the motion to modify the stay, has the burden of proof on the issue of the debtor's equity in the property. Therefore, the bank will be required to demonstrate the value of the property.

If the court determines that the property is worth more than the debt (so there is equity) and the property is not exempt, the court will deny the bank's motion and thus allow the trustee to sell the property, pay the bank (the mortgagee), and retain the equity for the bankruptcy estate. The equity will be deemed to be adequate protection even without mortgage payments being made.

Buffington's trustee, the party opposing the bank's motion, has the burden of proof on all other issues.

The parties may agree that the stay is not enforceable or will not be enforced with respect to certain property. The parties can also agree that certain conditions are required for the stay to remain in effect. Very often these agreements are strictly informal, without a writing. See Exhibit 5–31 for a sample motion for relief from the automatic stay.

b. Motion to Dismiss the Case The case may also be dismissed for cause, including unreasonable delay by the debtor that is prejudicial to creditors. 11 U.S.C.A. § 707(a)(1). All creditors, however, must be given notice as provided in Rule 2002(a). Fed. R. Bank. P. 1017(a). See Exhibit 5–32 for a sample motion to dismiss the case.

c. Motion for Abstention by the Court A party in interest may move for abstention by the court. The abstention may be from hearing the case or from hearing an issue. The motion to abstain may be necessary because another tribunal may be better suited to try the matter or because another solution to the debtor's financial problems may be possible and even preferable. Abstention is mandatory in some situations and permissive in others. 28 U.S.C.A. § 1334(c); 11 U.S.C.A. § 305.

d. Motion for a Change of Venue A party in interest may move for a change in venue of either the entire case or an issue in the case. After notice, a hearing will be conducted on whether the transfer is in the interest of justice or for the convenience of the parties. Compare 28 U.S.C.A. § 1412 with Fed. R. Bank. P. 1014(a)(1).

EXAMPLE

Carrie Yamauchi was a resident of Hawaii when she incurred a significant amount of debt. Carrie then moved from Hawaii to California, taking her exempt assets with her. She left her nonexempt assets in Hawaii. After living in California for several months, Carrie filed for bankruptcy under Chapter 7 in the United States Bankruptcy Court for the Southern District of California.

Upon receiving notice of Carrie's bankruptcy petition, First Bank of Hawaii filed a motion for a change of venue requesting the case be transferred to the United States Bankruptcy Court of Hawaii. Hawaii, of course, was where the debtor incurred the debt and where the debtor's nonexempt assets are located.

The bankruptcy court will grant First Bank's motion on the ground that since the administrative work with the estate will be in Hawaii, the trustee in Hawaii, rather than a trustee in California, will have an easier time administering the assets.

e. Motion for Disallowance of a Claim A proof of claim is deemed allowed unless there is an objection by a party in interest. 11 U.S.C.A. § 502(a). The Code prescribes nine grounds on which a claim may be disallowed. 11 U.S.C.A. § 502(b). If the objection involves the determination of the validity, priority, or extent of a lien or other interest in property, a complaint rather than a motion must be used. Fed. R. Bank. P. 7001.

f. Motion for Examination of Any Entity A party in interest may move for the examination of any entity. Fed. R. Bank. P. 2004. Attendance of a witness and production of documentary evidence may be compelled. Fed R. Bank. P. 9016. The examination may take place in the district in which the case is pending or in another district. An entity other than the debtor will receive mileage and a witness fee, of which payment for one day

EXHIBIT 5–31 Party in Interest's Motion for Relief from the Automatic Stay

UNITED STATES BANKRUPTCY COURT
____________________ DISTRICT OF ____________________

In re ______________________________ ,
Debtor

Case No. __________________
Chapter 7

MOTION FOR RELIEF FROM AUTOMATIC STAY AND NOTICE OF INTENT TO SEEK ABANDONMENT OF PROPERTY, OR ALTERNATIVELY SEEKING ADEQUATE PROTECTION AND RELIEF IN SUPPORT THEREOF

COMES NOW, __________________________ , [hereinafter referred to as movant] pursuant to 11 U.S.C.A. §§ 361, 362, and 554, and moves the court to grant it relief from the automatic stay and order abandonment of ______________________ [describe the collateral], or in the alternative, to require debtor to provide adequate protection of movant's interest in the collateral.

In support of its motion, movant alleges:

1.

That the maker, for consideration, issued to payee a promissory note which is attached, marked Exhibit A, and made a part of this motion.

2.

As a part of the same transaction, and to secure the payment of the note and the indebtedness represented by the note, the maker created a real estate mortgage in the following real estate in which he/she was the owner:

[description of the real estate]

A copy of the mortgage, marked Exhibit B, is attached and made a part of this motion.

3.

Movant is the current owner and holder of the note and mortgage.

4.

The note and mortgage are in default. After allowing all just credits, movant has due on the note and mortgage the sum of $ _________ , with _____ percent interest per annum from ____________________ , until paid; and the further sum of $ _________ for attorney fees.

5.

The mortgage is a valid first lien against the mortgaged property, prior and superior to any right, title, lien, estate, or interest of the debtor or any other party.

6.

The debtor has no equity in the mortgaged property.

7.

Movant will suffer irreparable injury, loss, and damage unless the automatic stay is terminated so as to permit movant to commence with its foreclosure action or, in the alternative, the debtor shall be required to provide movant with adequate protection of its interest in the mortgaged property.

8.

The mortgaged property is burdensome to the estate or is of inconsequential value to the estate and it is therefore in the best interest of the estate and the debtor that relief from the automatic stay be granted and that the mortgaged property be abandoned so as to permit movant to proceed in state court with an action for foreclosure.

(continued)

EXHIBIT 5–31 Party in Interest's Motion for Relief from the Automatic Stay, Continued

9.

Notice of the motion and a copy of Rules ____________________ of the Local Rules for Bankruptcy Practice and Procedure have been mailed to the trustee, the debtor, and all parties listed on the list of creditors filed by the debtor.

WHEREFORE, movant moves the court for an order vacating or modifying the automatic stay as provided by 11 U.S.C.A. § 362 and directing the trustee to abandon the mortgaged property as authorized by 11 U.S.C.A. § 554 as full satisfaction of the personal liability of debtor and so as to permit movant and other interested parties to enforce their liens against the mortgaged property.

____
Movant

By: ___________________________
Attorney for Movant

CERTIFICATE OF SERVICE

I hereby certify that I mailed a true and correct copy of this motion with postage thereon fully prepaid to: [*name and address of debtor*], [*name and address of debtor's attorney*], [*name and address of trustee*], and to all other creditors who claim an interest in this property, on ____________________, 20 _____ .

____
Attorney for Movant

must be tendered before the witness is required to attend. The debtor will receive mileage only (no witness fee) for attending an examination more than 100 miles from his or her residence for the amount over 100 miles. The scope of the examination is limited to the acts, conduct, property, liabilities, and financial condition of the debtor; to any matter that may affect the administration of the estate; or to the debtor's right to a discharge. Fed. R. Bank. P. 2004(b).

3. Motion by the United States Trustee to Dismiss the Case

The United States trustee may move to dismiss a case for the debtor's failure to file—within 15 days or such additional time as the court may have allowed—the schedules and statement of financial affairs. 11 U.S.C.A. § 707(a)(3).

The United States trustee also may move to dismiss a case filed by an individual debtor under Chapter 7 whose debts are primarily consumer debts. The court, after notice and a hearing, will dismiss the case if it finds that the granting of relief would be a substantial abuse of the provisions of Chapter 7. The presumption, however, is in favor of the debtor for granting the relief that he or she requested. 11 U.S.C.A. § 707(b).

EXHIBIT 5–32 Party in Interest's Motion to Dismiss the Bankruptcy Case

UNITED STATES BANKRUPTCY COURT
_______________ DISTRICT OF _______________

In re ______________________________,
Debtor

Case No. ____________________
Chapter 7

MOTION TO DISMISS THE BANKRUPTCY CASE

__________, moving party, moves the court:

1.

Debtor filed a petition under Chapter 7 of the Bankruptcy Code on ____________________, 20 _____ .

2.

The moving party is a creditor.

3.

The debtor's delay in ________________________ is unreasonable and is prejudicial to the moving party in that ________________________ .

4.

The moving party moves the court to dismiss this case.

WHEREFORE, the moving party prays for an order dismissing this case.

Dated: _______________, 20 _____ ________________________
Attorney for the Moving Party

CERTIFICATE OF SERVICE

I hereby certify that I mailed a true and correct copy of this motion with postage thereon fully prepaid to: [*name and address of debtor*], [*name and address of debtor's attorney*], [*name and address of trustee*], and to all parties in interest, on ______________________, 20 _____ .

____
Attorney for Movant

EXAMPLE

It is readily apparent that the McPhersons have substantial monthly income, after taxes, in excess of their monthly living expenses, particularly if they made a diligent effort to live within their means. Consequently, the paralegal should be mindful that if the McPhersons were to file bankruptcy under Chapter 7, there is a strong likelihood that either the court, on its own motion to show cause why the case should not be dismissed, or the United States trustee, in a motion to dismiss, may seek the dismissal of the case under 11 U.S.C.A. § 707(b) for substantial abuse. The McPhersons are individuals, their debts are primarily consumer debts, and they have sufficient regular disposable income as defined in 11 U.S.C.A. § 1325(b)(2) to fund a Chapter 13 plan. Even though the statute provides that there is a presumption in favor of granting the relief requested by the debtors (a Chapter 7 discharge), and even though any charitable contributions to be made by the McPhersons may not be considered in determining whether the case should be dismissed, their disposable income is large enough to present a potential problem for them. The effect of such a motion would be to cause the McPhersons to voluntarily convert their case to Chapter 13 to avoid the dismissal of the case since a debtor may not be put into Chapter 13 bankruptcy involuntarily.

Because of the vagueness of the statute, it is not surprising that the courts do not apply § 707(b) uniformly. One line of cases holds that a debtor's future ability to pay—having substantial disposable income—can alone constitute substantial abuse. *In re Kelly,* 841 F.2d 908 (9th Cir. 1988). The contrary view is that an ability to pay is just one factor to consider, among a totality of circumstances, in determining whether there is substantial abuse. Other factors include: the circumstances that precipitated the bankruptcy; the debtor's prebankruptcy financial behavior; whether the information filed by the debtors in the bankruptcy is accurate and complete; and whether the debtor's projected budget is reasonable. *In re Green,* 934 F. 2d 568 (4th Cir. 1991).

A paralegal's role in insuring that the debtor's schedules and statement of financial affairs are accurately and fully completed is therefore of critical importance. Although a paralegal cannot change the amount of income earned by the debtor or the circumstances that caused the debtor's financial problems, the paralegal can and should make sure that the expenses in Schedule J are within the limits the court may find acceptable and that the schedules and statements are otherwise accurate. Sloppy work may result in an unwarranted motion to dismiss for substantial abuse.

In re May involves a motion by the U.S. trustee to dismiss the case for substantial abuse of the provisions of Chapter 7 under 11 U.S.C.A. § 707(b). Jerry May was employed as a wastewater treatment plan operator and received some income as a general contractor. The debtor's non-filing spouse was employed by a water resource group. Their Schedules of Current Income and Expenditures indicate their expenses exceed their income. The U.S. Trustee, however, claimed that the debtors actually did have monthly disposable income and that they did have the ability to pay a substantial portion of their creditors.

In re May

261 B.R. 770 (Bankr. M.D. Fla. 2001)

ALEXANDER L. PASKAY, Bankruptcy Judge.

JERRY CURTIS MAY (Debtor) filed his Petition for Relief under Chapter 7 of the Bankruptcy Code on June 26, 2000. Schedule B attached to the Petition stated the total value of his assets as $118,911.82. Among the assets scheduled were a Variable Annuity IRA and a 401K plan valued at $81,414.65. The Debtor's total unsecured obligations per Schedule F total $63,132.79. The Debtor in his Schedule I, the Current Income Statement, indicated he is single and that his current gross income is $3,125.17 per month and with some overtime the total is $3,267.76. According to this Schedule, his total net monthly take home pay is $2,694.87. In his original Schedule of Current Expenses, Schedule J, the Debtor stated his expenses to be $1,787.71 per month. Thus, facially it first appeared that the Debtor has a surplus of income over expenses of $907.16.

On October 23, 2000, the United States Trustee filed a Motion pursuant to 11 U.S.C.A. § 707(b) and sought a dismissal of the Debtor's Chapter 7 case contending that to permit this Debtor to obtain a discharge in Chapter 7 would be a substantial abuse of the system. As noted earlier, the Debtor indicated on his Schedule I that he is single. However, he was in fact married to Beverly Stephenson who did not file a Petition for Relief. His claim of exemption as set forth in Schedule C listed the following items, which the Debtor seeks to immunize from administration:

A. "universal life" insurance policy with a monthly premium of $121.87 and a "variable life" insurance policy with a monthly premium of $121.87. The current market value of these policies combined is $26,145.60.
B. "fixed annuity IRA" with a current market value of $4,598.09.
C. variable annuity IRA with a monthly premium of $75.00 and a 401K plan. The current market value of these policies combined is $81,414.65.

The Schedule of Liabilities filed by the Debtor includes a secured debt owed to Sears in the amount of $3,119.00. However, the Debtor testified that this amount may no longer be owing. The Debtor has 13 general unsecured creditors, all or substantially all credit card debts totaling $63,132.79. The case was noticed as a no-asset case pursuant to Federal Rules of Bankruptcy Procedure 2002(e). However, because the Trustee recovered some assets, a claims bar date was set for December 6, 2000. Prior to the expiration of the bar date, the total unsecured claims filed were $31,863.05.

The Debtor has been and still is employed by Bonita Springs Utilities, Inc., as a wastewater treatment plant operator. In addition to his income from his employment, the Debtor also received some additional income from services he provides as an independent contractor. According to the record, the Debtor's level of income is consistent with the income he received in 1998 and 1999. The returns were filed jointly with his wife, Beverly Stephenson.

The Debtor's non-filing spouse is employed by MP Water Resources Group and had a gross salary in 1999 of $46,434.99. The Debtor's scheduled monthly gross income, as noted earlier, is $3,267.76. The Debtor's Schedule I reflects monthly payroll deductions totaling $572.89 which includes $273.52 for payroll taxes and social security, $28.47 for insurance and $270.90 for his contribution to his 401K plan.

On January 11, 2001, Schedule J was amended in which the expenses increased to $2,705.93. The increase is attributable to an increased listing in housing of $31.46, electricity of $5.00, home repairs of $100.00, his clothing allowance of $50.00, cost of transportation of $60.00 and additional expenses for dental of $112.50, cable of $45.00, car insurance of $67.00, anticipated car payment of $445.18, cell phone of $45.00 and payment to Associates National Bank credit card of $250.00. Therefore, the increase of expenses as reflected by Amendment to Schedule J, along with the net monthly income of $2,694.87 reported on Schedule I resulted in a deficit of $11.06.

At trial, the Debtor introduced a further revised budget in which life insurance increased by $8.00, anticipated car payment increased $4.82, and homeowners insurance of $41.25 was taken out, bringing his total monthly expenses to $2,677.50. Debtor also contended that his net monthly income is actually $2,492.94 based on the figures in the W-2 form provided by Bonita Springs Utilities for 1999 divided by 12. Income of $2,494.94 and expenses of $2,677.50 results in a deficit of $184.56.

If this Court accepts the valuation of the Debtor, he has no disposable income from which he could fund any Chapter 13 Plan; therefore, he is entitled to retain the benefits offered by the Chapter 7 case through the general bankruptcy discharge available pursuant to § 727(a).

Based on the foregoing, it is the contention of the U.S. Trustee that the twice revised budget of the Debtor is substantially overstated without any justification for his expenses, and if one eliminates or reduces certain items such as the excessive amount for transportation, home repairs and car expenses, the expenses should be substantially below what is now claimed. Moreover, that the Debtor continued to pay $270.90 per month into his 401K plan, and contributions to 401K plans are generally rejected as unnecessary and unreasonable to a debtor who seeks relief in bankruptcy court. See, e.g., In re Carlton, 211 B.R. 468 (Bankr.W.D.N.Y.1997) (considering that 401K contributions may be voluntary); In re Bicsak, 207 B.R. 657 (Bankr.W.D.Mo.1997) (including amounts that Chapter 7 debtor had deducted from his income each month for thrift savings plan and for savings account as part of hypothetical Chapter 13 disposable income calculation, for purposes of determining whether case should be dismissed for substantial abuse); In re Roth, 108 B.R. 78 (Bankr.W.D.Pa.1989) (finding $150.00 per month contributions to 401K plan not necessary to fund present needs).

This Debtor has no dependents and while his wife is not a debtor, she has a substantial annual income and no doubt would certainly be able to share in meeting the expenses incurred for the family unit, e.g., general household expenses, including assisting with the rent or mortgage payment. Trustee argues that if the budget were readjusted to expenses of an acceptable level, i.e., reducing the $300.00 allocated for food, $100.00 for recreation and also reducing the life insurance expense to $50.00 per month, then Debtor could fund $49,610.16 over 36 months under a Chapter 13 plan, enough to pay over 70% of all unsecured debts.

In opposing the Motion, counsel for the Debtor contends that the very language of Section 707(b) provides that there shall be a presumption in favor of granting the relief requested by the Debtor and cites In re Attanasio, 218 B.R. 180 (Bankr.N.D.Ala.1998). The Debtor contends that he could not meet his debts as they became due because there are substantial marital debts arising from a previous marriage and his former wife ran up bills to the extent of $30,000 after she herself filed bankruptcy. This $30,000, or half of the total $60,000 in debts were not caused by the Debtor and were not of his own making.

The majority of courts in dealing with this Section looked at the debtor's ability to repay the debts for which a discharge is sought. In re Kelly, 841 F.2d 908, 914 (9th Cir.1988); U.S. Trustee v. Harris, 960 F.2d 74 (8th Cir.1992); Fonder v. United States, 974 F.2d 996 (8th Cir.1992). All of these cases concluded that the Debtor's ability to pay creditors out of future income is sufficient to make the Chapter 7 liquidation case a substantial abuse. However, having income in excess of necessary expenses is not, by itself, sufficient to support a finding of substantial abuse of Chapter 7, and the bankruptcy court should engage in a "totality of the circumstances" analysis in determining whether a discharge would be a substantial abuse of Chapter 7. In re Green, 934 F.2d 568 (4th Cir.1991).

Applying the totality of circumstances, the Courts considered the following factors:

1. Whether the bankruptcy petition was filed because of sudden illness, calamity, disability, or unemployment;
2. Whether the debtor incurred cash advances and made consumer purchases far in excess of his ability to repay;
3. Whether the debtor's proposed family budget is excessive or unreasonable;
4. Whether the debtor's schedules and statement of current income and expenses reasonably and accurately reflect the true financial condition; and
5. Whether the petition was filed in good faith.

In re Green, 934 F.2d at 572.

This Court is satisfied that the ability to repay or fund the Chapter 13 plan is a factor, which must be considered although it is not an exclusive factor.

Debtor's budget first reflected a surplus of $907.16, then a deficit of $11.06 after Trustee's Motion to Dismiss was filed, and lastly it reflected a deficit of $184.56. The multiple revisions of the Debtor's budget that could be charitably described as creative budgeting casts some serious doubt on the Debtor's good faith. The good faith of the Debtor is certainly important and in this particular instance the Debtor's budget was amended twice. The most recent amendment just before trial is clearly indicative that it was done for the purpose of increasing the deficit to establish and to show that the Debtor has no surplus from which he can fund a meaningful Chapter 13 case. See In re Weber, 208 B.R. 575, 577 (Bankr.M.D.Fla.1997) (stating that a "telling sign and a red flag indicating bad faith is an inflated budget, especially an amended budget after the Debtor's right to remain in Chapter 7 is challenged").

Based on the foregoing, this Court is satisfied that the Trustee's Motion to Dismiss is well taken and to permit this Debtor to retain this Chapter 7 case and obtain a Chapter 7 discharge would be a substantial abuse of the system.

Accordingly, it is ORDERED, ADJUDGED AND DECREED that the U.S. Trustee's Motion to Dismiss be, and the same is hereby, granted. It is further ORDERED, ADJUDGED AND DECREED that the above-captioned Chapter 7 case be, and the same is hereby, dismissed unless the Debtor within ten (10) days from the date of entry of this Order files a notice of conversion to Chapter 13.

4. Motion by the Court to Dismiss the Case

The court on its own motion may, after notice and a hearing, dismiss a Chapter 7 case for cause, such as the debtor's unreasonable delay if the delay is prejudicial to creditors or the debtor's nonpayment of any fees or charges. The court may dismiss the debtor's petition, after hearing on notice to the debtor and the trustee, for failure to pay any installment of the filing fee. Within 30 days after dismissal for failure to pay the filing fee, all creditors appearing on the list of creditors and creditors who have filed claims must be given notice of the dismissal. This type of dismissal requires a hearing after notice to the debtor, the trustee, and other parties in interest as the court directs. This notice must advise the debtor of all matters that will be considered by the court at the hearing. 11 U.S.C.A. § 707(a); Fed. R. Bank. P. 1017.

The court on its own motion may also, after notice and a hearing, dismiss a Chapter 7 case filed by an individual debtor whose debts are primarily consumer debts if the court finds that the granting of relief would be a substantial abuse of the provisions of Chapter 7. 11 U.S.C.A. § 707(b).

B. COMPLAINTS

Complaints may be filed by a creditor, the trustee, the U.S. trustee, and the debtor.

1. Complaints by a Creditor

A creditor may file a complaint objecting to the debtor's discharge or objecting to the dischargeability of a debt.

a. Complaint Objecting to Debtor's Discharge At any time after the order for relief but not later than 60 days following the first date set for the section 341 meeting of creditors, a creditor may file a complaint objecting to the debtor's discharge. 11 U.S.C.A. § 727(c)(1); Fed. R. Bank. P. 4004(a), 7001.

With one exception, all the grounds for objecting to the debtor's discharge have to do with the debtor's action with respect to the bankruptcy case (postpetition activity). The only exception is the debtor's making a transfer of property within one year of the date of the filing of the petition in bankruptcy and with the actual intent to hinder, delay, or defraud creditors. See Exhibit 5–33 on pp. 259–260 for a sample complaint objecting to the debtor's discharge.

In the following case, *In re Cohen,* a creditor filed a complaint objecting to the debtor's discharge on five enumerated grounds. The court carefully examined each allegation in relation to the evidence the debtor presented to the court.

In re Cohen

47 B.R. 871
(Bankr. S.D. Fla. 1985)

FINDINGS OF FACT AND CONCLUSIONS OF LAW
SIDNEY M. WEAVER, Bankruptcy Judge

This cause came on before the Court upon an Amended Complaint Objecting to Discharge of the Debtor, and the Court, having reviewed the file, heard the testimony, examined the evidence presented, observed the candor and demeanor of the witnesses, considered the legal argument of counsel for the parties, and, being otherwise fully advised in the premises, does hereby make the following findings of fact and conclusions of law:

The Court has jurisdiction over this "core" matter, as defined in 28 U.S.C. 157.

Plaintiff objects to the Debtor's discharge under 11 U.S.C. 727(a)(2), (3), (4), and (5).

The facts are largely undisputed. Defendant is an auto mechanic by trade and has an eighth-grade formal education. Prior to his personal bankruptcy, Defendant owned real property on which he operated a truck repair business, known as T & M AUTO SERVICE, INC. ("T & M"). T & M is also a Chapter 7 Debtor, in proceedings pending in the Southern District of Florida. Defendant is the sole shareholder of T & M.

On or about October 22, 1982, Defendant entered into a somewhat complex business transaction with CARL PLATT, as Trustee. The business deal called for the sale of the property, with a lease back of the property to T & M. As a result of this transaction, Defendant was to receive cash at closing ($57,975.00), and, thereafter, payments on promissory notes ($121,175.00) and "credit units" ($162,000.00).

The Court finds, based upon the testimony presented, that Defendant received payments on account of the sale over a period of time prior to bankruptcy. While the payment checks were made to the Defendant personally, it was Defendant's regular practice to deposit the checks in the business checking account of T & M. From this account, Defendant would pay various corporate and personal obligations, including the debt owed to Plaintiff herein.

In the months following the sale, the business was robbed and vandalized in excess of 21 times. During this period, Defendant was faced with a situation wherein the bank would not immediately clear the checks deposited into the T & M account, and the Defendant began to cash his checks with his son. The cash was then deposited into the T & M account and checks were written on the available funds.

On or about May 2, 1983, a loan was arranged between Plaintiff and Defendant for $25,000.00. The loan was collateralized by Defendant's pledge of 4 promissory notes from third parties that were originally payable to Defendant. Plaintiff admits that $18,750.00 was repaid to her by the Defendant on account of the loan.

Ultimately, a fire occurred at the business premises of T & M which caused the final demise of the business. Thereafter, personal and corporate Chapter 7 Bankruptcies were filed by the Defendant herein and T & M AUTO SERVICE, INC.

The Debtor's Schedules, including the Statement of Financial Affairs, of which the Court has taken judicial notice, provide in part that the income received from the Debtor/Defendant's trade or profession during each of the two calendar years immediately preceding the filing of the Chapter 7 was: $13,200.00 for the calendar year 1982 and reflects no income for the year 1983. The Statement further requires information on income received from other sources during each of these two years, for which the Debtor/Defendant listed income for the year of 1982 only.

Plaintiff alleges several distinct grounds in support of her objection to discharge: (1) that Defendant has failed to explain loss or deficiency of assets to meet his liabilities; (2) that Defendant's Schedules and Statement of Affairs do not fully reflect monies received prior to Bankruptcy; (3) that Defendant has concealed or failed to keep books and records; (4) that Defendant has transferred his assets to insiders; and (5) that Defendant has acted with the intent to defraud, hinder or delay creditors of the estate.

Each of these allegations shall be examined in relationship to the evidence presented to the Court.

Section 727 provides that the Court will grant a discharge to a Chapter 7 debtor unless one or more of the specific grounds for the denial of discharge is proven to exist. The House Report accompanying the Bankruptcy Reform Act has described Section 727 as "the heart of the fresh start provisions of the bankruptcy law." H.R. Rep. No. 595, 95th Cong., 1st Sess. 384 (1977), U.S. Code Cong. & Admin. News 1978, pp.5787, 6340.

This Court observes that the Reform Bankruptcy Code offers to debtors what may well be the most extensive "fresh start" since the seven year release described in the *Old Testament.* Deuteronomy, 15:1 and 2. Traditionally, the debtor's fresh start is one of the primary purposes of bankruptcy law; consequently, exceptions to discharge must be strictly construed. *Matter of Vickers,* 577 F.2d 683, 687 (10th Cir.1978) citing to *Gleason v. Thaw,* 236 U.S. 558, 35 S.Ct. 287, 59 L.Ed. 717 (1915).

B.R. 4005 places the burden of proof upon the party objecting to discharge. This burden must be met with evidence that is clear and convincing. "It has always been fundamental that the conduct of mankind is presumed to be upright and those who allege to the contrary have the burden of strict proof as to every allegation." *In re Ashley,* 5 B.R. 262, 2 C.B.C.2d 949 (Bkrtcy. E.D.Tenn.1980).

The evidence must be such that, when considered in light of all the facts, it leads the Court to the conclusion that the debtor has violated the spirit of the bankruptcy laws and should therefore be denied the privilege of eliminating the legal obligation of his debts. Plaintiff has failed to carry the burden of proof in this case.

Plaintiff contends under 727(a)(5) that Defendant has failed to explain the loss or deficiency of assets to meet his liabilities. However, the Court finds that the Defendant's explanation of how the land sale payments were received and disbursed, including the partial repayment of Plaintiff's debt, is satisfactory.

A satisfactory explanation requires the debtor to demonstrate good faith in the conduct of his affairs and in explaining the loss of assets. 4 *Collier on Bankruptcy,* Section 727.08 (15th ed. 1983), *In re Shapiro & Ornish,* 37 F.2d 403 (D.C.Tex. 1929), aff'd, *Shapiro & Ornish v. Holliday,* 37 F.2d 407 (5th Cir.1930). In the *Shapiro* case, the Court found

> The word "satisfactorily," . . . may mean reasonable, or it may mean that the court, after having heard the excuse, the explanation, has that mental attitude which finds contentment in saying that he believes the explanation—he believes what the (debtors) say with reference to the disappearance or the shortage. . . . He no longer wonders. He is contented.

This Court adopts the *Shapiro* definition. The standard by which the explanation is measured may then be said to be one of reasonableness or credibility. *In re Wheeler,* 38 B.R. 842, 846 (E.D.Tenn.1984).

After careful review of the evidence and testimony, the Court finds that it is satisfied with the Defendant's explanation as to the disposition of his assets, and that there should be no denial of discharge under 727(a)(5).

Plaintiff next seeks to block Defendant's discharge under Section 727(a)(4). At issue is whether the Defendant's Schedules and Statement of Affairs fully reflected the monies received from the land sale.

Defendant is an unsophisticated man; he relied upon his accountant of some 20 years to assist him in answering the questions in the Statement of Affairs. The accountant was under the impression that the tax returns of the Defendant were to have been made a part of the Debtor's Schedules, and, in fact, the 1982 tax return does detail the land sale transaction proceeds.

It is well established that a debtor should be granted discharge under Section 727(a)(4) unless there is an *intentional* effort made to defraud. *In re Schnoll,* 31 B.R. 909, 912 (E.D.Wis.1983); *In re Kirst,* 37 B.R. 275 (E.D.Wis.1983). The record before this Court is devoid of any evidence which would indicate that errors in Defendant's Schedules were made with a fraudulent intent. As has been enunciated in the past by this Court,

> The basic rule in Bankruptcy Court in the Southern District of Florida is that any false oath must be made intentionally and must hinder the administration of the estate. . . . The element of fraud required to satisfy 727(a)(4) is established when statements are made "with a calculated disregard for the importance of the documents signed under penalty of perjury. . . ." *In re Wasserman,* 33 B.R. 779, 780 (S.D.Fla. 1983).

The omissions in the Defendant's Schedules do not reach a level of activity this Court would deem bad faith or fraud upon the Court and creditors of the debtor estate. Plaintiff has *not* shown any intentional design to defraud. The Court does not find that the Debtor's discharge should be denied under 727(a)(4).

The third basis for Plaintiff's objection to discharge is the allegation that the Defendant failed to keep books and records or that the Defendant has concealed his records.

The Court finds that the evidence presented does not prove that the Debtor concealed records.

On the question of failure to preserve records, Section 727(a)(3) of the Code recognizes that circumstances may occur which would justify such failure. The Court may in its discretion excuse any failure to keep or preserve records given justifiable circumstances. *In re Kirst,* Supra; *In re Kinney,* 33 B.R. 594, 9 C.B.C.2d 502 (N.D.OH 1983). In this case, it is unrefuted that robberies, vandalism and a fire occurred at the T & M Property where Defendant's personal records had been kept.

In view of the foregoing circumstances, the Court does not believe that Plaintiff has met her burden of proof to warrant denial of discharge under 727(a)(3).

In the next allegation of Plaintiff's Complaint, it is alleged that Defendant transferred his assets to family members or corporations controlled by relatives.

The Court finds the fact that the Debtor's son cashed checks does not rise to the level of proof required under Rule 4005 to impute a fraudulent intent by the Defendant.

Section 727(a)(2) provides in part that the act complained of must be done with the *intent* to hinder, delay or defraud a creditor or officer of the estate. "This intent must be an actual fraudulent intent as distinguished from constructive intent." *Colliers,* 15th Ed., Section 727.02.

The Court is satisfied with the Debtor's explanation as to why the practice of check cashing was used. It is reasonable to find that, in months preceding the Bankruptcy, the bank with whom the Defendant did business would hold checks for clearance, and that the Defendant was reluctant to issue checks against uncollected funds—hence the check cashing practice. Plaintiff has failed to prove the requisite intent and has therefore not proven all elements necessary to prevail under 727(a)(2).

Finally, Plaintiff has claimed that, under 727(a)(2), Defendant acted with the intent to defraud, hinder or delay Plaintiff, by failing to remit to Plaintiff monies received by Defendant from third parties.

After careful review of the evidence, the Court finds that Defendant used the proceeds from the land sale to pay business expenses, including periodic payments on his obligation to Plaintiff.

The Court further finds that there was no assignment of these notes to the Plaintiff, and that the agreement between Plaintiff and Defendant did not preclude Defendant from receiving payments on the third party notes.

In order to succeed in her efforts to prevent the granting of discharge, Plaintiff must prove that ". . . the transfer of the Debtor's property (has) been done with the intention to hinder, delay, or defraud a creditor or creditors." *In re Crane, Jr.*, 7 B.R. 859, 7 B.C.D. 36, 37 (N.D.Ala.1980). Based on the foregoing, the Court finds that no misrepresentations were made and there is no proof that the Debtor acted with the intention of transferring, removing, destroying or concealing his property.

The Court, upon review of the testimony of the witnesses and argument presented by respective counsel, and examination of the documentary evidence, finds that the Plaintiff has not presented clear, cogent and convincing evidence that this Debtor has conducted himself in such a manner as to warrant denial of a discharge under 727(a)(2), (3), (4) or (5).

The denial of a discharge of a debtor is not a step to be taken lightly and is not justified here.

This Memorandum shall constitute Findings of Fact and Conclusions of Law. As is required by B.R. 9021, a Final Judgment pursuant to these Findings and Conclusions is being entered this date.

In *Grogan v. Garner*, 498 U.S. 279 (1991), the United States Supreme Court held that the preponderance of the evidence standard, rather than the clear and convincing evidence standard, applies to all exceptions from dischargeability of debts contained in Bankruptcy Code, 11 U.S.C.A. § 523(a), including nondischargeability for fraud.

b. Complaint Objecting to the Dischargeability of a Debt At any time after the order for relief, a creditor may file a complaint objecting to the dischargeability of a debt. 11 U.S.C.A. § 523; Fed. R. Bank. P. 4007(a), 7001. See Exhibit 5–34 (See pp. 261–262) for a sample complaint objecting to the dischargeability of a debt.

In the following case, *In re Keenan*, a student loan foundation brought a complaint seeking a determination whether two loans insured by the foundation were dischargeable.

In re Keenan

53 B.R. 913 (Bankr. D. Conn. 1985)

MEMORANDUM OF DECISION

ALAN H.W. SHIFF, Bankruptcy Judge

The plaintiff, Connecticut Student Loan Foundation,[1] brought this adversary proceeding seeking a determination, pursuant to 11 U.S.C. § 523(a)(8),[2] that two loans insured by the plaintiff were not discharged by this court's July 6, 1983 order of discharge on the basis that the loans became due within five years of the debtor's petition for discharge. For the reasons set forth below, I conclude that these loans were discharged by that order.

BACKGROUND

In August 1975 and January 1976, the defendant obtained two student loans of $750.00 each from the Union Trust Company, a Connecticut banking institution, to finance vocational training. These loans were insured by the plaintiff. From September 1975 through June 1976, the defendant attended the New Haven Academy of Business for training as a keypunch operator. Under the terms of the notes signed by the defendant, the educational loans were to become due on the first day of the thirteenth month following the month in which the defendant completed her academic program, which in this case was July 1, 1977.

On February 10, 1983, the defendant filed a petition in this court, seeking relief under Chapter 7 of the 1978 Bankruptcy Code. Thus, absent any valid suspension of the repayment period, these loans became due more than five years prior to the defendant's petition for relief and would be dischargeable. The plaintiff, however, gave the defendant two six-month deferments,[3] to wit: July 1, 1977 to January 1, 1978, granted on October 26, 1977, and January 1, 1978 to July 1, 1978, granted on August 18, 1978. Both deferments were granted to the defendant as "unemployment deferments."

The issue here is the effect of those deferments. The plaintiff claims that the student loans were not discharged because the effect of those deferments was to suspend the repayment and cause the loans to become due less than five years prior to the defendant's petition. The defendant, on the other hand, asserts that the deferments were invalid, so that the loans were in fact due more than five years prior to the petition, and that the loans are, therefore, dischargeable. Moreover, the defendant asserts that the loans should be discharged as they impose an undue hardship on the defendant and her dependents.

DISCUSSION

A.
Burden of Proof

1.
Under § 523(a)(8)(A)

Neither Code § 523 nor the Bankruptcy Rules provides an allocation of the burden of proof in dischargeability proceedings. Thus, courts are guided by the construction of the particular part of section 523 under consideration, its legislative history and the evolving body of court decisions on that subject.

Although the court in *In re Wright,* 7 B.R. 197 (Bankr.N.D.Ala.1980) was not faced with the task of allocating the burden of proof on the five year issue in post discharge litigation under Code § 523(a)(8)(A), it did recognize that "there will be interesting questions raised involving the burden of proof depending on which party initiates the complaint." *Id.* at 200. The court then observed that "it would appear that the burden is on the creditor to show that the loan first became due before the date of filing the petition. Otherwise the loan is presumed discharged." *Id.* The court in *In re Norman,* 25 B.R. 545 (Bankr.S.D.Cal.1982), following *Wright* held:

> [T]he creditor must establish the existence of the debt, that it is owed to or insured or guaranteed by a governmental agency or a non-profit institution of higher education, and that it first became due less than five years prior to the date the bankruptcy petition was filed.

Id. at 548. *(citation omitted)*

A review of the legislative history of Code § 523(a)(8) disclosed the congressional view that, as a condition precedent to nondischargeability, the loan must have been made, insured, or guaranteed within five years of the filing of the bankruptcy petition. *See* Senate Report No. 96-230, 96th Cong., 1st Sess. 3 (1979), *reprinted in* 1979 U.S.Cong. and Admin.News 936. It therefore follows that a post discharge student loan creditor who asserts a right to payment on the basis that the debt was not discharged should have the burden of proving that the debt comes within the definition of student loans that are not discharged.

The same result may be reached from a different direction. Since a post discharge student loan creditor would be free to sue on the debt in either state or bankruptcy court, the bankruptcy court having concurrent jurisdiction on such debts, and since a student loan creditor as a plaintiff in a state court action would have the burden of proving that the debt was viable, it is not unfair to impose the same burden upon the creditor in bankruptcy court. *See In re Roberts,* 13 B.R. 832, 835 (Bankr.N.D.Ohio 1981). Moreover, this apportionment is consistent with the parties' relative access to information. A student loan creditor is in the best position to show, through the records which it is required to maintain, that a loan has in fact come due within five years of the filing of a petition. Placement of the burden upon the party in the best position to know the facts to be proven accords with considerations of fairness. *See Keyes v. School District No. 1, Denver, Colo.,* 413 U.S. 189, 210, 93 S.Ct. 2686, 2698, 37 L.Ed.2d 548 (1973); 9 Wigmore on Evidence § 2486 (3d ed. 1940).

Having concluded that the burden of proof is upon the creditor on the five year issue under Code § 523(a)(8)(A), it follows that the burden of proof is also upon the creditor on the issue involving the validity of any suspension of that five year period.

2. Under § 523(a)(8)(B)

Bankruptcy courts are in general agreement that in student loan dischargeability litigation based upon undue hardship, the burden of proof is upon the debtor for the reason that the assertion of undue hardship is in the nature of an affirmative defense or an exception to the exception of such a debt from discharge. In *In re Norman,* 25 B.R. 545 (Bankr.S.D.Ca.1982) the court quoted the reasoning of Justice Holmes on a similar question:

> By the very form of the law the debtor is discharged subject to an exception, and one who would bring himself within the exception must offer evidence to do so. [citation] But there is an *exception to the exception,* . . . and, by the same principle, if the debtor would get the benefit of that he must offer evidence to show his right.

Id. at 549, *quoting, Hill v. Smith,* 260 U.S. 592, 595, 43 S.Ct. 219, 220, 67 L.Ed. 419 (1923) (emphasis added by court in *Norman*). *See also In re Fitzgerald,* 40 B.R. 528, 529 (Bankr.E.D.Pa.1984); *In re Richardson,* 32 B.R. 5 (Bankr.S.D.Ohio1983).

This allocation is consistent with the legislative history of Code § 523(a)(8) which indicates that this "provision is intended to be self executing and the lender or institution is not required to file a complaint to determine the nondischargeability of any student loan." S.Rep. No. 95-989, 95th Cong., 2d Sess. 79 (1978), *reprinted in* 1978 U.S. Code Cong. & Admin.News 5787, 5865. The case law and legislative history of this Code section persuade me that the burden of proof on the issue of undue hardship should be on the debtor.

B. Dischargeability under Code § 523(a)(8)(A): Validity of Unemployment Extensions

John A. Kearns, the plaintiff's vice president, testified that at the time the second loan deferment was granted, the plaintiff had regulations which authorized unemployment deferments, but that such deferments would not apply to any period during which the loan recipient was actually employed.[4] Further, deferments would not be proper if the debtor did not request such treatment.[5]

It is apparent from the evidence that on August 18, 1978, the plaintiff granted the defendant a second retroactive unemployment deferment, effective from January 1, 1978 to July 1, 1978,[6] in reliance upon a July 5, 1978 letter[7] from the defendant. The plaintiff's reliance on that letter was misplaced. The letter stated:

> I am presently unemployed but I am seeking full-time employment. Whenever I secure employment, I will notify you immediately.

The letter does not state that the defendant had been unemployed during the period from January 1, 1978 to July 1, 1978. Nor does the letter request an extension, retroactive or otherwise, of her loan.

On the contrary, the defendant denied that she sought any deferment and specifically testified that she had been fully employed during five of the six months during which the plaintiff gave her the second unemployment deferment. The deferment was therefore not valid. *Cf. In re Crumley,* 21 B.R. 170, 172 (Bankr.E.D.Tenn.1982) (student loan creditor granted deferment for 19 months, 8 months longer than requested by the debtor).

An improper deferment does not suspend the time between the date an educational loan first comes due and the filing of a petition in bankruptcy. *In re Whithead,* 31 B.R. 381 (Bankr.S.D.Ohio1983); *In re Crumley,* 21 B.R. at 172. Since, here, the second deferment was invalid, the loans first became due more than five years before the defendant's petition was filed, and the debt arising out of those loans is therefore dischargeable.

The same result is reached upon an analysis of the first deferment. Even if the defendant was unemployed during the period from July 1, 1977 to January 1, 1978, the period of the first unemployment deferment, the applicable regulations did not authorize unemployment deferments during that period. Under the applicable regulations, deferments were allowable only for periods during which the borrower was in the Armed Forces of the United States, serving in the Peace Corps as a volunteer, or serving as a full-time volunteer under title VIII of the Economic Opportunity Act of 1964. *See* 45 C.F.R. § 177.46(f) (1978).[8]

C. Dischargeability under Code § 523(a)(8)(B): Undue Hardship

It is a well recognized principle of construction that statutes are to be construed so that they carry out legislative intent. That is, the language of a statute should be read with the assumption that the legislative branch chose particular words to accomplish a specific purpose. *Rockefeller v. Commissioner of Internal Revenue Service,* 676 F.2d 35, 36 (2d Cir.1982). Under the guidance of that rule, bankruptcy courts have uniformly applied Code § 523(a)(8)(B) narrowly. It is not enough that a student loan imposes a hardship upon the debtor and the debtor's dependents. Most, if not all, debtors could make such a claim in good faith. To qualify for discharge, the debt must be an "undue hardship."

As the court in *In re Brown,* 18 B.R. 219, 222 (Bankr.D.Ka.1982) observed:

> The Code does not define "undue hardship" . . . it seems universally accepted, however, that "undue hardship" contemplates unique and extraordinary circumstances. Mere financial adversity is insufficient, for that is the basis of all petitions in bankruptcy.

See also, In re Fischer, 23 B.R. 432, 433 (Bankr.W.D.Ky.1982); *In re Densmore,* 7 B.C.D. 271, 272, 8 B.R. 308 (Bankr.N.D.Cal. 1980).

The evidence in this proceeding demonstrates that the defendant supports herself and her three sons. One of the defendant's sons is unable to work because of a psychiatric disability. The defendant has endured many surgical procedures. She suffers from serious, chronic medical conditions, including hypertension, for which she cannot afford prescribed medication. The defendant's net income is well below the federal poverty guideline, and her expenses significantly exceed her monthly income. Moreover, it appears that the defendant's illnesses will continue to adversely affect her employability, and it appears highly unlikely that her monthly income will, in the foreseeable future, exceed her expenses.

Having analyzed the evidence in this proceeding, including the defendant's testimony, I am persuaded that the defendant has sustained the burden of proving that repayment of the student loans would impose an undue hardship upon her and upon her dependents, and therefore the debt arising out of the student loans is dischargeable. *Cf. In re La Chance,* 17 B.R. 1023 (Bankr. D.Me.1982) (impossible for debtor to generate enough income in foreseeable future to pay off loan and maintain debtor and dependents above poverty level); *In re Diaz,* 5 B.R. 253, 254 (Bankr.N.D.N.Y.1980) (debtor spending more money per week than she earns). *Cf. In re Dresser,* 33 B.R. 63 (Bankr.D.Me.1983) (no prospect for relief from medical symptoms adversely affecting debtor's employability); *In re Connolly,* 29 B.R. 978 (Bankr.M.D.Fla.1983).

CONCLUSION

For the foregoing reasons, the two educational loans insured by the plaintiff are dischargeable pursuant to Code § 523(a)(8)(A) and (B), they were discharged by the July 6, 1983 order of discharge, and judgment may enter accordingly.

---

[1]A nonprofit corporation formed for the purpose of improving educational opportunities by guaranteeing loans for post-secondary education. Conn.Gen.Stat. § 10a–201. (Formerly § 10–358)

[2]Code section 523(a) provides in pertinent part:

> A discharge under section 722 . . . of this title does not discharge an individual debtor from any debt—
>
> . . .
>
> (8) for an educational loan made, insured, or guaranteed by a governmental unit, or made under any program funded in whole or in part by a governmental unit or a nonprofit institution of higher education, unless—
>
> (A) such loan first became due before five years (exclusive of any applicable suspension of the repayment period) before the date of the filing of the petition; or
>
> (B) excepting such debt from discharge under this paragraph will impose an undue hardship on the debtor and the debtor's dependents.

[3]Plaintiff's Exhibits 3 and 6 are loan extension agreements purporting to show a request by the debtor for, and the granting of, unemployment extensions. The loan extension requests were submitted by Union Trust to CSLF, the guarantor of the loans, for its approval.

[4]Tr. Mar. 15, 1985 at 73.

[5]Tr. Mar. 15, 1985 at 78.

[6]Plaintiff's Exhibit 6.

[7]Plaintiff's Exhibit 5.

[8]45 C.F.R. § 177.46(f) reads:

> (f) *Deferment.* Periodic installments of principal need not be paid, but interest shall accrue and be paid, during any period (1) in which the borrower is pursuing a full-time course of study at an eligible institution, (2) not in excess of 3 years, during which the borrower is a member of the Armed Forces of the United States, (3) not in excess of 3 years during which the borrower is in service as a volunteer under the Peace Corps Act or (4) not in excess of 3 years during which the borrower is in service as a full-time volunteer under title VIII of the Economic Opportunity Act of 1964. Where repayment of the loan is deferred, the minimum or maximum periods allowed for repayment of the loan are provided for in paragraph (e) of this section.

EXHIBIT 5–33 Complaint Objecting to Debtor's Discharge

UNITED STATES BANKRUPTCY COURT
_________________________ DISTRICT OF _________________________

In re _________________________ ,)	
Debtor)	Case No. ____________________
)	
_________________________ ,)	Chapter ____________________
Plaintiff)	
)	
v.)	
)	
_________________________ ,)	Adv. Proc. No. _______________
Defendant)	

COMPLAINT OBJECTING TO DEBTOR'S DISCHARGE

The court has jurisdiction over this proceeding pursuant to 28 U.S.C.A. § 1334, 28 U.S.C.A. § 157, and 11 U.S.C.A. § 727. The plaintiff proceeds pursuant to Fed. R. Bank. P. 7001 and 4004.

1.

The plaintiff, ____________________________ , a creditor of ____________________________ ____________________________ , defendant, brings this action to object to the discharge of the defendant, all according to the following:

2.

The defendant filed a voluntary petition in bankruptcy on ___________ , 20____ , in the United States Bankruptcy Court for the ______________________ District of _________________________ , Bankruptcy No. __________ , in which the plaintiff was listed as a creditor.

3.

The defendant is indebted to the plaintiff in the principal amount of $___________ , plus interest, attorney fees, and costs, all as evidenced by the proof of claim filed in this case, marked Exhibit A, attached and incorporated in this complaint by reference.

4.

Plaintiff objects to the discharge of the defendant for the reasons stated in 11 U.S.C.A. § 727(a)(2)(A), in that the defendant, with intent to hinder, delay, or defraud the plaintiff, has transferred the following described real property within one year before the date of the filing of the bankruptcy petition and has failed to list the transfer of this real estate in his bankruptcy schedules.

The East One Hundred and Fifty (150) feet of Lots Five (5) through Ten (10), inclusive, GOLDEN MEADOWS ADDITION, City of Metropolis, State of Utopia.

The general warranty deed from the defendant to ____________________ , his wife, was filed with the county clerk of Metropolis County, Utopia, on ____________________ , 20_____ , and recorded at Book 2365, page 1269. A true and correct copy, marked Exhibit B, is attached to and incorporated in this complaint by reference.

5.

Plaintiff objects to the discharge of the defendant for the reasons stated in 11 U.S.C.A. § 727(a)(2)(A), in that the defendant, with intent to hinder, delay, or defraud the plaintiff, has transferred equipment, furniture, inventory, and accounts receivable to the _________________________________ Church within one year of bankruptcy.

(continued)

EXHIBIT 5–33 Complaint Objecting to Debtor's Discharge, Continued

6.

Plaintiff objects to the discharge of the defendant for the reasons stated in 11 U.S.C.A. § 727(a)(5), in that the defendant has failed to explain satisfactorily any loss of the assets described above.

7.

Plaintiff objects to the discharge of the defendant for the reasons stated in 11 U.S.C.A. § 727(a)(3) in that he failed to keep or preserve any recorded information, including books, documents, records, and papers, from which his financial condition might be ascertained.

8.

Plaintiff objects to the discharge of the defendant for the reasons stated in 11 U.S.C.A. § 727(a)(4)(A) in that he knowingly and fraudulently in connection with the case made the following false oaths.

(a) He failed to list a personal account that he had at East Park State Bank within the two years immediately preceding the filing of the bankruptcy petition.
(b) He failed to list a lawsuit in which he was a party at the time of filing the bankruptcy petition.
(c) He failed to list a lawsuit in which he was a party that was terminated within the year immediately preceding the filing of the bankruptcy petition.
(d) He stated that none of his property had been garnished within the year immediately preceding the filing of the bankruptcy petition. The plaintiff garnished the defendant's property within the year immediately preceding the filing of the bankruptcy petition in Case No. CJ-90-003476, Metropolis County District Court, Utopia. A true and correct copy, marked Exhibit C, is attached to and incorporated in this complaint by reference.
(e) He failed to disclose certain gambling losses that he incurred during the year immediately preceding the filing of the bankruptcy petition.

WHEREFORE, plaintiff respectfully requests:

1.

For a determination that the defendant be denied a discharge in bankruptcy;

2.

For a judgment in favor of plaintiff against the defendant in the principal sum of $____________, plus interest, reasonable attorney fees, and all costs of this action;

3.

For such further and additional relief as this court may deem to be just and equitable and to which the plaintiff may show himself/herself to be entitled.

____
Name of firm

By: __________________________
Attorney for the Plaintiff

EXHIBIT 5–34 Complaint Objecting to the Dischargeability of a Debt

UNITED STATES BANKRUPTCY COURT
______________________ DISTRICT OF ______________________

In re ____________________,)	
Debtor)	Case No. ______________
)	
____________________,)	Chapter ______________
Plaintiff)	
)	
v.)	
)	
____________________,)	Adv. Proc. No. __________
Defendant)	

COMPLAINT OBJECTING TO THE DISCHARGEABILITY OF A DEBT

The court has jurisdiction over this proceeding pursuant to 28 U.S.C.A. § 1334, 28 U.S.C.A. § 157, and 11 U.S.C.A. § 523(c). The plaintiff proceeds pursuant to Fed R. Bank. P. 7001 and 4007(a).

1.

Plaintiff ____________________ is an individual residing in ____________________ County, ____________________, within the ____________________ District of ____________________.

2.

Defendant ____________________ is an individual residing in ____________________ County, ____________________, and is the debtor in the above-captioned bankruptcy case.

3.

This bankruptcy case was initiated by the defendant by filing a voluntary petition on ____________________, 20 _____.

4.

On ________________, 20 _____, the defendant purchased ____________________ from the plaintiff and paid the plaintiff with a check for $ ______________ drawn on the First National Bank. Upon receipt of the check, plaintiff delivered the ____________________ to the defendant. The plaintiff presented the check for payment to First National Bank but the check was dishonored because the defendant no longer had an account with the bank. A copy of the dishonored check, marked Exhibit A, is attached to this complaint and made a part of this complaint by reference.

5.

Two weeks after the issuance of the check, the defendant filed a petition in bankruptcy under Chapter 7.

6.

When the plaintiff delivered ____________________ to the defendant, the defendant at no time intended to pay. By virtue of this fraud, the plaintiff's claim against defendant for $ ____________ is nondischargeable pursuant to 11 U.S.C.A. § 523(a)(2)(A).

(continued)

EXHIBIT 5–34 Complaint Objecting to the Dischargeability of a Debt, Continued

WHEREFORE, the plaintiff respectfully requests:

1.

For a determination that the indebtedness owed by the defendant to the plaintiff is nondischargeable;

2.

For a judgment in favor of the plaintiff against the defendant in the principal sum of $________ , plus interest reasonable attorney fees, and all costs of this action;

3.

For such further and additional relief as this court may deem to be just and equitable and to which the plaintiff may show himself/herself to be entitled.

____
Name of firm

By: ________________________________
Attorney for the Plaintiff

2. Complaint by the Trustee or the United States Trustee Objecting to Debtor's Discharge

At any time after the order for relief but not later than 60 days following the first date set for the section 341 meeting of creditors, the trustee or the United States trustee may file a complaint objecting to the debtor's discharge. 11 U.S.C.A. § 727(c)(1); Fed. R. Bank. P. 4004(a), 7001.

3. Complaint by the Trustee to Avoid Prepetition and Postpetition Transfers

The trustee has the power to avoid prepetition transfers that involve voidable preference and fraudulent transfer by filing a complaint. 11 U.S.C.A. §§ 547, 548. The trustee may also avoid postpetition transfers not authorized by the Bankruptcy Code or by the bankruptcy court. 11 U.S.C.A. § 549(a). The trustee has the rights of a hypothetical lien creditor, which enable the trustee to set aside unperfected security interests. 11 U.S.C.A. § 544(a). These powers were discussed in Section 3 of this chapter in relation to the appointment of an interim trustee.

4. Complaint by the Debtor Objecting to the Dischargeability of a Debt

The debtor may file a complaint objecting to the dischargeability of a debt. For example, the debtor may file a complaint against a former spouse seeking a determination whether alimony is in the nature of support or a property division. The debtor could also file a complaint against the IRS seeking a determination whether certain taxes are dischargeable, or the debtor could file a complaint against a creditor seeking a determination whether the debtor's student loans were dischargeable.

SECTION 7
ORDER AND NOTICE OF CHAPTER 7 BANKRUPTCY FILING, MEETING OF CREDITORS, AND FIXING OF DATES

Under the Federal Rules of Bankruptcy Procedure, the clerk, or some other person as the court may direct, is mandated to give the debtor, the trustee, all creditors, and indenture trustees notice by mail of the meeting of creditors. (See Exhibits 5–35 through 5–37.) The notice must be given not less than 20 days before the 341 meeting. Fed. R. Bank. P. 2002(a). If the court finds notice by mail is impracticable (perhaps due to large numbers of creditors) or if there is a need to supplement the notice, notice may be given by publication. Fed. R. Bank. P. 2002(l).

SECTION 8
OBJECTIONS BY A PARTY IN INTEREST TO DEBTOR'S CLAIM OF EXEMPTIONS

Any creditor or the trustee may object to the debtor's claim of exemptions. Ordinarily, an objection is made to an exemption if the property claimed as exempt is not within the exemption parameters allowed the debtor.

EXAMPLE

Debtor files for bankruptcy under Chapter 7 in State A. State A has opted out of the federal bankruptcy exemptions. Therefore the debtor's exemptions are those provided by State A and the federal nonbankruptcy exemptions.

Debtor claims an item of property as exempt when, in fact, it is not covered on the State A exemptions or on the federal nonbankruptcy exemptions although it would have been covered on the federal bankruptcy exemptions had State A not opted out.

An objection can be made to the exemption.

Objections may be filed within 30 days after the meeting of creditors or after the filing of either an amendment to the list of property claimed as exempt or supplemental schedules. The court may extend this period. The Rules require the party filing an objection to either mail or deliver a copy of this objection to the trustee, the person filing the list (usually the debtor), and the attorney for that person. Fed. R. Bank. P. 4003(b).

EXHIBIT 5–35 Official Form No. B9A (Notice of Chapter 7 Bankruptcy Filing, Meeting of Creditors, and Fixing of Dates) (Chapter 7 Individual or Joint Debtor No Asset Case)

FORM B9A (Chapter 7 Individual or Joint Debtor No Asset Case (12/03))

UNITED STATES BANKRUPTCY COURT ________ **District of** ____________________

Notice of Chapter 7 Bankruptcy Case, Meeting of Creditors, & Deadlines

[A chapter 7 bankruptcy case concerning the debtor(s) listed below was filed on ____________________ (date).]
or [A bankruptcy case concerning the debtor(s) listed below was originally filed under chapter __________ on ____________________ (date) and was converted to a case under chapter 7 on____________________.]

You may be a creditor of the debtor. **This notice lists important deadlines.** You may want to consult an attorney to protect your rights. All documents filed in the case may be inspected at the bankruptcy clerk's office at the address listed below. NOTE: The staff of the bankruptcy clerk's office cannot give legal advice.

See Reverse Side For Important Explanations.

Debtor(s) (name(s) and address):	Case Number:
	Last four digits of Soc. Sec. No./Complete EIN or other Taxpayer I.D.No.:
All Other Names used by the Debtor(s) in the last 6 years (include married, maiden, and trade names):	Bankruptcy Trustee (name and address):
Attorney for Debtor(s) (name and address): Telephone number:	Telephone number:

Meeting of Creditors:

Date: / / Time: ( ) A.M. ( ) P.M. Location:

Deadlines:

Papers must be *received* by the bankruptcy clerk's office by the following deadlines:

Deadline to File a Complaint Objecting to Discharge of the Debtor *or* to Determine Dischargeability of Certain Debts:

Deadline to Object to Exemptions: Thirty (30) days after the *conclusion* of the meeting of creditors.

Creditors May Not Take Certain Actions

The filing of the bankruptcy case automatically stays certain collection and other actions against the debtor and the debtor's property. If you attempt to collect a debt or take other action in violation of the Bankruptcy Code, you may be penalized.

Please Do Not File A Proof of Claim Unless You Receive a Notice To Do So.

Address of the Bankruptcy Clerk's Office:	For the Court:
Telephone number:	Clerk of the Bankruptcy Court:
Hours Open:	Date:

(continued)

EXHIBIT 5–35 Official Form No. B9A (Notice of Chapter 7 Bankruptcy Filing, Meeting of Creditors, and Fixing of Dates) (Chapter 7 Individual or Joint Debtor No Asset Case), Continued

EXPLANATIONS

FORM B9A (9/97)

Filing of Chapter 7 Bankruptcy Case	A bankruptcy case under chapter 7 of the Bankruptcy Code (title 11, United States Code) has been filed in this court by or against the debtor(s) listed on the front side, and an order for relief has been entered.
Creditors May Not Take Certain Actions	Prohibited collection actions are listed in Bankruptcy Code § 362. Common examples of prohibited actions include contacting the debtor by telephone, mail or otherwise to demand repayment; taking actions to collect money or obtain property from the debtor; repossessing the debtor's property; starting or continuing lawsuits or foreclosures; and garnishing or deducting from the debtor's wages.
Meeting of Creditors	A meeting of creditors is scheduled for the date, time and location listed on the front side. *The debtor (both spouses in a joint case) must be present at the meeting to be questioned under oath by the trustee and by creditors.* Creditors are welcome to attend, but are not required to do so. The meeting may be continued and concluded at a later date without further notice.
Do Not File a Proof of Claim at This Time	There does not appear to be any property available to the trustee to pay creditors. *You therefore should not file a proof of claim at this time.* If it later appears that assets are available to pay creditors, you will be sent another notice telling you that you may file a proof of claim, and telling you the deadline for filing your proof of claim.
Discharge of Debts	The debtor is seeking a discharge of most debts, which may include your debt. A discharge means that you may never try to collect the debt from the debtor. If you believe that the debtor is not entitled to receive a discharge under Bankruptcy Code § 727(a) *or* that a debt owed to you is not dischargeable under Bankruptcy Code § 523(a)(2), (4), (6), or (15), you must start a lawsuit by filing a complaint in the bankruptcy clerk's office by the "Deadline to File a Complaint Objecting to Discharge of the Debtor or to Determine Dischargeability of Certain Debts" listed on the front side. The bankruptcy clerk's office must receive the complaint and the required filing fee by that Deadline.
Exempt Property	The debtor is permitted by law to keep certain property as exempt. Exempt property will not be sold and distributed to creditors. The debtor must file a list of all property claimed as exempt. You may inspect that list at the bankruptcy clerk's office. If you believe that an exemption claimed by the debtor is not authorized by law, you may file an objection to that exemption. The bankruptcy clerk's office must receive the objection by the "Deadline to Object to Exemptions" listed on the front side.
Bankruptcy Clerk's Office	Any paper that you file in this bankruptcy case should be filed at the bankruptcy clerk's office at the address listed on the front side. You may inspect all papers filed, including the list of the debtor's property and debts and the list of the property claimed as exempt, at the bankruptcy clerk's office.
Legal Advice	The staff of the bankruptcy clerk's office cannot give legal advice. You may want to consult an attorney to protect your rights.

—Refer To Other Side For Important Deadlines and Notices—

(continued)

EXHIBIT 5–36 Official Form No. B9C (Notice of Chapter 7 Bankruptcy Filing, Meeting of Creditors, and Fixing of Dates (Chapter 7 Individual or Joint Debtor Asset Case)

FORM B9C (Chapter 7 Individual or Joint Debtor Asset Case) (12/03)

UNITED STATES BANKRUPTCY COURT ________ District of ____________________

Notice of
Chapter 7 Bankruptcy Case, Meeting of Creditors, & Deadlines

[A chapter 7 bankruptcy case concerning the debtor(s) listed below was filed on ____________________ (date).]
or [A bankruptcy case concerning the debtor(s) listed below was originally filed under chapter __________ on ____________________ (date) and was converted to a case under chapter 7 on____________________.]

You may be a creditor of the debtor. **This notice lists important deadlines.** You may want to consult an attorney to protect your rights. All documents filed in the case may be inspected at the bankruptcy clerkís office at the address listed below. NOTE: The staff of the bankruptcy clerkís office cannot give legal advice.

See Reverse Side For Important Explanations.

Debtor(s) (name(s) and address):	Case Number:
	Last four digits of Soc. Sec. No./Complete EIN or other Taxpayer I.D. No.:
All Other Names used by the Debtor(s) in the last 6 years (include married, maiden, and trade names):	Bankruptcy Trustee (name and address):
Attorney for Debtor(s) (name and address): Telephone number:	Telephone number:

Meeting of Creditors:

Date: / / Time: ( ) A.M. ( ) P.M. Location:

Deadlines: Papers must be *received* by the bankruptcy clerk's office by the following deadlines:

Deadline to File a Proof of Claim:

For all creditors (except a governmental unit): For a governmental unit:

Deadline to File a Complaint Objecting to Discharge of the Debtor or to Determine Dischargeability of Certain Debts:

Deadline to Object to Exemptions: Thirty (30) days after the *conclusion* of the meeting of creditors.

Creditors May Not Take Certain Actions:

The filing of the bankruptcy case automatically stays certain collection and other actions against the debtor and the debtorís property. If you attempt to collect a debt or take other action in violation of the Bankruptcy Code, you may be penalized.

Address of the Bankruptcy Clerk's Office:	**For the Court:**
	Clerk of the Bankruptcy Court:
Telephone number:	
Hours Open:	Date:

(continued)

EXHIBIT 5–36 Official Form No. B9C (Notice of Chapter 7 Bankruptcy Filing, Meeting of Creditors, and Fixing of Dates) (Chapter 7 Individual or Joint Debtor Asset Case), Continued

EXPLANATIONS

FORM B9C (9/97)

Filing of Chapter 7 Bankruptcy Case	A bankruptcy case under chapter 7 of the Bankruptcy Code (title 11, United States Code) has been filed in this court by or against the debtor(s) listed on the front side, and an order for relief has been entered.
Creditors May Not Take Certain Actions	Prohibited collection actions are listed in Bankruptcy Code § 362. Common examples of prohibited actions include contacting the debtor by telephone, mail or otherwise to demand repayment; taking actions to collect money or obtain property from the debtor; repossessing the debtor's property; starting or continuing lawsuits or foreclosures; and garnishing or deducting from the debtor's wages.
Meeting of Creditors	A meeting of creditors is scheduled for the date, time and location listed on the front side. *The debtor (both spouses in a joint case) must be present at the meeting to be questioned under oath by the trustee and by creditors.* Creditors are welcome to attend, but are not required to do so. The meeting may be continued and concluded at a later date without further notice.
Claims	A Proof of Claim is a signed statement describing a creditor's claim. If a Proof of Claim form is not included with this notice, you can obtain one at any bankruptcy clerk's office. If you do not file a Proof of Claim by the "Deadline to File a Proof of Claim" listed on the front side, you might not be paid any money on your claim against the debtor in the bankruptcy case. To be paid you must file a Proof of Claim even if your claim is listed in the schedules filed by the debtor.
Discharge of Debts	The debtor is seeking a discharge of most debts, which may include your debt. A discharge means that you may never try to collect the debt from the debtor. If you believe that the debtor is not entitled to receive a discharge under Bankruptcy Code § 727(a) *or* that a debt owed to you is not dischargeable under Bankruptcy Code § 523(a)(2), (4), (6), or (15), you must start a lawsuit by filing a complaint in the bankruptcy clerk's office by the "Deadline to File a Complaint Objecting to Discharge of the Debtor or to Determine Dischargeability of Certain Debts" listed on the front side. The bankruptcy clerk's office must receive the complaint and the required filing fee by that Deadline.
Exempt Property	The debtor is permitted by law to keep certain property as exempt. Exempt property will not be sold and distributed to creditors. The debtor must file a list of all property claimed as exempt. You may inspect that list at the bankruptcy clerk's office. If you believe that an exemption claimed by the debtor is not authorized by law, you may file an objection to that exemption. The bankruptcy clerk's office must receive the objection by the "Deadline to Object to Exemptions" listed on the front side.
Liquidation of the Debtor's Property and Payment of Creditors' Claims	The bankruptcy trustee listed on the front of this notice will collect and sell the debtor's property that is not exempt. If the trustee can collect enough money, creditors may be paid some or all of the debts owed to them, in the order specified by the Bankruptcy Code. To make sure you receive any share of that money, you must file a Proof of Claim, as described above.
Bankruptcy Clerk's Office	Any paper that you file in this bankruptcy case should be filed at the bankruptcy clerk's office at the address listed on the front side. You may inspect all papers filed, including the list of the debtor's property and debts and the list of the property claimed as exempt, at the bankruptcy clerk's office.
Legal Advice	The staff of the bankruptcy clerk's office cannot give legal advice. You may want to consult an attorney to protect your rights.

—Refer To Other Side For Important Deadlines and Notices—

EXHIBIT 5–37 Official Form No. B9D (Notice of Chapter 7 Bankruptcy Filing, Meeting of Creditors, and Deadlines) (Chapter 7 Corporation/Partnership Asset Case)

FORM B9D (Chapter 7 Corporation/Partnership Asset Case) (12/03)

UNITED STATES BANKRUPTCY COURT ________ District of ____________________

Notice of Chapter 7 Bankruptcy Case, Meeting of Creditors, & Deadlines

[A chapter 7 bankruptcy case concerning the debtor [corporation] *or* [partnership] listed below was filed on _________(date).]
or [A bankruptcy case concerning the debtor [corporation] *or* [partnership] listed below was originally filed under chapter ____ on _______________________ (date) and was converted to a case under chapter 7 on______________.]

You may be a creditor of the debtor. **This notice lists important deadlines.** You may want to consult an attorney to protect your rights. All documents filed in the case may be inspected at the bankruptcy clerk's office at the address listed below. NOTE: The staff of the bankruptcy clerk's office cannot give legal advice.

See Reverse Side For Important Explanations.

Debtor (name(s) and address):	Case Number:
	Last four digits of Soc. Sec. No./Complete EIN or other Taxpayer I.D. No.:
All Other Names used by the Debtor(s) in the last 6 years (include married, maiden, and trade names):	Bankruptcy Trustee (name and address):
Attorney for Debtor (name and address): Telephone number:	Telephone number:

Meeting of Creditors:

Date: / / Time: ( ) A.M. ( ) P.M. Location:

Deadline to File a Proof of Claim

Proof of Claim must be *received* by the bankruptcy clerk's office by the following deadline:

For all creditors (except a governmental unit): For a governmental unit:

Creditors May Not Take Certain Actions:

The filing of the bankruptcy case automatically stays certain collection and other actions against the debtor and the debtor's property. If you attempt to collect a debt or take other action in violation of the Bankruptcy Code, you may be penalized.

Address of the Bankruptcy Clerk's Office:	**For the Court:**
Telephone number:	Clerk of the Bankruptcy Court:
Hours Open:	Date:

(continued)

EXHIBIT 5–37 Official Form No. B9D (Notice of Chapter 7 Bankruptcy Filing, Meeting of Creditors, and Deadlines (Chapter 7 Corporation/Partnership Asset Case), Continued

EXPLANATIONS

FORM B9D (9/97)

Filing of Chapter 7 Bankruptcy Case	A bankruptcy case under chapter 7 of the Bankruptcy Code (title 11, United States Code) has been filed in this court by or against the debtor listed on the front side, and an order for relief has been entered.
Creditors May Not Take Certain Actions	Prohibited collection actions are listed in Bankruptcy Code § 362. Common examples of prohibited actions include contacting the debtor by telephone, mail or otherwise to demand repayment; taking actions to collect money or obtain property from the debtor; repossessing the debtor's property; and starting or continuing lawsuits or foreclosures.
Meeting of Creditors	A meeting of creditors is scheduled for the date, time and location listed on the front side. *The debtor's representative must be present at the meeting to be questioned under oath by the trustee and by creditors.* Creditors are welcome to attend, but are not required to do so. The meeting may be continued and concluded at a later date without further notice.
Claims	A Proof of Claim is a signed statement describing a creditor's claim. If a Proof of Claim form is not included with this notice, you can obtain one at any bankruptcy clerk's office. If you do not file a Proof of Claim by the Deadline to File a Proof of Claim listed on the front side, you might not be paid any money on your claim against the debtor in the bankruptcy case. To be paid you must file a Proof of Claim even if your claim is listed in the schedules filed by the debtor.
Liquidation of the Debtor's Property and Payment of Creditors' Claims	The bankruptcy trustee listed on the front of this notice will collect and sell the debtor's property. If the trustee can collect enough money, creditors may be paid some or all of the debts owed to them, in the order specified by the Bankruptcy Code. To make sure you receive any share of that money, you must file a Proof of Claim, as described above.
Bankruptcy Clerk's Office	Any paper that you file in this bankruptcy case should be filed at the bankruptcy clerk's office at the address listed on the front side. You may inspect all papers filed, including the list of the debtor's property and debts, at the bankruptcy clerk's office.
Legal Advice	The staff of the bankruptcy clerk's office cannot give legal advice. You may want to consult an attorney to protect your rights.

Refer To Other Side For Important Deadlines and Notices

SECTION 9
MEETING OF CREDITORS (THE SECTION 341 MEETING) AND MEETING OF EQUITY SECURITY HOLDERS

After the petition has been filed, the United States trustee must call a **meeting of creditors** and may call a **meeting of equity security holders.**

A. THE MEETING OF CREDITORS

The 341 meeting is to be held not less than 20 nor more than 40 days after the order for relief. Fed. R. Bank. P. 2003(a). Generally, the only parties who attend the meeting of creditors are the United States trustee, the debtor, the debtor's attorney, the Chapter 7 trustee, and secured creditors.

1. Examination of the Debtor

The debtor is required to appear at the meeting of creditors and to answer questions under oath. The oath will be administered by the United States trustee who will preside at the meeting. In some districts, the interim trustees appointed in Chapter 7 cases preside at the 341 meetings. The debtor may be examined by creditors, the trustee, an indenture trustee, or the United States trustee. 11 U.S.C.A. § 343. The scope of this examination is limited to the acts, conduct, property, liabilities, and financial condition of the debtor; to any matter that may affect the administration of the estate; or to the debtor's right to a discharge. Fed. R. Bank. P. 2004(b). The purpose of this examination is to aid the trustee and creditors in determining if any assets have been concealed or disposed of improperly. The trustee inquires about the accuracy of the schedules and the statement of financial affairs. The creditors inquire as to the status of their collateral and the debtor's desire to reaffirm their debts. Grounds for objection to discharge may surface at this meeting.

The examination of the debtor by the trustee at the meeting of creditors has been expanded. The trustee is now required to examine the debtor orally to determine the debtor's awareness on several points:

1. the potential consequences of seeking a discharge in bankruptcy, including the effects on credit history;
2. the debtor's ability to file a petition under a different chapter of this title;
3. the effect of receiving a discharge of debts under this title; and
4. the effect of reaffirming a debt, including the debtor's knowledge of the provisions of section 524(d) of this title. 11 U.S.C.A. § 341(d).

Any examination under oath at the 341 meeting must be recorded verbatim by electronic recording sound equipment or by other means by the United States trustee. Fed. R. Bank. P. 2003(c).

2. Election of a Trustee

Creditors who are allowed to vote under the Code may request the election of a trustee at the 341 meeting. 11 U.S.C.A. § 702(b). A trustee elected by the creditors will serve in the case rather than having the interim trustee continue as trustee. 11 U.S.C.A. § 702(d). The creditors may recommend to the court the amount of the elected trustee's bond.

The meeting of creditors may be adjourned from time to time without further written notice. An announcement at the meeting of the adjourned date and time is sufficient notice. Fed. R. Bank. P. 2003(e).

B. THE MEETING OF EQUITY SECURITY HOLDERS

The United States trustee may convene a meeting of any equity security holders. 11 U.S.C.A. § 341(b). The United States trustee shall fix a date for the meeting and shall preside at the meeting of equity security holders. Fed. R. Bank. P. 2003(b)(2). A meeting of equity security holders generally is not particularly beneficial in a Chapter 7 case, because Chapter 7 leads to liquidation and not to a reorganization plan. The equity security holders share in the distribution of the debtor's assets regardless of their input. The equity security holders, however, can play a role if they have the opportunity to increase the bankruptcy estate so that there will be more assets to distribute.

SECTION 10 REDEMPTION, DISCHARGE AND REAFFIRMATION

An individual debtor under Chapter 7 has two options by which to retain property encumbered by a lien that cannot be avoided: redemption or reaffirmation.

A. REDEMPTION

The Bankruptcy Code accords an individual debtor who has filed for bankruptcy under Chapter 7 the right to redeem certain property independent of any right of redemption accorded by state law or contract. Under 11 U.S.C.A. § 722, the debtor may redeem tangible personal property that is subject to a dischargeable consumer debt, if that property is intended primarily for person, family, or household use and the property is exempt property or has been abandoned by the trustee, by paying the lienholder the amount of the secured claim, regardless of the amount owed.

EXAMPLE

Maxine Yocum borrowed $5,000 from the Ready Cash Company and gave Ready Cash a security interest in two diamond rings and a pendant that were family heirlooms. Ready Cash property perfected its security interest.

Shortly thereafter, Maxine filed for bankruptcy under Chapter 7. She listed Ready Cash's secured claim on Schedule D as the amount of the loan, $5,000. Maxine then moved to redeem the heirlooms. Fed. R. Bank. P. 6008. The court granted her motion and required her to pay Ready Cash the amount a creditor would receive if the redemption did not occur and the creditor was forced to sell the collateral in a manner most beneficial to the creditor. The court determined that at auction, the heirlooms would bring $3,500. Therefore, Maxine was required to pay Ready Cash $3,500. The remainder of her loan was unsecured, from which she would be discharged.

B. DISCHARGE AND REAFFIRMATION

Prior to the 1986 amendments, a discharge and reaffirmation hearing was held in every case involving individuals entitled to discharge under 11 U.S.C.A. § 727. Any reaffirmation agreement the debtor wished to enter into was scrutinized by the court at this hearing. In 1986, the Code was changed from "shall hold a hearing" to "the court may hold a hearing." 11 U.S.C.A. § 524(d). The debtor, however, is still required to attend the hearing if the court holds one. Most courts no longer hold a discharge and reaffirmation hearing.

Over the past decade, the dynamics of reaffirmation have changed. The focus is no longer on the reaffirmation hearing but rather on strict compliance with 11 U.S.C.A. § 524(c)—the requirements for a reaffirmation agreement. This agreement must be signed by the debtor, attested to by the debtor's attorney, and filed with the clerk of the court. The emphasis, therefore, has shifted from the court's assuring the fairness of the reaffirmation agreement to the debtor's attorney's assuring the fairness of the reaffirmation agreement. By signing the reaffirmation agreement, the debtor's attorney states that he or she is satisfied that the reaffirmation agreement will not place a hardship on the debtor or the debtor's dependents. Court approval, however, is required to reaffirm a debt if the debtor has consumer debt secured by real property. 11 U.S.C.A. § 524(c)(6)(B).

If the debtor does enter into a reaffirmation agreement, the terms of the original agreement may be renegotiated between the debtor and creditor. Thus the terms of the original agreement may be modified. On the other hand, the creditor has the option not to enter into a reaffirmation agreement with the debtor. See Exhibit 5–38 for a **reaffirmation agreement** and Exhibit 5–39 for the motion for approval of a reaffirmation agreement.

A debtor may repay a debt, whether secured or unsecured, without reaffirming it.

> (f) Nothing contained in subsection (c) or (d) of this section prevents the debtor from voluntarily repaying any debt. 11 U.S.C.A. § 524(f).

It is important to remember that Chapter 7 has two aspects: (1) the debtor seeks a fresh start; and (2) the assets of the estate are administered. Each process goes down a separate, independent track with little convergence. Although one debtor could be denied a discharge and all his or her assets could be administered and distributed, another debtor could be granted a discharge although he or she has no assets to be administered. In some situations, however, the two processes may come together. For example, if a debtor conceals assets, his or her discharge will be denied.

If the discharge has been granted and if the debtor wants to enter into a reaffirmation agreement and was not represented by an attorney during the course of negotiating the agreement

> . . . the court shall hold a hearing at which the debtor shall appear in person and at such hearing the court shall
> (1) inform the debtor—
> (A) that such an agreement is not required under this title, under nonbankruptcy law, or under any agreement not made in accordance with the provisions of subsection (c) of this section; and
> (B) of the legal effect and consequences of—
> (i) an agreement of the kind specified in subsection (c) of this section; and
> (ii) a default under such an agreement; and
> (2) determine whether the agreement that the debtor desires to make complies with the requirements of subsection (c)(6) of this section, if the consideration for such agreement is based in whole or in part on a consumer debt that is not secured by real property of the debtor. 11 U.S.C.A. § 524(d).

C. REVOCATION OF DISCHARGE

A Chapter 7 discharge may be revoked by the filing of a complaint within one year for fraud in obtaining the discharge. For any other grounds, a complaint must be filed before one year after the discharge or the date the case was closed, whichever is later. The complaint may be filed by the trustee, a creditor, or the United States trustee. 11 U.S.C.A. §§ 727(d), (e).

EXHIBIT 5–38 Procedural Form B 240 (Reaffirmation Agreement)

Form B 240
3/99

United States Bankruptcy Court

________________ District Of ________________

Debtor's Name	Case No.
	Chapter
Creditor's Name and Address	

REAFFIRMATION AGREEMENT

Instructions: 1) Attach a copy of all court judgments, security agreements, and evidence of their perfection.
2) File all the documents by mailing them or delivering them to the Clerk of the Bankruptcy Court.

NOTICE TO DEBTOR:

This agreement gives up the protection of your bankruptcy discharge for this debt.

As a result of this agreement, the creditor may be able to take your property or wages if you do not pay the agreed amounts. The creditor may also act to collect the debt in other ways.

You may rescind (cancel) this agreement at any time before the bankruptcy court enters a discharge order or within 60 days after this agreement is filed with the court, whichever is later, by notifying the creditor that the agreement is canceled.

You are not required to enter into this agreement by any law. It is not required by the Bankruptcy Code, by any other law, or by any contract (except another reaffirmation agreement made in accordance with Bankruptcy Code § 524(c)).

You are allowed to pay this debt without signing this agreement. However, if you do not sign this agreement and are later unwilling or unable to pay the full amount, the creditor will not be able to collect it from you. The creditor also will not be allowed to take your property to pay the debt unless the creditor has a lien on that property.

If the creditor has a lien on your personal property, you may have a right to redeem the property and eliminate the lien by making a single payment to the creditor equal to the current value of the property, as agreed by the parties or determined by the court.

This agreement is not valid or binding unless it is filed with clerk of the bankruptcy court. If you were not represented by an attorney during the negotiation of this reaffirmation agreement, the agreement cannot be enforced by the creditor unless 1) you have attended a reaffirmation hearing in the bankruptcy court, and 2) the agreement has been approved by the bankruptcy court. (Court approval is not required if this is a consumer debt secured by a mortgage or other lien on your real estate.)

(continued)

EXHIBIT 5–38 Procedural Form B 240 (Reaffirmation Agreement), Continued

B 240
continued

REAFFIRMATION AGREEMENT

The debtor and creditor named above agree to reaffirm the debt described in this agreement as follows.

THE DEBT

Total Amount of Debt When Case was Filed $________

Total Amount of Debt Reaffirmed $ ________

Above total includes the following:

Interest Accrued to Date of Agreement $________
Attorney Fees $________
Late Fees $________
Other Expenses or Costs Relating to the Collection of this Debt (Describe) $________

Annual Percentage Rate (APR) __________ %

Amount of Monthly Payment $ ________

Date Payments Start ___________

Total Number of Payments to be made ___________

Total of Payments if paid according to schedule ___________

Date Any Lien Is to Be Released if paid according to schedule ___________

The debtor agrees that any and all remedies available to the creditor under the security agreement remain available.

All additional Terms Agreed to by the Parties (if any):

____

____

Payments on this debt [were][were not] in default on the date on which this bankruptcy case was filed.

This agreement differs from the original agreement with the creditor as follows:

____

____

(continued)

B 240
Continued

CREDITOR'S STATEMENT CONCERNING AGREEMENT AND SECURITY/COLLATERAL (IF ANY)

Description of Collateral. If applicable, list manufacturer, year and model. ______________

____

Value $ ______________

Basis or Source for Valuation ______________________________________

Current Location and Use of Collateral______________________________________

Expected Future Use of Collateral ______________________________________

Check Applicable Boxes:

☐ Any lien described herein is valid and perfected.

☐ This agreement is part of a settlement of a dispute regarding the dischargeability of this debt under section 523 of the Bankruptcy Code (11 U.S.C. § 523) or any other dispute. The nature of dispute is ______________________________________.

DEBTOR'S STATEMENT OF EFFECT OF AGREEMENT ON DEBTOR'S FINANCES

My Monthly Income (take home pay plus any other income received) is $ ______________.

My current monthly expenses total $ ______________, not including any payment due under this agreement or any debt to be discharged in this bankruptcy case.

I believe this agreement [will][will not] impose an undue hardship on me or my dependents.

DEBTOR'S STATEMENT CONCERNING DECISION TO REAFFIRM

I agreed to reaffirm this debt because ______________________________________

____

I believe this agreement is in my best interest because ______________________________

____

I [considered][did not consider] redeeming the collateral under section 722 of the Bankruptcy Code (11 U.S.C. §722). I chose not to redeem because ______________________________

____

I [was][was not] represented by an attorney during negotiations on this agreement.

(continued)

B 240
Continued

CERTIFICATION OF ATTACHMENTS

Any documents which created and perfected the security interest or lien [are][are not] attached. [*If documents are not attached*: The documents which created and perfected the security interest or lien are not attached because

____

____.]

SIGNATURES

____
(Signature of Debtor)

Date______________________________

____
(Signature of Joint Debtor)

Date______________________________

____
(Name of Creditor)

____
(Signature of Creditor Representative)

Date ______________________________

CERTIFICATION BY DEBTOR'S ATTORNEY (IF ANY)

I hereby certify that 1) this agreement represents a fully informed and voluntary agreement by the debtor(s); 2) this agreement does not impose a hardship on the debtor or any dependent of the debtor; and 3) I have fully advised the debtor of the legal effect and consequences of this agreement and any default under this agreement.

______________________________ ______________
(Signature of Debtor's Attorney, if any) Date

EXHIBIT 5–39 Procedural Form 240M (Motion for Approval of Reaffirmation Agreement)

B 240M
7/99

United States Bankruptcy Court

_______________ District Of _______________

In re ____________________
Debtor

Case No.____________

Chapter ___________

MOTION FOR APPROVAL OF REAFFIRMATION AGREEMENT

The debtor[s] named above and _______________, a creditor of the debtor[s], have made an agreement reaffirming the debtor's [debtors'] debt to the creditor. The agreement is dated __________ and [has][has not] been filed with the court [*if previously filed,* on _______________].

The court [has][has not] granted a discharge to the debtor[s].

The debtor was [debtors were] [not] represented by an attorney during the negotiation of this agreement.

The debt reaffirmed in the agreement [is][is not] an unsecured debt.

The reaffirmation agreement includes the debtor's[s'] statement that the debtor believes [debtors believe] that the reaffirmation agreement is in the best interest of the debtor[s].

The reaffirmation agreement includes the debtor's[s'] statement that the debtor believes [debtors believe] that the reaffirmation agreement does not impose an undue hardship on the debtor[s] or the dependents of the debtor[s].

I [We] ask the court to approve the reaffirmation agreement.

Date ______________ ______________________________________
(Signature of Debtor)

Date ______________ ______________________________________
(Signature of Joint Debtor)

Date ______________ ______________________________________
(*Signature of Creditor or Attorney for Creditor*)

SECTION 11
DISTRIBUTION OF THE PROPERTY OF THE ESTATE

Distribution of the property of the estate takes place after the trustee has collected the property and reduced it to money as required by the Code. 11 U.S.C.A. § 704(1). The trustee will file a final report and proposed distribution. The office of the bankruptcy court clerk will mail the notice to all creditors and other parties in interest. After the court's review and ruling on fees and objections to claims, the trustee distributes the assets of the estate.

The order in which distribution takes place in Chapter 7 cases is set forth in 11 U.S.C.A. § 726. Section 726 refers to section 507 for priorities and to section 503(b) for administrative expenses.

A. PRIORITY CLAIMS

Priority claims include administrative expenses; wages, salaries, or commissions; contributions to employee benefit plans; consumer deposits; farmer and fishermen claims; debts owed for alimony, maintenance, or support; certain governmental tax claims; and insured depository institution claims. 11 U.S.C.A. § 507.

1. Administrative Expenses

Administrative expenses are the actual, necessary costs of preserving and administering the estate. Trustees, examiners, professional persons employed by the estate with approval of the court, and the debtor's attorney are included in this category. 11 U.S.C.A. § 507(a)(1).

EXAMPLE

Sylvia Williams filed for bankruptcy under Chapter 7. Upon the filing of the petition, her second car, a 2004 Buick, became an asset of the bankruptcy estate. The trustee's administrative expenses for liquidating the car include the expense for picking the car up, storing it, preparing it for sale, and the auctioneer's fee for selling it.

2. Extension of Credit in an Involuntary Case

Claims arising in the ordinary course of the debtor's business or financial affairs after the commencement of an involuntary Chapter 7 bankruptcy but before the appointment of a trustee or the order for relief are priority claims.

EXAMPLE

On March 1, an involuntary Chapter 7 petition was filed against the Corner Store, a locally owned drug store. On March 5, the Corner Store placed a drug order with ABC Pharmaceutical Company, a drug manufacturer. The drugs were delivered on March 7. As in the past, the sale was made on credit with the Corner Store to pay within 30 days of receiving its monthly statement. On March 10, the bankruptcy court granted the order for relief and appointed a trustee. ABC Pharmaceutical Company has an unsecured, priority claim. 11 U.S.C.A. § 507(a)(2).

3. Wages, Salaries, or Commissions

Individuals with allowed unsecured claims for wages, salaries, or commissions, up to $4,650 for each individual, are included in this category. Vacation, severance, or sick leave pay is considered part of wages, salaries, or commissions. To be eligible for this priority, an individual must have earned what is claimed within 90 days before the filing of the petition or the date the debtor's business ceased, whichever occurred first. 11 U.S.C.A. § 507(a)(3).

EXAMPLE

On June 1, the Sun Valley Casino filed for bankruptcy under Chapter 7. For the 90 days preceding the filing of the petition, the Sun Valley employees had been paid only half of their wages. Therefore, at the time of the filing, Jerri Jackson, an employee, had a wage claim against the estate of $6,000 for this 90-day period. Of the $6,000 wage claim, $4,925 will be a priority claim and $1,075 will be an unsecured claim.

4. Contributions to Employee Benefit Plans

Allowed unsecured claims for contributions to an employee benefit plan must arise within 180 days before the date the debtor's petition was filed or the date the debtor's business ceased, whichever occurred first. These claims are only to the extent, for each plan, of the number of employees covered by the plan multiplied by $4,925, minus the aggregate amount paid to employees under the wages, salaries, or commissions provision, plus the aggregate amount paid by the estate on behalf of these employees to any other employee benefit plan. 11 U.S.C.A. § 507(a)(4).

EXAMPLE

On June 1, the Sun Valley Casino filed for bankruptcy under Chapter 7. The casino had a collective bargaining agreement with the Western States Casino Workers Union by which Sun Valley was to contribute to the employee retirement fund administered by the union. Five hundred Sun Valley employees were covered by the plan. During the 180 days preceding the filing of the petition, although Sun Valley was obligated to contribute $3,000,000 to the fund on behalf of its employees, it did not do so.

At the time of the filing of the petition, the union had an employee benefit claim against the estate for the unpaid benefit for this 180-day period. The union's priority claim will be $4,925 times the number of employees covered by the plan (500) or $2,462,500. Because the employees did not claim retirement contributions in their priority claims for unsecured wages, and no other employee benefit plan received money from the estate on behalf of these employees, the $2,462,500 stands without deduction and is the union's priority claim for the employee benefit plan. The balance of the union's claim ($537,500) will be unsecured.

5. Farmer and Fishermen Claims

The allowed unsecured claims of grain farmers and United States fishermen, to the extent of $4,925 for each individual, are priority claims. This priority was designed to protect the farmer and fisherman from loss when a grain storage facility or a fish storage or processing facility files bankruptcy. 11 U.S.C.A. §§ 507(a)(5)(A), (B).

6. Consumer Deposits

Individuals with allowed unsecured claims up to the extent of $2,225 arising from a deposit of money for consumer goods or services before the commencement of the case are included in this priority. The deposit of money could be in connection with the purchase of services that were not delivered or provided. The goods or services must have been intended for personal, family, or household use only. 11 U.S.C.A. § 507(a)(6).

EXAMPLE

During the fall, a number of customers of Cheryl's Department Store selected Christmas gifts and placed them on layaway. Over the next several months, each customer made monthly payments toward the purchase price. Three weeks before Christmas, Cheryl's filed a petition in bankruptcy under Chapter 7. Each customer is entitled to a priority claim of up to $2,225 for the money paid in connection with the purchase.

7. Alimony, Maintenance, and Support Claims

Allowed claims for debts to a spouse, former spouse, or child of the debtor for alimony, maintenance, or support are included in this category of priority claims. These claims arise in connection with a separation agreement, divorce decree, or other order of the court. 11 U.S.C.A. § 507(a)(7).

8. Certain Governmental Tax Claims

Allowed unsecured tax claims of governmental units for various taxes are included in this category. A tax on income or gross receipts is probably the tax most commonly owed by debtors. Other tax claims filed may be for property tax, sales tax, employee withholding such as social security and unemployment insurance, and customs duties. A penalty related to actual loss is also a priority claim, but a penalty that is punitive only is not a priority claim. 11 U.S.C.A. § 507(a)(8).

EXAMPLE

Last year Juanito's Restaurant failed to pay the United States Treasury its payroll taxes. Juanito's has filed a petition in bankruptcy under Chapter 7. The Internal Revenue Service has a priority claim for the unpaid taxes.

9. Insured Depository Institution Claims

This so-called S&L priority has been added to the list of priority claims because of the failure of financial institutions. Allowed unsecured claims that are based on a commitment of the debtor to the Federal Deposit Insurance Corporation (FDIC), the Resolution Trust Corporation (RTC), the Director of the Office of Thrift Supervision, the Comptroller of the Currency, or the Board of Governors of the Federal Reserve System, or their predecessors or successors, to maintain the capital of an insured depository institution, are priority claims. 11 U.S.C.A. § 507(a)(9).

B. NONPRIORITY CLAIMS

After distribution to priority claimants in the order set forth in 11 U.S.C.A. § 507, distribution is then made to the general unsecured creditors. 11 U.S.C.A. § 726.

1. Timely Filed Unsubordinated General Unsecured Claims and Tardily Filed Unsecured Claims Where Creditor Did Not Have Notice but Proof of Claim Filed in Time to Make Payment

Tardily filed unsecured claims are included in the same class as timely filed unsecured claims if the tardiness in filing came about because the creditor had neither notice nor knowledge of the bankruptcy case. Proof of the claim, however, must be filed in time to permit payment of the claim.

2. Other Tardily Filed Unsecured Claims

The tardily filed unsecured claim which comes about through failure of the creditor to timely act is subordinated to the timely filed and tardily filed claim due to lack of notice.

3. Penalty-Type Claims

A penalty-type claim, secured or unsecured, for any fine, penalty, or foreclosure, or punitive damages, to the extent that it is not compensation for actual pecuniary loss, arising before the order for relief or the appointment of a trustee, whichever is earlier, comes fourth in distribution of the estate. This type of claim will be paid only if there are assets left after distribution that would otherwise go to the debtor when the case is closed. 11 U.S.C.A. § 726(a)(4).

4. Interest on Priority and Nonpriority Prepetition Claims

Postpetition interest at the legal rate on prepetition claims, priority or nonpriority, will be paid only if a surplus of assets will be available to return to the debtor when the case is closed.

5. Debtor

If, when all claims have been paid, a surplus remains, it will be paid to the debtor.

EXAMPLE

Colleen O'Riley was involved in an automobile accident and has incurred numerous medical bills. In the meanwhile, she has been unable to work and bills, both medical and nonmedical, have been accumulating. Although Colleen will probably receive a significant settlement from the accident, she is hesitant to settle because the extent of her injuries and the costs of treatment and rehabitation is uncertain. Colleen files for bankruptcy under Chapter 7, thus gaining the protection of the automatic stay for both herself and her property. Her nonexempt, unsecured assets are sold by the trustee. Subsequently, her tort claim is settled and the money paid to her Chapter 7 trustee. The trustee pays the creditors who had claims as of the date of the bankruptcy petition and whose claims were not discharged by the bankruptcy. Any surplus created by the settlement of the tort claim is returned by the trustee to Colleen.

SECTION 12 CLOSING THE CASE

The **closing of a case** begins with the trustee's final report and proposed distribution of the assets of the bankruptcy estate. The office of the bankruptcy clerk mails notice to all creditors and other parties in interest. After the court's review and ruling on fees and objections to claims, the trustee distributes the assets of the estate. The trustee then reports his or her post-distribution activities and requests discharge from any further duties. The trustee is discharged and the case closed.

A. TRUSTEE'S FINAL REPORT AND PROPOSED DISTRIBUTION

Exhibit 5–40 is a sample of the trustee's final report and proposed distribution.

The creditors and other parties in interest are then notified of the Trustee's Final Report and Proposed Distribution. They are given 30 days in which to file a written objection. See Exhibit 5–41 on page 291 for the notice to creditors and parties in interest.

B. TRUSTEE'S FINAL ACCOUNT AFTER DISTRIBUTION AND REQUEST FOR DISCHARGE

After the court rules on the objections to the trustee's final report and proposed distribution, and after any adjustments are made, the court approves the trustee's final report and proposed distribution of the assets of the bankruptcy estate. The trustee then distributes the assets of the estate and files the trustee's final account after distribution. The trustee certifies to the court and the U.S. trustee that the estate has been fully administered and requests that the court order the case be closed and the trustee be discharged from any further duties. Exhibit 5–42 on page 292 is the trustee's declaration that the estate has been fully administered. Exhibit 5–43 on pages 293–294 is the trustee's final account after distribution and his request for discharge.

C. CLOSING THE CASE

After the court issues the final decree (See Exhibit 5–44 on page 295) the case file is reviewed by the office of the clerk of the bankruptcy court. After a period of time, the case file will be shipped to a central regional location for storage.

EXHIBIT 5–40 Trustee's Final Report and Proposed Distribution

IN THE UNITED STATES BANKRUPTCY COURT
FOR THE ______________ DISTRICT OF ______________

In re:	)	
	)	
	)	Chapter 7
	)	
	)	
Debtor (s).	)	Case No.

TRUSTEE'S FINAL REPORT
AND PROPOSED DISTRIBUTION

I. FINAL REPORT:

The petition commencing this case was filed on ______________________, 20____ , and the undersigned was (appointed) (elected) trustee on ______________________, 20____ . The amount of the trustee's bond is now $___________ .

The trustee certifies that the balance in his or her office account, bank account, bank account number _____________ at __________________ _____________ , is in the amount of $___________ . This amount includes all earned interest and is subject to check for payment to creditors.

All property of the estate, except that claimed exempt by the debtor(s), without objection, or determined by the Court as exempt, has been inventoried, collected and liquidated, or abandoned.

All claims have been examined and objections have been ruled on by the Court. Applications for approval of compensation and expenses of professional persons have been ruled on by the Court. Any property not abandoned by the trustee before is now abandoned and is scheduled on the attached Proposed Distribution. (See Section II.)

1. THE VALUE OF:

Administered property totals: $_____________________
Exempt property totals: $_____________________
Abandoned property totals: $_____________________
(Attached hereto as Form 1)

(continued)

2. The trustee adopts the schedules of the petition filed as his or her inventory.
   (YES) ____ (NO) ____
   (if "NO," inventory attached)

3. Final Account as of ________________, 20 ___ .

   RECEIPTS: (Attached hereto as Form 2) $________________

   DISBURSEMENTS: (Attached hereto as Form 2) $________________

   BALANCE OF FUNDS ON HAND: $________________

   ANALYSIS OF CLAIMS FILED (Attached hereto as Form 3)

   PROPOSED DISTRIBUTION (See Section II, entitled "Proposed Distribution")

4. The net estate upon which the trustee's compensation was computed is $________________ . This does not include any exemptions paid to the debtor(s) or any refunds to be made to the debtor(s).

The undersigned trustee certifies under penalty of perjury that the foregoing Final Report, and attached forms, are true and correct to the best of his or her knowledge and belief. The trustee hereby requests the United States trustee to approve this Final Report and requests the Court to provide for notice and opportunity for a hearing under 11 U.S.C.A. §§ 502(b) and 503(b) and thereafter to make final allowance for the purposes of distribution to claims, administrative expenses, and other payments stated in this Final Report and Proposed Distribution.

WHEREFORE, the trustee requests that this Final Report and Proposed Distribution be approved by this Court.

TRUSTEE NAME: ____________________ DATE: ____________________

SIGNED: ____________________ ADDRESS: ____________________

____

TELEPHONE: ____________________

(continued)

EXHIBIT 5–40 Trustee's Final Report and Proposed Distribution, Continued

Page 1

FORM 1

INDIVIDUAL ESTATE PROPERTY RECORD AND REPORT
ASSET CASES

Case No.: ________ Trustee Name: ____________

Case Name: ____________ Dates Submitted: ____________

	1	2	3	4	5	6
Ref. No.	Asset Description (Scheduled and Unscheduled Property)	Petition/ Unscheduled Values	Value Determined by Trustee Less Liens and Exemption	Property Abandoned	Sales/ Funds Received by the Estate	Asset Fully Administered/ Value of Remaining Assets (Yes or Dollar Amount of Remaining Assets)
1	Residence, Happy Rock MO	220,000.00	12,000		275,000	Yes
2	Cash on Hand	10.00	0			Yes
3	Deposits	250.00	0			Yes
4	Household Goods	1,000.00	0			Yes
5	Jewelry	2,000.00	1,360		5,000	Yes
6	1990 Cadillac	1,000.00	0	(1)		Yes
7	2000 Corvette	25,000.00	21,000		20,000	Yes
8	1996 BMW	12,000.00	1,500	(1)		Yes
9	Mach./Equipment	9,000.00	0	Yes		Yes
10	Air Compressor	1,500.00	0	(1)		Yes

* (1) Abandoned at close of case.

TOTALS ________ ________ Value of Remaining Assets ________

(Total Dollar Amount in Column 6)

Major activities affecting case closing which are not reflected above.

Matters Pending ________ Date of Hearing or Sale ________ Other Action ________

Projected Date of Final Report ____________

(continued)

EXHIBIT 5–40 Trustee's Final Report and Proposed Distribution, Continued

Page 1

FORM 2

CASH RECEIPTS AND DISBURSEMENT RECORD

Case No. __________

Case Name: ______________________________

Taxpayer ID #: __________

Bank Name :______________________________

Savings Account #: ______________________________

Checking Account #: ______________________________

Bond Amount: ______________________________

(indicate if blanket bond)

1	2	3	4	5	6	7	8
Trans. Date	**Check or Reference Number**	**Paid to/ Received From**	**Description of Transaction**	**Deposit $**	**Disburs. $**	**Checking Account Balance**	**Savings (s) Invest. (i) Balance**
7/29/04	5	ABC Jewelry	Sale of Jewelry	5,000.00		5,000.00	
7/30/04	101	J & M Buzzard	Exemption—jewelry		640.00(D)	4,360.00	
7/31/04	102	MO Western	Transfer to Savings		3,860.00(T)	500.00	3,860.00(S)
8/10/04	12	MO Sharpshooters	Sale of Guns	3,500.00		4,000.00	3,860.00(S)
8/11/04	103	ABC Bank	Lien on Guns		2,500.00	1,500.00	3,860.00(S)
8/15/04	104	Ins. Brokers	Trustee Bond		100.00	1,400.00	3,860.00(S)
8/16/04	7	Joe Cool	Sale of 90 Corv.	20,000.00		21,400.00	3,860.00(S)
8/16/04	105	XYZ Bank	Lien on 90 Corv.		3,500.00	17,900.00	3,860.00(S)
8/16/04	106	J & M Buzzard	Exemption—Corvette		500.00(D)	17,400.00	3,860.00(S)
8/16/04	107	MO Western	Transfer to Savings		16,900.00(T)	500.00	20,760.00(S)
8/31/04	—	MO Western	Interest 8/31/04	68.32		568.32	20,760.00(S)
9/3/04	14(u)	Smalltown Bank	Cert. of Deposit	10,000.00		10,568.32	20,760.00(S)
9/4/04	15(u)	Darrell Buzzard	1/2 Int. in Boat	50,000.00		60,568.32	20,760.00(S)
9/4/04	108	MO Western	Transfer to Savings		60,068.32(T)	500.00	80,828.32(S)
9/6/04	18(u)	Jackie Luft Eqpt	Preference	2,300.00		2,800.00	80,828.32(S)
9/6/04	19(u)	Goforth Mfg. Co.	Preference	5,000.00		7,800.00	80,828.32(S)
9/8/04	23(u)	Red Barn Ins. Co.	Insurance—barn	6,500.00		14,300.00	80,828.32(S)
9/15/04	1	Happy Rock Title	Sales of Residence	275,000.00		289,300.00	80,828.32(S)
9/15/04	109	Happy Rock Title	Closing Costs/Comm.		23,142.91	266,157.09	80,828.32(S)

(continued)

EXHIBIT 5–40 Trustee's Final Report and Proposed Distribution, Continued

Page 1

FORM 3
ANALYSIS OF CLAIMS REGISTER
DEBTOR NAME ____________

CASE # ________
BAR DATE FOR CLAIMS ____________
CLAIMS REVIEWED BY ____________

Number	Creditor	Date of Claim	Priority (Amount)	Taxes (Amount)	Liens (Amt.)	Secured (Amt.)	Unsecured (Amt.)	Abandon (Date)	Reaffirm (Date)	Other	Contest
1	Ace Carpenter	7/20/04	2,600.00								Objection (over $2,000)
1a	Ace Carpenter	8/10/04	2,000.00								
1b	Ace Carpenter	8/10/04					600.00				
2	Ben Easymark	7/21/04	20,000.00								Objection (over $900)
2a	Ben Easymark	8/11/04	900.00								
2b	Ben Easymark	8/11/04					19,100.00				
3	Justin Taken	7/22/04	10,000.00								Objection (over $900)
3a	Justin Taken	8/12/04	900.00								
3b	Justin Taken	8/12/04					9,100.00				
4	Sue Brown	7/22/04	9 1,200.00								
5	Bob Jones	7/22/04	700.00								
6	IRS	7/31/04		60,000.00							
7	Joseph Jones	8/1/04	500.00								

(continued)

EXHIBIT 5–40 Trustee's Final Report and Proposed Distribution, Continued

II. PROPOSED DISTRIBUTION: (*** Pursuant to Fed. R. Bank. P. 3010, all funds less than $5.00 will be paid into the Registry fund of this Court without further order.)

A. ADMINISTRATIVE EXPENSES (U.S.C.A. § 507(a)(1)):

1. Professionals (with date(s) appointed by Court order(s))

Professional (name(s) and date(s) appointed)	Amount(s) Paid (date(s) of Court order(s))
a. Trustee's Compensation	
b. Trustee's Expenses	
c. Attorney for Trustee's Compensation	
d. Attorney for Trustee's Expenses	
e. Accountant's Compensation	
f. Accountant's Expenses	
g. Appraiser's Compensation	
h. Appraiser's Expenses	
i. Attorney for Debtor's Compensation	
j. Attorney for Debtor's Expenses	
k. Attorney for Others' Compensation	
l. Attorney for Others' Expenses	
m. Auctioneer's Compensation	
n. Auctioneer's Expenses	
o. Harvester's Compensation	
p. Harvester's Expenses	
q. Real Estate Agent's Compensation	
r. Real Estate Agent's Expenses	
s. Other Professionals' Compensation (list)	
t. Other Professionals' Expenses (list)	

SUBTOTAL (Professionals) $______________

(continued)

EXHIBIT 5–40 Trustee's Final Report and Proposed Distribution,Continued

2. Other Administrative Expenses

Type	Amount of Claim	Amount to be Paid
a. Super-Priority Claims (list)		
b. Court costs, filing and notice fees		
c. Other (list)		

SUBTOTAL (Other Administrative Expenses) $__________
TOTAL ADMINISTRATIVE EXPENSES
(Professional and Other) $__________
Note: All 507(a)(1) Fees Share Pro Rata

B. SECURED CLAIMS

Claimant	Amount of Claim	Amount to be Paid
(list)		

TOTAL SECURED CLAIMS $__________

C. PRIORITY CLAIMS
1. Wage Claims (U.S.C. § 507(a)(3))

Claimant	Claim Amount	Dividend	Employee Share Fed. W/H	Employee Share Soc. Sec.	Soc. Sec. W/H	Net
(list)						
TOTALS	____	____	____	____	____	____

Net to Employees $__________
Total for IRS $__________
Total to be Paid $__________

Gross $__________
Employers FICA $__________
SUBTOTAL (Wage Claims) $__________

The trustee should issue a check payable to the Director of Internal Revenue in the appropriate amount, for each wage claimant, representing withholding for income tax, the Employee's portion of Social Security and the Employer's portion of Social Security.

(continued)

EXHIBIT 5–40 Trustee's Final Report and Proposed Distribution, Continued

2. Contributions To Employee Funds
(U.S.C.A. § 507(a)(4))

Claimant	Amount of Claim	Amount to be Paid
(list)		
SUBTOTAL (Contributions to Employee Funds)		$______________

3. Tax Claims (U.S.C.A. § 507 (a)(7))

Type	Amount of Claim	Amount to be Paid
a. Federal		
b. State		
c. County		
d. Employment		
e. Fuel		
f. Other (list)		
SUBTOTAL (Tax Claims)		$______________

4. Other Priority Claims

Claimant	Amount of Claim	Amount to be Paid
(list)		
SUBTOTAL (Other Priority Claims)		$______________
TOTAL PRIORITY CLAIMS (Wage + Tax + Contributions + Other)		$______________

D. GENERAL UNSECURED CLAIMS

Name and Address of Creditor	Amount of the Claim	% to be Paid	Amount to be Paid
______________________	$_______	_____%	$_______
______________________	$_______	_____%	$_______
______________________	$_______	_____%	$_______
______________________	$_______	_____%	$_______
______________________	$_______	_____%	$_______
______________________	$_______	_____%	$_______

(continued)

EXHIBIT 5–40 Trustee's Final Report and Proposed Distribution, Continued

____________	$______	_____%	$______
____________	$______	_____%	$______
____________	$______	_____%	$______
____________	$______	_____%	$______
____________	$______	_____%	$______
____________	$______	_____%	$______
____________	$______	_____%	$______
____________	$______	_____%	$______
____________	$______	_____%	$______
____________	$______	_____%	$______
____________	$______	_____%	$______
____________	$______	_____%	$______
____________	$______	_____%	$______
____________	$______	_____%	$______
____________	$______	_____%	$______
____________	$______	_____%	$______
____________	$______	_____%	$______
____________	$______	_____%	$______
TOTAL UNSECURED CLAIMS	$______		$______

If additional space is needed, continue on an attached page(s). Check here if additional page(s) is attached [ ].

E. ABANDONMENT OF ESTATE PROPERTY

Unless objection is made in writing to the Clerk of the Court and request for notice and hearing requested, the trustee, pursuant to 11 U.S.C.A. § 554, abandons the following property:

Property	Lienholder & Address	Stored at	Value	Reason for Abandonment

TOTAL PROPOSED DISTRIBUTION

Administrative Expenses	$______________
Secured Claims	$______________
Priority Claims	$______________
General Unsecured Claims	$______________
TOTAL	$______________

EXHIBIT 5–41 Notice to Creditors and Other Parties in Interest Concerning the Trustee's Final Report and Proposed Distribution

IN THE UNITED STATES BANKRUPTCY COURT
FOR THE ______________ DISTRICT OF ______________

In re:)
)
) Chapter 7
)
)
Debtor(s).) Case No.

NOTICE DIRECTING AFFECTED CREDITORS AND PARTIES IN INTEREST TO SHOW CAUSE IN WRITING WITHIN 30 DAYS OF THIS NOTICE WHY TRUSTEE'S FINAL REPORT SHOULD NOT BE APPROVED AND WHY TRUSTEE'S PROPOSED DISTRIBUTION SHOULD NOT BE MADE

Notice is hereby given to all affected creditors that any claimant may object to any of the foregoing statements or take exception to them or offer written evidence to contradict them and may object to the proposed distribution on any grounds available to them. If there are no objections, exceptions, or submissions of controverting evidence, the trustee will make distribution in accordance with the foregoing proposed distribution. It is therefore

DIRECTED that all affected creditors and parties in interest, or any of them, show cause within thirty (30) days of the mailing of this notice by filing with the court and simultaneously serving such on the trustee at the below address and on the Office of the United States trustee, ______________, ______________________, a written objection setting forth the reasons why the trustee's final account should not be approved and why the trustee's distribution should not be made.

______________________ ______________________
Date Trustee in bankruptcy

Address: ______________________
____

EXHIBIT 5–42 Trustee's Declaration That the Estate Has Been Fully Administered

IN THE UNITED STATES BANKRUPTCY COURT
FOR THE ______________ DISTRICT OF ______________

In re:	)	
	)	
	)	Chapter 7
	)	
	)	
Debtor(s).	)	Case No.

DECLARATION THAT ESTATE HAS BEEN FULLY ADMINISTERED,
THAT BANK ACCOUNT HAS A ZERO BALANCE, AND THAT UNCLAIMED
FUNDS ATTRIBUTABLE TO CERTAIN CLAIMANTS HAVE BEEN
DEPOSITED IN THE REGISTRY OF THE COURT

Comes now the trustee in bankruptcy of the above styled bankruptcy estate and hereby

DECLARES that the above estate has been fully administered; and further

DECLARES that the trustee's bank account formerly maintained as an account for this case now has a zero balance; and further

DECLARES that unclaimed funds attributable to the following claimants have been deposited in the registry of the court:

Name of Claimant	Last Known Address	Amount
____________________	____________________	__________
____________________	____________________	__________
____________________	____________________	__________
____________________	____________________	__________
____________________	____________________	__________
____________________	____________________	__________

[   ] Check here if additional pages are attached

________________ ______________________
Date Trustee in bankruptcy

EXHIBIT 5–43 Trustee's Final Account after Distribution and Request for Discharge

IN THE UNITED STATES BANKRUPTCY COURT
FOR THE ______________ DISTRICT OF ______________

In re:	)	Chapter 7
	)	Case No.
	)	
	)	FINAL ACCOUNT AFTER
	)	DISTRIBUTION AND REQUEST
Debtor(s).	)	FOR DISCHARGE OF TRUSTEE

The undersigned trustee reports:

1. The balance on hand has been distributed in accordance with the trustee's Final Report Before Distribution as amended (if any) by Court Order except for unclaimed dividends paid to the Court Registry Fund as follows:

Creditor (Name and Address)	Claim No.	Amount

2. Gross receipts of $______________ from liquidation of all property of the estate has been distributed under 11 U.S.C.A. § 726 as follows:

$____________________ a. Trustee Compensation
$____________________ b. Fee for Attorney for Trustee
$____________________ c. Fee for Attorney for Debtor
$____________________ d. Other Professionals
$____________________ e. *All* expenses, including Trustee and Court costs
$____________________ f. Secured Creditors
$____________________ g. Priority Creditors
$____________________ h. Unsecured Creditors
$____________________ i. Other Payments, *except to Debtor*
$____________________ j. SUBTOTAL (sum of lines a through i)
$____________________ k. Payments to Debtor
$____________________ l. TOTAL DISBURSEMENTS (sum of lines j and k)

3. The final bank statement of the estate and all canceled checks evidencing the distribution have been submitted to the United States trustee.

I hereby certify to the Court and the United States trustee, that this estate has been fully administered. A Final Report has been filed and proper disbursements completed. No funds or assets of the estate remain.

(continued)

EXHIBIT 5–43 Trustee's Final Account after Distribution and Request for Discharge, Continued

Therefore, pursuant to Fed. R. Bank. P. 5009, the trustee requests that this Final Account After Distribution be accepted, and that the Court order the case closed and discharge the trustee of any further duties.

____________________ ____________________
Date Trustee

____
Address

____

REVIEW BY UNITED STATES TRUSTEE

I have reviewed the trustee's Final Account After Distribution for Closing and Discharge.

____________________ ____________________
Date United States trustee

By: ____________________

SECTION 13
AFTER THE CASE IS CLOSED

After the case is closed, it may be amended without being reopened or it may be reopened.

A. AMENDING THE CASE WITHOUT REOPENING THE CASE

A case may be amended without being reopened to correct clerical errors in judgments, orders, and other parts of the record. Errors in the record caused by oversight or omission may also be corrected in a closed case.

B. REOPENING A CLOSED CASE

The two basic reasons for reopening a case are to administer assets or to include another creditor. A case may be reopened in the court in which it was closed.

In *In re Thompson,* after the debtor had received a discharge in a no-asset case and her case was closed, she petitioned the court to reopen her bankruptcy case and amend her schedule of liabilities to include an omitted creditor. The court stated that "The decision to reopen a case is within the sound discretion of the [bankruptcy court]."

EXHIBIT 5–44 Final Decree

UNITED STATES BANKRUPTCY COURT
______________ DISTRICT OF ______________

In re ______________________________ ,)
[Set forth here all names including married, maiden, and trade names used by debtor within last 6 years.])
Debtor) Case No. ________
) Chapter ________
Social Security No(s). ____________ and all)
Employer's Tax Identification Nos. *[if any]* _____)
____________)

FINAL DECREE

The estate of the above named debtor has been fully administered.

IT IS ORDERED THAT:

[name of the trustee]
is discharged as trustee of the estate of the above named debtor and the bond is canceled;
The Chapter 7 case of the above named debtor is closed.

____
Date

____
United States Bankruptcy Judge

In re Thompson

(Bankr. E.D.N.Y. 1993) 152 B.R. 24

MEMORANDUM AND ORDER
RAYMOND J. DEARIE, District Judge

Debtor Henrietta Thompson appeals from a bankruptcy court order, dated October 6, 1992, denying her motion to reopen her no-asset Chapter 7 bankruptcy case for the purpose of adding a creditor and extending such creditor's time to object to discharge. There is no opposition to the appeal. This Court finds that the denial of the debtor's motion was an abuse of discretion. Accordingly, the order is vacated, and the matter is remanded to the bankruptcy court.

BACKGROUND

On October 15, 1991, Henrietta Thompson, the debtor, filed a Chapter 7 petition pursuant to 11 U.S.C. § 301 for release from consumer debts. The debtor's estate contained no assets. Scheduled creditors were sent notice of the commencement of the case and of the creditors meeting to be held on November 15, 1991. The deadline to file a complaint objecting to the discharge of the debtor or to determine dischargeability of a debt was set for January 14, 1992. Because no assets were available for distribution, the creditors were advised not to file proofs of claim until receiving notice to do so. The case proceeded without incident, and on March 12, 1992, the debtor was released from all dischargeable debts.

Approximately three months after the discharge, the debtor discovered that she had inadvertently failed to list FCDB Preferred Charge/Spiegel, an unsecured creditor for $1,775.52, on her schedule. FCDB Preferred Charge/Spiegel was subsequently informed that the debtor had filed for bankruptcy. On September 9, 1992, the debtor moved to reopen her case to add the omitted creditor to her schedule and extend the creditor's time to object to discharge. The motion was made on notice to the omitted creditor, its attorney, the interim trustee and the United States trustee. At the oral argument on October 6, 1992, no one appeared in opposition to the motion. The bankruptcy court denied the motion orally, concluding that "the rule in th[e] District is even if [the court] granted [the] motion and even if the creditor did not file an objection the debt would not be discharged. . . . [I]f [the court] granted [the] motion it would be futile and a waste of time." The debtor now appeals the ruling of the bankruptcy court. Again, there is no opposition.

DISCUSSION

The decision to reopen a case is within "the sound discretion of the [bankruptcy court]. *In re McNeil,* 13 B.R. 743, 745 (Bankr.S.D.N.Y.1981). Therefore, the bankruptcy court's decision not to reopen a case may be vacated only "upon a showing that the failure to reopen was an abuse of discretion." *In re Candelaria,* 121 B.R. 140, 142 (E.D.N.Y.1990) (quoting *In re Sheerin,* 21 B.R. 438, 440 (BAP 1st Cir.1982)). The bankruptcy court below incorrectly concluded that, as a matter of law, the debt to FCDB Preferred Charge/Spiegel would not be discharged even if the debtor's motion to reopen her case were granted and the creditor did not object to discharge. Therefore, it abused its discretion in denying the debtor's motion to reopen.

Under the Bankruptcy Code, an individual who files for relief under Chapter 7 is not discharged from any debt that is "neither listed nor scheduled . . . in time to permit . . . timely filing of a proof of claim."[1] 11 U.S.C.A. § 523(a)(3)(A) (1979 & Supp. 1992). If a debt is of a kind specified in paragraph (2), (4), or (6) of section 523(a),[2] an individual is not discharged from such debt unless it is listed or scheduled "in time to permit . . . timely request for a determination of dischargeability" in addition to timely filing of a proof of claim.[3] 11 U.S.C.A. § 523(a)(3)(B) (1979 & Supp.1992).

Generally, "a proof of claim shall be filed within 90 days after the first date set for the meeting of creditors." 11 U.S.C.A.Bankr.Rule 3002(c) (Supp.1992). However, in a case in which no assets are available for distribution, creditors may be notified that it is unnecessary to file proofs of claim. 11 U.S.C.A.Bankr.Rule 2002(e) (Supp.1992). If they are so notified, they must be informed of any subsequent discovery of assets from which a dividend may be paid. They may then file proofs of claim within ninety days. 11 U.S.C.A.Bankr.Rule 3002(c)(5) (Supp.1992). Thus, in a no-asset case, section 523(a)(3)(A) does not preclude the discharge of an unscheduled debt until the expiration of the filing period following notice to the creditors of the existence of assets from which a dividend may be paid. *In re Candelaria,* 121 B.R. at 144; *see In re De Mare,* 74 B.R. 604, 605 (Bankr.N.D.N.Y. 1987); *In re Maddox,* 62 B.R. 510, 513 (Bankr.E.D.N.Y.1986); *In re Jensen,* 46 B.R. 578, 582 (Bankr.E.D.N.Y.1985); *In re Zablocki,* 36 B.R. 779, 782 (Bankr.D.Conn. 1984). Because no assets have been discovered in the estate of the debtor in this case, section 523(a)(3)(A) does not preclude the discharge of the debt to FCDB Preferred Charge/Spiegel.

Generally, a creditor contending that a debt is of a kind excepted from discharge pursuant to section 523(a)(2), (4), or (6)[4] must file a request for a determination of dischargeability within sixty days of the first date set for the meeting of creditors. 11 U.S.C.A. § 523(c) (Supp.1992) & Rule 4007(c) (Supp.1992). Under Rule 4007(c), motions to extend the time to file must be made within the sixty day period. However, the expiration of that period alone does not preclude the discharge of an unscheduled debt pursuant to section 523(a)(3)(B). To bring an unscheduled debt within section 523(a)(3)(B), the creditor must show that he had grounds for claiming the debt was of a kind specified in paragraph (2), (4), or (6) of section 523(a) in addition to showing that the debtor's omission deprived him of the opportunity to timely assert a claim of nondischargeability on such grounds. *In re Candelaria,* 121 B.R. at 144; *In re Zablocki,* 36 B.R. at 782.

Accordingly, the limitations of section 523(c) and Rule 4007(c) do not apply when the issue of exception to discharge pursuant to paragraph (2), (4), or (6) of section 523(a) arises in the context of exception to discharge pursuant to section 523(a)(3)(B). *In re Candelaria,* 121 B.R. at 144–45 (citing in accord *In re Jensen,* 46 B.R. at 583); *In re Zablocki,* 36 B.R. at 782. A creditor added to a debtor's schedule after the debtor is granted a discharge must be afforded a reasonable period of time to file a complaint to determine the dischargeability of the debt under section 523(a)(2), (4) or (6). *In re Candelaria,* 121 B.R. 140 at 145. If the creditor does not file a complaint, or if upon consideration of such complaint, the debt is determined to be dischargeable, the debt is then discharged. Thus, section 523(a)(3)(B) does not as a matter of law preclude the discharge of the debt to FCDB Preferred Charge/Spiegel.

CONCLUSION

Applicable law does not support the bankruptcy court's conclusion that granting the debtor's motion would have been futile. Accordingly, the Court finds that the bankruptcy court's refusal to reopen the debtor's case was an abuse of discretion. The order of the bankruptcy court is vacated, and the case is remanded for further proceedings consistent with this opinion.

SO ORDERED.

---

[1]If a creditor has notice or actual knowledge of the debtor's bankruptcy case in time for such timely filing of a proof of claim, the debt need not be listed or scheduled in order to be discharged. 11 U.S.C.A. § 523(a)(3)(A) (1979 & Supp.1992).

[2]Paragraph (2) specifies debts obtained by false pretenses, a false representation, or actual fraud, and debts obtained by use of a materially false statement of financial condition. Paragraph (4) specifies debts "for fraud or defalcation while acting in a fiduciary capacity, embezzlement, or larceny." Paragraph (6) specifies debts "for willful and malicious injury by the debtor to another entity or to the property of another entity." 11 U.S.C.A. § 523(a).

[3]If a creditor has notice or actual knowledge of the debtor's bankruptcy case in time to permit a timely request for a determination of dischargeability in addition to timely filing of a proof of claim, the debt need not be listed or scheduled in order to be discharged. 11 U.S.C.A. § 523(a)(3)(B) (1979 & Supp.1992).

[4]*See supra* text accompanying note 2.

KEY TERMS

Abandoned property of the estate
Administrative expenses
Automatic stay
Avoidance powers
Bankruptcy estate
Bankruptcy petition preparer
Clerk's notice
Closing of a case
Codebtor
Community property state
Contested matters
Contingent claim
Convert nonexempt property into exempt property
Creditor holding a secured claim
Current monthly expenditures of an individual debtor
Current monthly income of an individual debtor
Declaration Concerning the Debtor's Schedules
Disclosure of Attorney's Compensation Statement
Disputed claim
Distribution of the property of the estate
Executory contract
Exemptions (federal)
Exemptions (state)
Exempt property
Interim trustee
Joint case
Liquidation
List of creditors
Meeting of creditors
Meeting of equity security holders
Order for relief
Priority claims
Property of the estate
Reaffirmation Agreement
Setoff
Statement of Financial Affairs
Statement of Intention
Unexpired lease
Unliquidated claim

CHAPTER 6

The Chapter 13 Bankruptcy (Adjustment of Debts of an Individual with Regular Income)

CHAPTER OUTLINE

SECTION 1
THE INITIATION OF A CHAPTER 13 CASE

SECTION 2
THE CHAPTER 13 PLAN
A. Contents of a Chapter 13 Plan
B. The Debtor's Payments under the Plan
C. Modification of the Plan before Confirmation

SECTION 3
THE FILING OF THE PETITION

SECTION 4
THE SIGNIFICANCE OF FILING A PETITION
A. Possession and Control of Property of the Estate
B. Operation of the Debtor's Business
C. Exemptions

SECTION 5
APPOINTMENT AND DUTIES OF A CHAPTER 13 TRUSTEE

SECTION 6
MOTIONS AND COMPLAINTS AFTER THE ORDER FOR RELIEF
A. Motions
B. Complaints

SECTION 7
THE CLERK'S NOTICE

SECTION 8
MEETING OF CREDITORS (THE SECTION 341 MEETING)

SECTION 9
HEARING ON CONFIRMATION OF THE PLAN

SECTION 10
TRUSTEE'S DISTRIBUTION OF PAYMENTS UNDER THE PLAN

SECTION 11
MODIFICATION OF THE PLAN AFTER CONFIRMATION

SECTION 12
REVOCATION OF ORDER OF CONFIRMATION

SECTION 13
DISCHARGE

SECTION 14
REVOCATION OF THE DISCHARGE

SECTION 15
CLOSING THE CASE AND PROCEEDINGS AFTER THE CASE IS CLOSED

This chapter explores the Chapter 13 bankruptcy—adjustment of debts of an individual with regular income. Not all debtors may file a Chapter 13 petition. A debtor may file a Chapter 13 petition only if he or she is an individual with sufficiently stable and regular income to make payments under a Chapter 13 plan, with unsecured debts of less than $307,675 and secured debts of less than $922,975. 11 U.S.C.A. § 109(e). The dollar amounts for a Chapter 13 are adjusted every three years. 11 U.S.C.A. § 104(b). Future adjustment dates will be April 1, 2007 and April 1, 2010.

Chapter 13 gives individual debtors with regular income certain advantages not available under Chapter 7.

- Chapter 13 allows debtors to keep their nonexempt assets that would be surrendered to the trustee in a Chapter 7 case.
- Chapter 13 allows debtors to use their disposable income to pay creditors as much as they can over the term of the plan, whereas under Chapter 7, creditors are paid only from the liquidation of assets of the bankruptcy estate.
- Certain debts can be discharged in Chapter 13 that are potentially nondischargeable in Chapter 7.
- In Chapter 13, a debtor can cure defaults in order to keep property subject to a lien (e.g., curing a payment default on a loan secured by a residence).
- In Chapter 13, the automatic stay extends to codebtors on consumer loans.
- In Chapter 13, debtors can alter the payment terms on most secured debt if the debt is to be paid within the term of the Chapter 13 plan.
- In Chapter 13, debtors can pay nondischargeable claims, such as priority tax, and support alimony claims under the term of the Chapter 13 plan without the postpetition accrual of interest and penalties.
- A debtor may receive a discharge under Chapter 13 more often than every six years as permitted under Chapter 7.
- A Chapter 13 filing carries less stigma for the debtor than does a Chapter 7 filing.

Chapter 13 has disadvantages as well.

- A Chapter 13 debtor is in bankruptcy for three to fives years and will need to live under a tight budget with little room for contingencies.
- The Chapter 13 trustee is paid a fee under the Chapter 13 plan, thus reducing the amount available to pay creditors under the plan.

- Because of the additional work involved in a Chapter 13, attorneys will generally charge debtors higher fees for Chapter 13 than for Chapter 7.
- Creditors may be less willing to extend credit to a Chapter 13 debtor during the term of the plan because all of the debtor's disposable income is subject to the plan and is not available to postpetition creditors unless the plan is modified.

This chapter follows the Chapter 13 case from the time the potential client initiates contact with the bankruptcy attorney's office through the closing of the case and beyond. This chapter includes

- the initiation of the attorney/client relationship;
- the filing of the Chapter 13 petition;
- the significance of the filing;
- the Chapter 13 plan, its contents, the debtor's payments under the plan, and modification of the plan before confirmation;
- the appointment of the Chapter 13 trustee, as well as the various motions and complaints that could be filed after the order for relief;
- the clerk's notice and the meeting of creditors;
- the hearing on confirmation of the plan and the concept of the Chapter 13 cramdown;
- modification of the plan after confirmation and revocation of an order of confirmation;
- the debtor's full-compliance discharge after payments have been completed under the plan, and the hardship discharge for those debtors who may be unable to complete the payments under the plan;
- the closing of the case and further action available after the case is closed.

For those who would like to follow a Chapter 13 case in diagram form, the following flow chart in Exhibit 6–1 will prove useful.

SECTION 1
THE INITIATION OF A CHAPTER 13 CASE

The initiation of a Chapter 13 case closely resembles that of a Chapter 7 case. The main difference is that a Chapter 13 plan must be drafted. As noted earlier, all attorneys have their own ways of allocating responsibility to their paralegals and for dealing with debtor-clients. Some attorneys effectively use their paralegals by significantly involving them in the process. For example, an attorney may employ the following procedure:

- After the debtor has initiated contact with the attorney's firm, the paralegal sets up the client file, acquires a list of the debtor's creditors, and initiates a conflict of interest check.
- The paralegal gives the debtor a questionnaire (worksheets) that will help the debtor itemize his or her assets and liabilities as well as monthly income and monthly expenses.
- The paralegal requires the debtor to provide copies of relevant documents such as real estate deeds and mortgages, loan agreements, security agreements, vehicle titles, and tax returns.
- The debtor completes the questionnaire and returns it to the paralegal along with the documents requested by the paralegal.
- The paralegal meets with the debtor and reviews the questionnaire with the debtor to insure that it is completed fully and accurately and to identify any emergencies that may require the attorney's immediate attention.
- The attorney and paralegal meet with the debtor, and the attorney discusses the questionnaire adding, deleting, modifying, and verifying the debtor's entries.

EXHIBIT 6–1 Flowchart for Chapter 13

Filing the Chapter 13 Petition

The debtor files with the bankruptcy court clerk's office:

1. Filing fee
2. Voluntary petition, including Exhibit B, if the debtor is an individual whose debts are primarily consumer debts, and Exhibit C, if the debtor has some connection to hazardous waste
3. Clerk's notice (if an individual consumer debtor), if required by the court
4. Disclosure of attorney's compensation statement or disclosure of compensation statement by a non-attorney bankruptcy petition preparer
5. List of creditors
6. Schedules
   a. Summary of schedules
   b. Schedule A. Real property
   c. Schedule B. Personal property
   d. Schedule C. Property claimed as exempt
   e. Schedule D. Creditors holding secured claims
   f. Schedule E. Creditors holding unsecured priority claims
   g. Schedule F. Creditors holding unsecured nonpriority claims
   h. Schedule G. Executory contracts and unexpired leases
   i. Schedule H. Codebtors
   j. Schedule I. Current income of individual debtor(s)
   k. Schedule J. Current expenditures of individual debtor(s)
7. Statement of financial affairs
8. Chapter 13 plan

If the petition is accompanied by the list of creditors, the debtor has up to 15 days to file items 6, 7, and 8

The debtor has a duty to supplement the schedules for certain property acquired after the petition has been filed

Prior to the time the case is closed, the debtor may amend the petition, lists, schedules, and statement of financial affairs

Prior to confirmation, the debtor may modify his or her plan

Upon filing of the voluntary petition, which constitutes an order for relief, an estate is created and the automatic stay and the codebtor stay go into effect, protecting the estate from dismemberment and the debtor and the codebtor from collection procedures

The standing Chapter 13 trustee, or another individual if there is no standing Chapter 13 trustee, or the U.S. trustee will serve as the trustee in the case

The clerk of the bankruptcy court mails to the debtor, the debtor's attorney, the trustee, all creditors, and the U.S. trustee:

1. notice of the filing of the chapter 13 bankruptcy case,
2. an explanation of the automatic stay and the codebtor stay,
3. the date, time, and location of the meeting of creditors,
4. the deadline for filing proofs of claim,
5. the deadline for filing objections to the debtor's claim of exemptions, and
6. the date, time, and location of the meetings of creditors

(continued)

EXHIBIT 6–1 Filing the Chapter 13 Petition, Continued

An eligible debtor may convert the case to Chapter 7, 11, or 12

A party in interest may move to convert the case to Chapter 7, 11, or 12

The debtor or a party in interest may move to dismiss the case

The debtor or a party in interest may move for a change of venue

A party in interest may move for abstention by the court or for examination of any entity

Meeting of Creditors

The meeting of creditors is to be held not less than 20 nor more than 50 days after the Chapter 13 petition has been filed

The business of the meeting of creditors includes the examination of the debtor under oath

Fresh Start for the Debtor (Discharge)

Within 60 days after the first date set for the meeting of creditors, a creditor may file a complaint objecting to the dischargeability of a debt

While the case is open, the debtor may file a complaint to determine the dischargeability of a debt or may move to avoid a judicial lien or to avoid a nonpossessory, nonpurchase money security interest in certain items of personal property, to the extent that such lien impairs exceptions to which the debtor would have been entitled

Within 30 days after the conclusion of the meeting of creditors or within 30 days after any amendment is filed, whichever is later, a party in interest may object to the debtor's claim of exemptions

Administration of the Estate

The debtor remains in possession of the property of the estate

If the debtor is engaged in business, the debtor is required to file periodic reports on forms as required by the U.S. trustee or the court

Within 30 days of the filing of the plan, the debtor begins making payments as proposed by the plan

A creditor may file a proof of claim, subject to the statutory deadline

A creditor, trustee, U.S. trustee, or the debtor may move for disallowance of a claim

(continued)

EXHIBIT 6–1 Filing the Chapter 13 Petition, Continued

A creditor may move for relief from the automatic stay or for relief from the codebtor stay

A creditor, trustee, U.S. trustee, or the debtor may move for abandonment of an asset from the estate

The debtor may move for permission to use cash collateral or to use, sell, or lease property

In many jurisdictions, the trustee may file a complaint to avoid unperfected security interests, statutory liens that arise upon the debtor's insolvency, prepetition preferential transfers of property of the debtor, prepetition transfers of property of the debtor that are fraudulent under the Bankruptcy Code or state law, and postpetition transfers of property of the estate that are not authorized by the bankruptcy court or Bankruptcy Code

In some jurisdictions, a debtor may use the trustee's avoidance powers

The debtor may file a motion to assume or reject executory contracts or unexpired leases

Confirmation Hearing

The court shall conduct a confirmation hearing at which time the court may confirm or deny confirmation of the debtor's plan

Parties in interest may object to confirmation of the plan

(continued)

EXHIBIT 6–1 Filing the Chapter 13 Petition, Continued

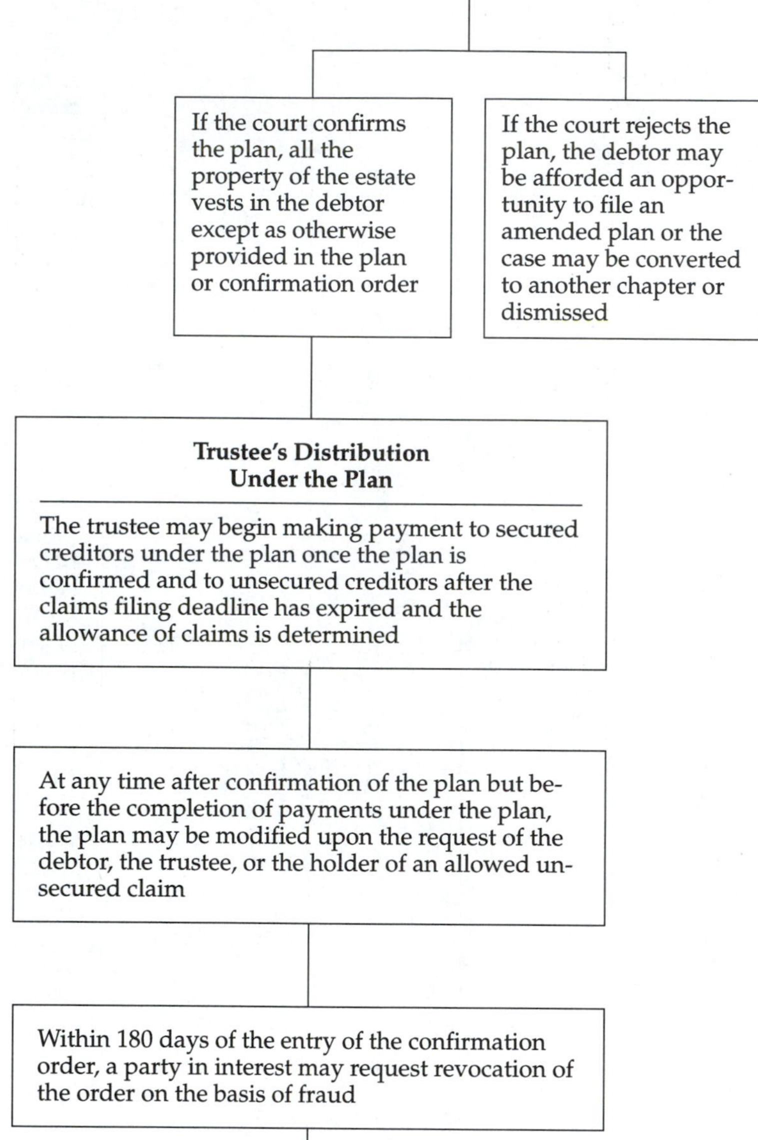

(continued)

EXHIBIT 6–1 Filing the Chapter 13 Petition, Continued

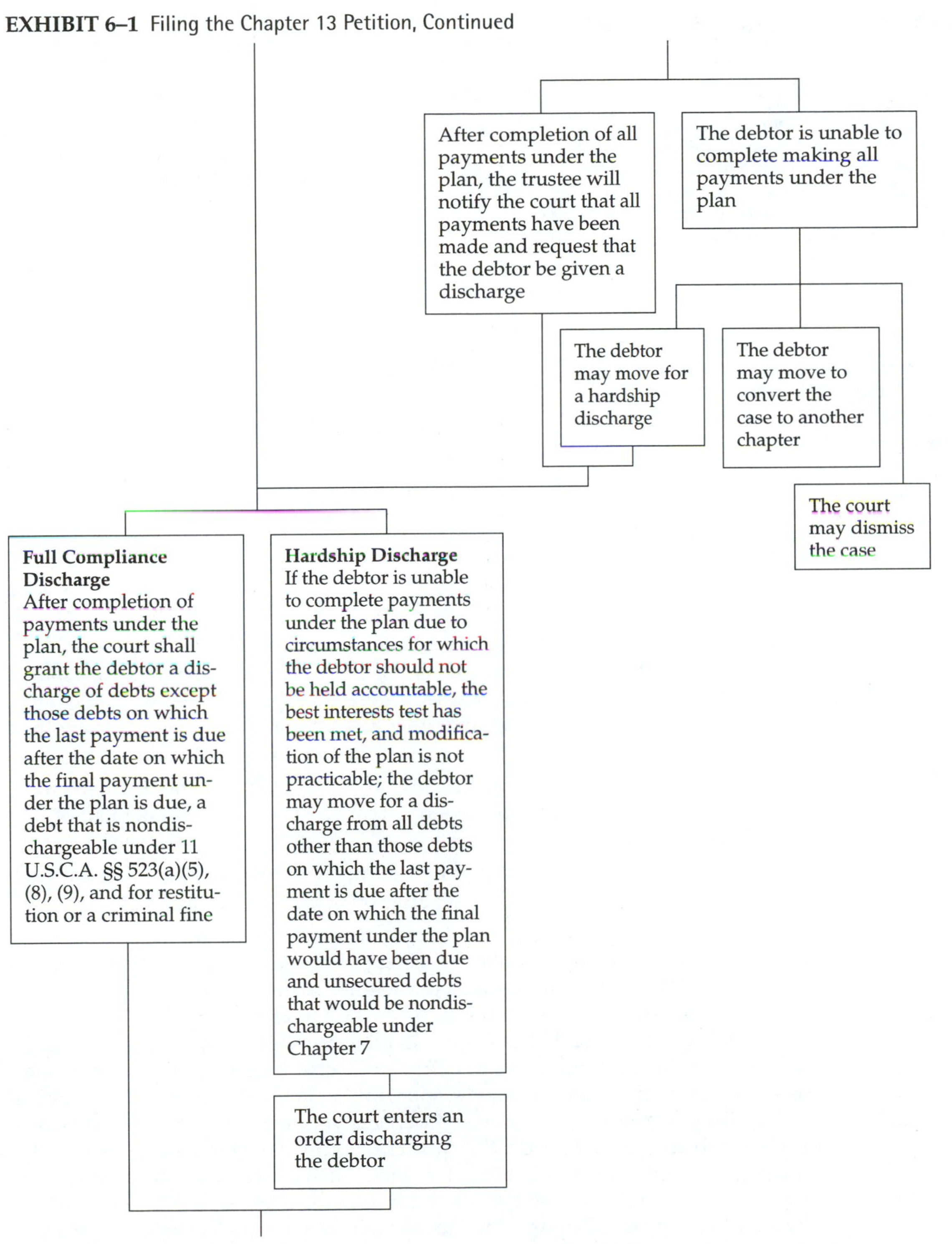

(continued)

EXHIBIT 6–1 Filing the Chapter 13 Petition, Continued

Upon the completion of payments under the plan, the trustee files a final report and final account certifying that the estate has been fully administered. Notice of the filing of the final report and the final account is given to all parties in interest. If there is no objection filed within 30 days, the case is closed.

A party in interest may request revocation of the discharge for fraud within one year after the discharge is granted

After the case is closed, it may be amended or reopened for cause with or without the appointment of a trustee

- The attorney advises the debtor whether bankruptcy is the appropriate course of action and, if so, whether the case should be filed under Chapter 7 or Chapter 13. The attorney explains the bankruptcy process to the debtor and discusses attorney fees and other aspects of the attorney/client contract for services.
- The paralegal completes the petition, the list of creditors, the disclosure of attorney's compensation statement, the schedules, and the statement of financial affairs.
- If the relief selected is a Chapter 13 bankruptcy, the attorney or an experienced paralegal under the attorney's supervision drafts the Chapter 13 plan.

To illustrate a Chapter 13 bankruptcy, the text will follow Jennifer and Eric McPherson, husband and wife, from Problem 4.5 and Chapter 5, Section 1. We will pick up the discussion with the meeting attended by the McPhersons, the attorney, and the paralegal. The discussion focuses on a Chapter 13 filing.

The attorney noted that a Chapter 13 filing requires that a Chapter 13 plan be submitted to and confirmed by the court. The Chapter 13 plan term may be as short as three years and, with the court's approval, as long as five years. 11 U.S.C.A. § 1322(d). During the life of the plan, the McPhersons's disposable income will be paid to the Chapter 13 trustee. 11 U.S.C.A. § 1325(b)(1)(B). Therefore, under the plan, the McPhersons will be on a strict budget and the difference between their income and their budget will be considered disposable income (11 U.S.C.A. § 1322(b)(2)) and will be distributed by the Chapter 13 trustee to their creditors under the terms of a confirmed plan. As an initial impression, the attorney notes that to be in good faith and to have enough disposable income to fund the plan, the McPhersons will need to cut back spending. For example, they have been spending $1,000 on food a month and this will need to be trimmed to about $600. The $800 a month for clothing will need to be reduced to about $500. The $400 a month on entertainment will need to be reduced to about $150. Contributions to the church may need to be reduced or eliminated, but they can discuss this as the plan develops. Dry cleaning will be reduced from $300 a month to about $35. Eric Jr. may need to take out student loans or find alternative avenues for financing his education (his allowance will be eliminated) and Irene may need to attend public school rather than the private school she now attends. The attorney also explains that the yard and cleaning services may need to be cancelled for the plan to be confirmed. The McPhersons failure to make these concessions may prevent their plan from being confirmed due to an absence of good faith and their failure to meet the best interests test.

The attorney calculates that the McPhersons have $3,750 of income a month and will need to reduce their monthly budget to $2,750 a month so they can provide the Chapter 13 trustee with $1,000 as disposable income a month.

Jennifer	
Salary	$1,250.00 per month
Child support (Irene)	$500.00 per month
Eric	
Salary	$2,000.00 per month
Net salary	$3,750.00 per month

The attorney and paralegal calculate that the McPhersons have reasonably necessary expenses totaling $2,730.00 a month.

Jennifer	
State license (LPN)	$24.00 per month
Books & CE	25.00 per month
Eric	
Child support (Bethany)	400.00 per month
Home mortgage payments (First Mortgage Company)	500.00 per month
Electricity	75.00 per month
Natural gas	100.00 per month
Water	25.00 per month
Telephone	50.00 per month
Food	600.00 per month
Clothing	300.00 per month
Recreation, clubs, & entertainment	10.00 per month
Laundry & dry cleaning	35.00 per month
Medical & dental expenses	40.00 per month
Automobile insurance (one vehicle)	200.00 per month
Safe deposit box	5.00 per month
Home maintenance	100.00 per month
Transportation	125.00 per month
Charitable contributions	45.00 per month
Life insurance	75.00 per month
	$2,730.00 per month

Therefore the McPhersons's disposable monthly income is $1,020.00.

Monthly Income	$3,750.00
Monthly Expenses	$2,730.00
	$1,020.00

Their attorney proposes paying $1,000 a month into the plan.

PROBLEM 6.1 The attorney felt that the McPhersons needed $1,000.00 a month in disposable income to make the Chapter 13 plan confirmable. This required the attorney to insist that the McPhersons whittle their monthly expenses down to $2,730.00. Debts to be paid under the plan (other than the payment to First Mortgage Company to be made directly by the McPhersons) are no longer considered as monthly expenses.

Compare the previous list totaling $2,730.00 with the list of monthly expenses found in Problem 5.3 (the McPhersons's list plus any items added during their discussion with the paralegal and attorney). What changes were made to bring the McPhersons monthly expenses down to $2,730.00? Do you agree with these changes or would you have made others?

After formulating a monthly budget, the paralegal, under the attorney's supervision, completes the voluntary petition, the disclosure of attorney's compensation statement, the list of creditors, and the schedules and statement of financial affairs. These documents, found in Chapter 5 of this text, are identical whether the case is filed as a Chapter 13 or a Chapter 7 with two exceptions: the documents will designate that the case is being filed under Chapter 13, rather than Chapter 7, and Schedule J will be modified.

PROBLEM 6.2 Complete Schedule J, Current Expenditures of Individual Debtor(s) for a Chapter 13 filing. The form is available at http://www.uscourts.gov. Link to U.S. Bankruptcy Courts and then to official bankruptcy forms.

Are your entries the same (same dollar amounts) as when you completed Schedule J for the Chapter 7 filing?

The attorney or an experienced paralegal, under the attorney's supervision, will then draft the Chapter 13 plan.

SECTION 2
THE CHAPTER 13 PLAN

The debtor must file a plan showing how he or she intends to repay part or all of the allowed claims. Generally, payment will be from future earnings and from the surrender of collateral to the creditor. Occasionally, however, the plan may provide for the sale of assets and payment from the sale proceeds. The plan must be filed not later than 15 days after the filing of the petition, although an extension may be granted by the court for cause shown. Fed. R. Bank. P. 3015. Only the debtor may file a plan in a Chapter 13 case. 11 U.S.C.A. § 1321.

A. CONTENTS OF A CHAPTER 13 PLAN

The contents of a Chapter 13 plan are delineated in the Code. 11 U.S.C.A. § 1322. Some provisions are mandatory; others are permissive. The mandatory provisions are noted in the Code by "shall" or "may not" and the permissive provisions by "may." Compare 11 U.S.C.A. § 1322(a) with 11 U.S.C.A. § 1322(b).

1. Mandatory Provisions

Because Chapter 13 is designed with flexibility in mind, the Code provides only four mandatory provisions in regard to the contents of the plan.

1. A Chapter 13 plan must provide for the trustee's supervision and control of that portion of the debtor's future income necessary for the implementation of the plan. 11 U.S.C.A. § 1322(a)(1).
2. A Chapter 13 plan must provide for the full payment of all priority claims (11 U.S.C.A. § 507) unless the holder of the claim agrees to a different treatment of that claim. 11 U.S.C.A. § 1322(a)(2).
3. If the Chapter 13 plan classifies claims into classes, the plan must provide the same treatment for each claim within a class. 11 U.S.C.A. § 1322(a)(3).
4. The payment period under the plan may not exceed three years unless the court, for cause, approves a longer period. If a longer time period is approved, it may not exceed five years. 11 U.S.C.A. § 1322(d).

2. Permissive Provisions

A Chapter 13 plan may

1. divide unsecured nonpriority claims (non-11 U.S.C.A. § 507 claims) into classes;
2. modify the rights of holders of secured and unsecured claims, except claims secured only by a security interest in real property that is the debtor's principal residence;
3. cure or waive any default;
4. propose payments on unsecured claims concurrently with payments on any secured claim or any other unsecured claim;
5. provide for curing any default on any secured or unsecured claim on which the final payment is due after the proposed final payment under the plan;
6. provide for payment of any allowed postpetition claim;
7. assume or reject any previously unrejected executory contracts or unexpired lease;
8. propose the payment of all or any part of any claim from property of the estate or property of the debtor;
9. provide for the vesting of property of the estate; and
10. include any other provision not inconsistent with other Title 11 provisions. 11 U.S.C.A. § 1322(b).

3. A Sample Chapter 13 Plan

The format of a **Chapter 13 plan** may vary from district to district. Exhibit 6–2 provides a sample Chapter 13 plan.

Following are the attorney's comments on why the plan was drafted as it was.

Drafting a Chapter 13 plan requires working backwards. First determine what the debtor's disposable monthly income is. Disposable monthly income is defined in the Bankruptcy Code at 11 U.S.C.A. § 1325(b)(2)(A) as "income which is received by the debtor and which is not reasonably necessary to be expended . . . for the maintenance or support of the debtor or a dependent of the debtor. . . ." The McPhersons had $3,750 a month of income. The attorney designed a budget of $2,730 a month, thus leaving approximately $1,000 in disposable monthly income.

Once the disposable monthly income has been calculated, the plan can be developed by considering the first rule of the day—priority claims must be paid in full. 11 U.S.C.A. § 507. One advantage of a Chapter 13 is that the priority claims can be paid under the plan without interest. 11 U.S.C.A. § 1322(a)(2). The priority claims in the McPherson plan are the McPhersons' attorney, IRS, the state tax commission, and the arrearages in child support and alimony to Eric's former spouse. No interest is paid to any of these creditors. 11 U.S.C.A. § 507(a). This plan shows a $1,000 attorney fee. The amount of a reasonable attorney fee varies from jurisdiction to jurisdiction. Ordinarily an attorney would require that a portion of the fee be paid in advance of filing (in case the debtor is unable to present a confirmable plan) and allow the balance to be paid under the plan. This plan, for convenience, includes the full $1,000 in the plan with no up-front payment, and the payments are taken over a period less than the life of the plan. The attorney will be paid in 20 months at $50 a month. This shows that not all creditors need to be paid over the entire length of the plan.

EXHIBIT 6–2 Sample Chapter 13 Plan

UNITED STATES BANKRUPTCY COURT
FOR THE ________________ DISTRICT OF ________________

In re:)
)
McPHERSON, Eric) Case Number: 03-00000-R
SS# ***-**-1277) (Chapter 13)
McPHERSON, Jennifer)
SS# ***-**-2787)
Debtors.)

CHAPTER 13 PLAN

LENGTH OF PLAN: 40 months

PLAN PAYMENT: Debtor(s) shall pay $1,000.00 per month. The Trustee shall deduct the Trustee's preset percentage fee from each payment.

DATE OF COMMENCEMENT: Plan payments shall commence on or before 45 days after the Chapter 13 Petition is filed.

PRIORITY CLAIMS: (To be paid in full without interest)

CLAIMANT	DESCRIPTION	CLAIM AMOUNT	MONTHLY PAYMENT AND HOW PAID
Attorney	Legal Fee	$1,000.00	$ 50.00 × 20 months
IRS	Taxes	8,000.00	$200.00 × 40 months
State Tax Commission	Taxes	3,500.00	$ 87.50 × 40 months
Former Spouse	Child Support and Alimony	1,400.00	$ 35.00 × 40 months

(continued)

EXHIBIT 6–2 Sample Chapter 13 Plan, Continued

SECURED CLAIMS: (Exclusive of debt secured only by home mortgages)

CLAIMANT	FILED OR SCHEDULED CLAIM	COLLATERAL	ALLOWED SECURED CLAIM	INTEREST RATE	MONTHLY PAYMENT AND HOW PAID
Second Mtg. Co.	$ 6,000.00	2nd Mortgage	$6,000.00	7.5%	$170.00 × 40 months
Sears	$850.00	Washer/Dryer	$500.00	10%	$14.75 × 40 months
Auto Finance Co.	$12,000.00	Chevrolet Blazer	$8,000.00	10%	$236.01 × 40 months
Rockwell Construction	$ 2,500.00	Lien on Residence	$2,500.00	7.5%	$70.83 × 40 months

Note: Secured creditors shall retain their liens to the extent of allowed secured claim stated above. The allowed secured claim of each secured creditor shall be the value of the collateral, as indicated above, or the amount of the claim, whichever is less, with the balance of the claim as scheduled or filed being allowed as an unsecured claim, with the lien of the creditor being avoided on the unsecured portion pursuant to 11 U.S.C.A. §§ 506(a) and (b).

HOME MORTGAGE(S): (Debtor's principal residence)

CLAIMANT	DESCRIPTION	ALLOWED CLAIM AMOUNT	INTEREST RATE	MONTHLY PAYMENT AND HOW PAID
First Mortgage Co.	Residence	$60,000.00	8.0%	Regular payments ($500) direct to Creditor
First Mortgage Co.	Arrearage	$1,575.00	N/A	$ 39.38 × 40 months

SPECIAL UNSECURED CLASS(ES):

CLAIMANT	DESCRIPTION	ALLOWED CLAIM AMOUNT	INTEREST RATE	MONTHLY PAYMENT AND HOW PAID
Friendly Finance Co.	Co-Debtor	$1,500.00	15.0%	$47.88 x 40 months

PROPERTY TO BE SURRENDERED: The following property shall be surrendered to the named claimant in full satisfaction of the secured claim stated below with the balance, if any, relegated to general unsecured status.

CLAIMANT	COLLATERAL	ALLOWED SECURED CLAIM	BALANCE RELEGATED TO UNSECURED
Capital Finance Co.	Buick Regal	$3,000.00	$4,000.00

(continued)

LIEN AVOIDANCE(S): The Debtor(s) shall file a separate Motion or Motions to avoid the liens or security interests of the following claimants pursuant to 11 U.S.C.A. § 522(f) and, if applicable, the claim(s) of such claimant(s) shall be relegated and treated as general unsecured claims below:

CLAIMANT	COLLATERAL
Second Mortgage Co.	Household Goods

UNSECURED CLAIMS: All claims not specifically provided for above and those relegated to unsecured status above shall be paid as general unsecured claims, without priority, on a pro rata basis.

Unsecured Claims per Schedule F:	$77,100.00
Unsecured portion of Secured Claims per Schedule D:	$ 8,350.00
Total Projected Unsecured Claims:	$85,450.00
Approximated Percentage Payback to Holders of Unsecured Claims (Unsecured Priority and Unsecured Nonpriority Claims) (per Schedules E and F)	18.75%

Note: The approximate payback to unsecured claims may be more or less depending on claims actually filed and allowed.

OTHER PROVISIONS:

1. All property of the estate under 11 U.S.C.A. § 1306 shall be and remain property of the estate and all stays shall remain in force and effect until conclusion of the case or other Order of the Court.
2. All claims will be treated as set forth above unless a creditor objects prior to the confirmation hearing and files a claim within ninety (90) days after the first date set for the meeting of creditors called pursuant to 11 U.S.C.A. § 341(a). Governmental units must file claims within 180 days after the order for relief.
3. Unsecured Creditors without priority who fail to file a claim within the time stated in Paragraph 2 above, will not receive any distribution under this Plan.
4. All secured creditors shall retain their liens until conclusion of the Plan (except as to long-term secured debt, if any) thereafter, all secured creditors shall release all liens.
5. The above named Debtor(s) is/are enjoined from incurring any debts without prior approval of the Court, except such debts as may be necessary for emergency medical or hospital care.

Dated: ______________________

Respectfully submitted,

____

Attorney
Bar #
Address
Telephone

(continued)

EXHIBIT 6–2 Sample Chapter 13 Plan, Continued

CALCULATION OF BEST INTERESTS OF CREDITORS TEST
11 U.S.C.A. § 1325(a)(4)

Assets Available for Administration in Chapter 7:

• Bass Boat	$16,000.00
• Savings Bonds	3,000.00
	$19,000.00

Amount to be Paid by Debtors Under Plan:

$40,000.00 ($1,000 × 40)

Amount Available to Pay Unsecured Claims (Unsecured Priority and Unsecured Nonpriority Claims) in Chapter 13:

$40,000.00	Amount to be paid by debtors under plan
−2,400.00	Trustee Fee (6 percent) − 11 U.S.C.A. § 326(a)
$37,600.00	Available for Distribution
−18,575.00	Secured Claims
$19,025.00	Amount to be paid on unsecured claims (unsecured priority and unsecured nonpriority claims) under the plan

$19,025.00 exceeds $19,000.00, so best interests of creditors test is met.

11 U.S.C.A. § 1322(b)(4). If the attorney were to be paid over the entire life of the plan, the payment would be $25 a month. So this plan has two intervals—months 1–20 and months 21–40. The monthly payments to other creditors change depending on whether they are made during the first 20 months or the last 20 months. The debtor could decide to pay secured creditors toward the end of the plan, and they could not prevent confirmation so long as they are paid in full with accrued interest. Priority claims can be paid in full before the debtor begins paying the unsecured, nonpriority claims—and a number of debtors do just that.

The second category under this plan involves the treatment of secured claims, exclusive of debt secured only by the debtor's principal residence. Four claimants have such secured claims—Second Mortgage Company (a second mortgage on the principal residence), Sears (a security interest on the washer and dryer), Auto Finance Company (the security interest on the Chevrolet Blazer) and Rockwell Construction Company (a lien on the principal residence). The secured portion of these creditors must be paid in full with interest.

If the amount of a claim exceeds the value of the collateral, the claimant will hold a secured claim up to the value of the collateral and an unsecured claim for the balance. 11 U.S.C.A. § 506(a). Both Sears and Auto Finance Company are secured by collateral valued at less than their respective claims. Therefore, each has a secured claim and an unsecured claim. Under the plan, they must be paid in full on their secured claim, although they will only be paid a portion of their unsecured claim along with other unsecured creditors. As to these four secured creditors, the plan calls for paying interest to the secured party, but not at the interest rate agreed upon when the respective loans were made. The interest rate may be modified so long as the claim is paid in full.

Rockwell Construction has been included as a secured creditor because the grace period in which Rockwell may file a lien against the house has not expired. The debtors anticipate that after the Chapter 13 petition has been filed, Rockwell will file its lien. This filing is not precluded by the automatic stay because of an exception in 11 U.S.C.A. § 362(b)(3)—within a grace period afforded under state law. Upon the filing of its lien, Rockwell's claim must be treated as a secured claim.

The third category of claims treated under the plan is the claim of First Mortgage Company, secured only by the McPhersons' residence. Special protection is afforded such claims under the Bankruptcy Code. 11 U.S.C.A. § 1322(b)(2). Claims secured only by a security interest in real property that is the debtors' principal residence may not be modified under the plan. That is, the term, interest rate and claim amount, for instance, may not be changed.

Upon filing the petition, the debtors may resume making their regular mortgage payments to the mortgagee. 11 U.S.C.A. § 1322(b)(5). Many courts will permit the debtors to make the mortgage payments directly to the creditor (the mortgagee) rather than to the Chapter 13 trustee. 11 U.S.C.A. § 1326(c). All other payments are made by the Chapter 13 trustee to the creditors. Remaining current on their home mortgage is important to the debtors because their home mortgage is an obligation that will extend beyond the terms of the Chapter 13 plan.

While the McPhersons resume making their mortgage payments to First Mortgage Company, the plan provides that they will cure the $1,575 arrearage over the 40 month life of the plan. Because the mortgage document does not provide for the payment of interest on the arrearage claim, the McPhersons are not required to pay interest in order to cure the default. 11 U.S.C.A. § 1322(e). The right to cure a default on a claim secured by the debtor's principal residence is particularly important if the secured creditor has initiated a mortgage foreclosure. Through Chapter 13, debtors have the right to cure such a default through a Chapter 13 plan until the mortgaged property has been sold at a foreclosure sale conducted in accordance with applicable nonbankruptcy law. 11 U.S.C.A. § 1322(c)(1). Of course, upon the filing of the petition, the secured creditor is stayed from conducting such a foreclosure sale, so it is imperative that debtors file their Chapter 13 petition before the foreclosure sale. 11 U.S.C.A. § 362(a)(5).

The fourth category of claims treated under the plan deals with a special unsecured claim. As a general rule, debtors may not discriminate in favor of one or more unsecured claims over others. 11 U.S.C.A. § 1322(b)(1). One exception to this rule applies to consumer debt in which an individual, like a relative, is liable on the debt with the debtor. Such a claim may be paid in full even though other unsecured claims are not. If the relative is required to pay the portion of the debt not paid by the debtor under the plan, the pressure on the debtor may impede the debtors' ability to perform under the plan. This provision is consistent with the codebtor stay, which precludes creditors from collecting a consumer debt from a codebtor as long as a plan provides for the payment of the claim in full. 11 U.S.C.A. § 1301. Since the McPhersons' debt to Friendly Finance is guaranteed by a relative, Eric's father, the McPhersons may treat that claim differently from other unsecured claims by paying it in full.

The fifth category involves property to be surrendered. The treatment of the claim of Capital Finance Company secured by the Buick Regal is in recognition that among the ways to pay a secured claim is to surrender the collateral to the creditor and relegate the balance of the claim, if any, to unsecured status. 11 U.S.C.A. § 1325(a)(5)(C). Here, the McPhersons chose to surrender the vehicle to Capital Finance Company because it is of minimal value, $3,000, and they believe that they can manage without it. The only reason Capital Finance Company may challenge the plan is if it believes the vehicle is not really worth $3,000, which has the effect of limiting the unsecured claim to $4,000.

The sixth category involves lien avoidances. Second Mortgage Company's claim is secured by a second mortgage on the McPhersons' residence and their household goods. Even though Second Mortgage Company's claim is secured by a mortgage on the residence, Second Mortgage's claim, unlike the claim of First Mortgage Company, may be modified because collateral in addition to the residence secures the claim. The McPhersons are entitled to avoid Second Mortgage Company's lien on their household goods because their household goods are exempt property, they are in the possession of the McPhersons, Second Mortgage Company's loan was not used by the McPhersons to purchase the household goods, and the household goods are among the category of assets subject to lien avoidance. 11 U.S.C.A. § 522(f)(1)(B). Once the lien on the household goods is avoided, Second Mortgage Company's claim will be secured only by the residence. Many courts require that the lien avoidance be accomplished by a separate motion rather than through the confirmed plan. Fed. R. Bank. P. 4003(d). A Motion to Avoid Security Interest of Second Mortgage Company is shown in Exhibit 6–3.

EXHIBIT 6–3 Motion of Debtors to Avoid Lien

IN THE UNITED STATES BANKRUPTCY COURT
FOR THE ______________ DISTRICT OF ______________

In re:	)	
	)	
McPHERSON, Eric	)	Case Number:
SS# ***-**-1277	)	(Chapter 13)
McPHERSON, Jennifer	)	
SS# ***-**-2787	)	
Debtors.	)	

MOTION OF DEBTORS TO AVOID LIEN
OF SECOND MORTGAGE BANK COMPANY,
AND NOTICE OF OPPORTUNITY FOR HEARING

Debtors, Eric and Jennifer McPherson, for this Motion to Avoid Lien of Second Mortgage Company, and Notice of Opportunity for Hearing, state as follows:

1. The Debtors filed with this Court their Voluntary Petition under Chapter 13 of the United States Bankruptcy Code on __________________ .

2. This Court has jurisdiction over the parties and subject of this core proceeding pursuant to 28 U.S.C.A. §§ 1334 and 157(b)(2)(K).

3. Included among the assets of the Debtors are household goods and furnishings that the Debtors value at $3,500.00. The household goods were claimed as exempt by the Debtors pursuant to __[applicable state law]__ . No objection to the exemption was timely filed. The exemption is therefore deemed allowed pursuant to 11 U.S.C.A. § 522(l) and Fed. R. Bank. P. 4003(b).

5. On, ______________________ , the Debtors made, executed, and delivered to Second Mortgage Company a security agreement by which they conveyed to Second Mortgage Company a security interest in, among other things, their household goods to secure a non-possessory, non-purchase money loan made by Second Mortgage Company to the Debtors.

6. Second Mortgage Company's security interest in the household goods is voidable pursuant to 11 U.S.C.A. § 522(f)(1)(B) and Fed. R. Bank. P. 4001(d).

Your rights may be affected. You should read this document carefully and consult your attorney about your rights and the effect of this document. If you do not want the Court to grant the requested relief, or if you wish to have your views considered, you must file a written response or objection to the requested relief, with the Clerk of the United States Bankruptcy Court for the ____________________________ District of _______________________ , _______________________ , ___________________ no later than fifteen (15) days from the date of filing of this request for relief. You should also mail a file-stamped copy of your response or objection to the undersigned movants attorney [and others who are required to be served] and file a certificate of service with the Court. If no response or objection is timely filed, the Court may grant the requested relief without a hearing or further notice. The fifteen (15) day period includes the three (3) days allowed for mailing provided for in Fed. R. Bank. P. 9006(f).

(continued)

EXHIBIT 6–3 Motion of Debtors to Avoid Lien, Continued

WHEREFORE, the Debtors request, in the absence of an objection or after a hearing on any objection, for an order voiding Second Mortgage Company's security interest in the household goods.

DATED at __________________________, this ______ day of ______________________, 20___ .

Respectfully submitted,

____

Attorney's Name, Bar #*****
Firm
Address
Phone
FAX
Attorney for Eric & Jennifer
McPherson, debtors

CERTIFICATE OF SERVICE

I do hereby certify that on ______ day of ________________, 20___ , a true, correct and exact copy of the above and foregoing document was served by placing same in the United States Mail, certified mail, return receipt requested, addressed as follows:

Second Mortgage Company

____

Attorney's Name

This same concept applies to the avoidance of judicial liens. If a creditor, such as one of the credit card companies, had sued the McPhersons prior to their filing the Chapter 13 petition and had received a judgment, but was unable to collect the judgment from the McPhersons, the judgment creditor had the opportunity to attach its judgment to any of the McPherson property that it could find. Assume that the judgment creditor attached its judgment to the McPherson home and then the McPhersons filed their Chapter 13 petition. The McPhersons could avoid the judicial lien because it impaired the exemption they had in their home. 11 U.S.C.A. § 522(f)(1)(A).

The seventh and final category of claims under the McPhersons' plan are the general unsecured claims. They consist of unsecured claims and the unsecured portion of a partially secured claim. 11 U.S.C.A. § 506(a). Unsecured claims merely get paid the balance of payments under the plan not otherwise paid on secured claims, priority claims, and codebtor claims. Generally, as long as the debtors are contributing all of their disposable income to the plan (11 U.S.C.A. § 1325(b)(1)(B)) and the best interests test is met (11 U.S.C.A. § 1325(a)(4)), the plan may be confirmed. Here, very little is available from the McPhersons' plan to pay general unsecured creditors primarily because of the size of their priority claims and, as previously noted, priority claims must be paid in full under the plan.

Unfortunately, this particular plan will not completely solve the McPhersons' financial problems. They owe $35,000 to Thrifty Credit Union for student loans guaranteed by the government, a debt that is nondischargable. 11 U.S.C.A. §§ 1328(a), 523(a)(8). Since claims for student loans are not afforded priority status (priority claims are paid in full under a plan) and are not guaranteed by an individual codebtor (codebtors may be paid in full under the plan), they are merely unsecured claims that must be paid *pro rata* with other unsecured claims. Consequently, when the McPhersons receive their discharge in 40 months, they must be prepared to deal with the balance of the student loan debt to Thrifty Credit Union.

The attorney selected a plan based on 40 months, a number between 36 and 60 and the minimum number of months required to meet the best interests of creditors test. The attorney used the following formula to calculate the minimum number of months required for the plan.

> The number of months of the plan equals [(the assets available for administration in a Chapter 7 case plus the amount of the secured claims) divided by (1.00 less the trustee's percentage)] divided by the dollars of disposable income per month.

EXAMPLE

For the McPhersons, the Number of months = [($19,000 + $18,575) divided by (1.00 − .06)] divided by $1,000.

or

The Number of months = [$37,575 divided by .94] divided by $1,000.

or

The Number of months = 39.97 months or rounded up to 40 months

	$40,000	amount to be paid by debtors under the plan
less	2,400	trustee's fee (6%)
	$37,600	available for distribution under the plan
less	$18,575	secured claims
	$19,025	amount to be paid on unsecured claims (i.e., unsecured priority and unsecured nonpriority claims) under the plan.

$19,025 (the amount to be paid to unsecured claims under the Chapter 13 plan) exceeds $19,000 (the amount to be paid to unsecured claims under Chapter 7 liquidation) so the best interests of creditors test is met.

Also, the amount to be paid on unsecured claims under the plan must exceed the amount of the unsecured priority claims, because the priority claims must be paid in full. The McPhersons have priority claims totaling $13,900, an amount less than the amount to be paid on unsecured claims under the plan ($19,025). Therefore, 40 months can be used to fund this plan.

At the end of the plan, the attorney has included footnotes to address the following issues:

1. Once the plan is confirmed, unless the plan or the order confirming plan provides otherwise, property of the estate revests in the debtor. 11 U.S.C.A. § 1327(b). The debtor wants the property to remain property of the estate because it will remain protected by the automatic stay and a postpetition creditor will still be subject to the automatic stay and cannot collect a judgment from property of the estate. 11 U.S.C.A. § 362(a)(3). Permitting a postpetition creditor from collecting a debt from property of the estate, by garnishing the debtor's wages, for instance, will impair the debtor's ability to perform under a plan.

2. & 3. Unsecured creditors who do not timely file claims will not receive a distribution under the plan. 11 U.S.C.A. § 502(b)(9). These creditors have not been considered when the payouts of the plan were formulated. Therefore, even if the plan is confirmed, the trustee must wait until the deadline for filing claims has expired before making payments to unsecured creditors under the plan.

4. All secured claims retain their liens throughout the plan and will release their liens once all payments have been made. This protects not only the creditor, but the debtor, as well.

5. Enjoins the debtors from incurring debt post-bankruptcy. By acquiring more debt, the plan is upset. If debtors need to incur more debt, they must return to court and receive a modification of the plan.

PROBLEM 6.3 What if, when the Chapter 13 trustee was reviewing the filed claims, she noticed that the All America Pawn Shop had filed a claim indicating that it had a perfected security interest in a 12-gauge shotgun recently purchased by Eric McPherson. Upon further investigation, the trustee discovered that the shotgun was purchased for $600, its current value is $400, and the balance owed to All America is $50. The trustee knows that the shotgun is nonexempt under state law. Would the 40-month plan be confirmable? (That is, does the introduction of the gun increase the amount of money that would be available to distribute to unsecured creditors in Chapter 7 and thus cause the plan not to meet the best interests of creditors test?) Return to the formula used by the attorney to compute the minimum number of months.

If 40 months would be inadequate, how many months would be adequate?

PROBLEM 6.4 Return to the original facts. What if the McPhersons told their attorney that they would rather be under the plan for 48 months and have more of their income to spend on a monthly basis. How much disposable monthly income would they need to contribute to a 48-month plan? [Suggestion: Return to the attorney's formula and insert 48 for the number of months and divide [(the assets available for administration in a Chapter 7 case plus the amount of the secured claims) by (1.00 less the trustee's percentage)] by 48 months, rather than by the dollars of disposable income per month.]

B. THE DEBTOR'S PAYMENTS UNDER THE PLAN

Starting within 30 days after the plan is filed and unless otherwise ordered by the court, the debtor begins making payments to the trustee. 11 U.S.C.A. § 1326(a)(1). The trustee retains these payments until confirmation or denial of confirmation of the plan. 11 U.S.C.A. § 1326(a)(2).

In some cases, the debtor may be unable to make even the first payment under the plan. Those cases will likely be converted to Chapter 7 or dismissed. 11 U.S.C.A. § 1307(c)(4).

C. MODIFICATION OF THE PLAN BEFORE CONFIRMATION

The debtor may modify his or her plan at any time before confirmation, but the plan, as modified, must meet the requirements of the Code. 11 U.S.C.A. § 1323(a). The plan, as modified, becomes the plan. 11 U.S.C.A. § 1323(b). A holder of a secured claim that has accepted or rejected the plan is deemed to have accepted or rejected the plan, as modified, unless the holder's rights have been changed by the modification and the holder has changed the previous acceptance or rejection. 11 U.S.C.A. § 1323(c).

SECTION 3
THE FILING OF THE PETITION

The same documents necessary for filing the petition in a voluntary Chapter 7 case are necessary in a Chapter 13 case. However, unlike a **Chapter 7 case,** which is a liquidation, a Chapter 13 case is not a liquidation and therefore does require a plan as described in the previous section of this chapter. The filing of a Chapter 13 case requires the following items:

1. Filing fee;
2. Voluntary Petition (Official Form No. 1);
3. Clerk's Notice (if an individual consumer debtor), if required by the court;

4. Disclosure of attorney's compensation statement or disclosure of compensation statement by a non-attorney bankruptcy petition preparer;

5. List of creditors;

6. Schedules (Official Form No. 6)

   a. Summary of Schedules
   b. Schedule A: Real Property
   c. Schedule B: Personal Property
   d. Schedule C: Property Claimed as Exempt
   e. Schedule D: Creditors Holding Secured Claims
   f. Schedule E: Creditors Holding Unsecured Priority Claims
   g. Schedule F: Creditors Holding Unsecured Nonpriority Claims
   h. Schedule G: Executory Contracts and Unexpired Leases
   i. Schedule H: Codebtors
   j. Schedule I: Current Income of Individual Debtor(s)
   k. Schedule J: Current Expenditures of Individual Debtor(s)

7. Statement of Financial Affairs (Official Form No. 7); and

8. Chapter 13 plan.

The Bankruptcy Code provides for reasonable compensation to the debtor's attorney in a Chapter 13 case for representing the interests of an individual debtor in connection with the case. 11 U.S.C.A. § 330(a)(4)(B). The Code also authorizes the court to order the return of any excess to the estate if interim compensation exceeds the final compensation awarded. 11 U.S.C.A. § 330(a)(5). Ordinarily, a debtor's attorney will require that a portion of the fee be paid before filing the petition and accept payment of the balance of the fee under the confirmed plan. Rather than requiring the attorney to file a fee application that is otherwise required under 11 U.S.C.A. § 330, courts will allow the fee if the amount does not exceed a set amount approved by the court.

If the petition is accompanied by the list of creditors, the debtor has 15 days from the date of the filing of the petition to file the schedules, the statement of financial affairs, and the Chapter 13 plan. Fed. R. Bank. P. 1007(c), 3015(b).

Prior to the time the case is closed, the debtor may amend the petition, lists, schedules, and statement previously filed. Fed. R. Bank. P. 1009(a). The debtor has a duty to supplement the schedules if, within 180 days after the date of filing the petition, property is acquired by bequest, devise, or inheritance or as a result of a property settlement agreement with the debtor's spouse or an interlocutory or final divorce decree. The debtor may also have acquired property as a beneficiary of a life insurance policy or a death benefit plan. 11 U.S.C.A. § 541(a)(5); Fed. R. Bank. P. 1007(h). The duty of the debtor to supplement the schedules may prove important to creditors who would otherwise be paid less or not at all. It prevents the debtor who may be discharged of his or her debts from walking away with potentially large sums of money that would otherwise increase the distribution under the plan.

SECTION 4
THE SIGNIFICANCE OF FILING A PETITION

The filing of the petition by a debtor constitutes an order for relief under Chapter 13. Upon the filing of the petition, the estate is created and the automatic stay goes into effect, protecting the estate from dismemberment and the debtor from collection procedures. This prevents the more aggressive creditors from taking what is owed to them to the detriment of other creditors.

The automatic stay in a Chapter 13 is the same as the automatic stay in a Chapter 7.

The automatic stay applies not only to the debtor and the property of the debtor but also to property of the estate. Since Chapter 13 property of the estate includes the debtor's postpetition earnings (11 U.S.C.A. § 1306(a)(2)), a postpetition creditor of the debtor, who is not precluded from garnishing a Chapter 7 debtor's wages, is affected by the automatic stay in Chapter 13. Although the postpetition creditor could obtain a judgment against the debtor without violating the stay, the creditor could not garnish a Chapter 13 debtor's wages or otherwise execute on the debtor's assets so long as the assets are property of the estate.

EXAMPLE

The McPhersons filed their Chapter 13 plan and it was confirmed by the bankruptcy court. The plan required the McPhersons to surrender their second car, the Buick Regal.

Several months after confirmation and with bankruptcy court approval, the McPhersons purchased a new car so Jennifer could get back and forth to work. They purchased a new VW from Import Motors for $18,000. The car was purchased with no money down and zero percent interest over five years. Payments were $300 a month. Import Motors financed the sale.

When the McPhersons were unable to make their payments, Import Motors repossessed the car and sued the McPhersons for the deficiency. Import Motors then sought to garnish Jennifer's wages.

Import Motors is a postpetition creditor because the McPhersons' obligation arose after they filed their petition in bankruptcy. Had they filed a Chapter 7 petition, Import Motors could garnish her wages because the bankruptcy estate would not have included her postpetition income. Thus the automatic stay would not have applied. However, since the McPhersons filed a Chapter 13 petition, the automatic stay bars Import Motors from garnishing Jennifer's wages, because her postpetition wages are part of their bankruptcy estate.

There is an additional stay in Chapter 13—a codebtor stay. The **codebtor stay,** which precludes collection of all or any part of a consumer debt of the debtor from a codebtor (usually a family member), also goes into effect at this time. 11 U.S.C.A. § 1301.

EXAMPLE

Since the McPhersons have been married, they have had financial problems. Eric was unemployed for a time before he found his current position at the local high school.

Six months ago, the McPhersons borrowed $1,500 from Friendly Finance at an annual rate of 15 percent. Eric's father, Benjamin Franklin McPherson, cosigned for the loan. Monthly payments are $100 a month.

When the McPhersons filed their Chapter 13 petition, they had not paid Friendly Finance for four months.

Upon the filing of the petition, the codebtor stay automatically went into effect, preventing Friendly Finance from attempting to collect on the loan from Eric's father.

The codebtor stay does not apply if the codebtor became liable in the ordinary course of the codebtor's business or if the case is closed, dismissed, or converted to Chapter 7 or 11. 11 U.S.C.A. § 1301(a). The codebtor stay does not preclude a creditor from presenting a negotiable instrument for payment and giving notice of dishonor. 11 U.S.C.A. § 1301(b).

A creditor with a claim based on a consumer debt of the Chapter 13 debtor may seek relief from the codebtor stay if the codebtor received the consideration for the claim held by the creditor, if the Chapter 13 plan does not propose to pay the creditor his or her claim, or if the creditor's interest would be irreparably harmed by continuation of the stay. 11 U.S.C.A. § 1301(c). To the extent that the Chapter 13 plan does not propose to pay a creditor's claim and that creditor has filed a request for relief from the codebtor stay, the debtor or codebtor has 20 days to file a written objection; otherwise, the codebtor stay is terminated as to that creditor's claim. 11 U.S.C.A. § 1301(d).

EXAMPLE

Change the facts from the McPherson problem so that Jennifer purchased her Buick Regal after her divorce and before her marriage to Eric McPherson. Jennifer financed the purchase through Capital Finance Company, and her Aunt Sarah cosigned her obligation to Capital Finance. Subsequently, she married Eric and they filed their Chapter 13 petition. Their Chapter 13 plan proposed surrender of the Buick to Capital Finance and valued the Buick at $3,000, although the outstanding debt was $7,000. The plan was confirmed and the Buick was surrendered to Capital Finance.

Assume instead that the McPhersons' Chapter 13 plan had proposed to pay Capital Finance on its unsecured deficiency claim, $1,600 or $.40 on a dollar on the debt. Capital Finance moved for relief from the codebtor stay. Upon receiving relief from the codebtor stay, Capital Finance could pursue Aunt Sarah for $2,400.

The codebtor stay only applies to the extent that the claim is being paid under the plan. If the plan only proposes to pay $.40 on a dollar on a debt where there is a co-obligor, as soon as the plan is confirmed, the creditor can get codebtor stay relief and collect the balance owed on the debt (in this instance $.60 on a dollar) from the codebtor.

After the order for relief, the various parties in interest may begin to assert their claims against the estate. A creditor or an indenture trustee may file a proof of claim subject to the time limitations found in the Rules. If a creditor does not timely file a proof of claim, the debtor, codebtor, or trustee may file a proof of claim within 30 days after expiration of the time for filing claims. 11 U.S.C.A. §§ 501(b), (c); Fed. R. Bank. P. 3004, 3005.

A. POSSESSION AND CONTROL OF PROPERTY OF THE ESTATE

Unlike a Chapter 7 where the trustee takes possession of nonexempt property, the debtor in a Chapter 13 case remains in possession of all property of the estate except as specified and provided in the confirmed plan or order confirming a plan. 11 U.S.C.A. § 1306(b). The right to retain possession and control of property of the estate are often the controlling factors in the debtor's decision to select a Chapter 13 filing. The estate in a Chapter 13 case includes all the property specified in section 541 and all the property that the debtor acquires after the commencement of the case but before the case is closed, dismissed, or converted to a case under Chapter 7, 11, or 12, whichever occurs first. Also included in the property of the estate are earnings from services performed by the debtor after the commencement of the case but before the case is closed, dismissed, or converted to a case under Chapter 7, 11, or 12, whichever occurs first. 11 U.S.C.A. § 1306(a).

The property of the estate in a Chapter 13 case that is converted to a case under another chapter will consist only of the property at the date of filing the Chapter 13 petition that remains in possession of or under control of the debtor on the date of conversion. The debtor not only retains the property acquired since the filing date but also benefits from postpetition payments made on secured claims. 11 U.S.C.A. § 348(f)(1). This provides an additional incentive for debtors to try Chapter 13 but only if the debtor converts to another chapter in good faith. 11 U.S.C.A. § 348(f)(2).

B. OPERATION OF THE DEBTOR'S BUSINESS

If the debtor is engaged in business, the Code contemplates that the debtor will operate the business unless the court orders otherwise. 11 U.S.C.A. § 1304(b). The court will enter an order for periodic reports from the debtor engaged in business. Fed. R. Bank. P. 2015(c)(1). The nature of these reports will vary depending on the debtor's business and how much information is required by the court. Most courts will have a regular format for this type of report.

C. EXEMPTIONS

Exemptions are treated the same in a Chapter 13 case as in a Chapter 7 case. The listing of exemptions and the valuation of exempt property, as well as the valuation of nonexempt property, should be considered carefully. What is exempt or nonexempt, and its value, will have a definite effect on the confirmation of a plan. The value, as of the effective date of the plan, of the property to be distributed under the plan to each allowed unsecured claim cannot be less than the amount that would have been paid on such claim if the petition had been filed under Chapter 7. 11 U.S.C.A. § 1325(a)(4). This is called the best interests of creditors test. Therefore, the more nonexempt assets the debtor has, the more the creditors holding unsecured claims will be paid.

EXAMPLE

The McPhersons had $19,000 in nonexempt assets and $47,100 in unsecured debt. If the McPhersons were to file a Chapter 7 petition, their creditors holding unsecured claims would receive $.403 on a dollar. If they were to file a Chapter 13 petition, their creditors holding unsecured claims would need to receive at least $.403 on a dollar to satisfy the best interests of creditors test.

Naturally, if the McPhersons had $30,000 rather than $19,000 in nonexempt assets, their creditors holding unsecured claims would receive $.637 on a dollar in a Chapter 7 case and at least $.637 in a Chapter 13 case. Thus, the more nonexempt assets the debtor has, the higher will be the threshold for the best interests of creditors test.

SECTION 5
APPOINTMENT AND DUTIES OF A CHAPTER 13 TRUSTEE

After the order for relief is entered, the standing Chapter 13 trustee, or another individual if there is no standing trustee, or the U.S. trustee will serve as the trustee in the case. 11 U.S.C.A. § 1302(a). The trustee in a Chapter 13 case is accountable for all property received and must perform some of the same duties as a Chapter 7 trustee. These duties include

1. investigate the financial affairs of the debtor;
2. examine proofs of claim and object to allowance of any claim that is improper if a purpose would be served;
3. oppose the discharge of the debtor if this is advisable;
4. upon the request of a party in interest, furnish information concerning the estate and its administration unless the court orders otherwise; and
5. make a final report and file a final account with the court and the United States trustee. 11 U.S.C.A. § 1302(b)(1).

The trustee must also appear and be heard at any hearing concerning the value of property subject to a lien, the confirmation of a plan, or the modification of the plan after confirmation. 11 U.S.C.A. § 1302(b)(2). The trustee may not advise the debtor on legal matters regarding the performance of the plan, but must advise and assist the debtor in other matters pertaining to performance of the plan. The trustee also has a duty to distribute payments to creditors as provided in the plan or the order confirming the plan. 11 U.S.C.A. § 1326.

Because the trustee's avoidance powers are spelled out in Chapter 5, a universal chapter, the trustee in a Chapter 13 case has most of the same avoidance powers as are granted to trustees in other types of cases. See 11 U.S.C.A. §§ 544–549. The fact that the Chapter 13 trustee may choose not to exercise the trustee's avoidance power should not be taken to mean that the trustee does not have the power to avoid fraudulent or preferential transfers. The essential role of a Chapter 13 trustee, however, differs from the role of a Chapter 7 trustee. The primary function of a Chapter 13 trustee is to review the Chapter 13 plan, to advise the court with respect to the plan, and to act as a disbursing agent under the confirmed plan. Therefore, the Chapter 13 trustee often does not use the trustee's avoidance powers.

The Code imposes a two-year statute of limitations on the trustee's avoidance powers that runs from the date of the order for relief. 11 U.S.C.A. § 546(a)(1)(A). A trustee elected or appointed before expiration of the two-year period specified in subparagraph (A) has only one year to begin an avoidance action or proceeding. 11 U.S.C.A. § 546(a)(1)(B).

If the debtor is engaged in business, the trustee has further duties. 11 U.S.C.A. § 1302(c). These include investigating the financial condition of the debtor, the operation of the debtor's business, the desirability of continuing the business, and any other matter relevant to the case or to the formulation of a plan. 11 U.S.C.A. § 1106(a)(3). The trustee is required to file a statement on this investigation that includes any information on fraud, dishonesty, incompetence, misconduct, mismanagement, or irregularity in the management of the debtor's affairs, or any cause of action available to the estate. 11 U.S.C.A. § 1106(a)(4)(A).

SECTION 6 MOTIONS AND COMPLAINTS AFTER THE ORDER FOR RELIEF

The manner in which claims will be treated is generally addressed in the debtor's plan. Some issues, however, must be presented in the form of a motion or a complaint.

A. MOTIONS

After the order for relief, the *debtor* may convert the case from Chapter 13 to Chapter 7, 11, or 12 (11 U.S.C.A. §§ 1307(a), (e)). The debtor may move to dismiss the case (11 U.S.C.A. § 1307(b); Fed. R. Bank. P. 1017); for a change of venue (Fed. R. Bank. P. 1014); for permission to use cash collateral (if engaged in business) (11 U.S.C.A. § 363(c)(2)); or to use, sell, or lease property (11 U.S.C.A. §§ 1303, 363(b)(1)). Fed. R. Bank. P. 6004.

As in Chapter 7, the Chapter 13 debtor may exercise 522(f) power to avoid a judicial lien on any property to the extent that the property could have been exempted in the absence of the lien (11 U.S.C.A. § 522(f)(1)(A)) and to avoid a nonpossessory, nonpurchase-money security interest in certain household and personal goods (11 U.S.C.A. § 522(f)(1)(B)). The Chapter 13 debtor may not avoid a judicial lien impairing an exemption if a debt for alimony, maintenance, or support is secured by the lien. 11 U.S.C.A. § 522(f)(1)(A).

In *In re Mulliken,* the debtor moved to avoid a lien under 11 U.S.C.A. § 522(f). The court noted that a debtor could avoid the fixing of a judicial lien on an interest of the debtor in property to the extent that such lien impairs an exemption to which the debtor would have been entitled under § 522(b). The court then investigated whether the debtor was entitled to the exemption.

In re Mulliken

1995 WL 70335. (Bankr. D. Idaho 1995)

Jim D. Pappas, Bankruptcy Judge

Debtors William and Gayle Mulliken filed for Chapter 13 relief on December 21, 1992. Prior to the filing, Creditor David Homolka obtained a judgment against Debtor William Mulliken. Creditor recorded the judgment which created a lien in the real property of Debtors including their homestead. Idaho Code §§ 10–1110 and 55–1009. Debtors' Chapter 13 plan was confirmed by the Court on March 22, 1993, and subsequently modified on June 28, 1994. Debtors then filed a Motion for approval of the sale of their home. After payment of the first priority lien held by First Security Bank and closing costs, there was expected to be net proceeds of $29,220 from the sale. The Motion states that Debtors would be claiming the net proceeds as exempt and would be using $15,200 therefrom to complete their performance under the plan. The $15,200 was to be paid directly to the Trustee out of the closing. The Court entered an Order on September 29, 1994 approving the sale of Debtors' residence free and clear of liens. The Order states, however, that after payment of the first priority lien held by Creditor and closing costs, all net proceeds of the sale were to be turned over to the Chapter 13 Trustee pending further order of the Court.

Debtors have now moved to avoid the judicial lien of Creditor claiming the lien impairs their homestead exemption claim in the proceeds. Creditor objects contending that since it is Debtors' intention to use a portion of the proceeds to "pre-pay" the plan that they in effect have waived their homestead exemption claim in the proceeds.

Section 522(f)(1) of the Bankruptcy Code provides that a debtor may avoid the fixing of a judicial lien on an interest of the debtor in property to the extent that such lien impairs an exemption to which the debtor would have been entitled under Section 522(b). "Thus, under § 522(f)(1), a debtor may avoid a lien if three conditions are met: (1) there was a fixing of a lien on an interest of the debtor in property; (2) such lien impairs an exemption to which the debtor would have been entitled; and (3) such lien is a judicial lien." *In re Catli,* 999 F.2d 1405, 1406 (9th Cir.1993). Debtors bear the burden of proving that they are entitled to avoid the lien under Section 522(f)(1). *Id.* The only condition at issue in this case is whether the lien impairs an exemption to which Debtors would have been entitled.

Under subsection (b) of Section 522, Idaho has "opted-out" of the federal exemptions, and Debtors are limited to the exemptions allowed under Idaho state law. 11 U.S.C. § 522(b); Idaho Code § 11–609; *In re Land,* 94 I.B.C.R. 225, 225–26. Pursuant to Idaho Code §§ 55–1004, residents of Idaho are entitled to an exemption in a homestead. In addition, residents are also allowed an exemption, for up to one year from the date of receipt, in the proceeds from the voluntary sale of the homestead in good faith for the purpose of acquiring a new homestead. Idaho Code § 55–1008. Creditor may contest the exemption claim in connection with the Section 522(f)(1) action even though it has not made a formal objection to the exemption claim. *In re Morgan,* 149 B.R. 147 (9th Cir. B.A.P.1993).

The purpose of the homestead provisions is to allow owners to keep their homes when they are beset by financial difficulties. *In re Fullerton,* 92 I.B.C.R. 22, 23. In other words, the homestead exemption is to protect "the property occupied as a home by the owner thereof or his or her family from attachment and execution." *In re Tomko,* 87 B.R. 372, 375 (Bankr.E.D.Pa. 1988) citing Riesenfeld, *Homestead and Bankruptcy in Colorado and Elsewhere,* 56 U.Colo.L.Rev. 175, 177 (1985). In addition, the Idaho legislature has adopted a rule that allows debtors to sell a homestead and purchase a different homestead and the new homestead will also be protected by the exemption statutes. Idaho Code § 55–1008. However, it is clear from the plain language of Idaho Code § 55–1008 that the proceeds from the voluntary sale of a home may only be claimed exempt if they are held for the "purpose of acquiring a new homestead." If the proceeds are to be used for any other purpose they may not be validly claimed as exempt.

In this case, Debtors' Motion for approval of the sale of their home requests that $15,200 of the proceeds be transferred to the Trustee to be applied to plan payments to their various creditors. As such, this portion of the proceeds will not be used for the purpose of acquiring a new homestead and therefore is not properly exempt under Idaho's homestead exemption statutes. Since Debtors are not entitled to an exemption in this portion of the proceeds, Debtors may not avoid Creditor's lien on these funds under Section 522(f)(1) because it does not impair an exemption to which Debtors would have been entitled under Section 522(b).

The remaining sale proceeds were to be turned over to Debtors after the sale. Debtors have not shown that this portion of the proceeds will be used for acquiring a new homestead and at this point they have failed to meet their burden in this regard. If within a reasonable time Debtors make an adequate showing to the Chapter 13 Trustee that the proceeds from the sale will be used to acquire a new homestead within one year from the date they receive them, Trustee may distribute the funds to Debtors. In such event, Debtors may submit an order signed by the Trustee and the lien will be avoided as to that portion of the proceeds. Until such time the Trustee shall retain the proceeds until further order of the Court subject to Creditor's lien.

This Memorandum constitutes the Court's findings of fact and conclusions of law. F.R.B.P. 7052. Counsel for Debtors may submit an appropriate order.

A *party in interest* may move for relief from the automatic stay (11 U.S.C.A. § 362(d); Fed. R. Bank. P. 4001, 9014); for abstention by the court (11 U.S.C.A. § 305); to dismiss the case (11 U.S.C.A. § 1307(c)); for a change of venue (Fed. R. Bank. P. 1014); for disallowance of a claim (11 U.S.C.A. § 502); to convert the case to Chapter 7, 11, or 12 (except if the debtor is a farmer) (11 U.S.C.A. §§ 1307(c)–(e)); for relief from the codebtor stay (11 U.S.C.A. § 1301(c)); or for examination of any person (Fed. R. Bank P. 2004).

The *trustee* or the *U.S. trustee* may file a motion objecting to confirmation of the plan. 11 U.S.C.A. § 1324. If the debtor is a farmer, the court may not convert a Chapter 13 case to Chapter 7, 11, or 12 upon the request of anyone except the debtor. 11 U.S.C.A. § 1307(e).

B. COMPLAINTS

After the order for relief, a creditor may file a complaint objecting to the dischargeability of a debt. 11 U.S.C.A. § 523; Fed R. Bank. P. 4007(a), 7001.

Proceedings brought by the *trustee* to avoid transfers are classified as adversary proceedings by Fed. R. Bank. P. 7001. This topic was discussed in Section 5 of this chapter.

Whether a Chapter 13 debtor may use the avoidance powers granted to the trustee is a question that has left the courts divided. The Chapter 13 provision that addresses the rights and powers of the Chapter 13 debtor does not address this issue. 11 U.S.C.A. § 1303. The legislative history, however, includes comments to the effect that section 1303 "does not imply that the debtor does not also possess other powers concurrently with the trustee." 124 Cong. Rec. H32,409 (Sept. 28, 1978, remarks of Rep. Edwards).

In *In re Mast,* the debtor attempted to exercise the Chapter 13 trustee's power to avoid a preferential transfer. The court discussed the division in the courts and the reasons for this division.

In re Mast

79 B.R. 981 (Bankr. W. D. Mich. 1987)

MEMORANDUM OPINION REGARDING AVOIDANCE POWERS IN CHAPTER 13 CASES
James D. Gregg, Bankruptcy Judge

On August 5, 1987, Mary L. Mast, "Debtor," filed her Petition for Relief Under Chapter 13 of the Bankruptcy Code. 11 U.S.C. § 301; 11 U.S.C. §§ 1301–1330.[1] Brett N. Rodgers, "Trustee," was subsequently appointed by the Court to serve as the trustee in connection with the case.

On August 5, 1987, the Debtor also filed a Complaint against Borgess Medical Center, "Defendant," which seeks to avoid an involuntary transfer, pursuant to Section 547 of the Bankruptcy Code, received by the Defendant as a result of a garnishment of the Debtor's bank account which allegedly took place within 90 days of the date of the filing of the Petition. The Trustee has not joined the adversary proceeding as a party plaintiff.[2] On August 24, 1987, the Defendant filed an Answer to Complaint.

On October 16, 1987, the Debtor filed a Motion for Summary Judgment. On October 28, 1987, the Defendant filed a Cross Motion for Summary Judgment. The Defendant asserts, among other things, as a matter of law, a Chapter 13 Debtor lacks the authority to avoid a preferential transfer. At the hearings respecting the cross motions for summary judgment, both parties, through their counsel, presented argument regarding their respective legal positions. Because of the importance of the legal issues presented, the Court took the matter under advisement pending issuance of this written opinion.

Section 547(b) of the Bankruptcy Code states "the trustee may avoid" a preferential transfer by proving the requisite elements. Section 1303 of the Bankruptcy Code explicitly enumerates the rights and powers of a Chapter 13 debtor. The debtor is empowered, exclusive of the trustee, to use, sell or lease property in accordance with Sections 363(b), 363(d), 363(e), 363(f) and 363(1) of the Bankruptcy Code. If a Chapter 13 debtor is engaged in business, Section 1304 grants additional powers to the debtor to enter into ordinary business transactions under Section 363(c) and to obtain credit pursuant to Section 364 of the Bankruptcy Code.

The Court has carefully reviewed all provisions contained in Chapter 13 and there does not exist any *statutory* authority for a Chapter 13 debtor to utilize avoidance powers granted to the trustee, including those powers listed in Sections 544, 545, 547 and 548 of the Bankruptcy Code. If Congress intended to grant avoidance powers to a Chapter 13 debtor, it could have explicitly done so.[3]

There exists a split of authority regarding whether a Chapter 13 debtor may utilize a trustee's avoidance powers. After careful consideration, this Court believes those cases which hold the Chapter 13 debtor lacks the power to unilaterally set aside avoidable transfers are better reasoned and more persuasive than those cases decided to the contrary. *In re Carter,* 2 B.R. 321 (Bankr.D.Colo.1980) (Chapter 13 debtors lack § 544 "strong arm" power); *In re Walls,* 17 B.R. 701 (Bankr.S.D.W.Va.1982) (Chapter 13 debtor lacked ability to exercise power to avoid preferential transfer under § 547); *In re Driscoll,* 57 B.R. 322 (Bankr.W. D.Wis.1986) (Chapter 13 debtor may not generally utilize the trustee's Chapter 5 avoidance powers); *cf. In re Colandrea,* 17 B.R. 568 (Bankr.D.Md.1982) (Chapter 13 trustee has authority to avoid preferential transfers under § 547).

Cases decided to the contrary recognize the "realities of bankruptcy practice" to justify a strained interpretation of the Bankruptcy Code and to conclude a Chapter 13 debtor is empowered to utilize a trustee's avoidance powers. See, e.g., *In re Ottaviano,* 68 B.R. 238, 240 (Bankr. D.Conn.1986), and the cases cited therein. As a matter of practice, a Chapter 13 debtor may easily request that the Chapter 13 trustee utilize his powers to set aside avoidable transfers.[4] If avoiding a transfer is in the interest of the estate, the trustee may unilaterally seek to avoid the transfer or consent to the debtor's possible intervention as an additional party plaintiff pursuant to Bankruptcy Rule 7024. Alternatively, the Chapter 13 Plan may propose that the debtor, on behalf of the estate, and in conjunction with the trustee, utilize avoidance powers to assure equality of distribution and no unfair discrimination among creditors. *In re Walls, supra* at 704.

The Court therefore concludes, as a matter of law, that a Chapter 13 Debtor has no independent standing to exercise the Trustee's power to avoid a preferential transfer under Section 547 of the Bankruptcy Code. The Debtor's motion for summary judgment is therefore denied. The Defendant's motion for summary judgment is granted[5] without prejudice to the Trustee to file a Complaint to avoid the alleged preferential transfer if the Trustee determines to do so in the exercise of his reasonable discretion.[6] An order shall be entered accordingly.

---

1 All future references to 11 U.S.C. §§ 1301–1330 herein shall be referred to as the "Bankruptcy Code" by reference to the applicable section thereof.

2 During argument, Debtor's counsel made an oral motion to join the Trustee as a party. The Court did not grant the motion. The Trustee was not present at the hearing and he has not consented or indicated a willingness to now be added as a party to this adversary proceeding.

3 In Sections 1107(a) and 1203 of the Bankruptcy Code, Chapter 11 and Chapter 12 debtors are granted all rights and powers of a trustee, subject to any limitations or conditions which the Court may prescribe.

4 It should be noted that when exempt property is involved, the debtor has certain avoidance powers which are independent of the trustee under Sections 522(f) and 522(h) of the Bankruptcy Code.

5 Because the issue of standing is dispositive, the Court has not addressed the other issues raised in the Defendant's Cross Motion for Summary Judgment.

6 In the exercise of his discretion, the Trustee may consider factors such as whether seeking to avoid a transfer will benefit the estate, whether the proposed Chapter 13 plan is confirmable absent avoidance of the transfer and the ultimate probability of success if an avoidance action is commenced.

If the debtor operates a business, the *debtor* may file a complaint against third parties to collect accounts receivable or to have property brought back into the estate. 11 U.S.C.A. §§ 542, 543; Fed. R. Bank. P. 7001.

SECTION 7
THE CLERK'S NOTICE

The official form for the clerk's notice in a Chapter 13 case is B9I. (See Exhibit 6–4.) The clerk must give the debtor, the trustee, all creditors, the indenture trustees, and the U.S. trustee not less than 20 days notice by mail of the date, time, and location of the meeting of creditors; an explanation of the automatic stay and the codebtor stay; the deadline for filing proofs of claim; and the deadline for objecting to the debtor's claim of exemption. This notice serves as the notice of the order for relief required by 11 U.S.C.A. § 342(a) and may also serve as the notice for the confirmation hearing in a Chapter 13 case. Either a copy or a summary of the plan must be included with notice of the confirmation hearing.

SECTION 8
MEETING OF CREDITORS (THE SECTION 341 MEETING)

The meeting of creditors (the section 341 meeting) is held not less than 20 nor more than 50 days after the order for relief. Fed. R. Bank. P. 2003. The business of the meeting includes the examination of the debtor under oath.

It is quite common for the trustee to conduct some type of examination of the debtor, asking questions directed toward any possible indication that the plan may not be feasible. The trustee must be assured that all debts and assets have been listed. Creditors with problems will have an opportunity to talk to both the trustee and the debtor about these problems. The trustee will probably give the debtor some indication of the trustee's recommendation on the confirmation of the plan. The trustee may suggest modification of the plan in an attempt to lead the debtor and the debtor's attorney toward a confirmable plan.

SECTION 9
HEARING ON CONFIRMATION OF THE PLAN

After the meeting of creditors, the stage is set for the **confirmation hearing.** 11 U.S.C.A. § 1324. The paralegal should check local court rules for confirmation hearing requirements. Courts may require the debtor to be present at the hearing on confirmation of the plan. The judge may ask the debtor's attorney to summarize the contents of the plan. The judge will also ask the trustee for comments on the plan. The trustee will advise the judge as to what the problems are and whether the plan can be confirmed. The trustee may suggest modifications to make the plan confirmable. The judge may decide to continue the hearing to give the debtor an opportunity to file an amended or a supplemental plan, or such changes may be provided for in the order of confirmation.

A party in interest may file a motion objecting to confirmation of the plan. 11 U.S.C.A. § 1324. The judge, on his or her own initiative, may determine that the plan is not confirmable. 11 U.S.C.A. § 1325.

To be confirmed by the court, the plan must comply with the provisions of 11 U.S.C.A. § 1325. Section 1325(a) mandates the following six requirements:

1. the plan must comply with the provisions of Chapter 13 and with other applicable provisions of U.S.C.A. title 11 (11 U.S.C.A. § 1325(a)(1));
2. the fees and charges required by U.S.C.A. title 28 or by the plan have been paid (11 U.S.C.A. § 1325(a)(2));

EXHIBIT 6–4 Official Form No. B9I (Notice of Chapter 13 Bankruptcy Case, Creditors, and Deadlines)

FORM B9I (Chapter 13 Case) (12/03)

UNITED STATES BANKRUPTCY COURT ________ District of ________________

Notice of Chapter 13 Bankruptcy Case, Meeting of Creditors, & Deadlines

[The debtor(s) listed below filed a chapter 13 bankruptcy case on ______________________ (date).]
or [A bankruptcy case concerning the debtor(s) listed below was originally filed under chapter __________ on ________________ (date) and was converted to a case under chapter 13 on________________.]

You may be a creditor of the debtor. **This notice lists important deadlines.** You may want to consult an attorney to protect your rights. All documents filed in the case may be inspected at the bankruptcy clerk's office at the address listed below. NOTE: The staff of the bankruptcy clerk's office cannot give legal advice.

See Reverse Side For Important Explanations.

Debtor(s) (name(s) and address):	Case Number: Last four digits of Soc. Sec. No./Complete EIN or other Taxpayer I.D. No.:
All Other Names used by the Debtor(s) in the last 6 years (include married, maiden, and trade names):	Bankruptcy Trustee (name and address): Telephone number:
Attorney for Debtor(s) (name and address): Telephone number:	

Meeting of Creditors:

Date: / / Time: ( ) A.M. ( ) P.M. Location:

Deadlines:

Papers must be *received* by the bankruptcy clerk's office by the following deadlines:

Deadline to File a Proof of Claim:

For all creditors (except a governmental unit): For a governmental unit:

Deadline to Object to Exemptions:

Thirty (30) days after the *conclusion* of the meeting of creditors.

Filing of Plan, Hearing on Confirmation of Plan

[The debtor has filed a plan. The plan or a summary of the plan is enclosed. The hearing on confirmation will be held:
Date: ________________ Time: ______________ Location: ______________________]
or [The debtor has filed a plan. The plan or a summary of the plan and notice of confirmation hearing will be sent separately.]
or [The debtor has not filed a plan as of this date. You will be sent separate notice of the hearing on confirmation of the plan.]

Creditors May Not Take Certain Actions:

The filing of the bankruptcy case automatically stays certain collection and other actions against the debtor, debtor's property, and certain codebtors. If you attempt to collect a debt or take other action in violation of the Bankruptcy Code, you may be penalized.

Address of the Bankruptcy Clerk's Office: Telephone number:	**For the Court:** Clerk of the Bankruptcy Court:
Hours Open:	Date:

(continued)

EXHIBIT 6–4 Official Form No. 9I (Notice of Chapter 13 Bankruptcy Case, Creditors, and Deadlines), Continued

EXPLANATIONS

FORM B9I (9/97)

Filing of Chapter 13 Bankruptcy Case	A bankruptcy case under chapter 13 of the Bankruptcy Code (title 11, United States Code) has been filed in this court by the debtor(s) listed on the front side, and an order for relief has been entered. Chapter 13 allows an individual with regular income and debts below a specified amount to adjust debts pursuant to a plan. A plan is not effective unless confirmed by the bankruptcy court. You may object to confirmation of the plan and appear at the confirmation hearing. A copy or summary of the plan [is included with this notice] *or* [will be sent to you later], and [the confirmation hearing will be held on the date indicated on the front of this notice] *or* [you will be sent notice of the confirmation hearing]. The debtor will remain in possession of the debtor's property and may continue to operate the debtor's business, if any, unless the court orders otherwise.
Creditors May Not Take Certain Actions	Prohibited collection actions against the debtor and certain codebtors are listed in Bankruptcy Code § 362 and § 1301. Common examples of prohibited actions include contacting the debtor by telephone, mail or otherwise to demand repayment; taking actions to collect money or obtain property from the debtor; repossessing the debtor's property; starting or continuing lawsuits or foreclosures; and garnishing or deducting from the debtor's wages.
Meeting of Creditors	A meeting of creditors is scheduled for the date, time and location listed on the front side. *The debtor (both spouses in a joint case) must be present at the meeting to be questioned under oath by the trustee and by creditors.* Creditors are welcome to attend, but are not required to do so. The meeting may be continued and concluded at a later date without further notice.
Claims	A Proof of Claim is a signed statement describing a creditor's claim. If a Proof of Claim form is not included with this notice, you can obtain one at any bankruptcy clerk's office. If you do not file a Proof of Claim by the "Deadline to File a Proof of Claim" listed on the front side, you might not be paid any money on your claim against the debtor in the bankruptcy case. To be paid you must file a Proof of Claim even if your claim is listed in the schedules filed by the debtor.
Discharge of Debts	The debtor is seeking a discharge of most debts, which may include your debt. A discharge means that you may never try to collect the debt from the debtor.
Exempt Property	The debtor is permitted by law to keep certain property as exempt. Exempt property will not be sold and distributed to creditors, even if the debtor's case is converted to chapter 7. The debtor must file a list of all property claimed as exempt. You may inspect that list at the bankruptcy clerk's office. If you believe that an exemption claimed by the debtor is not authorized by law, you may file an objection to that exemption. The bankruptcy clerk's office must receive the objection by the "Deadline to Object to Exemptions" listed on the front side.
Bankruptcy Clerk's Office	Any paper that you file in this bankruptcy case should be filed at the bankruptcy clerk's office at the address listed on the front side. You may inspect all papers filed, including the list of the debtor's property and debts and the list of property claimed as exempt, at the bankruptcy clerk's office.
Legal Advice	The staff of the bankruptcy clerk's office cannot give legal advice. You may want to consult an attorney to protect your rights.

—Refer To Other Side For Important Deadlines and Notices—

3. the plan must be proposed in good faith (11 U.S.C.A. § 1325(a)(3));
4. the payments of unsecured claims under the plan must fulfill the best interests of creditors test; that is, each unsecured claim must receive under the plan not less than it would have received had the claim been paid under Chapter 7 liquidation (11 U.S.C.A. § 1325(a)(4));
5. the secured claims are dealt with under the plan in one of three ways:
   a. the holder of the secured claim accepts the plan;
   b. the debtor surrenders the property to the holder of the secured claim; or
   c. the plan is crammed down on the creditors holding secured claims (11 U.S.C.A. § 1325(a)(5)); and
6. the debtor is able to make all payments under the plan and to comply with the plan (11 U.S.C.A. § 1325(a)(6)).

In re Letsche, 234 B.R. 208, 212 (D. Mass. 1999) provides the following guidance concerning the third requirement, **good faith.**

> Because the Bankruptcy Code does not define the term "good faith," courts have adopted a totality of the circumstances approach to evaluating whether a Chapter 13 plan has been proposed in good faith, and have looked to a variety of factors to assist them in determining the presence or absence of good faith, including the following:
>
> (1) the amount of the proposed payment and the amount of the debtor's surplus;
> (2) the debtor's employment history, ability to earn and likelihood of future increase in income;
> (3) the probable or expected duration of the plan;
> (4) the accuracy of the plan's statement of the debts, expenses and percentage repayment of unsecured debt and whether any inaccuracies are an attempt to mislead the court;
> (5) the extent of preferential treatment between classes of creditors;
> (6) the extent to which secured claims are modified;
> (7) the type of debt sought to be discharged and whether any such debt is nondischargeable in Chapter 7;
> (8) the existence of special circumstances such as inordinate medical expenses;
> (9) the frequency with which the debtor has sought relief under the Bankruptcy Reform Act;
> (10) the motivation and sincerity of the debtor in seeking Chapter 13 relief;
> (11) the burden which the plan's administration would place upon the trustee; and
> (12) whether the debtor is attempting to abuse the spirit of the Bankruptcy Code.

PROBLEM 6.5 The following are the facts from *In re Letsche:*

Marilyn and Paul Letsche, through false representations, induced Marilyn's elderly mother, Edith Connelly, to leave her home of 55 years.

Once Connelly moved to the Letsche home, Marilyn unduly influenced her to convey a one-half interest in her home to her and, without Connelly's authorization, signed reimbursement checks made payable to Connelly and obtained cash by signing Connelly's signature on various checks from Connelly's bank accounts. Marilyn also obtained the cash surrender value of various life and industrial insurance policies by forging Connelly's signature.

After moving into the Letsche home Connelly's contact with the outside world was cut off. The Letsches removed the telephone from Connelly's room and did not permit her access to theirs. Once when she was attempting to use the telephone, Marilyn grabbed the phone from her mother's hands with such force that Connelly fell to the floor. Marilyn told her mother that she would not have any visitors and that she would be "a lonely old lady." After this incident, Connelly made contact with a visiting nurse and requested that she be taken to the hospital. At the time of her admission to the hospital on August 16, 1996, Connelly was diagnosed as being volume depleted; malnourished; suffering from major depression, psychiatric disorders, and chronic pancreatitis; and suffering from chronic abdominal and mouth pain.

On September 19, 1997, Connelly obtained the judgment in Suffolk Superior Court for $77,077.70 against the Letsches for intentional infliction of emotional distress.

Two months later, the Letsches recorded a homestead with respect to their residence located in Hyde Park, Massachusetts.

In mid-June 1998, Connelly levied and suspended execution on a judgment she obtained against the Letsches from the Suffolk Superior Court.

One week later, June 25, 1998, the Letsches filed a voluntary petition under Chapter 13. The petition was filed without schedules, statement of financial affairs, or a Chapter 13 plan.

On July 8, 1998, the Debtors filed their schedules, statement of financial affairs, and Chapter 13 plan. With respect to the total unsecured claims, the Debtors listed the MBTA Credit Union as the holder of a claim in the sum of $2,180.93. The schedules did not disclose the existence of an MBTA Credit Union share account. Prior to the filing of the Chapter 13 petition, the amount of $310.96 was being deducted from Mr. Letsche's pension check for payment of two unsecured loans from the MBTA Credit Union. This sum was being applied to the satisfaction of two prepetition obligations: a personal loan in the amount of approximately $5,500.00 and a vacation loan in the amount of approximately $2,600.00. After the filing, the MBTA Credit Union began depositing the sum of $396.10 per month into the share account.

The Debtors' 60-month Chapter 13 plan provided for monthly payments to the Chapter 13 trustee in the sum of $269.00 and a 15 percent dividend for unsecured creditors, whose claims, according to the Debtors, totaled $97,014.00, a sum predicated upon the complete avoidance of Connelly's lien under 11 U.S.C.A. § 522(f). It also was predicated upon the Debtors' schedules I and J pursuant to which the Debtors disclosed joint monthly income of $2,530.00, joint monthly expenses of $2,168.00 and excess income of $362.00. The Debtors did not explain why they were contributing $269.00 per month toward plan payments, rather than $362.00. The difference of $93.00 per month over 60 months could have increased the dividend to unsecured creditors by 5.75 percent.

Approximately two months later, on September 4, 1998, Connelly filed her objection to confirmation of the Debtors' Chapter 13 plan.

On September 8, 1998, the Debtors filed an amended Schedule J.

On November 2, 1998, the Debtors filed amended schedules B, C, F, I, and J; an amended statement of financial affairs; and an amended Chapter 13 plan. The amended Chapter 13 plan was signed by the Debtors on September 17, 1998, and the amended statement of financial affairs was signed on October 31, 1998. The amended schedules were not dated and were not accompanied by a declaration signed under pains and penalties of perjury as to their truthfulness and correctness.

The amended schedule B disclosed the MBTA share account, as well as a joint account at the Hyde Park Cooperative Bank that Mr. Letsche had with his disabled son. On amended schedule F, the Debtors substantially increased the sum owed to the MBTA Credit Union, listing it as the holder of a claim in the amount of $7,412.93. The amended schedule I accounted for the increased monthly income in the amount of $396.10 that was being deducted from Mr. Letsche's pension prior to the filing of the bankruptcy petition.

The amended plan increased the monthly plan payment to the Chapter 13 trustee from $362.00 to $646.00, resulting in an increased dividend to unsecured creditors of 20 percent. In the amended plan, the unsecured claims totaled $104,713.00.

In late October 1998, the Debtors began making payments to the Chapter 13 trustee in the monthly amount of $646.00.

On March 10, 1999, the bankruptcy court conducted an evidentiary hearing on Connelly's objection to confirmation of the Debtors' Chapter 13 plan. The issue raised by the objection is whether the Debtors filed their Chapter 13 plan in good faith.

At the hearing, the Debtors admitted that they failed to list on any version of their schedules two credit card debts, one to Orchard Bank and the other to First Card, as well as debts arising from prepetition loans from their children. The Debtors admitted that they continued to make payments on these credit cards after the filing of their Chapter 13 petition. Consistent with the Debtors' failure to list the two credit card obligations, the Debtors' expenses listed on Schedule J do not include expenses for installment payments. Postpetition payments to these credit card companies totaled at least

$1,495.00. The full extent of the payments cannot be determined, however, because, despite a subpoena, Mr. Letsche failed to produce all the relevant credit card statements.

Also at the hearing, Mr. Letsche testified that he continued to borrow monies from his children and that he repaid the pre- and postpetition loans from sums deposited into the MBTA share account, which sums had been applied prepetition to reduce the outstanding loans from the MBTA Credit Union. During their testimony, neither Mr. nor Mrs. Letsche proffered any excuse for failing to list the credit card debts and loans from family members. Additionally, their financial affairs are not complicated in terms of the number of assets and liabilities, or debt structure. Accordingly, the Debtors have no excuse for failing to list their prepetition debts to Orchard Bank, First Card, and their children.

If you are the judge, would you confirm the Debtors' Chapter 13 plan and, if not, which factors would influence your decision?

The fourth and fifth requirements deal with unsecured and secured claims, respectively. In a Chapter 13 case, it is unnecessary to cramdown unsecured creditors because they have no vote. Although unsecured creditors may object to confirmation of the plan, the plan is confirmable in regard to unsecured claims if the holders of the unsecured claims will receive an amount not less than their claims or if the plan provides that all of the debtor's projected disposable income for three years from the date the first payment is due will be applied to make payments under the plan and if it meets the best interests of creditors test. 11 U.S.C.A. § 1325(b)(1). Note that the best interests test only requires that the holders of unsecured claims receive not less than they would receive under Chapter 7. Thus, if unsecured creditors would receive nothing in a Chapter 7 case (all assets are secured, exempt, or burdensome), a Chapter 13 plan may be confirmable even if no payment is to be made on nonpriority unsecured claims.

In *Flood v. Chrysler Financial Corp.*, Chrysler Financial had a perfected security interest in Flood's automobile. Flood filed a Chapter 13 petition. In her plan, she proposed a Chapter 13 **cramdown** for Chrysler Financial's secured claim.

Flood v. Chrysler Financial Corp.

2000 WL 356376 (E. D. Penn. 2000)

OPINION
Giles.

This is an appeal of an Order from the United States Bankruptcy Court for the Eastern District of Pennsylvania granting summary judgment to the defendant-creditor, Chrysler Financial Corporation ("Chrysler"). The issue before the court is whether the grant of summary judgment was proper. The bankruptcy court's judgment is affirmed.

I.

Appellant, Shirley L. Flood ("Flood") filed a voluntary petition for bankruptcy and a "cramdown"[1] plan under Chapter 13 of the Bankruptcy Code, 11 U.S.C. § 1301, *et seq.*, on October 15, 1998. Appellee, Chrysler, is a secured creditor of Flood because it possesses a perfected lien on her automobile, a 1998 Dodge Stratus. On December 8, 1998, Chrysler filed a Proof of Claim in Flood's case in which it sought the value of its collateral, the car, plus its contract rate of interest, 16.95%. Attached thereto was the original sales agreement for Flood's vehicle. On December 21, 1998, Flood filed an Adversary Complaint to determine the validity and extent of Chrysler's lien against her vehicle.[2] On January 20, 1999, Chrysler filed its Answer to Flood's Adversary Complaint.

Prior to the scheduled hearing on the Adversary Complaint, Chrysler filed a Motion for Summary Judgment. The motion asserted that there were two issues yet to be resolved in the case as a matter of law: the value of the vehicle and the appropriate interest rate. On August 26, 1999, the bankruptcy court held a hearing on Chrysler's summary judgment motion. There, Flood stated that there was no dispute over the collateral's value. However, Flood disagreed as to the applicable rate of interest. On September 13, 1999, the bankruptcy court granted Chrysler's motion for summary judgment. Flood immediately filed a Motion for Reconsideration, which was denied. On November 15, 1999, Flood filed a Notice of Appeal asserting that the proper interest rate was a genuinely disputed material fact which should have precluded the award of summary judgment.

II.

This court has jurisdiction over this matter pursuant to 28 U.S.C.A. § 157(a). The issue presented is a question of law, over which this court has plenary review. *In re Anes,* 195 F.3d 177, 180 (3d Cir.1999).

III.

Summary judgment is appropriate when there are no genuine disputes as to any material facts. *See* Fed.R.Civ.P. 56(c). If such is the case, a trial is unnecessary because a reasonable fact finder could not enter a judgment for the nonmoving party. *See Anderson v. Liberty Lobby, Inc.,* 477 U.S. 242, 248 (1986). In reviewing the bankruptcy court's grant of summary judgment, this court must "exercise plenary review, construing all evidence and resolving all doubts raised by affidavits, depositions, answers to interrogatories, and admissions on file in favor of the non-moving party." *Ciarlante v. Brown & Williamson Tobacco Corp.,* 143 F.3d 139, 145 (3d Cir.1998). Accordingly, this court must "lay out the substantive law governing the action, and then in light of that law determine whether there is a genuine dispute over dispositive facts." *Id.*

The proper interest rate to be charged in the Chapter 13 cramdown plan was a matter of law, and not a matter of factual dispute. Controlling law in this area was set out by the third circuit in *GMAC v. Jones,* 999 F.2d 63 (3d Cir.1993). The court held that, in order to be consistent with the statutory objective of section 1325(a)(5)(B)(ii), the cramdown section of the Bankruptcy Code, the appropriate interest rate to be charged under a plan is the "contract rate of interest," as it is the "rate that the creditor voluntarily agreed to accept at an earlier date." *Jones,* 999 F .2d at 70. Further, in recognition of the fact that interest may fluctuate over time, the third circuit established as the rule of practice that:

> [i]n the absence of a stipulation regarding the creditor's current rate for a loan of similar character, amount and duration, we believe it would be appropriate for bankruptcy courts to accept a plan utilizing the contract rate if the creditor fails to come forward with persuasive evidence that its current rate is in excess of the contract rate. Conversely, utilizing the same rebuttable presumption approach, if a debtor proposes a plan with a rate less than the contract rate, it would be appropriate, in the absence of a stipulation, for a bankruptcy court to require the debtor to come forward with some evidence that the creditor's current rate is less than the contract rate.

Id. at 70–71 (footnotes omitted). Thus, the third circuit has held that a bankruptcy court should assume that the proper interest rate for a cramdown plan is the contract interest rate and that if the debtor believes that the creditor's rate is less than the contract rate, she bears the burden of proving that fact. As such, it would not suffice for a debtor to try to prove other lenders may have lower rates. She must indeed establish that her creditor's current lending rate is lower than her contract rate.

IV.

This court holds that the bankruptcy court properly granted summary judgment to Chrysler. The appropriate interest was not a disputed material fact as the third circuit has held that, as a "rule of practice,"[3] the contract rate of interest is the proper interest rate in a cramdown. The contract rate of interest is what Chrysler requested and was a part of the record available to the bankruptcy court at the time it rendered its judgment, as it was attached to Chrysler's Proof of Claim. If Flood believed that a lesser interest rate was applicable, she had the affirmative duty "to come forward with some evidence that the creditor's current rate is less than the contract rate" for a loan of a similar character, amount, and duration in her response to Chrysler's motion.[4] Flood failed to do so. At the hearing on the summary judgment motion, she offered some newspaper articles which allegedly showed the "market rate for automobiles." (Summ. J. Hr'g Tr. at 5.). That proffer did not create a possible genuine issue of fact as to the rate Chrysler was then charging for loans like Flood's.

Flood's "mere assertion that at a further hearing, or on the ultimate date of trial she will be successful in presenting competent evidence to demonstrate that Chrysler's current rate is less than [her] contract rate,"[5] misconstrued her burden under *Jones* and was insufficient to withstand summary judgment at the time the motion was decided. The bankruptcy judge did not abuse his discretion by not putting off the resolution of the interest issue under these circumstances. The bankruptcy court appropriately concluded that the interest rate was the contract rate based on controlling law, and that Flood had proffered no evidence creating a genuine issue of fact.

Accordingly, the bankruptcy court's Order granting summary judgment in favor of Chrysler is affirmed.

An appropriate Order follows.

JUDGMENT

AND NOW, this __ day of April, 2000, the Order dated September 1, 1999 of the United States Bankruptcy Court for the Eastern District of Pennsylvania granting summary judgment in favor of Chrysler Financial Corporation is hereby AFFIRMED for the reasons stated in the attached Opinion.

---

[1] In a Chapter 13 "cramdown," the debtor retains the property in which the secured creditor has a security interest, even if the secured creditor would prefer to repossess and liquidate the property as it would be entitled to do in the absence of a bankruptcy filing. In exchange for giving the debtor a right to continue possession of the property, section 1325(a)(5)(B) mandates two things: (i) the secured creditor shall retain a continuing lien on the property; and (ii) the secured creditor shall receive from the debtor "the value, as of the effective date of the plan, of such property to be distributed under the plan on account of such claim [which shall be] not less than the allowed amount of such claim." 11 U.S.C. § 1325(a)(5)(B)(ii).

[2] 11 U.S.C. § 506(a) of the bankruptcy code enables a debtor to bifurcate a creditor's claim, treating the claim, up to the value of the collateral, as a secured claim while treating as unsecured the amount of the claim that exceeds the value of the collateral. Section 506(a) states in relevant part that "[a]n allowed claim of a creditor secured by a lien on property in which the estate has an interest . . . is a secured claim to the extent of the value of such creditor's interest in the estate's interest in such property . . . and is an unsecured claim to the extent that the value of such creditor's interest . . . is less than the amount of such allowed claim."

[3] *Jones*, 999 F.2d at 70.

[4] *Id.* at 71.

[5] *In re Shirley L. Flood*, No. Bankr.98-33272 (Bankr. Order Sept. 1, 1999).

The final provision of section 1325(a) is that the debtor be able to make all payments under the plan and to comply with the plan. 11 U.S.C.A. § 1325(a)(6). The plan should be specific enough so the trustee knows exactly to whom payment should be made, how much, and when.

The confirmation of a plan binds the debtor and each creditor to the provisions of the plan, whether or not the creditor's claim is provided for by the plan and whether or not the creditor has objected to, accepted, or rejected the plan. 11 U.S.C.A. § 1327(a).

The confirmation of a plan vests all of the property of the estate in the debtor except as provided in the plan or confirmation order. The property vested in the debtor is free and clear of any claim or interest of any creditor provided for by the plan. 11 U.S.C.A. §§ 1327(b), (c). Although the court can deny confirmation on legal grounds, such as nonpayment of a fee, creditors may object on legal grounds but have no vote on the confirmation itself.

If the plan is unconfirmable, the debtor may convert the case to Chapter 7 or may request the court to dismiss the case. 11 U.S.C.A. §§ 1307(a), (b). A party in interest may also request the court to dismiss the case. 11 U.S.C.A. § 1307(c)(5).

For the bankruptcy court's order confirming the McPhersons' Chapter 13 plan, see Exhibit 6–5.

EXHIBIT 6–5 Order Confirming a Chapter 13 Plan

IN THE UNITED STATES BANKRUPTCY COURT
FOR ________ DISTRICT OF ________

In re:	)	
	)	
McPHERSON, Eric	)	
SS# ***-**-1277	)	Case Number:
	)	(Chapter 13)
McPHERSON, Jennifer	)	
SS# ***-**-2787	)	
Debtors.	)	

ORDER CONFIRMING CHAPTER 13 PLAN

The Court has determined that the Chapter 13 Plan filed ____________, 20___, (the "Plan") by the Debtor(s) (hereinafter the "Debtor") meets the confirmation requirements of Chapter 13 of Title 11 of the United States Code and the Court finds that the Plan should be confirmed, subject to the provisions set forth below.

IT IS THEREFORE ORDERED AS FOLLOWS:

1. The Plan is hereby confirmed, subject to the provisions of this Order.

2. The plan payments shall be made to the Standing Chapter 13 Trustee (the "Trustee") under an Order for Wage Deduction issued to the Debtor's employer or other payment order ("Payment Order"). Prior to commencement of payments to the Trustee under an Order for Wage Deduction or a Payment Order, or at any time the employer or third party does not make the required plan payments, the Debtor shall timely pay all plan payments which become due to "______________, Trustee", by certified or cashier's check or money order, with the Debtor's name and case number legibly written thereon.

3. The Debtor shall immediately notify the Court and the Trustee, by written pleading, of any change of address or of any change in Debtor's place of employment. Notice of change of employment shall include the name and appropriate mailing address for the payroll department of the new employer.

4. Notwithstanding confirmation of the Plan, all property of the estate defined by 11 U.S.C.A. § 1306 shall remain property of the estate and shall not revest in the Debtor until a discharge is entered or the case is dismissed. If the case is converted to another chapter of Title 11 of the United States Code, property of the estate shall vest in accordance with applicable law. Only those funds returned to the Debtor by the Trustee, if any, shall revest in the Debtor. The Debtor shall remain in possession of property of the estate and is responsible for its preservation and protection. If required by the original contract between the parties, the Debtor shall maintain adequate insurance coverage for all property on which any creditor holds a lien unless such insurance coverage is specifically waived, in writing, by the secured creditor or by Order of the Court. The amount of insurance coverage shall not be less than the amount of the allowed secured claim of the secured creditor with respect to such property stated in the Plan and the amount of the deductible shall not exceed the amount of the deductible in the policy of insurance provided for in the original contract between

(continued)

the parties. The secured creditor shall be listed on the insurance policy as loss-payee and the Debtor shall provide such secured creditor with proof of such insurance. The Trustee shall have no responsibility for preservation or protection of property in possession of the Debtor. Further, the Trustee shall have no responsibility to obtain insurance for the Debtor or monitor the Debtor in obtaining or maintaining insurance as required by this Order.

5. The automatic stay provided by 11 U.S.C.A. § 362(a) shall remain in force and effect until the Court enters an order granting relief therefrom, or the case is closed, or the case is dismissed by order of the Court, or the Debtor is granted or denied a discharge. Further, the stay of action against codebtors provided by 11 U.S.C.A. § 1301(a) shall remain in force and effect until the Court specifically grants relief therefrom, or this case is closed, dismissed, or converted to a case under Chapter 7 or 11 of Title 11 of the United States Code, or the codebtor stay is terminated as provided in 11 U.S.C.A. § 1301(d). In the event the Plan provides that certain property is to be surrendered, the automatic stay is hereby modified or terminated to allow the creditor to whom such property is surrendered to exercise its rights with respect to such property.

6. The Debtor shall not incur any additional debts during the term of the Plan without prior order of the Court except such debts as may be necessary for emergency or routine medical, dental, optical or hospital care, or as may be necessary for emergency or routine automobile or home repair expenses. The Debtor may incur additional debt without prior order of the Court if necessary for the protection and preservation of life, health or property and prior permission cannot be readily obtained. If the Debtor is engaged in business, the Debtor may incur debt in the usual and ordinary course of Debtor's business operations.

7. During the pendency of this case, the Debtor is enjoined and prohibited from selling, encumbering or in any manner disposing of assets of the estate without prior order of the Court except as may be required in the ordinary course of Debtor's business if Debtor is engaged in a business.

8. All claims provided for in the Plan shall be treated for purposes of distribution as set forth in the Plan, except as stated below. Each secured creditor shall retain its lien to the extent of the value of its collateral stated in the Plan and shall have an allowed secured claim in the amount of that stated value, with any balance of its claim as actually filed being allowed as an unsecured claim. If the holder of a secured claim files a Proof of Claim for less than the value stated in the Plan for its collateral, the allowed secured claim of that creditor shall be in the amount filed and the Trustee is authorized to reamortize the payments due to that creditor, at the interest rate specified in the Plan, for the term of payments for that creditor under the Plan. If the Plan provides for a claim as a secured claim but the holder of the claim files the claim as an unsecured nonpriority claim, the Trustee shall pay that claim as an unsecured nonpriority claim. If the holder of an unsecured priority claim files a Proof of Claim for less than the amount stated in the Plan, the Trustee is authorized to pay the amount stated in the Proof of Claim over the term of payments provided under the Plan for that creditor.

9. In the event all allowed claims have been paid in full prior to the term of months stated in the Plan, the Trustee is hereby authorized to file a Motion for Entry of Early Discharge and the Plan shall be deemed completed and the Debtor shall be entitled to a full-compliance discharge upon the filing of such motion, unless the Court orders otherwise.

10. Creditors are enjoined and prohibited from assessing late charges, penalties or other fees by virtue of the manner in which payments are made or by virtue of the timing of payments under the Plan from the Trustee, without prior order of the Court.

(continued)

11. If this case is hereafter dismissed or converted to another chapter under Title 11 of the United States Code, all funds received by the Trustee prior to such dismissal or conversion shall be paid under the terms of the Plan to the creditors. Any funds received by the Trustee subsequent to dismissal or conversion of this case may be returned to the payor uncashed or may be cashed and refunded to the Debtor, in the sole discretion of the Trustee.

12. This Order supersedes any adequate protection orders previously entered in this case and any such orders shall be of no further force and effect.

13. If the Debtor is engaged in business, the Trustee shall not perform the duties stated in 11 U.S.C.A. § 1302(c) until further order of the Court. If the Debtor is engaged in business and if the Plan does not provide for payment of all claims in full, the Debtor is directed to file the reports required under 11 U.S.C.A. § 704(8) and ___ D. Bankr. Local R 2015(b), signed under penalty of perjury, at least quarterly (with the information therein contained compiled by month) and furnish a file stamped copy thereof to the Trustee.

14. The Trustee is authorized to make disbursements under the Plan and in accordance with 11 U.S.C.A. § 1326.

15. The Trustee is authorized to deduct and transfer to the Chapter 13 Expense Account the preset percentage fee fixed pursuant to 28 U.S.C.A. § 586(e)(1)(B) by Orders of the Attorney General.

16. Payment of Debtor's attorney fees as set forth in the Plan is approved.

17. If the Debtor fails to perform any provision of the Plan or this Order (other than the timely payments of plan payments), the Trustee may file a Declaration of Non-Compliance and give notice thereof to the Debtor and the Debtor's attorney. In the event the default is not cured by the Debtor within 15 days after the date the Declaration is filed, the Trustee is authorized to submit an Order Dismissing Case and this case may be dismissed without further notice or hearing.

Dated: ____________________

____
UNITED STATES BANKRUPTCY JUDGE

Prepared and submitted by:

____
Chapter 13 Standing Trustee

CERTIFICATE OF SERVICE

I hereby certify that on ______ day of __________________, 20___, I transmitted a true and correct copy of the foregoing Order Confirming Chapter 13 Plan to the parties listed below:

Eric R. McPherson
Jennifer E. McPherson
8110 S. Windsor Drive
Your City, XX *****

Chapter 13 Standing Trustee

United States Trustee

____

SECTION 10
TRUSTEE'S DISTRIBUTION OF PAYMENTS UNDER THE PLAN

If the plan is confirmed, the trustee will distribute payments to the creditors in accordance with the plan as soon as it is practicable to do so. This will depend upon how quickly a plan is confirmed and whether the bar date for filing claims has expired. Ordinarily the deadline for filing claims is 90 days after the first date set for the meeting of creditors. Fed. R. Bank. P. 3002(c). Since the trustee will not know which claims are allowed until the deadline for filing claims has expired and any objections to the claims are resolved, the trustee may not be able to make payments to unsecured creditors even though the plan is confirmed.

If the plan is not confirmed, the trustee will return the payments to the debtor, less any unpaid administrative expenses allowed under section 503(b). 11 U.S.C.A. § 13267(a)(2).

SECTION 11
MODIFICATION OF THE PLAN AFTER CONFIRMATION

At any time after the confirmation of the plan but before the completion of payments under the plan, the debtor, the trustee, or the holder of an allowed unsecured claim may request the court to modify the plan. The plan, upon notice and opportunity for a hearing, may be modified to increase or reduce the amount of payments on claims of a particular class provided for by the plan or to extend or reduce the time for such payments. The plan may also be modified to alter the amount of the distribution to a creditor provided for by the plan to the extent necessary to take into account any payment of such claim outside the plan. 11 U.S.C.A. § 1329(a).

In *In re Richardson,* the Debtor filed motion to modify her confirmed Chapter 13 plan to reduce percentage of distribution to unsecured creditors from 100 percent to 46 percent and to nominally increase plan payment from $300 to $375 per month. The Chapter 13 trustee filed motion to dismiss. The Bankruptcy Court discussed whether they meet her burden of showing that modification was warranted absent change in circumstances.

In re Richardson

192 B.R. 224 (Bankr. S. D. Cal. 1996)

MEMORANDUM DECISION
Peter W. Bowie, Bankruptcy Judge.

Debtor seeks to modify her Chapter 13 Plan to reduce the percentage of distribution to unsecured creditors, to nominally increase the plan payment by $75, all with the intent to allow completion of the plan within the sixty month maximum duration of a Chapter 13 plan. Most of the debt is unsecured, and debtor seeks to reduce the distribution from 100% to 46%, with no time remaining on the sixty month period.

This Court has jurisdiction to hear this matter pursuant to 28 U.S.C. § 1334 and General Order No. 312-D of the United States District Court for the Southern District of California. This is a core proceeding pursuant to 28 U.S.C. § 157(b)(2)(L).

FACTS

Hillary Richardson ("debtor") filed a Chapter 13 petition on August 26, 1990. On October 31, 1990, an order was entered confirming debtor's plan which provided for monthly payments of $300 to the trustee and a 100% repayment to unsecured creditors. Shortly thereafter, on January 15, 1991 the Chapter 13 Trustee filed a motion to dismiss because the debtor was not making her plan payments. In her opposition, the debtor acknowledged that she had missed payments because she had lost her job in September 1990. She stated in February 1991 that she was reemployed, wanted to continue with her plan, and she asked that the missed payments be added to the end of the plan. After a continuance to track performance, the motion to dismiss was ordered off calendar in June 1991.

In the meantime, the Chapter 13 Trustee issued a Notice of Claims Filed and Intent to Pay Claims. Including attorneys fees, the total claims were $18,275.69. Of that amount, $6,291.68 was a secured claim accruing interest at 10%. Without taking into account the accruing interest or the administrative fees of the Trustee, it would take 60.9 months at $300 per month to pay the allowed claims.

Approximately one year later, debtor amended her Statement of Affairs to add a small secured claim. Then, three months later, debtor added a student loan creditor owed $1,200. That amendment was filed in July 1992.

Presumably, debtor made a number of payments over the next two and one-half years. However, at some point payments became a problem, and on May 4, 1995 the Chapter 13 Trustee filed another motion to dismiss for failure to make payments. After the motion was filed, debtor filed opposition and made a payment of $375. At the hearing in late June 1995, the Trustee indicated that the only other payment in 1995 was in February. The Trustee also stated that approximately 24 more payments were necessary to complete the plan. The Court observed that the plan was rapidly approaching the sixty month maximum duration. The hearing on the motion to dismiss was continued to allow debtor and counsel to review the circumstances.

On August 10, 1995 debtor filed a notice of motion to modify her Chapter 13 plan. She proposed to increase the plan payment from $300 to $375 and to reduce the percentage distribution to unsecured creditors from 100% to 46%. Because the sixty-month period of 11 U.S.C. § 1322(d) had essentially run out by the time of the noticed hearing on the motion to modify, set for September, 1995, the proposed payment increase was illusory and in reality the debtor was seeking to modify to allow a percentage to unsecured creditors approximately equal to the amount already paid.

DISCUSSION

A debtor may bring a motion to modify a confirmed plan at any time after confirmation and before completion. *In re Solis,* 172 B.R. 530 (Bankr.S.D.N.Y.1994); 11 U.S.C.A. § 1329(a). Section 1329(a)(1) authorizes modification to increase or reduce the amount of payments on claims of a particular class provided for by the plan. 11 U.S.C.A. § 1329(a)(1). This section, however, does not grant an unfettered license to modify. The modification of a plan of reorganization is tantamount to a new confirmation and must be consistent with the statutory requirements for confirmation. *In re Louquet,* 125 B.R. 267 (9th Cir. BAP 1991). Therefore, all the good faith requirements needed to confirm a plan must be met in order to modify a plan. While the Code does not specifically set out what circumstances are sufficient to warrant modification, numerous courts have commented on the issue.

Many courts have limited post-confirmation modification to instances where there is some change in circumstance or occurrence that did not exist at the time the plan was originally confirmed. *In re Hutchins,* 162 B.R. 1014 (Bankr.N.D.Ill.1994). These courts have required that a debtor experience a significant and unexpected change in financial circumstances or in his or her ability to pay creditors. See *In re Gadlen,* 110 B.R. 341, 344 (Bankr.W.D.Tenn.1990) (confirmation is appropriate where a debtor has suffered a pay cut after the bankruptcy filing); *In re Klus,* 173 B.R. 51 (Bankr.D.Conn.1994) (significantly higher or lower proofs of claim that were not accounted for in plan, or significant change in debtor's financial condition is grounds for modification); *In re Bostwick,* 127 B.R. 419 (Bankr.N.D.Ill.1991) (change in circumstance is not limited to a change in financial condition, but may also include a change in the debtor's ability to pay creditors such as where several creditors do not file claims). This view comports with the legislative history suggesting that § 1329(a) was enacted to complement the "ability-to-pay" test of § 1325(b).[1] *In re Fitak,* 92 B.R. 243, 248 (Bankr.S.D.Ohio 1988).

The language of § 1329 does not expressly require a substantial or unexpected change in circumstance. *In re Powers,* 140 B.R. 476, 479 (Bankr.N.D.Ill.1992). However, the requirement is often based upon the view that without such a change in circumstance post-confirmation, the doctrine of res judicata would bar modification. *In re Bereolos,* 126 B.R. 313, 326 (Bankr.N.D.Ind.1990). In other words, a confirmed plan is res judicata as to all issues that could have been decided as of the confirmation date. *In re Moseley,* 74 B.R. 791, 799–800 (Bankr.C.D.Cal.1987).

Several courts have declined to require a change in circumstances in interpreting § 1329. See, e.g., *In re Klus,* 173 B.R. 51, 59 (Bankr.D.Conn.1994) (holding that a change in circumstances is not a threshold requirement for modification, but that the absence of such a change is a factor in the court's exercise in discretion to allow the modification). In a recent analysis, the Seventh Circuit also rejected a change in financial circumstances test. It concluded that a change in circumstance was not required by § 1329 and that the doctrine of res judicata did not apply to § 1329. *In re Witkowski,* 16 F.3d 739, 742–46 (7th Cir.1994). Interestingly, *Witkowski* involved a post-confirmation motion to modify brought by the trustee because a number of creditors had not filed claims. The trustee sought to increase the percentage payable to those creditors which had filed claims. The motion to modify was granted, and the debtor appealed. Both the district court and the Seventh Circuit affirmed. A recent case from this circuit court cited *Witkowski* favorably, with the proviso that it believed some change in circumstance should be necessary. *In re O'Brien,* 181 B.R. 71, 78–79 (Bankr.D.Ariz.1995).

As stated above, and in *Witkowski,* § 1329 does not specifically require a substantial or unanticipated change in circumstance as a prerequisite for modification. However, this Court does not agree that § 1329 gives a debtor, unsecured creditor, or trustee the absolute right to seek modification at any time or under any circumstances.

The Court of Appeals for the Ninth Circuit, in *In re Anderson,* 21 F.3d 355 (1994), faced the circumstance of a trustee seeking to extract a promise from debtors to commit all actual future disposable income to a plan, rather than the projected disposable income. The court found that approach "inconsistent with the procedures established for modifying a debtor's plan." 21 F.3d at 358. The court then wrote:

> Under § 1329, the trustee may request modification of the debtor's plan. 11 U.S.C. § 1329(a). If the debtor or a creditor objects to the modification, the trustee "must bear the burden of showing a substantial change in the debtor's ability to pay since the confirmation hearing and that the prospect of the change had not already been taken into account at the time of confirmation." [Citations omitted.] 21 F.3d at 358.

In the present case, debtor has proffered no changed circumstances, except inferentially that she is out of time to perform under the confirmed plan, and therefore would not receive the benefits of a Chapter 13 discharge. A plan cannot be confirmed that violates the sixty-month time limitation. *In re Dinsmore,* 141 B.R. 499, 505 (Bankr.W.D.Mich.1992); *In re Martin,* 156 B.R. 47, 50 (9th Cir. BAP 1993). This issue always exists at the time of any confirmation. The expiration of this period is not unexpected. The time limitation is statutorily mandated and the debtor is held to full knowledge of her responsibility to complete the plan within the time permitted by the Code. Therefore, inability to complete performance of a confirmed plan within the sixty months allowed by 11 U.S.C.A. § 1322(d) is not, by itself, a sufficient ground to support modification of a confirmed plan.

CONCLUSION

A Chapter 13 reorganization plan is a contract between the debtor and creditors. Both creditors and the debtor are bound by a plan's provisions. *In re Emly,* 153 B.R. 57 (Bankr.D.Idaho 1993). The creditors are bound by the terms of this contract and have a justifiable expectation that they will be treated in accordance with its terms. Where a debtor seeks to modify the contract after confirmation, to change the terms for treatment of the creditors, the debtor must show some change in circumstance not foreseeable at the time of confirmation to support that modification. Equally as important as the existence of changed circumstances is the timing of the motion to modify in conjunction with the changed circumstance. If a debtor proffers loss of employment for a period as the changed circumstance, but waits over four years to move to modify because of it, the debtor's good faith is implicated. Similarly, if claims are higher than originally scheduled, but debtor waits until the end of the plan term to move to modify, the circumstances should be closely scrutinized for a debtor's good faith.

In the present case, debtor has offered no change in circumstances. Instead, she tacitly acknowledges that she has not performed her side of the contract by providing payments to the trustee sufficient to distribute 100% to unsecured creditors within the maximum sixty months allowed. Notwithstanding her unilateral breach of the contract, she asks that it be ignored and that she be given the full benefit of the Chapter 13 discharge she bargained for, while reducing by more than 50% the consideration she promised to pay unsecured creditors for it over 5 years ago. She has failed to meet her burden under § 1329(a) and the decisions discussed above.

Accordingly, the debtor's motion to modify her plan is denied. The trustee's motion to dismiss is granted. Counsel for debtor is allowed fees of $530, payable as an administrative expense, and subject to funds held by the trustee. The Chapter 13 Trustee shall submit a separate order of dismissal.

IT IS SO ORDERED.

[1] "The ability-to-pay standard would be made applicable to plan modifications following confirmation, by the addition of a new subsection 1329(a), which would permit the debtor or the holder of an allowed unsecured claim to request modification of the plan in response to changes in the circumstances of the debtor substantially affecting the ability of the debtor to make future payments under the plan. New subsection 1329(a) would provide a measure of flexibility not presently available by permitting accommodation of the performance required under the chapter 13 plan to better suit the actual circumstances encountered during the course of the plan. . . .

The purpose of this amendment is to permit the debtor or the holder of an allowed unsecured claim to request modification of a confirmed chapter 13 plan in response to changes in circumstances of the debtor substantially affecting (favorably or unfavorably) the ability of the debtor to make payments under the plan, as determined by reference to the ability-to-pay test set forth in § 1325." *Fitak,* 92 B.R. at 249; citing Oversight Hearings on Personal Bankruptcy Before the Subcommittee on Monopolies and Commercial Law of the House Committee on the Judiciary, 97th Cong. 1st Sess. 181, 215–216, 221 (1981–82).

SECTION 12
REVOCATION OF ORDER OF CONFIRMATION

Upon request of a party in interest, the court may **revoke an order for confirmation** if the order was procured by fraud. The revocation must occur within 180 days after the order for confirmation and must follow notice and a hearing. 11 U.S.C.A. § 1330(a). If an order for confirmation has been revoked, the case will be converted or dismissed pursuant to Section 1307(c)(7) unless, within the time fixed by the court, the debtor proposes a modification of the plan that is confirmed by the court. 11 U.S.C.A. § 1330(b).

SECTION 13
DISCHARGE

After the payments have been completed under the plan, the court will grant the debtor a discharge of his or her debts. This is often called a full-compliance discharge. The debtor will not be discharged from

1. allowed claims that were not provided for by the plan;
2. any debt for the curing of any default on any secured or unsecured claim on which the final payment is due after the proposed final payment under the plan; and
3. any debt of the kind specified in 11 U.S.C.A. § 1328(a)(2). 11 U.S.C.A.§ 1328(a).

Therefore, with the exception of alimony and child support, educational loans owing to a governmental unit or a nonprofit institution of higher education, any debts for death or personal injury caused by the debtor's operation of a motor vehicle while intoxicated, and restitution included in a sentence on the debtor's conviction of a crime, the effect of a Chapter 13 full-compliance discharge is that the debtor can be discharged from debts that would be nondischargeable under Chapter 7. The Chapter 13 full-compliance discharge is the broadest discharge available to the debtor under the Bankruptcy Code and is designed to encourage debtors to repay at least part of their debts under Chapter 13 rather than to liquidate under Chapter 7.

PROBLEM 6.6 Jennifer borrowed $40,000 from Thrifty Credit Union to finance her nursing school education. After this debt was paid down to $35,000, Jennifer and Eric McPherson filed a petition in bankruptcy under Chapter 13.

Under the McPhersons' Chapter 13 plan, they propose to pay only a very small percentage of Jennifer's student loan. Could the McPhersons receive a discharge from the balance due on her student loan?

Under the McPhersons' Chapter 13 plan, they propose to pay the same small percentage of their other unsecured, nonpriority debts. Could the McPhersons receive a discharge from the balance due on these debts?

What is this percentage? Is interest accruing on each claim and, if so, how is this factored in?

The court may grant what is called a hardship or compassionate discharge to a debtor who has not completed payments under the plan. This type of discharge is granted only if the debtor's failure to complete the payments is due to circumstances for which the debtor should not justly be held responsible, the value of the payments made to creditors as of the effective date of the plan is not less than the amount that would have been paid on the claim if the debtor's estate had been liquidated under Chapter 7 (the best interests test is met), and modification of the plan is not practicable. 11 U.S.C.A. § 1328(b).

The debtor under a hardship discharge will not be discharged from any allowed secured claims, from allowed unsecured claims that were not provided for by the plan, from any debt for the curing of any default on any secured or unsecured claim on which the final payment is due after the proposed final payment under the plan, or from any nondischargeable claims under section 523(a). 11 U.S.C.A. § 1328(c). Therefore, the effect of a hardship discharge is that the debtor will not be discharged from any secured debts or from unsecured debts that would be nondischargeable under Chapter 7.

PROBLEM 6.7 After making payments for 30 weeks under the plan, Eric McPherson lost his job and the McPhersons were unable to continue making payments. If they received a hardship discharge, would they be discharged from any of their debts?

A debtor who has received either a full-compliance or a hardship discharge cannot receive a discharge in a Chapter 7 case filed within six years of the date of the Chapter 13 filing, unless payments under the Chapter 13 plan totaled 100 percent of the allowed unsecured claims, or totaled 70 percent of the allowed unsecured claims and the Chapter 13 plan was proposed by the debtor in good faith and was the debtor's best effort. 11 U.S.C.A. § 727(a)(9). A debtor who has received a discharge in a Chapter 13 case is not foreclosed from filing another Chapter 13 case or a Chapter 11 or 12 case at any time and receiving a discharge, if the debtor is otherwise eligible to file under any of these chapters and receive a discharge. 11 U.S.C.A. §§ 109, 1141, 1228, 1328.

PROBLEM 6.8 Five years after filing their Chapter 13 case and two years after their hardship discharge, Jennifer became ill and was unable to continue her nursing career. Once again, the McPhersons were unable to pay their creditors.

Are the McPhersons eligible to file a Chapter 7 petition? Are they eligible for a Chapter 7 discharge?

Are the McPhersons eligible to file another Chapter 13 petition? Are they eligible for a Chapter 13 discharge?

SECTION 14
REVOCATION OF THE DISCHARGE

A party in interest may request **revocation of the discharge** for fraud within one year after the discharge is granted if this party did not know about the fraud until after the discharge was granted. 11 U.S.C.A. § 1328(e).

SECTION 15
CLOSING THE CASE AND PROCEEDINGS AFTER THE CASE IS CLOSED

Upon completion of payments under the plan and discharge of the debtor, the trustee files a final report and account, certifying that the case has been fully administered. The case is presumed to have been fully administered unless the United States trustee or a party in interest files an objection within 30 days. If no objection is filed, the court may discharge the trustee and close the case without reviewing the final report and account. 11 U.S.C.A. § 350(a); Fed. R. Bank. P. 5009.

Even after the case is closed, it is still subject to further action. In certain situations, a case may be amended without being reopened. Clerical errors in judgments, orders, and other parts of the record or errors in the record caused by oversight or omission may be corrected. A closed case may be reopened to add a creditor or to distribute previously undistributed property of the estate. 11 U.S.C.A. § 350(b).

KEY TERMS

Chapter 7 case
Chapter 13 plan
codebtor stay
confirmation hearing
cramdown
good faith
revocation of the discharge
revoke an order for confirmation

CHAPTER 7

The Chapter 12 Bankruptcy (Adjustment of Debts of a Family Farmer with Regular Annual Income)

CHAPTER OUTLINE

SECTION 1
THE INITIATION OF A CHAPTER 12 CASE

SECTION 2
THE CHAPTER 12 PLAN

A. Contents of a Chapter 12 Plan
B. The Debtor's Payments under the Plan
C. Modification of the Plan before Confirmation

SECTION 3
THE FILING OF THE PETITION

SECTION 4
THE SIGNIFICANCE OF FILING A PETITION

A. Possession and Control of Property of the Estate: The Debtor in Possession
B. Operation of the Debtor's Business
C. Exemptions

SECTION 5
APPOINTMENT AND DUTIES OF A CHAPTER 12 TRUSTEE

SECTION 6
MOTIONS AND COMPLAINTS AFTER THE ORDER FOR RELIEF

A. Motions
B. Complaints

SECTION 7
THE CLERK'S NOTICE

SECTION 8
MEETING OF CREDITORS (THE SECTION 341 MEETING)

SECTION 9
HEARING ON CONFIRMATION OF THE PLAN

SECTION 10
TRUSTEE'S DISTRIBUTION OF PAYMENTS UNDER THE PLAN

SECTION 11
MODIFICATION OF THE PLAN AFTER CONFIRMATION

SECTION 12
REVOCATION OF ORDER OF CONFIRMATION, CONVERSION, OR DISMISSAL

SECTION 13
DISCHARGE

SECTION 14
REVOCATION OF THE DISCHARGE

SECTION 15
CLOSING THE CASE AND PROCEEDINGS AFTER THE CASE IS CLOSED

This chapter explores the Chapter 12 bankruptcy—adjustment of debts of a family farmer with regular annual income. Although Chapter 7 encompasses almost all debtors (any person is eligible to be a debtor under Chapter 7, with the exception of railroads, insurance companies, and certain banking institutions), Chapter 12 is only available to family farmers who have regular annual income (11 U.S.C.A. § 109(f)), that is, family farmers whose annual income is sufficiently stable and regular to enable them to make payments under a **Chapter 12 plan.** 11 U.S.C.A. § 101(19).

The term **family farmer** is further restricted because not all persons involved in **farming operations** are defined as family farmers under the Bankruptcy Code. For an individual or an individual and spouse to be considered a family farmer

1. the aggregate debts must not exceed $1,500,000;
2. at least 80 percent of the aggregate noncontingent, liquidated debts must arise out of the debtor's farming operation; and
3. more than 50 percent of the debtor's gross income for the preceding taxable year must have been received from the farming operation.

For a partnership or a corporation to be considered a family farmer

1. more than 50 percent of the partnership or the outstanding stock must be held by one family conducting the farming operation;
2. more than 80 percent of the value of the partnership or the corporate assets must consist of assets related to the farming operation;
3. the aggregate debts must not exceed $1,500,000; and
4. not less than 80 percent of its aggregate noncontingent, liquidated debts must arise out of the farming operation.

If the entity is a corporation that issued stock, the stock must not be publicly traded. 11 U.S.C.A. § 101(18).

In *In re Swanson,* the debtor received cash rent for his farm. To seek protection under Chapter 12, Swanson had to qualify as a family farmer, a classification that required that he obtain more than 50 percent of his gross income for the preceding taxable year from farming operations. His income for the year before filing the Chapter 12 reflected that a significant portion of his income came from the lease rent. The court had to determine whether or not the income Swanson earned from the lease constituted farm income.

In re Swanson

289 B.R. 372 (Bankr. C.D. Ill. 2003)

OPINION
THOMAS L. PERKINS, Bankruptcy Judge.

This matter came before the Court for an evidentiary hearing on several issues, including confirmation of the Chapter 12 plan filed by the Debtor, Paul R. Swanson, Sr., ("DEBTOR"), as well as three motions filed by Union Bank/Central (the "BANK"), for relief from the automatic stay, to dismiss the Chapter 12 case, and for the DEBTOR to show cause why he will not allow the BANK'S appraiser access to the farm property. Based on the evidence received at trial, the Court finds that the BANK'S motion to dismiss should be granted on the basis that the DEBTOR is not eligible for Chapter 12 relief since he is not a family farmer.

Only a family farmer with regular annual income may be a debtor under Chapter 12. 11 U.S.C. § 109(f). "Family farmer" is defined in Section 101(18) of the Bankruptcy Code, in pertinent part, as follows:

> (18) "family farmer" means—
> (A) individual or individual and spouse engaged in a farming operation whose aggregate debts do not exceed $1,500,000 and not less than 80 percent of whose aggregate noncontingent, liquidated debts (excluding a debt for the principal residence of such individual or such individual and spouse unless such debt arises out of a farming operation), on the date the case is filed, arise out of a farming operation owned or operated by such individual or such individual and spouse, and such individual or such individual and spouse receive from such farming operation more than 50 percent of such individual's or such individual and spouse's gross income for the taxable year preceding the taxable year in which the case concerning such individual or such individual and spouse was filed.

11 U.S.C. § 101(18)(A).

At issue is whether the DEBTOR earned from a farming operation more than fifty percent (50%) of his gross income for the taxable year 2001, which is conceded to be the taxable year preceding the taxable year in which his case was filed.

Based on the evidence received at trial, the Court finds that the DEBTOR'S gross income for 2001 is itemized as follows:

Amount	Source of Income
$39,750	Cash rent received from annual lease of DEBTOR'S farm real estate.
36,454	DEBTOR'S half interest in proceeds from sale of hogs, cattle and grain.
219	Interest income
7,992	Social Security
2,000 (est.)	Del Monte wages

There is no dispute that the $36,454 from the sale of livestock and grain is income derived from a farming operation, and that the income from social security, Del Monte and interest is not derived from a farming operation. Accordingly, the DEBTOR'S eligibility for Chapter 12 turns on whether the cash rent is or is not income received from a farming operation.

"Farming operation" is defined in Section 101(21) of the Bankruptcy Code, as follows:

> (21) "farming operation" includes farming, tillage of the soil, dairy farming, ranching, production or raising of crops, poultry, or livestock, and production of poultry or livestock products in an unmanufactured state.

11 U.S.C. § 101(21).

In support of its position that cash rent received from the lease of farm ground is not income from a farming operation, the BANK relies upon *In re Armstrong,* 812 F.2d 1024 (7th Cir.1987), *In re Ross,* 270 B.R. 710 (Bankr.S.D.Ill.2001) and *In re Seabloom,* 78 B.R. 543 (Bankr.C.D.Ill.1987) (Altenberger, J.).

The issue in *Armstrong* was whether the debtor was a "farmer" who, by virtue of that status, could not be forced into bankruptcy via an involuntary petition filed pursuant to Section 303. Since the Bankruptcy Code's definition of "farmer" at Section 101(17) [now 101(18)] is tied to the percentage of gross income received from a farming operation, it was necessary to the court's decision to construe the definition of "farming operation" at Section 101(18) [now 101(19)]. Specifically, the Seventh Circuit considered whether money received by the debtor from acreage rented to a third party was income received from a farming operation. Because the lease payment of approximately $17,000 was paid by the tenant "in cash and up front," the court reasoned that the traditional risks associated with growing crops were assumed entirely by the tenant. Rejecting the debtor's argument that he actively participated in the tillage of the crops and provided fertilizer, the court determined that the rental income was nonfarm income for the purpose of the Bankruptcy Code definitions of "farmer" and "farming operation." On this basis, the court held that the debtor did not meet the definition of a farmer and could be subjected to an involuntary filing.

In *Seabloom,* a case arising out of a voluntary Chapter 12 filing, the court held that the debtors failed to qualify as family farmers since less than fifty percent (50%) of their 1985 income was received from a farming operation and dismissed the petition. The debtors' cash rent lease called for a portion of the rent to be paid up front and the balance paid after sale of the crops. Judge Altenberger rejected the debtors' attempt, on that basis, to distinguish their lease from the lease in *Armstrong,* reasoning that since the obligation to pay the rent was absolute and not contingent upon the crop yields or prices, the risks were solely on the shoulders of the tenant. The issue in *Ross* was whether income derived from the *sale* of farmland was farm income. *Ross* did not involve a cash rent lease and is inapposite.

The DEBTOR argues that *Armstrong,* involving a question of eligibility for an involuntary filing, is not binding precedent on the issue before this Court. The DEBTOR would have this Court apply a totality of the circumstances analysis such as used by the bankruptcy courts in *In re Coulston,* 98 B.R. 280 (Bankr.E.D.Mich.1989) and *In re Hettinger,* 95 B.R. 110 (Bankr.E.D.Mo.1989). Rejecting *Armstrong's* "mechanistic risk analysis approach," the *Coulston* court held that cash rent could be farm income where the debtor "behaved historically as a farmer" and "had both an honest intention and a reasonable probability of returning to 'true' farming." 98 B.R. at 283. The court determined that Mr. Coulston met this two-part test and ruled that the cash rent he received in the year prior to bankruptcy was farm income thereby making him eligible for Chapter 12 relief.

Over the BANK'S objection, this Court allowed the DEBTOR to testify as to his farming history and future plans. The Court must now consider whether it is bound by *Armstrong's* determination that cash rent "paid in full and up front" is not farm income.

The binding precedent rule, that lower courts must follow the holdings of their court of appeals and the Supreme Court, affords a lower court no discretion where a higher court has already decided the issue before it. *Johnson v. DeSoto County Bd. of Com'rs,* 72 F.3d 1556, 1559 n.2 (11th Cir.1996). Lower courts are not bound to follow a higher court's dictum. *U.S. v. Crawley,* 837 F.2d 291 (7th Cir.1988). Generally, a court's statement is dictum if it is not necessary for its decision. *Id.* at 292. Statements that explain the court's rationale are part of its holding. *U.S. v. Bloom,* 149 F.3d 649, 653 (7th Cir.1998).

There is simply no doubt that the Seventh Circuit's determination in *Armstrong,* that cash rent, paid in full and up front, is not income received from a farming operation, is part of its holding. That determination was necessary to the result, and was in no way gratuitous. Both the definition of "farmer" at issue in *Armstrong* and the definition of "family farmer" at issue here, are measured by the same percentage of gross income test, even though the percentages are different. The key term of both definitions is "farming operation." Even though the ultimate issue in *Armstrong* was different than the one before this Court, the question of whether cash rent is income derived from a "farming operation," necessary to resolution of both cases, is identical.

Neither is *Armstrong* distinguishable on its facts. As in *Armstrong,* the DEBTOR'S lease was paid in full and up front. Although the DEBTOR could not recall if the rent was paid in one payment or two, it was fully paid at the beginning of the crop year 2001. On the facts in the record, even the argument rejected by Judge Altenberger in *Seabloom,* that a portion of the rent paid at the end of the year distinguishes *Armstrong,* is not available to the DEBTOR here.

Armstrong is binding precedent that controls the outcome here. Following that precedent, the cash rent received by the DEBTOR in 2001 is not income received from a farming operation. Less than fifty percent (50%) of the DEBTOR'S gross income for taxable year 2001 was received from a farming operation. Therefore, the DEBTOR was not a family farmer at the time he filed his Chapter 12 petition and the petition must be dismissed. Given this result, it is not necessary for the Court to address the other pending motions which are now moot.

This Opinion constitutes this Court's findings of fact and conclusions of law in accordance with Federal Rule of Bankruptcy Procedure 7052. A separate Order will be entered.

Chapter 12 gives family farmers with regular annual income certain advantages not available under Chapter 7.

- Chapter 12 allows debtors to keep their nonexempt assets that would otherwise be surrendered to, and liquidated by, the trustee in a Chapter 7 case.
- Chapter 12 allows debtors to use their disposable income to pay creditors as much as they can over the term of the plan whereas under Chapter 7, creditors are paid only from the liquidation of nonexempt assets of the bankruptcy estate.
- Certain debts can be discharged in Chapter 12 that are potentially nondischargeable in Chapter 7.
- A debtor can cure defaults in Chapter 12 in order to keep property subject to a lien (e.g., curing a payment default on a loan secured by a residence).
- The automatic stay extends to codebtors on consumer loans in Chapter 12.
- Debtors can alter the payment terms on most secured debt in Chapter 12 and, unlike Chapter 13, the debt need not be paid in full within the 36- to 60-month term of the Chapter 13 plan.
- In Chapter 12, debtors can pay nondischargeable debt such as priority tax and support alimony under the term of the Chapter 12 plan without the postpetition accrual of interest and penalties.
- A debtor may receive a discharge under Chapter 12 more often than every six years as permitted under Chapter 7.
- A Chapter 12 filing carries less stigma for the debtor than does a Chapter 7 filing.

Chapter 12 has disadvantages as well.

- A Chapter 12 debtor is in bankruptcy for three to five years and will need to live under a tight budget with little room for contingencies.
- The Chapter 12 trustee is paid a fee under the Chapter 12 plan, thus reducing the amount available to pay creditors under the plan.
- Because of the additional work involved in a Chapter 12, attorneys will generally charge debtors higher fees for Chapter 12 than for Chapter 7.
- Creditors may be less willing to extend credit to a Chapter 12 debtor during the term of the plan because all of the debtor's disposable income is subject to the plan and is not available to postpetition creditors unless the plan is modified.

This chapter deals exclusively with the Chapter 12 bankruptcy. A Chapter 12 case is developed in chronological order, beginning when a potential client approaches the law office for advice and continuing to the closing of the case. This chapter includes

- the initiation of a Chapter 12 case;
- the Chapter 12 plan—including who may file a plan, the contents of a plan, and modification of the plan before confirmation;
- the filing of the petition and the significance of filing a petition;
- the appointment and duties of a Chapter 12 trustee;
- motions and complaints after the order for relief;
- the clerk's notice;
- the meeting of creditors (the 341 meeting);
- the hearing on confirmation of the plan and the Chapter 12 cramdown;
- the debtor's payments under the plan and the trustee's distribution of payments under the plan;
- modification of the plan after confirmation;
- revocation of the order of confirmation, conversion, and dismissal;
- full-compliance and hardship discharge and revocation of discharge;
- the closing of the case and proceedings after the case is closed.

Exhibit 7–1 is a flow chart for a Chapter 12 case.

EXHIBIT 7–1 Flow Chart for Chapter 12

Filing the Chapter 12 Petition

The debtor files with the bankruptcy court clerk's office:
1. Filing fee
2. Voluntary petition, including Exhibit C, if the debtor has some connection to hazardous waste
3. Disclosure of attorney's compensation statement or disclosure of compensation statement by a non-attorney bankruptcy petition preparer
4. List of creditors
5. Schedules
   a. Summary of schedules
   b. Schedule A. Real property
   c. Schedule B. Personal property
   d. Schedule C. Property claimed as exempt
   e. Schedule D. Creditors holding secured claims
   f. Schedule E. Creditors holding unsecured priority claims
   g. Schedule F. Creditors holding unsecured nonpriority claims
   h. Schedule G. Executory contracts and unexpired leases
   i. Schedule H. Codebtors
   j. Schedule I. Current income of individual debtor(s)
   k. Schedule J. Current expenditures of individual debtor(s)
6. Statement of financial affairs
7. Chapter 12 plan

If the petition is accompanied by the list of creditors, the debtor has up to 15 days to file items 5 and 6 and has up to 90 days to file item 7

The debtor has a duty to supplement the schedules for certain property acquired after the petition has been filed

Prior to the time the case is closed, the debtor may amend the petition, lists, schedules, and statement of financial affairs

Prior to confirmation, the debtor may modify the plan

Upon filing of the voluntary petition, which constitutes an order for relief, an estate is created and the automatic stay and the codebtor stay go into effect, protecting the estate from dismemberment and the debtor and the codebtor from collection procedures

The standing Chapter 12 trustee, or another individual if there is no standing Chapter 12 trustee, or the U.S. trustee will serve as the trustee in the case

The debtor remains in possession of property of the estate as the debtor in possession (DIP)

(continued)

EXHIBIT 7–1 Filing the Chapter 12 Petition, Continued

The clerk of the bankruptcy court mails to the debtor, the debtor's attorney, the trustee, all creditors, and the U.S. trustee:
1. notice of the filing of the Chapter 12 bankruptcy case;
2. an explanation of the automatic stay and the codebtor stay;
3. the date, time, and location of the meeting of creditors;
4. the deadline for filing proofs of claim;
5. the deadline for filing objections to the debtor's claim of exemptions; and
6. the date, time, and location of the hearing on confirmation of the plan

An eligible debtor may convert the case to Chapter 7, 11, or 13 or the debtor may move to dismiss the case or move for a change of venue

A party in interest (including creditors, the trustee, and the U.S. trustee) may move to dismiss the case, for abstention by the court, for a change of venue, for examination of any entity, or to convert the case to Chapter 7, 11, or 13

Meeting of Creditors

The meeting of creditors is to be held not less than 20 nor more than 35 days after the Chapter 12 petition has been filed

The business of the meeting of creditors includes the examination of the debtor under oath

Fresh Start for the Debtor (Discharge)

Within 60 days after the first date set for the meeting of creditors, a creditor may file a complaint objecting to the dischargeability of a debt

While the case is open, the debtor may file a complaint to determine the dischargeability of a debt or may move to avoid a judicial lien or to avoid a nonpossessory, nonpurchase money security interest in certain items of personal property, to the extent that such lien impairs exceptions to which the debtor would have been entitled

Administration of the Estate

The debtor remains in possession of the property of the estate

The debtor is required to file periodic reports on forms as required by the U.S. trustee or the court

As the debtor receives income, the debtor begins making payments as proposed by the plan

(continued)

EXHIBIT 7–1 Filing the Chapter 12 Petition, Continued

Within 30 days after the conclusion of the meeting of creditors or within 30 days after any amendment is filed, whichever is later, a party in interest may object to the debtor's claim of exemptions

A creditor may file a proof of claim, subject to the statutory deadline

A creditor may move for relief from the automatic stay or for relief from the codebtor stay

A creditor, trustee, U.S. trustee, or the debtor may move for disallowance of a claim or for abandonment of an asset from the estate

The debtor may move for permission to use cash collateral or to use, sell, or lease property

The debtor in possession may file a complaint to avoid unperfected security interests, statutory liens that arise upon the debtor's insolvency, prepetition preferential transfers of property of the debtor, prepetition transfers of property of the debtor that are fraudulent under the Bankruptcy Code or state law, and postpetition transfers of property of the estate that are not authorized by the bankruptcy court or Bankruptcy Code

The debtor in possession may file a motion to assume or reject executory contracts or unexpired leases

Parties in interest may object to confirmation of the plan

(continued)

EXHIBIT 7–1 Filing the Chapter 12 Petition, Continued

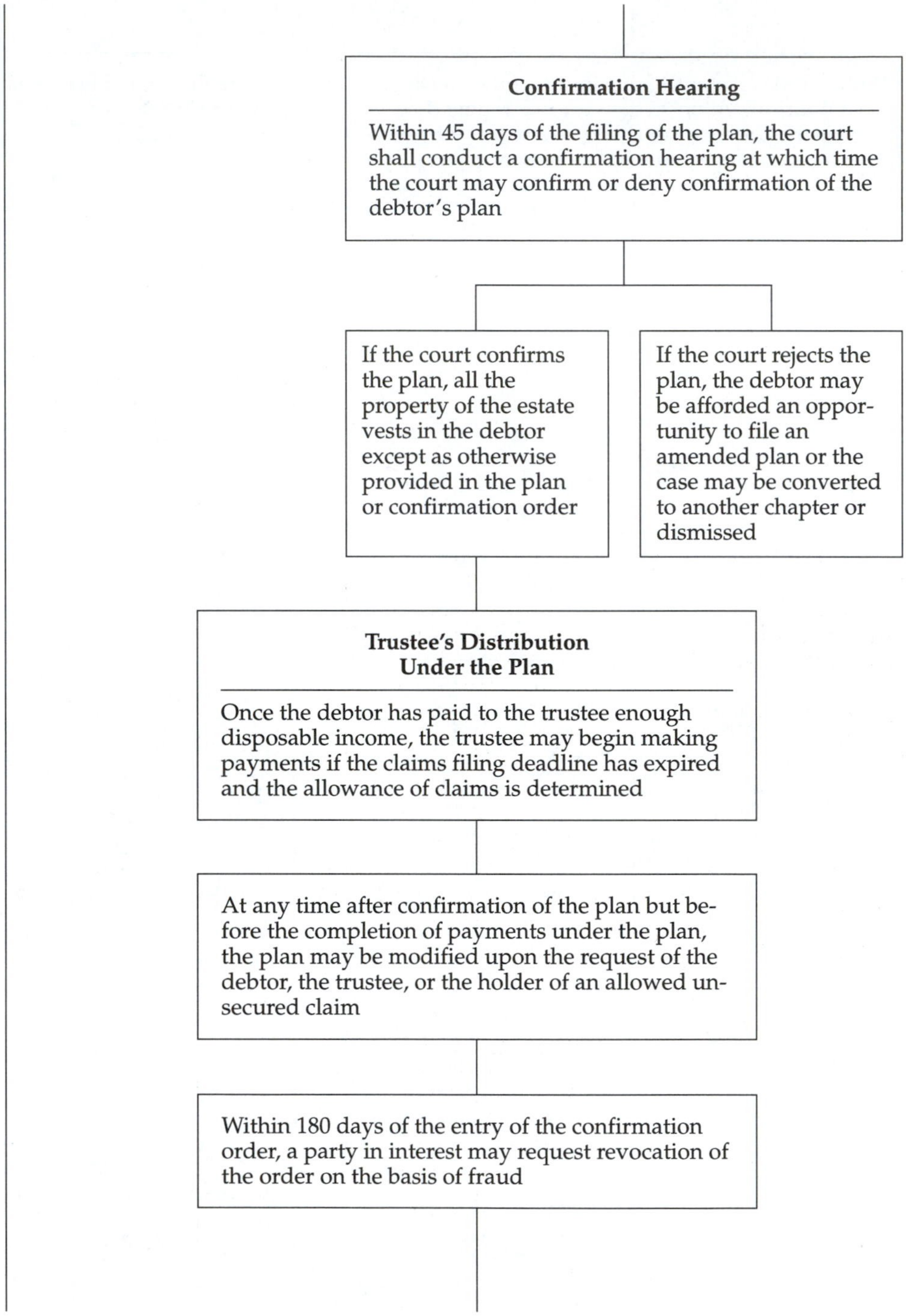

Confirmation Hearing

Within 45 days of the filing of the plan, the court shall conduct a confirmation hearing at which time the court may confirm or deny confirmation of the debtor's plan

If the court confirms the plan, all the property of the estate vests in the debtor except as otherwise provided in the plan or confirmation order

If the court rejects the plan, the debtor may be afforded an opportunity to file an amended plan or the case may be converted to another chapter or dismissed

Trustee's Distribution Under the Plan

Once the debtor has paid to the trustee enough disposable income, the trustee may begin making payments if the claims filing deadline has expired and the allowance of claims is determined

At any time after confirmation of the plan but before the completion of payments under the plan, the plan may be modified upon the request of the debtor, the trustee, or the holder of an allowed unsecured claim

Within 180 days of the entry of the confirmation order, a party in interest may request revocation of the order on the basis of fraud

(continued)

EXHIBIT 7–1 Filing the Chapter 12 Petition, Continued

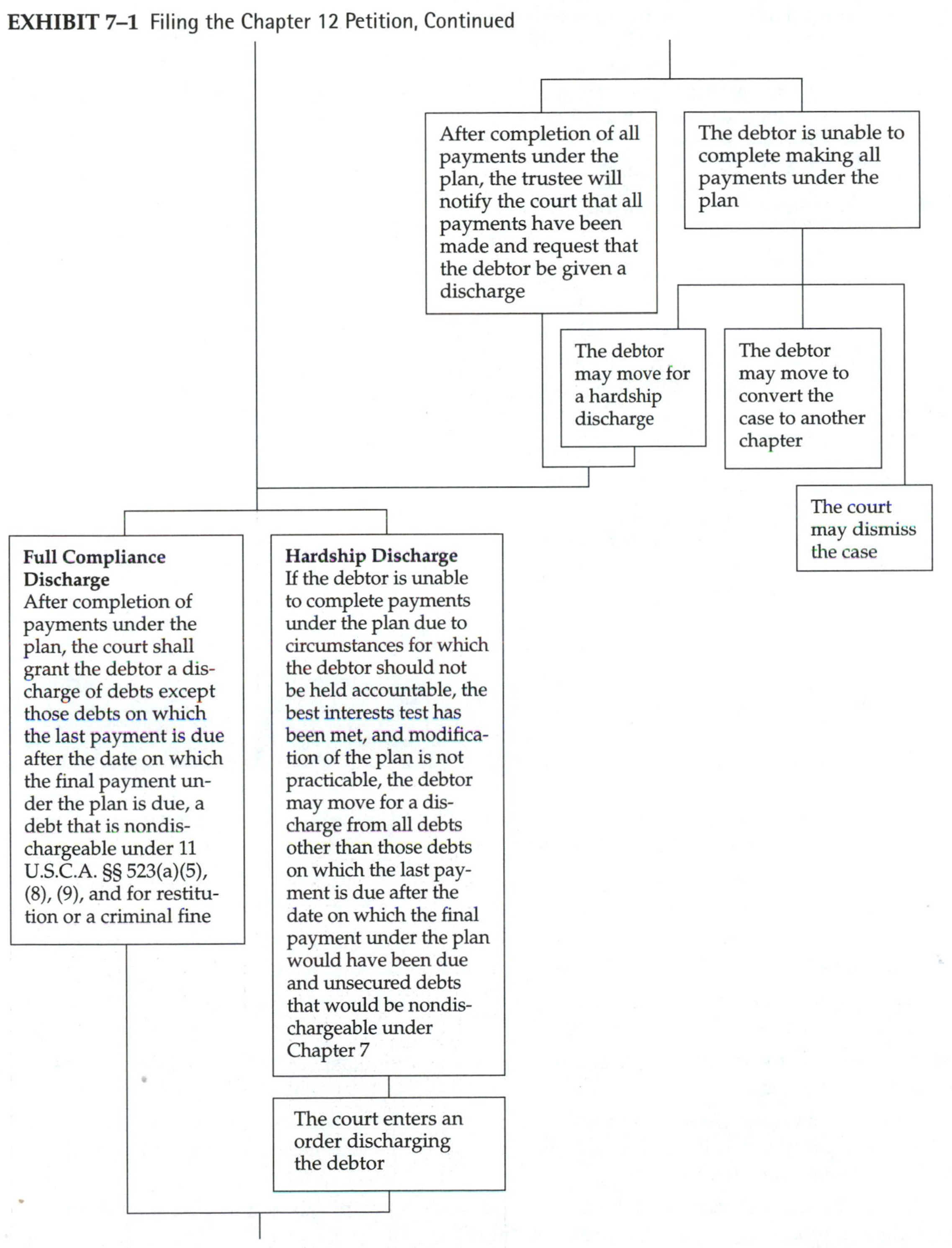

(continued)

EXHIBIT 7–1 Filing the Chapter 12 Petition, Continued

Upon the completion of payments under the plan, the trustee files a final report and final account certifying that the estate has been fully administered. Notice of the filing of the final report and the final account is given to all parties in interest. If there is no objection filed within 30 days, the case is closed.

A party in interest may request revocation of the discharge for fraud within one year after the discharge is granted

After the case is closed, it may be amended or reopened for cause with or without the appointment of a trustee

SECTION 1
THE INITIATION OF A CHAPTER 12 CASE

The initiation of a Chapter 12 case follows much the same path as the initiation of a Chapter 13 case. For example, an attorney may employ the following procedure:

- After the debtor has initiated contact with the attorney's firm, the attorney's paralegal sets up the client file, acquires a list of the debtor's creditors, and initiates a conflict of interest check.
- The paralegal gives the debtor a questionnaire (worksheets) that will help the debtor itemize his or her assets and liabilities as well as monthly income and monthly expenses.
- The paralegal requires the debtor to provide copies of relevant documents such as real estate deeds and mortgages, loan agreements, security agreements, vehicle titles, and tax returns.
- The debtor completes the questionnaire and returns it to the paralegal along with the documents requested by the paralegal.
- The paralegal meets with the debtor and reviews the questionnaire with the debtor to insure that the questionnaire is completed fully and accurately and to identify any emergencies that may require the attorney's immediate attention.
- The attorney and paralegal meet with the debtor, and the attorney discusses the questionnaire adding, deleting, modifying, and verifying the debtor's entries.
- The attorney advises the debtor whether bankruptcy is the appropriate course of action and, if so, whether the case should be filed under Chapter 7, Chapter 11, Chapter 12, or Chapter 13. The attorney will explain the process to the debtor and will discuss attorney fees and other aspects of the attorney/client contract for services.

- The paralegal completes the petition, the list of creditors, the disclosure of attorney's compensation statement, the schedules, and the Statement of Financial Affairs.
- If the relief selected is a Chapter 12 bankruptcy, the attorney drafts the Chapter 12 plan.

For the purpose of illustrating a Chapter 12 bankruptcy, the text will follow the plight of Ronald Milton Oliver, a local rancher. Mr. Oliver has contacted a law office and has spoken with the paralegal who works under the supervision of the bankruptcy attorney. After obtaining general information about Mr. Oliver, the paralegal asks him to submit a list of his creditors so the firm can initiate a conflict of interest check and decide whether it can take the case. The paralegal informs Mr. Oliver that once the conflict check has been completed, he will be required to complete a questionnaire concerning his assets and liabilities. The paralegal describes the procedure that the office will follow in preparing for his bankruptcy filing.

Mr. Oliver delivers the list of his creditors to the firm and the paralegal conducts a conflict of interest check. Finding no conflict, the paralegal sends Mr. Oliver the questionnaire that he must complete for the process to go forward.

The following is Mr. Oliver's personal history from which he will complete the questionnaire.

Ronald Milton Oliver

Ronald Milton Oliver owns and operates a feeder cattle operation on 1,490 acres of land located in Craig County, Oklahoma. This land is used for grazing cattle and has a barn and small cabin on it that is used as a workshop. The land has been in Oliver's family since statehood in 1907. For many years, Oliver worked for his father, who owned the land. Several years ago when Oliver's father decided to retire, he sold the land to Oliver for $425,000. The sale was financed with a 30-year loan from Federal Land Bank (FLB) for $400,000 at 4.5% interest per annum. The land has a current value of $425,000 and FLB is owed $350,000, which includes postpetition attorney fees, late charges, and other costs. FLB still holds the promissory note and mortgage. The loan is three months in arrears ($9,179.91).

Several years ago, Oliver borrowed $100,000 at 6.0% from Second National Bank (SNB) and gave SNB a promissory note and a second mortgage on the 1,490 acres of land. The collateral for this loan also includes Oliver's John Deere tractor with brush hog and bailer. Oliver still owes SNB $90,000. When the tractor was used as collateral for the SNB loan, Oliver had owned it for a number of years, and it was debt-free.

Oliver also owns a home on five acres, located several miles from his feeder cattle operation. He purchased this homestead for $175,000 and financed $150,000 of the purchase price with a 30-year loan from Homestead Bank (HB). The loan is at 9.25%. He signed a promissory note and gave the bank a real estate mortgage in his homestead. The present value of the homestead is $185,000 and the outstanding balance is $140,000.

In addition to his 1,490 acres, Oliver leases 640 acres of grazing land from Joseph and Sarah Smith. Under this pasture lease, Oliver is obligated to pay the Smiths $2,240 a year. Oliver is currently in the third year of this five-year lease.

In April of each year when the Bermuda grass begins to green, Oliver purchases 300 head of feeder cattle. The purchase price for the cattle is financed through a loan obtained from Farmers and Merchants Bank (F&M). When purchased, the cattle average 550 pounds a head. Once purchased, the cattle are turned loose to graze for the summer. They gain an average of two to three pounds a day, thus weighing about 900 pounds a head when sold in September when the grass begins to die out (roughly 150 days later). Each year Oliver anticipates losing about one percent of his herd and paying the vet about $10 per head. Oliver repays his loan from the bank in one lump sum (principal and interest) after the herd is sold in September.

This past April, Oliver borrowed $112,000 at 7.0 percent per annum from F&M to purchase his current herd (purchase price $123,750) and F & M took a promissory note and security interest in the herd of cattle. Oliver anticipates selling the herd for $229,878 (297 head times 900 pounds per head times $.86 a pound) if the price holds at $.86 a pound. The price is not always stable. For example, last year the price fell to $.75 a pound, which was more than the previous year when the price was $.65 a pound.

Since purchasing the land from his father, Oliver has been having a difficult time maintaining his feeder cattle operation. By the time he purchases his cattle, fattens and sells them, and pays his mortgage, other secured creditors, and his taxes, he never has enough money to pay his other creditors. Currently he owes $150,000 for medical and funeral expenses for his son, $25,000 in credit card debt, and $35,000 in trade debt.

Oliver's luck seemed to change last year when he was approached by the Astro Drilling Company for permission to explore for gas on his land. After drilling in several locations, Astro discovered gas. Oliver gave Astro a gas lease that permitted drilling for up to ten years. Under the lease, Oliver was to receive 3/18th of the gross revenue from each well. Astro drilled 20 wells, and each produces about 1000 mcf (metric cubic feet) per week. With the price of gas currently at $4 per mcf, Oliver expects to be paid $3,900 per well per year. He is paid quarterly.

In addition to the land, homestead, and cattle, Ronald Oliver owns two horses valued at $2,500; farm equipment and machinery valued at $5,000; a Chevrolet C-2500 Silverado pickup truck valued at $15,000; a Chevrolet C-2000 pickup valued at $1,000; a John Deere tractor with bush hog and bailer valued at $5,000; household goods valued at $10,000; wearing apparel valued at $750; a Beretta™ 12-gauge shotgun valued at $250; an IRA valued at $7,250; hand tools valued at $350; and hay valued at $3,200.

Oliver purchased his Silverado pickup from Great Plains Chevy Dealer and financed the sale through General Motors Acceptance Corporation (GMAC). The purchase price was $28,000 and the vehicle is now worth $15,350. When GMAC financed the sale at 0% interest, Oliver gave GMAC a promissory note and a security interest in the vehicle. His current balance with GMAC is $15,000. His monthly payments are $466.67.

Although Oliver paid some of his taxes last year, he still owes the Internal Revenue Service $8,000, the Oklahoma Tax Commission $4,500, and the Craig County Treasurer $845 (for ad valorem [property] tax). All three are accruing interest and penalty.

Oliver's monthly living and farm expenses are as follows:

Home Maintenance	$40
Electric	60
Natural gas	60
Telephone (including mobile phone)	40
Cable and Internet	70
Food	150
Clothing	60
Medical/Dental/Rx	21
Group Medical/Dental insurance	300
Auto Insurance	80
Recreation	30
Transportation, gasoline, repairs	420
Veterinary Services	250
Salt	33
Hay and Cake	916
Weed Control/Fertilizer	416

In addition to these expenses, Oliver calculates that this year he will owe the IRS $41,472; the OTC $11,629; and the Craig County Treasurer $960. He is paying the IRS and OTC estimated tax quarterly. He is current with this year's taxes.

The paralegal gave Mr. Oliver a questionnaire that resembles the questionnaire in Appendix A. He completed the questionnaire and returned it to the paralegal. The paralegal met with him to review the completed questionnaire to insure that it had been completed accurately and to identify any emergencies that would require the attorney's immediate attention.

The paralegal then met with Mr. Oliver and reviewed his questionnaire for accuracy and completeness.

Mr. Oliver then met with the attorney and the paralegal to discuss his answers to the questionnaire. The attorney verifies Mr. Oliver's answers and adds, deletes, and modifies where necessary.

Mr. Oliver explains to the attorney that he is desperate to keep his ranch.

The attorney then discusses the attorney/client contract with Mr. Oliver. The attorney noted that since Mr. Oliver would like to keep his ranch the initial impression was that he needed to file for bankruptcy and that a Chapter 12 filing would be appropriate. The attorney stated that the office would charge $4,000 for representing him in his Chapter 12 bankruptcy. The attorney also told them that in a Chapter 12 in this district, he can expect the Chapter 12 trustee fees to be 10 percent of each payment.

PROBLEM 7.1 Based on this information, is Mr. Oliver eligible to file a Chapter 12 petition? See 11 U.S.C.A. § 109(f) and 11 U.S.C.A. §§ 101(18)–(21).

PROBLEM 7.2 Based on this information, calculate Mr. Oliver's disposable annual income that will fund the Chapter 12 plan. See 11 U.S.C.A. § 109(f) and 11 U.S.C.A. §§ 101(18)–(21).

The attorney noted that a Chapter 12 filing requires that a Chapter 12 plan be submitted to, and confirmed by, the court. The Chapter 12 plan pay-out may be as short as three years and, with the court's approval, as long as five years. Under the plan Mr. Oliver will be on a strict budget. The difference between his income and his budget will be considered disposable income and will be distributed by the Chapter 12 trustee to his creditors under the terms of a confirmed plan. As an initial impression, the attorney notes that Mr. Oliver will need to cut back spending or the court will not confirm the plan.

After this meeting, the paralegal, under the attorney's supervision, completed the voluntary petition, the disclosure of attorney's compensation statement, the list of creditors, the schedules, and the statement of financial affairs. The attorney then drafted the following Chapter 12 plan.

SECTION 2
THE CHAPTER 12 PLAN

The debtor must file a Chapter 12 plan showing how he or she intends to repay part or all of the creditors' allowed claims from future earnings. The plan must be filed not later than 90 days after the order for relief (i.e., the filing of the petition), although an extension may be granted by the court if substantially justified. Only the debtor may file a plan in a Chapter 12 case. 11 U.S.C.A. § 1221. Creditors cannot file a plan nor can they vote on the debtor's plan. If the debtor does not file a plan within 90 days or within the allowed extension, the trustee or a creditor may request dismissal of the case. 11 U.S.C.A. § 1208(c)(3).

A. CONTENTS OF A CHAPTER 12 PLAN

The contents of a Chapter 12 plan are delineated in the Code. 11 U.S.C.A. § 1222. Some provisions are mandatory; others are permissive. The mandatory provisions are noted in the Code by "shall" and the permissive provisions by "may." Compare 11 U.S.C.A. § 1222(a) with 11 U.S.C.A. § 1222(b).

1. Mandatory Provisions

Because Chapter 12 is designed with flexibility in mind, the Code provides only a few mandatory provisions in regard to the contents of the plan.

1. A Chapter 12 plan must provide for the trustee's supervision and control of that portion of the debtor's future income necessary for the implementation of the plan. 11 U.S.C.A. § 1222(a)(1).
2. A Chapter 12 plan must provide for the full payment of all priority claims (11 U.S.C.A. § 507) unless the holder of the claim agrees to a different treatment of that claim. 11 U.S.C.A. § 1222(a)(2).

3. If the Chapter 12 plan divides claims and interests into classes, the plan must provide the same treatment for each claim or interest within a particular claim, unless the holder of a particular claim or interest agrees to less favorable treatment. 11 U.S.C.A. § 1222(a)(3).
4. The payment period under the plan may not exceed three years unless the court, for cause, approves a longer period. If a longer period is approved, it may not exceed five years. 11 U.S.C.A. § 1222(c).

2. Permissive Provisions

A Chapter 12 plan may

1. designate a class or classes of unsecured claims, but may not discriminate unfairly against a designated class (the plan may treat claims for a consumer debt of the debtor differently than other unsecured claims if there is a codebtor);
2. modify the rights of holders of secured and unsecured claims;
3. cure or waive any default;
4. propose payments on unsecured claims concurrently with payments on any secured claim or any other unsecured claim;
5. provide for curing any default on any secured or unsecured claim on which the final payment is due after the proposed final payment under the plan;
6. provide for assumption, rejection, or assignment of any previously unrejected executory contract, including the debtor's unexpired lease;
7. provide for the payment of all or any part of any claim from property of the estate or of the debtor;
8. provide for the sale of all or any part of the property of the estate or the distribution of all or any part of the property of the estate among those having an interest in such property;
9. provide for payments of allowed secured claims consistent with section 1225(a)(5) over a period exceeding the usual three years of the plan allowed for other payments under the plan;
10. provide for the vesting of property of the estate in the debtor or in any other entity; and
11. include any other provision not inconsistent with other Title 11 provisions. 11 U.S.C.A. § 1222(b).

Unlike Chapter 13, which does not give the debtor a method for dealing with long-term secured debts, Chapter 12 gives the family farmer a method for dealing with long-term secured debts owed on both farmland and equipment. Such secured debts may be paid out after the other payments under the three-year plan have been completed. 11 U.S.C.A. § 1222(b)(9). The length of this extended period is not specified by the Code. Chapter 12 was written specifically to allow the farmer to handle this type of long-term mortgage debt which is so much a part of farm life.

The value of nonexempt property, as of the effective date of the plan, plays a critical role in the confirmation of the plan. For a Chapter 12 plan to be confirmed, it must meet the best interests of creditors test.

3. A Sample Chapter 12 Plan

Chapter 12 plans vary from district to district. Exhibit 7–2 is a sample Chapter 12 plan. How does this Chapter 12 plan compare with the Chapter 13 plan in Chapter Six of this text?

B. THE DEBTOR'S PAYMENTS UNDER THE PLAN

As in a Chapter 13 case, the debtor makes payments to the trustee in a Chapter 12 case. There is, however, no time period set for beginning the payments in a Chapter 12. The trustee retains the payments until confirmation or denial of confirmation of the plan. 11 U.S.C.A. § 1226(a).

EXHIBIT 7–2 The Chapter 12 Plan

IN THE UNITED STATES BANKRUPTCY COURT
FOR THE NORTHERN DISTRICT OF OKLAHOMA

In re:	)	
	)	
OLIVER, Ronald Milton	)	Case No: 04-00000
SS# xxx-xx-xxxx	)	
	)	(Chapter 12)
Debtor.	)	
	)	

CHAPTER 12 PLAN

The Debtor submits this Chapter 12 Plan ("the Plan") pursuant to 11 U.S.C.A. § 1221:

I. **Income Subject to the Supervision and Control of the Trustee and Duration of the Plan.**

The Debtor shall pay to the Chapter 12 trustee all disposable income as defined in 11 U.S.C.A. § 1225(b)(2) for a period of 3 years from the effective date.

II. **Classification of Claims.**

Class 1: Administrative Claims. The costs and expenses associated with this bankruptcy case allowable under 11 U.S.C.A. § 503 and entitled to priority under 11 U.S.C.A. § 507(a)(1), including the fees of the Chapter 12 trustee pursuant to 12 U.S.C.A. § 586(e). The administrative claims include the fees and expenses of the professionals employed in this case, including the attorney and accountant.

Class 2: Other Priority Claims. Claims entitled to priority under 11 U.S.C.A. § 507(a) other than Class 1 administrative claims. These claims include the claim of the Internal Revenue Service in the amount of $8,000, the claim of the Oklahoma Tax Commission in the amount of $4,500, and the claim of the Craig County Treasurer in the amount of $850.

Class 3: General Motors Acceptance Corporation ("GMAC"). The allowed secured claim of GMAC in the amount of $15,000.00, secured by a security interest in a Chevrolet C-2500 Silverado Pickup.

Class 4: Federal Land Bank. The allowed secured claim of the Federal Land Bank in the amount of $350,000, secured by a mortgage on 1,490 acres of real estate located in Craig County, Oklahoma.

Class 5: Second National Bank. The allowed secured claim of Second National Bank in the amount of $90,000 secured by a second mortgage on 1,490 acres of real estate located in Craig County, Oklahoma, and a security interest in a John Deere tractor with brush hog and bailer.

Class 6: Farmers and Merchant's Bank. The allowed secured claim of Farmers & Merchants Bank ("F&M") in the amount of $112,000, secured by 300 head of cattle.

Class 7: Homestead Bank. The allowed secured claim of Homestead Bank in the amount of $140,000, secured by Oliver's home on 5 acres.

(continued)

EXHIBIT 7–2 The Chapter 12 Plan, Continued

Class 8: Allowed unsecured claims. All unsecured claims allowed under 11 U.S.C.A. § 502, including the deficiency portion of any class 3, 4, 5, and 6 claims, consisting of the difference between the allowed amount of such creditors' claims and the value of the collateral securing their claims.

III. Treatment of Claims.[1]

Class 1: The allowed class 1 administrative claims will be paid in full upon the entry of a final order allowing such claims.

Class 2: The allowed priority claims of the Internal Revenue Service, the Oklahoma Tax Commission, and the Craig County Treasurer will be paid in full in available funds after the payment of allowed class 3, 4, 5, and 6 claims.

Class 3: The allowed secured claim of GMAC will be paid in 30 monthly payments in the amount of $466.67, with interest at the rate of 0% per annum under the terms of the Retail Installment Contract.

Class 4: The allowed secured claim of Federal Land Bank in the amount of $350,000, which includes postpetition late charges, attorney fees, and costs, will be paid in full together with interest at the rate of 4.5% per annum, under the terms of the Promissory Note and Mortgage in consecutive monthly installments of $3,059.97 beginning on the effective date. The prepetition arrearage of $9,179.91 will be paid in three annual installments of $3,059.97 beginning on the effective date. 11 U.S.C.A. § 506(b).

Class 5: The allowed secured claim of Second National Bank in the amount of $75,000 will be paid in full with interest at the rate of 6% per annum in 12 consecutive annual installments of $8,945.78 beginning on November 15 each year after the effective date. The remaining portion of this claim will be treated as a Class 8 unsecured claim.

Class 6: The allowed secured claim of F&M Bank in the amount of $112,000 will be paid in full with interest at the rate of 7% per annum on or about November 15 after the effective date from the sale of all or a portion of the feeder cattle securing its claim.

Class 7: The allowed secured claim of Homestead Bank in the amount of $140,000 will be paid in full with interest at the rate of 5% per annum in 360 consecutive monthly installments of $751.55 beginning on the effective date.

Class 8: Allowed unsecured claims will be paid prorata from available funds after the payment of the Class 1 through 7 claims, in three annual payments on November 15 for the three years after the effective date.

IV. Summary of Debtor's Cattle Operations.

The Debtor operates a feeder cattle operation. In the early spring of each year the Debtor purchases approximately 300 head of feeder cattle, which are sold in the fall. The purchase price of the cattle is financed through a loan obtained from F&M Bank and is paid, with interest, in a single payment from the proceeds from the sale of the cattle. In addition, the Debtor receives periodic royalty income from oil and gas production under the terms of an Oil and Gas Lease with Astro Drilling Company.

V. Executory Contracts and Unexpired Leases.

On the effective date, the Oil and Gas Lease with Astro Drilling Company will be assumed pursuant to 11 U.S.C.A. § 1222(b)(6). The Pasture Lease between Joseph and Sarah Smith, as lessors, and the Debtor, as lessee, covering 640 acres of real estate in Craig County, Oklahoma, shall be assumed and assigned to Raymond Jones on the effective date, pursuant to 11 U.S.C.A.

[1] A Summary of Plan Payments is attached as Exhibit A.

(continued)

EXHIBIT 7–2 The Chapter 12 Plan, Continued

§ 222(b)(6), in consideration for which the Debtor shall receive $5,000. On the effective date, any unpaid pasture rent due Joseph and Sarah Smith will be paid to them together with interest on the amount of such payment at the rate of 6% per annum calculated from the date the payment was due on the Pasture Lease to the effective date. All other executory contracts and unexpired leases will be deemed rejected. Pursuant to Fed. R. Bank. P. 3002(c)(4), any claim for rejection damages must be filed within 60 days after the effective date.

VI. Lien Avoidance.

On or before the effective date, the Debtor shall file a Motion under 11 U.S.C.A. § 522(f)(1)(B) and Fed. R. Bank. P. 4003(d) to avoid the non-possessory, non-purchase money security interest of the Second National Bank in the John Deere tractor and implements.

VII. Implementation of Plan.

Pursuant to 11 U.S.C.A. § 1203, the Debtor shall continue to operate his ranching operation as Debtor in Possession. The Debtor will fund this Plan through three annual payments, consisting of all the Debtor's disposable income, made to the trustee on or by November 1 of each year beginning after the effective date. The disposable income will be generated from the sale of feeder cattle each fall and from royalty income on oil and gas production. Pursuant to 11 U.S.C.A. § 1222(b)(8), the Debtor may sell, in his discretion, as many cattle as necessary each year to fund this Plan. The Debtor may, without further Order of this Court, incur debt in the ordinary course of business during the term of this Plan as necessary to implement this Plan, including debt to acquire feeder cattle each year.

VIII. Liquidation Analysis.

Asset	Value	Secured Claim	Exemption
1,490 Acres	$425,000	$350,000 $90,000	–0–
Residence	185,000	140,000	45,000
Household goods	$10,000	–0–	$10,000
Wearing apparel	$750	–0–	$750
Beretta™ 12-gauge shotgun	$250	–0–	$250
IRA	$7,250	–0–	$7,250
Chevrolet C-2500 Silverado pickup	$15,350	$15,000	–0–
Chevrolet C-2000 pickup	$1,000	–0–	$1,000
300 head of cattle	$112,000	$112,000	–0–
Hand tools	$350	–0–	$350
2 horses with saddles and tack	$2,500	–0–	$2,500
John Deere Tractor with Bailer and Brush Hog	$5,000	$20,000	$5,000
Hay	$3,200	–0–	–0–

Value of non-exempt, unencumbered assets: $3,200 (Hay)
350 (Silverado Pickup)
$3,550

(continued)

EXHIBIT 7–2 The Chapter 12 Plan, Continued

IX. Other Provisions.

1. The effective date of this Plan shall be the date the Order Confirming Plan becomes final.
2. Available funds means those funds generated from the Debtor's disposable income that are available after the payment of the trustee's fee under 28 U.S.C.A. § 586(e) and Class 1 through Class 6 claims.
3. The terms of all agreements between the Debtor and the holders of all allowed secured claims, including the liens and security interests afforded therein, shall continue in effect except to the extent modified herein or by Order of the Court.
4. The Court shall retain jurisdiction over this chapter 12 case pursuant to and for the purposes of 11 U.S.C.A. § 1229, to determine the allowability of claims including administrative expenses, to determine the allowed amount of secured claims, and for such other purposes as may be provided in the Order Confirming Plan.
5. Upon the completion of all payments under this Plan, which shall occur approximately 3 years after the effective date, the Debtor shall receive a discharge under 11 U.S.C.A. § 1228(a).
6. Property of the estate shall not revest in the Debtor on the effective date as provided by 11 U.S.C.A. § 1227(b).
7. The actual payments to be made under this Plan will be based upon the allowed amount of each claim. The claim amounts reflected herein are estimates based upon information available to the Debtor. Pursuant to 11 U.S.C.A. § 502(b), the allowed amount of each claim will be the amount reflected in the Proof of Claim to which no objection is filed. If an objection filed by each creditor to a claim is filed, the allowed amount shall be the amount determined by a final order of the Court.
8. On or by November 15 for three years after the effective date, the Debtor shall file an operating report, on such form as required by the United States trustee, to reflect all income earned by the Debtor and all household and business expenses incurred and paid by the Debtor. The Debtor shall also file all State and Federal Income tax returns each year and provide copies to the trustee.

DATED this ______ day of ________________________, 20___ .

____

Attorney's Name (Bar #)
Address
Telephone number
Fax number

EXAMPLE

Peter Eckert filed a petition for bankruptcy relief under Chapter 12 on June 1. A Chapter 12 plan was filed along with the petition. The plan called for payments by the trustee to creditors on the first of each month.

On July 15, Eckert began making payments to the trustee. On September 10, the plan was confirmed by the bankruptcy court. On October 1, the trustee began to pay out under the plan.

C. MODIFICATION OF THE PLAN BEFORE CONFIRMATION

The debtor may modify the plan at any time before confirmation, but the plan, as modified, must meet the same requirements as the original plan. 11 U.S.C.A. § 1223(a). The plan, as modified, becomes the plan. 11 U.S.C.A. §1223(b). A holder of a secured claim that has accepted or rejected the plan is deemed to have accepted or rejected the plan, as modified, unless the holder's rights have been changed by the modification and the holder has changed the previous acceptance or rejection. 11 U.S.C.A. §1223(c).

EXAMPLE

On January 1, First Bank loaned Alice Whatley $22,000 so she could buy a John Deere tractor for her farm. On May 1, Whatley filed a petition in bankruptcy under Chapter 12. At the time of filing her petition, Whatley filed her Chapter 12 plan.

On May 10, First Bank accepted the plan. On May 20, Whatley modified the plan, but this modification did not affect First Bank's rights because Whatley's obligation to the Bank was fully secured by the tractor. First Bank, without further action, is deemed to have accepted the plan as modified.

The following are the attorney's comments on why the plan was drafted as it was:

Like Chapter 13, the process of drafting a Chapter 12 plan begins with the calculation of disposable income in Schedules I and J. Unlike Chapter 13, however, it is usually impossible to know precisely how much income the family farmer debtor will realize during the term of the plan. The debtor's income will fluctuate due to the ever-changing price of the commodity that is produced, whether it is crops, such as wheat, soybeans, corn, or tobacco, or livestock, such as cattle, chickens, or sheep. It is just as difficult to calculate the expenses that the debtor will incur over the course of the plan term; that is why Schedules I and J for family farmers are merely estimates. Nevertheless, because feasibility is one of the criteria for plan confirmation, the debtor must project sufficient disposable income to pay all administrative claims, to meet the debt service required under the plan for all secured claims, and to have enough income remaining to pay unsecured creditors in order to meet the best interests test.

Class 1: Priority claims, including administrative claims of professionals, must be paid in full under the plan. 11 U.S.C.A. § 1222(a)(2). They may be paid over the term of the plan, and like Chapter 13, they need not be paid with interest, although in fairness, if the debtor has sufficient cash, administrative claims should be paid promptly to ensure the attorney's and other professionals' continued interest in representing the debtor. For that reason, administrative claims are classified first and are to be paid when the administrative claims (which must be approved by the court under 11 U.S.C.A. § 330) are allowed by an order of the court.

Class 2: The allowed claims of the taxing authorities, the Internal Revenue Service, the Oklahoma Tax Commission, and the Craig County Treasurer (ad valorem tax), must likewise be paid in full under the plan, but since the claims may be paid without interest over the term of the plan, it is in the best interest of Oliver to use his discretion to pay those tax claims when the money is available in those years in which cattle operations are most profitable.

Class 3: Each secured claim must be treated in separate classes because the treatment for each claim within a class must be the same. 11 U.S.C.A. § 1222(a)(3). The first secured claim addressed in the plan is the claim of GMAC. The Retail Installment Contract with GMAC provides for a rate of interest (zero percent interest) that is more favorable than the current market rate, the claim is fully secured (the value of the collateral exceeds the amount owed [$15,350 vs. $15,000]), and the payments were current when the bankruptcy was filed. It is therefore in the debtor's best interest to leave unaffected the rights of GMAC. (11 U.S.C.A. § 1222(b)(2)). This will enable Oliver to enjoy the benefits of the zero interest rate for the 30 months remaining under the Retail Installment Contract. GMAC will probably consent to these plan terms. 11 U.S.C.A. § 1225(a)(5)(A).

Class 4: The 4.5 percent interest rate on the secured claim of Federal Land Bank is below market. Thus, like GMAC, the debtor will want to leave the claim unimpaired. 11 U.S.C.A. § 1222(b)(2). Unlike GMAC, however, the Federal Land Bank will incur substantial late charges, attorney fees, and costs during the bankruptcy case because the loan is in default. The claim is oversecured and the Promissory Note and Mortgage provide for the payment of late charges, costs, and attorney fees in the event of default. Thus, under 11 U.S.C.A. § 506(b) those charges are added to the amount of the allowed secured claim. At the time of the bankruptcy, filing the loan was three months past due. The arrearage may be cured during the term of the plan. The Promissory Note and Mortgage are silent about interest on a bankruptcy cure payment; therefore, interest need not be paid on the cure amount. 11 U.S.C.A. § 1222(d). The plan proposes to stretch the cure payment over the three-year term of the plan in order to ease the debtor's cash flow needs as much as possible. The Federal Land Bank will probably consent to these plan terms. 11 U.S.C.A. § 1225(a)(5)(A).

Class 5: The claim of Second National Bank is not fully secured. After the payment of Federal Land Bank, there is only $75,000 equity in the real estate to secure the $90,000 claim. The value of the John Deere tractor with brush hog and bailer are not included because the bank's security interest in those items is subject to lien avoidance under 11 U.S.C.A. § 522(f)(2)(B). The loan made by Second National Bank was not a purchase-money loan and the collateral is in the debtor's possession. Moreover, the tractor and implements are exempt under Oklahoma law and they constitute implements or tools of the trade of the debtor. Thus, a separate motion to avoid lien will be filed as required by Fed. R. Bank. P. 4003(d). The motion must be served upon Second National Bank in compliance with Fed. R. Bank. P. 7004(h). The allowed amount of the secured claim is therefore $75,000, which will be paid with interest at the current market rate (6 percent) over a 12-year term, which is reasonable based upon the nature of the collateral, real estate. Consequently, the repayment term extends beyond the life of the Plan. This is a significant advantage of Chapter 12 over Chapter 13. 11 U.S.C.A. § 1222(b)(5). This treatment can be crammed down over the bank's objection. 11 U.S.C.A. § 1225(a)(5)(B).

Class 6: The secured claim of F&M Bank, secured by the 300 head of feeder cattle is fully secured. Consistent with previous years, the loan will be paid in full with accrued interest at the 7 percent contract rate as the cattle are sold. The interest rate is higher than other interest rates, because this is a riskier loan. The interest rate will not be modified so as not to alienate the bank, because the debtor intends to borrow money each year from the bank to fund the purchase of the feeder cattle stock in the spring. As debtor in possession, Oliver may continue to operate the cattle operation in the ordinary course of business and may sell the cattle in the ordinary course of business without court approval. 11 U.S.C.A. § 1203. F&M Bank will probably consent to these plan terms. 11 U.S.C.A. § 1225(a)(5)(A).

Class 7: The claim of Homestead Bank, secured by Oliver's home on five acres, is fully secured. The payment terms will be modified under the plan to decrease the monthly payment by stretching the term to 30 years (360 months)—the original term of the loan—and reducing the interest rate to the current market rate, 5 percent. This treatment can be crammed down over the bank's objection. 11 U.S.C.A. § 1222(a)(5)(B).

Class 8: Allowed unsecured claims, including prepetition trade claims and the class 5—deficiency claim, will receive three annual payments from the disposable income remaining after the payment of class 1 through 7 claims. Since it is not known how much disposable income Oliver will have for the next three years, the exact amount to be paid on class 8 claims is unspecified. It must, however, appear to meet the best interests test of 11 U.S.C.A. § 1225(a)(4).

PROBLEM 7.3 Is there enough disposable income to fund this plan? If not, what would you suggest?

PROBLEM 7.4 Will this plan meet the best interests of creditors test?

SECTION 3 THE FILING OF THE PETITION

Although some of Chapter 12 has been patterned after Chapter 11, the procedural aspects of Chapters 12 and 13 are almost identical. Chapter 12 was patterned after Chapter 13 and is closer in form to Chapter 13 than to the other chapters.

The filing of the petition in a Chapter 12 case (and in a Chapter 13 case) is quite similar to the filing of the petition in a Chapter 7 case. Except for the filing of the Chapter 12 plan, the filing of a voluntary Chapter 12 bankruptcy case is substantially the same as the filing of a voluntary Chapter 7 bankruptcy case. The filing of a voluntary Chapter 12 case requires the following items:

1. Filing fee;
2. Voluntary Petition (Official Form No. 1);
3. Disclosure of attorney's compensation statement or disclosure of compensation statement by a non-attorney bankruptcy petition preparer;
4. List of creditors;
5. Schedules (Official Form No. 6)
   a. Summary of Schedules
   b. Schedule A: Real Property
   c. Schedule B: Personal Property
   d. Schedule C: Property Claimed as Exempt
   e. Schedule D: Creditors Holding Secured Claims
   f. Schedule E: Creditors Holding Unsecured Priority Claims
   g. Schedule F: Creditors Holding Unsecured Nonpriority Claims
   h. Schedule G: Executory Contracts and Unexpired Leases
   i. Schedule H: Codebtors
   j. Schedule I: Current Income of Individual Debtor(s)
   k. Schedule J: Current Expenditures of Individual Debtor(s)
   l. Schedule of Income and Expenditures of a Partnership or a Corporation, if applicable
6. Statement of Financial Affairs (Official Form No. 7); and
7. a Chapter 12 plan.

The Code provides for reasonable compensation to the debtor's attorney in a Chapter 12 case (if the debtor is an individual) for representing the interests of the debtor in connection with the case. 11 U.S.C.A. § 330(a)(4)(B). It also authorizes the court to order the return of any excess to the estate if interim compensation exceeds the final compensation awarded. 11 U.S.C.A. § 330(a)(5).

If the petition is accompanied by the list of creditors, the debtor has 15 days from the filing of the petition to file the schedules and the statement of financial affairs.

Prior to the time the case is closed, the debtor may amend the petition, lists, schedules, and statement previously filed. Fed. R. Bank. P. 1009. The debtor has a duty to supplement the schedules if, within 180 days after the date of filing the petition, property is acquired by bequest, devise, or inheritance; or as a result of a property settlement agreement with the debtor's spouse or of an interlocutory or final divorce decree. The debtor may also have acquired property as a beneficiary of a life insurance policy or a death benefit plan. 11 U.S.C.A. § 541(a)(5); Fed. R. Bank. P. 1007(h). The duty of the debtor to supplement the schedules may prove important to creditors who would otherwise be paid less or not at all. It prevents the debtor who has just been discharged of his or her debts from walking away with potentially large sums of money that could be distributed to creditors by the trustee.

The Chapter 12 plan provides for payment of creditors from the debtor's future earnings. The debtor must file a Chapter 12 plan not later than 90 days after the order for relief. 11 U.S.C.A. § 1221. The period for filing a plan may be extended by the court if an extension is substantially justified. 11 U.S.C.A. § 1221. The debtor may modify his or her plan before confirmation. 11 U.S.C.A. § 1223.

SECTION 4
THE SIGNIFICANCE OF FILING A PETITION

The significance of filing a petition in a Chapter 12 is much the same as in the filing of a Chapter 7. The filing of the case constitutes an order for relief, brings the automatic stay into operation, and creates the estate. The estate in Chapter 12, however, includes both earnings and property acquired by the debtor after the filing of the petition. 11 U.S.C.A. § 1207. The debtor is entitled to exemptions, and the automatic stay goes into effect to protect the estate from dismemberment and the debtor from collection procedures. This prevents the more aggressive creditors from taking what is owed to them to the detriment of other creditors. It also gives the debtor relief from harassment by these creditors.

The codebtor stay goes into effect when the case is filed. 11 U.S.C.A. § 1201. Although the codebtor stay was meant to protect family members of farmers, it only protects them on consumer debts. Since the next crop must be financed before the last crop begins to pay for itself, there is a great deal of borrowing to carry on farming operations. It is common practice for members of farming families to cosign for each other's loans. Unfortunately, the codebtor stay is in large measure ineffective in Chapter 12 cases because these debts are generally not consumer debts. The codebtor stay does not apply if the codebtor became liable in the ordinary course of the codebtor's business or if the case is closed, dismissed, or converted to Chapter 7. 11 U.S.C.A. § 1201(a).

The codebtor stay does not preclude a creditor from presenting a negotiable instrument for payment and giving notice of dishonor. 11 U.S.C.A. §1201(b). A creditor with a claim based on a consumer debt of the Chapter 12 debtor may seek relief from the codebtor stay to the extent that

1. the codebtor received the consideration for the claim held by the creditor;
2. the Chapter 12 plan does not propose to pay the creditor his or her claim; or
3. the creditor's interest would be irreparably harmed by continuation of the stay. 11 U.S.C.A. § 1201(c).

If the Chapter 12 plan does not propose to pay a creditor's claim and that creditor has filed a request for relief from the codebtor stay, the debtor or codebtor has 20 days to file a written objection; otherwise, the codebtor stay is terminated as to that creditor's claim. 11 U.S.C.A. § 1201(d).

In the case of *In re Smith,* the Smiths were farming land owned by Helen Gorham, Mrs. Smith's mother. Ms. Gorham mortgaged the farm to Wedge Bank (now Mercantile Bank) and the Smiths cosigned the note to the bank. The Smiths stopped making payments on the note and filed under Chapter 12 of the Bankruptcy Code. With the note in default, the bank filed a complaint for foreclosure against Ms. Gorham. The Smiths argued that the bank's foreclosure action violated the automatic stay as it applies to codebtors and therefore the bank should be sanctioned.

In re Smith

189 B.R. 11
(Bankr. C.D. Ill. 1995)

OPINION
Larry L. Lessen,
Bankruptcy Judge

The issue before the Court is whether a foreclosure action filed against a creditor of the Debtors violated the automatic stay of 11 U.S.C. § 362(a)(1) and (3).

The Debtors, Edward and Helen Smith, filed a petition pursuant to Chapter 12 of the Bankruptcy Code on March 21, 1995. In their schedule of Unexpired Leases, the Debtors listed a 60/40 crop share agreement with Helen Gorham. The Debtors also listed Helen Gorham as a creditor with an unsecured claim of $50,000.00. The Mercantile Bank of Illinois, formerly known as Wedge Bank, was listed as a creditor with a secured claim of $216,000.00. The security for the debt was machinery and the farm of Ms. Gorham, Mr. Smith's mother-in-law.

On July 17, 1995, Mercantile Bank of Illinois filed a Complaint for Foreclosure against Ms. Gorham. The Complaint is based on a January 15, 1992, mortgage wherein Ms. Gorham mortgaged her farm in Jersey County, Illinois, to the Mercantile Bank. Ms. Gorham is the sole owner of the farm. The Debtors are currently farming the land pursuant to their crop share agreement. The Debtors were not named in the foreclosure complaint. However, the Debtors have signed a note to the Bank as comakers, and their Chapter 12 Plan provides for full payment of the debt to Mercantile Bank. In fact, Ms. Gorham has never made payments to the Bank; the Debtors have farmed the property and made the payments to the Bank.

On August 16, 1995, the Debtors filed a Request for Sanctions which alleges that Mercantile Bank violated the automatic stay. A hearing was held on September 25, 1995, and the parties agreed that the material facts were not in dispute.

The Debtors argue that the Bank's foreclosure action violates the automatic stay of 11 U.S.C. § 362(a)(1) and (3) because it directly interferes with their Chapter 12 proceeding. They note that the Bank was aware of their tenancy and the fact that their Chapter 12 Plan proposes to pay the Bank's debt in full. The Debtors assert that the foreclosure action is an attempt to take possession of property of the bankruptcy estate in violation of the automatic stay.

The Bank responds that the foreclosure action is directed against Helen Gorham individually and not the Debtors. Ms. Gorham is equally liable with the Debtors on the debt which is the subject matter of the foreclosure action, and she is not protected by the codebtor stay of 11 U.S.C. § 1201 because the codebtor stay is limited to consumer debts. The Bank points out that while the Debtors may be tenants of Ms. Gorham, they were not made parties to the foreclosure action, and the mortgage foreclosure will be subject to the rights of the Debtors as tenants in possession.

The Debtors concede that the Bank has the right to proceed with the foreclosure action against Ms. Gorham, but the Debtors insist that the Bank erred in not first moving to lift the automatic stay. The Court agrees with the Debtors that it would have been prudent for the Bank to seek Court approval before filing the foreclosure action, but the Court finds that the failure to do so does not merit sanctions for violating the automatic stay. Ms. Gorham is not protected by the codebtor stay of § 1201, and the Bank is free to pursue its claim against Ms. Gorham. Moreover, the mortgage foreclosure does not affect the Debtors' rights under their lease with Ms. Gorham. Under the Illinois Mortgage Foreclosure Act,

> whoever takes possession can take only those rights that the mortgagor had. The Act also provides that a lease subordinate to a mortgage shall not be terminated during the pendency of a foreclosure solely by virtue of a mortgagee's entry into possession under the Act. (Ill.Rev.Stat., 1987, ch. 110, par. 15–1701(e).) . . . Since the lease is not terminated when a mortgagee takes possession, both the tenant and the mortgagee are bound by its terms. The mortgagee accedes only into the shoes of the mortgagor; hence, if the mortgagor would be bound by a lease, the mortgagee in possession would also be bound.

Kelley/Lehr & Associates v. O'Brien, 194 Ill.App.3d 380, 388, 141 Ill.Dec. 426, 551 N.E.2d 419 (1990). A bankruptcy court reached a similar conclusion in *In re Sauk Steel Co., Inc.*, 133 B.R. 431, 436 (Bankr. N.D.Ill.1991):

In Illinois, neither the mortgagee's entry into possession before foreclosure, nor the appointment of a receiver, automatically terminates a junior lease. Ill.Rev.Stat. ch. 110, 15–1701 (1989). After state court entry of an order for possession against a property owner, a lessee is in exactly the same position as it was in prior to such an Order.

Until a debtor is named as party-defendant, a foreclosure action does not generally affect the bankruptcy estate. *In re Comcoach Corp.*, 698 F.2d 571, 574 (2nd Cir.1983).

The automatic stay prohibits actions against the debtor, the property of the debtor, and the property of the estate. 11 U.S.C. § 362(a). Since the foreclosure action in the instant case was not against the Debtor . . . there was no violation of the automatic stay.

For the foregoing reasons, the Debtors' Request for Sanctions against Mercantile Bank of Illinois is denied.

This Opinion is to serve as Findings of Fact and Conclusions of Law pursuant to Rule 7052 of the Rules of Bankruptcy Procedure.

See written Order.

ORDER

For the reasons set forth in an Opinion entered this day,

IT IS THEREFORE ORDERED that Debtors' Request for Sanctions against Mercantile Bank of Illinois be and is hereby denied.

After the order for relief, the various parties in interest may begin to assert their interests in the property of the estate. An unsecured creditor or an equity security holder must file a proof of claim or interest subject to statutory limitations as to time. Fed. R. Bank. P. 3002. If, prior to distribution, a creditor does not timely file a proof of claim, the debtor or trustee may file a proof of claim within 30 days after the expiration of the time for filing claims. Fed. R. Bank. P. 3004.

A. POSSESSION AND CONTROL OF PROPERTY OF THE ESTATE: THE DEBTOR IN POSSESSION

The Chapter 12 debtor, unlike his or her Chapter 7 counterpart, is a **debtor in possession (DIP).** The debtor will retain possession of all property of the estate (unless he or she is removed for cause such as fraud or gross mismanagement), except as provided in a confirmed plan or in an order confirming a plan. 11 U.S.C.A. § 1204(a). The debtor in possession may be reinstated by the court on request of a party in interest and after notice and a hearing. 11 U.S.C.A. § 1204(b).

B. OPERATION OF THE DEBTOR'S BUSINESS

The Code contemplates that the debtor will operate the business unless the court orders otherwise. 11 U.S.C.A. § 1203. The court will enter an order for periodic reports. Fed. R. Bank. P. 2015(b) and committee notes. The nature of these reports will vary depending on the debtor's situation and on how much information is required by the court. Most courts have a regular format for this type of report.

Most of the administrative rights and powers that apply to the debtor in possession in a Chapter 11 case also apply to the debtor in a Chapter 12 case. 11 U.S.C.A. § 1203. These rights and powers include providing adequate protection to creditors to preserve the automatic stay (11 U.S.C.A. § 362(d)); using, selling, or leasing property, including cash collateral (11 U.S.C.A. § 363); and obtaining credit (11 U.S.C.A. § 364), as well as the ability to assume or reject executory contracts and unexpired leases (11 U.S.C.A. § 365) and to obtain continuation of utility services (11 U.S.C.A. § 366). The important difference between a Chapter 11 debtor in possession and a Chapter 12 debtor in possession is not whether they share the same rights and powers, which they do with several exceptions, but how **adequate protection** is provided. A Chapter 11 debtor in possession provides adequate protection by following 11 U.S.C.A. § 361. This section, however, does not apply to a Chapter 12 debtor in possession. 11 U.S.C.A. § 1205(a). A Chapter 12 debtor in possession provides adequate protection by following 11 U.S.C.A. § 1205(b).

> (b) In a case under this chapter, when adequate protection is required under section 362, 363, or 364 of this title of an interest of an entity in property, such adequate protection may be provided by
> (1) requiring the trustee to make a cash payment or periodic cash payments to such entity, to the extent that the stay under section 362 of this title, use, sale, or lease under section 363 of this title, or any grant of a lien under section 364 of this title results in a decrease in the value of property securing a claim or of an entity's ownership interest in property;
> (2) providing to such entity an additional or replacement lien to the extent that such stay, use, sale, lease, or grant results in a decrease in the value of property securing a claim or of an entity's ownership interest in property;
> (3) paying to such entity for the use of farmland the reasonable rent customary in the community where the property is located, based upon the rental value, net income, and earning capacity of the property; or
> (4) granting such other relief, other than entitling such entity to compensation allowable under section 503(b)(1) of this title as an administrative expense, as will adequately protect the value of property securing a claim or of such entity's ownership interest in property. 11 U.S.C.A. § 1205(b).

The provision for payment of the reasonable rent customary in the community as adequate protection for the use of farmland is very beneficial to the farmer. This means that only the actual value of the property must be protected. This approach to adequate protection costs the farmer far less than protecting the value of the creditor's interest in the property as required by the "indubitable equivalent" language of section 361(3). The periodic cash payments provided for in Chapter 12 are designed to give creditors necessary protection without stripping family farmers of their chance to stay in operation. 11 U.S.C.A. § 1205(b)(1).

C. EXEMPTIONS

The same exemptions that can be claimed in a Chapter 7 case can be claimed in a Chapter 12 case. The listing of exemptions and the valuation of exempt property, as well as the valuation of nonexempt property, should be considered carefully. The value of nonexempt property, as of the effective date of the plan, plays a critical role in the confirmation of the plan because it relates to the best interests of creditors test. Although the Chapter 12 debtor retains possession of nonexempt property, the unsecured creditors under a Chapter 12 plan must receive more than they would in a Chapter 7 liquidation.

SECTION 5
APPOINTMENT AND DUTIES OF A CHAPTER 12 TRUSTEE

After the order for relief, the standing Chapter 12 trustee, or another individual if there is no standing trustee, or the U.S. trustee will serve as the trustee in the case. 11 U.S.C.A. § 1202(a). The trustee in a Chapter 12 case is accountable for all property received and must perform some of the same duties as a Chapter 7 trustee. These duties include

1. examine proofs of claim and object to allowance of any claim that is improper if a purpose would be served;
2. oppose the discharge of the debtor if this is advisable;

3. upon the request of a party in interest, furnish information concerning the estate and its administration unless the court orders otherwise; and
4. make a final report and file a final account with the court and the United States trustee. 11 U.S.C.A. § 1202(b)(1).

The trustee in a Chapter 12 case also has duties that are required of a Chapter 11 trustee. These duties will be ordered by the court, for cause, if requested by a party in interest, the trustee, or the United States trustee. 11 U.S.C.A. § 1202(b)(2). These duties include

1. investigation of the acts, conduct, assets, liabilities, and financial condition of the debtor;
2. operation of the debtor's business and the desirability of continuing the business; and
3. any other matter which is relevant to the case or to the formulation of a plan. 11 U.S.C.A. § 1106(a)(3).

If the trustee conducts an investigation, he or she is required to file a statement on this investigation and to include any information on fraud, dishonesty, incompetence, misconduct, mismanagement, or irregularity in the management of the debtor's affairs, or any cause of action available to the estate. 11 U.S.C.A. § 1106(a)(4).

The trustee must appear and be heard at any hearing concerning the value of property subject to a lien, the confirmation of a plan, the modification of the plan after confirmation, or the sale of property of the estate. 11 U.S.C.A. § 1202(b)(3). The trustee also has a duty to ensure that the debtor begins making timely payments required by a confirmed plan. 11 U.S.C.A. § 1202(b)(4).

Because the trustee's avoidance powers are spelled out in Chapter 5, a universal chapter, the trustee in a Chapter 12 case has most of the same avoidance powers granted to trustees in other types of cases. See 11 U.S.C.A. §§ 544–549. The Code imposes a two-year statute of limitations, running from the date of the order for relief, on the trustee's avoidance powers. However, a trustee elected or appointed before expiration of the two-year period specified in subparagraph (A) has only one year to begin an avoidance action or proceeding. 11 U.S.C.A. § 546(a)(1).

The essential role of a Chapter 12 trustee, however, differs from the role of a Chapter 7 trustee but is similar to that of a Chapter 13 trustee. The primary function of a Chapter 12 trustee is to review the Chapter 12 plan, to advise the court with respect to the plan, and to act as a disbursing agent under the confirmed plan. The fact that the Chapter 12 trustee may choose not to exercise the trustee's avoidance power should not be taken to mean that the trustee does not have the power to avoid fraudulent and preferential transfers.

If the Chapter 12 debtor ceases to be a debtor in possession, the Chapter 12 trustee must file periodic reports and summaries of the operation of the business with the court, the United States trustee, and any governmental unit responsible for collection or determination of taxes arising from the business. 11 U.S.C.A. § 1202(b)(5). This is a duty "borrowed" from the duties of the Chapter 7 trustee. 11 U.S.C.A. § 704(8).

The trustee in a Chapter 12 case in which the debtor is no longer in possession also has other duties performed by a trustee in a Chapter 11 case. These duties include

1. filing the list, schedules, and statement required by section 521(1), if the debtor has not filed them;
2. filing a tax return for any year from which the debtor has not filed a return; and
3. filing reports after the confirmation of a plan. 11 U.S.C.A. § 1202(5).

SECTION 6 MOTIONS AND COMPLAINTS AFTER THE ORDER FOR RELIEF

In most districts, the debtor's plan will contain all the important issues relating to the case. The court will consider most issues at the hearing on confirmation of the plan because all of these issues will affect the plan. The Code does, however, provide for various motions and complaints that may be used to resolve issues as they arise in the case.

A. MOTIONS

After the order for relief, the *debtor* may move to convert the case from Chapter 12 to Chapter 7 (11 U.S.C.A. § 1208(a)); to dismiss the case (11 U.S.C.A. 1208(b); Fed. R. Bank. P. 1017); for a change of venue (Fed. R. Bank. P. 1014); or for permission to use cash collateral (11 U.S.C.A. § 363(c)(2)). The motion for permission to use cash collateral is often filed along with the petition. Without use of cash collateral, the debtor may be unable to carry on farming operations. Therefore, it is important to handle this aspect of the case immediately.

The Chapter 12 debtor may exercise 522(f) power to avoid a **judicial lien** on any property to the extent that the property could have been exempted in the absence of the lien and to avoid a **nonpossessory, nonpurchase money security interest** in certain household and personal goods. Fed. R. Bank. P. 4003(d).

In *In re Dykstra,* the debtor moved to avoid the nonpossessory, nonpurchase money lien of Security State Bank, claiming it was on exempt farm equipment. The court discussed the Chapter 12 debtor's power to avoid a lien under 522(f).

In re Dykstra

80 B.R. 128 (Bankr. N.D. Iowa 1987)

FINDINGS OF FACT, CONCLUSION OF LAW, AND ORDER RE: LIEN AVOIDANCE
Michael J. Melloy, Bankruptcy Judge

The matter before the Court is the Debtors' motion to avoid the lien of Security State Bank (Bank). The Court, being fully advised, makes the following Findings of Fact, Conclusion of Law and Order pursuant to Fed.R.Bankr.P. 7052. This is a core proceeding under 28 U.S.C. § 157(b)(2)(K).

FINDINGS OF FACT

The following facts are stipulated by the parties:

1. Henry and Carolyn Dykstra (Debtors), as individuals, filed a petition under Chapter 12 of the Bankruptcy Code on February 24, 1987.
2. The Security State Bank has a valid security interest in farm equipment, described in Exhibit A, owned by the Debtors as of the date of the filing of their petition.
3. The lien of Security State Bank is a nonpurchase-money, nonpossessory interest.
4. The Debtors have claimed an exemption to the extent of $20,000 in the farm equipment subject to the Bank's lien.
5. The Debtors, in their Substituted and Amended Plan of Reorganization, have reduced the Bank's secured claim by $20,000 to reflect avoidance of the lien on the Debtors' property claimed as exempt.
6. On June 10, 1987, the Debtors filed a motion to avoid the Bank's lien to the extent of $20,000 pursuant to 11 U.S.C. § 522(f).
7. The Bank filed an objection to the Debtors' Substituted and Amended Plan, objecting, among other things, to avoidance of their lien on Debtors' farm equipment.

DISCUSSION

The Bank contends that Chapter 12 does not permit the debtor to avoid a nonpossessory, nonpurchase-money lien pursuant to 11 U.S.C. § 522(f). The issue of applicability of the lien avoidance provision in a Chapter 12 case is one of first impression. Consequently, it must be analyzed on the basis of the following: (1) the purpose behind the lien avoidance provision, (2) applicability of 11 U.S.C. §522(f) in Chapter 13 cases, and (3) the legislative history of Chapter 12.

Purpose of 11 U.S.C. §522(f)

The Bankruptcy Act of 1898, which was repealed in 1978, contained no provision for the avoidance of liens by debtors. Under that Act, creditors were permitted to enforce blanket nonpurchase-money security interests in debtor's household goods. These blanket security clauses were used to encumber as much of the debtor's property as possible without regard to the relationship between the values of the property and the loan amount. Note, *Avoiding Liens under the New Bankruptcy Code: Construction and Application of Section 522(f)*, 15 U.Mich.J.L.Ref. 577 n.2 (1982), *citing* Federal Trade Commission, *Report of the Presiding Officer on Proposed Trade Regulation Rules: Credit Practices* 131, 133 (1973). The purpose behind securing these liens was not to provide the creditor with redeemable collateral but to frighten the debtor into repayment by threatening him with the loss of his household belongings. *Id.*

Congress attempted to remedy this situation in 1978 by providing debtors with a lien avoidance right. Section § 522(f) of the Bankruptcy Code provides:

Notwithstanding any waiver of exemptions, the debtor may avoid the fixing of a lien on an interest of the debtor in property to the extent that such lien impairs an exemption to which the debtor would have been entitled under subsection (b) of this section, if such lien is—

(2) a nonpossessory, nonpurchase-money security interest in any—

(A) household furnishings, household goods, wearing apparel, appliances, books, animals, crops, musical instruments, or jewelry that are held primarily for the personal, family, or household use of the debtor or a dependent of the debtor;

(B) implements, professional books, or tools, of the trade of the debtor or the trade of a dependent of the debtor; or

(C) professionally prescribed health aids for the debtor or a dependent of the debtor.

In addition to alleviating pressure from creditors, Congress intended that this provision allow debtors to retain enough property to make a fresh start after discharge. *In re Hall*, 752 F.2d 582, 588 (11th Cir.1985). Congress was also concerned that a balance be maintained between debtors and creditors. *In the Matter of Thompson*, 750 F.2d 628, 631 (8th Cir.1984). The lien avoidance provision was not deemed applicable to all property otherwise exempt, but only to items described in subsections (A), (B), and (C) above. *Id.* It is clear that, if the items claimed by the debtor constitute exempt property, the lien could be avoided to the extent of $20,000 had the case been filed under Chapter 7 of the Bankruptcy Code. *See In re Punke*, 68 B.R. 936 (Bankr.N.D.Iowa1987); Iowa Code § 627.6(11) (1987).

Lien Avoidance in Chapter 13

The courts which have addressed the applicability of § 522(f) in Chapter 13 cases are not in agreement. At least four bankruptcy courts, including this Court, have permitted § 522(f) to apply to Chapter 13 cases without legal analysis. *In re Hitts*, 21 B.R. 158 (Bankr.W.D.Mich.1982); *In re McKay*, 15 B.R. 1013 (Bankr.E.D.Pa.1981); *In re Graham*, 15 B.R. 1010 (Bankr.E.D.Pa.1981); *In re Clayborn*, 11 B.R. 117 (Bankr.E.D.Tenn.1981); *In re Ulrich*, No. 85–01042C (Bankr.N.D.Iowa March 3, 1986). Other courts have relied solely on Bankruptcy Code § 103(a) in allowing Chapter 13 debtors to avoid liens pursuant to § 522(f). Section 103(a) provides: "Except as provided in § 1161 of this title, Chapters 1, 3, and 5 of this title apply in a case under Chapter 7, 11, 12, or 13 of this title." *In re Jordon*, 5 B.R. 59 (Bankr.D.N.J.1980); *In re Primm*, 6 B.R. 142 (Bankr.D.Kan.1980); *In re Canady*, 9 B.R. 428 (Bankr.D.Conn.1981). Yet another group of courts has gone further to analyze the issue of whether or not there is a conflict between § 522(f) and § 1325(a)(5)(B)(i). A general rule of statutory construction is that where two provisions in a statute conflict, the more specific one will control. *Matter of Thornhill Way I*, 636 F.2d 1151 (7th Cir.1980). Section 1325(a)(5)(B)(i) states that a Chapter 13 plan can only be confirmed if it provides for the retention of liens held by secured creditors.

The overwhelming majority of courts addressing the issue of conflicting code provisions has determined that there is no conflict between § 522(f) and § 1325(a)(5)(B)(i). *Baldwin v. Avco Financial Services*, 22 B.R. 507 (Bankr.D.Del.1982); *In re Mattson*, 20 B.R. 382 (Bankr.W.D.Wis.1982); *Matter of Lantz*, 7 B.R. 77 (Bankr.S.D.Ohio1980); *In re Lincoln*, 26 B.R. 14 (Bankr.W.D.Mich.1982); *In re Mitchell*, 25 B.R. 406 (Bankr.N.D.Ga.1982); *In re Cameron*, 25 B.R. 410 (Bankr.N.D.Ga.1982); *In re Thurman*, 20 B.R. 978 (Bankr.W.D.Tenn.1982). The rationale for this is that once a lien has been avoided pursuant to § 522(f), the once secured claim becomes an unsecured claim, and therefore § 1325(a)(5)(B)(i) does not apply. *Mattson*, 20 B.R. at 384. Additionally, the legislative history was found to be void of any Congressional intent to deny the use of § 522(f) in a Chapter 13 case. *Lincoln*, 26 B.R. at 15. As further support, a finding that § 522(f) does not apply in Chapter 13 cases would make Chapter 7 the more desirable proceeding, thus defeating the efforts of Congress to encourage greater use of Chapter 13. *Baldwin*, 22 B.R. at 510.

The leading case which found that § 522(f) and § 1325(a)(5)(B)(i) conflict is *In re Aycock*, 15 B.R. 728 (Bankr.E.D.N.C.1981). The court stated:

Although Section 522(f) provides the debtor may avoid the fixing of a lien on the debtor's interest in certain property. Section 1325(a)(5)(B) conflicts by

> *mandating* that the plan contain a provision for the retention of the lien of a non-accepting holder of a secured claim, provided for in the plan, in order for the court to confirm the plan. (Emphasis added).

This decision has been criticized and is thought to be an incorrect decision. 5 *Collier on Bankruptcy,* ¶ 1300.81, 1300–158 (15th ed. 1987).

Another theory for not allowing a debtor in a Chapter 13 case to avoid liens pursuant to § 522(f) is that he keeps all of his property so there is no exemption which is being impaired. *In re Sands,* 15 B.R. 563 (Bankr.M.D.N.C.1981). However, *Collier's* states that a Chapter 13 debtor is entitled to claim the same exemptions as those allowed a Chapter 7 debtor, though exemptions are of less practical concern in a Chapter 13 proceeding than in a Chapter 7 liquidation. *Collier, supra* at 1300–157. The majority of courts have determined that exemptions are important to a Chapter 13 debtor. *In re Thurman,* 20 B.R. 978 (Bankr.W.D.Tenn.1982); *In re Ohnstad,* 6 B.C.D. 6 (Bankr.S.D.1980).

Legislative History of Chapter 12

The legislative history of Chapter 12 indicates that it was created because Congress felt that the bankruptcy system "did not afford an opportunity of financial rehabilitation to many family farmers since most of them had too much debt to qualify as debtors under Chapter 13 and many of them found the only remaining remedy, Chapter 11, to be needlessly complicated, unduly time-consuming, inordinately expensive, and, in too many cases, unworkable." *Bankr.Service L.Ed.,* Code Commentary and Analysis § 44.1:2 at 7 (1987), *citing* H.R. 958, 99th Cong., 2nd Sess., 132 Cong. Rec. H8986–(H)9002 (1986). Chapter 12 was closely modeled after Chapter 13 with changes being made in those provisions which were inappropriate for family farmers. *Id.*

The provisions of § 1225 are identical to those of § 1325. As the majority of courts have determined that there is no conflict between Code § 522(f) and § 1325(a)(5) (B)(i), it follows that there is no conflict between § 522(f) and § 1225(a)(5)(B)(i). Additionally, exemptions are important to Chapter 12 debtors who file as individuals.[1] J. Anderson and J. Morris, *Chapter 12 Farm Reorganizations,* § 5.16, 5–77 (1987). The legislative purposes of § 522(f) to protect debtors from unnecessary harassment of creditors and provide them with a fresh start should apply in Chapter 12 cases, the same as in Chapter 7 and Chapter 13 cases, where the family farmers are individual debtors.

CONCLUSION OF LAW

The nonpossessory, nonpurchase-money lien of Security State Bank in the Debtors' farm equipment claimed as exempt is avoidable pursuant to 11 U.S.C. § 522(f).

ORDER

Henry and Carolyn Dykstra, as individuals filing under Chapter 12 of the Bankruptcy Code, are entitled to avoid the nonpossessory, nonpurchase-money lien of Security State Bank in exempt farm equipment as described in Exhibit A to the extent of $20,000.

[1]Section 522(b) clearly states that only individual debtors may exempt property of the estate. This may explain why this Court could find no case in which a Chapter 11 debtor attempted to avoid a secured creditor's nonpossessory, non-purchase-money lien pursuant to 11 U.S.C. § 522(f).

A *party in interest* may move for relief from the automatic stay (11 U.S.C.A. § 362(d); Fed. R. Bank. P. 4001, 9014); for abstention by the court (11 U.S.C.A. § 305); to dismiss the case (11 U.S.C.A. §§ 1208(c), (d)); for a change of venue (Fed. R. Bank. P. 1014); for disallowance of a claim (11 U.S.C.A. § 502); to convert the case to Chapter 7 (11 U.S.C.A. § 1208(d)); for relief from the codebtor stay (11 U.S.C.A. § 1201(c)); for examination of any person (Fed. R. Bank. P. 2004); or for removal of the debtor as debtor in possession (11 U.S.C.A. § 1204(a)).

The *U.S. trustee* may move to dismiss the case. 11 U.S.C.A. §§ 307, 1208.

A *party in interest,* the *trustee,* or the *U.S. trustee* may move to object to confirmation of the plan. 11 U.S.C.A. § 1224.

B. COMPLAINTS

Proceedings brought by the *trustee* to avoid transfers are classified as adversary proceedings by Rule 7001. The trustee's avoidance powers were discussed in Section 5 of this chapter.

The *debtor* in a Chapter 12 case is granted powers nearly identical to those of a debtor in possession in Chapter 11, with only the investigation and distribution functions assigned exclusively to the Chapter 12 trustee. 11 U.S.C.A. § 1203. Therefore, a Chapter 12 debtor, as debtor in possession, may use the avoidance powers granted to the trustee. 11 U.S.C.A. § 1203.

The *debtor* may file a complaint against third parties to collect accounts receivable or to have property brought back into the estate. 11 U.S.C.A. §§ 542, 543.

A *creditor* may file a complaint objecting to the dischargeability of a debt. 11 U.S.C.A. § 523.

SECTION 7
THE CLERK'S NOTICE

The official forms for the clerk's notice in a Chapter 12 case are B9G and B9H. Official Form B9G is the clerk's notice in a Chapter 12 case filed by an individual or joint debtor family farmer. (See Exhibit 7–3.) Official Form B9H is the clerk's notice for a Chapter 12 case filed by a partnership or corporation family farmer. (See Exhibit 7–4.)

The clerk must give the debtor, the trustee, all creditors, and the indenture trustees not less than 20 days notice by mail of the date, time, and place of the meeting of creditors and of the time fixed for filing proofs of claim. Fed. R. Bank. P. 2002. This notice generally serves as the notice of the order for relief required by 11 U.S.C.A. § 342(a) and may also serve as the notice for the confirmation hearing in a Chapter 12 case if a plan has been filed in the case. In practice, this does not often happen. If this notice is to serve as notice for the confirmation hearing, a copy or a summary of the proposed plan will be included.

SECTION 8
MEETING OF CREDITORS (THE SECTION 341 MEETING)

The meeting of creditors (the section 341 meeting) is held not less than 20 nor more than 35 days after the order for relief. The business of the meeting includes the examination of the debtor under oath by the U.S. trustee, the trustee, and the creditors. Fed. R. Bank. P. 2003.

It is quite common for the trustee to conduct some type of examination of the debtor at the meeting of creditors. The trustee must be assured that all debts and assets have been listed. Creditors with problems will have an opportunity to talk to both the trustee and the debtor.

If a plan has been filed at the time of the meeting, the trustee may ask questions about the feasibility of the plan and may give the debtor some indication of the trustee's recommendation on the confirmation of the plan. The trustee may suggest modification of the plan in an attempt to lead the debtor and the debtor's attorney toward a confirmable plan.

In addition to the meeting of creditors, the Code authorizes the U.S. trustee to convene a meeting of equity security holders if the debtor is a corporation.

EXHIBIT 7–3 Official Form No. B9G (Notice of Chapter 12 Bankruptcy, Meeting of Creditors, & Deadlines)

FORM B9G (Chapter 12 Individual or Joint Debtor Family Farmer) (12/03)

UNITED STATES BANKRUPTCY COURT ________ District of ____________________

Notice of Chapter 12 Bankruptcy Case, Meeting of Creditors, & Deadlines

[The debtor(s) listed below filed a chapter 12 bankruptcy case on ______________________ (date).]
or [A bankruptcy case concerning the debtor(s) listed below was originally filed under chapter ________ on ______________ (date) and was converted to a case under chapter 12 on______________.]

You may be a creditor of the debtor. **This notice lists important deadlines.** You may want to consult an attorney to protect your rights. All documents filed in the case may be inspected at the bankruptcy clerk's office at the address listed below. NOTE: The staff of the bankruptcy clerk's office cannot give legal advice.

See Reverse Side For Important Explanations.

Debtor(s) (name(s) and address):	Case Number: Last four digits of Soc. Sec. No./Complete EIN or other Taxpayer I.D. No.:
All Other Names used by the Debtor(s) in the last 6 years (include married, maiden, and trade names):	Attorney for Debtor(s) (name and address): Telephone number:
Bankruptcy Trustee (name and address): Telephone number:	

Meeting of Creditors:

Date: / / Time: ( ) A.M. ( ) P.M. Location:

Deadlines: Papers must be *received* by the bankruptcy clerk's office by the following deadlines:

Deadline to File a Proof of Claim:

For all creditors (except a governmental unit): For a governmental unit:

Deadline to File a Complaint to Determine Dischargeability of Certain Debts:

Deadline to Object to Exemptions:

Thirty (30) days after the *conclusion* of the meeting of creditors.

Filing of Plan, Hearing on Confirmation of Plan

[The debtor has filed a plan. The plan or a summary of the plan is enclosed. The hearing on confirmation will be held:
Date: ________________ Time: ______________ Location: ____________________________]
or [The debtor has filed a plan. The plan or a summary of the plan and notice of confirmation hearing will be sent separately.]
or [The debtor has not filed a plan as of this date. You will be sent separate notice of the hearing on confirmation of the plan.]

Creditors May Not Take Certain Actions:

The filing of the bankruptcy case automatically stays certain collection and other actions against the debtor, the debtor's property, and certain codebtors. If you attempt to collect a debt or take other action in violation of the Bankruptcy Code, you may be penalized.

Address of the Bankruptcy Clerk's Office:	**For the Court:**
Telephone number:	Clerk of the Bankruptcy Court:
Hours Open:	Date:

(continued)

EXHIBIT 7–3 Official Form No. B9G (Notice of Chapter 12 Bankruptcy, Meeting of Creditors, & Deadlines), Continued

EXPLANATIONS

FORM B9G (9/97)

Filing of Chapter 12 Bankruptcy Case	A bankruptcy case under chapter 12 of the Bankruptcy Code (title 11, United States Code) has been filed in this court by the debtor(s) listed on the front side, and an order for relief has been entered. Chapter 12 allows family farmers to adjust their debts pursuant to a plan. A plan is not effective unless confirmed by the court. You may object to confirmation of the plan and appear at the confirmation hearing. A copy or summary of the plan [is included with this notice] *or* [will be sent to you later], and [the confirmation hearing will be held on the date indicated on the front of this notice] *or* [you will be sent notice of the confirmation hearing]. The debtor will remain in possession of the debtor's property and may continue to operate the debtor's business unless the court orders otherwise.
Creditors May Not Take Certain Actions	Prohibited collection actions against the debtor and certain codebtors are listed in Bankruptcy Code § 362 and § 1201. Common examples of prohibited actions include contacting the debtor by telephone, mail or otherwise to demand repayment; taking actions to collect money or obtain property from the debtor; repossessing the debtor's property; starting or continuing lawsuits or foreclosures; and garnishing or deducting from the debtor's wages.
Meeting of Creditors	A meeting of creditors is scheduled for the date, time and location listed on the front side. *The debtor (both spouses in a joint case) must be present at the meeting to be questioned under oath by the trustee and by creditors.* Creditors are welcome to attend, but are not required to do so. The meeting may be continued and concluded at a later date without further notice.
Claims	A Proof of Claim is a signed statement describing a creditor's claim. If a Proof of Claim form is not included with this notice, you can obtain one at any bankruptcy clerk's office. If you do not file a Proof of Claim by the "Deadline to File a Proof of Claim" listed on the front side, you might not be paid any money on your claim against the debtor in the bankruptcy case. To be paid you must file a Proof of Claim even if your claim is listed in the schedules filed by the debtor.
Discharge of Debts	The debtor is seeking a discharge of most debts, which may include your debt. A discharge means that you may never try to collect the debt from the debtor. If you believe that a debt owed to you is not dischargeable under Bankruptcy Code § 523(a)(2), (4), (6), or (15), you must start a lawsuit by filing a complaint in the bankruptcy clerk's office by the "Deadline to File a Complaint to Determine Dischargeability of Certain Debts" listed on the front side. The bankruptcy clerk's office must receive the complaint and the required filing fee by that Deadline.
Exempt Property	The debtor is permitted by law to keep certain property as exempt. Exempt property will not be sold and distributed to creditors, even if the debtor's case is converted to chapter 7. The debtor must file a list of all property claimed as exempt. You may inspect that list at the bankruptcy clerk's office. If you believe that an exemption claimed by the debtor is not authorized by law, you may file an objection to that exemption. The bankruptcy clerk's office must receive the objection by the "Deadline to Object to Exemptions" listed on the front side.
Bankruptcy Clerk's Office	Any paper that you file in this bankruptcy case should be filed at the bankruptcy clerk's office at the address listed on the front side. You may inspect all papers filed, including the list of the debtor's property and debts and the list of the property claimed as exempt, at the bankruptcy clerk's office.
Legal Advice	The staff of the bankruptcy clerk's office cannot give legal advice. You may want to consult an attorney to protect your rights.

—Refer To Other Side For Important Deadlines and Notices—

EXHIBIT 7–4 Official Form No. B9H (Notice of Bankruptcy Case, Meeting of Creditors, & Deadlines)

FORM B9H (Chapter 12 Corporation/Partnership Family Farmer) (12/03)

UNITED STATES BANKRUPTCY COURT ________ District of ____________________

Notice of Chapter 12 Bankruptcy Case, Meeting of Creditors, & Deadlines

[The debtor [corporation] *or* [partnership] listed below filed a chapter 12 bankruptcy case on ________________(date).]

or [A bankruptcy case concerning the debtor [corporation] *or* [partnership] listed below was originally filed under chapter ____ on ____________________ (date) and was converted to a case under chapter 12 on____________________.]

You may be a creditor of the debtor. **This notice lists important deadlines.** You may want to consult an attorney to protect your rights. All documents filed in the case may be inspected at the bankruptcy clerk's office at the address listed below. NOTE: The staff of the bankruptcy clerk's office cannot give legal advice.

See Reverse Side For Important Explanations.

Debtor (name(s) and address):	Case Number:
	Last four digits of Soc. Sec. No./Complete EIN or other Taxpayer I.D. No.:
All Other Names used by the Debtor(s) in the last 6 years (include married, maiden, and trade names):	Bankruptcy Trustee (name and address):
Attorney for Debtor (name and address): Telephone number:	Telephone number:

Meeting of Creditors:

Date: / / Time: ( ) A.M. ( ) P.M. Location:

Deadlines: Papers must be *received* by the bankruptcy clerk's office by the following deadlines:

Deadline to File a Proof of Claim:

For all creditors (except a governmental unit): For a governmental unit:

Deadline to File a Complaint to Determine Dischargeability of Certain Debts:

Filing of Plan, Hearing on Confirmation of Plan

[The debtor has filed a plan. The plan or a summary of the plan is enclosed. The hearing on confirmation will be held: Date: __________________ Time: ______________ Location: ______________________________]

or [The debtor has filed a plan. The plan or a summary of the plan and notice of confirmation hearing will be sent separately.]

or [The debtor has not filed a plan as of this date. You will be sent separate notice of the hearing on confirmation of the plan.]

Creditors May Not Take Certain Actions:

The filing of the bankruptcy case automatically stays certain collection and other actions against the debtor, the debtor's property, and certain codebtors. If you attempt to collect a debt or take other action in violation of the Bankruptcy Code, you may be penalized.

Address of the Bankruptcy Clerk's Office:	**For the Court:**
Telephone number:	Clerk of the Bankruptcy Court:
Hours Open:	Date:

(continued)

EXHIBIT 7–4 Official Form No. B9H (Notice of Bankruptcy Case, Meeting of Creditors, & Deadlines), Continued

EXPLANATIONS	FORM B9H (9/97)
Filing of Chapter 12 Bankruptcy Case	A bankruptcy case under chapter 12 of the Bankruptcy Code (title 11, United States Code) has been filed in this court by the debtor listed on the front side, and an order for relief has been entered. Chapter 12 allows family farmers to adjust their debts pursuant to a plan. A plan is not effective unless confirmed by the court. You may object to confirmation of the plan and appear at the confirmation hearing. A copy or summary of the plan [is included with this notice] *or* [will be sent to you later], and [the confirmation hearing will be held on the date indicated on the front of this notice] *or* [you will be sent notice of the confirmation hearing]. The debtor will remain in possession of the debtor's property and may continue to operate the debtor's business unless the court orders otherwise.
Creditors May Not Take Certain Actions	Prohibited collection actions against the debtor and certain codebtors are listed in Bankruptcy Code § 362 and § 1201. Common examples of prohibited actions include contacting the debtor by telephone, mail or otherwise to demand repayment; taking actions to collect money or obtain property from the debtor; repossessing the debtor's property; and starting or continuing lawsuits or foreclosures.
Meeting of Creditors	A meeting of creditors is scheduled for the date, time and location listed on the front side. *The debtor's representative must be present at the meeting to be questioned under oath by the trustee and by creditors.* Creditors are welcome to attend, but are not required to do so. The meeting may be continued and concluded at a later date without further notice.
Claims	A Proof of Claim is a signed statement describing a creditor's claim. If a Proof of Claim form is not included with this notice, you can obtain one at any bankruptcy clerk's office. If you do not file a Proof of Claim by the "Deadline to File a Proof of Claim" listed on the front side, you might not be paid any money on your claim against the debtor in the bankruptcy case. To be paid you must file a Proof of Claim even if your claim is listed in the schedules filed by the debtor.
Discharge of Debts	The debtor is seeking a discharge of most debts, which may include your debt. A discharge means that you may never try to collect the debt from the debtor. If you believe that a debt owed to you is not dischargeable under Bankruptcy Code § 523(a)(2), (4), or (6), you must start a lawsuit by filing a complaint in the bankruptcy clerk's office by the "Deadline to File a Complaint to Determine Dischargeability of Certain Debts" listed on the front side. The bankruptcy clerk's office must receive the complaint and the required filing fee by that Deadline.
Bankruptcy Clerk's Office	Any paper that you file in this bankruptcy case should be filed at the bankruptcy clerk's office at the address listed on the front side. You may inspect all papers filed, including the list of the debtor's property and debts, at the bankruptcy clerk's office.
Legal Advice	The staff of the bankruptcy clerk's office cannot give legal advice. You may want to consult an attorney to protect your rights.

—Refer To Other Side For Important Deadlines and Notices—

SECTION 9
HEARING ON CONFIRMATION OF THE PLAN

The hearing on confirmation of the plan must be concluded not later than 45 days after the filing of the plan. This time period may be extended for cause. 11 U.S.C.A. § 1224. Most courts will require the debtor to be present at the hearing on confirmation of the plan. The judge may ask the debtor's attorney to summarize the contents of the plan. The judge will ask the trustee for comments on the plan. The trustee will advise the judge of any problems and of whether or not the plan can be confirmed. The judge may ask questions of the debtor, the debtor's attorney, or the trustee to clarify the information being presented. The trustee may suggest modification to make the plan confirmable. The judge may decide to continue the hearing to give the debtor an opportunity to file an amendment or a supplemental plan.

The trustee, a creditor, or the U.S. trustee may file an objection to confirmation of the plan. 11 U.S.C.A. § 1224. The judge, on his or her own initiative, may determine that the plan is not confirmable. To be confirmed by the court, the plan must comply with the provisions of 11 U.S.C.A. § 1225. Section 1225 contains several requirements:

1. The plan must comply with Chapter 12 and other applicable provisions of the Code. 11 U.S.C.A. § 1225(a)(1).
2. The fees and charges required by Title 28 of the Code or by the plan must be paid. 11 U.S.C.A. § 1225(a)(2).
3. The plan must be proposed in **good faith.** 11 U.S.C.A. § 1225(a)(3).
4. The payments of unsecured claims must fulfill the best interests of creditors test. Under this test, each holder of an unsecured claim must receive under the plan not less than it would have received had the claim been paid under Chapter 7 liquidation. 11 U.S.C.A. § 1225(a)(4). In a Chapter 12 case, it is unnecessary to cramdown unsecured creditors because they have no vote. Although unsecured creditors may object to confirmation of the plan, the plan is confirmable in regard to unsecured claims if the holders of the unsecured claims will receive an amount not less than their claims. The plan is also confirmable if it provides that all of the debtor's projected disposable income for three years from the date the first payment is due will be applied to make payments under the plan. 11 U.S.C.A. § 1225(b)(1).
5. A secured claim in a Chapter 12 plan must be dealt with in one of three basic ways: get the holder of the secured claim to agree to accept the plan; have the debtor surrender the property to the secured party; or cram the plan down on the creditor. 11 U.S.C.A. § 1225(a)(5). If the holder of a secured claim does not accept the settlement stated in the plan, the debtor may surrender the property securing the claim to the creditor. If the value of the secured property does not fully cover the claim, there will be a deficiency. The deficiency becomes an unsecured claim. The attorney for the debtor may want to obtain a full release from the creditor when the property is surrendered. This may be provided for in the plan and is binding if the plan is confirmed.

   If the debtor cannot get a release upon surrender of the property, then the plan must provide that the creditor will retain the unsecured claim. This last option, in which the plan provides that the holder of each secured claim may retain the lien securing the claim and receive not less than the allowed amount of the secured claim, is the Chapter 12 cramdown and applies only to secured creditors. 11 U.S.C.A. § 1225(a)(5)(B)(ii).

   Cramdown under Chapter 12 is a simple cramdown without application of the fair and equitable doctrine. The debtor can retain everything and need only meet the best interests of creditors test. This may leave the unsecured creditors with little or nothing.

6. The debtor will be able to make all payments under the plan and to comply with the plan. 11 U.S.C.A. § 1225(a)(6).

In *Travelers Insurance Co. v. Bullington,* the Bullington brothers and their now-deceased father operated their individual farms as a constructive partnership. In February 1985, the Bullingtons took out a $520,000 mortgage from Travelers on their farmland and fixtures. Under the mortgage, the Bullingtons were to pay only interest (no principal) for the first four years and all of the principal on the fifth year (February 1990). The interest rate was fixed at 12.50 percent for the first year and one point above the AAA corporate bonds index for the next three years.

In January 1987, the Bullingtons filed for bankruptcy under Chapter 12. Their Chapter 12 plan split Travelers's claim into two parts: (1) a secured claim of $475,000 (the stipulated value of the collateral; i.e., the farmland and fixtures); and (2) an unsecured claim of $170,000 representing the balance (principal and unpaid interest). The Bullingtons's plan converted the five-year floating-rate mortgage into a $475,000 thirty-year fixed-rate (10.75 percent) mortgage. Travelers objected to the confirmation of the plan and the Court of Appeals discussed five issues:

1. Does 11 U.S.C.A. § 1225 prohibit a thirty-year payout to an objecting secured creditor?
2. Does the plan provide a present "value" to the creditor that is not less than the allowed amount of such claim, as section 1225(a)(5)(B)(ii) requires?
3. Did the debtors prove the feasibility of the plan, as section 1225(a)(6) requires?
4. Does Chapter 12 constitute an unconstitutional taking of property without due process?
5. Does Chapter 12 apply retroactively?

Travelers Insurance Co. v. Bullington

878 F.2d 354 (11th Cir. 1989)

Before KRAVITCH and COX, Circuit Judges, and MORGAN, Senior Circuit Judge
Phyllis A. Kravitch, Circuit Judge

This is an appeal by Travelers Insurance Co. from an order affirming the bankruptcy court's confirmation of plan under Chapter 12 (Family Farmer) of the bankruptcy code. 89 B.R. 1010. We affirm.

The Bullingtons were brothers who, together with their now-deceased father, operated their individual farms in a constructive partnership. Because of this the bankruptcy court effectively consolidated their individual petitions for Chapter 12 bankruptcy and their virtually identical reorganization plans are treated as one. [hereinafter the "plan"]

In February of 1985 the Bullingtons took out a mortgage from appellant on certain of their farm properties. It was a balloon-type mortgage under which the Bullingtons received $520,000 and were to pay interest (but no principal) in semi-annual installments for the first four years, and then the entire amount of the principal would be due in February of 1990. The interest rate was fixed at 12 1/2% for the first year; the rate then floated at one point above an index of AAA corporate bonds. The mortgage was secured by land and certain fixtures (pumps, motors, etc.). The Bullingtons used the funds from the mortgage loan in their farming operations.

In November of 1986 Congress enacted Chapter 12 of the bankruptcy code to provide special relief for family farmers.

In January, 1987 the Bullingtons petitioned for bankruptcy under Chapter 12. As of the date of the petition, the Bullingtons' debt to Travelers Insurance was $645,929.77, with interest accruing at $300 per day. The value of the land that secured the Travelers loan was stipulated to be $475,000.

The plan, submitted by the Bullingtons and approved over the objections of Travelers, split Travelers claim into two parts: a secured claim of $475,000 (the stipulated value of the collateral) and an unsecured claim of $170,000 representing the remainder. The plan converted the five-year floating-rate mortgage into a $475,000 thirty-year fixed-rate mortgage. The court set the interest rate on the mortgage at 10.75%. The unsecured claim of $170,000 would be treated as any unsecured claim: the Debtors' entire disposable income (if any) would be used over the four-year term of the plan to pay each unsecured claim on a pro rata basis. At the end of the four years of the plan, any part of the unsecured debt that had not been paid off would be discharged.

Travelers appealed the bankruptcy court's order to the district court raising, inter alia, statutory and constitutional issues. The district court affirmed[1] and this appeal ensued. We address each issue in turn.

Unlike Chapter 11, secured creditors in Chapter 12 do not "vote" on a plan. Instead, section 1225 provides that the bankruptcy court "shall" approve the plan if one of three conditions are met in the plan:[2]

> with respect to each allowed secured claim provided for by the plan—
>
> (A) the holder of such claim has accepted the plan;
>
> (B) (i) the plan provides that the holder of such claim retain the lien securing such claim; *and*
>
> (ii) the value, as of the effective date of the plan, of property to be distributed by the trustee or the debtor under the plan on account of such claim is not less that the allowed amount of such claim; or
>
> (C) the debtor surrenders the property securing such claim to such holder; . . .

Because Travelers did not accept the plan, section 1225(a)(5)(A) does not apply. Under § 1225(a)(5)(C) the court may also approve a plan if the debtor surrenders the property subject to the lien, i.e., forfeits the land. Here debtors have not done so, thus our focus is on section 1225(a)(5)(B).[3]

Travelers does not suggest that the plan fails under section 1225(a)(5)(B)(i), which requires that the plan give the creditor a lien in the amount of his secured claim. The allowed secured claim here is $475,000 (the stipulated value of the property) and the plan gives a lien in that amount, so this requirement is satisfied.

Travelers argues, however, that the plan fails to meet the requirements of section 1225(a)(5)(B)(ii) because it stretches out the payments for thirty years and because Travelers does not receive sufficient "value" under the plan.

1. DOES 11 U.S.C. § 1225 PROHIBIT A THIRTY-YEAR PAYOUT TO AN OBJECTING SECURED CREDITOR?

Travelers first objection is that the plan's thirty-year mortgage violates section 1225(a)(5)(B)(ii). Travelers reasons as follows: section 1225(a)(5)(B)(ii) requires that the value of the property distributed under the plan be not less than the allowed amount of the claim, and that it be distributed "under the plan." Yet section 1222(c) provides that—subject to only two exceptions—payments under a plan may never exceed five years. Thus, Travelers suggests that because the thirty-year rescheduled mortgage is longer than five years, the plan violates the code.

Travelers argument is colorable, but it ignores the two express exceptions to section 1222(c) that permit payments to exceed five years. Section 1222(c) provides as follows:

> Except as provided in subsections (b)(5) and (b)(9), the plan may not provide for payments over a period that is longer than three years unless the court for cause approves a longer period, but the court may not approve a period that is longer than five years.

Section 1222(b)(5), the first exception to the section 1222(c) five-year limit, permits a debtor to reinstate an old debt (cure default), and is not applicable to this appeal. Section 1222(b)(9), however, has direct bearing on this case:

> [the plan may] provide for payment of allowed secured claims consistent with section 1225(a)(5) of this title, over a period exceeding the period permitted under section 1222(c).

Thus, section 1222(b)(9), as an express exception to the section 1222(c) five-year limit, permits payments under a plan to extend over five years, but only when "consistent with section 1225(a)(5)."

We find section 1222(b)(9) explicit and dispositive of Travelers' objection: a plan may provide for a payout period greater than five years, provided that it is "consistent with section 1225(a)(5)." Travelers' argument that payments under a plan can never exceed five years would render section 1222(b)(9) a nullity. Thus, the mere fact that the plan provides for a thirty-year payment of Travelers' allowed secured claim does not violate section 1225.

2. DOES THE PLAN PROVIDE A PRESENT "VALUE" TO THE CREDITOR NOT LESS THAN THE ALLOWED AMOUNT OF SUCH CLAIM AS SECTION 1225(a)(5)(b)(II) REQUIRES?

Travelers next argues that the plan does not give it the full value of its allowed secured claim as § 1225(a)(5)(B)(ii) requires. Travelers frames this objection in two ways. First, Travelers stresses that to satisfy this section it must receive value equal to its allowed secured claim "under the plan." Arguing that under the plan means the same as "during the plan," Travelers concludes that the four-year length of the plan that the bankruptcy court confirmed is the proper time frame in which to apply the section 1225(a)(5)(B)(ii) "value" test, i.e., Travelers would have us total up the payments it is to receive over these four years, and if that amount is less than the $475,000 amount of its allowed secured loan, then the plan fails.

This objection need not detain us long. Section 1225(a)(5)(B)(ii) explicitly directs that the "value" is to be determined "as of the *effective date of the plan.*" (emphasis added) Under this section, therefore, we do not total the payments received "during the plan." Instead, the test is simply whether, as of the effective date of the plan, the present value of the property distributed—i.e., the new thirty-year mortgage—is equal to or greater than the amount of the allowed secured claim.

In addition to its argument that the value it receives under section 1225(a)(5)(B)(ii) must be within the term of the plan, Travelers also argues that the thirty-year mortgage itself is not of sufficient value.

Travelers frames this issue in terms of burdens of proof. Travelers asserts that there is insufficient proof to show that a thirty-year 10.75% mortgage is of a value not less than the allowed secured claim of $475,000. From a pure finance perspective, all Travelers seems to be saying is that the term of the mortgage is too long and/or the interest rate is too low.

The debtors presented to the district court a chart of then-current interest rate returns, which tends to support a finding that a 10.75% interest rate on a thirty-year mortgage is within the range of market rates. Travelers, on the other hand, presented no *objective* evidence to demonstrate that the term or interest rate of the mortgage was such that its present value did not equal or exceed $475,000.

Travelers put on a witness who testified that Travelers itself would never lend for a period longer than twenty years, and if it did it would be at a somewhat higher rate of interest. Yet this testimony regarding Travelers' subjective valuation does not sufficiently undermine the bankruptcy courts' implicit factual finding that the present value of the mortgage as of the effective date of the plan was not less than the value of the allowed secured claim.

"Value" must be determined objectively. Simply because a creditor subjectively would not extend a mortgage on the same terms does not mean that objectively the mortgage does not have a given value. Given that Travelers has pointed to no record evidence to show that the 10.75% interest rate does give the mortgage a present value of $475,000, while the debtors' chart does tend to support that interest rate, the bankruptcy court's finding that the thirty-year mortgage at 10.75% annual interest rate has a present value not less than the $475,000 value of Travelers' allowed secured claim is supported by sufficient evidence.

Accordingly, we reject appellants' statutory and constitutional challenges, and AFFIRM the order of the district court affirming the bankruptcy court's confirmation of the debtors' plan for reorganization.

[1] In the course of the proceedings the plan was amended slightly, but none of the amendments have anything to do with this appeal.

[2] Section 1225 provides in part:

(a) Except as provided in subsection (b), the court shall confirm a plan if—
  (1) the plan complies with the provisions of this chapter and with the other applicable provisions of this title;
  (2) any fee, charge, or amount required under chapter 123 of title 28, or by the plan, to be paid before confirmation, has been paid;
  (3) the plan has been proposed in good faith and not by any means forbidden by law;
  (4) the value, as of the effective date of the plan, of property to be distributed under the plan on account of each allowed unsecured claim is not less than the amount that would be paid on such claim if the estate of the debtor were liquidated under chapter 7 of this title on such date

[3] The plan does call for the debtors to surrender the personal property collateral, but does not provide for them to forfeit the real property.

The plan must be specific enough so that the trustee and the debtor know exactly who is to be paid, how much is to be paid, and when it is to be paid.

The **confirmation of the plan** binds the debtor, each creditor, each equity security holder, and each general partner in the debtor to the provisions of the confirmed plan, whether or not the claim is provided for by the plan and whether or not the party has objected to, accepted, or rejected the plan. 11 U.S.C.A. § 1227(a).

The confirmation of a plan vests all of the property of the estate in the debtor except as provided in section 1228(a), in the plan, or in the confirmation order. The property vested in the debtor is free and clear of any claim or interest of any creditor provided for by the plan. 11 U.S.C.A. §§ 1227(b), (c). This allows the debtor to use property not encumbered by the provisions of the plan as collateral for new loans. Although the court can deny confirmation on legal grounds, such as nonpayment of a fee, creditors may object on legal grounds but have no vote on the confirmation itself.

If the plan is confirmed, the trustee will distribute payments to the creditors in accordance with the plan. If the plan is not confirmed, the trustee will return the payments to the debtor, less any unpaid administrative expenses allowed under section 503(b) and the percentage fee fixed for a standing trustee, if a standing trustee is serving in the case. 11 U.S.C.A. § 1226(a).

If the plan is unconfirmable, the debtor may convert the case to Chapter 7 or may request the court to dismiss the case. 11 U.S.C.A. §§ 1208(a), (b). A party in interest may also request the court to dismiss the case. 11 U.S.C.A. § 1208(c)(5).

SECTION 10
TRUSTEE'S DISTRIBUTION OF PAYMENTS UNDER THE PLAN

If the plan is confirmed, the trustee will distribute payments to the creditors in accordance with the plan as soon as it is practicable to do so. This will depend upon how quickly a plan is confirmed and whether the bar date for filing claims has expired. Ordinarily the deadline for filing claims is 90 days after the first date set for the meeting of creditors. Fed. R. Bank. P. 3002(c). Since the trustee will not know which claims are allowed until the deadline for filing claims has expired and any objections to the claims are resolved, the trustee may not be able to make payments to unsecured creditors even though the plan is confirmed.

If the plan is not confirmed, the trustee will return the payments to the debtor, less any unpaid administrative expenses allowed under 11 U.S.C.A. § 503(b). 11 U.S.C.A. § 1226(a).

SECTION 11
MODIFICATION OF THE PLAN AFTER CONFIRMATION

At any time after the confirmation of the plan but before the completion of payments under the plan, the debtor, the trustee, or the holder of an allowed unsecured claim may request modification of the plan. The holder of a secured claim, however, may not request modification. The plan, upon notice and opportunity for a hearing, may be modified to increase or reduce the amount of payments on claims of a particular class provided for by the plan or to extend or reduce the time for such payments. The plan may also be modified to alter the amount of the distribution to a creditor provided for by the plan to the extent necessary to take into account any payment of such claim outside the plan. 11 U.S.C.A. § 1229(a).

In *In re Cooper,* the debtors' Chapter 12 plan, as amended, was confirmed on December 14, 1987. The plan provided for payments of $57,050 to unsecured creditors over the life of the plan. This amount represented the liquidation value of the debtors' unencumbered farm machinery and equipment as of November 1, 1987.

On May 6, 1988, the debtors filed an amendment to their plan in which they proposed to reduce the payments to unsecured creditors to $34,150 because the liquidation value of the debtors' unsecured farm machinery and equipment was only $34,150 as of the time of the proposed modification. The trustee objected on the ground that the liquidation value should not be reevaluated. The court needed to decide whether the unsecured farm machinery and equipment should be reevaluated as of the time of the proposed modification and how this modification would affect the unsecured creditors and their reliance on the confirmed plan.

In re Cooper

1989. 94 B.R. 550 (Bankr. S.D. Ill. 1989)

MEMORANDUM AND ORDER
Kenneth J. Meyers, Bankruptcy Judge

Debtors, Robert and Phyllis Cooper, filed a Chapter 12 bankruptcy petition on December 12, 1986, and filed their original plan of reorganization on March 12, 1987. They subsequently filed a first amendment to their plan on September 14, 1987, and a second amendment on October 13, 1987. On November 24, 1987, debtors filed a third amendment to their plan of reorganization, which was confirmed by order of the Court on December 14, 1987.

Debtors' plan as confirmed provides for payments to unsecured creditors over the life of the plan in the amount of $57,050. This amount represents the liquidation value of debtors' unencumbered farm machinery and equipment as of November 1, 1987. The plan defines the effective date of the plan as the "date the order confirming the plan becomes final and non-appealable," which was assumed to be November 1, 1987, in debtors' liquidation analysis.

On May 6, 1988, debtors filed a fourth amendment to their plan in which they seek to modify the confirmed plan of reorganization with regard to the treatment of unsecured claims. By this amendment, debtors propose to sell a portion of the farm machinery and equipment and to distribute the proceeds to unsecured creditors, after payment of trustee fees and unpaid attorney's fees. The amendment further proposes to reduce the amount of the yearly payments to unsecured creditors.

The trustee has filed two objections to debtors' proposed amendment, one of which—regarding the amount of trustee's fees to be paid under the amendment—has been settled. The trustee's remaining objection is that the amendment proposes to pay unsecured creditors $34,150 over the life of the plan, which is less than the liquidation value of $57,050 provided in the confirmed plan. The trustee prays that the plan as modified provide for total payments of $57,050 to unsecured creditors so as to comply with § 1225(a)(4), which requires that unsecured creditors receive at least as much under a Chapter 12 plan as they would receive in a Chapter 7 liquidation.[1]

In response to the trustee's objection, debtors state that the value of their unencumbered farm machinery and equipment is less than that set forth in their original liquidation analysis of November 1987 and assert that this lesser value should control in determining whether the proposed modification to their plan complies with the liquidation test of § 1225(a)(4). Debtors maintain that the appropriate time for determining the liquidation value of unencumbered assets in a post-confirmation modification is the time of the proposed modification rather than the time the original plan became effective. Debtors contend, therefore, that their modified plan should be approved over the trustee's objection because it proposes to pay unsecured creditors the value of unencumbered assets as of the date of their modified plan.

At hearing on the trustee's objection, debtors informed the court that the $57,050 liquidation value ascribed to their unencumbered farm machinery and equipment in November 1987 was an inflated value based on debtors' own estimates. Debtors have since obtained professional appraisals of this equipment in preparing to sell part of the equipment in order to reduce their farming operation. The liquidation value based on these appraisals is less than that originally estimated, and debtors assert that they are only required to pay the revised value of $34,150 over the life of the plan in order to comply with the confirmation standard of § 1225(a)(4).

Section 1229, dealing with modification of a Chapter 12 plan after confirmation, provides in pertinent part

> (a) At any time after confirmation of the plan but before the completion of payments under such plan, the plan may be modified . . . to—
>
> (1) increase or reduce the amount of payments on claims of a particular class provided for by the plan; . . .
>
> (b) (2) The plan as modified becomes the plan unless, after notice and hearing, such modification is disapproved.

11 U.S.C. § 1229.

Post-confirmation modification under Chapter 12, as under Chapter 13, is intended as a method of addressing unforeseen difficulties that arise during plan administration, and such modification is warranted only when an unanticipated change in circumstances affects implementation of the plan as confirmed. *Matter of Grogg Farms, Inc.*, 91 B.R. 482 (Bankr.N.D.Ind.1988); *In re Dittmer*, 82 B.R. 1019 (Bankr.D.N.D.1988). A debtor seeking to modify a confirmed Chapter 12 plan under § 1229 has the burden of proving that the modifications meet the confirmation requirements. *In re Hart*, 90 B.R. 150 (Bankr.E.D.N.C.1988). Absent a modification under § 1229, the provisions of a confirmed Chapter 12 plan are binding on both the debtor and his creditors. *See* 11 U.S.C. § 1227(a); *In re Grogg Farms, Inc.*

Debtors have cited no authority, and the Court has found none, in which modification of a Chapter 12 plan was allowed based on a lesser liquidation value than existed at the time of confirmation. Debtors, observing that a modified plan replaces the original plan, assert that modification has the effect of creating a new "effective date of the plan" as of which debtors' estate is to be valued to determine compliance with § 1225(a)(4). The court, however, need not reach this issue under the facts of the instant case. By debtors' own admission, there has been no change in the value of their unencumbered assets in the few months since confirmation. Rather, debtors have determined that their original estimate of value in the liquidation analysis of their confirmed plan was not accurate. While debtors seek to be relieved of the consequences of their mistaken valuation, it would be contrary to the purpose of § 1229 to allow debtors to change a term of their confirmed plan that could have and should have been properly determined at the time of confirmation. *Cf. In re Grogg Farms, Inc.*: confirmation is *res judicata* as to those issues which could and should have been raised prior to or in connection with confirmation.

In considering debtors' proposal to decrease the amount of payments to unsecured creditors, the Court must be aware of the legitimate expectations of the parties to the confirmed plan and the need for finality in determining their rights and duties. *See In re Grogg Farms, Inc.* Once debtors' Chapter 12 plan was confirmed, their creditors could rightfully expect that the new contractual arrangement represented by the plan would be complied with. Absent some unforeseen difficulty leading to debtors' inability to fulfill their obligations under the plan, the plan should be implemented as agreed. The Court finds, therefore, that debtors' proposed modification to their plan providing for payment to unsecured creditors in the amount of $34,150 over the life of the plan fails to comply with § 1225(a)(4) and cannot be approved as proposed.

At hearing, debtors stated that if the Court should find that the payments to unsecured creditors under their proposed fourth amendment to the plan were insufficient, the trustee and debtors have agreed that debtors would increase these payments by $4,500 per year in order to give the unsecured creditors the equivalent of the liquidation value of debtors' equipment as of November 1, 1987. Based upon this representation, the Court will approve debtors' proposed fourth amendment to allow debtors to sell a portion of their farm machinery and equipment and to distribute the proceeds pro rata to unsecured creditors after payment of trustee and attorney's fees. The amount of the trustee's fee to be paid from the sale proceeds is $2,300, as agreed at the time of hearing.

IT IS ORDERED, therefore, that debtors' fourth amendment to their Chapter 12 plan is APPROVED as modified by the agreement between the trustee and debtors regarding payments to unsecured creditors and the amount of the trustee's fee.

---

[1] Section 1225(a)(4) provides

(a) . . . [T]he court shall confirm a plan if—

> (4) the value, as of the effective date of the plan, of property to be distributed under the plan on account of each allowed unsecured claim is not less than the amount that would be paid on such claim if the estate of the debtor were liquidated under Chapter 7 of this title on such date.

This requirement is made applicable to post-confirmation modifications by 11 U.S.C. § 1229(b)(1).

SECTION 12
REVOCATION OF ORDER OF CONFIRMATION, CONVERSION, OR DISMISSAL

Upon request of a party in interest, the court may revoke an order for confirmation if the order was procured by fraud. The revocation must occur within 180 days after the order for confirmation and must follow notice and a hearing. 11 U.S.C.A. § 1230(a). The case in which an order for confirmation has been revoked will be dismissed pursuant to section 1208(c)(7), unless within the time fixed by the court the debtor proposes a modification of the plan which is confirmed by the court. 11 U.S.C.A. § 1230(b). A case under Chapter 12 may be converted to Chapter 7 or dismissed upon request of a party in interest only after notice and a hearing to show that the debtor has committed fraud in connection with the case. This is the only provision in the Code that allows for the involuntary liquidation of a farmer's assets. 11 U.S.C.A. § 1208(d).

SECTION 13
DISCHARGE

After the completion of payments under the plan, the debtor receives a discharge. The debtor will not be discharged from allowed claims, secured or unsecured, that were not provided for by the plan, from any debt for the curing of any default on any secured or unsecured claim on which the final payment is due after the proposed final payment under the plan, or from the nondischargeable debts listed in section 523(a). 11 U.S.C.A. § 1228(a).

The court may grant what is called a hardship or compassionate discharge to a debtor who has not completed payments under the plan. This type of discharge is granted only if the debtor's failure to complete the payments is due to circumstances for which the debtor should not justly be held responsible, the payments to creditors would not be less than they would have received if the debtor's estate had been liquidated under Chapter 7, and modification of the plan is not practicable. 11 U.S.C.A. § 1228(b).

The debtor under a hardship discharge will not be discharged from any allowed secured claims, from allowed unsecured claims that were not provided for by the plan, from any debt for the curing of any default on any secured or unsecured claim on which the final payment is due after the proposed final payment under the plan, or from any nondischargeable claims under section 523(a). 11 U.S.C.A. § 1228(c). Therefore, the effect of a hardship discharge is that the debtor will not be discharged from any secured debts or from unsecured debts not provided for by the plan or that would be nondischargeable under Chapter 7.

A debtor who has received either a full-compliance or a hardship discharge cannot receive a discharge in a Chapter 7 case filed within six years of the date of the Chapter 12 filing, unless payments under the Chapter 12 plan totaled 100 percent of the allowed unsecured claims, or payments under the Chapter 12 plan totaled 70 percent of the allowed unsecured claims and the Chapter 12 plan was proposed by the debtor in good faith and was the debtor's best effort. 11 U.S.C.A. § 727(a)(9). A debtor who has received a discharge in a Chapter 12 case is not foreclosed from filing another Chapter 12 case or a Chapter 11 case or a Chapter 13 case at any time if the debtor is otherwise eligible to file under these chapters.

SECTION 14
REVOCATION OF THE DISCHARGE

A party in interest may request revocation of the discharge for fraud within one year after the discharge is granted if this party did not know about the fraud until after the discharge was granted. 11 U.S.C.A. § 1228(d).

SECTION 15
CLOSING THE CASE AND PROCEEDINGS AFTER THE CASE IS CLOSED

Upon the completion of payments under the plan and the discharge of the debtor, the trustee files a final report and account, certifying that the case has been fully administered. There is a presumption that the case has been fully administered unless the United States trustee files an objection within 30 days. If no objection is filed, the court may discharge the trustee and close the case without reviewing the final report and account. 11 U.S.C.A. § 350(a); Fed. R. Bank. P. 5009.

Even after the case is closed, it is still subject to further action. In certain situations, a case may be amended without being reopened. Clerical errors in judgments, orders, and other parts of the record or errors in the record caused by oversight or omission may be corrected. A closed case may be reopened to add a creditor or to distribute previously undistributed property of the estate. 11 U.S.C.A. § 350(b).

KEY TERMS

Adequate protection
Chapter 12 plan
Confirmation of the plan
Debtor in possession (DIP)
Family farmer
Farming operations
Good faith
Judicial lien
Nonpossessory, nonpurchase money security interest

CHAPTER 8

The Voluntary Chapter 11 Bankruptcy (Reorganization)

CHAPTER OUTLINE

SECTION 1
THE INITIATION OF A CHAPTER 11 CASE

SECTION 2
THE CHAPTER 11 PETITION AND THE SIGNIFICANCE OF FILING A CHAPTER 11 PETITION
A. The Filing of the Chapter 11 Petition
B. The Significance of Filing a Petition
C. Evidence of Debtor in Possession (DIP) Status
D. Exemptions

SECTION 3
THE CHAPTER 11 PLAN
A. Strategies Utilized in Reorganization Plans
B. Contents of a Chapter 11 Plan
C. Modification of a Chapter 11 Plan
D. Chapter 11 Plan Filed by Parties Other Than the Debtor

SECTION 4
DISCLOSURE STATEMENT OR EVIDENCE SHOWING COMPLIANCE WITH 11 U.S.C.A. § 1126(b)

SECTION 5
ORDER AND NOTICE OF CHAPTER 11 BANKRUPTCY FILING, MEETING OF CREDITORS, AND FIXING OF DATES

SECTION 6
MOTIONS AND COMPLAINTS
A. Motions
B. Complaints

SECTION 7
APPOINTMENT OF A COMMITTEE OF UNSECURED CREDITORS AND A COMMITTEE OF EQUITY SECURITY HOLDERS

SECTION 8
MEETING OF CREDITORS (THE SECTION 341 MEETING) AND MEETING OF EQUITY SECURITY HOLDERS

SECTION 9
HEARING ON THE DISCLOSURE STATEMENT

SECTION 10
HEARING ON CONFIRMATION OF THE PLAN

SECTION 11
EFFECT OF CONFIRMATION OF THE PLAN

SECTION 12
DISTRIBUTION UNDER THE PLAN AND REPORTING BY DEBTOR IN POSSESSION OR CHAPTER 11 TRUSTEE

SECTION 13
Revocation of an Order of Confirmation

SECTION 14
Final Report and Final Decree

The voluntary Chapter 11 bankruptcy, called **reorganization,** is covered in this chapter. A person that may proceed under Chapter 7 may be a debtor under Chapter 11, with two exceptions. Stockbrokers and commodity brokers cannot proceed under Chapter 11, although they can proceed under Chapter 7. Railroads, which are excluded from Chapter 7, may file under Chapter 11.

Chapter 11 gives debtors who desire to reorganize certain advantages not available under Chapter 7.

- Chapter 11 allows individual debtors as debtors in possession to keep their nonexempt assets that would otherwise be surrendered to the trustee in a Chapter 7 case.
- Business debtors can use Chapter 11 as a business planning tool, but Chapter 7 involves the liquidation of the business.
- Chapter 11 provides a discharge to individuals, partnerships, and corporations, but Chapter 7 only provides a discharge to individuals.
- Chapter 11 allows debtors to use future income to pay creditors as much as they can over the term of the plan, whereas under Chapter 7, creditors are paid only from the liquidation of assets of the bankruptcy estate.
- In Chapter 11, debtors can alter the payment terms on most secured debt if the debt is to be paid within the term of the Chapter 11 plan.
- Debtors may receive a discharge under Chapter 11 more often than every six years as permitted under Chapter 7.

Chapter 11 has disadvantages as well.

- Chapter 11 debtors whose accounts receivable and inventory are subject to a lien may only use the cash proceeds under a cash collateral order.
- Chapter 11 trustees, if appointed, are paid a fee under the Chapter 11 plan, thus reducing the amount available to pay creditors under the plan.
- Because of the additional work involved in a Chapter 11, more professionals are involved who charge debtors substantially higher fees for Chapter 11 than for Chapter 7.
- Creditors may be less willing to extend postpetition credit to a Chapter 11 debtor.
- Court approval is needed by a Chapter 11 debtor in possession or trustee for actions outside the ordinary course of business.
- A creditors' committee may be appointed whose professionals are paid from the bankruptcy estate.
- In addition to the initial filing fee, there is a quarterly fee that must be paid based on the amount of money disbursed each quarter.

The chronological order of a Chapter 11 case is not as fixed as that of the Chapter 7 case because of the more complex nature of the proceedings in a Chapter 11. For example, the re organization plan may be filed along with the petition or at a much later time.

This chapter follows the Chapter 11 case from the time the potential client initiates contact with the bankruptcy attorney's office through the closing of the case. This chapter includes

- the initiation of the attorney/client relationship;
- the filing of the Chapter 11 petition and its significance, including the possession and control of the property of the estate, the operation of the debtor's business, and exemptions;

- the Chapter 11 plan and some of the strategies considered when drafting the plan;
- the requirements of the disclosure statement;
- the order and notice of Chapter 11 bankruptcy filing, meeting of creditors, and fixing of dates;
- motions and complaints, including first day motions;
- the appointment of a creditors committee and equity security holders committee;
- the meeting of creditors (the section 341 meeting) and the meeting of equity security holders;
- the hearing on the disclosure statement;
- the hearing on confirmation of the plan and the effect of confirmation of the plan, including discharge;
- a brief discussion of distribution under the plan and reporting requirements for the debtor in possession or the Chapter 11 trustee;
- revocation of an order of confirmation and the final decree.

The ultimate success of a bankruptcy reorganization will hinge on the debtor's ability to use the Bankruptcy Code sections discussed in this chapter. Exhibit 8–1 presents a flow chart for this chapter.

SECTION 1 THE INITIATION OF A CHAPTER 11 CASE

All attorneys have their own ways of allocating responsibility to their paralegals and for dealing with debtor clients. Some attorneys effectively use their paralegals by significantly involving them in the process. For example, an attorney may employ the following procedure:

- After the debtor has initiated contact with the attorney's firm, the paralegal sets up the client file, acquires a list of the debtor's creditors, and initiates a conflict of interest check.
- The paralegal gives the debtor a questionnaire (worksheets) that will help the debtor itemize his or her assets and liabilities as well as monthly income and monthly expenses.
- The paralegal requires the debtor to provide copies of relevant documents such as real estate deeds and mortgages, loan agreements, security agreements, vehicle titles and tax returns.
- The debtor completes the questionnaire and returns it to the paralegal along with the documents requested by the paralegal.
- The paralegal meets with the debtor and reviews the questionnaire with the debtor to insure that it is completed fully and accurately and to identify any emergencies that may require the attorney's immediate attention.
- The attorney and paralegal meet with the debtor, and the attorney discusses the questionnaire adding, deleting, modifying, and verifying the debtor's entries.
- The attorney advises the debtor whether bankruptcy is the appropriate course of action and, if so, under which chapter the case should be filed. The attorney will explain the bankruptcy process to the debtor and will discuss attorney fees and other aspects of the attorney/client contract for services.
- The paralegal completes the petition, the list of creditors, the disclosure of attorney's compensation statement, the schedules and the statement of financial affairs.
- The paralegal searches for connections between the law firm to be employed by the debtor in possession and the creditors, their professionals, the U.S. trustee, and persons employed in the office of the U.S. trustee to prepare the declaration and corresponding retention application.
- If the relief selected is a Chapter 11 bankruptcy, the attorney ultimately drafts the Chapter 11 plan and the disclosure statement.

EXHIBIT 8–1 Flow Chart for Chapter 11

Filing the Chapter 11 Petition

The debtor files with the bankruptcy court clerk's office:

1. Filing fee
2. Voluntary petition (Official Form No. 1)
3. Exhibit "A," to Official Form No. 1, if the debtor is a corporation
4. Corporate resolution authorizing the filing of a Chapter 11, if the debtor is a corporation
5. Disclosure of attorney's compensation statement or disclosure of compensation statement by a non-attorney bankruptcy petition preparer
6. List of creditors
7. Schedules (Official Form No. 6)
   a. Summary of schedules
   b. Schedule A. Real property
   c. Schedule B. Personal property
   d. Schedule C. Property claimed as exempt
   e. Schedule D. Creditors holding secured claims
   f. Schedule E. Creditors holding unsecured priority claims
   g. Schedule F. Creditors holding unsecured nonpriority claims
   h. Schedule G. Executory contracts and unexpired leases
   i. Schedule H. Codebtors
   j. Schedule I. Current income of individual debtor(s), if applicable
   k. Schedule J. Current expenditures of individual debtor(s), if applicable
   l. Schedule of current income and expenditures of a partnership or corporation, if applicable
8. List of creditors holding 20 largest unsecured claims (Official Form No. 4)
9. List of debtor's equity security holders, if the debtor is a corporation or partnership
10. Statement of financial affairs

If the petition is accompanied by a list of all creditors, the debtor has up to 15 days to file items 7, 9, and 10.

Prior to the time the case is closed, the debtor may amend the petition, lists, schedules, and statement. The debtor has a duty to supplement the schedules for certain property acquired after the petition has been filed.

Upon the filing of a voluntary petition, which constitutes an order for relief, the estate is created and the automatic stay goes into effect, protecting the estate from dismemberment and the debtor from collection procedures. The debtor becomes the **debtor in possession (DIP)**.

Upon the filing of a case or sometime thereafter, the U.S. trustee's office will, under local rules, give the debtor an order relating to reporting requirements.

As soon as practicable after the filing of the petition, the U.S. trustee appoints a committee of unsecured creditors.

If the debtor is a small business, a party in interest may request the court to order that a committee not be appointed.

A party in interest may file an application for the appointment of additional committees of creditors or of equity security holders.

(continued)

EXHIBIT 8–1 Filing the Chapter 11 Petition, Continued

The clerk of the bankruptcy court mails to the debtor, the debtor's attorney, the trustee, all creditors, all equity security holders, the indenture trustees, and the U.S. trustee not less than 20 days notice of

1. the filing of the chapter 11 bankruptcy case
2. an explanation of the automatic stay
3. the date, time, and location of the meeting of creditors
4. the deadline for filing objections to the debtor's claim of exemptions

---

A party in interest or the U.S. trustee may request appointment of a trustee or an examiner.

A party in interest or the U.S. trustee may request termination of the trustee's appointment.

The debtor in possession may dismiss the case; convert the case to Chapter 7, 12, or 13; or move for a change of venue.

The U.S. trustee may move to dismiss the case or to convert the case to Chapter 7.

A party in interest may move to dismiss the case, to convert the case to Chapter 7, for a change of venue, for abstention by the court, or for examination of any person.

The debtor in possession or the trustee may assume or reject executory contracts, including collective bargaining agreements.

Meeting of Creditors

To be held not less than 20 nor more than 40 days after the order for relief.

The business of the meeting includes the examination of the debtor under oath.

The U.S. trustee may also convene a meeting of equity security holders.

(continued)

EXHIBIT 8–1 Filing the Chapter 11 Petition, Continued

Fresh Start for the Debtor (Discharge)

A creditor may file a complaint objecting to the dischargeability of a debt.

A party in interest may object to the debtor's claim of exemptions.

The trustee, if one has been appointed, a creditor, or the U.S. trustee may file a complaint objecting to the debtor's discharge.

Administration of the Estate

The debtor remains in possession of property of the estate unless a trustee has been appointed.

If the debtor is engaged in business, the debtor is required to file periodic reports on forms as required by the U.S. trustee.

Subject to the bar date set by the court, a creditor or an indenture trustee may file a proof of claim and an equity security holder may file proof of interest.

If a creditor does not timely file a proof of claim, the debtor or trustee may file a proof of claim within 30 days after expiration of the time for filing claims.

The trustee, if one has been appointed, or a party in interest (including a debtor in possession) may move to object to a claim.

The DIP, the trustee, or the creditors committee may file a complaint for turnover of property of the estate, to compel a custodian to turn over property of the estate and for an accounting, or to avoid a fraudulent transfer or preferential transfer.

A party in interest may move for relief from the automatic stay.

A party with an interest in property to be used, sold or leased by the trustee or DIP may ask the court to condition such use, sale or lease as necessary to provide adequate protection.

(continued)

EXHIBIT 8–1 Filing the Chapter 11 Petition, Continued

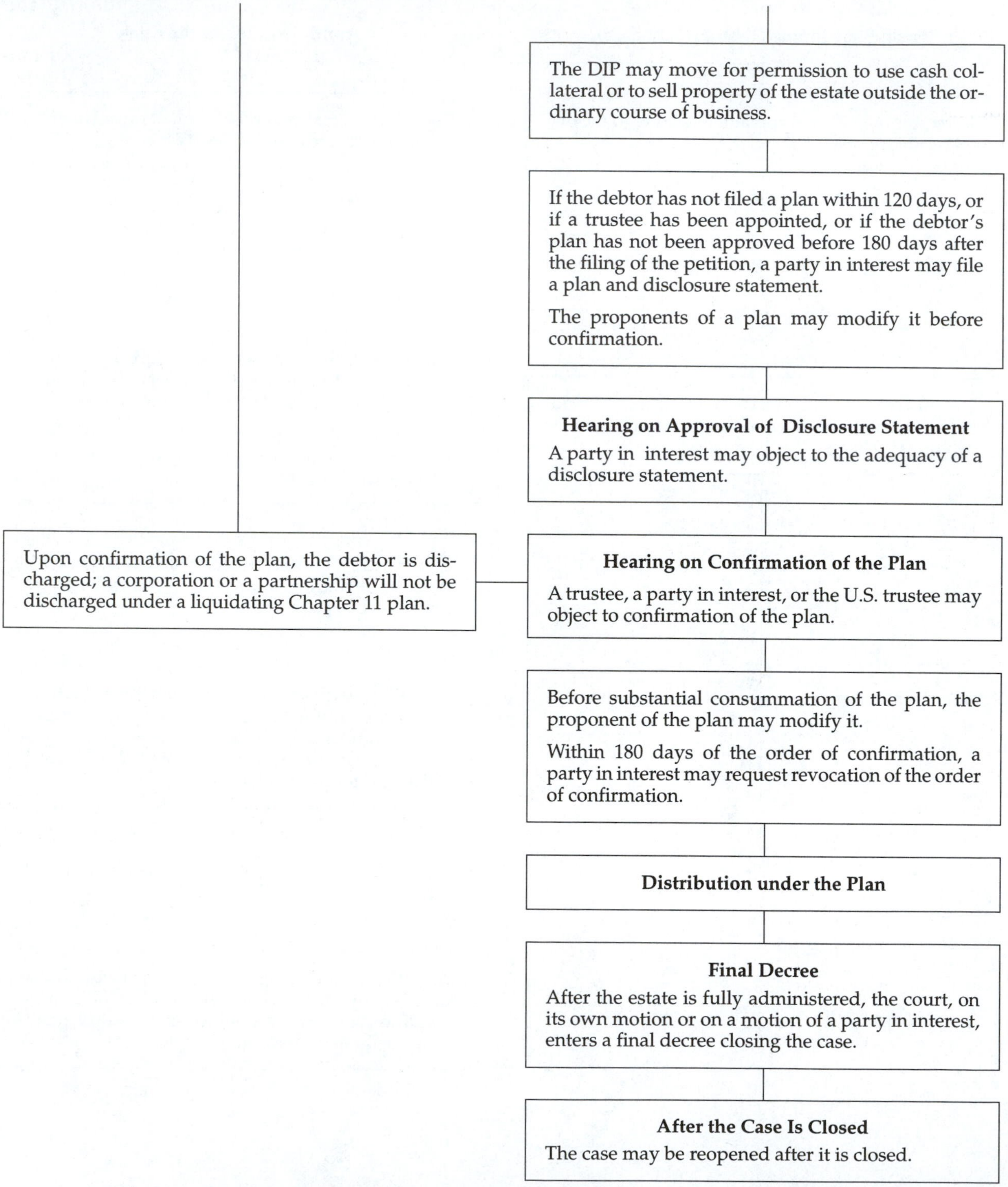

The DIP may move for permission to use cash collateral or to sell property of the estate outside the ordinary course of business.

If the debtor has not filed a plan within 120 days, or if a trustee has been appointed, or if the debtor's plan has not been approved before 180 days after the filing of the petition, a party in interest may file a plan and disclosure statement.

The proponents of a plan may modify it before confirmation.

Hearing on Approval of Disclosure Statement

A party in interest may object to the adequacy of a disclosure statement.

Hearing on Confirmation of the Plan

A trustee, a party in interest, or the U.S. trustee may object to confirmation of the plan.

Upon confirmation of the plan, the debtor is discharged; a corporation or a partnership will not be discharged under a liquidating Chapter 11 plan.

Before substantial consummation of the plan, the proponent of the plan may modify it.

Within 180 days of the order of confirmation, a party in interest may request revocation of the order of confirmation.

Distribution under the Plan

Final Decree

After the estate is fully administered, the court, on its own motion or on a motion of a party in interest, enters a final decree closing the case.

After the Case Is Closed

The case may be reopened after it is closed.

For the purpose of illustrating a Chapter 11 bankruptcy, the text will follow a corporate debtor. We will pick up the discussion with the meeting attended by the CFO and CEO of the company, the attorney, and the paralegal. The discussion focuses on a Chapter 11 filing.

The attorney noted that a Chapter 11 filing requires that a Chapter 11 plan be submitted to and confirmed by the court. The Chapter 11 plan term may be short or long, depending on the complexity of the debtor's situation and the debtor's objectives. The debtor will remain in possession of all the assets of the corporation, unless the plan calls for sale or lease. A creditors' committee will be appointed by the U.S. trustee to oversee the process. The debtor will have the exclusive right for 120 days from the date of filing its Chapter 11 petition to file a Chapter 11 plan for reorganization. If the debtor does not file a plan within this time, the creditors may file a plan. The plan must be confirmed by the bankruptcy court.

After a number of meetings, the concept of the plan may be formulated and the paralegal, under the attorney's supervision, will complete the voluntary petition, the disclosure of attorney's compensation statement, the list of creditors, and the schedules and the statement of financial affairs. These documents are found in Chapter 5 of this text. They are identical whether the case is filed as a Chapter 11 or Chapter 7 with two exceptions: the documents will designate that the case is being filed under Chapter 11, rather than Chapter 7, and the documents will include the list of the 20 largest creditors.

The attorney will then, with numerous consultations with the debtor, draft the Chapter 11 plan and the disclosure statement.

SECTION 2 THE CHAPTER 11 PETITION AND THE SIGNIFICANCE OF FILING A CHAPTER 11 PETITION

A. THE FILING OF THE CHAPTER 11 PETITION

The same documents necessary for filing the petition in a voluntary Chapter 7 case are also necessary in a voluntary Chapter 11 case, with the exceptions of the clerk's notice and a statement of intention, both of which are required in a Chapter 7 case if the debtor is an individual with consumer debts. A Chapter 11 filing also requires Exhibit "A" to the voluntary petition if the debtor is a corporation, a list of the debtor's 20 largest unsecured creditors, and a list of equity security holders if the debtor is a corporation or partnership. Therefore, filing a voluntary Chapter 11 case requires the following items:

1. Filing fee
2. Voluntary Petition (Official Form No. 1)
3. Exhibit "A" to voluntary petition, if the debtor is a corporation
4. Corporate resolution authorizing the filing of a Chapter 11, if the debtor is a corporation
5. Disclosure of attorney's compensation statement or disclosure of compensation statement by a non-attorney bankruptcy petition preparer
6. List of creditors
7. Schedules (Official Form No. 6)
   a. Summary of Schedules
   b. Schedule A: Real Property
   c. Schedule B: Personal Property
   d. Schedule C: Property Claimed as Exempt
   e. Schedule D: Creditors Holding Secured Claims

f. Schedule E: Creditors Holding Unsecured Priority Claims
g. Schedule F: Creditors Holding Unsecured Nonpriority Claims
h. Schedule G: Executory Contracts and Unexpired Leases
i. Schedule H: Codebtors
j. Schedule I: Current Income of Individual Debtor(s), if applicable
k. Schedule J: Current Expenditures of Individual Debtor(s), if applicable
l. Schedule of Current Income and Expenditures of a Partnership or Corporation, if applicable

8. List of Creditors Holding 20 Largest Unsecured Claims (Official Form No. 4)
9. List of debtor's equity security holders
10. Statement of Financial Affairs
11. Application to employ attorney for debtor in possession with attorney's declaration

If the debtor is a corporation filing under Chapter 11, Exhibit "A" to the voluntary petition must be completed and attached to the petition. (See Exhibit 8–2.)

Not all of these documents must be filed at once. If the petition is accompanied by the list of creditors, the debtor has up to 15 days from the date of the filing of the petition to file the schedules, a statement of financial affairs, and a list of the debtor's equity security holders.

The debtor could file a plan at any time during the case unless the court orders otherwise. The debtor's right to file a plan is exclusive for the first 120 days after the petition is filed unless a trustee has been appointed. If the debtor files a plan, the debtor must also file a disclosure statement or evidence showing compliance with 11 U.S.C.A. § 1126(b).

In a Chapter 11 case, as in a Chapter 7 case, the debtor has a duty to supplement the schedules. A supplemental schedule is not necessary, however, in a Chapter 11 case for property acquired after the order confirming the plan has been entered. Fed. R. Bank. P. 1007(h). A Chapter 11 debtor also has a right to amend the petition, lists, schedules, and statement of financial affairs. Fed. R. Bank. P. 1009(a).

The List of Creditors Holding the 20 Largest Unsecured Claims (Official Form No. 4) is required to enable the United States trustee to appoint a committee of unsecured creditors. The information concerning each creditor expedites the formation of the committee and assures adequate creditor representation. 11 U.S.C.A. § 1102; Fed. R. Bank. P. 1007(d). (See Exhibit 8–3.)

Instructions for Completing Official Form No. 4 (List of Creditors Holding the 20 Largest Unsecured Claims)

The List of Creditors Holding the 20 Largest Unsecured Claims should not include insiders. Insiders include persons who are related to the debtor, such as relatives, partners, directors, officers, affiliates, or others in control of the debtor. See 11 U.S.C.A. § 101 (31). A creditor holding a secured claim can be listed only if the claim is undersecured and the unsecured portion of the claim would place it among the 20 largest unsecured claims.

A State the name of each of the debtor's creditors holding the 20 largest unsecured claims. State the creditor's complete name and complete mailing address, including zip code. Although the form does not call for a telephone number, a telephone number for each creditor would be helpful.

B For each creditor listed in "A," state the name, telephone number, and complete mailing address, including zip code, of the employee, agent, or department of the creditor familiar with the claim. This information must be complete so the U.S. trustee's office can find the creditors for the creditors' committee.

C State the nature of the claim.

Example: Trade debt for merchandise or supplies
purchase of computers
purchase of inventory
Institutional debt
bank loan

EXHIBIT 8–2 Official Form No. 1, Exhibit "A" (Exhibit "A" to the Voluntary Petition)

Form B1, Exh.A (9/97)

Exhibit "A"

[If debtor is required to file periodic reports (*e.g.*, forms 10K and 10Q) with the Securities and Exchange Commission pursuant to Section 13 or 15(d) of the Securities Exchange Act of 1934 and is requesting relief under chapter 11 of the Bankruptcy Code, this Exhibit "A" shall be completed and attached to the petition.]

United States Bankruptcy Court

______________ District of ______________

Exhibit "A" to Voluntary Petition

1. If any of the debtor's securities are registered under Section 12 of the Securities Exchange Act of 1934, the SEC file number is ______________.

2. The following financial data is the latest available information and refers to the debtor's condition on ______________.

a. Total assets $ ______________

b. Total debts (including debts listed in 2.c., below) $ ______________

					Approximate number of holders
c.	Debt securities held by more than 500 holders.				
	secured / /	unsecured / /	subordinated / /	$ ______________	______________
	secured / /	unsecured / /	subordinated / /	$ ______________	______________
	secured / /	unsecured / /	subordinated / /	$ ______________	______________
	secured / /	unsecured / /	subordinated / /	$ ______________	______________
	secured / /	unsecured / /	subordinated / /	$ ______________	______________
d.	Number of shares of preferred stock			______________	______________
e.	Number of shares common stock			______________	______________

Comments, if any: ____

3. Brief description of debtor's business: ____

4. List the names of any person who directly or indirectly owns, controls, or holds, with power to vote, 5% or more of the voting securities of debtor:

____

EXHIBIT 8–3 Official Form No. 4 (List of Creditors Holding 20 Largest Unsecured Claims)

Official Form 4
11/92

United States Bankruptcy Court

_______________ District of _______________

In re ______________________________,
Debtor

Case No. ________________

Chapter ___________

LIST OF CREDITORS HOLDING 20 LARGEST UNSECURED CLAIMS

Following is the list of the debtor's creditors holding the 20 largest unsecured claims. The list is prepared in accordance with Fed. R. Bankr. P. 1007(d) for filing in this chapter 11 [*or* chapter 9] case. The list does not include (1) persons who come within the definition of "insider" set forth in 11 U.S.C. § 101, or (2) secured creditors unless the value of the collateral is such that the unsecured deficiency places the creditor among the holders of the 20 largest unsecured claims.

(1)	(2)	(3)	(4)	(5)
Name of creditor and complete mailing address including zip code	*Name, telephone number and complete mailing address, including zip code, of employee, agent, or department of creditor familiar with claim who may be contacted*	*Nature of claim (trade debt, bank loan, government contract, etc.)*	*Indicate if claim is contingent, unliquidated, disputed or subject to setoff*	*Amount of claim [if secured also state value of security]*
A	**B**	**C**	**D**	**E**

Date: ______________________

F
____
Debtor

DECLARATION UNDER PENALTY OF PERJURY ON BEHALF OF A CORPORATION OR PARTNERSHIP

I, [the president *or* other officer *or* an authorized agent of the corporation] [*or* a member *or* an authorized agent of the partnership] named as the debtor in this case, declare under penalty of perjury that I have read the foregoing list and that it is true and correct to the best of my information and belief.

Date ____________________

Signature ______________________

____
(Print Name and Title)

Debt based on a judgment
  money judgment from negligence action
  money judgment for breach of contract
Debt for services
  installation of fence
  maintenance contract
  security services
  repairs to the company's automobile fleet

D Indicate if the claim is contingent, unliquidated, disputed, or subject to setoff. If the claim is not, state "no."

E State the amount of the claim. If the claim is secured, also state the value of the security.

Example: $50,000 claim
secured by present
and after-acquired
equipment valued
at $40,000

F Have the debtor sign and date the form. The debtor's name should appear as it appears on the petition.

Although there is no official form for the list of equity security holders, the list enables the United States trustee to appoint a committee of equity security holders. An **equity security holder** is a holder of an equity security of the debtor. 11 U.S.C.A. § 101(17). Equity security is defined as

1. the share in a corporation, whether or not transferable or denominated "stock," or a similar security;
2. an interest of a limited partner in a limited partnership; or
3. a warrant or a right, other than a right to convert, to purchase, sell, or subscribe to a share, security, or interest of a kind previously specified. 11 U.S.C.A. § 101(16).

Therefore, the two most common holders of equity security are stockholders of a corporation and limited partners of a partnership.

Rule 1007(3) requires the debtor to file a list of the debtor's equity security holders within 15 days after entry of the order for relief. The list must contain

1. the name of each holder;
2. the last known address or place of business of each holder;
3. the kind of interest registered in the name of each holder; and
4. the number of interests registered in the name of each holder.

See also 11 U.S.C.A. § 1102.
(See Exhibit 8–4.)

Instructions for Completing List of Equity Security Holders

The list of the debtor's equity security holders can be derived from the Debtor-Client Questionnaire and the Statement of Financial Affairs (Official Form No. 7). Equity security holders who are limited partners will be listed in the Debtor-Client Questionnaire § VII, question 21.a, and in the Statement of Financial Affairs, question 21.a. Equity security holders who hold 5 percent or more of the voting securities of the corporation will be listed in the Debtor-Client Questionnaire § VII, question 21.b, and in the Statement of Financial Affairs, question 21.b. Equity security holders holding less than 5 percent of the voting securities are listed in the Debtor-Client Questionnaire § VII, question 21.c.

A State the name of equity security holder and complete mailing address, including zip code. The address should be the last known address or place of business of the equity security holder.

EXHIBIT 8–4 List of Equity Security Holders

UNITED STATES BANKRUPTCY COURT
_______________ **DISTRICT OF** _______________

In re _______________,
Debtor

Case No. _______________

Chapter _______________

LIST OF EQUITY SECURITY HOLDERS

The following list of the debtor's equity security holders is prepared in accordance with Fed. R. Bank. P. 1007(a)(3) for filing in this Chapter 11 case.

(1) Name of equity security holder and complete mailing address, including zip code	(2) Kind of interest registered in the name of each holder	(3) Number of shares or percentage of ownership	(4) Par value, if applicable

A **B**

Date: _______________ _______________
Debtor

If completed by an individual debtor, or husband and wife filing a joint petition, use the following sworn declaration.

I declare under penalty of perjury that I have read the answers contained in the foregoing list of equity security holders and any attachments thereto and that they are true and correct.

_______________ _______________
Date Signature of Debtor

_______________ _______________
Date Signature of Joint Debtor (if any)

If completed on behalf of a partnership or corporation, use the following sworn declaration.

I declare under penalty of perjury that I have read the answers contained in the foregoing list of equity security holders and any attachments thereto and that they are true and correct to the best of my knowledge, information, and belief.

_______________ _______________
Date Signature

____
Print Name

____
Title **C**

B Identify the kind of interest registered in the name of each holder.

Examples: limited partner

preferred stock

common stock

C An individual signing on behalf of a partnership or a corporation must indicate his or her position or relationship to the debtor.

B. THE SIGNIFICANCE OF FILING A PETITION

The significance of filing a petition under Chapter 11 is similar in many ways to the significance of filing a petition under Chapter 7. The filing of the case constitutes an order for relief, bringing the automatic stay into effect and creating the bankruptcy estate.

1. Possession and Control of Property of the Estate

Unlike Chapter 7 bankruptcy in which a trustee is appointed to take control over and administer the bankruptcy estate, in Chapter 11, there is no trustee appointed at the outset. Rather, the debtor, as debtor in possession (commonly called "DIP") continues in control over the assets of the estate. Debtor in possession is defined as a debtor in a Chapter 11 bankruptcy case in which no trustee has been appointed. 11 U.S.C.A. § 1101(1). If the debtor is a corporation, the United States trustee will require that the debtor designate a person responsible for performing the duties of the debtor in possession. Control over the bankruptcy estate, including the debtor's business, may determine whether the debtor can reorganize and under what terms. The prospects for a debtor to reorganize are usually improved if the debtor remains in control. Thus, in adopting the Bankruptcy Code, Congress chose to give a debtor, as debtor in possession, the opportunity to reorganize without the disruption that would result if a bankruptcy trustee was appointed.

Because no trustee is appointed, the debtor in possession has the rights, powers, and duties of a **Chapter 11 trustee** except the right to compensation and the duty to investigate the acts, conduct, assets, liabilities, and financial condition of the debtor. 11 U.S.C.A. §§ 1107(a), 1106(a)(3), (4). With few exceptions, all references to "trustee" in the Bankruptcy Code apply equally to a debtor in possession. Consequently, the debtor in possession effectively serves as its own bankruptcy trustee and is expected to manage the business, file the quarterly reports required by the United States trustee (see Fed. R. Bank. P. 2015(a)(5)) and pay the quarterly fee required by 28 U.S.C.A. § 1930(a)(6), make whatever operational changes are necessary to develop a plan of reorganization (such as returning the business to profitability or identifying assets that can be sold), and perform the fiduciary duties of a bankruptcy trustee, including avoiding preferential transfers and fraudulent conveyances made prior to the bankruptcy filing. The exercise of the trustee's fiduciary duties is oftentimes not easy because it may entail taking actions that are adverse to the person who is charged with performing the duties of the debtor in possession. For instance, a debtor in possession may, as a fiduciary, be required to file a complaint against a creditor to avoid a preferential payment, even though the person in charge of the debtor in possession has guaranteed the debt owed to the creditor.

A debtor in possession will not always be allowed to remain in control of the assets of the estate. At the request of a party in interest, including the United States trustee, the court may order the United States trustee to appoint a trustee for cause (such as fraud, dishonesty, incompetence, or gross mismanagement, either before or after the commencement of the case), or simply because the court determines that the appointment is in the best interests of creditors, equity security holders or the bankruptcy estate. 11 U.S.C.A. § 1104(a). When a trustee is appointed, the debtor ceases to be a debtor in possession. The trustee's duties are outlined in 11 U.S.C.A. § 1106. The appointment of a Chapter 11 trustee is a drastic measure, particularly at the early stages of a Chapter 11 case, but if the court determines that it is in the best interests of the estate to do so, the court has the authority to order the appointment of a trustee.

Once the court orders the appointment of a trustee, the Chapter 11 trustee is actually appointed by the United States trustee. Upon the request of a party in interest, however, made not later than 30 days after the court orders the appointment of a trustee, the United States trustee shall convene a meeting of creditors to afford creditors the opportunity to elect a trustee under the same procedure as in a Chapter 7 case. 11 U.S.C.A. §§ 1104(b), 702.

If the court is not convinced that the appointment of a Chapter 11 trustee is warranted, the court may, instead, order the appointment of an examiner to conduct an investigation of the debtor and to report to the court. However, upon the request of a party in interest, the court shall appoint an examiner if the debtor's fixed, liquidated, unsecured debts, other than debts for goods, services, or taxes, or owing to an insider, exceed five million dollars. 11 U.S.C.A. § 1104(c).

2. Operation of the Debtor's Business

Unless the court orders otherwise, the debtor in possession may continue to operate the debtor's business without any specific court approval. 11 U.S.C.A. § 1108. The Code allows this because it would simply be too cumbersome to require court approval of every transaction by the debtor in possession. A trustee or debtor in possession may also use, sell, or lease property of the estate, in the ordinary course of business, without court approval. 11 U.S.C.A. § 363(b). Because of the fundamental policy of treating all creditors equally and because the date the petition is filed is known as the point of cleavage, there is a strict prohibition against paying any prebankruptcy debt after the bankruptcy filing outside of a confirmed Chapter 11 plan or without specific court approval. The relationship between the debtor and creditors is fixed as of the time of the filing of the petition, and the Bankruptcy Code strives to maintain that status despite the debtor's operation of its business and the resulting postpetition use of assets.

3. Use of Cash Collateral

Special rules apply if the property to be used by a debtor in possession is cash collateral, defined in 11 U.S.C.A. § 363(a). Cash collateral is cash or cash equivalents generated from collateral secured to a creditor of the debtor. For instance, the cash generated from the sale of inventory or cash generated from the collection of accounts receivable are cash collateral if the inventory or accounts are subject to a lien or security interest. The debtor in possession may not use the cash in the operation of its business without either the consent of the creditor or an order of the court. 11 U.S.C.A. § 363(c)(2). Therefore, even though, in the ordinary course of its business, the debtor may sell the inventory or collect the accounts, it may not use the money generated therefrom without the consent of the secured creditor or the court. The purpose of this requirement is to prevent the dissipation of the creditor's collateral without protecting the creditor's interest in the collateral—in bankruptcy terms, providing adequate protection. Because cash is so easily dissipated, the burden is on the debtor in possession to provide adequate protection as a condition of using cash collateral.

4. Adequate Protection

Creditors with a lien or security interest in property of the estate are entitled to adequate protection even if their collateral is not cash collateral. At the request of an entity with an interest—such as a security interest—in property that the debtor in possession uses, sells, or leases in the operation of its business, the court will prohibit or condition the use, sale, or lease of such property unless the creditor's interest is adequately protected. 11 U.S.C.A. § 363(e). **Adequate protection** is defined in 11 U.S.C.A. § 361. Generally, adequate protection is whatever protection is needed to maintain the value of the creditor's interest in the collateral despite the debtor's postpetition use, sale, or lease of it. The form of adequate protection will differ depending upon the type of collateral involved. For instance, adequate protection of the inventory of a store requires that the inventory be adequately insured and that the value of the inventory during the pendency of the Chapter 11 bankruptcy case not fall below the lesser of the amount of the creditor's claim or the value of the inventory when the bankruptcy petition was filed. Conversely, if the collateral is a delivery truck, adequate protection requires that the vehicle be adequately insured against loss and, if there is no equity in the vehicle, that the creditor receive periodic payments for the depreciation of the vehicle. A debtor is not required to pay interest on an undersecured claim (the value of the collateral is less than the amount owed to the creditor) as a condition of adequate protection. *United Savings Ass'n of Texas v. Timbers of Inwood Forest Associates, Ltd.*, 484 U.S. 365 (1988).

5. Employment of Professionals

The debtor in possession will need the assistance of attorneys and other professionals to navigate the minefield of Chapter 11 bankruptcy. An attorney that represents a debtor under any chapter of the Bankruptcy Code must file a Statement of Attorney's Compensation, indicating the amount paid to the attorney and the terms of the representation. 11 U.S.C.A. § 329(a), Fed. R. Bank. P. 2016(b).

Since the attorney and other professionals effectively represent the bankruptcy estate, the court must approve their employment by the debtor in possession. 11 U.S.C.A. § 327(a); Fed. R. Bank. P. 2014(a). The person to be employed must not hold or represent an interest adverse to the estate, and must be disinterested as that term is defined in 11 U.S.C.A. § 101(14) meaning generally that they may not be themselves a creditor of the debtor. 11 U.S.C.A. § 327(a). The application to employ the professional must disclose the necessity for the employment, the reason for the person's selection, the professional services to be rendered, the terms of compensation, and all the persons connections with the debtor, creditors, any other parties in interest, their respective attorneys, accountants, the United States trustee, and any person employed in the office of the United States trustee. A verified statement of the professional to be employed that contains this information must accompany the application. Fed. R. Bank. P. 2014(a). The purpose for the disclosure is to permit the court to determine that the professional is truly disinterested.

The professional may be employed under any terms that are reasonable, including a fixed fee, hourly fee, or contingency fee. Regardless of whether the court approved the terms of employment, if such terms prove to be improvident in light of developments not known at the time of the employment, the court may alter the terms of compensation. 11 U.S.C.A. § 329(a). If it is later discovered that the professional was not disinterested or represents an interest adverse to the estate, the court may deny compensation to the professional and may order the disgorgement of fees previously allowed and paid. 11 U.S.C.A. § 329(c).

A professional who seeks to be paid from the bankruptcy estate must file a fee application and have it approved by the court under the standards of 11 U.S.C.A. § 330. The fees must be reasonable for services and expenses actually rendered and incurred that were necessary at the time. Unless the court orders otherwise, an application for compensation may be filed not more than once every 120 days after the order for relief. Fees and expenses that are approved by the court are allowed as administrative claims. 11 U.S.C.A. § 503(b)(2). Administrative claims must be paid on the effective date of a Chapter 11 plan unless the holder of the claim agrees to a different treatment. 11 U.S.C.A. § 1129(a)(9)(A).

6. Obtaining Credit

The DIP or the trustee authorized to operate the business of the debtor may obtain unsecured credit and incur unsecured debt in the ordinary course of business unless the court orders otherwise. Court authorization is necessary, however, for the debtor to obtain unsecured credit or incur unsecured debt out of the ordinary course of business. Creditors in both instances have an administrative expense priority, which makes it easier for the DIP to obtain credit. 11 U.S.C.A. §§ 364, 503(b)(1). If the debtor is unable to obtain unsecured credit allowable as an administrative expense, other more complex alternatives are afforded by the Code. 11 U.S.C.A. §§ 364(c), (d).

7. Utility Services

The uninterrupted continuation of utility services is imperative to the survival of a debtor's business. For this reason the Code affords protection from loss of such services that might otherwise occur because of the filing of a bankruptcy case or because the debtor had not paid, when due, a debt owed for service rendered before the order for relief. 11 U.S.C.A. § 366(a). The DIP or the trustee, however, must furnish adequate assurance of payment, in the form of a deposit or other security, within 20 days after the order for relief has been entered. Modification of the amount necessary for adequate assurance may be made by the court, after notice and a hearing, upon request of a party in interest.

8. Shedding Burdensome Collective Bargaining Contracts

The Chapter 11 DIP or the trustee may, subject to the court's approval, assume or reject any executory contract or unexpired lease of the debtor. 11 U.S.C.A. § 365(a). This provision of the Code has proved invaluable to the DIP in shedding burdensome collective bargaining agreements and in assuming leases of real property essential to a reorganization plan or rejecting such leases that are unnecessary to the plan.

The creative use of reorganization under the bankruptcy laws to deal with burdensome collective bargaining contracts is best illustrated by the *Continental Airlines* case. *In re Continental Airlines Corp.*, 38 B.R. 67 (Bankr.S.D.Tex.1984). On September 24, 1983, Continental Airlines filed a petition for reorganization under Chapter 11. Continental admitted that a primary motivation for its filing was a desire to reduce operating costs in addition to its inability to negotiate concessions from its employees' unions. At the time of the filing, Continental was still flying and had substantial net worth and working capital. It had not been forced by a cash flow crisis into a "nonoperating" Chapter 11, as had been the case with Braniff Airways. Upon filing, Continental rejected its collective bargaining agreements with its employees and imposed unilateral wage reductions and work rule changes.

When the unions moved to dismiss the petition, the bankruptcy judge denied their motion. The judge found that Continental was, in fact, in a severe and terminal financial crisis. The judge found that Continental had a long and continuing history of mounting financial losses, was shortly going to run out of operating capital, had no credit or unencumbered assets, and had no prospects for raising cash sufficient to continue operating for a reasonable time. Because management had no alternative to filing the petition, except almost certain operational failure and possible liquidation, the filing of the petition was proper and necessary.

9. Dealing with Pending and Future Litigation

Another creative use of reorganization under the bankruptcy laws is to deal with pending and future litigation. This strategy is best illustrated by the *Manville* case. *In re Johns-Manville Corp.*, 26 B.R. 420 (Bankr.S.D.N.Y.1983). The Johns-Manville Corporation, a Fortune 500 company, was a diversified manufacturing, mining, and forest products company that conducted its business through five principal operating subsidiaries. Manville was the world's largest miner, processor, manufacturer, and supplier of asbestos and asbestos-containing products. After the link between asbestos and cancer became well known, Manville became the target of thousands of products liability claims. By September 1982, 16,500 asbestos-related lawsuits had been filed against the Manville Corporation. The company estimated that this was less than one-third of a projected 52,000 asbestos-related lawsuits that could be brought against it in the next 20 years. Manville projected that the lawsuits could cost the company $2 billion.

On September 2, 1982, Johns-Manville Corporation and 20 of its subsidiaries or affiliates, in an attempt to reduce the burdens placed on them by these suits, filed for reorganization under Chapter 11. At the time of the filing, Manville was a profitable, solvent corporation with 25,000 employees. Its net worth exceeded $1.1 billion, its long-term debt was less than $500 million, its short-term debt was just over $100 million, and its sales for 1981 exceeded $2 billion. By filing for reorganization, the Manville Corporation hoped to find an orderly manner of dealing with these cases and a method of providing a finite sum (a fund) for dealing with the cases arising in the future.

The Manville strategy provided an orderly manner of dealing with the asbestos cases and a cap on its aggregate liability, and saved the company. Some analysts, however, predicted that the cost of the reorganization strategy to the stockholders of the Manville Corporation could be high.

On October 3, 1988, the United States Supreme Court refused to hear the last appeal on Manville's reorganization plan. The plan required Johns-Manville Corporation to establish two trust funds. The first, a trust fund for property damage claims, would start with $330 million in cash and receive $250,000 a year from the Manville Corporation. The second, a trust fund for personal injury claims, would have a role in selecting company directors and would start with $675 million in cash and receive $160 million from Manville's insurers over the next three years; $1.85 billion in notes and bonds, repayable in regular installments by 2014; and 20 percent of Manville's net income, beginning in 1992. If the Manville payments to the fund do not meet claims as they are settled, the trust could claim 50 percent of the outstanding shares in the corporation (estimated at $180 million). The trust's claim could be increased to 80 percent.

The Manville strategy has had a profound effect on all asbestos-related tort claims and has led the way for other solvent companies who face massive tort liability. Industries producing tobacco, chemicals, or pharmaceutical products, if threatened by large-scale products liability claims, may find comfort, however cold, in a reorganization filing to limit the aggregate size of their current and future liability.

The Code now includes a procedure for dealing with the future personal injury claims in a Chapter 11 case that arise from exposure to asbestos-containing products. This procedure involves the creation of a trust to pay the future claims, coupled with an injunction to prevent future claimants from suing the debtor. 11 U.S.C.A. § 524(g).

C. EVIDENCE OF DEBTOR IN POSSESSION (DIP) STATUS

The debtor often needs evidence of debtor in possession status to continue business operations. After all, the debtor in possession is its own fiduciary and has the powers of a bankruptcy trustee. Lending institutions and suppliers, however, may be reluctant to deal with the Chapter 11 debtor without some official assurance of the debtor's status. The clerk of the bankruptcy court may certify the DIP status of the debtor. This certificate constitutes conclusive evidence of such status. Fed. R. Bank. P. 2011. Procedural Form No. B207 serves this purpose. (See Exhibit 8–5.)

D. EXEMPTIONS

Only individuals are eligible for exemptions. Partnerships and corporations are not allowed exemptions. The scheduling and determination of exemptions in a Chapter 11 case are done in the same way as exemptions in a Chapter 7 case. There is, however, an important difference in the way nonexempt property is handled in Chapter 7 and in Chapter 11 cases. In a Chapter 7 case, property that exceeds the limits on exemptions is sold by the trustee, who then uses the proceeds to pay creditors. A DIP in a Chapter 11 case retains possession of *all* property, except as otherwise provided by the plan. The best interests of creditors test, however, must be met before confirmation of a plan. This test is determined by the amount of property that would be nonexempt under Chapter 7 and therefore available for payment of creditors. "Best interests of creditors" means that a creditor or an interest holder whose claim is impaired under a Chapter 11 plan must accept the plan *or* must receive no less under the plan than it would receive under Chapter 7. 11 U.S.C.A. § 1129(a)(7).

If, however, a party in interest in a case in which the debtor is a small business (defined in 11 U.S.C.A. § 101(51C)) requests, for cause shown, the court may order that no committee be appointed. 11 U.S.C.A. § 1102(a)(3).

EXHIBIT 8–5 Procedural Form B 207 (Certificate of Retention of Debtor in Possession)

B 207
(6/91)

United States Bankruptcy Court

_______________ District Of _______________

In re

Case No. __________

Debtor*
Social Security No.:
Employer's Tax I.D. No. [if any]:

Chapter ________

CERTIFICATE OF RETENTION OF DEBTOR IN POSSESSION

I hereby certify that the above-named debtor continues in possession of its estate as debtor in possession, no trustee having been appointed.

____
Clerk of the Bankruptcy Court

______________________ By: ______________________________
Date Deputy Clerk

**Set forth all names, including trade names, used by the debtor within the last 6 years. (Fed. R. Bankr. P. 1005). For joint debtors set forth both social security numbers.*

SECTION 3
THE CHAPTER 11 PLAN

A **Chapter 11 reorganization plan** must be filed showing how the debtor intends to surmount its financial difficulties so it can once more become a viable business and how the debtor intends to pay debt. In a voluntary Chapter 11 case, the debtor may file a reorganization plan along with the petition or at any time after the filing of the petition. 11 U.S.C.A. § 1121(a).

The debtor has the exclusive right to file a plan for 120 days after the filing of the petition (i.e., after the order for relief) unless the court has appointed a trustee or the court, for cause, has reduced or increased this exclusive time period. 11 U.S.C.A. §§ 1121(b)–(d). If the debtor files a plan within this 120-day period, the debtor has an additional 60 days to obtain acceptance of the plan by each class of claims or interests impaired under the plan. Therefore, the debtor's exclusive period expires if the debtor does not file a plan within 120 days after the filing of the petition or does not obtain the required acceptances of the plan within 180 days after the filing of the petition. If the debtor obtains the necessary acceptances within the 180-day exclusive period, no other party in interest may file a plan.

EXAMPLE

Fern Nicholson, dba Fern's Graphics and Design, filed a petition in bankruptcy under Chapter 11 on March 1. Fern has the exclusive right to file a plan through June 28, which is 120 days from March 1. If Fern files a plan on June 1, a date within the 120-day period, she will have through August 27, which is 180 days from March 1, to obtain the required acceptances of the plan.

PROBLEM 8.1 If Fern files a plan on June 28, by what date must she have obtained the required acceptance of the plan?

The filing and acceptance of the plan are independent of the confirmation of the plan. This is important to the debtor because the confirmation hearing may not take place until long after the exclusive period has elapsed.

If a debtor requests an increase in the exclusive filing period for the plan, an increase in the time period for obtaining the acceptances should also be requested to get the full benefit of the extension.

EXAMPLE

Fern Nicholson, dba Fern's Graphics and Design, filed a petition in bankruptcy under Chapter 11 on March 1. Fern has the exclusive right to file a plan through June 28, which is 120 days from March 1. On June 1, Fern requested a 30-day extension in the exclusive filing period. Fern did not request an extension in the time period required to obtain the acceptances of the plan. If Fern files a plan on July 20, she will still have only through August 27, which is 180 days from March 1, to obtain the required acceptances of the plan.

28 U.S.C.A. § 148(a)(2) has been amended to cut down on excessive extensions of the debtor's exclusive 120-day period in which to file a reorganization plan. This amendment allows an immediate appeal to the district court from an extension or a reduction of that period.

A. STRATEGIES UTILIZED IN REORGANIZATION PLANS

A proponent of a reorganization plan may use one or more strategies in designing a plan. The strategy or strategies chosen by the proponent should be based on a realistic assessment of the debtor's activities and future. Commonly used strategies are

1. recapitalization by selling some assets, borrowing some money, or issuing securities;
2. rejection or assumption of executory contracts;

3. dealing with pending and future litigation;
4. merger or consolidation;
5. bootstrap; or
6. liquidation of all assets.

Recapitalization may be managed by the sale of some of the debtor's assets or by borrowing more money. For either to be successful, the debtor must have unencumbered assets that may be sold or pledged as security for new loans. If incorporated, the debtor may issue company stock to investors to fund a plan. Stock may also be issued to creditors in lieu of cash payments. If stock is issued, the debtor is exempt from federal, state, or local securities laws under the Code. 11 U.S.C.A. § 1145. For this reason, the debtor is required to file with the court and to transmit to each holder of a claim or interest a disclosure statement providing "adequate information" to allow an informed judgment to be made on the proposed plan. 11 U.S.C.A. § 1125.

Executory contracts, including unexpired leases and collective bargaining agreements, may be rejected by a debtor in possession or a trustee. 11 U.S.C.A. §§ 365, 1113. If the executory contract is a collective bargaining agreement, the employees affected under an agreement must have an authorized representative to evaluate the proposed modifications. Meetings will be held by the DIP or trustee with the employees' representative to attempt to reach mutually satisfying modifications of the agreement. The application for rejection of a collective bargaining agreement must be ruled on by the bankruptcy court. 11 U.S.C.A. § 1113.

The debtor may seek reorganization to deal with pending and future litigation. The risks that emanate from pending and future litigation might threaten the existence of the debtor. By filing a petition in bankruptcy under Chapter 11, a plan can be developed for controlling the litigation process and a cap can be placed on the debtor's liability.

The debtor might reorganize by a merger with a related or unrelated company or consolidation with a related company. The debtor's net operating losses may benefit the other company as a tax write-off. Tax consequences of a proposed plan should always be determined before going forward.

The **bootstrap plan** will not require new money from outside sources. As the name implies, a bootstrap plan involves funding a plan through the debtor's ability to produce income either through ongoing activities or by a partial liquidation of assets. This is sometimes called an internal plan and is the most difficult to implement because of the debtor's reluctance to change operating methods. Many debtors engage in a type of magical thinking, imagining that the methods that may have worked in the past will work in the future, even though they are not working in the present.

A plan involving liquidation of all assets will be a last resort in many Chapter 11 cases and will be proposed only if the debtor has no realistic hopes of regaining its status as a viable operation. As a general rule, a debtor clearly has a right to proceed to terminate its business as it wishes, and to use Chapter 11 as the basis for filing a liquidating plan. In most cases there is little prospect of dissent from creditors to the confirmation of the liquidating plan. Creditors rarely, if ever, believe that a business should continue if its managers have concluded otherwise.

Liquidation under Chapter 11 may be more beneficial to creditors than liquidation under Chapter 7. The debtor in possession is in a better position than a trustee would be to collect accounts receivable and to sell assets, particularly such things as inventory. Although the DIP may not be able to get the prices for assets normally available to an operating business, the amount obtained to pay creditors will generally still exceed what might be obtained in a Chapter 7 auction. For this reason, some Chapter 11 cases are filed with the intention of proposing a liquidating plan. This is permitted under the Code even though Chapter 11 is entitled "Reorganization." 11 U.S.C.A. § 1123(b)(4).

There are cases in which some of the assets of the debtor may be sold prior to confirmation of a plan. There may even be distribution of the proceeds from such a sale prior to confirmation if the creditor can establish extraordinary circumstances to justify immediate distribution.

In the following case, *In re Conroe Forge & Manufacturing Corporation,* the debtor filed an emergency motion to sell a piece of heavy equipment, free and clear of liens, and the bankruptcy court granted this request. After the sale, Mellon Bank, a creditor holding an unsecured claim, requested the immediate payment of the proceeds from the sale. The court, in *Conroe,* evaluated whether extraordinary circumstances existed that would require the immediate payment of proceeds.

In re Conroe Forge & Manufacturing Corporation

1988. 82 B.R. 781 (Bankr. W.D. Pa. 1988)

MEMORANDUM OPINION
Judith K. Fitzgerald, Bankruptcy Judge

The matter presently before the Court is secured creditor Mellon Bank's oral request, made at a hearing on Debtor's motion to sell free and clear, to receive immediate payment of proceeds of sale of a piece of heavy machinery.

Mellon Bank has submitted a "Memorandum of Law In Support of the Proposition that, When a Secured Creditor's Collateral is Sold Pursuant to 11 U.S.C. § 363 in a Liquidating Chapter 11 Case, the Proceeds of Sale May Be Distributed Immediately to the Secured Creditor." The Court finds the facts to be as follows.

Conroe Forge & Manufacturing Corporation (Debtor) is a corporation formerly engaged in the business of manufacturing die forgings. The Debtor's sole manufacturing facility is located in Conroe, Texas.

Debtor filed a petition for relief under Chapter 11 of the Bankruptcy Code in the United States Bankruptcy Court for the Western District of Pennsylvania on November 6, 1987, after having ceased operations. Debtor is a Debtor-in-Possession and does not intend to resume its manufacturing operations.[1] According to the Debtor's schedules, Mellon Bank holds a security interest in Debtor's land, buildings, machinery and equipment and is owed $2,254,004.51. The Debtor has valued these assets in its schedules at $1,909,360.77. Of this amount $440,831.69 represents the value of real estate pursuant to a tax assessment which may or may not reflect the fair market value of the realty.

In early December, the Debtor filed an emergency motion to sell certain machinery free and clear of liens, claims and encumbrances and a request that the Court shorten the notice period and conduct an expedited hearing. Mellon Bank did not oppose and the Court granted the requests. A hearing was held on December 23, 1987, because Interstate Drop Forge Company (Buyer) had an immediate need for the equipment and its offer would expire if it was not able to transport the machinery to Wisconsin before the Wisconsin Frost Laws went into effect. The Wisconsin Frost Laws prohibit movement of heavy machinery and the like over Wisconsin roads during certain winter months. From these facts, the absence of any relationship between Debtor and Buyer, the utilization of an independent broker and Mellon Bank's consent to the sale, the Court finds that a bona fide emergency existed and that the Buyer acted in good faith.

The gross sales price offered by Buyer was $149,000.00 which was represented without contradiction to be a fair and reasonable price. There were no other bidders at the hearing. At the request of the Debtor and with the consent of all parties who were present at the sale and hearing on this motion, the Court confirmed the sale and directed that a 10% (ten percent) brokerage commission be paid out of these gross receipts and an additional amount be placed in escrow pending resolution of the broker's claim for reimbursement of expenses.

Also escrowed was $7,200.00 representing a claim by Victoria Machine Works for repair charges allegedly secured by a repairman's possessory lien on a component of one of the presses. Victoria Machine Works agreed to turn over the piece in order that the Buyer would complete the sale inasmuch as the component increases the useful life of the machinery and, therefore, its absence would affect the sale. Debtor filed an adversary action to require Victoria Machine Works to turn over the component. Victoria Machine Works did not have an opportunity to respond to the adversary complaint prior to the sale but did agree to release the component to facilitate the sale. Victoria Machine Works has asserted that its response to the adversary complaint will claim that approximately $43,000 is due for repair work on the machinery sold. Therefore, at the hearing on December 23, 1987, Victoria Machine Works argued that the amount of its entire claim should be escrowed pending the outcome of the trial on the adversary proceeding. Thus, there is a dispute concerning the appropriate disposition to be made of these funds.

Mellon Bank argued that in order to adequately protect its interest, the Court must apply either 11 U.S.C. § 361(1) or the "indubitable equivalen[ce]" language of 11 U.S.C. § 361(3) and must authorize the immediate payment to Mellon Bank of the net proceeds of sale. Mellon Bank did not deny the Court's suggestion that 11 U.S.C. § 361(2), which permits a lien substitution to proceeds, would provide that protection; rather, Mellon Bank's position is that it would benefit more from immediate payment. The motion to sell free and clear specifically provided for the transfer of all liens to proceeds. On January 13, 1988, this Court entered an Order requiring that all proceeds be escrowed except for amounts previously authorized to be paid to the broker.

DISCUSSION

Bankruptcy Rule 3021 provides:

> After confirmation of a plan, distribution shall be made to creditors whose claims have been allowed. . . .

This provision is the successor to former Bankruptcy Rule 10–405(a) which is derived from § 224(3) of the Bankruptcy Act. Rule 10–405(a) provided that ". . . after confirmation of a plan distribution shall be made . . . to . . . creditors whose claims have been allowed. . . ." The problem in the case at bar arises from Bankruptcy Code § 1123(b)(4) which enables Debtors to structure a liquidation through a plan and states, in substance, that a plan *may* provide for the sale of all or substantially all estate assets and the distribution of proceeds.

The general rule is that distribution should not occur except pursuant to a confirmed plan of reorganization, absent extraordinary circumstances. *Abbotts Dairies of Pennsylvania, Inc.*, 788 F.2d 143 (3d Cir. 1986). *See* 6A Collier on Bankruptcy, ¶ 11.14 (14th ed. 1977). *See also* 11 U.S.C. § 1123(a)(5) (plan must provide adequate means for implementation); and Bankruptcy Rule 3021.

It is within the discretion of the Bankruptcy Court to determine whether extraordinary circumstances exist so that sale proceeds may be paid to creditors outside the confines of a plan. *Cf. In re Lilly C. Anderson*, 833 F.2d 834, 836 (9th Cir.1987) (concerning award of postpetition interest but denial of "lost opportunity" compensation to oversecured creditor after sale of collateral by Trustee appointed to conduct sale in apparent Chapter 11 where no plan had been confirmed). *See also, In re Industrial Office Building Corp.*, 171 F.2d 890, 892 (3d Cir.1949) (authorizing interim distribution of funds in excess of those needed for reorganization).

In re Braniff Airways, Inc., 700 F.2d 935 (5th Cir.1983) (rehearing and rehearing en banc denied), concerned a sale of a substantial portion of Debtor's assets before a plan had been confirmed. The appellate court found that the terms of sale would have dictated the plan provisions without circulation of a proposed plan. The sale was not permitted. Although the facts of the case at bar are not on point with those of *Braniff*, this court finds persuasive the Fifth Circuit's opinion that, first, Chapter 11's confirmation requirements (herein a plan and disclosure statement) should not be short-circuited and, second, approval of preplan distributions in liquidating Chapter 11 cases would leave little incentive for completing the requirements of the disclosure statement and plan preparatory to a reorganization by way of liquidation. *Id.* at 940.

The policy behind Chapter 11 reorganization is successful rehabilitation. *NLRB v. Bildisco and Bildisco*, 465 U.S. 513, 527, 104 S.Ct. 1188, 1196, 79 L.Ed.2d 482 (1984). However, the concept of reorganization includes liquidation. *In re Koopmans*, 22 B.R. 395, 398 (Bank.D.Utah1982). *See also In re Industrial Office Building Corp., supra*, 171 F.2d at 892. This Court, therefore, must determine whether the property, herein proceeds, is necessary for an effective reorganization. *See In re Keller*, 45 B.R. 469, 471 (Bank.N.D.Iowa1984). In a liquidating Chapter 11 where Debtor has ceased operations and collateral value is not decreasing, ordinarily all property will be necessary for an effective reorganization. "Necessary" property has been defined as that which " 'will contribute' to a plan of reorganization." *In re 6200 Ridge, Inc.*, 69 B.R. 837, 843 (BankE.D.Pa.1987). If, as in this case, circumstances require confirmation of a sale before a liquidating plan has been confirmed, the proceeds, which will be earning interest, are necessary to the plan which presumably will provide for the sale of the rest of Debtor's assets and distribution of proceeds.[2] *Cf.* 11 U.S.C. § 1123(a)(5) (plan must provide adequate means for implementation).

If distribution is made to creditors in a liquidating Chapter 11 before confirmation of a plan there will be little incentive for parties in interest to prosecute the case in an expeditious manner much less to perform the work required to issue and obtain approval of a disclosure statement and plan. *See In re Braniff Airways, Inc., supra*, 700 F.2d at 940; *In re Jartran, Inc.*, 71 B.R. 938, 942 and n. 6 (Bank.N.D.Ill.,E.D.1987) (court rejected argument that because debtor's case was a liquidating Chapter 11 it should be treated as a Chapter 7 for distribution purposes). In addition, if distribution of assets occurs before confirmation, there will exist no means by which a plan may be implemented. Such a course would violate § 1123(a)(5).

Moreover, Bankruptcy Rule 3021 provides that distribution pursuant to a Chapter 11 plan is authorized only with respect to *allowed* claims. The amount of Mellon Bank's allowed claim has not been determined and could depend on many factors, including, *inter alia,* the terms of a proposed plan, whether or not the plan is accepted, and whether or not the case suffers conversion to a Chapter 7.

The crux of Mellon Bank's argument is that even if it eventually receives the proceeds of sale plus interest it would receive a much greater return if it is paid the proceeds now and is able to use them in the ordinary course of its business. In support of this position, Mellon Bank relies on *In re American Mariner Industries, Inc.,* 734 F.2d 426 (9th Cir.1984), where, in deciding a motion for relief from stay, the court held that the secured creditor was entitled to compensation for the delay it had suffered in enforcing its rights in order to give it, as nearly as possible, the benefit of its bargain.

The United States Supreme Court recently discussed the concept that an undersecured creditor is not entitled to compensation for the delay occasioned by the automatic stay provisions of the Code. In *United Savings Association of Texas v. Timbers of Inwood Forest Associates, Ltd.,* ___U.S.___, 108 S.Ct. 626, 98 L.Ed.2d 740 (1988), the Court stated that "the undersecured petitioner [creditor] is not entitled to interest on its collateral during the stay to assure adequate protection under 11 U.S.C. § 362(d)(1)." *Id.* at ___, 108 S.Ct. at 635. In the case at bar, as in *Timbers of Inwood,* the undersecured creditor has not sought relief from stay under § 362(d)(2) or on any other ground, but merely raised the issue of what constitutes adequate protection.[3] To the extent that *Timbers of Inwood* discussed the payment of interest for use of an undersecured creditor's collateral during the automatic stay period, this Court finds it apposite to the instant case, and finds that *American Mariner,* which discussed a similar premise after a creditor applied for relief from stay, to be inapposite.[4] Even so, Mellon Bank's interest in the value of its collateral is preserved because the sale itself determined the value of the collateral and the sales proceeds, to which Mellon Bank's lien now attaches, are escrowed.

At the hearing in the instant matter Mellon Bank's counsel indicated that it was his opinion that Mellon Bank is undersecured and not secured in all assets and probably would sustain a deficiency. Furthermore, counsel did not know whether Debtor's obligation to Mellon Bank had been accelerated by reason of default. These factors, coupled with those discussed above, lead the Court to find that escrowing the proceeds at interest adequately protects Mellon Bank's interest. In addition, Mellon Bank has shown no basis upon which immediate payment of the net proceeds of sale would be required to afford it adequate protection nor why substitution of liens denies adequate protection. Whether or not Mellon Bank receives the indubitable equivalent of its claim, as argued at the hearing, is a matter for determination at the time of plan confirmation, *Timbers of Inwood, supra,* __U.S. at __, 108 S.Ct. at 632–33, especially where the value of its security has not been determined and where there is, as in this case, Debtor's assurance that it has prepared a liquidating plan.[5]

This Court also notes that case law in the Third Circuit which construed certain provisions of former Chapter XI of the Bankruptcy Act established that a sale of assets before confirmation of a plan is permissible only on the basis of a demonstrated emergency. "Emergency" was defined as an "imminent danger that the assets of the ailing business will be lost if prompt action is not taken." *In re Solar Manufacturing Corp.,* 176 F.2d 493, 494 (3d Cir.1949). *Compare In re White Motor Credit Corp.,* 14 B.R. 584, 4 C.B.C.2d 1562 (Bank.N.D.Ohio1981). *And see Matter of Mesta Machine Co.,* 30 B.R. 178 (Bank.W.D.Pa.1983) (concerning a Code case filed in the Western District of Pennsylvania pursuant to Chapter 11).[6] If the sale itself is permissible only in the most exigent circumstances absent confirmation of a Chapter 11 plan, distribution of the proceeds will require, at minimum, a showing of similar immediate need. That a creditor could receive a better return through immediate payment does not mean that the creditor is not adequately protected by substitution of liens to proceeds especially where the proceeds are escrowed at interest pending confirmation of a liquidating plan, and when the secured creditor agreed to the Debtor's motion for sale providing for transference of liens to proceeds.

Mellon Bank cites various Code provisions in support of its argument that this Court may order immediate payment; however, whether or not the Court may so order is not the issue. The issue is whether the best interests of all parties in interest will be served by the course of action requested. *See Matter of Realty Associates Securities Corp.,* 58 F.Supp. 220 (E.D.N.Y.1944) (regarding distribution of excess cash). *See also In re Industrial Office Building Corp.,*

171 F.2d at 893. At the time of the hearing on the sale a creditor's committee had not been appointed in this case. Furthermore, this case was only a few weeks old and, in this Court's view, an adequate opportunity to examine Debtor's affairs and/or negotiate and/or form a plan of reorganization had not been provided. There is no dispute that the sale was for a fair and reasonable price and in the best interest of creditors because a delay would have meant either the loss of the sale or a postponement until after the winter months with corresponding loss to the value of the collateral itself. In addition, a liquidating plan has been proposed which includes suggested distribution of proceeds to classes of creditors. Thus creditors are provided an opportunity to examine the proposal for liquidation pursuant to the plan and disclosure statement in accordance with the policy and spirit of Chapter 11 of the Bankruptcy Code. *See* H.R. No. 95–595 (1977), U.S.Code Cong. & Admin.News 1978, p. 5787 (Chapter 11 "incorporates the essence of the protection features of . . . Chapter X").

Furthermore, § 1106 provides, in pertinent part:

(a) A trustee shall—

(5) . . . file a plan . . . a report of why the trustee will not file a plan, or recommend conversion . . . or dismissal. . . .

Pursuant to § 1107(a) a debtor-in-possession is charged with the obligations of a trustee. No justification exists, based on the instant facts and the provisions and policies of the Bankruptcy Code, to order remittance of proceeds to Mellon Bank before confirmation of a plan or reorganization.

CONCLUSION

In accordance with the foregoing, this Court holds that in this liquidating Chapter 11 case where there has been a sale of assets prior to confirmation of a plan and an undersecured creditor has not established that immediate payment to it of proceeds of sale is required for adequate protection, there will be no distribution until a plan is confirmed. *See* H.R. No. 95–595, 95th Cong., 1st Sess. (1977) (the purpose of reorganization "is to form and have confirmed a plan of reorganization").

If Mellon Bank believes that it is suffering unduly through the pendency of this Chapter 11, it has many courses of action to choose from under the Bankruptcy Code. At this point and in this particular matter Mellon Bank is adequately protected by the substitution of liens to proceeds and payment of proceeds prior to plan confirmation will be and hereby is denied in accordance with the Order of this Court dated January 13, 1988.

---

[1]In fact, albeit after the sale involved herein, Debtor filed a disclosure statement and a liquidating Chapter 11 plan. As yet, there has been no hearing on the disclosure statement or plan.

[2]The plan proposed by Debtor but as yet uncirculated to creditors does precisely this.

[3]The Court emphasizes that this issue was raised by the creditor after it consented to a sale free and clear of liens and encumbrances with transfer of liens and encumbrances to proceeds.

[4]Of further note is that the Bankruptcy Court for the Eastern District of Pennsylvania has chosen to disagree with *American Mariner* insofar as that case may require compensation for delay to every undersecured creditor in every case. *In re Grant Broadcasting of Philadelphia, Inc.*, 71 B.R. 376, 388 (Bank.E.D.Pa.1987). This court agrees that adequate protection depends on the circumstances of each case.

[5]Debtor's liquidating plan was filed with the court while this opinion was pending.

[6]This Court is aware of the opinion of the Bankruptcy Court for the Eastern District of Pennsylvania in *In re Industrial Valley Refrigeration and Air Conditioning Supplies, Inc.*, 77 B.R. 15 (Bank.E.D.Pa.1987), which held that the Third Circuit's decision in *Abbotts Dairies* implicitly overruled *Solar Manufacturing* and that therefore "the Third Circuit has . . . abandoned the 'emergency-only' standard . . . enunciated in *Solar Manufacturing*," adopting instead a test which includes as an element a showing of a "sound business purpose." 77 B.R. at 20, 21. This Court's examination of *Abbotts Dairies* revealed that an emergency sale was the event which triggered the appeal, 788 F.2d at 144–45, that the question of exigent circumstances was not at issue having been found by the district court to exist, and that the only issue before the Third Circuit and on remand was the existence of good faith between Debtor and Buyer. Nonetheless, this Court finds that the more stringent test of *Solar Manufacturing* was met in the case at bar, and it is not necessary to choose between the two standards. *McLaughlin v. Arco Polymers, Inc.*, 721 F.2d 426, 430 n. 5 (3d Cir.1983) (Third Circuit panel is bound by reported circuit opinions "unless and until they are reversed by the in banc court"); *Gardner v. Com. of Pa. Dept. of Public Welfare*, 685 F.2d 106, 108 (3d Cir.), *cert. denied*, 459 U.S. 1092, 103 S.Ct. 580, 74 L.Ed.2d 939 (1982) (a panel of the Third Circuit "is not free . . . to overrule a governing precedent in this circuit"). *See Penn Central Transportation Co., Inc. v. Celotex Corp.*, 403 F.Supp. 70, 74 (E.D.Pa.1975), *aff'd*, 538 F.2d 320 (3d Cir.1976) (on a statute of limitations question, the court stated "to overrule prior [judicial] authority is not lightly to be presumed, especially an overruling *sub silentio*") (citations omitted).

B. CONTENTS OF A CHAPTER 11 PLAN

The contents of a Chapter 11 reorganization plan are delineated in the Code. 11 U.S.C.A. § 1123. Some provisions are mandatory while others are permissive. The mandatory provisions are noted in the Code by "shall" language. 11 U.S.C.A. § 1123(a). The permissive provisions are set forth in "may" language. 11 U.S.C.A. § 1123(b).

1. Mandatory Provisions

A plan must divide the creditors into classes of claims and classes of interests. 11 U.S.C.A. § 1123(a)(1). A creditor holding an undersecured claim will have two claims, one secured and the other unsecured, and thus will be in two classes of claims. 11 U.S.C.A. § 506.

EXAMPLE

The XYZ Corporation borrowed $1,000,000 from First Bank and gave First Bank a perfected security interest in all of its present and after-acquired inventory. Shortly thereafter, XYZ Corporation filed a petition in bankruptcy under Chapter 11. At that time, XYZ's inventory had a value of $750,000. First Bank's secured claim for $750,000 will be in one class, and its unsecured claim for $250,000 will be in another class.

The usual classification of holders of claims or interests will include creditors holding secured claims, creditors holding unsecured priority claims, creditors holding unsecured nonpriority claims, and holders of equity security interests. In order to formulate a reorganization plan, it is necessary to classify the claims or interests. The Code has a general rule and an exception for classification. As a general rule, claims or interests may be included in a particular class only if substantially similar to the other claims or interests in that class. 11 U.S.C.A. § 1122(a). The exception to the general rule provides for a plan to designate a separate class of smaller claims for administrative convenience. This class would consist of every unsecured claim that is less than an amount, or that is reduced to an amount, that the court approves as reasonable and necessary for administrative convenience. 11 U.S.C.A. § 1122(b); Fed. R. Bank. P. 3013.

EXAMPLE

The XYZ Corporation has filed a petition in bankruptcy under Chapter 11. XYZ has 10 creditors with claims of $2,000 or more and 100 creditors with claims under $2,000. If XYZ were required to classify both groups of claims together, it could ruin a plan. In the plan, XYZ could utilize the exception and designate a separate class of smaller claims. The plan could then pay cash in full to the 100 creditors holding claims under $2,000 whose claims are in one class and give stock to the 10 creditors holding claims of $2,000 or more whose claims are in the other class.

This exception was provided as a practical matter. A Chapter 11 plan must be accepted by a majority in number of claims and two-thirds in amount of claims. A plan in a case with many small claims that were not to be paid in full might experience difficulty in gaining acceptance by a majority in numbers if only substantially similar claims were included in a class.

The ultimate meaning of the general rule that a claim or interest may be placed in a particular class only if substantially similar to the other claims or interests of the class is best demonstrated by security interests in specific assets or judgment liens. Each of these will usually be in a class by itself.

The next class, creditors holding unsecured claims whose claims are entitled to priority, is set forth in the Code. 11 U.S.C.A. § 507.

Creditors holding unsecured claims are third in the line-up. They hold a claim only against the general assets of the bankruptcy estate.

Equity security holders are last in line in the classification and payoff of creditors. They may consist of one or more classes depending on ownership, that may be at more than one level.

EXAMPLE

The XYZ Corporation has issued 1,500 shares of common stock and 1,000 shares of preferred stock. The claims of holders of the common stock will be in one class, and the claims of holders of the preferred stock will be in another class.

The Chapter 11 plan must specify any class of claims or class of interests not impaired under the plan. 11 U.S.C.A. § 1123(a)(2). The plan must also specify the treatment of any class of claims or interests impaired under the plan. 11 U.S.C.A. § 1123(a)(3). The Code describes when a class of claims or interests is impaired. 11 U.S.C.A. § 1124. As a general rule, a class of claims or interests is treated as impaired (i.e., when contractual rights of creditors or interest holders are affected by the plan) unless it falls within one of two enumerated exceptions.

1. If the plan proposes not to alter the legal, equitable, or contractual rights to which the claim or interest entitles its holder, the claim or interest is unimpaired. 11 U.S.C.A. § 1124(1).
2. If the plan proposes to restore a holder of a claim or interest to his or her original position by curing the effect of a default or by reinstating the original terms of an obligation when maturity was brought on or accelerated by the default, the claim or interest is unimpaired. 11 U.S.C.A. § 1124(2).

Each claim or interest within a class must be provided the same treatment unless the holder of the claim or interest agrees to a less favorable treatment. 11 U.S.C.A. § 1123(a)(4).

The plan must provide adequate means for implementation of its provisions. The Code sets out examples of such means:

> (A) retention by the debtor of all or any part of the property of the estate;
> (B) transfer of all or any part of the property of the estate to one or more entities, whether organized before or after the confirmation of such plan;
> (C) merger or consolidation of the debtor with one or more persons;
> (D) sale of all or any part of the property of the estate, either subject to or free of any lien, or the distribution of all or any part of the property of the estate among those having an interest in such property of the estate;
> (E) satisfaction or modification of any lien;
> (F) cancellation or modification of any indenture or similar instrument;
> (G) curing or waiving of any default;
> (H) extension of a maturity date or a change in an interest rate or other term of outstanding securities;
> (I) amendment of the debtor's charter; or
> (J) issuance of securities of the debtor, or of any entity referred to in subparagraph (B) or (C) of this paragraph, for cash, for property, for existing securities, or in exchange for claims or interests, or for any other appropriate purpose, ... 11 U.S.C.A. §§ 1123(a)(5)(A)–(J).

The means of implementing the plan will vary greatly from debtor to debtor, and the plan must be designed to fit the particular situation.

The plan must stipulate that certain provisions will be included in the charter of the debtor and in the charter of any corporation acquiring assets of the debtor or merging with or consolidating with the debtor. These provisions are designed to prohibit issuance of nonvoting equity securities and to provide an appropriate distribution of voting power among the classes having such power, including provisions for the election of directors representing preferred stockholders in the event of default in payment of preferred stock dividends. 11 U.S.C.A. § 1123(a)(6).

Every provision of the plan must be consistent with the interests of creditors and equity security holders and with public policy in the selection of any officer, director, or trustee (or their successors) under the plan. 11 U.S.C.A. § 1123(a)(7).

2. Permissive Provisions

A Chapter 11 plan may impair or leave unimpaired any class of claims (secured or unsecured) or interests. 11 U.S.C.A. § 1123(b)(1).

EXAMPLE

The XYZ Corporation provided its president with a company car, which was financed by First Bank. Several weeks before XYZ filed its petition in bankruptcy under Chapter 11, the president's car was involved in an accident. The car was repaired by Joe's Body Shop. At the time of the filing of the petition, the body shop's $1,500 bill had not been paid.

The plan placed First Bank's secured claim in one class and the body shop's unsecured claim in another class. In the plan, if the XYZ Corporation continues its payments to the creditors in the secured class, the bank's claim is unimpaired. If the plan provides for less than full payment to the class of unsecured claims, the body shop's claim is impaired under the plan.

A Chapter 11 plan may provide for the assumption or rejection of executory contracts. 11 U.S.C.A. § 1123(b)(2). In a Chapter 11 case, the debtor or the trustee may, at any time before the plan is confirmed, assume or reject an executory contract, including an unexpired lease of the debtor. The court, however, on request of a party to the contract or lease, may order a decision on rejection or assumption to be made within a specified time period. 11 U.S.C.A. § 365(d)(2).

EXAMPLE

The XYZ Corporation leased a warehouse from the ABC Property Company and subsequently filed a petition in bankruptcy under Chapter 11. In its plan, the XYZ Corporation decided to consolidate its operation, and the leased warehouse became expendable. The XYZ Corporation could reject the unexpired lease of the warehouse.

Under the Code, a Chapter 11 plan may provide for settlement or adjustment of any claim or interest belonging to the estate or for the retention and enforcement of any such claim or interest. 11 U.S.C.A. § 1123(b)(3).

EXAMPLE

The XYZ Corporation sold the ABC Company goods on credit. The ABC Company subsequently refused to pay, claiming that the goods failed to comply with the contract. Shortly after this, the XYZ Corporation filed its petition in bankruptcy under Chapter 11. XYZ negotiated with the ABC Company concerning the settlement of its claim. The settlement agreement provided that ABC would pay XYZ 75 percent of the original purchase price. XYZ's Chapter 11 plan may provide for settlement of XYZ's claim along the lines of the settlement agreement worked out between the parties.

Under the Code, a plan may be a liquidating plan, providing for sale of all or substantially all of the property of the estate with the proceeds of the sale to be distributed among the holders of claims or interests. 11 U.S.C.A. § 1123(b)(4).

A plan may modify the rights of holders of secured claims, with the exception of a claim secured only by the debtor's principal residence. The plan may also modify the rights of holders of unsecured claims or leave unaffected the rights of holders of any class of claims. 11 U.S.C.A. § 1123(b)(5).

A plan may also include any appropriate provision that is not inconsistent with Code provisions. 11 U.S.C.A. § 1123(b)(6).

3. A Sample Chapter 11 Plan

Exhibit 8–6 presents a sample Chapter 11 plan. Most Chapter 11 plans are much longer and more complex than the one shown here. This plan has been selected because it is relatively short but still shows what a Chapter 11 plan might look like. It may be helpful to compare the Chapter 11 plan with the Chapter 12 and Chapter 13 plans. How are they the same, and how do they differ?

This Chapter 11 plan, like all Chapter 11 plans, is accompanied by an extensive disclosure statement. (See Section 4.)

C. MODIFICATION OF A CHAPTER 11 PLAN

A Chapter 11 plan may be modified by the proponent at any time before confirmation. The modified plan must meet the Code's requirements regarding the classification of claims or interests and the contents of a plan. 11 U.S.C.A. §§ 1122, 1123. After a modification is filed, the plan as modified becomes the plan. 11 U.S.C.A. § 1127(a).

EXHIBIT 8–6 A Chapter 11 Plan

UNITED STATES BANKRUPTCY COURT
_____________________ DISTRICT OF _____________________

In re *[debtor's name]*	)	
[set forth here all names including	)	
married, maiden, and trade names,	)	
used by debtor within last 6 years]	)	
	)	Case No. ____________
Debtor	)	
	)	Chapter 11
Address _________________________	)	
Last four digits of Social Security No. ***-**-	)	
Employer's Tax Identification Nos. [if any]	)	
_________________________	)	

PLAN OF REORGANIZATION

The debtor in possession, *[debtor's name]*, dba *[name of debtor's business]* ("debtor"), a sole proprietorship, proposes the following plan pursuant to Chapter 11 of the Bankruptcy Code of 1978, as amended.

ARTICLE I
DEFINITIONS

For the purposes of this plan of reorganization ("plan"), the following terms shall mean:

1.01. *Allowed Claim* shall mean a claim (a) in respect of which a proof of claim has been filed with the Court within the applicable period of limitation fixed by Rule 3001; or (b) scheduled in the list of creditors prepared and filed with the Court pursuant to Rule 1007(b) and not listed as disputed, contingent, or unliquidated as to amount, in either case as to which no objection to the allowance thereof has been interposed within any applicable period of limitation fixed by Rule 3001 or an order of the Court, or as to which any such objection has been determined by an order or judgment which is no longer subject to appeal or certiorari proceeding and as to which no appeal or certiorari proceeding is pending.

1.02. *Allowed Secured Claim* shall mean an allowed claim secured by a lien, security interest, or other charge against or interest in property in which the debtor has an interest, or which is subject to setoff under 11 U.S.C.A. § 553, to the extent of the value (determined in accordance with 11 U.S.C.A. § 506(a)) of the interest of the holder of such allowed claim in the debtor's interest in such property or to the extent of the amount subject to such setoff, as the case may be.

1.03. *Allowed Small Claim* shall mean an allowed claim (a) the amount of which (prior to any subdivision or assignment thereof after the petition date) is not more than $300.00 or (b) the holder of which has irrevocably elected prior to the confirmation date to reduce the amount thereof to $300.00 and to have such allowed claim included in Class 4 by indicating such election on the form utilized for purposes of acceptance or rejection of the plan.

(continued)

1.04. *Claim* shall mean any right to payment, or right to an equitable remedy for breach of performance if such breach gives rise to a right to payment, against the debtor in existence on or as of the petition date, whether or not such right to payment or right to an equitable remedy is reduced to judgment, liquidated, unliquidated, fixed, contingent, matured, unmatured, disputed, undisputed, legal, secured, or unsecured.

1.05. *Class* shall mean any class into which allowed claims or allowed interests are classified pursuant to Article III.

1.06. *Class 1 Claims, Class 2 Claims, Class 3 Claims, Class 4 Claims,* and *Class 5 Claims* shall mean the allowed claims so classified in Sections 3.01 through 3.05 of this plan.

1.07. *Code* shall mean the Bankruptcy Code, 11 U.S.C.A. § 101 et seq., as amended.

1.08. *Confirmation Date* shall mean the date upon which the order of confirmation is entered by the Court.

1.09. *Court* shall mean the United States Bankruptcy Court for the *[name the district]* District of *[name the state],* in which the debtor's Chapter 11 case, pursuant to which this plan is proposed, is pending, and any court having competent jurisdiction to hear an appeal or certiorari proceeding therefrom.

1.10. *Debtor* shall mean the debtor sole proprietorship, the debtor in this Chapter 11 case, or any successor thereto or any transferee of all or substantially all of its assets.

1.11. *Distribution Account* shall mean the consideration to be distributed to holders of allowed claims and allowed interests on the distribution date (and the corresponding consideration payable to holders of claims and interests which have not been allowed as of the distribution date) and any account or accounts into which such consideration has been deposited.

1.12. *Distribution Date* shall mean the date upon which the order of confirmation is no longer subject to appeal or certiorari proceeding, on which date no such appeal or certiorari proceeding is then pending and on which date all of the conditions to the effectiveness of the plan expressly set forth in the plan have been satisfied fully or effectively waived.

1.13. *Fiscal Year* shall mean the fiscal year of debtor and its subsidiaries, which is the 12-month period ending December 31.

1.14. *Indebtedness* as applied to any person shall mean:

(a) all indebtedness or other obligations of the person for borrowed money or for the deferred purchase price of property or services;

(b) all indebtedness of the person, contingent, direct, or otherwise, secured (or for which the holder of such indebtedness has an existing right (contingent or otherwise) to be secured) by any mortgage, pledge, lien, security interest, or vendor's interest under any conditional sale or other title retention agreement existing on any property indebtedness secured thereby shall have been assumed by the person (hereinafter "secured"); or

(c) all indebtedness of others, secured or unsecured, directly or indirectly guaranteed, endorsed, or discounted with recourse by the person, or in respect of which the person is otherwise directly or indirectly liable, including without limitation, indebtedness in effect guaranteed by the person through any agreement (contingent or otherwise) to purchase, repurchase, or otherwise acquire such indebtedness or any security therefor, or to provide funds for the payment or discharge of such indebtedness (whether in the form of loans, advances, stock purchases, capital contributions, or otherwise), or to maintain the solvency or any balance sheet or other financial condition of the obligor of such indebtedness, or to make payment for any products, materials, or supplies or for any transportation or services, regardless of the nondelivery or nonfurnishing thereof.

(continued)

1.15. *Order of Confirmation* shall mean the order entered by the Court confirming the plan in accordance with the provisions of Chapter 11 of the Code, which order is no longer subject to appeal or certiorari proceeding and as to which no appeal or certiorari proceeding is pending.

1.16. *Person* shall mean an individual, corporation, partnership, joint venture, trust, estate, unincorporated organization, or a government or any agency or political subdivision thereof.

1.17. *Petition Date* shall mean [month, day,] 20__ , the date on which debtor filed its Chapter 11 petition with the Court.

1.18. *Plan* shall mean this Chapter 11 plan, as amended in accordance with the terms hereof or modified in accordance with the Code.

1.19. *Prorate* shall mean, with respect to any holder of plan debt, in the same proportion that the amount of such plan debt bears to the aggregate amount of the plan debt.

1.20. *Rules* shall mean the Federal Rules of Bankruptcy Procedure as supplemented by local rules adopted by the Court.

ARTICLE II
ADMINISTRATION AND PRIORITY CREDITORS

Unless otherwise ordered by the Court, the administrative expenses of the debtor's Chapter 11 case allowed pursuant to 11 U.S.C.A. § 503(b) and each allowed claim entitled to priority pursuant to 11 U.S.C.A. § 507(a)(2) or (6) shall be paid in full in cash on the distribution date or as soon thereafter as is practicable.

ARTICLE III
CLASSIFICATION OF CLAIMS AND INTERESTS

The claims and interests are classified as follows:

3.01. *Class 1.* Class 1 shall include the allowed secured claims of *[name the mortgagees].*

3.02. *Class 2.* Class 2 shall include the allowed secured claims of *[name the claimants].*

3.03. *Class 3.* Class 3 shall include the allowed secured claims of *[name the claimants].*

3.04. *Class 4.* Class 4 shall include the allowed small claims.

3.05. *Class 5.* Class 5 shall include all allowed claims other than those claims included in Classes 1 through 4.

ARTICLE IV
TREATMENT OF CLAIMS AND INTERESTS

4.01. *Class 1.* The Class 1 claims are impaired and shall be fully satisfied by execution of a deed in lieu of foreclosure or consent to an *in rem* decree of foreclosure with respect to the real property which secures the Class 2 claims. The holders of Class 2 claims shall have no recourse directly against the debtor or his spouse.

4.02. *Class 2.* The Class 2 claims are not impaired and shall be paid in accordance with the terms of the notes or contracts evidencing such claims.

(continued)

4.03. *Class 3.* The Class 3 claims are not impaired and shall be paid in full in deferred cash payments which, as of the distribution date of the plan, equal the allowed amount of such claims. The Class 3 claims shall be paid as follows:

Claimant	Amount of Secured Claim	Payment Terms
[name of claimant]	$________	____ consecutive monthly installments of principal and interest (at ____ Bank's prime plus ____ percent), commencing on the first day of the calendar month following 30 days from the distribution date
[name of claimant]	$________	____ consecutive monthly installments of principal and interest; interest rate on $____ is ____ Bank's prime plus ____ percent; interest rate on balance of principal is *[name the city]* prime less ____ percent; payments commence on the first day of the calendar month following 30 days from the distribution date

4.04. *Class 4.* Each holder of a Class 4 claim is impaired and shall be paid ____ percent of the amount of such claim upon the distribution date.

4.05. *Class 5.* Each holder of a Class 5 claim is impaired and shall be paid ____ percent of the amount of such claim, which payments shall be made by deferred cash payments commencing *[month, day]*, 20____ and thereafter at *[specify the intervals]* month intervals for a period of *[specify the total number]* years, without interest.

ARTICLE V
RETENTION OF JURISDICTION

The Court shall retain jurisdiction of this Chapter 11 case pursuant to and for the purpose set forth in 11 U.S.C.A. § 1127(b) and to

1. hear and determine objections to claims and interests;
2. fix allowances of compensation and other administrative expenses allowable under the Code;
3. hear and determine causes of action by or against the debtor arising prior to the commencement of or during the pendency of this proceeding;
4. hear and determine disputes arising under or relating to this plan;
5. hear and determine causes of action by or against the debtor relating to questions of what constitutes property of the estate; and
6. for such other matters as may be set forth in the order of confirmation or as may be appropriate under the Code.

ARTICLE VI
EXECUTORY CONTRACTS

6.01. *Assumption of Certain Executory Contracts.* The debtor hereby assumes, pursuant to 11 U.S.C.A. § 1123(b)(2), the executory contracts set forth on Exhibit "A" attached to this plan.

6.02. *Rejection of Certain Executory Contracts.* The debtor hereby rejects, pursuant to 11 U.S.C.A. § 1123(b)(2), the executory contracts set forth on Exhibit "B" attached to this plan.

(continued)

ARTICLE VII
MISCELLANEOUS

7.01. *Headings.* The headings in the plan are for convenience of reference only and shall not limit or otherwise affect the meanings hereof.

7.02. *Notices.* All notices required or permitted to be made in accordance with the plan shall be in writing and shall be delivered personally or by telex or other telegraphic means or mailed by registered or certified mail, return receipt requested:

(a) if to the debtor at *[mailing address]*, Attention: *[debtor's name]* with a copy to the debtor's counsel, *[debtor's attorney's name]*, *[mailing address]*;

(b) if to a holder of an allowed claim or allowed interest, at the address set forth in its proof of claim or proof of interest or, if none, at its address set forth in the debtor's schedules prepared and filed with the Court;

(c) notice shall be deemed given when received. Any person may change the address at which it is to receive notices under the plan by sending written notice pursuant to the provisions of this paragraph 7.02 to the debtor, with a copy to the debtor's counsel.

7.03. *Paragraph and Article References.* Unless otherwise specified, all references in the plan to paragraphs and articles are to paragraphs and articles of the plan.

7.04. *Reservation of Rights.* Neither the filing of this plan, nor any statement or provision contained herein, nor the taking by any creditor of any action with respect to this plan shall (a) be or be deemed to be an admission against interest and (b) until the distribution date, be or be deemed to be a waiver of any rights which any creditor might have against the debtor or any of its properties or any other creditor of the debtor, and until the distribution date all such rights are specifically reserved. In the event that the distribution date does not occur, neither this plan nor any statement contained in it, may be used or relied upon in any manner in any suit, action, proceeding, or controversy within or outside of the reorganization case involving the debtor.

[city], [state] ______________________________

Dated this ____ day of ____, 20____

[debtor's name], dba
[debtor's business name]
By: *[signature of debtor]*

[name of debtor's attorney], Esq.
[firm name]
[mailing address]
[telephone number]

ATTORNEY FOR THE DEBTOR

(continued)

EXHIBIT 8–6 A Chapter 11 Plan, Continued

EXHIBIT "A" TO PLAN OF REORGANIZATION
OF *[debtor's name]*, dba *[debtor's business name]*

ASSUMED EXECUTORY CONTRACTS

1. Lease agreement dated *[month, day]*, ______, from *[name the creditor]* to debtor covering a ______ *[make, model] [automobile, truck]*.

EXHIBIT "B" TO PLAN OF REORGANIZATION
OF *[debtor's name]*, dba *[debtor's business name]*

REJECTED EXECUTORY CONTRACTS

1. Lease agreement dated *[month, day]*, ______, from *[name the creditor]* to debtor covering a ______ *[make, model] [automobile, truck]*. (Assigned to *[name the assignee]*.)

EXAMPLE

The XYZ Corporation filed a petition in bankruptcy under Chapter 11. At the time of filing the petition, the XYZ Corporation filed its Chapter 11 plan. Prior to filing the plan, the XYZ Corporation hired an appraiser who valued XYZ's real property at $2,000,000, which was the market value listed in the plan. The real property was mortgaged to First Bank. When First Bank had the real property appraised, its appraiser valued the property at $2,500,000. XYZ and First Bank negotiated an agreed upon value of $2,200,000. XYZ filed a modification of the plan, amending the value of the real property to $2,200,000. The plan as modified became the plan.

The proponent of a Chapter 11 plan may file a modification of the plan after acceptance but before confirmation. The modification may not adversely change the rights of a creditor or an equity security holder, as those rights were fixed in the accepted plan before modification, unless the entities adversely affected have accepted the modification in writing. This rule allows for minor modifications to be made without submission to creditors and equity security holders if their rights are not affected. The modification is deemed accepted by all creditors and equity security holders who have previously accepted the plan. Fed. R. Bank. P. 3019.

Although not often done, the proponent of a plan or the debtor may modify the plan after confirmation but before substantial consummation of the plan. Such a modification must also meet the Code's requirements. 11 U.S.C.A. §§ 1122, 1123. This modified plan becomes the plan only if circumstances warrant the modification and if the Court, after notice and a hearing, confirms the plan as modified. 11 U.S.C.A. §§ 1127(b), 1129.

The proponents of a modification must meet the Code's disclosure requirements. 11 U.S.C.A. §§ 1125, 1127(c). This would require an amended disclosure statement unless an amendment to the disclosure statement met the requirements.

Any holder of a claim or interest that has accepted or rejected a plan is deemed to have accepted or rejected the modified plan unless this holder changes its vote within the time fixed by the court. 11 U.S.C.A. § 1127(d). The creditor or stockholder whose interests have been materially and adversely affected by the modification therefore has an opportunity to change its vote. This opportunity is necessary to meet the requirements regarding disclosure and solicitation of votes. 11 U.S.C.A. § 1125.

D. CHAPTER 11 PLAN FILED BY PARTIES OTHER THAN THE DEBTOR

Parties in interest, other than the debtor, may file a Chapter 11 plan under certain conditions. Parties who may file a plan include the trustee, a creditor, a creditors' committee, an equity security holder, an equity security holders' committee, or an indenture trustee. These parties may file a plan only if

(1) a trustee has been appointed under this chapter;

(2) the debtor has not filed a plan before 120 days after the date of the order for relief under this chapter; or

(3) the debtor has not filed a plan that has been accepted, before 180 days after the date of the order for relief under this chapter, by each class of claims or interests that is impaired under the plan. 11 U.S.C.A. §§ 1121(c)(1)–(3).

The 120-day period or the 180-day period may be reduced or increased by the court for cause upon request by a party in interest and after notice and a hearing.

SECTION 4
A DISCLOSURE STATEMENT OR EVIDENCE SHOWING COMPLIANCE WITH 11 U.S.C.A. § 1126(b)

A **disclosure statement** (see Exhibit 8–7) must provide "adequate information" to enable those voting on the plan to make an informed judgment about the plan. A disclosure statement is a written document that must be transmitted to each holder of a claim or interest, along with the reorganization plan or a summary of the plan, before acceptance of the plan may be solicited. The disclosure statement, however, must be approved by the court, after notice and a hearing, before it is transmitted to the creditors. The court will only approve a disclosure statement if it is found to contain **adequate information.** Adequate information can mean different things for different classes of creditors. The Code definition of "adequate information" is set forth in 11 U.S.C.A. § 1125.

(a) In this section—

(1) "adequate information" means information of a kind, and in sufficient detail, as far as is reasonably practicable in light of the nature and history of the debtor and the condition of the debtor's books and records, that would enable a hypothetical reasonable investor typical of holders of claims or interests of the relevant class to make an informed judgment about the plan, but adequate information need not include such information about any other possible or proposed plan; and

(2) "investor typical of holders of claims or interests of the relevant class" means investor having—
 (A) a claim or interest of the relevant class;
 (B) such a relationship with the debtor as the holders of others claims or interests of such class generally have; and
 (C) such ability to obtain such information from sources other than the disclosure required by this section as holders of claims or interests in such class generally have. 11 U.S.C.A. §§ 1125(a)(1), (2).

Although the same disclosure statement must be transmitted to each holder of a claim or interest of a particular class, different disclosure statements may be sent to other classes. Adequate information for one class may differ in amount, detail, or kind from that required for another class. 11 U.S.C.A. § 1125(c).

EXAMPLE

The debtor's plan provides for issuing stock to one class of unsecured creditors and paying cash in the full amount of the claim to another class of unsecured creditors. The class of creditors receiving stock will receive an extensive disclosure statement

EXHIBIT 8–7 A Chapter 11 Disclosure Statement

UNITED STATES BANKRUPTCY COURT
____________________ DISTRICT OF ____________________

In re *[debtor's name]* __________________ *[Set forth here all names including married, maiden, and trade names, used by debtor within last 6 years]*	))))	
	)	Case No. ____________
Debtor	))	Chapter 11
Address ________________________ Last four digits of Social Security No. ***-**- Employer's Tax Identification Nos. [if any] ______________________________	))))	

DISCLOSURE STATEMENT
FOR
[NAME OF THE DEBTOR]

The creditors should read the Disclosure Statement and the Plan carefully to determine into which class their claims are classified and how their claims are treated under the Plan. Classes 1, 4, and 5 are impaired under the Plan and therefore are entitled to vote on the Plan. A ballot accompanies this Disclosure Statement. Each creditor in the classes entitled to vote should properly complete the ballot and return it to the Bankruptcy Court as instructed on the ballot.

Capitalized terms used in this Disclosure Statement have the meanings as defined herein or in Article I of the Plan.

I. *PURPOSE*

A. *Introduction*

On *[month, day]*, 20____, the Debtor in Possession, *[debtor's name]*, dba *[name of business]* ("Debtor"), a sole proprietorship, filed its Voluntary Petition for Reorganization under Chapter 11 of the United States Bankruptcy Code. The Debtor has proposed a plan of reorganization which is provided simultaneously for your review.

B. *Acceptance of the Plan*

The Bankruptcy Court has set the ____ day of *[month]*, 20____ at _____ o'clock __.m. for hearing on acceptance of the Plan. A creditor may vote to accept the Plan by filling out and mailing the ballot which is provided with this Disclosure Statement to *[name and mailing address of debtor's attorney]*. A creditor may also vote in person at the hearing on acceptance, which will be held at the above time and date in Room _______ of *[name of the building or address]* in *[city, state]*. Whether a creditor votes on the Plan or not, the creditor will be bound by the terms and treatment set forth in the Plan if the Plan is accepted by the requisite majorities of creditors and is confirmed by the Court.

(continued)

Absent objection, any claim timely filed is deemed allowed. However, absent an affirmative act constituting a vote accepting or rejecting the Plan, a nonvoting creditor and that creditor's claim will not be included for purposes of determining whether or not the requisite number of votes is obtained. (Allowance or disallowance of a claim for voting purposes does not necessarily mean that all or a portion of the claim will not be allowed or disallowed for distribution purposes.)

In order for the Plan to be accepted by creditors, a majority in number and two-thirds in amount of claims filed and allowed (for voting purposes), and actually voting, of each affected class of creditors must vote to accept the Plan. You are therefore urged to complete, date, sign, and promptly mail the enclosed ballot. Please be sure to properly complete the form and legibly identify the name of the claimant.

C. *Solicitation*

The Debtor may solicit your vote. No one soliciting votes shall receive any compensation for any solicitation.

No representations concerning the Debtor or the Plan of Reorganization are authorized, other than those set forth in this Disclosure Statement. Any representations or inducements made by any person to secure your vote, other than those contained in this Disclosure Statement, should not be relied upon, and such representations or inducements should be reported to counsel for the Debtor, who shall deliver such information to the Bankruptcy Court.

D. *Requirement of Disclosure Statement*

Pursuant to the terms of the Code, this Disclosure Statement has been presented to and approved by the Bankruptcy Court. Such approval is required under the Code to provide assurance that this Statement contains information adequate to enable the holders of claims to make an informed judgment about the Plan. Court approval does not, in any way, constitute a judgment by the Court as to the desirability of the Plan or as to the value of any consideration offered thereby. Interested parties are referred to Section 1125 of the Bankruptcy Code (11 U.S.C.A. § 1125), which reads, in part

(b) An acceptance or rejection of a plan may not be solicited after the commencement of a case under this title from a holder of a claim or interest with respect to such claim or interest, unless, at the time of or before such solicitation, there is transmitted to such holder the plan or a summary of the plan, and a written disclosure statement approved, after notice and a hearing, by the court as containing adequate information. The court may approve a disclosure statement without a valuation of the debtor or an appraisal of the debtor's assets.

(c) . . . .

(d) Whether a disclosure statement required under subsection (b) of this section contains adequate information is not governed by any otherwise applicable nonbankruptcy law, rule, or regulation, but an agency or official whose duty is to administer or enforce such a law, rule, or regulation may be heard on the issue of whether a disclosure statement contains adequate information. Such an agency or official may not appeal from, or otherwise seek review of, an order approving a disclosure statement.

(e) A person that solicits acceptance or rejection of a plan, in good faith and in compliance with the applicable provisions of this title, or that participates, in good faith and in compliance with the applicable provisions of this title, in the offer, issuance, sale, or purchase of a security, offered or sold under the plan, of the debtor, of an affiliate participating in a joint plan with the debtor, or of a newly organized successor to the debtor under the plan, is not liable, on account of such solicitation or participation, for violation of any applicable law, rule, or regulation governing solicitation of acceptance or rejection of a plan or the offer, issuance, sale, or purchase of securities.

(continued)

EXHIBIT 8–7 A Chapter 11 Disclosure Statement, Continued

E. *Limitation of Disclosure Statement*

The Debtor has prepared the Disclosure Statement in order to disclose that information which, in the opinion of Debtor, is material, important, and necessary to an evaluation of the Plan. The information herein contained is intended to be used solely for the use of known creditors of the Debtor and, accordingly, may not be relied upon for any purpose other than the determination of how to vote on the Plan. In addition, materials contained in this Disclosure Statement are not intended to be adequate for the formation of a judgment by any creditor as to the preferability of any alternative to the Plan. Materials referring to alternatives to the Plan are limited by both the practical considerations of space and the opinion of the Debtor regarding same.

Certain of the materials contained in this Disclosure Statement are taken directly from other, readily accessible instruments or documents or are digests of other instruments or documents. While the Debtor has made every effort to retain the meaning of such other instruments or the portions thereof, it urges that any reliance on the contents of such other instruments should depend on a thorough review of the instruments themselves.

II. *BACKGROUND INFORMATION*

A. *Organization of Debtor*

Debtor is a sole proprietorship operated by *[debtor's name]*. *[Debtor's name]* purchased *[name of business]* from *[name of former owner]* on *[month, day]*, 20__ , for a purchase price of $xxx,xxx.xx. Debtor's place of business is located at *[street address]*.

B. *Business of the Debtor*

Debtor is in the business of *[describe debtor's business]* in the *[geographic]* market area.

C. *Economic Factors Affecting the Plan*

The Debtor believes that the Plan as proposed is fair and equitable and that each class of creditors will receive at least what it would realize if the Debtor were liquidated.

1. *Value of Debtor's Assets*. The Debtor has business assets having the liquidation values set forth below:

Asset	Liquidation Value
Land and buildings *[address]*	$xxx,xxx.xx
Office equipment	x,xxx.xx
Machinery, fixtures, equipment (excluding office equipment, and supplies	xx,xxx.xx
Inventory	xx,xxx.xx
Accounts receivable	x,xxx.xx

(continued)

The Debtor has non-business, personal assets owned by himself and his spouse having the liquidation values set forth below:

Asset	Liquidation Value
Residence *[address]*	$xxx,xxx.xx
Bank deposits	x,xxx.xx
Household goods	xx,xxx.xx
Wearing apparel and personal possessions	x,xxx.xx
[description of motor vehicle]	x,xxx.xx
[description of motor vehicle]	x,xxx.xx
[description of motor vehicle]	x,xxx.xx

2. *Liens and Debts.* The Debtor's business real property, inventory, and equipment are subject to claims of lien held by *[name of creditor]* in a total sum of approximately $xxx,xxx.xx. *[Name of creditor]* holds a lien in the approximate amount of $x,xxx.xx against Debtor's ____ *[make, model]* automobile. *[Name of creditor]* holds a lien on Debtor's ____ *[make, model]* automobile in the approximate amount of $x,xxx.xx. *[Name of creditor]* holds a lien on Debtor's ____ *[make, model]* truck in the approximate amount of $x,xxx.xx. *[Name of creditor]* holds a lien on Debtor's telephone system in the approximate amount of $x,xxx.xx. *[Name of creditor]* holds a lien on Debtor's pneumatic forklift in the approximate amount of $xxx.xx. The Debtor owes approximately $xx,xxx.xx on unsecured, prepetition indebtedness.

   The personal residence of Debtor and his spouse is encumbered by two mortgages, one held by *[name the mortgagee]* in the approximate sum of $xxx,xxx.xx, and one held by *[name the mortgagee]* in the approximate sum of $xx,xxx.xx.

   Since the filing of the petition, Debtor has paid for its inventory on a prepaid basis. Wages and taxes have been timely paid. Debtor has not borrowed any funds or incurred any credit after the petition date.

   Expenses of administration, including professional fees of attorneys and accountants, have been incurred and either have been or will be entitled to priority by the Bankruptcy Court. As of this date, counsel for the Debtor has incurred unpaid legal fees and expenses of approximately $x,xxx.xx. Incurred and unpaid accounting fees are presently in the sum of approximately $x,xxx.xx.

   It should be emphasized that the above estimates of debts and expenses are estimates only. The final determination of claims against the Debtor will be made by the Bankruptcy Court. There may be legitimate claims which are not reflected on the Debtor's books of account. In addition, final allowed claims may be more or less than the amounts shown on the books. The Debtor has accrued additional expenses since the preparation of this disclosure statement and will continue to accrue expenses in the future.

D. *Summary of Debtor's Assets and Liabilities*

The business assets of the Debtor have a total liquidation value of approximately $xxx,xxx.xx. Of this sum, $xxx,xxx.xx represents the value of land and buildings constituting Debtor's place of business at *[street address]*. The value of such real estate was established by *[name]* of *[name of company]*, who testified as to the value of such property on behalf of *[name the creditor]* at a hearing in Bankruptcy

(continued)

Court to determine if *[name the creditor]* should be allowed relief from the automatic stay to foreclose its real estate mortgages and security agreements.

The Debtor's business liabilities are in the total sum of approximately $xxx,xxx.xx, of which $xx,xxx.xx is due to unsecured creditors and $xxx,xxx.xx is due to holders of asserted secured claims. Debtor has filed objections to the secured claims of *[name the creditor]*. If such objections are upheld by the Court, $xxx,xxx.xx of asserted secured claims would be classified and treated as unsecured claims.

The personal assets of the Debtor and his spouse are approximately equal in value to their joint liabilities.

E. *Events Leading to the Bankruptcy Proceeding*

In *[month]* 20___ , *[name the mortgagee]* commenced an action in the *[name the court]* to foreclose its second real estate mortgage and security agreements on the business assets of the Debtor. At that time, the interest of *[name the mortgagee]* in the assets was subordinate to the lien of *[name the mortgagee]* in the amount of approximately $xxx.xxx.xx. *[Name the mortgagee]* paid the Debtor's indebtedness to *[name the mortgagee]* and became subrogated to the first lien position held by *[name the mortgagee]*.

As stated previously, the Debtor had purchased *[name of business]* from *[name the seller]* in *[month]* of _____ for $xxx,xxx.xx. Debtor paid $xx,xxx.xx of the purchase price down, and the balance of $xxx,xxx.xx was financed through *[name the creditor]* and *[name the creditor]*. Because the business of the Debtor is seasonal and Debtor had the burden of servicing substantial indebtedness, Debtor was unable to timely pay the sums owing to *[name the creditor]* in late 20___ and early 20___ .

To avert *[name the creditor's]* foreclosure action and to reorganize his financial affairs, the Debtor filed for relief under Chapter 11 of the Bankruptcy Code on *[month, date]*, 20___ .

F. *Events Subsequent to Filing*

The Debtor has continued to operate his business as a debtor in possession since the date of the filing of the Petition, *[month, date]*, 20___ . A committee of unsecured creditors was appointed by the Court. The names, addresses, and phone numbers of the members of the committee are shown on Exhibit "A" to this Disclosure Statement.

On *[month, date]*, 20___ , the Debtor obtained an order of the Bankruptcy Court authorizing the Debtor to use cash collateral in the operation of his business during the bankruptcy proceeding. The effect of the order was to allow the Debtor to use inventory and accounts receivable, and the proceeds thereof, in the operation of his business notwithstanding the security interests of *[name the creditor]* in such assets. On *[month, date]*, 20___ , the Bankruptcy Court denied the motion of *[name the mortgagee]* for relief from the automatic stay provided that the Debtor pay to *[name the mortgagee]* the accrued interest on the first mortgage indebtedness of approximately $x,xxx.xx previously held by *[name the mortgagee]* and subsequently transferred to *[name the mortgagee]*.

On *[month, date]*, 20___ , *[name the second mortgagee]* moved for removal of the automatic stay to allow *[name the second mortgagee]* to foreclose its second mortgage on the Debtor's personal residence. With the consent of the Debtor, the Bankruptcy Court subsequently entered an order allowing *[name the second mortgagee]* to proceed with a foreclosure action in state court. Under the order of the Bankruptcy Court, *[name the second mortgagee]* could not proceed to establish a personal judgment against the Debtor, but may only assert its interest against the Debtor's property. The Debtor consented to the Order Granting Relief from the Stay because Debtor's total monthly mortgage payments amount to approximately $x,xxx.xx. By surrendering the residence to the mortgage holders, Debtor can acquire

(continued)

replacement housing at a substantially lower cost, which will in turn allow the Debtor to reduce his compensation from *[name of business]* and facilitate the performance by the Debtor of his obligations under the Plan of Reorganization.

G. *Development of the Plan*

The Plan has been discussed by the Debtor in a general fashion with the committee of unsecured creditors and the Debtor's primary secured creditor, *[name the creditor]*. Such parties were advised by the Debtor that the purchase price which the Debtor paid for *[name of business]* was excessive in view of the value of the assets and earning potential of *[name of business]*. The Debtor advised such parties that his secured debt would have to be adjusted to conform to the true value of the assets which constituted the collateral for the secured indebtedness. The primary objective of the Plan is to reduce the Debtor's secured indebtedness, which will necessarily result in an increase of the Debtor's unsecured indebtedness. However, the unsecured indebtedness can then be paid on the basis of an amount which exceeds what the unsecured creditors would obtain in the event of a liquidation.

III. THE PLAN

A. *Principal Elements of the Plan*

The Plan essentially provides that secured creditors will receive payments equalling 100% of the allowed amount of their secured claims. Unsecured claims of $300.00 or less will be paid 15% of their claims, and other unsecured creditors will be paid 10% of their claims. Since there are no priority claims other than claims for administrative expenses, only the professional fees incurred by the Debtor and approved by the Court will have to be paid prior to making the payments to secured and unsecured creditors.

B. *Classification of Creditors*

The claims of the Debtor's creditors are divided into five classes: Class 1, Class 2, Class 3, Class 4, and Class 5. The following table shows the approximate amount of the claims in each class as reflected on the amended schedules filed in the Chapter 11 proceeding by the Debtor, exclusive, unless otherwise noted, of: (i) interest, if any; (ii) amounts paid previously pursuant to court order; and (iii) contingent, disputed, or unknown portions of claims. These amounts are for illustration only and do not include all claims.

Class Number	Claims Included	Unless Otherwise Indicated, Approximate Class Amount as of *[month, day]*, 20__
1	*[name of creditor]*, *[name of creditor]*	$xxx,xxx.xx
2	*[name of creditor]*, *[name of creditor]*, *[name of creditor]*, *[name of creditor]*	xx,xxx.xx
3	*[name of creditor]*, *[name of creditor]*	xxx,xxx.xx
4	Unsecured creditors having claims less than or equal to $300.00	xxx.xx
5	Unsecured claims in excess of $300.00	xxx,xxx.xx

(continued)

C. Treatment of Various Classes

Article 4 of the Plan details the treatment of the various classes under the Plan. It is important to realize that the Plan, if accepted and confirmed, binds each creditor and in some cases, in particular with regard to the holders of Class 4 and 5 claims, may result in the reduction and settlement of their claims for less than the full amount thereof. However, the liquidation of the Debtor would, in the opinion of the Debtor, result in settlement of these claims for far less than the full amount thereof and would result in Classes 4 and 5 receiving less than they would under the Plan.

Generally, the Plan impairs the Class 1, 4, and 5 Claims. Class 1 claims shall be satisfied by a deed in lieu of foreclosure or an agreed judgment of foreclosure with respect to the real property which secures such claims. Class 4 and Class 5 claims will be satisfied by the payment of a percentage of the full amount of such claims which, as to Class 5 Claims, shall be paid on a deferred basis.

The Class 2 Claims are not impaired and will be paid in accordance with the terms of promissory notes or contracts evidencing such claims. The Class 3 Claims shall be paid in full in deferred cash payments equal to the allowed amount of the claims plus accrued interest at the rates of interest specified in the notes evidencing the Class 3 Claims.

IV. *EFFECT OF ACCEPTANCE OF PLAN*

If a majority in number and two-thirds in amount of claims filed, allowed, and actually voting of each affected class of creditors vote to accept the Plan, the Plan will become effective and will be confirmed by the Court. Upon confirmation, all of the prepetition debts of the Company will be modified into the indebtedness as described in the Plan with respect to each class of claims.

The allowed amounts of Class 3, Class 4, and Class 5 Claims have not been completely resolved, and some objections to such claims have been or may be asserted. No final determination of the validity of these objections will be made until after the date of confirmation. Accordingly, some of the claims may be totally or partially disallowed.

Attached to this Disclosure Statement as Exhibit "B" is a projection of the Debtor's income and expenses for the period of *[month]* 20___, through *[month]* 20___. The projection reflects the payments to secured and unsecured creditors under the Plan. The sales projections are based upon actual sales for 20___, less ___%. The projections reflected in Exhibit "B" are based upon estimated revenues of the Debtor, and, while such projections are based upon the most reliable sources available, they are only estimates.

V. *GENERAL CONSIDERATIONS IN ACCEPTING A CHAPTER 11 PLAN*

A. *Operation of Chapter 11*

The confirmation of a Plan of Reorganization is the ultimate goal of a Chapter 11 proceeding. Consequently, the decision of the creditors to accept the Plan must be made in the context fixed by the law for Chapter 11 proceedings.

In a Chapter 11, the Debtor is the only possible proponent of a Plan of Reorganization during the initial 120 days of the proceedings unless certain special conditions, not present in this case, are met. After that 120-day period (unless the Bankruptcy Court extends it), any party in interest may propose a Plan of Reorganization. In this case, the 120-day period has expired.

(continued)

Chapter 11 of the Bankruptcy Code permits the adjustment of secured debt, unsecured debt, and equity interests. A Chapter 11 plan may provide less than full satisfaction of senior indebtedness and payment to junior indebtedness or may provide for return to equity owners absent full satisfaction of indebtedness so long as no impaired class votes against the Plan. ("Impaired" is defined in § 1124 of the Bankruptcy Code.)

If an impaired class votes against the Plan, this does not necessarily make implementation of the Plan impossible so long as the Plan is fair and equitable and the affected class is afforded "adequate protection." Adequate protection may be very broadly defined as providing to a creditor (or interest holder) the full value of his claim. Such value is determined by the Court and balanced against the treatment afforded the creditor. If the protection afforded to the creditor under the Plan is equal to or greater than the protection which the creditor otherwise has, the Plan may be confirmed over the dissent of that class. In the event a class is unimpaired, it is automatically deemed to accept the Plan. A class is unimpaired, in essence, if (1) its rights after confirmation are equal to what existed (or would have existed absent defaults) before the commencement of the Chapter 11 and any existing defaults are cured or provided for and the class is reimbursed actual damages, or (2) the class is paid its full claim as though matured.

If there is not a dissenting class, the test for approval by a court of a Chapter 11 plan (i.e., confirmation) is whether the Plan is feasible and is in the best interests of creditors and interest holders. In simple terms, a Plan is considered by the court to be in the best interests of creditors and interest holders if the Plan will provide a better recovery to the creditors than they would obtain if the Debtor were liquidated and the proceeds of liquidation were distributed in accordance with bankruptcy liquidation priorities. In other words, if the Plan provides creditors with money or other property of a value exceeding the probable distributions in liquidation bankruptcy, then the Plan is in the best interests of creditors. The Court, in considering this factor, is not required to consider any alternative to the Plan other than liquidation bankruptcy.

In considering feasibility, the court is only required to determine whether the obligations of the Plan can be performed. This entails determining: (1) the availability of cash for payments required at confirmation; (2) the ability of the Debtor to generate future cash flow sufficient to make payments called for under the Plan to continue in business; and (3) the absence of any other factor which might make it impossible for the Debtor to accomplish what is proposed in the Plan.

B. Alternatives to the Plan

Although this Disclosure Statement is intended to provide information to assist in the formation of a judgment whether to vote for or against the Plan, and although creditors are not being offered through that vote an opportunity to express an opinion concerning alternatives to the Plan, a brief discussion of alternatives to the Plan may be useful. These alternatives include: (1) continuation of the Chapter 11 proceedings and development of another, different Plan; (2) transfer to liquidation bankruptcy; or (3) dismissal of these proceedings. The Debtor believes the proposed Plan to be in the best interests of creditors and the Debtor. Thus, it does not favor any of the alternatives to the proposed Plan discussed below. In arriving at that conclusion, the alternative courses are assessed as follows:

1. Continuation of the Chapter 11 proceedings would be advisable if greater advantage could thereby be attained by improving the position of the Debtor and arranging a better plan of operations. While continuation of the Chapter 11 proceedings may result in an alternative

(continued)

Plan of Reorganization being developed, the Debtor does not believe, based upon his experience in the *[name the business]* business, that there can be material changes in the operation of *[name of company]*. The payments provided for under the proposed Plan are consistent with the past and projected income of *[name of company]*. Accordingly, the Debtor is unaware of any benefits that might result from continuation of the Chapter 11 proceedings and is unaware of any improvements which could be made to the Plan of Reorganization.

2. It is believed that liquidation proceedings would be contrary to the best interests of all interested parties. Market prices for assets of the Debtor are somewhat depressed at this time. Based upon the information available to the Debtor, the creditors will receive more under the Plan than they would recover in a liquidation.
3. Dismissal of the proceedings would lead to an unsatisfactory result. Should the proceedings be dismissed, secured creditors would pursue foreclosure actions against the Debtor which would ultimately result in the termination of the Debtor's business with no distribution to its unsecured creditors and a reduced distribution to secured creditors.

The assessment of these alternatives is provided solely for the purpose of full disclosure, and creditors are cautioned that a vote must be for or against the Plan. The vote on the Plan does not include a vote on alternatives to the Plan. There is no assurance of what results will occur if the Plan is not accepted. If you believe one of the alternatives referred to above, or some other alternative, is preferable to the Plan and you wish to urge it (them) upon the Court, you should consult counsel as to the appropriate action.

C. *Additional Specific Considerations in Voting*

All of the foregoing give rise in the instant case to the following implications and risks concerning the Plan.

While the Plan provides for some payments at or shortly after confirmation, such payments will be limited to Allowed Claims. Under the Bankruptcy Code, a claim may not be paid until it is allowed. A claim will be allowed in the absence of objection. A claim, including claims arising from defaults, which has been objected to will be heard by the Court at a regular evidentiary hearing and allowed in full or in part or disallowed. While the Debtor bears the principal responsibility for claim objections, any interested party, including the Creditors' Committee, may file claim objections. Accordingly, payment on some claims, including claims arising from defaults, may be delayed until objections to such claims are ultimately settled or a decision is made not to object to such a claim.

VI. *BINDING EFFECT UPON CREDITORS; DISCHARGE*

Upon confirmation, the Plan will bind all creditors and interest holders, including their heirs, successors, and assigns. All such creditors and interest holders will be legally obligated to execute and deliver any and all documents that may be required to effectuate the Plan. All debt, whether liquidated, contingent, or disputed and whether scheduled by the Debtor, except as provided in § 1141 of the Bankruptcy Code and except as same either is not impaired under the Plan or is payable as provided in the Plan, shall on confirmation of the Plan be discharged and thereby released and no longer recoverable from the company.

(continued)

VII. *RELEVANT INFORMATION—FURTHER INFORMATION*

In addition to the Exhibits attached hereto, the following additional documents pertain to the Debtor, or to the Plan and its implementation, and are referred to in order that any creditor who so desires may review a part or all of such documents in addition to the summaries or descriptions of them as contained in this disclosure statement:

1. Initial Financial Report filed with Bankruptcy Court by Debtor; and
2. Monthly Financial Reports filed in *[month]*, *[month]*, and *[month]* of 20___ .

Copies of the foregoing documents (or, if they are not yet in final form, then copies of the latest available drafts thereof) may be obtained from

[Name of Debtor's Attorney]
[mailing address]
[telephone number]

In addition, any creditor who desires any further information of any type regarding the Company or the Plan should direct his or her inquiry to the above address and telephone number. No person, other than Debtor and Debtor's counsel, is authorized to furnish any information on which a creditor is entitled to rely in connection with such creditor's acceptance or rejection of the Plan.

CONCLUSION

This disclosure statement contains information intended to assist the Debtor's creditors in evaluating the Plan of Reorganization. If the Plan is accepted, all creditors of the Debtor will be bound by its terms.

The Debtor urges each creditor to read the plan carefully and to use this Disclosure Statement, the other exhibits hereto, and such other information as may be available to the creditor in order to make an informed decision on the Plan.

[city], [state]

Dated this ____ day of __________, 20___

[debtor's name], dba
[debtor's business name]
By: *[signature of debtor]*

[name of debtor's attorney], Esq.
[firm name]
[mailing address]
[telephone number]

ATTORNEY FOR THE DEBTOR

(continued)

EXHIBIT 8–7 A Chapter 11 Disclosure Statement, Continued

EXHIBIT "A" TO DISCLOSURE STATEMENT
OF *[name]* **dba** *[name of business]*

UNSECURED CREDITORS' COMMITTEE

[Name]	*[Name]*
[mailing address]	*[mailing address]*
[telephone number]	*[telephone number]*
[Name]	*[Name]*
[mailing address]	*[mailing address]*
[telephone number]	*[telephone number]*
[Name]	*[Name]*
[mailing address]	*[mailing address]*
[telephone number]	*[telephone number]*

that looks like a prospectus but is not as detailed and would not meet securities regulations. The class of creditors receiving cash will receive only a brief disclosure statement that basically discloses the source of the cash that will be used to pay these creditors.

What adequate information consists of is not governed by any otherwise applicable nonbankruptcy law, rule, or regulation. An agency or official charged with administering or enforcing such a law, rule, or regulation may be heard on the subject but may not appeal an order approving a disclosure statement.

One of the areas most likely to cause problems for the proponent of a plan involves the issuing or transferring of stock. Adequate information may be difficult to glean from the records available. For this reason, the Code has what is known as the "safe harbor" provision. This provision permits freedom from liability for violations of securities laws made by a person, in good faith and in compliance with Code provisions, in the offer, issuance, sale, or purchase of a security under the plan. 11 U.S.C.A. § 1125(e).

In spite of the fact that the debtor issuing or transferring stock under the plan need not comply with state and federal securities laws to have a disclosure statement approved by the court, it may be desirable to do so. If the securities are to be traded soon after confirmation, they will have to meet securities regulations to be registered for trading. Preparation of a disclosure statement by the debtor issuing or transferring stock will be time and resource consuming if it is to be approved by the court. The extra effort expended at this time to meet securities regulations could pay off if the stock is ready to be registered for trading immediately upon certification.

A disclosure statement should contain a section stating the nature of the business and enough of the debtor's history to show why a Chapter 11 petition was filed. There should be a full discussion of any changes to be made that will permit the debtor to reorganize. Both financial data and a narrative discussion should be included. The creditor or the equity security holder must be able to determine from the disclosure statement if it will receive "not less" under the plan than it would receive under Chapter 7 liquidation. The best interests of creditors test is required for confirmation of the Chapter 11 plan. 11 U.S.C.A. § 1129(a)(7).

The plan will not be confirmed unless sufficient financial information is presented in the disclosure statement to show that the plan is a feasible one and will not be followed by liquidation or another attempt at reorganization.

The debtor may have solicited acceptances of a plan before the commencement of the Chapter 11 case. The holder of a claim or interest that has accepted or rejected the plan before the debtor has filed the case is deemed to have accepted or rejected the plan if

(1) the solicitation of such acceptance or rejection was in compliance with any applicable nonbankruptcy law, rule, or regulation governing the adequacy of disclosure in connection with such solicitation; or

(2) if there is not any such law, rule, or regulation, such acceptance or rejection was solicited after disclosure to such holder of adequate information, as defined in section 1125(a) of this title. 11 U.S.C.A. §§ 1126(b)(1), (2).

If the debtor has complied with these requirements and can provide evidence of this fact to the court, it will not be necessary to file any further disclosure statement.

SECTION 5 ORDER AND NOTICE OF CHAPTER 11 BANKRUPTCY FILING, MEETING OF CREDITORS, AND FIXING OF DATES

The clerk gives the debtor, the trustee, all creditors, the indenture trustees, and the U.S. trustee not less than 20 days notice by mail of the date, time, and place of the meeting of creditors and the time for filing objections to the debtor's claim of exemptions. This notice also serves as the notice of the order for relief required by 11 U.S.C.A. § 342(a). Fed. R. Bank. P. 2002.

The Bankruptcy Reform Act of 1994 requires that notice be given by the debtor to a creditor (Official Forms No. 9E and 9F, Notice of Commencement of Case Under Chapter 11 of the Bankruptcy Code, Meeting of Creditors, and Fixing of Dates) that contains the debtor's name, address and taxpayer identification number. 11 U.S.C.A. § 342(c). Procedural forms B 205, B 206, and B 207 would also appear to be affected by this requirement. These procedural forms, however, have not been changed.

Official Forms No. 9E and 9F have also been revised for the new period (180 days after the order for relief) allowed under 11 U.S.C.A. § 502(b)(9) for governmental units to file proofs of claim and for the time period (60 days) for filing a domestic relations property settlement dischargeability complaint under 11 U.S.C.A. § 523(c)(1). Fed. R. Bank. P. 4007(c).

Parties in interest, who may object to the debtor's claim of exemptions, will probably begin to do so on receipt of the clerk's notice unless they have had prior notice from the debtor's attorney or from another source.

SECTION 6 MOTIONS AND COMPLAINTS

Unlike a Chapter 7 case, which often is more or less routine, every Chapter 11 case is unique. Therefore, the motions and complaints must be tailored to the individual case. In practice, fewer complaints are filed in some districts in a Chapter 11 case than would appear to be necessary under the Code due to the willingness of attorneys to bypass such filings. Attorneys for both sides may agree to the filing of a motion and response in order to expedite a hearing. This section sets forth both motions and complaints as they appear in the Code. This is not meant to be a comprehensive list.

A. MOTIONS

After the order for relief, the debtor in possession may file a series of motions, known as "first day motions," designed to keep the business operating. Depending on the facts and the complexity of the case, they include a motion to hire counsel or other professionals, a motion to pay the prepetition claims of employees and critical vendors, and a motion to use cash collateral.

In addition to "first day motions," the debtor in possession may move to dismiss the case (Fed. R. Bank. P. 1017); for a change of venue (28 U.S.C.A. § 1412); for disallowance of a claim (11 U.S.C.A. § 502); to convert the case from a Chapter 11 to a Chapter 7, 12, or 13 (11 U.S.C.A. §§ 1112(a), (d)); or for permission to use cash collateral (11 U.S.C.A. § 363(c)(2)).

A party in interest may move for relief from the automatic stay (11 U.S.C.A. § 362(d); Fed. R. Bank. P. 4001, 9014); to convert the case to Chapter 7 (11 U.S.C.A. § 1112(b)); to dismiss the case (11 U.S.C.A. § 1112(b); Fed. R. Bank. P. 1017); for a change of venue (28 U.S.C.A. § 1412); for abstention by the court (11 U.S.C.A. § 305); or for examination of any person (Fed. R. Bank. P. 2004).

A party in interest or the U.S. trustee may move to appoint a trustee or an examiner. 11 U.S.C.A. §§ 1104(a), (c). Any time after a Chapter 11 case has been commenced but before a plan has been confirmed, the court may order the appointment of a trustee on request of either a party in interest or the U.S. trustee for cause, including fraud, dishonesty, incompetence, or gross mismanagement, that occurred either before or after the case was commenced. 11 U.S.C.A. § 1104(a)(1). A trustee may also be appointed if it is in the interests of the creditors, equity security holders, and other interests of the estate. 11 U.S.C.A. § 1104(a)(2). Neither the number of holders of securities nor the amount of the debtor's assets or liabilities is to have any bearing on the appointment of a trustee.

The U.S. trustee may move to dismiss the case or to convert the case to Chapter 7. 11 U.S.C.A. § 1112(e).

A motion objecting to a claim is usually filed by the DIP or the trustee but can be filed by a party in interest. 11 U.S.C.A. § 502(a); Fed. R. Bank. P. 3007.

B. COMPLAINTS

The trustee, a creditor, or the U.S. trustee may file a complaint objecting to the debtor's discharge in a Chapter 11 case. Fed. R. Bank. P. 4004, 7001. Such a complaint must be filed no later than the first date set for the hearing on confirmation of the plan. This timing is based on the fact that confirmation of the plan discharges the Chapter 11 debtor. 11 U.S.C.A. § 1141(d). A debtor or any creditor may file a complaint to determine the dischargeability of a particular debt in a Chapter 11 case involving an individual debtor. 11 U.S.C.A. § 523; Fed. R. Bank. P. 4007.

A complaint to determine the dischargeability of a debt under section 523(c) must be filed no later than 60 days after the first date set for the meeting of creditors. Fed. R. Bank. P. 4007(c). An objection to discharge may be filed if the plan is a liquidating plan, if the debtor does not continue to engage in business, *and* if the debtor would be denied a discharge under section 727(a) if the case were a case under Chapter 7. A dischargeability complaint will be filed by a creditor and will usually be based on the debtor's fraudulently obtaining goods or services or trying to discharge spousal support or an educational loan. Although the successful dischargeability complaint will deprive the debtor of a discharge of only the particular debt in question, a successful objection to discharge will prevent discharge of any and all debts.

The DIP, the trustee, or the creditors' committee may file a complaint for turnover of property of the estate (11 U.S.C.A. § 542), to compel a custodian to turn over property of the estate and for an accounting (11 U.S.C.A. § 543; Fed. R. Bank. P. 6002), or to avoid a fraudulent transfer (11 U.S.C.A. § 548).

The DIP or the trustee may file a complaint to avoid transfer of property. 11 U.S.C.A. § 544.

The trustee may file a complaint to avoid a preferential transfer of property. 11 U.S.C.A. § 547(b).

SECTION 7
APPOINTMENT OF A COMMITTEE OF UNSECURED CREDITORS AND A COMMITTEE OF EQUITY SECURITY HOLDERS

The Code requires appointment of a committee of creditors holding unsecured claims as soon as practicable after the order for relief in a Chapter 11 case. The United States trustee appoints this committee and may appoint additional committees of creditors or of equity security holders if they are needed. 11 U.S.C.A. § 1102(a)(1). If, however, a party in interest in a case in which the debtor is a small business (defined in 11 U.S.C.A. § 101(51C)) requests, for cause shown, the court may order that no committee be appointed. 11 U.S.C.A. § 1102(a)(3).

Upon the request of a party in interest, the court may order the U.S. trustee to appoint additional committees of creditors or equity security holders. This would only be done to assure adequate representation of creditors or equity security holders. 11 U.S.C.A. § 1102(a)(2).

A committee of creditors usually consists of the seven persons holding the largest claims of the kinds represented on the committee. 11 U.S.C.A. § 1102(b)(1). Sometimes one or more such persons are unwilling to serve on a committee. When this occurs, another person or persons among those holding the top 20 unsecured claims will be appointed.

Occasionally, a committee has been organized by creditors before the commencement of the Chapter 11 case. This committee, if fairly chosen and representative of the different kinds of claims, will be appointed to serve as the committee in the case.

Selection of a committee of equity security holders works in the same way as selection of the committee of creditors. The persons holding the seven largest amounts of equity securities of the debtor will be appointed by the U.S. trustee to the committee, provided they are willing to serve.

An unsecured creditors' committee has several powers and duties. The committee may employ attorneys, accountants, or other agents to represent or perform services for it. The selection and authorization of employment of such persons must, however, take place at a scheduled meeting of the committee and must have court approval. 11 U.S.C.A. § 1103(a). The Code has a conflict of interest provision that prevents an attorney or an accountant from representing any other entity having an adverse interest in the case. 11 U.S.C.A. § 1103(b).

SECTION 8
MEETING OF CREDITORS (THE SECTION 341 MEETING) AND MEETING OF EQUITY SECURITY HOLDERS

The meeting of creditors (the section 341 meeting) is held not less than 20 nor more than 40 days after the order for relief. The business of the meeting includes the examination of the debtor under oath by the U.S. trustee, the trustee (if one has been appointed), and the creditors. If the debtor is a corporation, the Code authorizes the U.S. trustee to convene a meeting of equity security holders.

SECTION 9
HEARING ON THE DISCLOSURE STATEMENT

Once the plan and disclosure statement are filed, the court will set a hearing on at least 25 days notice to consider the adequacy of the disclosure statement. If, however, the debtor is a small business (defined in 11 U.S.C.A. § 101(51C)), and has elected under 11 U.S.C.A. § 1121(e) to be considered a small business, the court may conditionally approve a disclosure statement. 11 U.S.C.A. § 1125(f). In that event, there will be no separate hearing on the disclosure statement; the adequacy of the disclosure statement will be considered at the hearing on plan confirmation. Otherwise, notice of the hearing on the disclosure statement and the deadline for objections, must be given to the debtor, creditors, equity security holders, and other parties in interest (including those persons who have entered an appearance and requested notices in the case and the U.S. trustee). The plan, disclosure statement, and Order and Notice of Hearing on Disclosure Statement (Official Form No. 12) must be mailed to the debtor, trustee, or any committee appointed, the Securities and Exchange Commission, the U.S. Trustee, and any persons who have entered an appearance and requested notices in the case. Objections to the disclosure statement must be made in writing, filed with the court, and served upon the debtor, the trustee (if any), any committee appointed, the U.S. trustee and any persons who have entered an appearance and requested notices in the case. Fed. R. Bank. P. 3017(a). Exhibit 8–8 (See p. 441) is the official notice of the hearing on the disclosure statement. Exhibit 8–9 (See p. 442) is the official order approving the disclosure statement and fixing the time for filing acceptances or rejections of the plan.

In re Scioto Valley Mortgage Company involves a hearing on a disclosure statement and the problems the court found with the debtor's disclosure statement.

In re Scioto Valley Mortgage Company

88 B.R. 168
(Bankr. S.D. Ohio 1988)

ORDER ON FIRST AMENDED DISCLOSURE STATEMENT

R. Guy Cole, Jr.,
Bankruptcy Judge

I. PRELIMINARY CONSIDERATIONS

This matter is before the Court upon the request of Scioto Valley Mortgage Company (the "Debtor") for approval of its First Amended Disclosure Statement ("Disclosure Statement"). Objections to the Debtor's request for approval have been filed by William G. Hayes, Jr., Trustee for Beacon Securities, Inc. and its consolidated affiliates; R. Dale Smith; BancOhio National Bank; and the United States Trustee. Upon conclusion of an actual, evidentiary hearing, the Court ruled orally that the Disclosure Statement omits adequate information as that term is defined in 11 U.S.C. § 1125(a). The Court hereby supplements its oral ruling with this Order.

The Court has jurisdiction over this matter pursuant to 28 U.S.C. § 1334(b) and the General Order of Reference entered in this judicial district. This is a core proceeding which the Court may hear and determine. 28 U.S.C. § 157(b)(1) and (2)(A). The following opinion constitutes the Court's finding of fact and conclusions of law pursuant to Bankruptcy Rule 7052.

II. FACTS

No interest would be served by the recitation of the numerous facts which were adduced at the nearly four-hour hearing on this matter. Suffice it to say, testimony was elicited from several witnesses and numerous documents were introduced into evidence. On the basis of the record made at the hearing, the Court finds that the Disclosure Statement does not contain information of a kind, and in sufficient detail, as far as is reasonably practicable in light of the nature and history of the Debtor and the condition of the Debtor's books and records, that would enable a hypothetical reasonable investor typical of the holders of claims or interests to make an informed judgment about the plan.

III. DISCUSSION

One of the fundamental policies underlying the Chapter 11 reorganization process is disclosure. The disclosure statement was intended by Congress to be the primary source of information upon which creditors and shareholders could rely in making an informed judgment about a plan of reorganization. *See In re Egan,* 33 B.R. 672, 675 (Bankr.N.D.Ill.1983). No simple method exists for determining whether a disclosure statement contains adequate information. A determination as to what constitutes adequate information in any particular instance must occur on a case-by-case basis under the facts and circumstances presented. Generally, the disclosure statement should set forth "all those factors presently known to the plan proponent that bear upon the success or failure of the proposals contained in the plan." *In re The Stanley Hotel, Inc.,* 13 B.R. 926, 929 (Bankr.D.Colo.1981). Although the term "adequate information" is not susceptible to precise definition, 11 U.S.C. § 1125 provides the framework for the Court's determination. Section 1125(b) of the Bankruptcy Code provides as follows:

> (b) An acceptance or rejection of a plan may not be solicited after the commencement of the case under this title from a holder of a claim or interest with respect to such solicitation, unless, at the time of or before such solicitation, there is transmitted to such holder the plan or a summary of the plan, and a written disclosure statement approved, after notice and a hearing, by the court as containing adequate information. The court may approve a disclosure statement without a valuation of the debtor or an appraisal of the debtor's assets. (emphasis added)

"Adequate information" is defined in 11 U.S.C. § 1125(a)(1) to mean:

> . . . information of a kind, and in sufficient detail, as far as is reasonably practicable in light of the nature and history of the debtor and the condition of the debtor's books and records, that would enable a hypothetical reasonable investor typical of holders of claims or interests of the relevant class to make an informed judgment about the plan, but adequate information need not include such information about any other possible or proposed plan.

A number of courts have provided a list of the type of information which should be addressed by a disclosure statement. Such information includes the following:

1. The circumstances that gave rise to the filing of the bankruptcy petition;
2. A complete description of the available assets and their value;
3. The anticipated future of the debtor;
4. The source of the information provided in the disclosure statement;
5. A disclaimer, which typically indicates that no statements or information concerning the debtor or its assets or securities are authorized, other than those set forth in the disclosure statement;
6. The condition and performance of the debtor while in Chapter 11;
7. Information regarding claims against the estate;
8. A liquidation analysis setting forth the estimated return that creditors would receive under Chapter 7;
9. The accounting and valuation methods used to produce the financial information in the disclosure statement;
10. Information regarding the future management of the debtor, including the amount of compensation to be paid to any insiders, directors, and/or officers of the debtor;
11. A summary of the plan of reorganization;
12. An estimate of all administrative expenses, including attorneys' fees and accountants' fees;
13. The collectibility of any accounts receivable;
14. Any financial information, valuations or *pro forma* projections that would be relevant to creditors' determinations of whether to accept or reject the plan;
15. Information relevant to the risks being taken by the creditors and interest holders;

16. The actual or projected value that can be obtained from avoidable transfers;
17. The existence, likelihood and possible success of non-bankruptcy litigation;
18. The tax consequences of the plan; and
19. The relationship of the debtor with affiliates.

See In re Inforex, Inc., 2 C.B.C.2d 612 (Bankr.D.Mass.1980); *In re William F. Gable Co.*, 10 B.R. 248, 249 (Bankr.N.D.W.Va.1981); *In re A.C. Williams Co.*, 25 B.R. 173, 176 (Bankr.N.D.Ohio 1982); *In re Malek*, 35 B.R. 443, 444 (Bankr.E.D.Mich. 1983); *In re Metrocraft Publishing Services, Inc.*, 39 B.R. 567, 568 (Bankr.N.D.Ga. 1984); *In re Jeppson*, 66 B.R. 269, 292 (Bankr.D.Utah 1986).

Disclosure of all the aforementioned information is not necessary in every case. Conversely, the list is not exhaustive; and a case may arise in which disclosure of all the foregoing type of information is still not sufficient to provide adequate information upon which the holders of claims or interests may evaluate a plan. Nevertheless, this list provides a useful starting point for the Court's analysis of the adequacy of information contained in the Disclosure Statement under review. *See In re Metrocraft Publishing Services, Inc.*, 39 B.R. at 568 (Bankr.N.D.Ga.1984).

While complete disclosure is integral to the Chapter 11 process, "overly technical and extremely numerous additions" to a disclosure statement suggested by an objecting party may be rejected if such additions decrease the clarity and understandability of the disclosure statement to the claimholders who will be called upon to accept or reject the plan. *In re Waterville Timeshare Group*, 67 B.R. 412, 413 (Bankr.D.N.H.1986). Further, it is noteworthy that a creditor only has standing to object to the adequacy of a disclosure statement as to its own class and not as to the adequacy of the statement as it affects another class. *In re Adana Mortgage Bankers, Inc.*, 14 B.R. 29, 30 (Bankr.N.D.Ga.1981). And, as one author warns, "reorganization is not to be doomed by meaningless disclosure paperwork." Trost, *Business Reorganization under Chapter 11 of the New Bankruptcy Code*, 34 Bus. Law. 1309, 1339 (1979).

Obviously, it would be impossible for the Court to instruct any plan proponent as to the entire spectrum of information which should properly be included in a disclosure statement. As a starting point, however, the Court directs the Debtor to the aforementioned types of information which numerous courts have noted are most often included in a disclosure statement. The Court also refers the Debtor to the various objections filed by the parties since, for the most part, they contain valid complaints about the adequacy of the information contained in the Disclosure Statement. The use of such guideposts would appear to mandate, at a minimum, the disclosure of the following information: (1) matters pertaining to an Agreement and Note entered into by and between the Debtor and an entity known as Quail Marsh Partnership, including the status of the parties' relationship and the existence and collectibility of a possible account receivable from Quail Marsh Partnership; (2) a more-detailed liquidation analysis, including the potential impact upon claimholders in the event of a hypothetical Chapter 7 liquidation (particularly if the sale of a partnership property were treated as an event of dissolution under the particular partnership agreements); (3) additional information concerning the status of various partnerships in which the Debtor may have an interest, including the nature and extent of any such interest or relationship; (4) the status of negotiations with Kinder-Care regarding future business opportunities of the Debtor; (5) information regarding the future ownership and management of the Debtor, including compensation to be paid to any insiders, directors, and/or officers of the Debtor; (6) all significant assets of the Debtor, including payments—whether they are periodic, lump-sum, or "balloon" payments—which the Debtor is entitled to receive in the future pursuant to any agreements with corporations, partnerships, individuals and other entities; (7) more detailed information concerning the Debtor's ability to make the payments proposed in the plan; (8) all accounting and valuation methods used in the preparation of the Disclosure Statement; (9) whether the Debtor can sell or alienate its interest in various partnerships, as proposed by the plan; and (10) whether the Debtor has any executory contracts it intends to assume under the plan.

The Court-suggested list is, by its very nature, nonexhaustive. In reality, the Debtor and affected creditors are better situated than is the Court to assess the extent of disclosure needed to satisfy the standard imposed by § 1125 because they possess a breadth of information which is unavailable to the Court. It is not the Court's intention to require the disclosure of burdensome and unnecessary information. Nor is it the Court's desire to give any holder of a claim or interest a strategic advantage by making it difficult for the Debtor to obtain ultimate review of a proposed plan. It is imperative, however, that the Debtor disclose all pertinent information so that such holders can cast an informed vote accepting or rejecting the plan. That is all the Code requires. If the creditors oppose their treatment in the plan, but the Disclosure Statement contains adequate information, issues respecting the plan's confirmability will await the hearing on confirmation. Therefore, the Debtor need not obtain the creditors' approval of the plan; it need only provide them with adequate information as that term is defined in 11 U.S.C. § 1125(a)(1).

Based upon the foregoing, the First Amended Disclosure Statement is hereby DISAPPROVED. The Debtor shall have forty-five (45) days from the entry of this Order to file a second amended disclosure statement. Failure to file a second amended disclosure statement in the time provided may result in the imposition of sanctions, including dismissal of the case, conversion to a case under Chapter 7, or appointment of a Chapter 11 trustee or examiner.

IT IS SO ORDERED.

SECTION 10
HEARING ON CONFIRMATION OF THE PLAN

After notice, the court holds a hearing on confirmation of the plan. The trustee, a party in interest, or the U.S. trustee may object to confirmation of the plan. 11 U.S.C.A. § 1128(b). The plan will be confirmed only if it meets all of the following requirements of the Code.

1. The plan and the proponent of the plan must comply with all of the applicable provisions of Title 11.
2. The plan must be proposed in good faith.
3. Any payment for services or for costs and expenses in connection with the case or the plan is subject to approval by the court as reasonable.
4. The identity and affiliation of any individual who is to serve as a director, an officer, or a voting trustee, after confirmation of the plan, must be disclosed and must be consistent with the best interests of creditors and equity security holders and with public policy. The identity of, and compensation for, an insider to be employed or retained by the reorganized debtor must be disclosed.
5. Any rate change provided for in the plan that is subject to approval of any governmental regulatory commission must be approved.
6. The plan must meet the best interests of creditors test by demonstrating that the creditor or equity security holder will not receive less under the plan than it would under a Chapter 7 liquidation.
7. The plan may not discriminate unfairly and must be fair and equitable with respect to impaired classes of claims or interests that have not accepted the plan. 11 U.S.C.A. § 1129.

At the hearing on confirmation of the Chapter 11 plan, the court reviews the case for acceptance by ballots or rejection by ballots and whether the plan can be "crammed down." **Cramdown** is a concept that permits confirmation of a plan if certain standards of fairness are met, even if some creditors or equity security holders do not accept the plan. The plan must be fair and equitable and may not discriminate unfairly. 11 U.S.C.A. § 1129(b)(1). For a Chapter 11 plan to be fair and equitable, it must meet certain criteria for each dissenting class.

1. The holder of a secured claim must retain its lien and receive deferred cash payments of at least the allowed amount of the claim. If the value of the claim is determined as of the effective date of the plan,

EXHIBIT 8–8 Official Form No. 12 (Order and Notice for Hearing on Disclosure Statement)

Official Form 12
(12/03)

United States Bankruptcy Court

_______________ District of _______________

ORDER AND NOTICE FOR HEARING ON DISCLOSURE STATEMENT

To the debtor, its creditors, and other parties in interest:

A disclosure statement and a plan under chapter 11 [*or* chapter 9] of the Bankruptcy Code having been filed by ______________________________ on ______________________________,

IT IS ORDERED and notice is hereby given, that:

1. The hearing to consider the approval of the disclosure statement shall be held at: ____________________, on ____________________, at ______________ o'clock __.m.

2. ____________________ is fixed as the last day for filing and serving in accordance with Fed. R. Bankr. P. 3017(a) written objections to the disclosure statement.

3. Within ____________ days after entry of this order, the disclosure statement and plan shall be distributed in accordance with Fed. R. Bankr. P. 3017(a).

4. Requests for copies of the disclosure statement and plan shall be mailed to the debtor in possession [*or* trustee *or* debtor *or* ____________________] at * ____________________.

Dated: ____________________

BY THE COURT

____
United States Bankruptcy Judge

* State mailing address

EXHIBIT 8–9 Official Form No. 13 (Order Approving Disclosure Statement and Fixing Time for Filing Acceptances or Rejections of Plan, Combined with Notice Thereof)

Official Form 13
(12/03)

United States Bankruptcy Court

_______________ District of _______________

ORDER APPROVING DISCLOSURE STATEMENT AND FIXING TIME FOR FILING ACCEPTANCES OR REJECTIONS OF PLAN, COMBINED WITH NOTICE THEREOF

A disclosure statement under chapter 11 of the Bankruptcy Code having been filed by ______________________________, on ____________________ [*if appropriate*, and by ______________________________, on ____________________], referring to a plan under chapter 11 of the Code filed by ________________________, on ________________ [*if appropriate*, and by ________________________, on ________________ respectively] [*if appropriate*, as modified by a modification filed on ________________]; and

It having been determined after hearing on notice that the disclosure statement [*or* statements] contain[s] adequate information:

IT IS ORDERED, and notice is hereby given, that:

A. The disclosure statement filed by ________________________ dated _____________ [*if appropriate*, and by ________________________, dated _______________ is [are] approved.

B. ______________________ is fixed as the last day for filing written acceptances or rejections of the plan [*or* plans] referred to above.

C. Within ___________ days after the entry of this order, the plan [*or* plans] *or* a summary *or* summaries thereof approved by the court, [and [*if appropriate*] a summary approved by the court of its opinion, if any, dated _____________, approving the disclosure statement [*or* statements]], the disclosure statement [*or* statements], and a ballot conforming to Official Form 14 shall be mailed to creditors, equity security holders, and other parties in interest, and shall be transmitted to the United States trustee, as provided in Fed. R. Bankr. P. 3017(d).

D. If acceptances are filed for more than one plan, preferences among the plans so accepted may be indicated.

E. *[If appropriate]* _____________ is fixed for the hearing on confirmation of the plan [*or* plans].

F. *[If appropriate]* ______________ is fixed as the last day for filing and serving pursuant to Fed. R. Bankr. P. 3020(b)(1) written objections to confirmation of the plan.

Dated: ____________________

BY THE COURT

____

United States Bankruptcy Judge

[If the court directs that a copy of the opinion should be transmitted in lieu of or in addition to the summary thereof, the appropriate change should be made in paragraph C of this order.]

the lien of the creditor attaches to the proceeds, or the holder of a claim may receive the **indubitable equivalent** of its claim. 11 U.S.C.A. § 1129(b)(2)(A).

2. The holder of an unsecured claim must receive property of a value equal to the allowed amount of the claim. The value of the claim is determined as of the effective date of the plan. If the holder of an unsecured claim does not receive property of a value equal to the allowed amount of its claim, the holder of a junior claim or interest receives nothing. This is called the **absolute priority rule.** 11 U.S.C.A. § 1129(b)(2)(B).
3. There is also an absolute priority rule for interest holders. 11 U.S.C.A. § 1129(b)(2)(C). The holder of an interest receives or retains property of a value (as of the effective date of the plan) equal to the greatest of the allowed amount of any fixed liquidation preference, any fixed redemption price, or the value of such interest. If this requirement is not met, the holder of any junior interest will not receive or retain anything.

The mere threat of cramdown appears to obviate the need for its actual use in most cases. The risks inherent in a possible cramdown tend to encourage settlement. Negotiations by the debtor, creditors, and equity security holders facilitate the development of a plan that can be accepted by all classes. Thus, the purpose of cramdown (to secure confirmation of a plan in spite of the dissent of one or more classes holding impaired claims or interests) is often accomplished through compromise and settlement. Exhibit 8–10 (see p. 452) presents the ballot used in confirmation of the plan.

In *In re Edgewater Motel, Inc.*, the debtor sought confirmation of its Chapter 11 plan. The court discussed the best interests of creditors test, the feasibility requirement, and cramdown.

In re Edgewater Motel, Inc.

85 B.R. 989 (Bankr. E.D. Tenn. 1988)

MEMORANDUM
Richard Stair, Jr.,
Bankruptcy Judge

The debtor seeks confirmation of its "Amended Plan of Reorganization" (Plan) filed August 6, 1987. Union Planters National Bank (Union Planters), holder of the first mortgage indebtedness encumbering the debtor's real property in Gatlinburg, Tennessee, filed "Objections To Confirmation" on September 25, 1987. A hearing on confirmation was held October 1, 1987.[1]

This is a core proceeding. 28 U.S.C.A. § 157(b)(2)(L) (West Supp. 1987).

I

The debtor, Edgewater Motel, Inc., a corporation, owns and operates a motel in the resort town of Gatlinburg, Tennessee. Subsequent to the 1983 tourist season, the debtor demolished its 39-unit motel and commenced construction of its present facility—a 209-room mid-rise resort hotel[2] known as the Edgewater Motel. Union Planters loaned the debtor the construction money for this project; Security Federal Savings and Loan Association, Nashville, Tennessee, was to provide permanent financing and "take out" Union Planters at the conclusion of construction.

In connection with its construction loan, the debtor executed a promissory note in favor of Union Planters on March 1, 1984, in the original principal amount of $7,605,000 bearing interest at the rate of one and one-half percent (1 1/2%) above the Union Planters prime rate.[3] This note, secured by a mortgage encumbering the debtor's real estate, matured on September 30, 1985. Construction of the Edgewater Motel was substantially completed on April 30, 1985; however, conditions essential to the funding of the permanent financing were not met and the commitment of the permanent lender expired. No permanent financing was obtained by the debtor prior to the filing of its voluntary petition under Chapter 11 on March 24, 1986. Union Planters' fully matured claim as of October 1, 1987, approximated $8,400,000.[4] It is undisputed that Union Planters is a fully secured.[5]

In its Plan the debtor designates ten classes of claims and interests. Union Planters is the sole creditor comprising Class II. Class I, consisting of administrative expense claims, represents the only unimpaired class under the Plan. All impaired classes, excepting the Class II creditor, Union Planters, have accepted the Plan.[6] The claim of Union Planters is dealt with under the Plan as follows:

> Treatment of Class II Creditors. The only creditor under Class II of the Plan is Union Planters National Bank. The Debtor proposes to amortize the debt due to Union Planters National Bank on a twenty five (25) year amortization schedule at nine (9%) percent interest with a ten (10) year balloon payment for all principal remaining due and owing at the end of the said period of time. As indicated above, the first payment shall be due on October 1, 1987 and the balloon payment would be due on September 30, 1997.
>
> During the first year of the Plan the Debtor shall pay Union Planters only One Hundred Eighty Thousand ($180,000.00) Dollars of the amount that would be due to Union Planters under the provisions of Paragraph 1 of this Subsection. Debtor will defer the remaining portion of the first year's payments to be paid in the eighth year of the Plan in equal monthly installments. Interest will be paid on the deferred portion of first year's payments at nine (9%) percent per annum. Interest on this deferred portion will accumulate for the first Plan year and will be paid in equal monthly installments during the second year of the Plan. Interest for the second year and interest thereafter until the deferred portion of payments due for the first year of the Plan are paid in full will be paid on a monthly basis at nine (9%) percent per annum.
>
> During the second year of the Plan Union Planters will be paid only Six Hundred Thousand ($600,000.00) Dollars of the amount that would otherwise be due under Paragraph 1 of this Subsection. This deferred portion of the second year's payments shall be paid in the eighth year of the Plan. Interest on the deferred payment for the second year of the Plan shall be paid in equal monthly installments during the second year of the Plan. Interest on the deferred portion of the second year's payments under the Plan for the third year and successive years until paid in full shall be paid in equal monthly installments at the rate of nine (9%) percent per annum.
>
> During the third year of the Plan Union Planters will be paid only Seven Hundred Thousand ($700,000.00) Dollars of the amount that would otherwise be due under Paragraph 1 of this subsection. The deferred portion of the third year's payments will be paid in the eighth Plan year. Interest on the deferred payment for the third year of the Plan shall be paid in equal monthly installments during the third year of the Plan. Interest on the deferred portion of the third year's payment for the fourth year and successive years shall be paid in equal monthly installments at the rate of nine (9%) percent per annum.
>
> Beginning with the fourth year of the Plan and thereafter until the balloon payment is due, the Debtor shall pay payments in accordance with the amortization schedule set forth in Paragraph 1 above.
>
> Union Planters National Bank shall retain its security interest and all security which it presently holds for payment of its claim. Union Planters National Bank is impaired under the terms of the Plan.

It is undisputed that the claim of Union Planters is impaired within the meaning of § 1124 of the Bankruptcy Code.

Union Planters grounds its objections to confirmation on the following allegations: (1) the Plan does not meet the best interest of creditors test required by § 1129(a)(7); (2) the Plan does not offer a reasonable prospect of success and therefore does not meet the feasibility standard required by § 1129(a)(11); and (3) the Plan discriminates unfairly against Union Planters and does not meet the "fair and equitable" test required by § 1129(b)(2)(A).

II

The debtor's Plan can be confirmed only if the court determines that the debtor has complied with all the requirements of Bankruptcy Code § 1129. The salient provisions of § 1129 which are at issue as a result of the Union Planters' objections are as follows:

§ 1129. Confirmation of plan.

(a) The court shall confirm a plan only if all of the following requirements are met:

....

(7) With respect to each impaired class of claims or interests—

(A) each holder of a claim or interest of such class—

(i) has accepted the plan; or

(ii) will receive or retain under the plan on account of such claim or interest property of a value, as of the effective date of the plan, that is not less than the amount that such holder would so receive or retain if the debtor were liquidated under chapter 7 of this title on such date; or

....

(11) Confirmation of the plan is not likely to be followed by the liquidation, or the need for further financial reorganization, of the debtor or any successor to the debtor under the plan, unless such liquidation or reorganization is proposed in the plan.

(b)(1) Notwithstanding section 510(a) of this title, if all of the applicable requirements of subsection (a) of this section other than paragraph (8) are met with respect to a plan, the court, on request of the proponent of the plan, shall confirm the plan notwithstanding the requirements of such paragraph if the plan does not discriminate unfairly, and is fair and equitable, with respect to each class of claims or interests that is impaired under, and has not accepted, the plan.

(2) For the purpose of this subsection, the condition that a plan be fair and equitable with respect to a class includes the following requirements:

(A) With respect to a class of secured claims, the plan provides—

(i)(I) that the holders of such claims retain the liens securing such claims, whether the property subject to such liens is retained by the debtor or transferred to another entity, to the extent of the allowed amount of such claims; and

(II) that each holder of a claim of such class receive on account of such claim deferred cash payments totaling at least the allowed amount of such claim, of a value, as of the effective date of the plan, of at least the value of such holder's interest in the estate's interest in such property;

(ii) for the sale, subject to section 363(k) of this title, of any property that is subject to the liens securing such claims, free and clear of such liens, with such liens to attach to the proceeds of such sale, and the treatment of such liens on proceeds under clause (i) or (iii) of this subparagraph; or

(iii) for the realization by such holders of the indubitable equivalent of such claims.

11 U.S.C.A. § 1129 (West 1979 & Supp.1987).

III. BEST INTEREST OF CREDITORS TEST: § 1129(a)(7)

Under the provisions of § 1129(a)(7)(A)(ii), the court, if it is to confirm the Plan, must find the Union Planters, the holder of a secured claim which has not accepted the Plan, "will receive or retain under the plan on account of such claim . . . property of a value, as of the effective date of the plan, that is not less than the amount that [Union Planters] would so receive or retain if the debtor were liquidated under chapter 7 of this title on such date."

The House Report describes § 1129(a)(7) as follows:

> Paragraph (7) incorporates the former "best interest of creditors" test found in chapter 11, but spells out precisely what is intended. With respect to each class, the holders of the claims or interests of that class must receive or retain under the plan on account of those claims or interest property of a value, as of the effective date of the plan, that is not less than the amount that they would so receive or retain if the debtor were liquidated under chapter 7 on the effective date of the plan.

H.R. Rep. No. 595, 95th Cong., 1st Sess. 412 (1977), U.S.Code Cong. & Admin.News 1978, p.5787.

In summary, the court must compare what Union Planters would receive upon liquidation to what it will receive under the Plan. Absent a determination that the Plan provides for Union Planters to receive as much as or more than it would receive upon liquidation under Chapter 7, the confirmation requirements of § 1129(a)(7) will not be met and the Plan cannot be confirmed.

Upon liquidation of the debtor under the provisions of Chapter 7 of Title 11, Union Planters would receive in cash the value of its fully secured claim, $8,400,000.[7]

The effect of the debtor's treatment of Union Planters under the Plan is to totally restructure the Union Planters loan. The debtor's obligation to Union Planters matured on September 30, 1985; the Plan provides that Union Planters will be paid on a twenty-five year amortization schedule at nine percent (9%) interest, with a balloon payment in the tenth year consisting of the remaining unpaid balance. However, the Plan further provides that actual payments to Union Planters during the first three years of the Plan will be substantially less than those required by the debtor's proposed twenty-five year amortization schedule: $180,000 will be paid in the first year; $600,000 will be paid in the second year; and $700,000 will be paid in the third year. The payment deficiencies in the first three years are deferred to the eighth year of the Plan and interest at nine percent (9%) on these deficiencies is to be paid monthly beginning in the second year of the Plan. The debtor's Plan payments to Union Planters, actual and deferred, are summarized as follows:[8]

Payments Due Union Planters under Plan

First Year—October 1, 1987—September 30, 1988		
Due in Year 1	$845,909.88	
Paid in Year 1	180,000.00	
Deferred to Year 8	665,909.88	
Total Paid		$180,000.00
Second Year—October 1, 1988—September 30, 1989		
Due in Year 2	$845,909.88	
Paid in Year 2	600,000.00	
Deferred to Year 8	245,909.88	
Interest Paid On Deferred Payments—(two years interest on Year 1 deferral; one year on Year 2 deferral)	104,799.03	
Total Payment		704,799.03
Third Year—October 1, 1989—September 30, 1990		
Due in Year 3	$845,909.88	
Paid in Year 3	700,000.00	
Deferred to Year 8	145,909.88	
Interest Paid On Deferred Payments	89,176.60	
Total Payment		789,176.60
Fourth Year—October 1, 1990—September 30, 1991		
Due and paid	$845,909.88	
Interest Paid On Deferred Payments[9]	95,195.67	
Total Payment		941,105.55
Fifth Year—October 1, 1991—September 30, 1992		
Due and paid	$845,909.88	
Interest Paid On Deferred Payments	95,195.67	
Total Payment		941,105.55
Sixth Year—October 1, 1992—September 30, 1993		
Due and paid	$845,909.88	
Interest Paid On Deferred Payments	95,195.67	

Total Payment		941,105.55
Seventh Year—October 1, 1993–September 30, 1994		
Due and paid	$845,909.88	
Interest Paid On Deferred Payments	95,195.67	
Total Payment		941,105.55
Eighth Year—October 1, 1994–September 30, 1995		
Due and paid	$845,909.88	
Deferred Payments Years 1, 2, and 3	1,057,729.64	
Interest Paid on Deferred Payments	52,270.60	
Total Payment		1,955,910.12
Ninth Year—October 1, 1995–September 30, 1996		
Due and paid		845,909.88
Tenth Year—October 1, 1996–September 30, 1997		
Due and paid	$845,909.88	
Balloon payment due September 30, 1997	6,950,096.16	
Total Payment		7,796,006.04

The dispositive issue for resolution by the court in determining whether the Plan meets the best interest of creditors test as to the Class II claim of Union Planters is the present value of the stream of payments provided Union Planters under the Plan. Most of the cases concerning present value arise in the context of "cram down" under the provisions of § 1129(b)(2)(A)(i) or under § 1325(a)(5)(B). Nonetheless, the principle is the same under § 1129(a)(7).

The court has determined that within the context of this Chapter 11 case present value assumes a current market rate of interest on Union Planters' claim based on comparative loans as distinguished from a rate of interest, as argued by the debtor, established pursuant to 28 U.S.C.A. § 1961(a) (West Supp.1987), or in reliance upon the Federal Reserve Bulletin for September, 1987, containing the weighted average during the week of May 4–8, 1987, for long-term loans with a fixed rate where the loan was for $1,000,000 or more. As has recently been noted by Judge Morton, Senior District Judge for the United States District Court for the Middle District of Tennessee:

> Sections 1129(a)(7)(A)(ii) and 1129(b)(2)(A)(i) require the Bankruptcy Court to analyze the present value of the stream of payments or other consideration provided by a plan. This concept of present value assumes the use of *market* rates of interest (as distinguished from the rate specified in the contract) for loans of similar duration, with similar security, and with similar risks. 5 *Collier on Bankruptcy* (15th ed. 1985) ¶ 1129.03[i]; see *Memphis Bank & Trust Co. v. Whitman*, 692 F.2d 427 (6th Cir. 1982) (construing 11 U.S.C. § 1325(a)(5)(B), the language of which is virtually identical to that contained in § 1129).
>
> In determining the allowed amount of the claim of a full-secured creditor, the creditor is entitled to his contract rate of interest up the effective date of the plan by virtue of 11 U.S.C. § 506(b), ... But this rule has no application to the present value analysis required by § 1129, or to the interest payable on claims after the effective date of a plan. 3 *Collier on Bankruptcy* (15th ed. 1985) ¶ 506.05 at 506–43.

Federal Land Bank of Louisville v. Gene Dunavant and Son Dairy (In re Gene Dunavant and Son Dairy), 75 B.R. 328, 335–36 (U.S.D.C.M.D.Tenn.1987) (emphasis in original).

The debtor's Plan contemplates the payment of interest on any deferred amounts at nine percent (9%). In support of its contention that nine percent (9%) represents a current market rate of interest, the debtor elicited testimony from Michael L. Harmon, a certified public accountant and president of a concern known as TexLaMiss Corp. (TexLaMiss). Mr. Harmon testified that TexLaMiss purchased the River Terrace Hotel in Gatlinburg, Tennessee, on July 8, 1987; that the purchase price was $8,850,000; that $20,000 was paid down; and that the sum of $8,830,000 was financed for a period of five (5) years at nine and four-tenths percent (9.4%) interest with the interest rate to be renegotiated at the end of the five year period.

Mr. Harmon further testified as to the involvement of TexLaMiss in negotiating several projects throughout the South with interest rates ranging from four percent (4%) fixed for five years to eleven percent (11%). Of the various loans discussed by Mr. Harmon, it is apparent that the only loan bearing any similarity to the debtor's proposed treatment of Union Planters' claim under the Plan is that loan involving the River Terrace Hotel. The basic similarity between the River Terrace loan and the debtor's proposed treatment of Union Planters' claim under its Plan are the amounts of the two obligations and their identical geographic locations. However, the debtor's own proof, through Mr. Harmon, establishes a current market rate of nine and four-tenths percent (9.4%), four-tenths percent (.4%) higher than the nine percent (9%) envisioned under the Plan.[10]

Mr. James G. Howell, a partner in the certified public accounting firm of Pannell, Kerr and Forster, testified that the prevailing market rate on October 1, 1987, for a twenty-five year loan with a ten year call providing a payout similar to that set forth in the debtor's Plan for the Union Planters' claim, approximated twelve percent (12%). Richard K. Howarth, a senior consultant with Pannell, Kerr and Forster, testified that the present value of the payments proposed to be made to Union Planters under the Plan, based upon the debtor's nine percent (9%) interest factor, assuming a market rate of twelve percent (12%) for similar loans, approximates $7,000,000.

This court doubts the availability under any current market setting of a loan envisioning the deferred repayment plan such as is provided Union Planters under the debtor's Plan. Nonetheless, considering the criteria espoused by Judge Morton in *In re Gene Dunavant and Son Dairy, supra,* the court, having considered the use of a market rate of interest for "loans of similar duration, with similar security, and with similar risks" concludes that the market rate of interest testified to by Mr. Howell, i.e., twelve percent (12%), represents a current market rate of interest for comparable loans.

As is noted in a leading treatise on bankruptcy:

> It is submitted that deferred payment of an obligation under a plan is a coerced loan and the rate of return with respect to such loan must correspond to the rate which would be charged or obtained by the creditor making a loan to a third party with similar terms, duration, collateral, and risk. It is therefore submitted that the appropriate discount rate must be determined by reference to the "market" interest rate.

5 *Collier on Bankruptcy,* ¶ 1129.03, at 1129–62, 63 (15th ed. 1987) (footnote omitted).

As the debtor's Plan contemplates interest at nine percent (9%), the Plan's discount rate is nine percent (9%). The Plan cannot be confirmed because it does not meet the best interest of creditors test required under § 1129(a)(7)(A)(i).

IV. FEASIBILITY REQUIREMENT: § 1129(a)(11)

As a confirmation requirement, § 1129(a)(11) mandates a determination by the court that "the plan is not likely to be followed by the liquidation, or the need for further financial reorganization, of the debtor. . . ." The court will not expend a considerable amount of time analyzing the debtor's projections in support of its claim of feasibility. The lack of feasibility appears to be self-evident by the deferred payment method provided in the Plan for payment of the Class II Union Planters claim, the Class III claim of Borg-Warner Leasing, and the Class IV claims of Blaine-Hays Construction Company and First National Bank of Gatlinburg.[11]

The debtor proposes a ten year Plan at the conclusion of which it will sell the Edgewater Motel or refinance the first mortgage claim of its largest creditor, Union Planters. At the end of the ten year Plan period the principal balance of Union Planters' claim will have been reduced by $1,449,903.84, from $8,400,000 to $6,950,096.16. During this ten year period the debtor will defer $1,057,729.64 in payments due in Plan years one through three to Plan year eight.

"[T]he longer a debtor intends to take in retiring plan obligations, the more difficult it may be to prove feasibility." *In re White,* 36 B.R. 199, 204 (Bankr.D.Kan.1983). The ability of the debtor to retire the claim of its major secured creditor is at best speculative. While the debtor projects a sufficient income to meet the payments proposed to various classes of creditors, the court, in view of the substantial amount of payments deferred by the debtor to Plan years six through eight, is not satisfied as to the ability of the debtor to meet these projections. The court cannot make a finding that confirmation "is not likely to be followed by the liquidation, or the need for further financial reorganization, of the debtor. . . ." 11 U.S.C.A. § 1129(a)(11) (West 1979).

The debtor's Plan does not meet the confirmation requirements of § 1129(a)(11).

V. CRAM DOWN: § 1129(b)(2)(A)

The court also finds that the Plan violates the "fair and equitable" standard of § 1129(b)(2)(A)(i). The § 1129(b) "cram down" provisions are available to a debtor only "if all of the applicable requirements of subsection (a) of . . . [§ 1129] other than paragraph (8) are met with respect to a plan, ..." Under such circumstances, § 1129(b) further provides that if all the confirmation requirements of § 1129(a) are met except that of § 1129(a)(8) "the court . . . shall confirm the plan notwithstanding the requirements of . . . [§ 1129(a)(8)] if the plan does not discriminate unfairly, and is fair and equitable, with respect to each class of claims or interests that is impaired under, and has not accepted, the plan."

Although the court's finding that the debtor's Plan does not meet the confirmation requirements of § 1129(a)(7) and (11) precludes the debtor from proceeding to "cram down," the court will nonetheless consider the debtor's Plan within the confines of § 1129(b)(2)(A).

For the debtor's Plan to be "fair and equitable" under the provisions of § 1129(b)(2)(A)(i), the Plan, with respect to the impaired non-accepting Class II claim of Union Planters, must provide (1) that Union Planters retain the lien securing its claim; and (2) that Union Planters receive on account of its claim "deferred cash payments totaling at least the allowed amount of such claim, of a value, as of the effective date of the plan, of at least the value of . . . [Union Planters] interest in the estate's interest in [the Edgewater Motel]. . . ."

As has been discussed within the context of the best interest of creditors test under § 1129(a)(7)(A), the inquiry to be made by the court is that of present value:

> If the proponent of a plan attempts to cram down a class of secured claims by means of making deferred cash payments under section 1129(b)(2)(A)(i), the court is required to value the future cash stream so as to establish the present value of the deferred payments provided for under the plan.

5 Collier on Bankruptcy, ¶ 1129.03[f], at 1129–60 (15th ed. 1987). Thus, if the Plan proposes to pay interest on the fully secured claim of Union Planters at a rate less than the current market rate, the Plan does not satisfy the "fair and equitable" requirement of § 1129(b)(2)(A)(i). *In re Sullivan,* 26 B.R. 677 (Bankr.W.D.N.Y.1982) (debtor's nine and one-half percent (9 1/2%) interest rate on mortgage balance did not satisfy the "fair and equitable" requirement in a market where the prime rate of interest was in excess of sixteen percent (16%)).

As is further noted in *5 Collier on Bankruptcy,* ¶ 1129.03, at 1129–62 (15th ed. 1987):

> The concept of "present value" is of paramount importance to an understanding of section 1129(b). Simply stated, "present value" is a term of art for an almost self-evident proposition: a dollar in hand today is worth more than a dollar to be received a day, a month or a year hence. Part of the "present value" concept may be expressed by a corollary proposition: a dollar in hand today is worth exactly the same as (1) a dollar to be received a day, a month or a year hence plus (2) the rate of interest which the dollar would earn if invested at an appropriate interest rate.

While the debtor's Plan provides that Union Planters will retain the lien securing its claim, the Plan, as has been noted in the court's discussion of the § 1129(a)(7)(A) confirmation requirement, does not meet the "fair and equitable" test of § 1129(b)(2)(A)(i). The current market rate of interest on October 1, 1987, the date of the hearing on confirmation, approximated twelve percent (12%); the debtor's Plan proposes to pay Union Planters interest at a rate of nine percent (9%). Further, the Plan does not provide for Union Planters to receive the "indubitable equivalent" of its claim under § 1129(b)(2)(A)(iii). "[T]reatment which is less favorable than the treatment specified in section 1129(b)(2)(A)(i) and (ii) would not satisfy the ["indubitable equivalent"] test." *5 Collier on Bankruptcy,* ¶ 1129.03[c], at 1129–56 (15th ed. 1987).

The court further notes that § 1129(b)(2), in defining the requirements utilized by the court to determine whether the Plan is "fair and equitable," uses the word "includes." Bankruptcy Code § 102(3) entitled "Rules of construction" provides that "includes" is not limiting. 11 U.S.C.A. § 102(3) (West 1979). The implication in reference to the "fair and equitable" doctrine of § 1129(b)(2) is that the use of the term "includes" is open-ended. The court accordingly finds, irrespective of the statutory definition of "fair and equitable," that the debtor's Plan, in its treatment of the claim of Union Planters, is not "fair and equitable."

Union Planters' claim matured on September 30, 1985. The debtor's Plan converts the Union Planters construction loan to a twelve year loan (two years since the September 30, 1985, maturity of its loan plus ten years under the Plan) with Union Planters to occupy substantially the same position at the end of the ten year life of the Plan as it occupies today. The debtor presently owes Union Planters $8,400,000; at the end of the ten year Plan period it will owe Union Planters $6,950,096.16 against resort property subject to the use and abuse of the public, which at that time will be almost thirteen years old. In the interim, the debtor will defer until the eighth year of the Plan payment of more than forty-one percent (41%) of those payments due Union Planters during the first three Plan years. In fact, the Plan requirements for liquidating the Union Planters Class II claim, while a panacea for the debtor, causes Union Planters' claim to increase from $8,400,000 on October 1, 1987, to $9,149,393.30 at the end of Plan year three, with a modest reduction to $8,585,401.98 at the end of Plan year seven.[12] Only at the end of Plan year eight, after satisfaction of those payments deferred from Plan years one through three, will the Union Planters prepetition claim of $8,400,000 reflect a reduction.

The debtor's Plan does not meet the "fair and equitable" test with respect to the claim of Union Planters and thus cannot be confirmed under the "cram down" provisions of § 1129(b).

For the reasons set forth herein, confirmation of the debtor's "Amended Plan Of Reorganization" filed August 6, 1987, will be denied.

This Memorandum constitutes findings of fact and conclusions of law as required by Fed.R.Bankr.P. 7052.

---

[1] In addition to the evidence introduced at the confirmation hearing, the court has also considered portions of the debtor's amended disclosure statement filed August 6, 1987, approved as containing adequate information on September 4, 1987.

[2] The terms "hotel" and "motel" are used interchangeably by the debtor in its amended disclosure statement and Plan and also by witnesses testifying at the hearing on confirmation. The court draws no distinction between the use of these two terms.

[3] Under the permanent financing arrangement contemplated by the debtor, Union Planters, and Security Federal Savings and Loan Association, the permanent loan was to bear interest at a minimum rate of fourteen and one-half percent (14 1/2%).

[4] In its pre-hearing memorandum Union Planters reflects a principal and interest balance on October 1, 1987, amounting to $8,329.857.30. The debtor estimates an additional liability for attorney fees approximately $75,000. The parties agree that $8,400,000 represents the amount of Union Planters claim.

[5] This court in a Memorandum filed October 29, 1986, after consideration of a motion filed by Union Planters seeking relief from the automatic stay and abandonment, determined the fair market value of the Edgewater Motel, including land and improvements, to be not less than $11,500,000. At the October 1, 1987, confirmation hearing, Jack Mann, an MAI appraiser, testified that the fair market value of the debtor's property is $11,000,000.

[6] Pursuant to the provisions of 11 U.S.C.A. § 1126(f) (West Supp.1987), the holders of unimpaired Class I claims are conclusively presumed to have accepted the Plan.

[7] Jack Mann, the MAI appraiser testifying on behalf of the debtor, testified that liquidation value "severely restricted to, say, two weeks or a month . . . will run between 60 and 75 percent of market value." As has been noted, Mr. Mann testified that the market value of the Edgewater Motel is $11,000,000. The issue of liquidation value was not further explored by the debtor's attorney on direct examination and was only briefly alluded to by the attorney for Union Planters on cross examination. The debtor, in its amended disclosure statement and at the hearing on confirmation, has consistently represented that Union Planters is fully secured. The court cannot and will not now conclude from the undeveloped testimony of Mr. Mann that the liquidation value of the debtor's real estate is less than $8,400,000.

[8] This analysis has been prepared from an exhibit to the testimony of Stuart Rispler, controller of The LeConte Company, entitled "Projected Payments Under Amended Plan as Modified." The LeConte Company has managed the Edgewater Motel since mid-1986.

[9] Payments deferred during Plan years one through three total $1,057,729.64. These deferred payments remain unpaid through Plan year seven. Interest on these deferred payments is reflected in this chart for Plan years four through eight; the total amount of deferred payments is not reflected except in Plan year eight, the year of payment.

[10] The court further notes that the nine and four-tenths percent (9.4%) interest rate testified to by Mr. Harmon is not truly indicative of the current market rate of interest. Mr. Harmon testified that TexLaMiss purchased the River Terrace Hotel from First Federal Savings and Loan Association, which had acquired the hotel through foreclosure proceedings. As acknowledged by Mr. Harmon, the River Terrace Hotel was financed by a seller with an apparent need to divest itself of property due to regulations requiring it to charge that property off against its earnings. The court also notes that Mr. Harmon is the vice-president for finance for The LeConte Company, the entity presently managing the Edgewater Motel.

[11] In addition to the $1,057,729.64 due Union Planters during Plan years one through three, payment of which is deferred to Plan year eight, the debtor defers payment of the Borg-Warner Leasing Class III claim totaling $372,240.72 to Plan year six, and payment of Blaine-Hays Construction Company and First National Bank of Gatlinburg's Class IV

claims totaling $410,000 and $375,000, respectively, to Plan year seven.

[12] Under the twenty-five year amortization schedule proposed by the debtor, Union Planters will be entitled to receive $845,909.88, inclusive of principal and interest, during each Plan year, for a total of $2,537,729.64 during Plan years one through three. However, the Plan provides that $1,057,729.64 of the first three years payments will be deferred for payment in Plan year eight. This will affect the amount of the Union Planters claim as follows:

End of Plan Year	Amortized Balance	Deferred Payment	Total Claim
1	$8,306,287.03	$698,372.70 (includes deferred payment of $665,909.88 and interest on deferred payment of $32,462.82)	$9,004,659.73
2	8,203,783.13	911,819.76	9,115,602.89
3	8,091,663.66	1,057,729.64	9,149,393.30
4	7,969,026.63	1,057,729.64	9,026,756.27
5	7,834,885.37	1,057,729.64	8,892,615.01
6	7,688,160.75	1,057,729.64	8,745,890.39
7	7,527,672.34	1,057,729.64	8,585,401.98
8	7,352,129.03	1,057,729.64	8,409,858.67
9	7,160,118.54	—0—	7,160,118.54
10	6,950,096.16	—0—	6,950,096.16

SECTION 11 EFFECT OF CONFIRMATION OF THE PLAN

Upon **confirmation of the Chapter 11 plan,** the property of the estate, except as otherwise provided in the plan or in the order confirming the plan, vests in the debtor. 11 U.S.C.A. § 1141(b). The confirmed plan is a contract that binds the debtor, creditors, and interest holders. 11 U.S.C.A. § 1141(a). The payment or issuing of stock by the debtor to its creditors under the plan is a substitute for the debtor's legal obligation to these parties prior to the filing of the bankruptcy petition.

The confirmation of a Chapter 11 plan discharges the debtor and releases it from all claims and interests of creditors, equity security holders, and general partners, whether or not the claims and interests are impaired or whether or not their holders have accepted the plan. 11 U.S.C.A. § 1141(a). This is a very broad discharge which includes all debts arising prior to the filing of the Chapter 11 and some debts arising after the filing. Corporations and partnerships will not, however, be discharged under a liquidating plan. This prevents the corporate or partnership debtor from accomplishing a discharge under Chapter 11 that would be forbidden under Chapter 7. The individual debtor will be discharged whether it remains in business or liquidates its assets, unless it would be denied a discharge under section 727(a). It will not be discharged from any debt that is excepted from section 523 of the Code. 11 U.S.C.A. § 1141(d). These exceptions include spousal or child support, educational loans, and debts incurred through fraud.

The court shall hold the discharge or reaffirmation hearing not more than 30 days following the confirmation of a plan in a Chapter 11 reorganization case concerning an individual. Fed. R. Bank. P. 4008. The form used to confirm a Chapter 11 plan appears as Exhibit 8–11 (see p. 454).

EXHIBIT 8–10 Official Form No. 14 (Ballot for Accepting or Rejecting the Chapter 11 Plan)

Official Form 14
(12/03)

United States Bankruptcy Court

_______________ District of _______________

In re ________________________________, *Set forth here all names including married, maiden, and trade names used by debtor within last 6 years.]* Debtor	)	Case No. ____________
Address ________________________________ ________________________________	)	Chapter ________
Employer's Tax Identification (EIN) No(s). [if any]:________ ________________________________	)	
Last four digits of Social Security No(s).:____________	)	

CLASS *[ ]* BALLOT FOR ACCEPTING OR REJECTING PLAN OF REORGANIZATION

[Proponent] filed a plan of reorganization dated *[Date]* (the "Plan") for the Debtor in this case. The Court has *[conditionally]* approved a disclosure statement with respect to the Plan (the "Disclosure Statement"). The Disclosure Statement provides information to assist you in deciding how to vote your ballot. If you do not have a Disclosure Statement, you may obtain a copy from *[name, address, telephone number and telecopy number of proponent/proponentís attorney.]* Court approval of the disclosure statement does not indicate approval of the Plan by the Court.

You should review the Disclosure Statement and the Plan before you vote. You may wish to seek legal advice concerning the Plan and your classification and treatment under the Plan. Your *[claim] [equity interest]* has been placed in class *[ ]* under the Plan. If you hold claims or equity interests in more than one class, you will receive a ballot for each class in which you are entitled to vote.

If your ballot is not received by [*name and address of proponentís attorney or other appropriate address]* on or before *[date]*, and such deadline is not extended, your vote will not count as either an acceptance or rejection of the Plan.

If the Plan is confirmed by the Bankruptcy Court it will be binding on you whether or not you vote.

ACCEPTANCE OR REJECTION OF THE PLAN

[At this point the ballot should provide for voting by the particular class of creditors or equity holders receiving the ballot using one of the following alternatives;]

[If the voter is the holder of a secured, priority, or unsecured nonpriority claim:]

(continued)

EXHIBIT 8–10 Official Form No. 14 (Ballot for Accepting or Rejecting the Chapter 11 Plan), Continued

Official Form 14 continued
(12/03)

The undersigned, the holder of a Class *[ ]* claim against the Debtor in the unpaid amount of Dollars ($)

[or, if the voter is the holder of a bond, debenture, or other debt security:]

The undersigned, the holder of a Class *[ ]* claim against the Debtor, consisting of Dollars ($) principal amount of *[describe bond, debenture, or other debt security]* of the Debtor (For purposes of this Ballot, it is not necessary and you should not adjust the principal amount for any accrued or unmatured interest.)

[or, if the voter is the holder of an equity interest:]

The undersigned, the holder of Class *[ ]* equity interest in the Debtor, consisting of ______ shares or other interests of *[describe equity interest]* in the Debtor

[In each case, the following language should be included:]

(Check one box only)

[ ] ACCEPTS THE PLAN [ ] REJECTS THE PLAN

Dated: ____________________

Print or type name: __________________________

Signature: ___________________________________

Title (if corporation or partnership) _____________

Address: ______________________________

____

RETURN THIS BALLOT TO:

[Name and address of proponent's attorney or other appropriate address]

EXHIBIT 8–11 Official Form No. 15 (Order Confirming the Chapter 11 Plan)

United States Bankruptcy Court

_______________ District of _______________

In re ____,)
Set forth here all names including married, maiden, and trade names used by debtor within last 6 years.])
Debtor) Case No. _______________
)
Address ____)
____) Chapter __________
)
Employer's Tax Identification (EIN) No(s). [if any]:________)
____)
Last four digits of Social Security No(s).:______________)

ORDER CONFIRMING PLAN

The plan under chapter 11 of the Bankruptcy Code filed by ________________________________, on ________________ [*if applicable*, as modified by a modification filed on ____________________,] or a summary thereof, having been transmitted to creditors and equity security holders; and

It having been determined after hearing on notice that the requirements for confirmation set forth in 11 U.S.C. § 1129(a) [*or, if appropriate,* 11 U.S.C. § 1129(b)] have been satisfied;

IT IS ORDERED that:

The plan filed by ____, on ______________, *[If appropriate, include dates and any other pertinent details of modifications to the plan]* is confirmed. *[If the plan provides for an injunction against conduct not otherwise enjoined under the Code, include the information required by Rule 3020.]*

A copy of the confirmed plan is attached.

Dated: ______________________

BY THE COURT

____
United States Bankruptcy Judge

SECTION 12
DISTRIBUTION UNDER THE PLAN AND REPORTING BY DEBTOR IN POSSESSION OR CHAPTER 11 TRUSTEE

Upon confirmation of the plan, distribution is made to creditors and equity security holders whose claims have been allowed under the confirmed plan. Either the debtor in possession or the trustee in the case will usually handle distribution under the plan. The court, however, may appoint a person designated as agent to handle the money. In some cases, the court appoints a "trustee" to administer the plan. This is not the trustee in the Chapter 11 case. The court might also place some conditions on how the money is to be handled, who will handle it, and in what manner it is to be handled.

The debtor in possession or the trustee, after confirmation of the plan, is required to file such reports as are necessary or as the court orders. 11 U.S.C.A. § 1106(a)(7).

SECTION 13
REVOCATION OF AN ORDER OF CONFIRMATION

A party in interest may request revocation of an order of confirmation within 180 days of the order on the basis of fraud. 11 U.S.C.A. § 1144; Fed. R. Bank. P. 7001.

SECTION 14
FINAL REPORT AND FINAL DECREE

Confirmation of the plan does not end the case. The bankruptcy case remains open until the court formally enters an order closing the case. 11 U.S.C.A. § 350. After the estate is fully administered, a party in interest—usually the debtor, trustee, or proponent of the plan—files a final report and requests that the case be closed. Fed. R. Bank. P. 3022. The case is eligible to be closed once the plan has been substantially consummated. Substantial consummation is defined in 11 U.S.C.A. § 1101(2). The court retains jurisdiction over the plan until the case is closed. Closing the case at the earliest opportunity causes the quarterly fees to the U.S. trustee under 28 U.S.C.A. § 1930(a)(6) to stop.

If the debtor in possession or the trustee does not request the court to enter a final decree, a party in interest may move the court to enter a final decree or the court, on its own motion may enter a final decree closing the case. The form used to enter a final decree is shown in Exhibit 8–12.

Even after the case is closed, it is still subject to further action. In certain situations, a case may be amended without being reopened. For example, clerical errors in judgments, orders, and other parts of the record or errors in the record caused by oversight or omission may be corrected without reopening the case. A closed case may be reopened to add a creditor or to distribute previously undistributed property of the estate.

EXHIBIT 8–12 Sample Final Decree

B 271
(8/96)

United States Bankruptcy Court

_________________ District Of _________________

In re

Case No. ___________

Debtor*
Last four digits of Social Security No.:
Employer Tax I.D. No.:

Chapter ___________

FINAL DECREE

The estate of the above named debtor has been fully administered.

☐ The deposit required by the plan has been distributed.

IT IS ORDERED THAT:

☐ ____
(*name of trustee*)
is discharged as trustee of the estate of the above-named debtor and the bond is cancelled.

☐ the chapter _____ case of the above named debtor is closed; and

☐ [other provisions as needed]

_______________________ Date

_______________________ Bankruptcy Judge

**Set forth all names, including trade names, used by the debtor within the last 6 years. (Fed. R. Bankr. P. 1005). For joint debtors set forth both social security numbers.*

KEY TERMS

Absolute priority rule
Adequate information
Adequate protection
Bootstrap plan
Chapter 11 reorganization plan
Chapter 11 trustee
Confirmation of the Chapter 11 plan
Cramdown
Debtor in possession (DIP)
Disclosure statement
Equity security holder
Indubitable equivalent
Reorganization

Selecting the Appropriate Type of Bankruptcy Filing

CHAPTER OUTLINE

SECTION 1
ELIGIBILITY

SECTION 2
SELECTING THE CHAPTER IF THE DEBTOR IS ELIGIBLE UNDER MULTIPLE CHAPTERS

A. The Business Debtor
  1. Choosing to Liquidate under Chapter 7 or Reorganize under Chapter 11
  2. Choosing to Liquidate under Chapter 7 or Liquidate under Chapter 11
  3. Choosing to Reorganize under Chapter 11 or Adjust Debt under Chapter 12 or 13

B. The Nonbusiness Debtor
  1. Choosing to Liquidate under Chapter 7 or Adjust Debt under Chapter 13
  2. Choosing to Liquidate under Chapter 7 or Reorganize under Chapter 11
  3. Choosing to Reorganize under Chapter 11 or Adjust Debt under Chapter 13

After the debtor is interviewed, all pertinent financial information gathered, and the decision made by the debtor to file a petition in bankruptcy, the attorney must determine which bankruptcy chapter best fits the debtor's needs. The Bankruptcy Code provides four choices—Chapter 7, liquidation; Chapter 11, reorganization; Chapter 12, adjustment of debts of a family farmer with regular annual income; and Chapter 13, adjustment of debts of an individual or individual and spouse with regular income. Not every debtor is eligible for every chapter. If the debtor is eligible to file under more than one chapter, the debtor's choice is often clear.

SECTION 1 ELIGIBILITY

The Bankruptcy Code defines who may be a debtor under each operative chapter. 11 U.S.C.A. § 109(b)–(f). It is, of course, to be expected that the drafters of the Bankruptcy Code would make some bankruptcy relief available to virtually all entities. Certain entities such as insurance companies, banks, savings and loan associations, and credit unions, however, are excluded entirely from eligibility under the Bankruptcy Code. The liquidation or reorganization of those entities is governed by laws other than the Bankruptcy Code.

When a debtor comes to see an attorney, the debtor either operates a business or does not. Some business debtors prefer and are able to reorganize their business rather than liquidate. Others either are not good candidates for reorganization or for some other reason prefer to liquidate. In the twelve months ending on September 30, 2002, 1,547,669 bankruptcy petitions were filed in the 94 bankruptcy courts across the country. Exhibit 9–1 compares the numbers of business and nonbusiness filings and the numbers of Chapter 7, 11, 12, and 13 filings. This exhibit also may be found at http://www.uscourts.gov.

Of these 1,547,669 bankruptcy cases, only 39,091 or 2.5 percent were business filings. For statistical purposes, a bankruptcy is considered a business filing when the debts are primarily business debts regardless of whether the debtor is operating a business when the bankruptcy petition is filed.

EXAMPLE

If Joe, who owned and operated Joe's Garage, stopped operating his garage a year before filing for bankruptcy, and if most of his debt is the product of that failed business, the filing is considered a business filing.

If the debtor operates a business and either is not a good candidate or does not want to reorganize, the bankruptcy options are Chapter 7 and a liquidating Chapter 11. All business debtors, except railroads, insurance companies, banks, savings and loan associations, and credit unions are eligible for Chapter 7. All business debtors, except insurance companies, banks, savings and loan associations, credit unions, stockbrokers, and commodity brokers, are eligible for Chapter 11. Therefore, while railroads are only eligible for Chapter 11 and stockbrokers and commodity brokers are only eligible for Chapter 7, all other business debtors are eligible to file under either chapter.

If the debtor operates a business and wants to reorganize, the bankruptcy options are Chapters 11, 12, and 13. A business debtor that is eligible to file a Chapter 11 petition is also eligible to file a Chapter 13 petition if the debtor also meets the eligibility requirements for Chapter 13. First, because the eligibility for Chapter 13 is limited to an individual or an individual and spouse, the business must be owned and operated by an individual or an individual and spouse. If the debtor is a partnership or a corporation, it cannot file a Chapter 13. Second, Chapter 13 has a debt limit for both secured and unsecured debts, and these limits are relatively low for a business. 11 U.S.C.A. § 109(e). Most businesses, even if owned and operated by an individual or individual and spouse, cannot qualify because of the large amount of the debt owed. Third, the debtor's income must exceed his or her business and living expenses to produce sufficient disposable income to pay creditors under the Chapter 13 plan. Moreover, the disposable income must be regular enough to enable a debtor to make payments to the Chapter 13 trustee as often as every month.

A few business debtors that are eligible to file under Chapter 11 are also eligible to file under Chapter 12. To be eligible to file under Chapter 12, the debtor must qualify as a family farmer as defined by the Code. 11 U.S.C.A. § 109(f). Many farmers are not eligible under Chapter 12 because the definition of family farmer includes a debt limit. If a debtor is not eligible to file under Chapter 12, reorganization under Chapter 11 remains available.

In even fewer situations, business debtors that are eligible to file under Chapter 11 are also eligible to file under Chapter 12 and Chapter 13. To be eligible to file under Chapters 12 and 13, the debtor must meet the requirements for both chapters. First, while the family farmer in Chapter 12 could be an individual, partnership, or corporation, Chapter 13 restricts eligibility to an individual or an individual and spouse. Therefore, only a family farmer who is an individual or individual and spouse can be eligible under both chapters. Second, although both chapters have debt limits, the debt limits differ. The debt limit for Chapter 13 distinguishes between unsecured and secured debt, but the Chapter 12 debt limit is based on the aggregate debt of the debtor. Third, the Chapter 13 debtor must have regular disposable income to support payment to creditors under the Chapter 13 plan, usually monthly. The Chapter 12 debtor must only have regular annual income. Because of the very nature of farming, income may be received only once, twice, or three times a year and may vary greatly from year to year. Therefore, a debtor need not make payments

EXHIBIT 9–1 U.S. Bankruptcy Courts—Business and Nonbusiness Cases Commenced, by Chapter of the Bankruptcy Code, During the 12-Month Period Ending September 30, 2002

Circuit and District	Total Filings	Total Chapter 7	Total Chapter 11	Total Chapter 12	Total Chapter 13	Total Business Filings*	Business Chapter 7	Business Chapter 11	Business Chapter 12	Business Chapter 13	Total Nonbusiness Filings	Non-business Chapter 7	Non-business Chapter 11	Non-business Chapter 13
TOTAL	1,547,669	1,084,336	11,669	322	451,258	39,091	22,574	10,702	322	5,414	1,508,576	1,061,762	967	445,844
DC	2,521	1,770	34	—	717	58	26	29	—	3	2,463	1,744	5	714
1ST	44,149	30,578	390	7	13,173	1,226	712	358	7	150	49,921	29,866	32	13,023
ME	4,467	4,059	18	2	388	101	69	18	2	12	4,366	3,990	—	376
MA	17,069	14,363	199	3	2,503	433	232	195	3	2	16,636	14,131	4	2,501
NH	3,903	3,517	31	—	355	233	196	29	—	8	3,670	3,321	2	347
RI	4,830	4,430	6	—	394	68	60	6	—	2	4,762	4,370	—	392
PR	13,880	4,209	136	2	9,533	393	155	110	2	126	13,487	4,054	26	9,407
2ND	83,234	65,495	1,916	10	15,785	2,869	842	1,829	10	160	80,365	64,653	87	15,625
CT	11,456	9,513	122	—	1,821	179	69	107	—	3	11,277	9,444	15	1,818
NY, N	15,941	12,688	87	5	3,161	357	191	83	5	78	15,584	12,497	4	3,083
NY, E	25,098	19,296	182	—	5,620	315	140	169	—	6	24,783	19,156	13	5,614
NY, S	15,914	12,586	1,473	1	1,827	1,635	177	1,422	1	8	14,279	12,409	51	1,819
NY, W	13,051	9,851	45	4	3,150	282	189	41	4	47	12,769	9,662	4	3,103
VT	1,774	1,561	7	—	206	101	76	7	—	18	1,673	1,485	—	188
3RD	98,214	64,333	1,626	3	32,231	3,054	1,214	1,569	3	247	95,160	63,119	57	31,984
DE	3,966	1,960	892	—	1,094	981	55	890	—	16	2,985	1,905	2	1,078
NJ	40,708	25,611	357	—	14,739	702	363	326	—	12	40,006	25,248	31	14,727
PA, E	24,390	13,541	114	2	10,733	304	175	105	2	22	24,086	13,366	9	10,711
PA, M	12,495	9,499	66	—	2,930	620	391	64	—	165	11,875	9,108	2	2,765
PA, W	16,596	13,693	192	1	2,710	439	227	180	1	31	16,157	13,466	12	2,679
VI	59	29	5	—	25	8	3	4	—	1	51	26	1	24
4TH	139,082	88,505	682	6	49,888	2,701	1,814	590	6	290	136,381	86,691	92	49,598
MD	34,963	23,353	171	—	11,439	636	393	150	—	93	34,327	22,960	21	11,346
NC, E	14,820	7,310	63	6	7,441	232	139	55	6	32	14,588	7,171	8	7,409
NC, M	11,668	4,869	26	—	6,773	269	201	26	—	42	11,399	4,668	—	6,731
NC, W	9,429	4,840	54	—	4,535	98	51	46	—	1	9,331	4,789	8	4,534
SC	15,531	6,776	96	—	8,659	183	99	82	—	2	15,348	6,677	14	8,657
VA, E	30,141	21,168	169	—	8,804	391	226	134	—	31	29,750	20,942	35	8,773
VA, W	12,509	10,780	35	—	1,693	566	460	34	—	71	11,943	10,320	1	1,622
WV, N	4,200	3,912	23	—	265	108	78	20	—	10	4,092	3,834	3	255
WV, S	5,821	5,497	45	—	279	218	167	43	—	8	5,603	5,330	2	271

(continued)

EXHIBIT 9–1 U.S. Bankruptcy Courts—Business and Nonbusiness Cases Commenced, by Chapter of the Bankruptcy Code, During the 12-Month Period Ending September 30, 2002, *(continued)*

Circuit and District	Total Filings	Total Chapter 7	Total Chapter 11	Total Chapter 12	Total Chapter 13	Total Business Filings*	Business Chapter 7	Business Chapter 11	Business Chapter 12	Business Chapter 13	Total Nonbusiness Filings	Non-business Chapter 7	Non-business Chapter 11	Non-business Chapter 13
5TH	**128,684**	**72,092**	**1,212**	**47**	**55,329**	**4,009**	**2,110**	**1,102**	**47**	**746**	**124,675**	**69,982**	**110**	**54,583**
LA, E	9,579	6,478	66	—	3,035	177	115	59	—	3	9,402	6,363	7	3,032
LA, M	3,678	2,595	54	—	1,029	68	17	50	—	1	3,610	2,578	4	1,028
LA, W	13,583	7,269	47	12	6,255	470	267	44	12	147	13,113	7,002	3	6,108
MS, N	8,080	5,372	47	2	2,659	122	67	45	2	8	7,958	5,305	2	2,651
MS, S	14,019	8,920	85	6	5,008	173	87	70	6	10	13,846	8,833	15	4,998
TX, N	28,195	13,572	290	13	14,319	1,142	645	276	13	207	27,053	12,927	14	14,112
TX, E	12,243	6,555	77	2	5,609	358	167	73	2	116	11,885	6,388	4	5,493
TX, S	20,812	11,112	364	3	9,332	815	369	325	3	117	19,997	10,743	39	9,215
TX, W	18,495	10,219	182	9	8,083	684	376	160	9	137	17,811	9,843	22	7,946
6TH	**218,300**	**149,170**	**1,046**	**18**	**68,066**	**3,556**	**2,128**	**953**	**18**	**457**	**214,744**	**147,042**	**93**	**67,609**
KY, E	11,905	10,310	107	—	1,488	246	129	105	—	12	11,659	10,181	2	1,476
KY, W	14,934	11,920	57	1	2,956	126	67	51	1	7	14,808	11,853	6	2,949
MI, E	37,517	25,551	184	3	11,779	442	230	177	3	32	37,075	25,321	7	11,747
MI, W	15,012	11,326	72	3	3,611	325	202	69	3	51	14,687	11,124	3	3,560
OH, N	40,341	33,090	128	—	7,123	1,035	782	125	—	128	39,306	32,308	3	6,995
OH, S	35,781	27,532	106	5	8,138	557	329	99	5	124	35,224	27,203	7	8,014
TN, E	19,466	11,904	74	4	7,484	320	189	70	4	57	19,146	11,715	4	7,427
TN, M	15,360	9,500	194	—	5,666	273	104	154	—	15	15,087	9,396	40	5,651
TN, W	27,984	8,037	124	2	19,821	232	96	103	2	31	27,752	7,941	21	19,790
7TH	**157,125**	**121,383**	**724**	**52**	**34,963**	**2,874**	**1,880**	**677**	**52**	**263**	**154,251**	**119,503**	**47**	**34,700**
IL, N	55,985	39,360	385	1	16,237	831	466	356	1	6	55,154	38,894	29	16,231
IL, C	15,353	13,071	41	21	2,220	193	125	39	21	8	15,160	12,946	2	2,212
IL, S	8,859	6,304	26	8	2,521	286	173	23	8	82	8,573	6,131	3	2,439
IN, N	20,591	17,239	48	2	3,302	215	142	47	2	24	20,376	17,097	1	3,278
IN, S	32,095	25,156	159	—	6,780	491	304	153	—	34	31,604	24,852	6	6,746
WI, E	16,079	13,076	16	7	2,979	229	186	16	7	20	15,850	12,890	—	2,959
WI, W	8,163	7,177	49	13	924	629	484	43	13	89	7,534	6,693	6	835
8TH	**98,774**	**74,601**	**350**	**53**	**23,768**	**3,203**	**2,382**	**319**	**53**	**447**	**95,571**	**72,219**	**31**	**23,321**
AR, E	14,546	7,646	22	2	6,876	131	72	14	2	43	14,415	7,574	8	6,833
AR, W	8,148	5,489	18	1	2,639	109	53	15	1	39	8,039	5,436	3	2,600
IA, N	4,451	4,272	15	2	162	198	173	14	2	9	4,253	4,099	1	153
IA, S	7,022	6,568	11	4	439	136	113	11	4	8	6,886	6,455	—	431
MN	19,655	16,337	56	6	3,256	1,825	1,501	55	6	263	17,830	14,836	1	2,993
MO, E	17,538	11,651	79	5	5,802	216	123	72	5	15	17,322	11,528	7	5,787
MO, W	15,270	12,319	84	2	2,865	228	107	81	2	36	15,044	12,212	3	2,829
NE	7,443	5,844	52	19	1,528	132	55	44	19	14	7,311	5,789	8	1,514
ND	2,028	1,940	8	9	71	108	87	8	9	4	1,920	1,853	—	67
SD	2,673	2,535	5	3	130	122	98	5	3	16	2,551	2,437	—	114

(continued)

EXHIBIT 9–1 U.S. Bankruptcy Courts—Business and Nonbusiness Cases Commenced, by Chapter of the Bankruptcy Code, During the 12-Month Period Ending September 30, 2002, *(continued)*

Circuit and District	Total Filings	Total Chapter 7	Total Chapter 11	Total Chapter 12	Total Chapter 13	Total Business Filings*	Business Chapter 7	Business Chapter 11	Business Chapter 12	Business Chapter 13	Total Nonbusiness Filings	Non-business Chapter 7	Non-business Chapter 11	Non-business Chapter 13
9TH	**279,561**	**226,434**	**2,163**	**58**	**50,890**	**9,319**	**5,502**	**1,891**	**58**	**1,854**	**270,242**	**220,932**	**272**	**49,036**
AK	1,432	1,291	18	—	123	112	80	16	—	16	1,320	1,211	2	107
AZ	28,738	22,788	323	6	5,620	733	372	271	6	83	28,005	22,416	52	5,537
CA, N	20,719	14,512	260	—	5,945	1,277	706	241	—	329	19,442	13,806	19	5,616
CA, E	31,455	26,584	117	20	4,733	1,265	823	104	20	317	30,190	25,761	13	4,416
CA, C	84,936	70,142	614	1	14,170	2,545	1,806	561	1	169	82,391	68,336	53	14,001
CA, S	12,844	10,336	64	—	2,443	223	159	50	—	13	12,621	10,177	14	2,430
HI	4,684	4,181	21	—	482	57	38	19	—	-	4,627	4,143	2	482
ID	8,686	7,440	64	8	1,174	287	171	52	8	56	8,399	7,269	12	1,118
MT	4,102	3,584	19	8	491	122	87	15	8	12	3,980	3,497	4	479
NV	19,095	14,000	312	—	4,782	447	147	281	—	18	18,648	13,853	31	4,764
OR	24,034	20,626	70	10	3,327	1,515	679	70	10	755	22,519	19,947	—	2,572
WA, E	10,059	7,596	87	5	2,371	295	169	62	5	59	9,764	7,427	25	2,312
WA, W	28,349	22,980	187	—	5,182	409	241	143	—	25	27,940	22,739	44	5,157
GUAM	400	350	6	—	44	26	19	5	—	2	374	331	1	42
NMI	28	24	1	—	3	6	5	1	—	—	22	19	—	3
10TH	**91,306**	**74,488**	**413**	**53**	**16,350**	**2,750**	**1,987**	**390**	**53**	**318**	**88,556**	**72,501**	**23**	**16,032**
CO	20,303	17,666	110	4	2,523	560	416	107	4	33	19,743	17,250	3	2,490
KS	14,519	11,790	48	18	2,663	243	148	45	18	32	14,276	11,642	3	2,631
NM	8,975	8,084	54	2	835	665	549	51	2	63	8,310	7,535	3	772
OK, N	6,374	5,808	24	—	542	322	275	21	—	26	6,052	5,533	3	516
OK, E	4,500	4,143	10	3	344	79	52	10	3	14	4,421	4,091	—	330
OK, W	12,959	10,985	41	20	1,912	252	173	39	20	19	12,707	10,812	2	1,893
UT	21,444	13,922	116	6	7,399	590	347	108	6	128	20,854	13,575	8	7,271
WY	2,232	2,090	10	—	132	39	27	9	—	3	2,193	2,063	1	129
11TH	**206,719**	**115,487**	**1,113**	**15**	**90,098**	**3,470**	**1,977**	**995**	**15**	**479**	**203,249**	**113,510**	**118**	**89,619**
AL, N	24,514	11,336	105	3	13,068	194	100	81	3	8	24,320	11,236	24	13,060
AL, M	9,552	4,900	12	—	4,640	133	99	10	—	24	9,419	4,801	2	4,616
AL, S	7,256	3,112	29	—	4,115	63	29	28	—	6	7,193	3,083	1	4,109
FL, N	6,394	5,047	36	—	1,311	74	40	34	—	—	6,320	5,007	2	1,311
FL, M	51,706	37,314	304	2	14,085	961	555	280	2	124	50,745	36,759	24	13,961
FL, S	32,230	22,789	323	—	9,115	840	520	293	—	25	31,390	22,269	30	9,090
GA, N	41,945	19,169	213	—	22,563	914	489	186	—	239	41,031	18,680	27	22,324
GA, M	17,832	7,625	60	7	10,140	160	72	55	7	26	17,672	7,553	5	10,114
GA, S	15,290	4,195	31	3	11,061	131	73	28	3	27	15,159	4,122	3	11,034

*THESE FIGURES INCLUDE THE FOLLOWING CASES NOT REFLECTED ELSEWHERE:

MA—SECTION 304	= 01	NY.S—SECTION 304	= 27	NY.W—SECTION 304	= 01
DE—SECTION 304	= 20	NJ—SECTION 304	= 01	VA.W—SECTION 304	= 01
TX.N—CHAPTER 9	= 01	TX.S—CHAPTER 9	= 01	TX.W—SECTION 304	= 02
IL.N—SECTION 304	= 02	WI, E—SECTION 304	= 01	AR.W—CHAPTER 9	= 01
MO.E—CHAPTER 9	= 01	AZ—SECTION 304	= 01	CA.N—SECTION 304	= 02
CA.E—CHAPTER 9	= 01	CA.C—CHAPTER 9	= 01	CA.C—SECTION 304	= 06
CA.S—SECTION 304	= 01	NV—SECTION 304	= 01	OR—SECTION 304	= 01
OK.W—SECTION 304	= 01	UT—SECTION 304	= 01	AL.N—CHAPTER 9	= 02
FL, M—SECTION 304	= 01	FL, S—SECTION 304	= 03		

EXHIBIT 9–2 Business Filings during Twelve Months Ending September 30, 2002

Chapter	No. of Filings
7	22,574
11	10,702
12	322
13	5,414
Total	39,012

under Chapter 12 as often as monthly. If the debtor is not eligible under both chapters, it is still eligible for the chapter under which it does qualify. And if the debtor does not qualify under either, it is still eligible under Chapter 11.

Exhibit 9–1 provides the data for Exhibit 9–2 that compares the number of business bankruptcy filings by chapter for the twelve month period ending September 30, 2002. Note that the Chapter 7 business filings outnumber the Chapter 11 business filings by more than two to one; the Chapter 11 business filings outnumber the Chapter 13 business filings by almost two to one; and the number of Chapter 12 filings is less than one percent of the total number of business filings.

If the debtor does not operate a business, it may consider Chapter 7 for liquidation, Chapter 13 for adjustment of debt, and in a rare case, Chapter 11 for reorganization. Chapter 12 is not available because a family farmer by definition is a business. As with the business debtor, the selection of which chapter or chapters are available to a nonbusiness debtor initially comes down to eligibility.

All nonbusiness debtors are eligible for Chapter 7 because the only entities not qualified for Chapter 7 (i.e., railroads, insurance companies, banks, savings and loan associations, and credit unions) are all business debtors. 11 U.S.C.A. § 109(b). Also, all nonbusiness debtors are eligible for Chapter 11, because the Chapter 11 exclusions (i.e., insurance companies, banks, savings and loan associations, credit unions, and stockbrokers and commodity brokers) are all business debtors. Neither Chapter 7 nor Chapter 11 has a debt limit.

A nonbusiness debtor that is eligible to file a Chapter 7 or 11 petition will also be eligible to file a Chapter 13 petition if the debtor meets the eligibility requirements for Chapter 13. First, the debtor must be an individual or an individual and spouse. The debtor satisfies this requirement by being a nonbusiness debtor. Second, Chapter 13 has a debt limit for both secured and unsecured debts. Most nonbusiness debtors do not exceed these debt limits. Third, the debtor's income must exceed his or her living expenses to produce sufficient disposable income to pay creditors under the Chapter 13 plan. The disposable income must also be regular enough for the debtor to make payments to the Chapter 13 trustee as often as every month. If the nonbusiness debtor is not eligible for a Chapter 13 filing, the debtor may still file under Chapter 7 or 11.

Of the 1,547,669 bankruptcy cases filed during the twelve months ending September 30, 2002, 1,508,578 or 97.5 percent were nonbusiness filings. Exhibit 9–1 provides the data for Exhibit 9–3 that compares the nonbusiness bankruptcy filings by chapters for the twelve-month period ending September 30, 2002. Note that the Chapter 7 filings exceeded the Chapter 13 filings by more than two to one and the Chapter 11 filings were slightly more than five hundredth of a percent of the total number of nonbusiness bankruptcy filings.

EXHIBIT 9–3 Nonbusiness Filings during Twelve Months Ending September 30, 2002

Chapter	No. of Filings
7	1,061,762
11	967
13	445,844
Total	1,508,573

From this discussion, it becomes apparent that many business debtors have only a choice between liquidation under Chapter 7 and liquidation or reorganization under Chapter 11, and nonbusiness debtors have no choice but to liquidate under Chapter 7. But some debtors are eligible under more than one chapter and it is these choices that are explored in the following section.

SECTION 2 SELECTING THE CHAPTER IF THE DEBTOR IS ELIGIBLE UNDER MULTIPLE CHAPTERS

This section deals with situations in which the debtor is eligible to file under more than one chapter of the Bankruptcy Code. The discussion first addresses the business debtor and then the nonbusiness debtor.

A. THE BUSINESS DEBTOR

Generally, a debtor who operates a business and who wants to reorganize is eligible for reorganization under Chapter 11. In a limited number of situations, a debtor may also be eligible to adjust debt under Chapter 12, Chapter 13, or both. Some business debtors who strive to reorganize under Chapter 11 or adjust debt under Chapter 12 or 13 ultimately liquidate under Chapter 7 because of their inability to become sufficiently profitable. Not all business debtors, however, seek reorganization or adjustment of debt. Those who would like to liquidate may choose Chapter 7 or Chapter 11 and propose a liquidating plan.

1. Choosing to Liquidate under Chapter 7 or Reorganize under Chapter 11

The ultimate choice for the debtor between filing Chapter 7 or Chapter 11 hinges on whether the debtor truly wants to continue the business and whether it can realistically reorganize. The desire to continue business operations may be based on a practical assessment of reorganization possibilities or an emotional tie to the business.

In many cases, debtors file under Chapter 11 in an effort to reorganize but they fail for a number of reasons. They may be undercapitalized. They may run out of cash. They may suffer from a lack of business acumen. They may be in a business that will never be profitable. Bankruptcy provides a mechanism through which debtors can restructure their debt but it will not make an unprofitable business profitable.

The attorney's role is to evaluate whether it is feasible for the debtor to attempt a reorganization. What is the problem with the business; why does it have financial problems; and is the debtor capable of performing the fiduciary duties of a debtor in possession?

Filing a Chapter 11 has always been an expensive and cumbersome process for the smaller business, and is often a mistake. Small businesses may file under Chapter 11 in a last gasp effort to keep the business going, when there is no realistic hope of reorganization. A number of small businesses are prolonged by filing under Chapter 11 when they should have filed under Chapter 7. The results obtained in such cases do not warrant the time and money spent on a Chapter 11, because creditors wind up with less than they would have received under Chapter 7 and the process takes an emotional toll on the debtor. Some small businesses merely want to keep operating until a buyer is found in the hope that the sale will provide them with sufficient cash to pay existing creditors. This strategy nearly always fails, and the business usually liquidates through Chapter 7.

If the debtor does have the will to reorganize and the business can become profitable, reorganization under Chapter 11 provides the debtor with several beneficial features. Partnerships and corporations may discharge unsecured debt under Chapter 11 through confirmation of a plan. A confirmed Chapter 11 plan will discharge all debts of a partnership or a corporation except those to be repaid under the plan.

The Chapter 11 plan can be confirmed with the consent of all impaired classes or by cramdown over the objections of creditors. The plan, however, must meet the best interests of creditors test (i.e., unsecured creditors would receive no less than they would receive in a Chapter 7) and the fair and equitable test for unsecured creditors (i.e., unless the creditors agree otherwise, that going down the line of priorities, the creditors with subordinate claims or ownership interests receive nothing unless the group with a higher priority is paid in full). Cramdown, the best interests of creditors test, and the fair and equitable test, as they relate to a Chapter 11 case, were discussed in Chapter Eight of this text.

2. Choosing to Liquidate under Chapter 7 or Liquidate under Chapter 11

Most business debtors are eligible under both Chapter 7 and Chapter 11 and therefore could liquidate under Chapter 11. However, Chapter 7 is generally used unless the debtor has a complex business that extends beyond the expertise of a Chapter 7 trustee or it is believed that a greater return for creditors will be obtained if the business is sold as a going concern. Large Chapter 11 cases involving corporate debtors will usually be filed for the purpose of reorganization, yet it is entirely permissible for debtors to liquidate under a liquidating plan. 11 U.S.C.A. § 1123(b)(4). It is possible to liquidate in Chapter 11 so that some or all of the assets are sold during the pendency of the case free and clear of liens and interests with the liens and interests attaching to the proceeds. 11 U.S.C.A. § 363(f). The plan then determines how the proceeds are to be paid.

If liquidation is inevitable, it may be important for the debtor to try to control who will oversee it. Unless a trustee is appointed, the debtor in possession in a Chapter 11 will manage the liquidation. It would be advantageous to handle it this way, because the debtor has special incentive to maximize the amount received for the liquidation of the debtor's business. In these instances, time may be needed to sell off the assets of the estate to maximize return, or the business may need to continue because an operating business may bring more than a piecemeal sale of the assets.

3. Choosing to Reorganize under Chapter 11 or Adjust Debt under Chapter 12 or 13

The business debtor who wants to reorganize and who is eligible for a Chapter 13 (an individual or individual and spouse whose debts are within the debt limits and who have regular disposable income to pay creditors under the Chapter 13 plan) has a choice between Chapter 11 and Chapter 13. Although Chapter 11 allows the debtor to pay creditors over a period longer than three to five years, to pay under more flexible terms than under Chapter 13, and, by being the debtor in possession, to control the prosecution of avoidance actions, the individual debtor will usually find it in his or her best interest to use Chapter 13 rather than Chapter 11. Chapter 13 was specifically designed for such a debtor.

A Chapter 13 is less expensive than a Chapter 11. A small business may wish to continue to operate but find Chapter 11 too expensive. The Chapter 11 process takes longer than Chapter 13 and is far more complicated. A Chapter 13 plan is less complex and can usually be confirmed within a few months while a Chapter 11 plan may not be confirmed for many more months. Consequently, the professional fees and court costs are much higher in Chapter 11.

EXAMPLE

The filing fee for a Chapter 11 exceeds the filing fee for a Chapter 13. The fact that there may be a creditors' committee and a prolonged confirmation process involving a more complex plan in a Chapter 11 increases attorney's fees. The Chapter 11 also includes a quarterly U.S. trustee's fee. 28 U.S.C.A. § 1930(a)(6).

Since the debtor is in possession in a Chapter 11, the attorney for the debtor will be required to do substantially more work than the attorney for the Chapter 13 debtor, thus increasing the costs for a Chapter 11. Also, the debtor, by being a debtor in possession, may need to hire additional professionals, such as accountants, to prepare the reports required by the U.S. trustee.

In a Chapter 13, the plan may not be less than three years (36 months) nor more than five years (60 months). In a Chapter 11, the plan need not fit within a 36- to 60-month framework. A Chapter 11 reorganization may be completed in less than three years or in some cases, may require more than five years to complete.

In a Chapter 13, the debtor retains more control over the business. There is no creditors' committee, only the debtor may file a Chapter 13 plan (in Chapter 11, the debtor has the exclusive right to file a plan for only 120 days), and the creditors do not vote on the plan. Because they do not have a vote in Chapter 13, creditors can block confirmation only by objecting. Under the absolute priority rule in Chapter 11, the debtor may usually retain ownership in the business only if the class of unsecured creditors votes in favor of the plan as a class. Otherwise, the debtor cannot confirm a plan under circumstances where the debtor retains ownership.

Adequate protection, an issue in Chapter 11, is not as much of an issue in Chapter 13. Because Chapter 13 moves at a quicker pace, creditors have less concern about the preservation of their collateral. One of the key fights in a Chapter 11 will be for control of collateral. If the debtor in possession keeps the property and uses it, the question becomes what the debtor will have to pay the creditor to use the collateral and under what terms.

In a Chapter 13, all priority claims must be paid in full under the plan but may be paid without the accrual of interest over the term of the plan. In some cases, the total amount required to be paid on priority claims exceeds what the debtor can pay over the length of a Chapter 13 plan. In that event the debtor must consider Chapter 11, which will allow certain priority claims to be paid with interest over a longer term with the creditors' consent.

EXAMPLE

Jeri Baldwin is a divorced mother of three. Her former husband has full custody of the children and Jeri is obligated to pay $750 a month child support. Jeri's unsecured debt (mostly business debt) is $75,000 and her secured debt is $25,000. She operates her own business, a florist shop, and nets $3,000 a month. Her living expenses total $2,000 a month. She is three months in arrears on her child support payments and owes the IRS $6,000 in back taxes.

If Jeri were to file under Chapter 13, she would have $250 a month of disposable income to contribute to the plan after the payment of her monthly child support. Under a 60-month plan, she would contribute $15,000. Under a Chapter 13 plan, Jeri's priority claims would be back child support ($750 × 3) or $2,250, back taxes of $6,000, attorney fees of $1,000, and Chapter 13 trustee fees of 6% of the total she contributes to fund the plan, or $900 ($15,000 × .06). Thus the total of her priority claims would be $10,150 and her Chapter 13 plan would be confirmable.

PROBLEM 9.1 If Jeri's net were $2,750 a month and her expenses were $2,000 a month, would her Chapter 13 plan be confirmable?

PROBLEM 9.2 If Jeri's net were $3,000 a month and her expenses were $2,000 a month, would a 48-month plan be confirmable?

In a Chapter 13, the debtor gets relief from interest accumulating on priority claims. The Chapter 13 debtor need not pay interest on priority claims as long as the priority claims are paid in full under the plan.

EXAMPLE

Juanita and Carlos Montoya owed the IRS $13,000 in back taxes on their mom & pop business. The $13,000 represented taxes owed, accumulated interest, and penalties as of the time the Montoyas filed their petition in bankruptcy under Chapter 13. Under their Chapter 13 plan, they must pay the IRS all of its priority claim, $13,000, but no further interest or penalties will accumulate on the IRS's priority claim.

The business debtor who is both a family farmer under Chapter 13 and an individual or an individual and spouse, within the debt limit for a Chapter 13, and has regular disposable income to pay creditors under the Chapter 13 plan, has the choice to adjust debt under Chapter 12 or Chapter 13. There is, however, no reason why a farmer would choose Chapter 13 over Chapter 12. Chapter 12 was drafted using Chapter 13 as a model, but Chapter 12 provides the debtor with greater flexibility in paying debt. Under a Chapter 12, secured claims may be paid over a term beyond the five-year limit of a Chapter 13 plan. 11 U.S.C.A. § 1222(b)(9). Chapter 12 also gives the debtor flexibility in the timing of the plan payments that is not available in Chapter 13.

B. THE NONBUSINESS DEBTOR

A debtor who does not operate a business may liquidate under Chapter 7 and, if eligible, may adjust his or her debt under Chapter 13. The nonbusiness debtor is eligible to file for reorganization under Chapter 11, but for reasons discussed shortly, will most likely not select that option.

1. Choosing to Liquidate under Chapter 7 or Adjust Debt under Chapter 13

Nonbusiness debtors who are eligible under Chapter 13 have a choice beyond liquidation under Chapter 7. Whether this choice is viable depends on whether a filing of a Chapter 7 petition will be substantial abuse under 11 U.S.C.A. § 707(b) and whether the debtor has the incentive to fund the Chapter 13 plan for three to five years.

The Bankruptcy Code contains incentives for eligible debtors to file Chapter 13, rather than liquidate under Chapter 7. Moreover, the Bankruptcy Code and official forms are designed to identify those debtors who could file Chapter 13 but, for whatever reason, choose not to. For instance, Schedules I and J construed together reveal a debtor's disposable income; the clerk's notice, required by 11 U.S.C.A. § 342(b) tells debtors which operative chapters of the Bankruptcy Code are available to them; and, by virtue of 11 U.S.C.A. § 342(d) the trustee in a Chapter 7 case is required at the meeting of creditors to make sure that the debtor is aware of, among other things, the debtor's ability to file under a different chapter of the Bankruptcy Code. Of course, under 11 U.S.C.A. § 707(b) a court may dismiss a Chapter 7 case filed by an individual debtor if the court finds that affording the debtor relief under Chapter 7 would constitute substantial abuse. Having sufficient disposable income to fund a Chapter 13 plan is indicative of substantial abuse.

PROBLEM 9.3 Return to Exhibit 9–1. What is the ratio between the nonbusiness filings under Chapter 7 and Chapter 13?

In what region of the country is Chapter 13 most prevalent? Why do you think so many more Chapter 13 cases are filed in that region than in other regions? Do you think that some of the nonbankruptcy options discussed in Chapter 4 might play a role and, if so, which ones?

If a nonbusiness debtor has enough disposable income to fund a Chapter 13 plan but not enough disposable income to face a dismissal of a Chapter 7 petition under 11 U.S.C.A. § 707(b), the debtor should consider a number of factors when making a choice between Chapter 7 and Chapter 13.

Because Chapter 7 is liquidation, it does not involve a payment plan. Chapter 13, however, is adjustment of debt under a plan. Only the debtor is allowed to file a Chapter 13 plan. The creditors have no vote but they may object if certain requirements are not met. This gives the debtor control over the formulation of the plan.

The debtor must comply with all the provisions of Chapter 13 to get a plan confirmed. For instance, the debtor must pay all priority claims (including administrative claims) in full and must pay the unsecured creditors not less than they would receive under Chapter 7 (i.e., the best interests of creditors test). 11 U.S.C.A. § 1325(a)(4).

A separate requirement for confirmation of a Chapter 13 plan is that a plan must be proposed in good faith. 11 U.S.C.A. § 1325(a)(3). It takes extreme circumstances to find an absence of good faith. The absence of good faith is established by a number of factors known as the totality of the circumstances test. Those factors include the duration of the plan, the accuracy of the debtor's schedules, the extent to which secured claims are to be modified by the plan, whether the debt to be discharged includes debt nondischargeable in Chapter 7, and the frequency of the debtor's bankruptcy filings. Failure to pay nondischargeable debt may not, by itself, be sufficient to demonstrate an absence of good faith. One reason for an expanded discharge in Chapter 13 that is available without the six-year waiting period applicable to Chapter 7 is to encourage debtors that have nondischargeable debt to file for relief under Chapter 13. The fact that a debtor is contributing all of his or her disposable income into the plan for three to five years should be enough to demonstrate good faith even though the debtor has not paid his or her nondischargeable debt. The debtor is doing all that he or she could do outside of bankruptcy.

EXAMPLE

Sarah Jane Stuart, a divorced woman with a 15-year-old daughter at home, works for the ABC Packing Company as a secretary. She earns a gross salary of $1,500 a month with a take-home paycheck of $1,281. Sarah also receives $300 a month for child support from her former husband. She rents an apartment. She owns an automobile, which is financed, some household furnishings, and her wearing apparel. Everything she owns is exempt property under the applicable law of the state where she resides. Her daughter has continuing medical problems because of arthritis, but most of these medical expenses are covered by insurance. Sarah is finding it extremely difficult to meet her financial obligations and is considering filing bankruptcy. Her attorney has advised her to file under Chapter 13.

The statement of income and expenditures reflects monthly expenses of $1,203, giving Sarah $378 a month as disposable income in accordance with the required calculation method. (See Fed. R. Bank. P 1007(b)(1). This refers to Official Form No. 6, Schedules I and J. See also 11 U.S.C.A. § 1325(b)(2) defining "disposable income." Note the requirement for inclusion of the support payment as a part of income.) The living expense items on the income and expense statement are based on what the debtor will be paying over the plan period. Obligations to be paid under the plan are not included in the budget in Schedule J; therefore, certain items that may have been installment payments will be paid under the plan. These items are part of the plan, not part of the monthly living expenses.

The district in which Sarah will file her Chapter 13 case requires that installment payments for automobiles be made under the plan and through the trustee. Basically, the debtor in a Chapter 13 case must pay disposable income for 36 months to the trustee. See 11 U.S.C.A. § 1325(b)(1)(B). The $378 a month will, for the first 24 months, be applied to the payment of administrative costs (including the trustee's fees of 10 percent and the balance of the fee owed to the attorney), to the $280 monthly car payment, and then to other creditors. The car will be paid off in 24 months, at which point the entire payment to the trustee will be applied to the administrative costs and other creditors. The only secured creditor is First Bank for the car payment. There are unsecured debts of $9,417. The car is worth a little more than the debt against it, and Sarah will propose in the plan to make the payments as scheduled in her original loan agreement. If the car were worth an amount less than the loan amount, the loan could be restructured in the Chapter 13 plan by reducing the banks' secured claim to the value of the vehicle and adding the difference to the unsecured claims. Up to this point, the case is a routine situation without a substantial problem.

This particular debtor, however, does have a problem. While Sarah's situation might point to the filing of a Chapter 13 case without this problem, the fact that she has a debt that may not be dischargeable under Chapter 7 makes filing under Chapter 13 even more desirable. About one year ago, Sarah and her former husband borrowed money from Friendly Finance Company, a consumer finance company, for the purpose (according to the loan application) of buying furniture for their home. An invoice was issued by a local furniture company and was taken with the loan application to the Friendly Finance office. The furniture was to be collateral for the loan. Everything was signed and the money was received from Friendly Finance, but the furniture was never purchased.

If Sarah files a Chapter 7 case, Friendly Finance would probably sue her by filing a complaint in the bankruptcy court claiming a nondischargeable debt on account of obtaining money by false pretenses. 11 U.S.C.A. § 523(a)(2)(A). This indebtedness is for $3,000, and the possibility of defending against a nondischargeability claim does not appear to be good. The effect of a Chapter 7 case would be that Sarah would not be paying the other unsecured creditors, people whom she would really like to pay. She would have to discharge those debts to be able to pay the cost of defending the nondischargeability case. The $3,000 debt would very likely be declared nondischargeable, and Sarah would ultimately have to pay it. Chapter 13 would permit her to pay less than 100 percent on her unsecured debt and the broad Chapter 13 discharge would allow her to discharge a debt that would be nondischargeable in a Chapter 7.

Assuming a plan based on these considerations, the unsecured creditors, including Friendly Finance, would receive about 50 cents on the dollar, the automobile would be paid off in two years, and the problem of the nondischargeable debt would be solved. Therefore, in this case, it would appear to be a good strategic move to recommend a Chapter 13 filing.

The percentage needed to be paid on an unsecured debt to meet the good faith requirement will probably depend on the particular district or even the attitude of each bankruptcy judge within the district. The majority of the cases in which all the debts are either secured or exempt, however, do not require any payment on unsecured claims to meet the best interests test, and the Code requires only that all the debtor's disposable income be committed for three to five years.

In a Chapter 13, it is unnecessary to cramdown unsecured creditors because they have no vote. Cramdown in a Chapter 13 applies only to secured creditors. If the secured creditor does not accept the settlement, the debtor may surrender the property securing the claim to the creditor. 11 U.S.C.A. § 1325(a)(5)(C). If the value of the collateral does not fully cover the claim, there will be a deficiency. The deficiency becomes an unsecured claim. The attorney for the debtor may want to obtain a full release from the creditor when the property is surrendered. This should be provided for in the plan. The full release in the plan eliminates the deficiency claim. If the debtor cannot get a release upon surrender of the property, then the plan must provide that the creditor will retain the unsecured claim to be treated with other unsecured claims. Alternatively, the debtor may have a secured claim (equal to the value of the collateral) over the term of the plan with interest. 11 U.S.C.A. § 1325(a)(5)(B).

Cramdown under Chapter 13 is a simple cramdown without application of the fair and equitable doctrine applicable in Chapter 11. The debtor can retain all assets and only meet the best interests of creditors test. This may result in the unsecured creditors being paid nothing. Cramdown and the fair and equitable doctrine, as they relate to a Chapter 13 case, are discussed in Chapter Six of this text.

The debtor's ability to pay out a Chapter 13 plan will require personal motivation and disposable income. The debtor's personal motivation encompasses a number of factors. One debtor may be motivated to pay off his or her debts because of a desire to maintain personal integrity or because of social pressures exerted by family or friends. An important factor may be the debtor's obligations to family members or friends who are cosigners on some of the debts owed. On the other hand, debtor may simply not care about what others will think if he or she files a Chapter 7 bankruptcy petition. This type of debtor may also have no qualms about leaving cosigners holding the bag. Paying creditors may not be high on his or her list of priorities either.

The highly motivated debtor may be able to pay off creditors in a Chapter 13 with no more disposable income than the poorly motivated debtor who would simply not have the discipline to do so. The most highly motivated debtor, however, cannot successfully pay out a Chapter 13 plan without adequate disposable income. Thus, if the debtor lacks either sufficient disposable income or the necessary motivation to pay out a Chapter 13 plan, a Chapter 7 filing is in order.

Chapter 13 provides an avenue for the debtor to obtain a discharge (even a superdischarge) while retaining possession of the property of the estate. Under Chapter 13, the debtor remains in possession of all of the property of the estate unless the plan calls for the debtor to sell property or surrender collateral to the secured party. Under Chapter 7, all property of the estate that is not secured or exempt is liquidated by the Chapter 7 trustee and the proceeds used to pay creditors.

EXAMPLE

When Eric and Jennifer McPherson filed for bankruptcy, they wanted to keep their bass boat. The bass boat was not subject to a creditor's security interest and could not be claimed as exempt property. Under Chapter 7, the bass boat, as nonexempt property of the estate would be surrendered to the Chapter 7 trustee who would have it sold. Under Chapter 13, the McPhersons would retain possession of their nonexempt property, including their bass boat, as long as they paid unsecured creditors an amount not less than the value of the bass boat.

Debt based upon fraud, embezzlement, larceny, or conversion is nondischargeable in Chapter 7. 11 U.S.C.A. §§ 523(a)(2), (4), and (6). Such debt is dischargeable in Chapter 13 (referred to as a superdischarge) if the other confirmation requirements can be met. 11 U.S.C.A. § 1328(a). A discharge under Chapter 7 is generally not available to debtors who have received a discharge within six years. 11 U.S.C.A. § 727(a)(8). The same restriction is not applicable to a Chapter 13 discharge. *Johnson v. Home State Bank,* 501 U.S. 78 (1991).

EXAMPLE

The debtor gets a Chapter 7 discharge, thus discharging him from all of his dischargeable debt. Three months later, debtor has, due to his own negligence, an automobile accident. The debtor has no insurance and is unable personally to pay the other party for the injury to that party's car and person.

Faced with this new claim, the debtor files for bankruptcy under Chapter 13 of the Bankruptcy Code. He proposes to pay all of his disposable income into a plan for 36 months. The bankruptcy court confirms the plan. At the end of 36 months, the debtor receives a full compliance discharge, thus discharging him from the automobile accident claim.

In Chapter 7, if a debtor has given a security interest in collateral and is in default for nonpayment, the debtor's only options are to surrender the collateral or find another source of financing if the creditor will not modify the repayment terms. One option that Chapter 13 affords the debtor is the right to resume making the regular payments while curing the default (the missed payments) through payments under the plan. 11 U.S.C.A. § 1322(a)(5). Interest need not be paid on the arrearage payments unless the agreement specifically requires it. 11 U.S.C.A. § 1322(e).

EXAMPLE

Willie Washington purchased a home for $150,000. To finance his purchase, Willie paid $30,000 down and borrowed $120,000 from First Bank, thus giving First Bank a mortgage on his home. After paying for three years, Willie was involved in an automobile accident and missed three months of work. Since half of Willie's pay was based on commissions, he lost significant income for not only the time he was unable to work but also for the several months after he came back to work. During this time, Willie failed to make three mortgage payments. The mortgage was silent about whether interest would accrue on the missed payments.

If Willie files a Chapter 13 petition, he could resume making his regular mortgage payments directly to First Bank (designated as a monthly expense under Schedule J) and include in the plan the payment of the arrearage without interest.

If Willie files a Chapter 7 petition, First Bank would not need to give Willie time to cure his default (the three past due payments) because Willie has equity in the house and First Bank knows that it can foreclose and get paid in full.

Every time a lender makes the determination to lend money, the risk that the borrower will be unable to repay the loan is assessed. As the risk of nonpayment increases, the lender may ask the borrower to provide a cosigner for the loan. In a Chapter 7, a cosigner is liable for the obligations for which he or she cosigns. When the borrower files for bankruptcy under Chapter 7, the lender may seek repayment from the cosigner.

EXAMPLE

The McPhersons borrowed $1,500 from Friendly Finance Company and Eric's father, Benjamin Franklin McPherson, cosigned their note. If Eric and Jennifer had filed their petition in bankruptcy under Chapter 7, Friendly Finance could seek payment from Eric's father. Chapter 7 does not provide codebtors protection from the debtors' creditors.

If the filing were under Chapter 13, a codebtor stay would go into effect as soon as the Chapter 13 petition was filed. 11 U.S.C.A. § 1301. The codebtor stay protects codebtors on consumer loans. The codebtor stay protects the codebtors if the debt is to be paid under the debtor's Chapter 13 plan. If, however, the debtor's Chapter 13 plan proposes to pay less than all of the creditor's claim, the codebtor would be liable for the remainder.

EXAMPLE

The McPhersons borrowed $1,500 from Friendly Finance Company and Eric's father, Benjamin Franklin McPherson, cosigned their note. When Eric and Jennifer filed their Chapter 13, their plan proposed paying Friendly Finance 100% of its unsecured claim. When the Chapter 13 petition was filed, the codebtor stay went into effect protecting Eric's father from collection efforts. When the McPherson plan proposed paying 100 percent of the claim, the codebtor stay remained in effect.

If the plan had proposed paying only 75 percent of the claim. Friendly Finance could seek relief from the codebtor stay. Once the bankruptcy court grants relief, Friendly Finance could seek the remaining 25 percent from Eric's father.

In Chapter 7, a debtor's only option with respect to secured debt is to surrender the collateral to the creditor, redeem the collateral (by paying a lump sum payment equal to the value of the collateral), or reaffirm the debt. The creditor may not modify the repayment terms and cannot be compelled to do so. Ordinarily a creditor will not do so except to avoid being stuck with a large deficiency claim. In concept, Chapter 13 allows a debtor to modify the amount of the secured claim (equal to the value of the collateral), the payment term (up to five years) and possibly even the interest rate. 11 U.S.C.A. § 1325(a)(5)(B).

EXAMPLE

Geraldine purchased a Chevy Impala from South Park Motors for $20,000. She paid $2,000 down and financed the balance with a loan from Second Bank documented by a note and security agreement. After driving the vehicle for several years, it is now worth $6,000. Second Bank is still owed $10,000.

If Geraldine files a Chapter 13 petition, she could design her Chapter 13 plan so Second Bank is paid $6,000 (the value of the vehicle) and only a fraction of the unsecured portion of its claim (the $4,000 difference between the claim amount and value of the vehicle). The payments under the plan could extend for the duration of the plan, even though only a few months remained under the original note and security agreement.

Debt that is nondischargeable survives a Chapter 7 debtor's discharge.

EXAMPLE

Tom Baker owed the IRS $10,000 when he filed his Chapter 7 petition. Tom's bankruptcy estate had no assets to distribute and he received a Chapter 7 discharge. After the discharge, Tom still owed the IRS $10,000 because the IRS's claim is nondischargeable.

Some unsecured claims are priority claims. These claims must be paid in full under a Chapter 13 plan. Some unsecured priority claims are also nondischargeable. Therefore, they will be paid in full under the Chapter 13 plan, so there is no need to discharge the debtor from these debts because they have been paid in full. There is no debt to discharge.

EXAMPLE

Return to Tom Baker in the previous example. If Tom had filed a Chapter 13 petition, the IRS claim would have been included in his plan as an unsecured priority claim and would have been paid in full by the end of the plan's term.

PROBLEM 9.4 What if Tom Baker had owed his ex-wife, Gwen, $4,000 in back alimony and child support. What would be the status of Gwen's claim if Tom filed a Chapter 7 petition and received a discharge and his case was a no-asset case?

What would be the status of Gwens' claim if Tom filed a Chapter 13 petition?

PROBLEM 9.5 What if Tom Baker had owed South Bank $15,000 for his student loans (that were government insured). What would be the status of South Bank's claim if Tom filed a Chapter 7 petition and received a discharge, and his case was a no-asset case?

What would be the status of South Bank's claim if Tom filed a Chapter 13 petition?

Finally, some debt that is nondischargeable under Chapter 7 is dischargeable under Chapter 13. The super discharge in Chapter 13 refers to four categories of debt that are nondischargeable in Chapter 7 if the creditor timely objects. These categories include fraud, larceny and embezzlement, intentional torts, and conversion. See 11 U.S.C.A. § 1328(a)(2) and 11 U.S.C.A. § 523(a). Note that the latter only refers to 11 U.S.C.A. § 1328(b), the Chapter 13 hardship discharge, and not to the full compliance Chapter 13 discharge of 11 U.S.C.A. § 1328(a).

2. Choosing to Liquidate under Chapter 7 or Reorganize under Chapter 11

Unlike the business debtor whose choice between filing Chapter 7 or Chapter 11 probably hinges on whether the debtor really wants to continue the business, the nonbusiness debtor, by definition, suffers no such dilemma. The debtor's choice is to liquidate now or to design a plan, retain possession of the property of the estate, and pay creditors (some not in full) over time. While Chapter 11 is available to nonbusiness debtors, Chapter 13 has been designed especially for the nonbusiness debtor who seeks to restructure his or her debt.

PROBLEM 9.6 Return to Exhibit 9–1. How many nonbusiness Chapter 11 filings occurred during the 12 months ending September 30, 2002? How does this number compare with other nonbusiness filings during this same period? How do you explain the differences?

3. Choosing to Reorganize under Chapter 11 or Adjust Debt under Chapter 13

The nonbusiness debtor who wants to reorganize and who is eligible under Chapter 13, has a choice between Chapter 11 and Chapter 13. Such a debtor, however, would find it in his or her best interest to use Chapter 13 rather than Chapter 11. Chapter 13 was specifically designed for such a debtor.

Although the Chapter 13 plan can be no less than 36 and no more than 60 months and the Chapter 11 plan is open ended as to duration, Chapter 13 is less expensive than Chapter 11. Chapter 11 expenses include additional attorney's fees because of the greater complexity of the case, the creditors' committee, and the monthly reports to the court.

In a Chapter 13, the debtor retains more control since there is no creditors' committee, only the debtor may file a Chapter 13 plan, and the creditors do not vote on the plan.

Unlike the Chapter 11 cramdown, the Chapter 13 cramdown is a simple one without application of the fair and equitable doctrine. The debtor needs only to meet the best interests of creditors test and pay all disposable income for at least three years in order to retain nonexempt assets. This may result in unsecured creditors being paid nothing.

The debtor in a small Chapter 11 will almost always find that the secured creditors will ask to have the stay modified so they can repossess the collateral. The court may then order adequate protection payments. One of the key fights in a Chapter 11 will be for control of collateral. If the debtor in possession keeps the property and uses it, the question becomes what the debtor will have to pay the creditor to use the collateral and under what terms.

In a Chapter 11, priority claims must be paid in full with interest. In a Chapter 13, all priority claims must be paid in full, but the debtor gets relief from interest accumulating on priority claims.

The nonbusiness debtor who is eligible for both Chapter 11 and Chapter 13 and whose friends or relatives have cosigned consumer loans, can obtain codebtor protection for these cosigners by filing Chapter 13. This codebtor stay is not available under Chapter 11.

CHAPTER 10

The Involuntary Bankruptcy: Chapter 7 or Chapter 11

CHAPTER OUTLINE

SECTION 1
LIMITATIONS ON FILING AN INVOLUNTARY PETITION
A. Debtors Who May Be Subject to an Involuntary Petition
B. Requirements of a Petitioning Creditor

SECTION 2
FLOW CHART FOR THE INVOLUNTARY PETITIONS

SECTION 3
THE FILING OF THE CREDITORS' PETITION

SECTION 4
THE SIGNIFICANCE OF FILING A PETITION
A. The Order for Relief, the Bankruptcy Estate, and the Automatic Stay
B. Appointment of a Trustee
C. Gap Period Creditors

SECTION 5
THE DEBTOR'S ANSWER

SECTION 6
HEARING AND DISPOSITION OF AN INVOLUNTARY PETITION
A. The Order for Relief
B. Dismissal of an Involuntary Petition

Not all petitions in bankruptcy are filed by the debtor. Those filed by the debtor are known as voluntary petitions. A creditor may force a debtor into bankruptcy by filing an **involuntary petition.** Why would a creditor want to put a debtor into bankruptcy involuntarily? Doing so is ordinarily against a creditor's desire to be the first to reach a debtor's limited resources. By reaching the debtor's assets before other creditors, a creditor will receive a disproportionate share of the debtor's assets. Nevertheless, a creditor will sometimes want to put a debtor into bankruptcy involuntarily, despite being stayed from pursuing further collection efforts, because the creditor believes that the debtor may be engaging in fraud by concealing assets or by transferring assets to third parties. Putting a debtor in bankruptcy will enable a creditor to take advantage of the avoidance powers that exist only in the Bankruptcy Code. For example, if a creditor learns that the debtor has made a preferential transfer within the past 90 days (or within the past year if the transfer was made to an insider), creditors may file an involuntary petition in bankruptcy, thus permitting the transfer to be avoided. Upon avoidance, the transferred assets are brought back into the debtor's estate and the creditors can share proportionately in the distribution of these assets.

SECTION 1 LIMITATIONS ON FILING AN INVOLUNTARY PETITION

There are limitations on the chapters in which an involuntary petition may be filed, as well as restrictions on the types of debtors against whom an involuntary case may be commenced. The number of creditors and the aggregate amount of their claims necessary to the filing of an involuntary petition are also circumscribed by the Code.

A. DEBTORS WHO MAY BE SUBJECT TO AN INVOLUNTARY PETITION

The creditors' options in bankruptcy court are limited to an **involuntary Chapter 7 (liquidation)** or an **involuntary Chapter 11 (reorganization).** In addition, there are limitations regarding the types of debtors against whom such a petition may be filed. An involuntary case may be commenced only against a person that may be a debtor under the chapter in which the case is filed. Furthermore, an involuntary petition may not be filed against a farmer, a family farmer, or a corporation that is not a moneyed, business, or commercial corporation. 11 U.S.C.A. § 303(a).

B. REQUIREMENTS OF A PETITIONING CREDITOR

An involuntary petition to be filed against a debtor who has more than twelve creditors requires that three creditors must join in the petition. The claims of the three creditors must aggregate at least $12,300 more than the value of any lien on the debtor's property securing these claims. The claims must not be contingent or the subject of a **bona fide dispute.** 11 U.S.C.A. § 303(b)(1). The claims may include the under-secured or deficiency portions of secured claims. 11 U.S.C.A. § 303(b)(1). If the debtor has fewer than twelve creditors, one or more creditors may file an involuntary petition with aggregate claims of at least $12,300. 11 U.S.C.A. § 303(b)(2). Beginning on April 1, 1998, the dollar amount for an involuntary case is adjusted every three years. 11 U.S.C.A. § 104(b)(1). Future adjustment dates will be April 1, 2007, and April 1, 2010.

After the petition has been filed but before relief is ordered or the case is dismissed, a creditor holding an unsecured, noncontingent claim who was not one of the original petitioning creditors may join in the petition. This will have the same effect as if the joining creditor had been one of the original petitioners. 11 U.S.C.A. § 303(c); Fed. R. Bank. P. 1003(b). Adding additional creditors can prevent dismissal of a case, if the claim of one of the original petitioners is disallowed, by enabling the petition to meet the requirements of three creditors and $12,000 in claims.

In *In re Faberge Restaurant of Florida, Inc.*, an involuntary Chapter 7 petition was filed by three creditors of Faberge Restaurant. They were later joined by three other creditors. Faberge, the debtor, moved to dismiss the petition on the ground that two of the original three creditors were holders of claims that were the subject of a *bona fide* dispute, and paying postpetition the claims of two of the three creditors who joined in the petition prevented the creditors from meeting the three-creditor requirement. Therefore, the petition should be dismissed.

In re Faberge Restaurant of Florida, Inc.

222 B.R. 385
(Bankr. S. D. Fla. 1997)

MEMORANDUM DECISION
A. JAY CRISTOL, Chief Judge

On May 23, 1997, an involuntary petition was filed under Chapter 7 by three petitioners against the Debtor, Faberge Restaurant of Boca, Inc., ("Faberge"), and after having a full evidentiary hearing on July 1, 1997 which was continued to July 2, 1997, and upon observing the candor and demeanor of the witnesses, and reviewing the documentation presented into evidence, the Court enters this ruling on the Motion to Dismiss as filed by Faberge which asserted only that two of the original three creditors were holders of claims which were the subject of a *bona fide* dispute.

Factual Background

The three original petitioners to this involuntary Chapter 7 petition are the following corporations:

G.S.P.C. Enterprises, Inc.	$528,000.00
A.R.T., Inc.	$ 2,230.00
Keystone Creations, Inc.	$ 4,502.50

On June 11, 1997, a motion to dismiss was filed by Faberge which disputed the debt owed to Keystone Creations, Inc. and A.R.T., Inc. and claimed those creditors were the subject of a *bona fide* dispute. No defense was raised as to G.S.P.C. Subsequently, three more creditors joined this petition:

Marina Polvay Associates	$ 4,777.19
Entertainment News & Views, Inc.	$ 480.00
Millward & Co.	$ 380.80

Subsequent to the joinder, but prior to the completion of the hearing, which commenced on July 2, 1997 at 1:45 p.m., Faberge approached three creditors and paid them. First, on or about July 1, 1997, Faberge paid $2,700.00 to Keystone as a settlement of the dispute between the parties. Second, on July 2, 1997, a Faberge check was delivered to Entertainment News & Views for the sum of $480.00. Third, on July 2, 1997, cash was received by Millward & Co. for $380.80.

None of the creditors who were paid withdrew their joinder in the petition.

Prior to the filing of this petition, but in the month of May of 1997, the Debtor created a list of its accounts payable. That list included the following creditors: (1) Marina Polvay for $550.68; (2) Millward & Co. for $370.60; (3) Entertainment News & Views for $480.00; and (4) A.R.T., Inc. for $974.34.

In addition, the Debtor had listed numerous loans on the reverse side of the accounts payable list, which included: (1) Verzura for $100,000.00; (2) American Foods for $72,547.76; (3) Lynka Adams Kroll for $20,000.00; (4) Total Bank for $100,000.00; (5) Payroll to Giulio Santillo for $27,000.00; (6) Pierro Filpi for $30,000.00; (7) Agnolotti for $160,000.00; and (8) rent for the premises $11,000.39. This excluded the amount owed to G.S.P.C. of $528,000.00 as indicated in the petition filed before this court.

Conclusions of Law

Section 303 of the Bankruptcy Code governs the filing of involuntary petitions and provides stringent tests which must be satisfied before a debtor may be adjudicated and an order for relief be entered by the Court.

First, the Court must determine whether the Debtor has generally not been paying its debts as they become due. As reflected in trial, the following creditors were not paid: (a) sales taxes; (b) liquor taxes; (c) Department of Revenue for the state of Florida taxes; (d) 941 withholding taxes; (e) insurance; (f) most of the loans mentioned above; and (g) the rent for the premises. The principal of the Debtor, Giulio Santillo, stated that he could not make payments to numerous creditors because he didn't have the money. It is clear that Faberge was not making payments as they became due in light of the fact that no less than $965,000.00 was owed to various loans as well as G.S.P.C. and that the inability of Faberge to pay rent, tax liabilities and insurance, between the time of the petition and the time of a 2004 exam held on June 20, 1997, proves that this Debtor is not generally paying its debts as they became due.

Second, if the Debtor has more than twelve creditors, then standards under 11 U.S.C. § 303(b)(1) require that there be three creditors who are not the subject of a *bona fide* dispute or holders of contingent claims. In addition, the party who is a Debtor must be a party who could file voluntarily under Chapter

7 or Chapter 11. In this instance, Faberge, a restaurant, has the ability to file bankruptcy voluntarily under Chapters 7 or 11, and therefore qualifies as a party against whom an involuntary petition may be filed. There is no doubt that more than twelve creditors exist pursuant to the accounts payable ledger [Trial Exhibit 8] which was delivered to the court and had an alphabetical listing of trade and other small creditors which approximately numbered 39 entities, excluding the eight (8) loan creditors, the landlord, the numerous taxing authorities, and G.S.P.C.

G.S.P.C. is an undisputed creditor. G.S.P.C.'s debt also provides the requisite debt of $10,000.00 as required under 11 U.S.C. § 303(b)(1). Therefore, the only issue for the Court to review as to the other five (5) petitioners is whether or not two of the five other creditors qualify to file an involuntary petition. Two are listed on the accounts payable ledger and were paid July 2, 1997 ("Entertainment News and Views" and "Millward & Co."). One was not listed on the accounts payable ledger, but was paid on or about July 1, 1997 ("Keystone"). The other two were listed on the accounts payable ledger and were not paid ("Marina Polvay Associates" and "A.R.T., Inc.").

(A) A Party Who Is Claimed To Be the Subject of a Bona Fide Dispute but Who Is Partially Paid after the Filing of the Petition

The mere existence of a counterclaim is insufficient to create a *bona fide* dispute. *See In Re Data Synco, Inc.* 142 B.R. 181 (Bankr.N.D.Ohio 1992) as cited in *IBM Credit Corp. v. Compuhouse Systems, Inc.*, 179 B.R. 474 (W.D.Pa.1995). Further, if a portion of the debt is not a subject of a *bona fide* dispute, then the part that is not subject to a *bona fide* dispute is sufficient to create a debt under 11 U.S.C. § 303(b)(1) so as to permit a creditor to have standing to be a petitioning creditor in an involuntary proceeding. *See IBM Credit Corp. v. Compuhouse Systems, Inc.* at 479 citing *In re Willow Lake Partners II L.P.*, 156 B.R. 638, 643 (Bankr.W.D.Mo.1993), and *In re F.R.P. Indus., Inc.*, 73 B.R. 309, 312 (Bankr.N.D.Fla.1987).

Keystone, an original petitioner for the sum of $4,502.50, received $2,700.00 on or about July 1, 1997. That payment, as made by the Debtor, indicates that at least a portion of the debt was not the subject of a *bona fide* dispute and is an admission of the liability by the Debtor. Keystone was not the subject of a *bona fide* dispute for $2,700.00. Keystone has standing to file an involuntary petition as it is undisputed that it was owed no less than $2,700.00 on May 23, 1997.

(B) Full Payment Made after Filing of the Petition

Keystone, Entertainment News & Views, and Millward & Co. all received payment after the filing of the bankruptcy. It is the contention of Faberge that payment to those creditors eliminated those parties' standing or eligibility to be creditors under 11 U.S.C. § 303(b)(1). This issue has been reviewed by numerous courts. Policy reasons, and other considerations, dictate that the postpetition payments will not deprive the court of jurisdiction or require dismissal of the petition. *See Reed v. Thornton*, 43 F.2d 813 (9th Cir.1930); *Matter of Sjostedt*, 57 B.R. 117, 120 (Bankr.M.D.Fla.1986); *In re Claxton*, 21 B.R. 905 (Bankr.E.D.Va.1982), *In re Carvalho Industries, Inc.* 68 B.R. 254, (Bankr.Or.1986). *Claxton* and *Carvalho* held that the involuntary petition protects all creditors of the Debtor and not only those presently before the Court. *See Claxton*, at 909, and *Carvalho*, at 256.

In *Matter of Sjostedt, supra* at 120, the parties who had joined in the petition *withdrew their joinder* by affidavits submitted to the court after receiving payment. Judge Paskay, in his decision, determined that:

> It is well settled that the fact that a creditor is paid post petition and withdraws his joinder in an involuntary case does not render the petition insufficient for lack of sufficient number of eligible creditors under § 303(b)(1).
>
> *See Matter of Sjostedt*, at 120.

Because of the policy considerations enumerated in *Carvalho Industries, Inc.* which incorporate the Ninth Circuit's decision of *Reed v. Thornton*, and those same considerations recited in *Matter of Sjostedt* by the Middle District of Florida Bankruptcy Court, it is deemed by this Court that payment made postpetition will not permit a Debtor to dismiss an involuntary petition because of the postpetition payment. Instead, the postpetition payment evidences that there is no *bona fide* dispute between the Debtor and petitioning creditor as to the amount paid. This permits a creditor, either an original petitioner or a joining petitioner, not to be the subject of a *bona fide* dispute or a holder of a contingent claim.

The Debtor's July 1, 1997 and July 2, 1997 payments evidence that there was an existing debt on May 23, 1997, the date of the filing of the involuntary petition, to Keystone, Entertainment News & Views, and Millward & Co.

(C) Creditor Who Is Listed in the Accounts Payable Ledger and Who Is Not Paid

The accounts payable ledger, a document created by the Debtor, is a statement against the Debtor's interest. That document, by itself, constitutes adequate proof that Faberge acknowledged the debts to listed parties and the debts are not the subject of a *bona fide* dispute. Two such creditors were not paid: (a) Marina Polvay Associates and (b) A.R.T. Inc. By reviewing the document reflecting debt owed to Marina Polvay & Associates and A.R.T. Inc., the Debtor made a statement against its interest. By thereupon proclaiming those particular parties to be the subject of a *bona fide* dispute after receiving a summons in this involuntary proceeding is inadequate. The Debtor bears the burden to prove the dispute is *bona fide*. *See In re Rimell*, 111 B.R. 250, 258 (Bankr.E.D.Mo.1990).

Conclusion

None of the petitioning creditors are the subject of a *bona fide* dispute. One was conceded at the outset, G.S.P.C. Enterprises, Inc., for $528,000.00. The joining petitioners who were paid, Entertainment News & Views, Inc. which received $480.00, and Millward & Co. which received $380.80, are also not the subject of a *bona fide* dispute in light of the fact that they received payment for their entire claim. Lastly, Keystone Creations, Inc., by receiving $2,700.00, is not the subject of a *bona fide* dispute for a sum of $2,700.00.

The two unpaid creditors, Marina Polvay Associates and A.R.T., Inc., were listed on the accounts payable ledger. They also are probably not the subject of a *bona fide* dispute because of the Debtor's representation of debt owed to these parties in the accounts payable ledger. Self-serving testimony cannot create a *bona fide* dispute when the Debtor's records reflect the opposite.

Accordingly, it is,

ORDERED AND ADJUDGED that the Motion to Dismiss as filed by the Debtor in the above-captioned involuntary is denied and a separate order for relief shall be entered by this court and this order, as issued, shall be immediately delivered to the U.S. Trustee's Office to assure that a panel trustee be appointed in all due haste to handle the affairs of this restaurant.

SECTION 2
FLOW CHART FOR THE INVOLUNTARY PETITIONS

Exhibit 10–1 is the flow chart for the involuntary Chapter 7 case and the involuntary Chapter 11 case.

SECTION 3
THE FILING OF THE CREDITORS' PETITION

Because a creditor or a group of creditors, rather than the debtor, is filing the petition in an involuntary case, the form of the petition to commence an involuntary case is slightly different from a voluntary petition. The petition must conform substantially to Official Form No. 5. (See Exhibit 10–2.) The involuntary petition is filed in the bankruptcy court clerk's office and submitted with the appropriate filing fee.

Upon the filing of an involuntary petition, the clerk issues a summons to be served on the debtor. The summons must conform to Procedural Form B 250E, Summons and to Debtor in Involuntary Case. A copy is served with a copy of the petition. (See Exhibit 10–3.) The manner of service is provided by Rule 7004(a) or (b), which requires personal service or service by first class mail. If service cannot be accomplished in this manner, the court may authorize service by mailing copies of the summons and petition to the party's last known address and at least one publication, as directed by the court. The summons and petition may be served on the party anywhere. Fed. R. Bank. P. 1010.

EXHIBIT 10–1 Flow Chart for the Involuntary Chapter 7 Case and the Chapter 11 Case

Initiating the Involuntary Chapter 7 or Chapter 11 Case

The creditor files with the bankruptcy court clerk's office
1. Filing fee
2. Involuntary petition

Upon filing the petition, the estate is created and the automatic stay goes into effect, protecting the estate from dismemberment and the debtor from collection procedures. Unless the court orders otherwise or until the order for relief is entered, any business of the debtor may continue to operate and the debtor may continue to use, acquire, or dispose of property as if the case had not been commenced.

Upon the filing of the petition, the clerk issues a summons which, along with the petition, is served on the debtor

After the petition has been filed, a creditor holding an unsecured claim may join the petition

The debtor, or a general partner in a partnership debtor, that did not join in the petition, may file an answer to the petition

At any time after the commencement of an involuntary case under Chapter 7, but before the order for relief, the court, upon request of a party in interest, may order the U.S. trustee to appoint an interim trustee to take possession of the property of the estate and to operate any business of the debtor in order to preserve the property of the estate or to prevent loss of the estate

(continued)

EXHIBIT 10–1 Flow Chart for the Involuntary Chapter 7 Case and the Chapter 11 Case, Continued

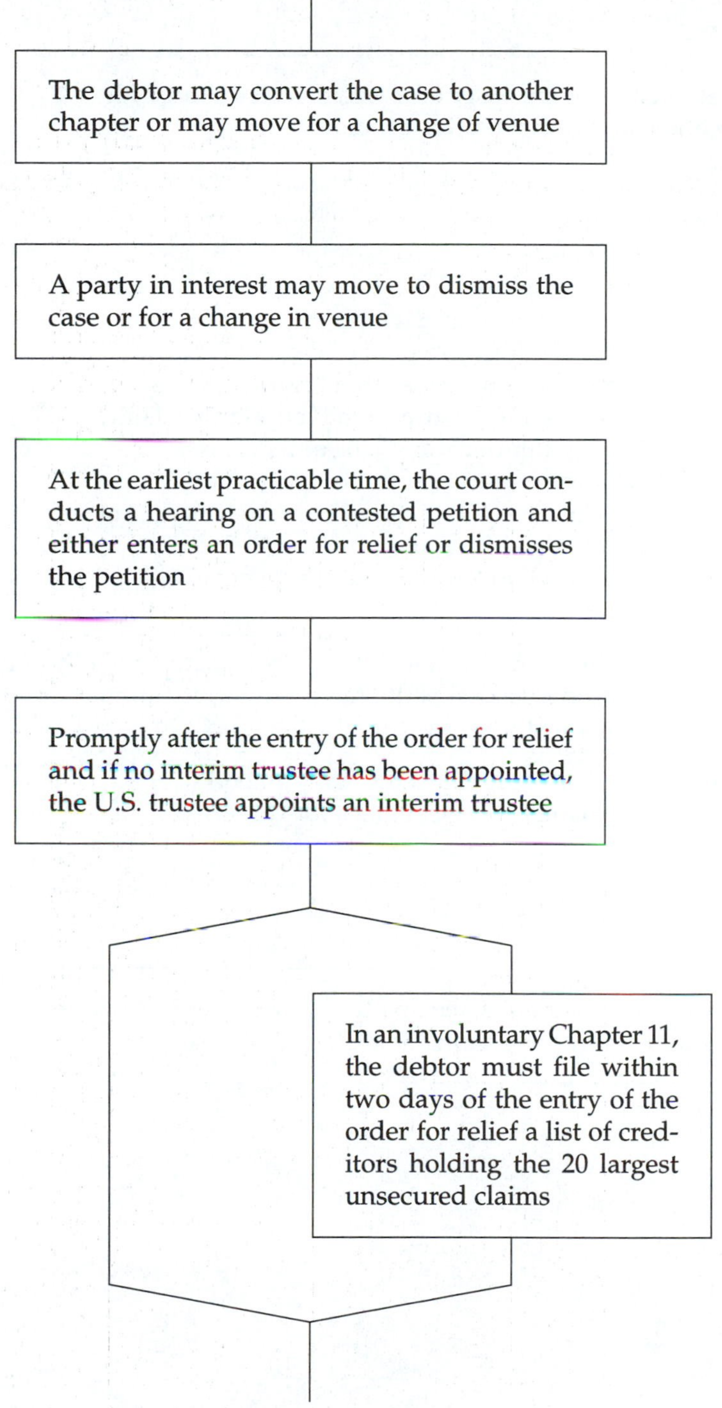

(continued)

EXHIBIT 10–1 Flow Chart for the Involuntary Chapter 7 Case and the Chapter 11 Case, Continued

Within 15 days after entry of the order for relief, the debtor must file:
1. Disclosure of attorney's compensation statement
2. List of creditors
3. Schedules (Official Form No. 6)
   a. Summary of schedules
   b. Schedule A: Real Property
   c. Schedule B: Personal Property
   d. Schedule C: Property Claimed as Exempt
   e. Schedule D: Creditors Holding Secured Claims
   f. Schedule E: Creditors Holding Unsecured Priority Claims
   g. Schedule F: Creditors Holding Unsecured Nonpriority Claims
   h. Schedule G: Executory Contracts and Unexpired Leases
   i. Schedule H: Codebtors
   j. Schedule I: Current Income of Individual Debtor(s), if applicable
   k. Schedule J: Current Expenditures of Individual Debtor(s), if applicable
   l. Schedule of Income and Expenditures of a Partnership or a Corporation, if applicable
4. Statement of financial affairs

If the debtor does not prepare and file a list, schedule, or statement, other than a statement of intention, the court may order the trustee, a petitioning creditor, committee, or other party to prepare and file any of these documents within a time fixed by the court.

Prior to the time the case is closed, the debtor may amend the lists, schedules, and statements. The debtor has a duty to supplement the schedules for certain property acquired after the petition has been filed.

From the entry of the order for relief, the involuntary Chapter 7 or Chapter 11 case proceeds in exactly the same manner as a voluntary Chapter 7 or Chapter 11 case

EXHIBIT 10–2 Official Form No. 5 (Involuntary Case: Creditors Petition)

FORM B5
(12/03)

United States Bankruptcy Court

District of ____________________

INVOLUNTARY PETITION

IN RE (Name of Debtor - If Individual: Last, First, Middle)

ALL OTHER NAMES used by debtor in the last 6 years (Include married, maiden, and trade names.)

LAST FOUR DIGITS OF SOC. SEC. NO./Complete EIN or other TAX I.D. NO. (If more than one, state all.)

STREET ADDRESS OF DEBTOR (No. and street, city, state, and zip code)

COUNTY OF RESIDENCE OR PRINCIPAL PLACE OF BUSINESS

MAILING ADDRESS OF DEBTOR (If different from street address)

LOCATION OF PRINCIPAL ASSETS OF BUSINESS DEBTOR (If different from previously listed addresses)

CHAPTER OF BANKRUPTCY CODE UNDER WHICH PETITION IS FILED

☐ Chapter 7 ☐ Chapter 11

INFORMATION REGARDING DEBTOR (Check applicable boxes)

Petitioners believe:
☐ Debts are primarily consumer debts
☐ Debts are primarily business debts

TYPE OF DEBTOR
☐ Individual ☐ Stockbroker
☐ Partnership ☐ Commodity Broker
☐ Corporation ☐ Railroad
☐ Other: ____________________

BRIEFLY DESCRIBE NATURE OF BUSINESS

VENUE

☐ Debtor has been domiciled or has had a residence, principal place of business, or principal assets in the District for 180 days immediately preceding the date of this petition or for a longer part of such 180 days than in any other District.

☐ A bankruptcy case concerning debtor's affiliate, general partner or partnership is pending in this District.

FILING FEE (Check one box)

☐ Full Filing Fee attached

☐ Petitioner is a child suport creditor or its representative, and the form specified in § 304(g) of the Bankruptcy Reform Act of 1994 is attached.

PENDING BANKRUPTCY CASE FILED BY OR AGAINST ANY PARTNER OR AFFILIATE OF THIS DEBTOR (Report information for any additional cases on attached sheets.)

Name of Debtor	Case Number	Date
Relationship	District	Judge

ALLEGATIONS
(Check applicable boxes)

1. ☐ Petitioner(s) are eligible to file this petition pursuant to 11 U.S.C. § 303(b).
2. ☐ The debtor is a person against whom an order for relief may be entered under title 11 of the United States Code.

3.a. ☐ The debtor is generally not paying such debtor's debts as they become due, unless such debts are the subject of a bona fide dispute;

or

b. ☐ Within 120 days preceding the filing of this petition, a custodian, other than a trustee, receiver, or agent appointed or authorized to take charge of less than substantially all of the property of the debtor for the purpose of enforcing a lien against such property, was appointed or took possession.

COURT USE ONLY

If a child support creditor or its representative is a petitioner, and if the petitioner files the form specified in § 304(g) of the Bankruptcy Reform Act of 1994, no fee is required.

(continued)

EXHIBIT 10–2 Official Form No. 5 (Involuntary Case: Creditors Petition), Continued

FORM 5 Involuntary Petition
(6/92)

Name of Debtor ____________________

Case No. ____________________
(court use only)

TRANSFER OF CLAIM

☐ Check this box if there has been a transfer of any claim against the debtor by or to any petitioner. Attach all documents evidencing the transfer and any statements that are required under Bankruptcy Rule 1003(a).

REQUEST FOR RELIEF

Petitioner(s) request that an order for relief be entered against the debtor under the chapter of title 11, United States Code, specified in this petition.

Petitioner(s) declare under penalty of perjury that the foregoing is true and correct according to the best of their knowledge, information, and belief.

X ____________________ Signature of Petitioner or Representative (State title) ____________________ Name of Petitioner — Date Signed Name & Mailing Address of Individual Signing in Representative Capacity ____________________	X ____________________ Signature of Attorney — Date ____________________ Name of Attorney Firm (If any) ____________________ Address ____________________ Telephone No.
X ____________________ Signature of Petitioner or Representative (State title) ____________________ Name of Petitioner — Date Signed Name & Mailing Address of Individual Signing in Representative Capacity ____________________	X ____________________ Signature of Attorney — Date ____________________ Name of Attorney Firm (If any) ____________________ Address ____________________ Telephone No.
X ____________________ Signature of Petitioner or Representative (State title) ____________________ Name of Petitioner — Date Signed Name & Mailing Address of Individual Signing in Representative Capacity ____________________	X ____________________ Signature of Attorney — Date ____________________ Name of Attorney Firm (If any) ____________________ Address ____________________ Telephone No.

PETITIONING CREDITORS

Name and Address of Petitioner	Nature of Claim	Amount of Claim
Name and Address of Petitioner	Nature of Claim	Amount of Claim
Name and Address of Petitioner	Nature of Claim	Amount of Claim
Note: If there are more than three petitioners, attach additional sheets with the statement under penalty of perjury, each petitioner's signature under the statement and the name of attorney and petitioning creditor information in the format above.		Total Amount of Petitioners' Claims

______continuation sheets attached

EXHIBIT 10–3 Summons to Debtor in Involuntary Case

B 250E
(6/91)

United States Bankruptcy Court

_________________ District Of _____________

In re ______________________
Debtor

Case No. ________

Chapter ________

SUMMONS TO DEBTOR IN INVOLUNTARY CASE

To the above named debtor:

A petition under title 11, United States Code was filed against you on ____________________ (date) in this bankruptcy court, requesting an order for relief under chapter ______ of the Bankruptcy Code (title 11 of the United States Code).

YOU ARE SUMMONED and required to file with the clerk of the bankruptcy court a motion or answer to the petition within 20 days after the service of this summons. A copy of the petition is attached.

Address of Clerk

At the same time, you must also serve a copy of your motion or answer on petitionerís attorney.

Name and Address of Petitioner's Attorney

If you make a motion, your time to serve an answer is governed by Federal Rule of Bankruptcy Procedure 1011(c).

If you fail to respond to this summons, the order for relief will be entered.

____
Clerk of the Bankruptcy Court

_________________ Date

By: ____________________________________
Deputy Clerk

**Set forth all names, including trade names, used by the debtor within the last 6 years. (Fed. R .Bankr. P. 1005).*

(continued)

Case No.________________________

CERTIFICATE OF SERVICE

I
of**
certify:

That I am, and at all times hereinafter mentioned was more than 18 years of age;
That on the day of ,19
I served a copy of the within summons, together with the petition filed in this case, on

the debtor in this case, by *[describe here the mode of service]*

the said debtor at

I certify under penalty of perjury that the foregoing is true and correct.

Executed on ________________________ ________________________________
[Date] *[Signature]*

**State mailing address.

SECTION 4
THE SIGNIFICANCE OF FILING A PETITION

When a voluntary petition is filed, an order for relief is automatically entered because the debtor volunteers for bankruptcy relief. The significance of filing an involuntary petition is somewhat different.

A. THE ORDER FOR RELIEF, THE BANKRUPTCY ESTATE, AND THE AUTOMATIC STAY

When an involuntary petition is filed, the order for relief is not automatically entered. The debtor may not want bankruptcy relief and may dispute the allegations contained in the creditors' petition. Therefore, the order for relief is entered after a determination that all of the elements of the petition are admitted by the debtor or proven to the court. The order for relief is tantamount to a judgment in a lawsuit.

At any time during what is called the gap period—the time between the filing of an involuntary petition and the order for relief—the debtor may consent to the entry of an order for relief under the chapter requested in the involuntary petition or the debtor may convert the case to any other chapter of the Bankruptcy Code for which it is eligible.

Unless the court orders otherwise, until an order for relief has been entered in an involuntary case, any business of the debtor may continue to operate and the debtor may continue to use, acquire, or dispose of property as if the case had not been filed. This means the debtor in an involuntary case is not limited by the constraints of Section 363 until the order for relief has been entered. 11 U.S.C.A. § 303(f).

Upon the filing of the petition in an involuntary case, however, the estate is created and the automatic stay goes into effect, protecting the estate from dismemberment just as it does in a voluntary case. This prevents the more aggressive creditors from taking what is owed to them to the detriment of other creditors. The creditors filing the involuntary petition are attempting to protect their interests from the actions of the other creditors as well as from the actions of the debtor. The involuntary petition also gives the debtor relief (albeit unsolicited) under the automatic stay from harassment by creditors. 11 U.S.C.A. § 362(a).

B. APPOINTMENT OF A TRUSTEE

In a Chapter 7 case, an interim trustee is always appointed upon the entry of an order for relief. In a voluntary Chapter 7 case, the order for relief is entered upon the filing of the petition and therefore an interim trustee is appointed when the petition is filed. In an involuntary Chapter 7 case, since the order for relief is not entered upon the filing of the petition, a gap period exists (i.e., the period between the filing of the petition and the order for relief). A creditor may have cause to worry about the debtor's conduct during this period. The Bankruptcy Code authorizes a creditor to request appointment of an interim trustee during this period. 11 U.S.C.A. § 303(g).

The Bankruptcy Code, however, makes no provision for the appointment of a trustee in an involuntary Chapter 11 case during this gap period. The Code only provides that a trustee may be appointed in a Chapter 11 case at any time after the entry of an order for relief. 11 U.S.C.A. § 1104(a).

C. GAP PERIOD CREDITORS

Creditors who hold claims that arise between the filing of an involuntary petition and the order for relief are called **gap creditors.** This group may be comprised of both existing creditors and creditors who have only begun to deal with the debtor postpetition.

Creditors may be unaware of the filing of the involuntary petition until the court clerk notifies them that the order for relief has been entered. Even though these claims arise after the filing of the petition, they are not given administrative claim status. These creditors do have some protection under the Code. If their claims arise in the ordinary course of the debtor's business or financial affairs after the commencement of the case but before the earlier of the appointment of a trustee or the order for relief, they are given a second priority and their claims are treated as if they had arisen before the date of the filing of the petition. 11 U.S.C.A. §§ 502(f), 507(a)(2).

SECTION 5 THE DEBTOR'S ANSWER

The debtor named in an involuntary petition may contest the petition. In an involuntary petition against a partnership, a nonpetitioning general partner, or a person who is alleged to be a general partner but denies the allegation, may contest the petition. Fed. R. Bank. P. 1011(a). Defenses and objections to the petition must be presented in accordance with Rule 12 of the Federal Rules of Civil Procedure and are to be filed and served within 20 days after service of the summons. If service is made by publication on a party or partner not residing or found in the state in which the court sits, the time for filing and serving the response is fixed by the court. Fed. R. Bank. P. 1011(b). No claim may be asserted in the answer against a petitioning creditor except for the purpose of defeating the petition. Fed. R. Bank. P. 1011(d).

If the debtor claims to have twelve or more creditors in its answer to a petition filed by fewer than three creditors, the debtor must file a list of all creditors with the answer. The list must include addresses, a brief statement of the nature of the claims, and the amounts of the claims. Fed. R. Bank. P. 1003(b). This information is to allow other creditors to join in the involuntary petition, if they so desire.

SECTION 6 HEARING AND DISPOSITION OF AN INVOLUNTARY PETITION

If the petition in an involuntary case is not timely controverted, the court will enter an order for relief without a trial. Fed. R. Bank P. 1013(b). However, if the debtor contests the petition, a trial will be held at the court's earliest opportunity. Fed. R. Bank. P. 1013(a).

A. THE ORDER FOR RELIEF

Relief against the debtor will be ordered after the trial only if

(1) the debtor is generally not paying such debtor's debts as such debts become due unless such debts are the subject of a bona fide dispute; or
(2) within 120 days before the date of the filing of the petition, a custodian, other than a trustee, receiver, or agent appointed or authorized to take charge of less than substantially all of the property of the debtor for the purpose of enforcing a lien against such property, was appointed or took possession. 11 U.S.C.A. §§ 303(h)(1), (2).

In *In re Palace Oriental Rugs, Inc.*, an involuntary Chapter 7 case, the debtor's answer to the involuntary complaint asserted that the creditors' claims were subject to *bona fide* disputes, that debts were being paid as they came due, and that the involuntary petition was filed in bad faith.

In re Palace Oriental Rugs, Inc.

193 B.R. 126 (Bankr. D. Conn. 1996)

MEMORANDUM OF DECISION ON INVOLUNTARY PETITION
ALBERT S. DABROWSKI, Bankruptcy Judge.

I. INTRODUCTION

In this involuntary Chapter 7 case the parties have called upon the Court to determine (1) whether the Petitioning Creditors' claims are "the subject of bona fide dispute" within the meaning of 11 U.S.C. § 303(b)(1); and/or (2) whether the Alleged Debtor, an oriental rug retailer, is "generally not paying . . . [its] debts as such debts become due . . ." within the meaning of 11 U.S.C. § 303(h)(1).

II. JURISDICTION

The United States District Court for the District of Connecticut has subject matter jurisdiction over the instant case by virtue of 28 U.S.C. §§ 1334(a), (b). This Court derives its authority to hear and determine this matter on reference from the District Court pursuant to 28 U.S.C. §§ 157(a), (b)(1). This Memorandum of Decision shall constitute this Court's Findings of Fact and Conclusions of Law pursuant to Federal Rule of Bankruptcy Procedure 7052(a).

III. BACKGROUND

The instant case was commenced by the December 9, 1993 (hereinafter, the "Petition Date") filing of an involuntary petition against the Alleged Debtor by the following petitioning creditors: (1) MER Corp., (2) Kelaty International, Inc., and (3) Amir Aziz & Son, Inc. (hereinafter collectively referred to as the "Petitioning Creditors"). On January 21, 1994, the Alleged Debtor filed an Answer with Counterclaim, asserting that the Petitioning Creditors' claims were subject to bona fide disputes, that the Alleged Debtor was generally paying its debts as they came due, and claiming that the Involuntary Petition was commenced by the Petitioning Creditors in bad faith. On February 18, 1994, the Petitioning Creditors filed their Reply to Counterclaim, generally denying the allegations contained in the Alleged Debtor's counterclaim. After a rather contentious period of discovery, this case was tried before the Court.

IV. DISCUSSION

The adjudication of involuntary bankruptcy petitions is governed by 11 U.S.C. § 303 and the Federal Rules of Bankruptcy Procedure. Section 303, as applicable to this case, provides in relevant part, as follows:

> (b) An involuntary case against a person is commenced by the filing with the bankruptcy court of a petition under chapter 7 or 11 of this title—
>
> (1) by three or more entities, each of which is . . . a holder of a claim against such person that is not contingent as to liability or the subject of a bona fide dispute . . . if such claims aggregate at least $5,000 more than the value of any lien on property of the debtor securing such claims held by the holders of such claims. . . .
>
> * * * * * *
>
> (h) . . . [A]fter trial, the court shall order relief against the debtor in an involuntary case under the chapter under which the petition was filed, only if—
>
> (1) the debtor is generally not paying such debtor's debts as such debts become due unless such debts are the subject of a bona fide dispute. . . .

11 U.S.C. § 303 (1992).

A. Burden of Proof Petitioning creditors bear the ultimate burden of proving that all statutory requirements of Bankruptcy Code Section 303 have been met. 2 *Collier on Bankruptcy* § 303.15[7], at pp. 303–80 (15th ed. 1995). Specifically, they bear the burden of establishing the "jurisdictional" prerequisites of Section 303(b). *See, e.g., In re Charon,* 94 B.R. 403, 405–406 (Bankr.E.D.Va.1988). Likewise, they bear the ultimate burden of proving by a preponderance of the evidence that the Alleged Debtor is generally not paying its debts as such debts become due.

B. Reference Date for Claims Analysis The petition filing date is the appropriate reference date for the determination of whether an alleged debtor is generally not paying its debts as they come due. *See In re B.D. Int'l Discount Corp. v. Chase Manhattan Bank,* 701 F.2d 1071, 1076 n. 9 (2d Cir.1983). Similarly, under the creditor qualification standards of Section 303(b)(1), the relevant question is whether the claims of petitioning creditors were the subject of a bona fide dispute on the petition date. However, in determining the petition date status of claims, the Court is not precluded from considering post-petition evidentiary developments.

C. "Generally Not Paying" Analysis Having heard and reviewed the testimonial and documentary evidence in this case, and after a thorough review of the entire case record, including the written and oral arguments of counsel for the respective parties, this Court concludes that the Petitioning Creditors have failed to sustain their burden of proving that the Alleged Debtor was "generally not paying" its debts "as such debts become due" on the Petition Date within the intent of Section 303(h)(1).

In reaching this conclusion the Court proceeds without a great deal of specific guidance from legislative sources or judicial authorities. *See generally B.D. Int'l Discount Corp., supra.* However, these sources are supportive of the following analytical approach in this case. The Court must first undertake a rough calculus of the number and amount of the Alleged Debtor's delinquent and current debts on the Petition Date. The Court then utilizes the results of that calculus to determine if the ratio of delinquent to current debts is supportive of a pattern of "generally not paying." On the evidence presented in this case, that pattern is not difficult to divine.

Even if the Court were to include as "delinquent" the debts allegedly owed to the Petitioning Creditors by the Alleged Debtor, *i.e.* conclude that such debts exist without bona fide dispute in the amounts asserted by the Petitioning Creditors, the Petitioning Creditors have failed to convince the Court that the nonpayment of those debts constitutes a majority, or even a substantial minority, of the Alleged Debtor's debts, in either number or amount.

The Petitioning Creditors presented payment history evidence relative to only one debt other than their own, namely utility charges due to the Southern New England Telephone Co. (hereinafter referred to as "SNET"). The Court finds that despite its introduction by the Petitioning Creditors, the evidence as to the SNET debt is supportive of that debt's "current" status on the Petition Date.

The only evidence of the existence and payment history of debts other than those allegedly owed to the Petitioning Creditors and SNET (hereinafter referred to as the "Third Party Debts") came from a witness offered by the Alleged Debtor. Hashem Hashemi, an officer and agent of the Alleged Debtor, testified credibly as to the status of the Third Party Debts on the Petition Date. That testimony established to the Court's satisfaction that with the possible exception of the Petitioning Creditors, the Alleged Debtor was generally "current" with all of its creditors on the Petition Date. In essence, the Court concludes that the genesis of this case was not the generalized financial dislocation of the Alleged Debtor, but rather its isolated disputes—bona fide or not—with the Petitioning Creditors. Such a situation does not constitute "generally not paying . . . [one's] debts as such debts become due . . .", and is not necessarily an appropriate precipitant to an involuntary bankruptcy.

D. Bona Fide Dispute Analysis Given the foregoing findings and conclusions on the ultimate issue of "generally not paying" under Section 303(h)(1), it is unnecessary to consider issues of petitioning creditor qualification, such as whether the claims of the Petitioning Creditors were "the subject of a bona fide dispute" on the Petition Date.

E. The Alleged Debtor's Counterclaim A claim in favor of an alleged debtor for costs, attorneys' fees and/or damages under Section 303(i) ripens upon the dismissal of the involuntary petition. *See In re Ross,* 135 B.R. 230, 234 (Bankr.E.D.Pa.1991). Although during the course of the trial of this case the Court heard isolated testimony relevant to the Alleged Debtor's Counterclaim for costs, attorneys' fees and damages, the Court is not convinced that the parties viewed that dispute as sufficiently ripe to elucidate a full and fair presentation of all evidence deemed material to issues arising therein. It is also unclear whether an alleged debtor may plead and prosecute a "counterclaim" prior to dismissal of the involuntary petition. *See* Fed.R.Bank.P. 1011(d), (e); *In re Contemporary Mission, Inc.,* 30 B.R. 369 (Bankr.D.Conn.1983). Therefore, it is the Court's view that a supplemental evidentiary hearing be held to consider the existence of the Petitioning Creditors' liability, if any, to the Alleged Debtor, and the extent of any consequential financial awards for costs, attorneys' fees and/or damages.

V. CONCLUSION

Having failed to meet their burden of proof under Section 303(h), the Petitioning Creditors are not entitled to an Order for Relief on their Involuntary Petition; and said Petition shall be dismissed by separate Order. A hearing shall be held upon the Alleged Debtor's Counterclaim under Section 303(i) on April 19, 1996 at 10:00 A.M.

An order for relief must substantially conform to Procedural Form No. B 253, Order for Relief in an Involuntary Case. (See Exhibit 10–4) After an order for relief has been entered, the debtor has 15 days to file the schedules, lists, and statements that would have been filed by the debtor in a voluntary case. From the date of the order for relief, the case proceeds in exactly the same manner as a voluntary case.

EXHIBIT 10–4 Procedural Form B 253 (Order for Relief in an Involuntary Case)

B 253
(8/96)

United States Bankruptcy Court

__________________ District Of __________________

In re

Case No. ____________

Debtor*
Address:
Social Security No.:
Employer Tax I.D. No.:

Chapter _________

ORDER FOR RELIEF IN AN INVOLUNTARY CASE

On consideration of the petition filed on ______________________________ (date) against the above-named debtor, an order for relief under chapter ____ of the Bankruptcy Code (title 11 of the United States Code) is granted.

____________________ Date

____________________ Bankruptcy Judge

*Set forth all names, including trade names, used by the debtor within the last 6 years. (Fed. R. Bankr. P. 1005).

B. DISMISSAL OF AN INVOLUNTARY PETITION

The court may dismiss an involuntary petition after notice and a hearing on the motion of a petitioner, on consent of all petitioners and the debtor, or for want of prosecution. 11 U.S.C.A. § 303(j). Upon the filing of a motion to dismiss, the debtor or some other entity designated by the court will be required to file a list of creditors with their addresses. This will afford all creditors an opportunity to object to the dismissal. Fed. R. Bank. P. 1017.

Dismissal of an involuntary petition may be a costly business for the petitioners. After notice and a hearing, and for cause, the court may require petitioning creditors to post a bond to indemnify the debtor against damages the court may allow later if the petition is dismissed under section 303(i). 11 U.S.C.A. § 303(e). If the court dismisses an involuntary petition for any reason other than on consent of all petitioners and the debtor, and if the debtor does not waive the right to judgment, the court may grant judgment against the petitioners for costs or a reasonable attorney's fee. 11 U.S.C.A. § 303(i)(1). The court may grant judgment against any petitioner found to have filed the petition in bad faith for any damages proximately caused by the filing or for punitive damages. 11 U.S.C.A. § 303(i)(2). This serves as a deterrent to creditors who might otherwise file an involuntary petition merely to harass the debtor.

The following case illustrates a situation in which the petitioner was found to have acted in bad faith. Ackerman filed a collection action in state court seeking payment for a debt he claimed the Runyons owed. A month after the state court granted the Runyons a continuance in that action, Ackerman filed an involuntary petition in the bankruptcy court against the Runyons, using an identical debt to support his standing in the involuntary action. The bankruptcy court found Ackerman had acted in bad faith and entered judgment against him for punitive damages and attorney's fees.

In re Runyon

1994 WL 259770 (9th Cir. 1994)

MEMORANDUM
Before: D.W. Nelson and Beezer, Circuit Judges and J. Spencer Letts, District Judge

Ackerman appeals the Bankruptcy Appellate Panel's affirmance of a bankruptcy court's order awarding the Runyons $15,000 in attorney's fees and $10,000 in punitive damages for Ackerman's "bad faith" filing of an involuntary petition within the meaning of 11 U.S.C. § 303(i). Ackerman challenges the punitive damages award, arguing that the bankruptcy court erred in finding that he filed in "bad faith." He also challenges the award of attorney's fees, contending that the bankruptcy court abused its discretion by holding him solely responsible for all of the fees, including those incurred after he withdrew from the involuntary bankruptcy action. The Runyons seek the imposition of sanctions for a frivolous appeal. We have jurisdiction pursuant to 28 U.S.C. § 158(d). We affirm.

I

Ackerman challenges the bankruptcy court's award of punitive damages, contending that the court erred in finding that he filed the petition against the Runyons in "bad faith" within the meaning of § 303(i). Specifically, Ackerman argues that the record does not support the predicate findings that he knew or had reason to know that he was an ineligible creditor, that he failed to disclose the disputed nature of his debt to his co-petitioners, and that he wrongfully induced petitioner Garaway to participate by misrepresenting material facts. He concludes that absent these challenged findings, the remaining facts cannot sustain the bankruptcy court's ultimate finding of "bad faith."

We review de novo decisions of the Bankruptcy Appellate Panel. *In re Dewalt,* 961 F.2d 848, 850 (9th Cir.1992). We review de novo the bankruptcy court's conclusions of law and its findings of fact for clear error. *Id.* We review the finding that an involuntary petition was filed in "bad faith" for clear error. *See In re Wavelength,* 61 B.R. 614, 620 (9th Cir.BAP1986).

Ackerman's argument is without merit. Even absent many, if not most, of the challenged findings, the record amply supports the bankruptcy court's ultimate finding of "bad faith." Ackerman filed an involuntary petition only one month after the state court granted the Runyons a continuance in a pending collection action seeking payment for the identical debt Ackerman relied on to support his standing in the involuntary action. The Runyons had filed a general denial to Ackerman's complaint, and trial was already set when Ackerman filed. At a minimum, Ackerman reasonably should have known that he would be required to demonstrate that the debt was not subject to a "bona fide dispute" or face dismissal. *See In re Rubin,* 769 F.2d 611, 615 (9th Cir. 1985) (burden on petitioner to prove that a claim is not subject to a "bona fide dispute"); *cf. In re Nordbrock,* 772 F.2d 397, 399 (8th Cir.1985). Despite this requirement, Ackerman supported his standing by claiming an unliquidated and contested debt of $356,000 rather than the $37,000 that Runyon had previously admitted he owed. This factor, considered in tandem with the fact that the unliquidated sum Runyon admitted owing was far smaller than the funds already subject to Ackerman's writ of attachment, provides ample support for the bankruptcy court's inference that Ackerman filed the petition with an eye toward harassing the Runyons or for gaining an advantage in the settlement of the collection action. *See In re Johnston Hawks, Ltd.,* 72 B.R. 361, 366 (Bkrtcy.D.Haw.1987). There was ample record support for the position that Ackerman's participation in the filing was merely another battle in his personal war with the Runyons. *See In re Willow Lake Partners II, L.P.,* 156 B.R. 638, 644–45 (W.D.Mo.1993).

In reaching this conclusion we reject Ackerman's argument that the lack of clarity in the case law on whether the "bona fide dispute" requirement of § 303(b) attached to the liability or to the amount of the alleged debt undermined the ultimate finding of "bad faith." Although Ackerman is correct that the case law was unclear at the time of filing, *see In re Dill,* 731 F.2d 629, 631 (9th Cir.1984), his argument is a red herring. Any lack of clarity in the case law regarding the eligibility of creditors fails to negate the inference of "bad faith" established by the facts recited above.

A

We also reject the contention that res judicata principles barred the bankruptcy court's predicate finding concerning the existence of a written retainer agreement between Ackerman and Runyon.

We review de novo the question of the availability of res judicata and collateral estoppel. *Clark v. Bear Sterns & Co., Inc.,* 966 F.2d 1318, 1320 (9th Cir.1992). Ackerman provides no basis for the proposition that the state collection action and the instant adversary proceeding to determine whether he filed an involuntary petition in "bad faith" involved the same "claim." *See Parklane Hosiery Co. v. Shore,* 439 U.S. 322, 326, n.5 (1979); *Hulsey v. Koehler,* 218 C.A.2d 1150, 1157 (1990). The judgment entered pursuant to the settlement agreement did not, moreover, incorporate any findings pertaining to the existence of a written retainer agreement. Collateral estoppel cannot bar a matter that was not actually litigated in a prior proceeding. *Shore,* 439 U.S. at 326, n.5; *Lucido v. Superior Court,* 51 Cal.3d 335, 341 (1990).

II

Ackerman challenges the bankruptcy court's award of attorney's fees. He argues that the award is excessive because it singles Ackerman out as being solely responsible for all of the Runyons' attorney's fees. He contends that he is, at most, responsible for one-third of the fees incurred for the period between the filing of the initial and the amended petitions.

We uphold the bankruptcy court's award of attorney's fees unless the court abused its discretion or erroneously applied the law. *Southwestern Media, Inc. v. Rau,* 708 F.2d 419, 422 (9th Cir.1983).

In *In re Reid,* 854 F.2d 156, 160 (7th Cir. 1988), the Seventh Circuit concluded that the bankruptcy court may properly employ a prior determination that a petitioner filed in "bad faith" to guide its discretion in imposing costs and fees pursuant to § 303(i)(1)(A) and (1)(B). We adopt this reasoning in concluding that the bankruptcy court did not abuse its discretion by holding Ackerman solely responsible for all of the fees incurred. The instant facts, moreover, support the award. Ackerman explained the value of filing an involuntary petition to Wiens and Gordon when they met to discuss their options. Ackerman also helped induce Garaway to join the petition by telling him that he had paid a retainer large enough to see the matter through to the end.

III

Although Ackerman has already had one proverbial bite at the apple before the Bankruptcy Appellate Panel, *see In re Nordbrock*, 772 F.2d at 400, the Panel did not fully address the question concerning the scope of the bankruptcy court's discretion in awarding attorney's fees pursuant to § 303(i)(1)(B). We consequently deny the Runyons' apparent request for Rule 38 sanctions. This appeal was not frivolous. *See McConnell v. Critchlow*, 661 F.2d 116, 118 (9th Cir.1981).

AFFIRMED.

KEY TERMS

Bona fide dispute
Gap creditor
Involuntary Chapter 7 (liquidation)
Involuntary Chapter 11 (reorganization)
Involuntary petition

Interview Questionnaire for the Debtor-Client

For us to properly handle your case, it is necessary that you complete this questionnaire. It is essential that you list every debt that you owe and every claim that any person or entity asserts that you owe.

Please list all real and personal property you own or own an interest in, including property you believe is exempt. If a bankruptcy petition is filed on your behalf, we will claim, in the schedules which will be prepared for you, the proper exemptions. We will discuss this with you before filing your case.

In listing real property, it is necessary that you include the full legal description. This may require you to search for deeds or other legal documents, but it is important that this information be furnished.

Each item on the following parts of the questionnaire must be answered. Complete these parts only:

- ❑ **I. A.** General Information—Individual Debtor and a Husband and Wife Filing a Joint Petition
- ❑ **I. B.** General Information—Partnership Debtor
- ❑ **I. C.** General Information—Corporate Debtor
- ❑ **II.** Assets
- ❑ **III.** Debts
- ❑ **IV.** Executory Contracts and Unexpired Leases
- ❑ **V.** Current Income and Current Expenditures of Individual Debtor(s)
- ❑ **VI.** Current Income and Current Expenditures of a Partnership or Corporation
- ❑ **VII.** Statement of Financial Affairs
- ❑ **VIII.** Property Status—Real and Personal

If additional space is needed, write the information on a separate sheet of paper and attach it to this questionnaire. Indicate to which question this information relates.

If your answer to any question should change during the period when we are handling your case, you must contact this office and advise us of any such change.

Our paralegal, __________________________________, will be assisting you in completing this questionnaire.

by __________________________________
Attorney at Law

Complete all parts of this questionnaire. If a question does not apply to you, indicate "n.a."

I. GENERAL INFORMATION

If the debtor is an individual or the debtors are a husband and wife filing a joint petition, complete question A.
If the debtor is a partnership, complete question B.
If the debtor is a corporation, complete question C.

At times a debtor may file as both an individual and a partnership or a corporation. If this may be your situation, complete question A and either question B or C, depending on whether you are a partnership or a corporation.

A. If the debtor is an individual or a husband and wife filing a joint petition, complete this question.

1. Information concerning the debtor

a. State your full name (last name, first name, middle name):
Debtor: ____
Last First Middle

b. Telephone number: ______________________________ (home)
______________________________ (work)

c. Have you used, or been known by, any other name or names within the immediately preceding six years?
yes _____ no _____
If yes, give particulars. Include maiden names, prior married names, nicknames, and trade names.
____
____
____

d. Social Security Number: ________________

e. Tax ID No., if any: ____________________

f. Address: ____
street
____
city state zip code
____
county of residence

g. Have you lived there longer than three months?
yes_____no______

h. Mailing address if different from the street address:
____
____
city state zip code

i. If business debt, briefly describe the nature of the business.
____
____

j. Marital status:
_____ single
_____ married
date: ______________________
place of marriage: ______________________
_____ divorced
date: ______________________
place of divorce: ______________________

_____widowed
date: ______________________
place of spouse's death: ______________________

2. Information concerning the debtor's spouse
   a. State your spouse's full name (last name, first name, middle name):
      Spouse: ____
      Last First Middle
   b. Telephone number: ______________________ (home)
      ______________________ (work)
   c. Has your spouse used, or been known by, any other name or names within the immediately preceding six years?
      yes_____no_____
      If yes, give particulars. Include maiden names, prior married names, nicknames, and trade names.
      ____
      ____
      ____
   d. Social Security Number: ______________
   e. Tax ID No., if any: ______________
   f. Address: ____
      street
      ____
      city state zip code
      ____
      county of residence
   g. Has your spouse lived there longer than three months?
      yes_____no_____
   h. Mailing address if different from the street address:
      ____
      ____
      city state zip code
   i. If business debt, briefly describe the nature of the business.
      ____
      ____

B. If the debtor is a partnership, complete this question.
   1. State the name of the partnership:
      ____
   2. Name of the individual authorized to file the petition:
      ____
   3. Title: ____
   4. Telephone number (include area code): ______________________
   5. Is the partnership known, or has it been known, by any other name or names within the immediately preceding six years?
      yes _____ no _____
      If yes, state the names and dates when the names were used.
      ____
      ____
      ____
      ____
   6. Partnership's Tax ID No.: ______________________

7. Street address of the partnership:

   ____
   street
   ____
   city   state   zip code
8. County of principal place of business:______________________
9. Mailing address of the partnership if different from the street address:
   ____
10. Location of principal assets of the partnership if different from the street address:
   ____
11. Nature of the partnership's business: ______________________
   ____
12. If a prior bankruptcy case has been filed within the last six years, provide the following information:
   a. Location where filed: ______________________
   b. Case number: ______________________
   c. Date filed: ______________________
13. If a pending bankruptcy case has been filed by a partner or an affiliate of the partnership, provide the following information.
   a. Name of the debtor: ______________________
   b. Case number: ______________________
   c. Date filed: ______________________
   d. Relationship: ______________________
   e. District where case was filed: ______________________
   f. Judge: ______________________

C. If the debtor is a corporation, complete this question.
   1. State the name of the corporation:
      ____
   2. Name of the individual authorized to file the petition:
      ____
   3. Title: ______________________
   4. Telephone number (include area code): ______________________
   5. Is the corporation known, or has it been known, by any other name or names within the immediately preceding six years?
      yes _____ no _____
      If yes, state the names and dates when the names were used.
      ____
      ____
      ____
   6. Corporation's Tax ID No.: ______________________
   7. Street address of the corporation:
      ____
      street
      ____
      city   state   zip code
   8. County of principal place of business: ______________________
   9. Mailing address of the corporation if different from the street address:
      ____
   10. Location of principal assets of the corporation if different from the street address:
      ____

11. Is the corporation publicly held or privately held?
____
12. Nature of the corporation's business:
____
13. If a prior bankruptcy case has been filed within the last six years, provide the following information.
    a. Location where filed: _______________
    b. Case number: _______________
    c. Date filed: _______________
14. If a pending bankruptcy case has been filed by an affiliate of the corporation, provide the following information.
    a. Name of the debtor: _______________
    b. Case number: _______________
    c. Date filed: _______________
    d. Relationship: _______________
    e. District where case was filed: _______________
    f. Judge: _______________

II. ASSETS

All debtors must complete this Part. Complete each question based on the assets of the debtor. All questions must be answered.

If you are answering as an individual, provide information for all questions that relate to you as an individual. Use "none" or "n.a." as your answer to a question if you have no assets or if the question is inapplicable to you as an individual.

If you are answering for a partnership, provide information for all questions that relate to the partnership. Use "none" or "n.a." as your answer to a question if the partnership has no assets or if the question is inapplicable to the partnership.

If you are answering for a corporation, provide the information for all questions that relate to the corporation. Use "none" or "n.a." as your answer to a question if the corporation has no assets or if the question is inapplicable to the corporation.

A. Real Property

State the legal description and the mailing address of all real property in which you have an interest, including all equitable and future interests, estates by the entirety, community property, life estates, leaseholds, and any power exercisable for your own benefit relating to real property. State the nature of your interest in each item of real property. If the debtor is an individual or a husband and wife filing a joint petition, state whether the property is owned by the husband, the wife, jointly, or as community property. State the current market value of your interest in the real property without deducting the mortgages or exemptions. If the property is mortgaged, state the amount of the mortgage.

If you do not have an interest in any real property, indicate "none."

1. Legal description:

____

lot #, block # addition

____

city county state

2. Mailing address:

____
street
____
city state zip code

3. The nature of the debtor's interest in the property (e.g., fee simple, option to purchase, three-year lease, life estate):

____

4. If the debtor is an individual who is married or a husband and wife filing a joint petition, check who owns the property:
_____ husband
_____ wife
_____ jointly
_____ community property

5. State the current market value of the debtor's interest in the property. (Do not deduct any secured claim or exemption.):
$ ______________

6. If the real property has a secured claim (e.g., a mortgage), state the amount of the claim:
$ ______________

B. Personal Property

If the debtor is an individual or a husband and wife filing a joint petition, list your personal property and, if married, your spouse's personal property, and its location. If the debtor is married, indicate who owns the property (e.g., husband, wife, jointly, community) by circling the appropriate letter. Also state the current market value of your interest in the property, without deducting for secured claims or exemptions. If the property normally spends part of the day at your residence, list "at residence." EACH BLANK MUST BE FILLED IN.

If the debtor is a partnership or a corporation, list all personal property of the partnership or the corporation.

If the assets are a mixture of individual and partnership or corporate assets, list all assets and designate whether they are individual, partnership, or corporate assets.

Description	Location	Ownership	Market Value of Debtor's Interest
1. Cash on hand	________	H W J C	$________
2. Checking, savings, and other financial accounts			
a. Banks			
______________	________	H W J C	$________
______________	________	H W J C	$________
b. Savings and loans			
______________	________	H W J C	$________
______________	________	H W J C	$________
c. Credit unions			
______________	________	H W J C	$________
______________	________	H W J C	$________
d. Brokerage houses			
______________	________	H W J C	$________
______________	________	H W J C	$________

e. Others

______	______	H	W	J	C	$______
______	______	H	W	J	C	$______

3. Security deposits

a. Public utilities

______	______	H	W	J	C	$______
______	______	H	W	J	C	$______

b. Telephone company

______	______	H	W	J	C	$______

c. Landlord

______	______	H	W	J	C	$______
______	______	H	W	J	C	$______

d. Others

______	______	H	W	J	C	$______
______	______	H	W	J	C	$______
______	______	H	W	J	C	$______

4. Household goods and furnishings

a. Living room, dining room, and family room

1) sofa	______	H	W	J	C	$______
2) chairs	______	H	W	J	C	$______
3) tables	______	H	W	J	C	$______
4) TVs	______	H	W	J	C	$______
5) VCRs	______	H	W	J	C	$______
6) stereos	______	H	W	J	C	$______
7) lamps	______	H	W	J	C	$______
8) carpets	______	H	W	J	C	$______
9) bookcases	______	H	W	J	C	$______
10) piano	______	H	W	J	C	$______
11) other musical instruments	______	H	W	J	C	$______
12) radios	______	H	W	J	C	$______
13) buffet	______	H	W	J	C	$______
14) china closet	______	H	W	J	C	$______
15) china	______	H	W	J	C	$______
16) silverware	______	H	W	J	C	$______
17) sewing machine	______	H	W	J	C	$______
18) other	______	H	W	J	C	$______

b. Kitchen

1) table and chairs	______	H	W	J	C	$______
2) stove	______	H	W	J	C	$______
3) microwave	______	H	W	J	C	$______
4) refrigerator	______	H	W	J	C	$______
5) freezer	______	H	W	J	C	$______
6) dishwasher	______	H	W	J	C	$______
7) washer	______	H	W	J	C	$______
8) dryer	______	H	W	J	C	$______
9) telephones	______	H	W	J	C	$______
10) misc. appliances	______	H	W	J	C	$______
11) misc. furnishings	______	H	W	J	C	$______

c. Bedrooms and study

1) bedroom suites	______	H	W	J	C	$______

2) cedar chest ________ H W J C $________
3) bureaus ________ H W J C $________
4) desks ________ H W J C $________
5) computer equipment ________ H W J C $________
6) TVs ________ H W J C $________
7) VCRs ________ H W J C $________
8) CD player ________ H W J C $________
9) radios ________ H W J C $________
10) stereos ________ H W J C $________
11) lamps ________ H W J C $________
12) telephones ________ H W J C $________
13) other ________ H W J C $________

d. Garage
1) tools ________ H W J C $________
2) bicycles ________ H W J C $________
3) other ________ H W J C $________

e. Other areas, including storage facilities
________________ ________ H W J C $________
________________ ________ H W J C $________
________________ ________ H W J C $________

5. a. Books, pictures, and other art objects
1) books ________ H W J C $________
2) pictures ________ H W J C $________
3) other art objects ________ H W J C $________

b. Collections and collectibles
1) antiques ________ H W J C $________
2) stamps ________ H W J C $________
3) coins ________ H W J C $________
4) records ________ H W J C $________
5) tapes ________ H W J C $________
6) compact discs ________ H W J C $________
7) other collections or collectibles ________ H W J C $________

6. Wearing apparel (exclude furs and jewelry)
List any item that exceeds $200 in market value.
________________ ________ H W J C $________
________________ ________ H W J C $________
Other clothing ________ H W J C $________

7. Furs and jewelry
List any item that exceeds $200 in market value.
________________ ________ H W J C $________
________________ ________ H W J C $________
________________ ________ H W J C $________
________________ ________ H W J C $________
Other jewelry ________ H W J C $________

8. a. Firearms
________________ ________ H W J C $________
________________ ________ H W J C $________
________________ ________ H W J C $________
________________ ________ H W J C $________

b. Sports equipment
List any item that exceeds $200 in market value.

____________	________	H W J C	$________
____________	________	H W J C	$________
____________	________	H W J C	$________
____________	________	H W J C	$________
Other sports equipment	________	H W J C	$________

c. Photographic equipment

____________	________	H W J C	$________
____________	________	H W J C	$________
____________	________	H W J C	$________

d. Other equipment
List any item that exceeds $200 in market value.

____________	________	H W J C	$________
____________	________	H W J C	$________
____________	________	H W J C	$________

9. Interests in insurance policies (list the surrender or refund value of each policy)

Type of insurance	**Insurance company**	**Location**	**Ownership**	**Surrender or refund value**
________	________	________	H W J C	$________
________	________	________	H W J C	$________
________	________	________	H W J C	$________
________	________	________	H W J C	$________
________	________	________	H W J C	$________

10. Annuities

Type of annuity	**Name of fund**	**Location of fund**	**Ownership**	**Current market value**
________	________	________	H W J C	$________
________	________	________	H W J C	$________
________	________	________	H W J C	$________
________	________	________	H W J C	$________
________	________	________	H W J C	$________

11. Interests in IRA, ERISA, Keogh, and other pension or profit-sharing plans

Description	**Location of institution**	**Ownership**	**Current market value**
________	________________	H W J C	$________
________	________________	H W J C	$________

12. Stock and interests in incorporated and unincorporated businesses

Shares or interests	**Name of business**	**Location of business**	**Ownership**	**Current market value**
________	________	________	H W J C	$________
________	________	________	H W J C	$________
________	________	________	H W J C	$________
________	________	________	H W J C	$________

13. Interests in partnerships or joint ventures

Interest	**Name of partnership**	**Location**	**Ownership**	**Current market value**
________	________	________	H W J C	$________
________	________	________	H W J C	$________

14. Government and corporate bonds and other negotiable and non-negotiable instruments

Description	**Location**	**Ownership**	**Current market value**
________	____________________	H W J C	$________
________	____________________	H W J C	$________

15. Accounts receivable

Description (account no.)	**Name of account debtor**	**Date first due**	**Ownership**	**Current market value of the amount due**
________	________	________	H W J C	$________
________	________	________	H W J C	$________
________	________	________	H W J C	$________
________	________	________	H W J C	$________

16. Alimony, maintenance, support, and property settlements to which the debtor is or may be entitled

Description of the obligation	**Address of the person owing the obligation**	**Ownership**	**Current market value of the total amount due or the amount of the monthly payments and duration**
________	________	H W J C	$________
________	________	H W J C	$________

17. Other liquidated debts owing debtor, including tax refunds

Description of the debt	**Address of the entity owing the obligation**	**Ownership**	**Current market value of the amount due**
________	________	H W J C	$________
________	________	H W J C	$________

18. Equitable or future interests, life estates, and rights or powers exercisable for the benefit of the debtor, other than those listed under "Real Property"

Description of the interest	**Address of the trustee, if any**	**Ownership**	**Current market value of the interest**
________	________	H W J C	$________
________	________	H W J C	$________

19. Contingent and noncontingent interests in estate of a decedent, death benefit plan, life insurance policy, or trust

Description of the interest	**Address of the administrator**	**Ownership**	**Current market value of the interest**
________	________	H W J C	$________
________	________	H W J C	$________

20. Other contingent and unliquidated claims of every nature, including tax refunds, counterclaims of the debtor, and rights to setoff claims

Description of the claim	**Address of the defendant**	**Ownership**	**Current market value of the claim**
________	________	H W J C	$________
________	________	H W J C	$________

21. Patents, copyrights, and other intellectual property

Description of the property	Address where documentation is kept	Ownership	Current market value of the property
________	________	H W J C	$________
________	________	H W J C	$________

22. Licenses, franchises, and other general intangibles

Description of the property	Address where documentation is kept	Ownership	Current market value of the property
________	________	H W J C	$________
________	________	H W J C	$________

23. Automobiles, trucks, trailers, and other vehicles

	Location	Ownership	Current market value
a. Automobile Year: ________ Make: ________ Model: ________ Serial No.: ________	________	H W J C	$________
b. Automobile Year: ________ Make: ________ Model: ________ Serial No.: ________	________	H W J C	$________
c. Automobile Year: ________ Make: ________ Model: ________ Serial No.: ________	________	H W J C	$________
d. Automobile Year: ________ Make: ________ Model: ________ Serial No.: ________	________	H W J C	$________
e. Automobile Year: ________ Make: ________ Model: ________ Serial No.: ________	________	H W J C	$________
f. Recreational Vehicle Year: ________ Make: ________ Model: ________ Serial No.: ________	________	H W J C	$________

24. Boats, motors, and their accessories

Description of the property	Address where the property is kept	Ownership	Current market value of the property
________	________	H W J C	$________
________	________	H W J C	$________

25. Aircraft and their accessories

Description of the property	Address where the property is kept	Ownership	Current market value of the property
________	________	H W J C	$________
________	________	H W J C	$________
________	________	H W J C	$________

26. Office equipment, furnishings, and supplies

Description of the property	Address where the property is kept	Ownership	Current market value of the property
________	________	H W J C	$________
________	________	H W J C	$________
________	________	H W J C	$________
________	________	H W J C	$________
________	________	H W J C	$________
________	________	H W J C	$________

27. Machinery, fixtures, equipment, and supplies used in business

Description of the property	Address where the property is kept	Ownership	Current market value of the property
________	________	H W J C	$________
________	________	H W J C	$________
________	________	H W J C	$________
________	________	H W J C	$________
________	________	H W J C	$________
________	________	H W J C	$________

28. Inventory

Description of the inventory	Address where the inventory is located	Ownership	Current market value of the inventory
________	________	H W J C	$________
________	________	H W J C	$________
________	________	H W J C	$________
________	________	H W J C	$________

29. Animals (including pets)

Description of the animal(s)	Address where the animal is located	Ownership	Current market value of the animal
________	________	H W J C	$________
________	________	H W J C	$________
________	________	H W J C	$________
________	________	H W J C	$________

30. Crops—growing or harvested

Description of the crops	Address where the crops are located	Ownership	Current market value of the crops
________	________	H W J C	$________
________	________	H W J C	$________

______________	______________	H W J C	$______________
______________	______________	H W J C	$______________

31. Farming equipment and implements

Description of the equipment or implements	**Address where located**	**Ownership**	**Current market value of the equipment or implements**
______________	______________	H W J C	$______________
______________	______________	H W J C	$______________
______________	______________	H W J C	$______________
______________	______________	H W J C	$______________

32. Farm supplies, chemicals, and feed

Description of the supplies, chemicals, or feed	**Address where located**	**Ownership**	**Current market value of the supplies, chemicals, or feed**
______________	______________	H W J C	$______________
______________	______________	H W J C	$______________
______________	______________	H W J C	$______________
______________	______________	H W J C	$______________

33. Other personal property of any kind not already listed

Description of the property	**Address where located**	**Ownership**	**Current market value of the property**
______________	______________	H W J C	$______________
______________	______________	H W J C	$______________
______________	______________	H W J C	$______________
______________	______________	H W J C	$______________

III. DEBTS

All debtors must complete Part III of the questionnaire. Complete each question based on the debts of the debtor. All questions must be answered.

If you are answering as an individual, provide information for all questions that relate to you as an individual. Use "none" or "n.a." as your answer to a question if you have no debts or if the question is inapplicable to you as an individual.

If you are answering for a partnership, provide information for all questions that relate to the partnership. Use "none" or "n.a." as your answer to a question if the partnership has no debts or if the question is inapplicable to the partnership.

If you are answering for a corporation, provide information for all questions that relate to the corporation. Use "none" or "n.a." as your answer to a question if the corporation has no debts or if the question is inapplicable to the corporation.

If the debts are a mixture of individual and partnership or corporate debts, list all debts and designate whether they are individual, partnership, or corporate debts.

A. Secured Creditors

List in alphabetical order the name, mailing address, account number, if any, and telephone number of each secured creditor, the date when the security interest (lien) was given, the nature of the lien (i.e., judgment lien, garnishment, mechanic's lien, real estate mortgage, deed of trust, UCC art. 9 security interest), a description of collateral subject to the lien, the market value of the collateral, and the amount of the claim without deducting the value of the collateral. Do not deduct the value of the collateral from the balance owed.

Creditor's name: ______________________________
Creditor's mailing address: ______________________________
street
____
city state zip code
Account number, if any: ______________________________
Telephone number (including area code): ______________________________
Date claim was incurred: ______________________________
Nature of the lien: ______________________________
Name of codebtor, if any: ______________________________
Address of codebtor: ______________________________
street
____
city state zip code
Whose debt: H W J C (circle one)
Description of the property subject to the lien:
____
Value of the property subject to the lien: $______________________________
Amount of the claim (do not deduct the value of the collateral): $ ______________________________
Creditor's name: ______________________________
Creditor's mailing address: ______________________________
street
____
city state zip code
Account number, if any: ______________________________
Telephone number (including area code): ______________________________
Date claim was incurred: ______________________________
Nature of the lien: ______________________________
Name of codebtor, if any: ______________________________
Address of codebtor: ______________________________
street
____
city state zip code
Whose debt: H W J C (circle one)
Description of the property subject to the lien:
____
Value of the property subject to the lien: $ ______________________________
Amount of the claim (do not deduct the value of the collateral): $ ______________________________
Creditor's name: ______________________________
Creditor's mailing address: ______________________________
street
____
city state zip code
Account number, if any: ______________________________
Telephone number (including area code): ______________________________
Date claim was incurred: ______________________________
Nature of the lien: ______________________________
Name of codebtor, if any: ______________________________

Address of codebtor: ______________________________
street

____
city state zip code
Whose debt: H W J C (circle one)
Description of the property subject to the lien:

____
Value of the property subject to the lien: $______________________________
Amount of the claim (do not deduct the value of the collateral): $ ______________________________

B. Priority Creditors

1. Has an involuntary petition in bankruptcy been filed against you?

   yes _____ no _____

2. Do you owe any wages, salaries, or commissions, including vacation, severance, or sick pay, to any employee which were earned within the immediately preceding 90 days or within 90 days of the cessation of business?

   yes _____ no _____

   If yes, provide the following information for each creditor and each claim.

   Creditor's name: ______________________________

   Creditor's mailing address: ______________________________
   street

   ____
   city state zip code

   Account number, if any: ______________________________

   Telephone number (including area code): ______________________________

   Name of codebtor, if any: ______________________________

   Address of codebtor: ______________________________
   street

   ____
   city state zip code

   Whose debt: H W J C (circle one)

   Date claim was incurred: ______________________________

   Consideration for the claim: ______________________________

   Amount of the claim: $ ______________________________

3. Do you owe any contributions to employee benefit plans for services rendered by your employees within the last 180 days or within the last 180 days prior to the cessation of business?

   yes _____ no _____

   If yes, provide the following information for each creditor and each claim.

   Creditor's name: ______________________________

   Creditor's mailing address: ______________________________
   street

   ____
   city state zip code

   Account number, if any: ______________________________

Telephone number (including area code): ____________________
Name of codebtor, if any: ____________________
Address of codebtor: ____________________
street
____
city state zip code
Whose debt: H W J C (circle one)
Date claim was incurred: ____________________
Consideration for the claim: ____________________
Amount of the claim: $ ____________________

4. Do you owe any claims to farmers or fishermen?
yes _____ no _____
If yes, provide the following information for each creditor and each claim.
Creditor's name: ____________________
Creditor's mailing address: ____________________
street
____
city state zip code
Account number, if any: ____________________
Telephone number (including area code): ____________________
Name of codebtor, if any: ____________________
Address of codebtor: ____________________
street
____
city state zip code
Whose debt: H W J C (circle one)
Date claim was incurred: ____________________
Consideration for the claim: ____________________
Amount of the claim: $ ____________________

5. Have you received any deposits from any individual for the purchase, lease, or rental of property or services for personal, family, or household use that were not delivered or provided?
yes _____ no _____
If yes, provide the following information for each creditor and each claim.
Creditor's name: ____________________
Creditor's mailing address: ____________________
street
____
city state zip code
Account number, if any: ____________________
Telephone number (including area code): ____________________
Name of codebtor, if any: ____________________

Address of codebtor: ______________________________
street

____
city state zip code

Whose debt: H W J C (circle one)

Date claim was incurred: ______________________________

Consideration for the claim: ______________________________

Amount of the claim: $ ______________________________

6. Do you owe an obligation to a spouse, a former spouse, or a child for alimony, maintenance, or support in connection with a separation agreement, divorce decree, or other order of a court of record?

To a spouse: yes _____ no _____

To a former spouse: yes _____ no _____

To a child: yes _____ no _____

If yes, provide the following information for each claimant.

Claimant's name: ______________________________

Claimant's mailing address: ______________________________
street

____
city state zip code

Nature of the claim: ______________________________

Amount of the claim: $ ______________________________

7. Do you owe taxes to any of the following entities?

To the United States: yes _____ no _____

To any state: yes _____ no _____

To any other taxing authority: yes _____ no _____

If yes, provide the following information for each creditor and each claim.

Creditor's name: ______________________________

Creditor's mailing address: ______________________________
street

____
city state zip code

Account number, if any: ______________________________

Telephone number (including area code): ______________________________

Name of codebtor, if any: ______________________________

Address of codebtor: ______________________________
street

____
city state zip code

Whose debt: H W J C (circle one)

Date claim was incurred: ______________________________

Consideration for the claim: ______________________________

Amount of the claim: $ ______________________________

8. Have you made a commitment to the Federal Deposit Insurance Corporation, the Director of the Office of Trust Supervision, the Comptroller of the Currency, or the Board of Governors of the Federal Reserve System, or their predecessors or successors, to maintain the capital of an insured depository institution?

   yes _____ no _____

   If yes, provide the following information for each creditor and each claim.

   Creditor's name: ______________________________

   Creditor's mailing address: ______________________________
   street

   ____
   city state zip code

   Account number, if any: ______________________________

   Telephone number (including area code): ______________________________

   Name of codebtor, if any: ______________________________

   Address of codebtor: ______________________________
   street

   ____
   city state zip code

   Whose debt: H W J C (circle one)

   Date claim was incurred: ______________________________

   Consideration for the claim: ______________________________

   Amount of the claim: $ ______________________________

C. Unsecured Creditors

List in alphabetical order the name, address, and account number, if any, of each unsecured creditor, the date the debt was incurred, the consideration for the claim, whether the claim is subject to setoff, and the amount of the claim. Include all open accounts with book and record clubs, credit cards, department stores, doctors, gasoline companies, hospitals, mail order houses, utilities, and signature loans at banks, savings and loan associations, credit unions, and finance companies. Show the exact name and address of the creditor, including zip code, and the creditor's telephone number. If a creditor has turned the account over to a collection agency or an attorney for collection, show the name, address, and telephone number of the collection agency or attorney and any additional amounts known to be owed to the collection agency or attorney for collection fees or costs.

Creditor's name: ______________________________

Creditor's mailing address: ______________________________
street

____
city state zip code

Account number, if any: ______________________________

Telephone number (including area code): ______________________________

Name of codebtor, if any: ______________________________

Address of codebtor: ______________________________
street

____
city state zip code

Whose debt: H W J C (circle one)

Date claim was incurred: ______________________________

Consideration for the claim: ______________________________

Was the claim subject to a setoff? yes _____ no _____

Amount of the claim: $ ______________________________

Creditor's name: ______________________________

Creditor's mailing address: ______________________________
street

____
city state zip code

Account number, if any: ______________________________

Telephone number (including area code): ______________________________

Name of codebtor, if any: ______________________________

Address of codebtor: ______________________________
street

____
city state zip code

Whose debt: H W J C (circle one)

Date claim was incurred: ______________________________

Consideration for the claim: ______________________________

Was the claim subject to a setoff? yes _____ no _____

Amount of the claim: $ ______________________________

Creditor's name: ______________________________

Creditor's mailing address: ______________________________
street

____
city state zip code

Account number, if any: ______________________________

Telephone number (including area code): ______________________________

Name of codebtor, if any: ______________________________

Address of codebtor: ______________________________
street

____
city state zip code

Whose debt: H W J C (circle one)

Date claim was incurred: ______________________________

Consideration for the claim: ______________________________

Was the claim subject to a setoff? yes _____ no _____

Amount of the claim: $ ______________________________

IV. EXECUTORY CONTRACTS AND UNEXPIRED LEASES

For each executory contract (a contract that has duties still to be performed by both contracting parties) and unexpired lease, provide the following information.

Name of the other party to the contract or lease: ______________________________

Mailing address of the other party: ______________________________
street

____
city state zip code

Telephone number (including area code): ______________________________

Description of the contract or lease: ______________________________

Nature of the debtor's interest: ______________________________

If a lease, is it for nonresidential real property? yes _____ no _____

If a government contract, state the contract number: ______________________________

Name of the other party to the contract or lease: ______________________________

Mailing address of the other party: ______________________________
street

____
city state zip code

Telephone number (including area code): ______________________________

Description of the contract or lease: ______________________________

Nature of the debtor's interest: ______________________________

If a lease, is it for nonresidential real property? yes _____ no _____

If a government contract, state the contract number: ______________________________

Name of the other party to the contract or lease: ______________________________

Mailing address of the other party: ______________________________
street

____
city state zip code

Telephone number (including area code): ______________________________

Description of the contract or lease: ______________________________

Nature of the debtor's interest: ______________________________

If a lease, is it for nonresidential real property? yes _____ no _____

If a government contract, state the contract number: ______________________________

V. CURRENT INCOME AND EXPENDITURES OF INDIVIDUAL DEBTOR(S)

Complete Part V if the debtor is an individual or if the debtors are husband and wife filing a joint petition.

A. Estimated average monthly income of the debtor and spouse, if applicable
   1. Total average monthly income for the debtor
      a. Net monthly take-home pay
         1) Gross monthly take-home pay

a) Current monthly gross wages, salaries, and commissions (pro rate if not paid monthly) $ _______
b) Estimated monthly overtime $ _______
2) Payroll deductions
a) Payroll taxes, including Social Security $ _______
b) Insurance $ _______
c) Union dues $ _______
d) Other: Specify ________________________ $ _______
________________________ $ _______

b. Other monthly income
1) Regular income from operation of business, profession, or farm $ _______
2) Income from real property $ _______
3) Investment income, including interest and dividends $ _______
4) Alimony, maintenance, or support payments payable to the debtor for the debtor's use $ _______
5) Support payable to the debtor for the support of another person
Specify name: ________________________ $ _______
Specify name: ________________________ $ _______
6) Social Security benefits $ _______
7) Other governmental assistance
Specify the type of assistance:
________________________ $ _______
________________________ $ _______
8) Pension and other retirement income $ _______
9) Income from ownership of personal property $ _______
10) Money provided by debtor's spouse to the debtor, excluding amounts listed above $ _______
11) Other monthly income:
Specify: ________________________ $ _______
Specify: ________________________ $ _______

2. Total average monthly income for the debtor's spouse, if the debtor is married
a. Net monthly take-home pay
1) Gross monthly take-home pay
a) Current monthly gross wages, salaries, and commissions (pro rate if not paid monthly) $ _______
b) Estimated monthly overtime $ _______
2) Payroll deductions
a) Payroll taxes, including Social Security $ _______
b) Insurance $ _______
c) Union dues $ _______
d) Other: Specify ________________________ $ _______
________________________ $ _______

b. Other monthly income
1) Regular income from operation of business, profession, or farm $ _______
2) Income from real property $ _______
3) Investment income, including interest and dividends $ _______
4) Alimony, maintenance, or support payments payable to the debtor for the debtor's use $ _______

5) Support payable to the debtor for the support of another person
Specify name: ________________ $ ______
Specify name: ________________ $ ______
6) Social Security benefits $ ______
7) Other governmental assistance
Specify the type of assistance:
________________ $ ______
________________ $ ______
8) Pension and other retirement income $ ______
9) Income from ownership of personal property $ ______
10) Money provided by debtor's spouse to the debtor, excluding amounts listed above $ ______
11) Other monthly income:
Specify: ________________ $ ______
Specify: ________________ $ ______

B. Estimated average current monthly expenditures of the debtor and the debtor's family, if the debtor has a family. Exclude payments on debts owed as of this date unless a debt is specifically listed below.

If the debtor is married, does the debtor's spouse maintain a separate household?

yes _____ no _____

If the debtor's spouse maintains a separate household, include those current expenses in B.2 rather than in B.1.

1. Estimated average current monthly expenses.
   a. Rent or home mortgage payment (include lot rented for mobile home and condominium fee) $ ______
      Are real estate taxes included? yes_____ no _____
      Is property insurance included? yes_____ no _____
   b. Utilities:
      1) Electricity $ ______
      2) Gas, oil, or coal $ ______
      3) Water $ ______
      4) Sewer $ ______
      5) Telephone $ ______
      6) Refuse removal $ ______
      7) Other ________________ $ ______
   c. Routine home maintenance (repairs and upkeep) $ ______
   d. Food $ ______
   e. Clothing $ ______
   f. Laundry and dry cleaning $ ______
   g. Medical and dental expenses (include drugs) $ ______
   h. Transportation, excluding automobile payments $ ______
   i. Recreation, clubs, and entertainment $ ______
   j. Newspapers, periodicals, and books, including school books $ ______
   k. Religious and charitable contributions $ ______
   l. Insurance not deducted from wages or included in home mortgage payments
      1) Homeowners or renters insurance $ ______
      2) Life insurance $ ______
      3) Medical insurance $ ______

4) Automobile insurance $ _______
5) Other ______________________________ $ _______

m. Taxes that are not deducted from wages or included in home mortgage payments
Specify: ______________________________ $ _______
Specify: ______________________________ $ _______

n. Installment payments:
1) Automobile: ______________________________ $ _______
2) Automobile: ______________________________ $ _______
3) Home improvements: ______________________________ $ _______
4) ______________________________ $ _______
5) ______________________________ $ _______
6) ______________________________ $ _______
7) ______________________________ $ _______

o. Alimony, maintenance, or support paid to others $ _______
p. Other payments for support of additional dependents not living at your home $ _______
q. Regular expenses from operation of business, profession, or farm $ _______
r. Union, professional, social, and other dues that are not deducted from wages $ _______
s. Other expenses: ______________________________ $ _______
______________________________ $ _______
______________________________ $ _______
______________________________ $ _______

2. Estimated average current monthly expenses for the debtor's spouse who maintains a separate household.

a. Rent or home mortgage payment (include lot rented for mobile home and condominium fee)
$ _______
Are real estate taxes included? yes _____ no _____
Is property insurance included? yes _____ no _____

b. Utilities:
1) Electricity $ _______
2) Gas, oil, or coal $ _______
3) Water $ _______
4) Sewer $ _______
5) Telephone $ _______
6) Refuse removal $ _______
7) Other $ _______

c. Routine home maintenance (repairs and upkeep) $ _______
d. Food $ _______
e. Clothing $ _______
f. Laundry and dry cleaning $ _______
g. Medical and dental expenses (include drugs) $ _______
h. Transportation, excluding automobile payments $ _______
i. Recreation, clubs, and entertainment $ _______
j. Newspapers, periodicals, and books, including school books $ _______
k. Religious and charitable contributions $ _______
l. Insurance not deducted from wages or included in home mortgage payments
1) Homeowners or renters insurance $ _______
2) Life insurance $ _______
3) Medical insurance $ _______
4) Automobile insurance $ _______
5) Other ______________________________ $ _______

m. Taxes that are not deducted from wages or included in home mortgage payments
   Specify: ______________________________ $ ______
   Specify: ______________________________ $ ______

n. Installment payments:
   1) Automobile: ______________________________ $ ______
   2) Automobile: ______________________________ $ ______
   3) Home improvements: ______________________________ $ ______
   4) ______________________________ $ ______
   5) ______________________________ $ ______
   6) ______________________________ $ ______
   7) ______________________________ $ ______

o. Alimony, maintenance, or support paid to others $ ______

p. Other payments for support of additional dependents not living at your home $ ______

q. Regular expenses from operation of business, profession, or farm $ ______

r. Union, professional, social, and other dues that are not deducted from wages $ ______

s. Other expenses: ______________________________ $ ______
   ______________________________ $ ______
   ______________________________ $ ______
   ______________________________ $ ______
   ______________________________ $ ______

VI. CURRENT INCOME AND CURRENT EXPENDITURES OF A PARTNERSHIP OR A CORPORATION

Complete Part VI if the debtor is a partnership or a corporation.

1. How are the debtor's accounting records kept?

   cash basis _____ accrual method _____

   If the debtor's accounting records are kept on a cash basis, complete question 2.

   If the debtor's accounting records are kept on an accrual method, complete question 3.

2. Summarize the debtor's cash flow for a 90- to 120-day period which ends no more than 30 days prior to the commencement of this case.
   a. Beginning date: ______________________________
   b. Ending date: ______________________________
   c. Cash balance at the beginning date: $ ______________________________
   d. Cash disbursements during this period: $ ______________________________
   e. Cash balance at the ending date: $ ______________________________

3. Summarize the debtor's revenue and expenses on an accrual method for a 90- to 120-day period which ends no more than 30 days prior to the commencement of this case.
   a. Beginning date: ______________________________
   b. Ending date: ______________________________
   c. Revenue during this period: $ ______________________________
   d. Expenses during this period: $ ______________________________
   e. Net gain or (loss) during this period: $ ______________________________

4. Attach to this questionnaire a copy of the most recent financial statement (audited or unaudited) which has been prepared by or for the debtor.

VII. STATEMENT OF FINANCIAL AFFAIRS

Questions 1–15 must be completed by all debtors.

1. Income from employment or operation of business.

   Question 1.a. applies to the debtor. Question 1.b. applies to the debtor's spouse, if a joint petition is filed. Answer question 1.b. only if a joint petition is filed.

   a. Debtor's gross income
      1) Debtor's financial records
         a) How are your financial records maintained or how have they been maintained?
            (1) fiscal year basis? yes _____ no _____
            (2) calendar year basis? yes _____ no _____
            If your answer is fiscal year, you may report fiscal year income.
         b) If fiscal year, identify the beginning and ending dates of your fiscal year.
            (1) beginning date: ____________________
            (2) ending date: ____________________
      2) For this calendar [fiscal] year to the date this case was commenced
         a) Beginning with this calendar [fiscal] year to the date this case was commenced, did you receive gross income from
            (1) employment
            (2) trade
            (3) profession or
            (4) operation of your business?
            yes _____ no _____
         b) If yes, state the gross amount of income you received during this period and the source of this income.

Amount	Source
$ _____	____________________
$ _____	____________________
$ _____	____________________
$ _____	____________________
$ _____	____________________
$ _____	____________________

      3) For the two years immediately preceding this calendar [fiscal] year
         a) During the two years immediately preceding this calendar [fiscal] year, did you receive gross income from
            (1) employment
            (2) trade
            (3) profession or
            (4) operation of your business?
            yes_____no_____
         b) If yes, state the gross amount of income you received during this period and the source of this income.

Amount	Source
$ _____	____________________
$ _____	____________________
$ _____	____________________
$ _____	____________________
$ _____	____________________
$ _____	____________________

b. The following questions apply to the debtor's spouse, if a joint petition is filed.
   1) Debtor's spouse's financial records
      a) How are your spouse's financial records maintained or how have they been maintained?
         (1) fiscal year basis? yes _____ no _____
         (2) calendar year basis? yes _____ no _____
         If your answer is fiscal year, you may report fiscal year income.
      b) If fiscal year, identify the beginning and ending dates of the spouse's fiscal year.
         (1) beginning date: ______________________________
         (2) ending date: ______________________________
   2) For this calendar [fiscal] year to the date this case was commenced
      a) Beginning with this calendar [fiscal] year to the date this case was commenced, did your spouse receive gross income from
         (1) employment
         (2) trade
         (3) profession or
         (4) operation of your business?
         yes_____no_____
      b) If yes, state the gross amount of income your spouse received during this period and the source of this income.
         Amount Source
         $ _____ ____________________
         $ _____ ____________________
         $ _____ ____________________
         $ _____ ____________________
         $ _____ ____________________
         $ _____ ____________________
   3) For the two years immediately preceding this calendar [fiscal] year
      a) During the two years immediately preceding this calendar [fiscal] year, did your spouse receive gross income from
         (1) employment
         (2) trade
         (3) profession or
         (4) operation of your business?
         yes_____no_____
      b) If yes, state the gross amount of income your spouse received during this period and the source of this income.
         Amount Source
         $ _____ ____________________
         $ _____ ____________________
         $ _____ ____________________
         $ _____ ____________________
         $ _____ ____________________
         $ _____ ____________________

2. Income other than from employment or operation of business.

   Question 2.a. applies to the debtor. Question 2.b. applies to the debtor's spouse, if a joint petition is filed. Answer question 2.b. only if a joint petition is filed.

   a. The following questions apply to all debtors.
      During the two years immediately preceding the commencement of this case, did you receive income *other than from*
      1) employment
      2) trade

3) profession or
4) operation of your business?
yes _____ no _____
If yes, state the amount of income you received during this period and the source of this income.

Amount Source
$ _____ _____________________
$ _____ _____________________
$ _____ _____________________

b. The following questions apply to the debtor's spouse, if a joint petition is filed.
During the two years immediately preceding the commencement of this case, did your spouse receive income *other than from*
1) employment
2) trade
3) profession or
4) operation of your business?
yes_____no_____
If yes, state the amount of income your spouse received during this period and the source of this income.

Amount Source
$ _____ _____________________
$ _____ _____________________
$ _____ _____________________

3. Payments to creditors.
a. Within 90 days immediately preceding the commencement of this case
1) Within 90 days immediately preceding the commencement of this case, did you make any payments of
a) loans
b) installment purchases of goods or services
c) other debts aggregating more than $600 to any creditor?
yes_____no_____
2) If yes, provide the following information.
Name of creditor: _____________________
Address: _____________________
Dates of payment: _____________________
Amount paid: $ _____________________
Amount still owing: $ _____________________
Name of creditor: _____________________
Address: _____________________
Dates of payment: _____________________
Amount paid: $ _____________________
Amount still owing: $ _____________________
Name of creditor: _____________________
Address: _____________________
Dates of payment: _____________________
Amount paid: $ _____________________
Amount still owing: $ _____________________
b. Within one year immediately preceding the commencement of this case
1) Within one year immediately preceding the commencement of this case, did you make any payments to or for the benefit of creditors who are or were insiders?
yes _____ no _____

The term "insider" includes but is not limited to
a) relatives of the debtor;
b) general partners of the debtor and their relatives;
c) corporations of which the debtor is an officer, director, or person in control;
d) officers, directors, and any persons in control of a corporate debtor and their relatives;
e) affiliates of the debtor and insiders of such affiliates;
f) any managing agent of the debtor.

2) If yes, provide the following information.
Name of creditor: ______________________
Address: ______________________
Relationship to the debtor: ______________________
Dates of payment: ______________________
Amount paid: $ ______________
Amount still owing: $ ______________
Name of creditor: ______________________
Address: ______________________
Relationship to the debtor: ______________________
Dates of payment: ______________________
Amount paid: $ ______________
Amount still owing: $ ______________

4. Suits, executions, garnishments, and attachments.
a. Lawsuits (include divorce proceeding)
1) Pending lawsuits
a) At the present time, are you a party to any lawsuit?
yes_____no_____
b) If yes, provide the following information.
Caption of the suit: ______________________
Case number: ______________________
Nature of the proceeding: ______________________
The Court: ______________________
The Court's location: ______________________
The status of the suit: ______________________
Caption of the suit: ______________________
Case number: ______________________
Nature of the proceeding: ______________________
The Court: ______________________
The Court's location: ______________________
The status of the suit: ______________________
2) Suits no longer pending
a) Within one year immediately preceding the filing of this bankruptcy case, were you a party to any lawsuit that is no longer pending?
yes_____no_____
b) If yes, provide the following information.
Caption of the suit: ______________________
Case number: ______________________
Nature of the proceeding: ______________________
The Court: ______________________
The Court's location: ______________________
The disposition of the suit: ______________________
Caption of the suit: ______________________
Case number: ______________________

Nature of the proceeding: ______
The Court: ______
The Court's location: ______
The disposition of the suit: ______

b. Attachments, seizures, and garnishments
   1) Within one year immediately preceding the filing of this bankruptcy case, has any of your property been attached or seized under any legal or equitable process or subjected to garnishment?
   yes_____no_____
   2) If yes, provide the following information.
   Name of the person for whose benefit the property was attached, seized, or subjected to garnishment: ______
   Address: ______
   Date of attachment, seizure, or garnishment: ______
   Description of the property: ______
   Value of the property: $ ______
   Name of the person for whose benefit the property was attached, seized, or subjected to garnishment: ______
   Address: ______
   Date of attachment, seizure, or garnishment: ______
   Description of the property: ______
   Value of the property: $ ______

5. Repossessions, foreclosures, and returns.
   a. Within one year immediately preceding the commencement of this case, has any of your property been repossessed by a creditor, sold at a foreclosure sale, transferred through a deed in lieu of foreclosure, or returned to the seller?
   yes_____no_____
   b. If yes, provide the following information.
   Name of the creditor or seller: ______
   Address: ______
   Date of repossession, foreclosure sale, transfer, or return: ______
   Description of the property: ______
   Value of the property: $ ______
   Name of the creditor or seller: ______
   Address: ______
   Date of repossession, foreclosure sale, transfer, or return: ______
   Description of the property: ______
   Value of the property: $ ______

6. Assignments and receiverships.
   a. Assignments
   1) Within 120 days immediately preceding the commencement of this case, has any of your property been assigned for the benefit of creditors?
   yes_____no_____

2) For each assignment, provide the following information.
Name of assignee: ____________________
Address: ____________________
Date of assignment: ____________________
Terms of assignment or settlement: ____________________
____
____

Name of assignee: ____________________
Address: ____________________
Date of assignment: ____________________
Terms of assignment or settlement: ____________________
____
____

b. Receiverships
1) Within one year immediately preceding the commencement of this case, has any of your property been in the hands of a custodian, receiver, or court-appointed official?
yes_____no_____
2) For any such property, provide the following information.
Name of custodian: ____________________
Address: ____________________
Name of the Court: ____________________
Location of the Court: ____________________
Case title: ____________________
Case number: ____________________
Date of the order: ____________________
Description of the property: ____________________
Value of the property: $ ____________________

7. Gifts.
a. Gifts
1) Within one year immediately preceding the commencement of this case, have you made any gifts other than ordinary and usual gifts to family members totaling less than $200 in value per individual family member?
yes_____no_____
2) For any such gift, provide the following information.
Name of the person receiving the gift: ____________________
____
Address: ____________________
____
Relationship to the debtor, if any: ____________________
Date of the gift: ____________________
Description of the gift: ____________________
Value of the gift: $ ____________________
Name of the person receiving the gift: ____________________
____
Address of the person receiving the gift: ____________________
____
Relationship to the debtor, if any: ____________________
Date of the gift: ____________________
Description of the gift: ____________________
Value of the gift: $ ____________________

b. Charitable contributions
   1) Within one year immediately preceding the commencement of this case, have you made any charitable contributions other than charitable contributions totaling less than $100 per recipient?
      yes_____no_____
   2) For any such contribution, provide the following information.
      Name of the recipient receiving the charitable contribution:
      ____
      Address: ______________________________
      ____
      Relationship to the debtor, if any: ______________________________
      Date of the contribution: ______________________________
      Description of the contribution: ______________________________
      Value of the contribution: $ ______________________________
      Name of the recipient receiving the charitable contribution:
      ____
      Address: ______________________________
      ____
      Relationship to the debtor, if any: ______________________________
      Date of the contribution: ______________________________
      Description of the contribution: ______________________________
      Value of the contribution: $ ______________________________

8. Losses.
   a. Within one year immediately preceding the commencement of this case, have you suffered any losses from fire, theft, other casualty, or gambling?
      yes_____no_____
   b. For each such loss, provide the following information.
      Description of the property: ______________________________
      Value of the property: $ ______________________________
      Description of the circumstances surrounding the loss: ______________________________
      ____
      Date of the loss: ______________________________
      Description of the property: ______________________________
      Value of the property: $ ______________________________
      Description of the circumstances surrounding the loss: ______________________________
      ____
      Date of the loss: ______________________________
   c. Was the loss covered in whole or in part by insurance?
      yes_____no_____
   d. Give particulars of the insurance coverage.
      ____
      ____

9. Payments related to debt counseling or bankruptcy.
   a. Payments made
      1) Within one year immediately preceding the commencement of this case, have payments been made by you or on your behalf to any persons, including attorneys, for
         a) consultation concerning debt consolidation
         b) relief under the bankruptcy law
         c) preparation of a petition in bankruptcy?
         yes _____ no _____

2) For any such payment, provide the following information.
Name of the payee: ______________________________
Address: ______________________________
____
Date of payment: ______________________________
Name of payor, if other than you: ______________________________
Amount of money paid: $ ______________________________

b. Property transferred
1) Within one year immediately preceding the commencement of this case, has property been transferred by you or on your behalf to any persons, including attorneys, for
a) consultation concerning debt consolidation
b) relief under the bankruptcy law
c) preparation of a petition in bankruptcy?
yes _____ no _____
2) For any such transfer, provide the following information.
Name of the transferee: ______________________________
Address: ______________________________
____
Date of transfer: ______________________________
Name of transferor, if other than you: ______________________________
____
Description of the property transferred: ______________________________

10. Other transfers.
a. Within one year immediately preceding the commencement of this case, have you transferred any other property, either absolutely or as security, which was not transferred in the ordinary course of your business or financial affairs?
yes _____ no _____
b. For such transfers, provide the following information.
Name of the transferee: ______________________________
Address: ______________________________
____
Relationship to you: ______________________________
Date of the transfer: ______________________________
Description of the property transferred: ______________________________
____
Value received for the property: $ ______________________________
Name of the transferee: ______________________________
Address: ______________________________
____
Relationship to you: ______________________________
Date of the transfer: ______________________________
Description of the property transferred: ______________________________
____
Value received for the property: $ ______________________________

11. Closed financial accounts.
a. Within one year immediately preceding the commencement of this case, were there any financial accounts or instruments (including checking accounts, savings accounts, other financial ac-

counts, certificates of deposit, shares and share accounts held in banks, credit unions, pension funds, cooperatives, associations, brokerage houses, and other financial institutions) held in your name or for your benefit which were closed, sold, or otherwise transferred?
yes_____no_____

b. For any such financial account or instrument, provide the following information.
Name of the institution: ____________________
Address: ____________________
____
Name under which the account was carried: ____________________
____
Type and account number: ____________________
Amount of the final balance: $ ____________________
Amount and date of sale or closing: $ ____________________
Name of the institution: ____________________
Address: ____________________
____
Name under which the account was carried: ____________________
____
Type and account number: ____________________
Amount of the final balance: $ ____________________
Amount and date of sale or closing: $ ____________________

12. Safe deposit boxes.

a. Within one year immediately preceding the commencement of this case, have you kept or used for your cash, securities, or other valuables a safe deposit box or other depositories?
yes _____ no _____

b. For each box or depository, provide the following information.
Name of the bank or other depository: ____________________
____
Address: ____________________
____
____
Name and address of every person who had the right of access to the box or depository: ________
____
____
____
____
Brief description of the contents: ____________________
____
____
If the box or other depository has been transferred, state the transfer date: ____________
If the box or other depository has been surrendered, state the date of surrender: ____________
____

13. Setoffs.

a. Within 90 days preceding the commencement of this case, were there any debts you owed to any creditor, including any bank, which were setoff by that creditor against a debt or deposit the creditor owed you?
yes _____ no _____

b. If there has been such a setoff, provide the following information.
Name of the creditor: ______
Address: ______
______
Date of setoff: ______
Amount of the debt you owed the creditor: $ ______
Amount of the setoff: $ ______
Name of the creditor: ______
Address: ______
______
Date of setoff: ______
Amount of the debt you owed the creditor: $ ______
Amount of the setoff: $ ______

14. Property held for another person.
a. Do you hold or control property that is owned by another person?
yes ____ no ____
b. For such property held or controlled by you, provide the following information.
Name of the owner: ______
Address: ______
______
Description of the property: ______
______
Value of the property: $ ______
Location of the property: ______
______
Name of the owner: ______
Address: ______
______
Description of the property: ______
______
Value of the property: $ ______
Location of the property: ______
______
Name of the owner: ______
Address: ______
______
Description of the property: ______
______
Value of the property: $ ______
Location of the property: ______
______

15. Prior address of debtor.
a. Within the two years immediately preceding the commencement of this case, have you moved from one address to another?
yes ____ no ____
b. For each such address, provide the following information.
Former address: ______
______
Name under which the premises was occupied: ______
______

Dates of occupancy: ____________________

____

Former address: ____________________

____

Name under which the premises was occupied: ____________________

____

Dates of occupancy: ____________________

____

Former address: ____________________

____

Name under which the premises was occupied: ____________________

____

Dates of occupancy: ____________________

____

c. If a joint petition, also provide separate addresses of either spouse during this period.
Separate address: ____________________

____

Name under which the premises was occupied: ____________________

____

Dates of occupancy: ____________________

____

Separate address: ____________________

____

Name under which the premises was occupied: ____________________

____

Dates of occupancy: ____________________

____

16. Spouses and former spouses

a. Within the six years immediately preceding the commencement of this case, did you reside in one of the following community property states, commonwealths, or territories: Alaska, Arizona, California, Idaho, Louisiana, Nevada, New Mexico, Puerto Rico, Texas, Washington, or Wisconsin?
yes _____ no _____

b. If your answer was yes, were you married at any time during these six years?
yes _____ no _____

c. If your answer was yes, identify the name of your spouse or any former spouse whom you were married to during this time:

____

____

____

17. Environmental information

a. Have you received a written notice from a governmental unit that you may be liable or potentially liable for an environmental law violation?
yes _____ no _____
If your answer was yes, list the site name and address, the name and address of the governmental unit, the date of the notice, and the environmental law cited in the notice.

____

____

____

____

b. Have you ever received a written notice from a governmental unit that you have released hazardous material?
yes _____ no _____
If yes, list the site name and address, the name and address of the governmental unit, the date of the notice, and the environmental law cited in the notice.
____
____
____

c. Were you ever a party to any judicial or administrative proceedings, including settlements or orders, under any environmental law?
yes _____ no _____
If yes, list the name and address of the governmental unit, the docket number, and the status or disposition of the proceeding.
____
____
____

Questions 18–23 are to be completed by every debtor that is
(a) a corporation;
(b) a partnership;
(c) an individual debtor who is or has been, within the two years immediately preceding the commencement of this case, any of the following:
(1) an officer, director, managing executive, or owner of more than 5 percent of the voting securities of a corporation;
(2) a partner, other than a limited partner, of a partnership;
(3) a sole proprietor or otherwise self-employed.

18. Nature, location, and name of business.
a. Answer this question if you are filing your petition as an individual.
1) Within the two years immediately preceding the commencement of this case, were you
a) an officer
b) a director
c) a partner
d) a managing executive of
(1) a corporation
(2) a partnership
(3) a sole proprietorship or
e) a self-employed professional?
yes _____ no _____
2) For each operation, provide the following information.
Name of the operation: _______________
Address: _______________
____
Nature of the business: _______________
____
Beginning date of operation: _______________
Ending date of operation: _______________
Name of the operation: _______________
Address: _______________
____
Nature of the business: _______________
____

Beginning date of operation: ______
Ending date of operation: ______

3) Within the two years immediately preceding the commencement of this case, did you own 5 percent or more of the voting or equity securities of a business?
yes _____ no _____

4) For each business in which you owned 5 percent or more of the voting or equity securities, provide the following information.
Name of the business: ______
Address: ______
______
Nature of the business: ______
______
Beginning date of ownership interest: ______
Ending date of ownership interest: ______
Name of the business: ______
Address: ______
______
Nature of the business: ______
______
Beginning date of ownership interest: ______
Ending date of ownership interest: ______

b. Answer this question if you are filing your petition as a partnership.

1) Within the two years immediately preceding the commencement of this case, were you a partner in a business?
yes _____ no _____

2) For each business, provide the following information.
Name of the business: ______
Address: ______
______
Nature of the business: ______
Beginning date of operation: ______
Ending date of operation: ______
Name of the business: ______
Address: ______
______
Nature of the business: ______
Beginning date of operation: ______
Ending date of operation: ______

3) Within the two years immediately preceding the commencement of this case, did the partnership own 5 percent or more of the voting securities of a business?
yes _____ no _____

4) For each business, provide the following information.
Name of the business: ______
Address: ______
______
Nature of the business: ______
Beginning date of ownership interest: ______
Ending date of ownership interest: ______
Name of the business: ______
Address: ______
______

Nature of the business: ______________________________

____

Beginning date of ownership interest: ______________________________
Ending date of ownership interest: ______________________________

c. Answer this question if you are filing your petition as a corporation.
   1) Within the two years immediately preceding the commencement of this case, was the corporation a partner in a business?
      yes _____ no _____
   2) For each business, provide the following information.
      Name of the business: ` ______________________________
      Address: ______________________________

      ____

      Nature of the business: ______________________________
      Beginning date of operation: ______________________________
      Ending date of operation: ______________________________
      Name of the business: ______________________________
      Address: ______________________________

      ____

      Nature of the business: ______________________________
      Beginning date of operation: ______________________________
      Ending date of operation: ______________________________
   3) Within the two years immediately preceding the commencement of this case, did the corporation own 5 percent or more of the voting securities of a business?
      yes _____ no _____
   4) For each business, provide the following information.
      Name of the business: ______________________________
      Address: ______________________________

      ____

      Nature of the business: ______________________________

      ____

      Beginning date of ownership interest: ______________________________
      Ending date of ownership interest: ______________________________
      Name of the business: ______________________________
      Address: ______________________________

      ____

      Nature of the business: ______________________________
      Beginning date of ownership interest: ______________________________
      Ending date of ownership interest: ______________________________

d. If you listed a business, did you have a "single asset real estate"; that is, one real property or project, excluding residential real property of less than four residential units, that generates substantially all of the debtor's gross income and on which the debtor does not conduct a substantial business other than the business of operating the property or activities incidental to operating the property and having aggregate noncontingent, liquidated secured debts of no more than $4,000,000?
   yes _____ no _____
   If yes, identify the real property or project by name and address.

   ____

   ____

19. Books, records, and financial statements.
   a. Bookkeepers and accountants
      1) Within the six years immediately preceding the filing of this bankruptcy case, did you use a bookkeeper or an accountant to keep or supervise the keeping of your account books and records?
         yes _____ no _____
      2) For any such bookkeeper or accountant, provide the following information.
         Name: ____________________
         Address: ____________________

         The dates the services were rendered: ____________________
   b. Audits and preparation of financial statements
      1) Within the two years immediately preceding the filing of this bankruptcy case, has a firm or an individual audited your books of account and records or prepared a financial statement for you?
         yes _____ no _____
      2) For any such services, provide the following information.
         Name: ____________________
         Address: ____________________
         ____
         The dates the services were rendered: ____________________
         ____
   c. Possession of books and records
      1) Provide the following information concerning the firms or individuals who currently have possession of your books of account or records.
         Name: ____________________
         Address: ____________________
         ____
      2) Are any of these books or records unavailable?
         yes _____ no _____
      3) Explain the circumstances surrounding the unavailability of these books or records: ________
         ____
         ____
         ____
         ____
         ____
         ____
   d. Financial statements
      1) Within the two years immediately preceding the commencement of this case, have you issued any written financial statements?
         yes _____ no _____
      2) For the persons to whom written financial statements have been issued (including mercantile and trade agencies), provide the following information.
         Name of the person receiving the written financial statement: ____________________
         ____
         Address: ____________________
         ____
         Date the financial statement was issued: ____________________
         Name of the person receiving the written financial statement: ____________________
         ____

Address: ______________________________

____

Date the financial statement was issued: ______________________________

20. Inventories.
    a. The last two inventories of your property
        1) The last inventory of your property
        Date of the last inventory: ______________________________
        Name of the person who took the inventory or under whose supervision the inventory was taken: ______________________________
        Dollar amount of the inventory: $ ______________________________
        Basis for the inventory: cost, market, other (specify): ______________________________
        2) The next-to-last inventory of your property
        Date of the next-to-last inventory: ______________________________
        Name of the person who took the inventory or under whose supervision the inventory was taken: ______________________________
        Dollar amount of the inventory: $ ______________________________
        Basis for the inventory: cost, market, other (specify): ______________________________
    b. Custodian of the inventory records
        1) The last inventory
        Name of the custodian of the inventory records: ______________________________

        ____

        Address: ______________________________

        ____

        2) The next-to-last inventory
        Name of the custodian of the inventory records: ______________________________

        ____

        Address: ______________________________

        ____

21. Current partners, officers, directors, and shareholders.

    If the debtor is a partnership, answer question a. If the debtor is a corporation, answer question b.

    a. For each member of the partnership, provide the following information.
    Name of the partner: ______________________________
    Address: ______________________________

    ____

    Nature of the partner's interest: ______________________________
    Percentage of the partnership interest: ____________ %
    Name of the partner: ______________________________
    Address: ______________________________

    ____

    Nature of the partner's interest: ______________________________
    Percentage of the partnership interest: ____________ %
    Name of the partner: ______________________________
    Address: ______________________________

    ____

    Nature of the partner's interest: ______________________________
    Percentage of the partnership interest: ____________ %
    b. For each officer or director of the corporation and each stockholder who directly or indirectly owns, controls, or holds 5 percent or more of the voting securities of the corporation, provide the following information.

Name of the officer, director, or stockholder: ______________________________

____

Address: ______________________________

____

Title: ______________________________

Nature of stock ownership: ______________________________

____

Percentage of stock ownership: ______________ %

Name of the officer, director, or stockholder: ______________________________

____

Address: ______________________________

____

Title: ______________________________

Nature of stock ownership: ______________________________

____

Percentage of stock ownership: ______________ %

Name of the officer, director, or stockholder: ______________________________

____

Address: ______________________________

____

Title: ______________________________

Nature of stock ownership: ______________________________

____

Percentage of stock ownership: ______________ %

c. For each officer or director of the corporation and each stockholder who directly or indirectly owns, controls, or holds less than 5 percent of the voting securities of the corporation, provide the following information.

Name of the officer, director, or stockholder: ______________________________

____

Address: ______________________________

____

Title: ______________________________

Nature of stock ownership: ______________________________

____

Percentage of stock ownership: ______________ %

Name of the officer, director, or stockholder: ______________________________

____

Address: ______________________________

____

Title: ______________________________

Nature of stock ownership: ______________________________

____

Percentage of stock ownership: ______________ %

Name of the officer, director, or stockholder: ______________________________

____

Address: ______________________________

____

Title: ______________________________

Nature of stock ownership: ______________________________

____

Percentage of stock ownership: ______________ %

22. Former partners, officers, directors, and shareholders. If the debtor is a partnership, answer question a. If the debtor is a corporation, answer question b.
  a. Partnership
    1) Has a member of the partnership withdrawn from the partnership within one year immediately preceding the commencement of this case?
       yes _____ no _____
    2) For each member of the partnership who withdrew from the partnership within one year immediately preceding the commencement of this case, provide the following information.
       Name of the former partner: _______________
       Address: _______________
       ____
       Date of withdrawal from the partnership: _______________
       Name of the former partner: _______________
       Address: _______________
       ____
       Date of withdrawal from the partnership: _______________
       Name of the former partner: _______________
       Address: _______________
       ____
       Date of withdrawal from the partnership: _______________
  b. Corporation
    1) Did an officer or a director of the corporation terminate his or her relationship with the corporation within one year immediately preceding the commencement of this case?
       yes _____ no _____
    2) For each officer or director of the corporation whose relationship with the corporation terminated within one year immediately preceding the commencement of this case, provide the following information.
       Name of the officer or director: _______________
       Address: _______________
       ____
       Title: _______________
       Date of termination of the relationship: _______________
       Name of the officer or director: _______________
       Address: _______________
       ____
       Title: _______________
       Date of termination of the relationship: _______________
       Name of the officer or director: _______________
       Address: _______________
       ____
       Title: _______________
       Date of termination of the relationship: _______________
23. Withdrawals from a partnership or distributions by a corporation.
  a. During one year immediately preceding the commencement of this case, were there any withdrawals of money or distributions of property credited or given to an insider, including compensation in any form, bonuses, loans, stock redemptions, options exercised, or any other perquisites?
     yes _____ no _____

b. For each insider recipient, provide the following information.
Name of the recipient: ____________________
Address: ____________________
____
Relationship to the debtor: ____________________
Date of the withdrawal: ____________________
Purpose of the withdrawal: ____________________
Amount of money withdrawn: $ ____________________
Description and value of the property distributed: ____________________
____________________ $ ____________________
Name of the recipient: ____________________
Address: ____________________
____
Relationship to the debtor: ____________________
Date of the withdrawal: ____________________
Purpose of the withdrawal: ____________________
Amount of money withdrawn: $ ____________________
Description and value of the property distributed: ____________________
____________________ $ ____________________
Name of the recipient: ____________________
Address: ____________________
____
Relationship to the debtor: ____________________
Date of the withdrawal: ____________________
Purpose of the withdrawal: ____________________
Amount of money withdrawn: $ ____________________
Description and value of the property distributed: ____________________
____________________ $ ____________________

24. Tax consolidation group

a. Within the six years immediately preceding the commencement of this case, did you reside in one of the following community property states, commonwealths, or territories: Alaska, Arizona, California, Idaho, Louisiana, Nevada, New Mexico, Puerto Rico, Texas, Washington, or Wisconsin?
yes _____ no _____

b. If your answer was yes, were you married at any time during these six years?
yes _____ no _____

c. If your answer was yes, identify the name of your spouse or any former spouse whom you were married to during this time:
____
____
____

25. Pension funds

a. Were you an employer within the six-year period immediately preceding the commencement of this case?
yes _____ no _____
If your answer was yes, list the name and federal taxpayer identification number of any pension fund to which you, as an employer, have been responsible for contributing at any time within this period.
Name of the pension fund: ____________________
Federal taxpayer identification number of the pension fund: ____________________

VIII. PROPERTY STATUS—REAL AND PERSONAL

A. Real Property

1. Real property debtor would like to surrender
   a. ______________________________
   Description of the property
   ____
   Creditor's name
   b. ______________________________
   Description of the property
   ____
   Creditor's name
   c. ______________________________
   Description of the property
   ____
   Creditor's name
   d. ______________________________
   Description of the property
   ____
   Creditor's name
2. Real property debtor would like to retain
   a. ______________________________
   Description of the property
   ____
   Creditor's name
   b. ______________________________
   Description of the property
   ____
   Creditor's name
   c. ______________________________
   Description of the property
   ____
   Creditor's name
   d. ______________________________
   Description of the property
   ____
   Creditor's name

B. Personal Property

1. Personal property debtor would like to surrender
   a. ______________________________
   Description of the property
   ____
   Creditor's name

b. ______________________________
Description of the property
____
Creditor's name

c. ______________________________
Description of the property
____
Creditor's name

d. ______________________________
Description of the property
____
Creditor's name

2. Personal property debtor would like to retain

a. ______________________________
Description of the property
____
Creditor's name

b. ______________________________
Description of the property
____
Creditor's name

c. ______________________________
Description of the property
____
Creditor's name

d. ______________________________
Description of the property
____
Creditor's name

e. ______________________________
Description of the property
____
Creditor's name

f. ______________________________
Description of the property
____
Creditor's name

g. ______________________________
Description of the property
____
Creditor's name

APPENDIX B

Interview Questionnaire for the Creditor-Client

1. Name, address (including zip code), and telephone number (including area code) of the creditor.
   Creditor's name: ______________________________
   Address: ______________________________
   ____
   city state zip code
   Telephone number (including area code): ______________________________
2. What is the nature of the creditor's business? ______________________________
   ____
3. Name, address (including zip code), and telephone number (including area code) of the debtor.
   Debtor's name: ______________________________
   Address: ______________________________
   ____
   city state zip code
   Telephone number (including area code): ______________________________
4. When and how did the claim arise? ______________________________
   ____
   ____
5. What is the amount of the claim?
   Original amount: $ ______________
   Current amount: $ ______________
6. Is the claim secured?
   yes _____ no _____
   If yes, state the collateral. ______________________________
   ____

7. Is the claim secured by collateral that is not the debtor's?

   yes _____ no _____

   If yes, provide details. ______________________________

8. Is there a guarantor or co-obligor to the debt?

   yes _____ no _____

   If yes, provide details. ______________________________

9. Have there been transfers of money or property from the debtor to the creditor?

   yes _____ no _____

   If yes, give the dates of each transfer and describe what was transferred.

10. Does the debtor have counterclaims?

    yes _____ no _____

    If yes, explain. ______________________________

11. Does the creditor have an insider relationship with the debtor?

    yes _____ no _____

    If yes, explain. ______________________________

12. Does the creditor have evidence or even suspicions that the debtor is hiding assets?

    yes _____ no _____

    If yes, explain. ______________________________

13. Has the debtor filed for bankruptcy?

    yes _____ no _____

    If yes, under which chapter did the debtor file, when, and in which Court?

    Chapter _____ Date of filing: ______________________________

    Court where filed: United States Bankruptcy Court for the ______________________________

    District of ______________________________

14. Describe any attempted settlement. ______________________________

Chapter 9—Debts of Municipalities

Chapter 9, a rarely used chapter, applies to financially troubled municipalities. A municipality is defined as a "political subdivision or public agency or instrumentality of a State." 11 U.S.C.A. § 101(40).

The Chapter 9 bankruptcy has a history of its own, apart from the rest of the Code. There were no bankruptcy provisions for the adjustment of debts of municipalities prior to 1934. Because of the problems created by the Great Depression, emergency legislation entitled "Provisions for the Emergency and Temporary Aid of Public Debtors" was passed in 1934. This was the beginning of what would ultimately become Chapter 9.

In 1936, the United States Supreme Court, in *Ashton v. Cameron County Water Improvement District No. 1*, 298 U.S. 513 (1936), found this statute unconstitutional on the ground that it "might materially restrict respondent's control over its fiscal affairs." Under pressure by distressed cities, Congress enacted a new statute the following year. It was entitled Chapter IX, "Composition of Indebtedness of Certain Taxing Agencies or Instrumentalities." The United States Supreme Court, in *United States v. Bekins*, 304 U.S. 27 (1938), held the new law constitutional because it provided for no restrictions on the control of the fiscal affairs of a state. This statute, due to expire in 1940, was extended several times. Finally, in 1946, Chapter IX became a permanent part of bankruptcy law.

The municipal bankruptcy chapter remained in the same form from 1946 until it was amended in 1976. Improved economic conditions after the Depression brought about a decline in municipal debtors, and Chapter IX apparently was sufficient for municipalities that found it necessary to file during this intervening period.

The financial crisis of New York City in the early 1970s caused renewed congressional interest in municipal bankruptcy. In 1975, New York City was near default several times due to a large bureaucracy, tuition-free open enrollment at City University, and high payments and services for welfare recipients. Default was avoided only by bailouts from the city teachers' pension fund, the New York state government, and the federal government.

The requirements of Chapter IX would have been cumbersome or even impossible for a large city such as New York to meet. The 1976 amendments facilitated a bankruptcy filing by such a city. The requirement to file the plan (to be accepted by creditors prior to filing the petition) along with the petition was changed to "with the petition or thereafter, but not later than a time fixed by the court." Bankruptcy Rule 9–22. The Bankruptcy Code contains a provision that is quite similar to this 1976 amendment to the Bankruptcy Act. 11 U.S.C.A. § 941.

It was also necessary under Chapter IX of the Act to file a list of creditors by names and addresses, with a description of each claim or type of securities held, at the time of filing the petition. The filing of such a list, along with the petition, could become an overwhelming clerical burden for a large city, which might have hundreds or even thousands of creditors, and could substantially delay filing of the petition. The 1976 amendments required filing of the list of creditors "within such time as the court may fix." Bankruptcy Rule 9–1. Under the Code, the list of creditors and equity security holders "shall be filed by the debtor in a Chapter 9 municipality case within such time as the court shall fix." Fed. R. Bank. P. 1007(e).

Although these changes in filing requirements have considerably lessened the burden of a municipality wishing to file a Chapter 9 bankruptcy, it is statistically remote that a paralegal will ever be involved in such a case. The number of municipal bankruptcies filed nationwide average less than ten per year.

GLOSSARY

abandonment of property of the estate The transfer of property from the estate to the debtor that is burdensome or of inconsequential value to the estate. 11 U.S.C.A. § 554.

absolute priority rule The requirement that a class of claims or interests be paid or satisfied in full before the next lower ranking class of claims or interests receives anything on account of such claim or interest. 11 U.S.C.A. §§ 1129(b)(2)(B),(C).

abstention The decision by a United States district court or a bankruptcy court to refrain from hearing matter in a case or a proceeding in a case that should be heard in another court, such as a state court or a tax court. 11 U.S.C. § 305; 28 U.S.C.A. § 1334(c).

account (account receivable) A right to payment of a moneyed obligation for property that has been or is to be sold, leased, assigned, or otherwise disposed of for services rendered or to be rendered that is not evidenced by an instrument or chattel paper. UCC § 9–102(a)(2).

adequate information The information to be included in a disclosure statement to enable holders of claims and holders of equity interests to make an informed decision about voting on a Chapter 11 plan. 11 U.S.C.A. § 1125(a).

adequate protection The protection afforded a creditor, such as a secured creditor, with an interest in property of the bankruptcy estate, as a condition of the trustee's or debtor in possession's use, sale, or lease of such property. The form of the adequate protection depends upon the nature of the collateral and is designed to protect the value of the creditor's interest in the collateral during the pendency of the bankruptcy case. 11 U.S.C.A. § 361.

administrative cost A reasonable and necessary expense of preserving the estate that arises after the commencement of the case. 11 U.S.C.A. § 503.

adversary proceeding A lawsuit in bankruptcy that is commenced by the filing of a complaint. Fed. R. Bank. P. 7001.

assignment A transfer of a right. The term assignment is also used when both a right is transferred and a duty delegated.

assignment for the benefit of creditors A voluntary transfer by a debtor of all of the debtor's property to a trustee of the debtor's own selection for administration, liquidation, and equitable distribution among the debtor's creditors. It is distinguishable from a bankruptcy proceeding in that the debtor does not receive a discharge from his or her obligations to creditors. Such an assignment is regulated by state law.

assumption of executory contract or unexpired lease A decision made by a debtor, debtor in possession, or trustee after the commencement of the case, subject to bankruptcy court approval, to retain the benefits of an executory contract or unexpired lease. 11 U.S.C.A. § 365(b)(1).

attachment The prejudgment seizure of property by legal process.

attachment of a security interest Under Article 9 of the UCC, a security interest attaches to personal property or fixtures when the security interest becomes enforceable against the debtor with respect to the collateral (the personal property or fixtures). UCC § 9–203(a). A security interest becomes enforceable against the debtor and third parties with respect to the collateral when value has been given, the debtor has rights in the collateral, and the debtor has authorized a security agreement or the secured party has possession of the collateral. UCC §§ 9–203(b), (c).

attorney's compensation statement (disclosure of attorney's compensation statement) A statement filed by the debtor's attorney that specifies the amount and source of compensation paid or agreed to be paid for services rendered in connection with the debtor's bankruptcy case. 11 U.S.C.A. § 329(a). Fed. R. Bank. P. 2016(b).

automatic stay A stay that goes into effect upon the filing of a bankruptcy petition that precludes a creditor from collecting a prepetition claim against the debtor or the bankruptcy estate. 11 U.S.C.A. § 362(a).

avoidance powers The power of a trustee, debtor in possession, or debtor to avoid certain transfers made or obligations incurred by a debtor.

bankruptcy A federal system whereby the debtor is given a "fresh start" (usually in the form of a discharge) and the creditors receive an equitable distribution of the debtor's nonexempt assets.

Bankruptcy Act The Bankruptcy Act of 1898, replaced by the Bankruptcy Reform Act of 1978 (Bankruptcy Code).

Bankruptcy Appellate Panel (BAP) An appellate body consisting of three bankruptcy judges of the district of the circuit in which the bankruptcy appeal originated. Whether a BAP exists depends on the Circuit, and whether the case is appealed to the BAP rather than the United States District Court depends on the parties. 28 U.S.C.A. § 158(b).

Bankruptcy Code (Title 11 of the United States Code) Title I of the Bankruptcy Reform Act of 1978, as amended from time to time.

bar date The deadline for filing proofs of claim or interests as set by the bankruptcy court. Fed. R. Bank. P. 3002(c).

best interests of creditors test The requirement that creditors holding allowed unsecured claims receive, under a Chapter 11, 12, or 13 plan, an amount not less than what they would have received if the bankruptcy estate were liquidated under Chapter 7. 11 U.S.C.A. §§ 1129(a)(7)(A), 1225(a)(4), 1325(a)(4).

bona fide dispute A dispute where there is some arguable defense to the claim.

bootstrap plan A plan that uses only the resources of the debtor that existed at the time of the filing of the petition for the payment of creditor claims.

cash collateral Cash or other cash equivalents in which the estate and an entity other than the estate have an interest. 11 U.S.C.A. § 363(a).

change of venue Transferring a bankruptcy case or adversary proceeding from one bankruptcy court to another. 28 U.S.C. § 1412; Fed. R. Bank. P. 1014.

Chapter 7 A liquidation case under the Bankruptcy Code.

Chapter 9 The adjustment of debts of a municipality or a governmental unit under the Bankruptcy Code.

Chapter 11 A reorganization, usually of a business, under the Bankruptcy Code that is accomplished through a plan.

Chapter 12 An adjustment of debts by a family farmer with regular annual income that is accomplished through a plan under the Bankruptcy Code.

Chapter 13 An adjustment of debts of an individual with regular income that is accomplished through a plan under the Bankruptcy Code.

chattel paper A record or records that evidence both a monetary obligation and a security interest in, or a lease of specific goods. UCC § 9–102(a)(11).

claim A right to payment or a right to an equitable remedy for breach of performance if such breach gives right to payment. 11 U.S.C.A. § 101(5).

clerk's notice Notice given by the clerk of the bankruptcy court of the filing of a bankruptcy case. It includes, if applicable, the deadline for filing objections to discharge and dischargeability and the date and time of the meeting of creditors. 11 U.S.C.A. § 342(a).

codebtor stay Upon the filing of a petition, creditors are prohibited from commencing or continuing any action to collect a consumer debt from any individual jointly liable with the debtor or any individual who secured such debt even though that individual is not the debtor in the bankruptcy case. 11 U.S.C.A. §§ 1201, 1301.

cognovit note (confession of judgment note) A note containing a provision appointing the creditor as the debtor's agent to admit liability and to confess judgment.

collateral The property that may be repossessed by the creditor if the debtor does not meet the terms of an agreement.

collective bargaining agreement A contract between an employer and a labor union that regulates the terms and conditions of employment.

complaint A pleading that commences an adversary proceeding in a bankruptcy court. Fed. R. Bank. P. 7003.

composition An agreement between the debtor and his or her creditors in which the creditors agree to accept in full satisfaction of their claims something less than full payment.

confirmation hearing The hearing before the bankruptcy court to determine whether the plan in a Chapter 11, 12, or 13 case will be approved by the court. 11 U.S.C.A. §§ 1128, 1224, 1324.

confirmation of the plan The determination by the bankruptcy court that the proposed plan in a Chapter 11, 12, or 13 case meets the confirmation requirements of the Bankruptcy Code.

consensual lien A lien created by agreement of the parties.

consideration The "price" paid for a promise. A contract has two "considerations"—the "price" sought by the promisor for his or her promise and the "price" sought by the promisee for his or her promise or performance.

consolidation loan A loan in which the debtor uses the proceeds to pay off other debts.

consumer debt A debt incurred by an individual primarily for a personal, family, or household purpose. 11 U.S.C.A. § 101(8).

contested matter A dispute in bankruptcy, other than an adversary proceeding, that is brought by motion rather than by complaint. Fed. R. Bank. P. 9014.

contingent claim A claim that is dependent on the occurrence of a future event that may never happen.

conversion of a case The conversion of a bankruptcy case from one chapter to another.

core proceedings Proceedings in bankruptcy in which the bankruptcy judge may enter a final order. 28 U.S.C.A. § 157(b)(1). Examples of core proceedings are found in 28 U.S.C.A. § 157(b)(2).

corporate shell An entity that has a corporate identity but not a corporate purpose.

cramdown The confirmation of a plan over the objection of one or more creditors holding secured claims.

credit counseling centers Licensed and bonded agencies that analyze the debtor's obligations and negotiate with creditors for the repayment of the debtor's bills on a schedule the debtor can manage. Credit Counseling Centers do not lend money but only educate the debtor and distribute the debtor's money to the debtor's creditors under an agreement with those creditors.

creditor An entity that has a claim against the debtor that arose prior to or at the time of the filing of the bankruptcy petition. 11 U.S.C.A. § 101(10).

creditor's bill An action in equity by a judgment creditor to reach property that could not be reached by execution at law.

creditors' committee The committee that is formed in a Chapter 11 case from the list of creditors holding the twenty largest unsecured claims. The function of the committee is to consult with the trustee, the U.S. trustee, and the debtor's attorney regarding the bankruptcy case. 11 U.S.C.A. § 1102.

debtor in bankruptcy A party for or against whom a case has been commenced. 11 U.S.C.A. § 101(13). In a nonbankruptcy context, the party who owes payment or other performance of an obligation.

debtor engaged in business A self-employed debtor who incurs trade credit in the production of income from this employment. 11 U.S.C.A. § 1304.

debtor in possession (DIP) A debtor in a Chapter 11 case in which a trustee has not been appointed to serve in the case. 11 U.S.C.A. § 1101(1). A debtor in a Chapter 12 case who has not been removed. 11 U.S.C.A. § 1204(a).

default The failure to perform a legal duty, such as the failure to pay a debt when it becomes due.

DIP An abbreviation for "debtor in possession."

discharge An order entered by a bankruptcy court that voids judgments rendered against a debtor and that enjoins the collection of a debt as a personal liability of a debtor. 11 U.S.C.A. § 524(a).

disclosure statement A written document containing adequate information to enable those voting on a Chapter 11 reorganization plan to make an informed decision about how to vote on the plan. 11 U.S.C.A. § 1125.

dismissal The termination of a bankruptcy case or adversary proceeding.

disputed claim A claim that is challenged as to either its enforceability or its amount.

entity Includes a person, estate, trust, governmental unit, or U.S. trustee. 11 U.S.C.A. § 101(15).

equitable lien A right, not recognized by law, to have a fund or a specific property or its proceeds applied, in whole or in part, to the payment of a particular debt or class of debts.

equity security Share of stock or other evidence of an ownership interest in a firm. 11 U.S.C.A. § 101(16).

estate The entity that is created upon the filing of a bankruptcy petition. 11 U.S.C.A. § 541.

examiner An individual whose appointment is ordered by the bankruptcy court to investigate the financial affairs of a Chapter 11 debtor. 11 U.S.C.A. § 1104.

execution A method of collecting on a judgment.

execution lien A lien acquired by a judgment creditor upon the issuance of an execution.

execution sale A sale under judicial process.

executory contract A contract in which performance has not been completed by either party.

exemptions Property that a debtor may claim under state or federal law free from the claims of unsecured creditors. 11 U.S.C.A. § 522.

ex parte An application made by one party to a proceeding in the absence of and without notice to the other party.

fair and equitable test A requirement for confirming a Chapter 11 plan by cramdown. 11 U.S.C.A. § 1129(b)(2)(A).

family farmer See 11 U.S.C.A. § 101(18).

family farmer with regular annual income A family farmer whose annual income is sufficiently stable and regular to enable the family farmer to make payments under a Chapter 12 plan. 11 U.S.C.A. § 101(19).

farmer A person who receives more than 80 percent of such person's gross income during the taxable year immediately preceding the taxable year in which the case was filed from a farming operation owned or operated by that person. 11 U.S.C.A. § 101(20).

farming operation Activities include farming; soil tilling; dairy farming; ranching; producing or raising crops, poultry, or livestock; and producing poultry or livestock products in an unmanufactured state. 11 U.S.C.A. § 101(21).

Federal Rules of Bankruptcy Procedure (Fed. R. Bank. P.) Rules promulgated by the Supreme Court, pursuant to 28 U.S.C.A. § 2075, that govern the process and procedure in bankruptcy cases. Fed. R. Bank. P. 1001. The Federal Rules of Bankruptcy Procedure are divided into nine parts: Rules 1002–1020 (Commencement of Case; Proceedings Relating to Petition and Order for Relief; Rules 2001–2020 (Officers and Administration; Notice; Meetings; Examinations; Elections; Attorneys and Accountants); Rules 3001–3022 (Claims and Distribution to Creditors and Equity Interest Holders; Plans); Rules 4001–4008 (The Debtor: Duties and Benefits); Rules 5001–5011 (Bankruptcy Courts and Clerks); Rules 6001–6010 (Collection and Liquidation of the Estate); Rules 7001–7087 (Adversary Proceedings); Rules 8001–8020 (Appeals to District Court or Bankruptcy Appellate Panel); and Rules 9001–9036 (General Provisions). In addition to the Federal Rules of Bankruptcy Procedure, each district court may adopt local rules that are consistent with the Bankruptcy Code, the Federal Rules of Bankruptcy Procedure, and the official forms. Fed. R. Bank. P. 9029.

final decree An order by the bankruptcy court determining that the case has been fully administered, that the trustee in the case has been discharged, and that the case is closed.

fixtures Goods that have become so related to particular real property that an interest in them arises under real property law. UCC § 9–102(a)(41).

fraudulent transfer A prepetition transfer of property by the debtor that is voidable under bankruptcy law or state law based upon actual or constructive fraud. 11 U.S.C.A. §§ 544(b), 548.

gap creditors Creditors who hold claims that arise after the filing of an involuntary Chapter 7 or Chapter 11 petition and the entry of the order for relief.

garnishment The legal or equitable procedure through which the earnings of an individual are required to be withheld for payment of a debt.

general intangible The catchall classification under the Uniform Commercial Code for personal property. Personal property is classified as a general intangible if it is not accounts, chattel paper, commercial tort claims, deposit accounts, documents, goods, instruments, investment property, letter-of-credit rights, letters of credit, money, and oil, gas, or other minerals before extraction. UCC § 9–102(a)(42).

good faith Good faith may be defined as "honesty in fact and the observance of reasonable commercial standards of fair dealing." UCC § 1–201(b)(20), 2–103(1)(b), 3–103(a)(4), and 9–102(a)(43).

goods All things that are movable but not including accounts, chattel paper, commercial tort claims, deposit accounts, documents, general intangibles, instruments, investment property, letter-of-credit rights, letters of credit, money, or oil, gas, or other minerals before extraction. UCC § 9–102(a)(44).

indenture See U.S.C.A. § 101(28).

indenture trustee A trustee under an indenture. 11 U.S.C.A. § 101(29).

indubitable equivalent A form of adequate protection, which is a substitute for the actual collateral or its cash equivalent, that will result in the creditor's realization of the value of its interest in the collateral securing its claim.

insider A party who has a close relationship to the debtor, including those parties listed in 11 U.S.C.A. § 101(31).

insolvent Under the Bankruptcy Code, when the sum of an entity's debts is greater than the value of all the entity's property, at a fair valuation, exclusive of property exempted or fraudulently transferred, including a general partner's nonpartnership property in a partnership. 11 U.S.C.A. § 101(32). Under the Uniform Commercial Code, when an individual or an organization ceases to pay its debts in the ordinary course of business, cannot pay its debts as they become due, or is insolvent under the Bankruptcy Code. UCC § 1–201(33).

instrument A writing that evidences a right to the payment of a monetary obligation and includes a negotiable instrument (check, note, draft, or certificate of deposit) and a certificated security (stocks and bonds). UCC § 9–102(a)(47).

interim trustee The trustee appointed by the U.S. trustee in a Chapter 7 case after the entry of the order for relief who will continue to serve as trustee, unless a different trustee is elected at the meeting of creditors.

Involuntary Chapter 7 (Liquidation) A Chapter 7 bankruptcy case that is initiated against a debtor by its creditors that seeks the administration of the bankruptcy estate by the Chapter 7 trustee.

Involuntary Chapter 11 (Reorganization) A Chapter 11 bankruptcy case that is initiated against a debtor by its creditors that seeks the restructuring of the debtor's business or financial affairs under Chapter 11.

involuntary petition A bankruptcy petition that is filed by three or more creditors against a debtor. 11 U.S.C.A. § 303.

judicial lien A lien obtained by judgment, levy, sequestration, or other legal or equitable process or proceeding. 11 U.S.C.A. § 101(36).

jurisdiction The power of a court to hear and decide the issues raised in a case or proceeding.

lien A claim against property to secure payment of an obligation. 11 U.S.C.A. § 101(37).

limited partner A partner whose liability for partnership debts extends only to the amount of his or her investment.

liquidated claim A claim, the amount of which is certain.

liquidation The sale of the nonexempt, nonburdensome assets of a bankruptcy estate.

list of creditors The list of creditors required to be filed in a bankruptcy case. Fed. R. Bank. P. 1007(a).

local bankruptcy rules The rules adopted by a United States district court or by a United States bankruptcy court relating to bankruptcy practice and procedure, which apply only in the court issuing the rules. Fed. R. Bank. P. 9029.

meeting of creditors (The Section 341 Meeting) A meeting at which the creditors or other parties in interest may examine the debtor under oath concerning matters that relate to the bankruptcy estate and to the debtor's discharge. 11 U.S.C.A. § 341(a).

meeting of equity security holders A meeting at which the equity security holders can discuss their rights and methods for enforcing those rights. 11 U.S.C.A. § 341(b).

mortgage A grant of an interest in real estate to secure payment of a debt.

motion A request made to a court to obtain an order of the court. A motion initiates a contested matter that is not an adversary proceeding.

noncontingent claim A claim that is not dependent on the occurrence of a future event that may never happen.

nonpossessory, nonpurchase money security interest A security interest in which the creditor neither retains possession of the collateral nor advances the purchase price to the debtor to enable the debtor to acquire the collateral.

notice and a hearing A notice appropriate for the particular circumstances and an opportunity for a hearing. 11 U.S.C.A. § 102.

official forms Forms prescribed by the United States Supreme Court as part of the Federal Rules of Bankruptcy Procedure. 28 U.S.C.A. § 2075.

operative chapters The chapters of the Bankruptcy Code under which petitions in bankruptcy may be filed. The operative chapters are Chapters 7, 9, 11, 12, and 13.

opt out The right afforded a state to make the federal exemptions in the Bankruptcy Code unavailable to debtors who reside in that State. 11 U.S.C.A. § 522(b)(1).

order for relief The relief afforded a debtor upon the filing of a voluntary petition and the relief afforded creditors when the court grants the relief requested by an involuntary petition.

party in interest A party who has an interest in a bankruptcy case.

perfected security interest A security interest as to which notice is given so as to give a creditor protection against interests acquired by third parties. For personal property and fixtures, see UCC §§ 9–308–9–316.

person Includes an individual, a partnership, and a corporation, but does not include a governmental unit. 11 U.S.C.A. § 101(41).

personal property Property that is not real property and includes accounts (accounts receivable), chattel paper, commercial tort claims, deposit accounts, general intangibles, documents, goods, instruments, investment property, letter-of-credit rights, letter of credit, money, and oil, gas, or other minerals before extraction.

petition The document filed by a debtor to initiate a voluntary bankruptcy case or by creditors to initiate an involuntary bankruptcy case.

plan The document filed in a Chapter 11, 12, or 13 case that dictates the terms under which claims and interests will be paid. See 11 U.S.C.A. §§ 1123, 1222, 1322.

postpetition transfer A transfer of property of the estate that occurs after the commencement of the case.

preferential transfer (voidable preference) A transfer of property of the debtor, made to or for the benefit of a creditor, on an antecedent debt, within 90 days or one year (if the transferee was an insider of the debtor) of the filing of the petition, while the debtor was insolvent, and which enabled the creditor to receive more than the creditor would have received had the transfer not been made. 11 U.S.C.A. § 547(b).

priority claim (unsecured priority claim) An unsecured claim, such as a claim for administrative expenses or wages, that is paid before other unsecured claims. 11 U.S.C.A. § 507.

proof of claim A document filed in the bankruptcy court stating the nature and amount of the claim. 11 U.S.C.A. § 501; Fed. R. Bank. P. 3001.

proof of interest A document filed in the bankruptcy court by equity security holders stating the nature and amount of the interest.

property of the estate All of the legal and equitable interests in property of the debtor that are included in a bankruptcy estate on or after the commencement of the case. 11 U.S.C.A. § 545.

purchase money security interest A security interest conveyed by a debtor to a creditor furnishing funds for the purchase of the collateral that secured the claim.

reaffirmation agreement A written agreement filed with the bankruptcy court to pay a prebankruptcy debt to enable the debt to survive the discharge in bankruptcy. 11 U.S.C.A. § 524(c).

real property Land and whatever is erected, growing on, or permanently attached to the land. Real property is defined by state law.

receivership A state court proceeding in which a fiduciary is appointed to hold in trust and administer property that is in litigation.

redemption The process by which a debtor, to obtain the release of a security interest in personal property, pays in a lump sum an amount equal to the value of the collateral securing a dischargeable consumer debt. 11 U.S.C.A. § 722.

rejection of executory contracts A decision by a debtor, debtor in possession, or trustee after the commencement of a case, subject to bankruptcy court approval, to not assume (retain the benefits of) an executory contract or unexpired lease. The rejection creates a prebankruptcy claim in favor of the nondebtor party to the executory contract or unexpired lease. 11 U.S.C.A. § 365(a).

relief from automatic stay An order entered by the bankruptcy court to terminate, annul, modify or place a condition on the automatic stay to permit the creditor to proceed against the property of the estate or property of the debtor.

reorganization The restructuring of the debtor's business or financial affairs.

replevin The proceeding in which a party holding a special interest in personal property seeks to gain possession of that property from another party.

revocation of discharge The bankruptcy court's rescission of its order discharging the debtor from certain debts.

schedules Documents to be filed in a bankruptcy case, disclosing a debtor's assets and liabilities, Official Form No. 6, consisting of the following:

Summary of Schedules

Schedule A—Real Property

Schedule B—Personal Property

Schedule C—Property Claimed as Exempt

Schedule D—Creditors Holding Secured Claims

Schedule E—Creditors Holding Unsecured Priority Claims

Schedule F—Creditors Holding Unsecured Nonpriority Claims

Schedule G—Executory Contracts and Unexpired Leases

Schedule H—Codebtors

Schedule I—Current Income of Individual Debtor(s)

Schedule J—Current Expenditures of Individual Debtor(s)

Although not an official form, a partnership or a corporation must complete a Schedule of Current Income and Current Expenditures of a Partnership or Corporation.

secured claim The claim of a creditor holding a lien against property of the estate.

secured party A lender, seller, or other person in whose favor a security interest is created or provided for under a security agreement. The definition of secured party also includes a person who holds an agricultural lien, a consignee, and a buyer of accounts, chattel paper, payment intangibles, and promissory notes. UCC § 9–102(a)(72). A secured party may also be a mortgagee of real property.

security agreement A lien created by an agreement. 11 U.S.C.A. § 101(50). An agreement that creates or provides for a security interest in personal property or fixtures. UCC § 9–102(a)(73).

security interest A lien created by an agreement. 11 U.S.C.A. § 101(51). An interest in personal property or fixtures that secures payments or performance of an obligation. UCC § 1–201(b)(35).

self-help repossession A procedure by which a creditor with a secured claim takes possession of the collateral upon the default of the debtor without the aid of a judicial proceeding. UCC § 9–609(b)(2).

setoff The crediting of one claim against another without an actual exchange of money between the parties.

standing trustee A trustee with a permanent appointment to serve in Chapter 12 or Chapter 13 cases in a district.

statement of financial affairs An official form containing information concerning a debtor's financial affairs.

statement of intention An individual consumer debtor's notification of the debtor's intention with respect to property of the estate that secures his or her consumer debts. 11 U.S.C.A. § 521(2).

statutory lien A lien arising solely by force of a statute on specified circumstances or conditions. 11 U.S.C.A. § 101(53).

subordinated claim A claim that is subordinated in payment to other claims of the same class.

summons A legal notice giving the defendant in an adversary proceeding notification of an action filed against him or her and specifying the time given in which to file a response.

Title 11 (11 U.S.C.A.) The title in the United States Code that contains the Bankruptcy Code.

transfer Every mode of disposing of or parting with property or an interest in property, whether it be direct or indirect, absolute or conditional, voluntary or involuntary. 11 U.S.C.A. § 101(54).

trustee A person appointed by the United States Trustee to administer the bankruptcy estate.

Uniform Commercial Code (UCC) A code drafted by the American Law Institute and the National Conference of Commissioners on Uniform State Laws that includes the sale of goods, lease of goods, commercial paper, bank deposits and collections, funds transfers, letters of credit, bulk transfers, documents of title (bills of lading and warehouse receipts), investment securities, and secured transactions. In order for the UCC to become state law, the state's legislature must enact it. The District of Columbia and the Virgin Islands have enacted the UCC. Louisiana has enacted Articles 1, 3, 4, 4A, 5, 7, 8, and 9 of the UCC. Each state has its own variations of the official text.

United States Code (U.S.C.) The official compilation of federal statutes. U.S.C. is printed and sold by the United States Government Printing Office.

United States Code Annotated (U.S.C.A.) West Group Publishing Company's annotated version of the United States Code.

United States trustee A person appointed by the attorney general of the United States to oversee the administration of bankruptcy cases and to appoint and supervise the trustees. 28 U.S.C.A. §§ 581–586.

universal chapters Chapters 1, 3, and 5 of the Bankruptcy Code, which contain definitional and administrative provisions that generally apply to all operative chapters of the Bankruptcy Code.

unliquidated claim A claim in which the amount owed is uncertain.

unperfected security Interest A security interest as to which notice has not been deemed to have been given so as to notify third parties of the secured party's interest in the collateral.

unsecured claim A claim that is not protected by a lien or security interest on property.

unsworn declaration An unsworn statement made under penalty of perjury, such as the declaration contained in the schedules of assets and liabilities and statement of financial affairs. Fed. R. Bank. P. 9011(e).

usury An interest rate charged for the use of money that exceeds the rate permitted by law.

venue The proper court in which to hear a bankruptcy case or adversary proceeding.

voluntary petition A bankruptcy petition that is filed by a debtor.

workout A noncourt arrangement between the debtor and his or her creditors to satisfy the debtor's obligations.

INDEX

A

Abandon property of estate, 213–214
Absolute priority rule, 443
Abstention by court, 245
Adequate information, 422
Adequate protection
- Chapter 11 case, 402–403
- Chapter 12 case, 369

Adjustment of debts
- family farmer. *See* Chapter 12 bankruptcy
- individual, *See* Chapter 13 bankruptcy
- municipality, 18, 73

Administrative expenses, 37, 278
Administrative Office (AO), 41
Adversary proceedings, 233. *See also* Complaints
"After notice and a hearing," 16
Alimony, 279
A.L.R.Fed, 27
Alternatives if no bankruptcy filed, 80–84
- attachment, 81
- cognovit judgment, 82
- consensual lien, 83
- creditor's bill, 83
- disposition of collateral, 82
- equitable lien, 83
- execution lien, 83
- execution sale, 83
- fraudulent conveyance, 83
- garnishment, 81, 83
- involuntary bankruptcy choices, 84
- judgment lien, 82–83
- private alternative, 80
- receivership, 81
- replevin, 82
- retention of collateral, 82
- self-help repossession, 82
- state court alternative, 80
- supplementary procedures, 83
- UCC 2-702, 81

Alternatives to bankruptcy filing, 66–70
- assignment for benefit of creditors, 70
- consolidation loan, 69
- credit counseling, 69–70
- negotiation, 66–69

American Jurisprudence 2d, 27
American Law Reports, 27
American Law Reports, Federal, 27
Analysis (bankruptcy *vs.* nonbankruptcy), 65–75
Answer (involuntary case), 486
AO, 41
Appeal, 22–24
Articles of Confederation, 2
Assignment for benefit of creditors, 70
Attachment, 81
Attorney. *See* Creditor's attorney; Debtor's attorney
Automatic stay. *See* Stay
Avoidance powers, 207
Avoiding transfers, 215–229
- claims voidable under state law, 220–222
- fraudulent transfers, 226
- statutory liens, 222
- unauthorized postpetition transfers, 228–229
- unperfected security interests, 215–220
- voidable preferences, 222–225

B

Banca rotta, 1
Bankruptcy appellate panel (BAP), 22
Bankruptcy choices, 70–75
Bankruptcy Code, 4–5, 12–13
- adjustment of dollar amount, 6
- amendments, 5–6
- Chapter 1 (general provisions), 14–16
- Chapter 3 (case administration), 16–17
- Chapter 5 (creditors, debtor, estate), 17
- Chapter 7, 18. *See also* Chapter 7 liquidation
- Chapter 9, 18
- Chapter 11, 18. *See also* Chapter 11 reorganization
- Chapter 12, 19. *See also* Chapter 12 bankruptcy
- Chapter 13, 19. *See also* Chapter 13 bankruptcy
- definitions, 14–15
- operative chapters, 17–19
- universal chapters, 13–17

Bankruptcy Code, Rules and Forms, 21
Bankruptcy court, 22
Bankruptcy court clerk, 43–44
Bankruptcy Court Decisions, 22
Bankruptcy court rules, 22
Bankruptcy estate. *See also* Property of estate
- Chapter 7 case, 194–200
- Chapter 11 case, 401
- Chapter 12 case, 366
- Chapter 13 case, 319
- Involuntary bankruptcy, 485

Bankruptcy estate—Chapter 7, 194–200
- after-acquired property, 198–199
- location of property, 198
- possession/control of property, 200
- property of estate, 194–198
- transferability of property, 200

Bankruptcy filings, compared. *See* Selecting type of bankruptcy filing
Bankruptcy judge, 42–43
Bankruptcy Law Reporter, 22

Bankruptcy loose-leaf services, 25
Bankruptcy petition preparer, 33–34
Bankruptcy reform, 7
Bankruptcy Reform Act of 1928. *See* Bankruptcy Code
Bankruptcy Reporter, 22
Bankruptcy treatises, 25–26
Bankruptcy *vs.* nonbankruptcy, 65–75
BAP, 22
Best interests of creditors test, 445–448
Bona fide dispute, 474
Bootstrap plan, 408
Business debtor, options, 464–467
Business filings, number of, 463

C

Carter, Jimmy, 4
Case reports, 24
Cash collateral, 402
Cast of characters, 29–49
  Administrative office, 41
  bankruptcy judge and staff, 42–43
  bankruptcy petition preparer, 33–34
  clerk's office, 43–44
  court reporter, 43
  creditor's, 34–39. *See also* Creditor.
  debtor, 30–31. *See also* Debtor.
  debtor's attorney, 31. *See also* Debtor's attorney.
  equity security holder, 39
  indenture trustee, 39
  lessor, 40
  paralegal, 32–33
  regulatory authorities, 41
  statutory lienholders, 39–40
Change of venue
  debtor's motion, 234–237
  party in interest's motion, 245
Chapter 1 (general provisions), 14–16
Chapter 3 (case administration), 16–17
Chapter 5 (creditors, debtor, estate), 17
Chapter 7 liquidation, 18, 71–73, 88–297
  amending case, 294
  automatic stay, 207–212
  bankruptcy estate, 194–200. *See also* Bankruptcy estate—Chapter 7
  Chapter 11 liquidation, compared, 465
  Chapter 11 reorganization, compared, 464–465, 472
  Chapter 13 bankruptcy, compared, 467–471
  closing the case, 281–294
  complaints, 252–262
  discharge and reaffirmation, 271–277
  distribution of property of estate, 278–281
  exemptions, 201–207, 263
  filing the petition, 100–193. *See also* Filing the petition—Chapter 7.
  final accounts, 281–294
  final decree, 295
  initiation of proceeding, 90, 95–100
  interim trustee, 212–229. *See also* Interim trustee
  meeting of creditors, 270
  meeting of equity security holders, 271
  motions, 234–252. *See also* Motions—Chapter 7.
  nonpriority claims, 280–281
  notice of meeting of creditors, etc., 263–269
  order for relief, 194
  overview, 91–94
  priority claims, 278–280
  proof of claim, 229–230
  proof of interest, 229–230
  redemption, 271
  reopening case, 294–297
  revocation of discharge, 272
  341 meeting, 270
  trustee's final accounts, 281–294
Chapter 7 trustee, 46–47
Chapter 9 (municipalities), 18, 73
Chapter 11 cramdown, 443, 449–450
Chapter 11 liquidation, 408, 465
Chapter 11 reorganization, 18, 73–74, 388–457
  absolute priority rule, 443
  actions of creditor's attorney, 84
  adequate protection, 402–403
  best interests of creditors test, 445–448
  cash collateral, 402
  Chapter 7 liquidation, compared, 389, 464–465, 472
  Chapter 12 bankruptcy, compared, 465–467, 472
  Chapter 13 bankruptcy, compared, 465–467, 472
  clerk's notice, 434
  collective bargaining contracts, 404
  committee of equity security holders, 436
  committee of unsecured creditors, 436
  complaints, 435
  confirmation hearing, 440–451
  confirmation of plan, 451–454, 455
  cramdown, 443, 449–450
  disclosure statement, 422–434, 437–442
  distribution under plan, 455
  exemptions, 405
  feasibility requirement, 448–449
  filing of petition, 395–401
  final report and decree, 455, 456
  hearing on disclosure statement, 437–440
  initiation of proceeding, 390, 395
  involuntary, 84
  list of creditors with largest unsecured claims, 396–398
  list of equity security holders, 399–401
  meeting of creditors, 436
  motions, 435
  obtaining credit, 403
  operation of debtor's business, 402
  overview, 391–394
  pending/future litigation, 404–405, 408
  plan. *See* Chapter 11 reorganization plan.
  professionals, 403
  revocation of order of confirmation, 455
  341 meeting, 436
  utility services, 404
Chapter 11 reorganization plan
  bootstrap plan, 408
  commonly used strategies, 407–408
  confirmation, 451–454, 455
  executory contracts, 408
  liquidation, 408
  mandatory provisions, 413–414
  merger or consolidation, 408
  modification, 415, 421
  pending/future litigation, 408
  permissive provisions, 414–415
  recapitalization, 408
  sample plan, 416–421
  who can file, 422
Chapter 12 bankruptcy, 19, 74–75, 344–387
  actions of creditor's attorney, 79

Chapter 7 liquidation, compared, 348
Chapter 11 reorganization, compared, 465–467, 472
clerk's notice, 374, 375–378
closing the case, 387
complaints, 374
confirmation hearing, 379–383
cramdown, 379
definitions, 74, 345
DIP, 368
discharge, 386
distribution of payments, 383
exemptions, 369
filing of petition, 365–366
initiation of proceeding, 354–357
lien avoidance, 371
meeting of creditor, 374
motions, 371–373
operation of debtor's business, 368–369
overview, 349–354
plan, 357–364. *See also* Chapter 12 plan
proceedings after case closed, 387
property of estate, 368
revocation, 386
revocation of discharge, 387
341 meeting, 374
trustee, 369–370

Chapter 12 cramdown, 379
Chapter 12 plan, 357–364
debtor's payments, 358, 363
filing deadline, 357
mandatory provisions, 357–358
modification, 363–364, 383–385
permissive provisions, 358
sample plan, 358, 359–362

Chapter 12 trustee, 369–370
Chapter 13 bankruptcy, 19, 75
actions of creditor's attorney, 79–80, 298–343
automatic stay, 320
Chapter 7 liquidation, compared, 299–300, 467–471
Chapter 11 reorganization, compared, 465–467, 472
clerk's notice, 327, 328–329
closing the case, 343
codebtor stay, 320
complaints, 325–326
confirmation hearing, 327–337
consumer debt, 320
cramdown, 332–334
discharge, 341–342
distribution of payments, 338
exemptions, 321–322
filing of petition, 318–319
initiation of proceeding, 300, 306–308
lien avoidance, 315–316
meeting of creditors, 327
motions, 323–325
operation of debtor's business, 321
overview, 301–306
plan, 308–318. *See also* Chapter 13 plan
proceedings after case closed, 343
property of estate, 321
revocation of discharge, 342
revocation of order of confirmation, 341
341 meeting, 327
trustee, 322–323

Chapter 13 cramdown, 332–334
Chapter 13 plan
debtor's payments, 318
mandatory provisions, 308–309
modifications, 318, 338–341
permissive provisions, 309
sample plan, 309–318

Chapter 13 trustee, 322–323
Chattel paper, 36
Choosing type of filing. *See* Selecting type of bankruptcy filing
Circuit court, 22–24
Claim. *See* Proof of claim
Clerk's notice
Chapter 7 case, 263–269
Chapter 11 case, 434
Chapter 12 case, 374, 375–378
Chapter 13 case, 327, 328–329
individual consumer debtor, 115–116

Code, 4. *See also* Bankruptcy Code
Codebtor, 154–156
Codebtor stay, 320
Cognovit judgment, 82
Collateral
cash, 402
defined, 35
disposition, 82
retention, 82

Collective bargaining contracts, 404
Collier's Bankruptcy Cases, 22
Commissions (wages, salaries), 278–279
Committee of equity security holders, 436. *See also* Equity security holders
Committee of unsecured creditors, 436
Commodity Futures Trading Commission, 41
Community property state, 154
Compassionate discharge, 342
Complaints, 230, 233
Chapter 7 case, 252–262
Chapter 11 case, 435
Chapter 12 case, 374
Chapter 13 case, 325–326
rule 7001, 233

Composition, 67, 68
Confirmation
Chapter 11 case, 440–451, 451–454, 455
Chapter 12 case, 379–383
Chapter 13 case, 327–337, 341

Congressional Record, 24
Consensual lien, 83
Consolidation (merger), 408
Consolidation loan, 69
Constitution, 2, 9–10
Constructive fraud, 226–228
Consumer debt/debtor, 7, 56, 115–116, 320
Consumer deposits, 279
Contested matter, 230, 233. *See also* Motions
Contingent claim, 229
Corporate resolution, authorizing filing of Chapter 7 petition, 117
Corporation, 54
Corpus Juris Secundum, 27
Counseling
creditor-client, 85
debtor-client, 76, 85

Court personnel. *See* Cast of characters
Court reporter, 43
Court rules, 21–22
Courtroom deputy, 43
Cramdown
Chapter 11, 443, 449–450
Chapter 12, 379
Chapter 13, 332–334

Credit, obtaining, 403
Credit counseling, 69–70
Creditor
attorney. *See* Creditor's attorney.
cause of distress, 77
gap, 485–486
involuntary bankruptcy. *See* Involuntary bankruptcy.
options if no bankruptcy filed, 84
secured claims, 34–37
unsecured nonpriority claims, 38–39

unsecured priority claims, 37–38
Creditor lists, 59–60, 121, 396–398
Creditor's attorney
counseling, 85
drafting of bankruptcy forms, 85
information gathering, 77
procedure, 77–80
Creditor's bill, 83

D
Debt adjustment. *See* Adjustment of debts
Debtor, 30–31
address, 54–56
answer (involuntary case), 486
attorney. *See* Debtor's attorney.
cause of problems, 56–58
DIP. *See* Debtor in possession (DIP).
eligibility, 458–464
employment situation, 56
expectations, 61
financial condition, 58–59
identity, 53–54
involuntary bankruptcy, 85–86. *See also* Involuntary bankruptcy
motions, 234–241
nonbankruptcy solution, 60–61, 66–70
pending lawsuits, 61
Debtor in possession (DIP)
Chapter 11 case, 401
Chapter 12, case 368
Debtor's attorney
analysis (bankruptcy *vs.* nonbankruptcy), 65–75
counseling, 76
drafting of bankruptcy forms, 76
fees, 62–65
information gathering, 52–65. *See also* Debtor
typical procedure, 51–52
Debtor's petition, 103–111
Declaration Concerning Debtor's Schedules, 166–168
Deputy clerks, 44
Digests, 25
DIP. See, Debtor in possession (DIP)
Discharge
Chapter 7 case, 271–277
Chapter 12 case, 342, 386, 387
Chapter 13 case, 341–342
hardship, 342
objecting to, 252–255, 262
revocation, 272, 387
Disclosure of attorney's compensation statement, 118–121
Disclosure statement, 422–434, 437–442
Dismissal of case. *See* Motion to dismiss case
Disposition of collateral, 82
Disputed claim, 229
Distribution of property of estate
Chapter 7 case, 278–281
Chapter 11 case, 545
Chapter 12 case, 383
Chapter 13 case, 338
District court, 22
District court rules, 21–22
Drafting of bankruptcy forms, 76, 85
Dual nature of bankruptcy, 7–8

E
Eligibility, 458–468
Employee benefit plans, contributions, 279
Encyclopedias, 27
Equitable lien, 83
Equity security, 39
Equity security holders
Chapter 7 case, 271
Chapter 11 case, 399–401, 436
defined, 39
proof of claim, 230
Examination (motion to examine), 245, 247
Examiner, 49
Execution lien, 83
Execution sale, 83
Executory contract
Chapter 11 case, 408
interim trustee, 214–215
Schedule G (Executory Contracts and Unexpired Leases), 152–154
Exemptions
Chapter 7 case, 201–207, 263
Chapter 11 case, 405
Chapter 12 case, 369
Chapter 13 case, 321–322
Schedule C (Property Claimed as Exempt), 135–137
waiver, 206–207
Extension of credit (involuntary case), 278

F
Family farmer, 74, 345. *See also* Chapter 12 bankruptcy
Family farmer with regular annual income, 74
Farmer/fishermen claims, 279
Farming operation, 74
Feasibility requirement, 448–449
Federal bankruptcy exemptions. *See also* Exemptions
Chapter 7 liquidation, 201–206
opting out, 204
Federal Practice Digest 3d, 25
Federal Practice Digest 4th, 25
Federal Reporter, 24
Federal Rules of Bankruptcy Procedure, 20–21
Federal Supplement, 22
Fees
attorney, 62–65
filing, 112–115
Filing of petition
Chapter 7 case. *See also* Filing the petition—Chapter 7
Chapter 11 case, 395–401
Chapter 12 case, 365–366
Chapter 13 case, 318–319
Filing the petition—Chapter 7, 100–193
amendment, 193
clerk's notice, 115–116
corporate resolution authorizing filing, 117
debtor's duty to supplement schedules, 192–193
debtor's petition, 103–111
Declaration Concerning Debtor's Schedules, 166–168
disclosure of attorney's compensation statement, 118–121
filing fee, 112–115
list of creditors, 121
Schedule A (Real Property), 122–125
Schedule B (Personal Property), 125–135
Schedule C (Property Claimed as Exempt), 135–137
Schedule D (Creditors Holding Secured Claims), 137–142
Schedule E (Creditors Holding Unsecured Priority Claims), 142–148
Schedule F (Creditors Holding Unsecured Nonpriority Claims), 148–152
Schedule G (Executory Contracts and Unexpired Leases), 152–154
Schedule H (Codebtors), 154–156
Schedule I (Current Income of Individual Debtor(s)), 156–159

Schedule J (Current Expenditures of Individual Debtor(s)), 159–163
Schedule of Current Income and Current Expenditures of Partnership or Corporation, 163–166
Statement of Financial Affairs, 168–190
Statement of Intention of Individual Debtor, 191–192
Summary of Schedules, 123
Final accounts and reports, 281–294
Final decree
Chapter 7 case, 295
Chapter 11 case, 456
Final report and decree (Chapter 11), 455, 456
First day motions, 435
Fishermen claims, 279
Fixtures, 35
Forms of business organization, 53–54
Fraudulent conveyance, 83, 226
Future bankruptcy reform, 7
Future litigation, 404–405, 408

G
Gap creditors, 485–486
Gap period, 485
Garnishment, 81, 83
General partnership, 53
Good faith, 330–332
Government Printing Office, 21
Governmental regulatory authorities, 41
Governmental tax claims, 279–280

H
Hardship discharge, 342
Hearing on disclosure statement, 437–440
Historical overview, 1
Bankruptcy Code, 4–6. *See also* Bankruptcy Code.
early American statutes, 2–4
Early English law, 2

I
Indenture, 39
Indenture trustee, 39, 230
Individual debtor. *See* Chapter 13 bankruptcy
Indubitable equivalent, 443
Information gathering
creditor's attorney, 77
debtor's attorney, 52–65, 85–86. *See also* Debtor
Information sources. *See* Secondary authority
Insured depository institution claims, 280
Interim trustee, 48, 212–229
abandon property of estate, 213–214
avoiding transfers, 215–229. *See also* Avoiding transfers
executory contracts, 214–215
Internet resources, 27–28
Involuntary bankruptcy, 473–492
answer, 486
automatic stay, 485
bankruptcy estate, 485
bona fide dispute, 474
creditor's options, 84
creditor's petition, 477, 481–482
debtor's attorney, 85–86
dismissal of petition, 489
extension of credit, 278
gap creditors, 485–486
gap period, 485
order for relief, 485, 486, 489, 492
overview, 478–480
trustee, 485

J
Joint case, 154
Judge, 42
Judge's staff, 43
Judgment lien, 82–83
Judicial assistant, 43
Judicial lien, 238–241

L
Labor unions (collective bargaining contract), 404
Law clerk, 43
Law reviews, 26
Lawyer. *See* Creditor's attorney; Debtor's attorney
Lease, 40, 152–154
Legal authority, 9
Legal encyclopedias, 27
Legal periodicals, 26–27
Legislative authority, 24
Lessee, 40
Lessor, 40
Lien
consensual, 83
equitable, 83
execution, 83
judgment, 82–83
judicial, 238–241
statutory, 39–40, 222
Lien avoidance
Chapter 12 case, 371
Chapter 13 case, 315–316
Limited liability company (LLC), 54
Limited liability partnership (LLP), 54
Limited partnership, 54
Liquidation
Chapter 7. *See* Chapter 7 liquidation
Chapter 11, 408
List of creditors, 59–60, 121, 396–398
List of creditors with largest unsecured claims, 396–398
List of equity security holders, 399–401
LLC, 54
LLP, 54
Local rules, 21–22
Loislaw, 24
Loose-leaf services, 25

M
Maintenance (support claims), 279
Mandatory authority, 9
Mandatory provisions
Chapter 11 reorganization plan, 413–414
Chapter 12 plan, 357–358
Chapter 13 plan, 308–309
Meeting of creditors. *See* 341 meeting
Meeting of equity security holders, 271. *See also* Equity security holders
Merger or consolidation, 408
Morris, Robert, 3
Motion, 231, 233
Chapter 7 case, 234–252
Chapter 11 case, 435
Chapter 12 case, 371–373
Chapter 13 case, 323–325
court, by, dismiss case, 251–252
debtor, by, 234–241
dismiss. *See* Motion to dismiss case
first day, 435
party in interest, by, 242–247
rule 9014, 233

U.S. trustee, by, dismiss case, 247–251
venue. *See* Change of venue
Motion to convert to Chapter 11, 12, or 13, 234
Motion to dismiss case
court, 251–252
debtor, 234
party in interest, 245
U.S. trustee, 247–251
Municipalities, 18, 73

N
National Bankruptcy web sites, 27–28
Negotiation, 66–69
No bankruptcy filed
creditor's options, 80–84. *See also* Creditor's options.
debtor's options, 66–70
Nonbankruptcy alternatives. *See* Alternatives to bankruptcy filing
Nonbankruptcy *vs.* bankruptcy, 65–75
Nonbusiness debtor, options, 467–472
Nonbusiness filings, number of, 464
Nonpossessory, nonpurchase money security interest, 371
Notice. *See* Clerk's notice

O
Objecting to discharge
creditor, 252–255
trustee, 262
Objecting to dischargeability of debt
creditor, 255–261
debtor, 262
Obtaining credit, 403
Office of the clerk of the bankruptcy court, 43–44
Official forms, 21. *See also* Table of exhibits
Operation of debtor's business
Chapter 11 case, 402
Chapter 12 case, 368–369
Chapter 13 case, 321
Order for relief
Chapter 7 case, 94
Chapter 11 case, 401
Chapter 12 case, 366
Chapter 13 case, 319
involuntary bankruptcy, 485, 486, 489, 492

P
Paralegal, 32–33, 48–49
Parties in interest. *See* Cast of characters
Partnership, 53–54
Penalty-type claim, 280
Pending/future litigation, 61, 404–405, 408
Periodicals, 26–27
Permissive provisions
Chapter 11 reorganization plan, 414–415
Chapter 12 plan, 358
Chapter 13 plan, 309
Personal Property (Schedule B), 125–135
Persuasive authority, 9
Petition. *See* Filing of petition
Petition preparer, 33–34
Postjudgment garnishment, 83
Prejudgment garnishment, 81
PREMISE CD-ROM ed., 24
Primary authority, 9–12
Priority claims
administrative expenses, 278
alimony, maintenance, support claims, 279
consumer deposits, 279
employee pension plans, contributions, 279
extension of credit (involuntary case), 278
farmer/fishermen claims, 279
governmental tax claims, 279–280
S&L priority, 280
wages, salaries, commissions, 278–279
Private law, 12
Private nonbankruptcy alternatives. *See* Alternatives to bankruptcy filing
Private trustee, 46–49
Proof of claim
contingent claim, 229
creditors, 230
disputed claim, 229
equity security holders, 230
general rule, 229
indenture trustees, 230
motion for disallowance, 245
official form, 231–232
unliquidated claim, 229
voidable under state law, 220–222
Proof of interest, 229–230
Property of estate. *See also* Bankruptcy estate
abandon, 213–214
Chapter 7 case 194–198
Chapter 12 case, 368
Chapter 13 case, 321
distribution. *See* Distribution of property of estate
involuntary bankruptcy, 485
Public law, 12
Public Law 95-598, 12. *See also* Bankruptcy Code
Public Law 99-554, 13

R
Reaffirmation agreement, 273–276
Real property (Schedule A), 122–125
Recapitalization, 408
Receivership, 81
Regulatory authorities, 41
Reorganization. *See* Chapter 11 reorganization
Reorganization plan. *See* Chapter 11 reorganization plan
Replevin, 82
Repossession, 82
Retention of collateral, 82
Revocation
Chapter 11 case, 386, 387
discharge, of, 272, 342, 387
order of confirmation, of, 341, 455
Rules
bankruptcy court, 22
district court, 21–22
federal, 20–21

S
Salaries (commissions), 278–279
Schedule A (Real Property), 122–125
Schedule B (Personal Property), 125–135
Schedule C (Property Claimed as Exempt), 135–137
Schedule D (Creditors Holding Secured Claims), 137–142
Schedule E (Creditors Holding Unsecured Priority Claims), 142–148
Schedule F (Creditors Holding Unsecured Nonpriority Claims), 148–152
Schedule G (Executory Contracts and Unexpired Leases), 152–154

Schedule H (Codebtors), 154–156
Schedule I (Current Income of Individual Debtor(s)), 156–159
Schedule J (Current Expenditures of Individual Debtor(s)), 159–163
Schedule of Current Income and Current Expenditures of Partnership or Corporation, 163–166
SEC, 41
Secondary authority, 9
  American Law Reports, 27
  digests, 25
  Internet resources, 27–28
  legal encyclopedias, 27
  legal periodicals, 26–27
  legislative authority, 24
  loose-leaf services, 25
  treatises, 25–26
Section 341 meeting. *See* 341 meeting
Secured claims, 34–37, 137–142
Secured party, 35
Securities and Exchange Commission (SEC), 41
Securities Investor Protection Corporation (SIPC), 41
Security agreement, 35
Security interest, 35
Selecting type of bankruptcy filing
  business debtor, 464–467
  Chapter 7 liquidation *vs.* Chapter 11 liquidation, 465
  Chapter 7 liquidation *vs.* Chapter 11 reorganization, 464–465, 472
  Chapter 7 liquidation *vs.* Chapter 13 bankruptcy, 467–471
  Chapter 11 reorganization *vs.* Chapter 12 or 13 bankruptcy, 465–467, 472
  eligibility, 458–468
  nonbusiness debtor, 467–472
Self-help repossession, 82
Shepardizing, 24
Shepard's Bankruptcy Citations, 24
SIPC, 41
S&L priority, 280
Sources of information. *See* Secondary authority
Standing trustee, 48
State securities commission, 41
Statement of Financial Affairs, 168–190
Statement of intention, 190–192
Statistics (number of filings), 459–464
Statutory lien/lienholders, 39–40, 222
Stay
  Chapter 7 case, 207–212
  Chapter 11 case, 401
  Chapter 12 case, 366
  Chapter 13 case, 320
  codebtor, 320
  involuntary bankruptcy, 485
Strong-arm power, 215
Summary of Schedules, 123
Supplementary procedures, 83
Support claims, 279
Supreme Court of United States, 24

T
Tax claims, 279–280
341 meeting
  Chapter 7 case, 270
  Chapter 11 case, 436
  Chapter 12 case, 374
  Chapter 13 case, 327
Treatises, 25–26
Trustee
  Chapter 7, 46–47
  Chapter 12, 369–370
  Chapter 13, 322–323
  eligibility, 46–47
  final accounts/report, 281–294
  indenture, 39, 230
  interim, 48, 212–229. *See also* Interim trustee
  involuntary bankruptcy, 485
  objecting to discharge, 262
  private, 46–49
  selection/qualification, 47
  standing, 48
  U.S., 45–46
Trustee panel, 46–47

U
Unauthorized postpetition transfers, 228–229
Unions (collective bargaining contract), 404
United States bankruptcy court, 22
United States circuit court, 22–24
United States Code (U.S.C.), 12
United States Code Annotated (U.S.C.A.), 12
United States Code Service (U.S.C.S.), 12
United States district court, 22
United States Law Week, 24
United States Reports, 24
United States Supreme Court, 24
United States Supreme Court Bulletin, 24
United States Supreme Court Reports, 24
United States Trustee Pilot Program, 45
United States trustees, 13, 45–46
Unliquidated claim, 229
Unperfected security interests, 215–220
Unsecured creditors
  list, 396–398
  nonpriority claims, 38–39, 148–152
  priority claims, 37–38, 142–148
Unsecured creditors committee, 436
U.S. Constitution, 2, 9–10
U.S. Government Printing Office, 21
U.S.C., 12
U.S.C.A., 12
U.S.C.S., 12
Utility services, 404

V
Venue, 237. *See also* Change of venue
Voidable preferences, 222–225

W
Wages, salaries, commissions, 278–279
Waiver
  avoidance powers, 207
  exemptions, 206–207
West's Bankruptcy Digest, 25
Wilson, James, 3